AMERICAN**BAR**ASSOCIATION

Cybersecurity Legal
Task Force

THE ABA
CYBERSECURITY
HANDBOOK

A RESOURCE FOR ATTORNEYS, LAW FIRMS, AND BUSINESS PROFESSIONALS

——— THIRD EDITION ———

JILL D. RHODES, ROBERT S. LITT, AND PAUL ROSENZWEIG, EDITORS

This edition is dedicated to Holly McMahon, Director, ABA Standing Committee on Law and National Security, and Director, ABA Cybersecurity Legal Task Force. For more than three decades, Holly's tireless and invaluable efforts have quietly facilitated and enabled the advancement of these organizations and the field of national security law. We are forever grateful for her leadership.

Table of Contents

CHAPTER 3
Understanding Technology: What Every Lawyer Needs to Know about the Cyber Network 71
Paul Rosenzweig and Bryson Bort

CHAPTER 6
Lawyers' Obligations to Provide Data Security
Arising from Ethics Rules and Other Laws

CHAPTER 7
Occasions When Counsel Should Consider Initiating
a Conversation about Cybersecurity with the Client

CHAPTER 12

Why Public Interest Attorneys Should Care about Cybersecurity

Edward Marchewka and Ozoda Usmanova

CHAPTER 13

Get SMART on Data Protection Training and How to Create a Culture of Awareness

Ruth Hill Bro and Jill D. Rhodes

"There are only two types of companies: those that have been hacked, and those that will be."

—Robert Mueller

"If you think technology can solve your security problems, then you don't understand the problems and you don't understand the technology."

—Bruce Schneier

Foreword

As we write this foreword to the third edition of the Cybersecurity Handbook, the threats associated with cybercrime, cyber espionage, and cyber warfare loom even larger in our headlines and daily lives than when the second edition was published in 2018. The Cybersecurity Legal Task Force remains just as committed to enabling the legal profession to do all that we can to protect ourselves and our clients. It is our goal that this third edition of the Handbook will continue to serve as a resource for lawyers and others in both private and public sectors as they grapple with cyber issues and seek trusted guidance.

As we embark on a new ABA year, the Task Force has grown to include ABA presidential appointee/representatives from 28 ABA entities, as well as technical and private sector representation—all with expertise in cybersecurity. Our goals are to examine ways we can help lawyers protect both their practices and their clients' confidential information and intellectual property during cyber events, and at the same time position the ABA to contribute to the increasing national dialogue about how to address cyber issues, be it through legislation, enforcement, or the implementation of the growing body of international and national standards and best practices. The Task Force accomplishes these goals by:

- facilitating collaboration and information exchange among constituent ABA entities, relevant public agencies, and private organizations;
- serving as a clearinghouse regarding cybersecurity activities, policy proposals, advocacy, publications, and resources;
- studying and analyzing executive and legislative branch cybersecurity proposals;

- identifying cyber-related issues for appropriate action by the ABA, including filling gaps in policy; encouraging ABA entities to develop new policies as appropriate; and sharing best practices with the bench, the bar, and those non-lawyers with interest; and
- advising on ABA cybersecurity advocacy and responses to government actions.

The Task Force hosts and sponsors educational programs and events designed for government officials and private sector representatives involved in cybersecurity issues. We also develop resources to assist practitioners, including, more notably, the recently updated Vendor Cybersecurity Checklist. The Checklist is designed to assist law firms and lawyers advising other procuring organizations and vendors about how to address cybersecurity risks through implementation of information security requirements in their transactions. With this second edition of the Checklist, we focused on the perspective of solo practitioners and smaller firms that may lack the resources of larger firms and organizations. The Checklist frames the issues that parties should consider consistent with common principles for managing cybersecurity risk by due diligence and vendor selection through contracting and vendor management. The Checklist suggests that cybersecurity provisions are not "one size fits all," but should instead be informed by parties' assessment of risk and strategies to mitigate risk. The Checklist has been widely disseminated throughout the public and private sector, and we encourage you to use it as a resource. It is available on our website at https://www.americanbar.org/groups/cybersecurity

In terms of policy, the Task Force has been actively engaged with its cyber advocacy. In its nine years of existence, it has proposed, and the ABA House of Delegates has approved, eight resolutions.[1] The first built upon the amendment of Model Rules of Professional Conduct Rules 1.0, 1.6, and 4.4 to provide guidance on confidentiality and technology (August 2012). The second condemned intrusions into law firms' systems and networks and encouraged the government to examine and amend laws to

---

1. https://www.americanbar.org/groups/cybersecurity/aba-policy-initiatives/.

fight such intrusions (August 2013). The third encouraged the private and public sectors to maintain cybersecurity programs in line with legal and ethical obligations, tailored to the needs of the organization, and able to protect all data and systems (August 2014). The fourth resolution urged the government to fund cyber programs and training for the courts (August 2015). The fifth stressed the importance of cyber preparedness and identified actions that should be taken to prevent a cyberattack from occurring (February 2017). The sixth urged Congress to protect the security and integrity of U.S. federal elections by enacting legislation that authorizes and appropriates necessary funding for NIST (February 2020). And the seventh and eighth resolutions urged (1) Congress to preserve and protect each American citizen's right to vote in federal elections by enacting legislation that prohibits the use of false, deceptive, or misleading statements, information, acts, or practices by a foreign principal or its agent; and (2) federal, state, local, territorial, and tribal governments, and private sector entities, to promote digital literacy, civic education, and public awareness to build societal resilience to domestic and foreign malign disinformation operations (August 2020). Additionally, in November 2012, the ABA Board of Governors approved a set of principles proposed by the Task Force. The principles emphasize the importance of (1) public–private frameworks to protect U.S. assets, infrastructure, and economic interests; (2) information sharing between government agencies and private industry; (3) modernizing legal and policy environments; (4) privacy and civil liberties; and (5) cybersecurity training, education, and workforce development of senior leadership, technical operators, and lawyers. These ABA policies and principles are even more critical today. Needless to say, we have been an active group.

The Task Force is proud to be a leading partner in the national cyber dialogue and we invite you to visit our website at https://www.americanbar.org/groups/cybersecurity, which we update regularly to include cybersecurity resources and cyber-related events and programs. We both feel privileged to co-chair the Task Force leading this ABA-wide effort, leveraging the assistance and input of all ABA entities and the many government and private entities with which we partner in offering recommendations for how we can best protect against and be resilient in the face of the ongoing threats cyber threats.

We also are quite proud to follow in the footsteps of the Task Force's prior chairs: Harvey Rishikof, Judith Miller, Vince Polley, Ruth Hill Bro, and Thomas Smedinghoff. We are thankful for the strong continued support the Task Force has received from each ABA president since the Task Force's inception, especially Laurel Bellows, who helped establish the Task Force in 2012.

We extend our very special thanks to the editors and authors of this book for assisting in furthering this important conversation, as well as our ABA team members Holly McMahon and Sally Heuker and all the current members and liaisons without whom the Task Force simply would not be able to accomplish its many initiatives.

Maureen Kelly and Claudia Rast
Co-Chairs, Cybersecurity Legal Task Force

Acknowledgments

The ABA Cybersecurity Legal Task Force was initiated by Laurel Bellows at the beginning of her term as ABA president in 2012. In 2013, the first edition of *The ABA Cybersecurity Handbook: A Resource for Attorneys, Law Firms, and Business Professionals* (Handbook) was published to provide attorneys a basic understanding of cybersecurity and its implications. The second edition received the 2018 ACLEA Award of Outstanding Achievement. This third edition reunites many of the previous authors, bringing unique perspectives from across ABA Sections and industry, to assess how our cybersecurity risks and obligations have expanded. While the ABA Cybersecurity Legal Task Force remains an ad hoc assembly, nothing related to cybersecurity is ad hoc. The technology will continue to evolve at a pace faster than we can manage; our clients' business practices will change; and the law will develop. As it does, the ABA will endeavor to update many of the online resources referenced in this Handbook. Of course, many ABA entities also will continue to address these issues. In particular, work by these ABA entities merits attention:

Business Law Section
Science & Technology Law Section
Tort Trial and Insurance Practice Section
Solo, Small Firm and General Practice Division
Standing Committee on Law & National Security
Special Committee on Disaster Response & Preparedness
Center for Professional Responsibility
Section of Administrative Law and Regulatory Practice
Antitrust Law Section
Section on Civil Rights and Social Justice

Criminal Justice Section
Section of Environment, Energy, and Resources
Section of Intellectual Property Law
Section of International Law
Forum on Communications Law
Health Law Section
Judicial Division
Law Practice Division
Standing Committee on Lawyers' Professional Liability
Section of Litigation
Section of Public Contract Law
Infrastructure and Regulated Industries Section
Standing Committee on Technology and Information Systems
Section of State and Local Government Law
Rule of Law Initiative
Young Lawyers Division
Senior Lawyers Division
Law Student Division

We recommend that readers reach out to these organizations to learn more about the subject.

This Handbook would not be possible without the commitment of almost 30 legal practitioners from across the American Bar Association who volunteered their time and expertise to educate the legal community.[2] We offer a special thanks to each one of them, who worked under an extremely tight schedule in a collaborative group environment, during a global pandemic, to make this Handbook a reality. As experts in their fields, each of them brought together the literature, sharpened focus on the issues, and offered concrete advice to practitioners. As a result, we hope this Handbook will prove a valuable resource to practitioners at all levels, in various types of practices.

---

2. All author biographies are available in the Author Biographies section at the end of this Handbook.

In addition to its authors, many people have worked hard to help build this resource. As always, the ABA Staff have enabled and facilitated this Handbook. We offer a special thanks to Holly McMahon and Sally Heuker, who have provided endless support, organizational management, and direction, without which this book would not have been brought to fruition. We also want to thank our law student volunteers, Sydney Huppert, Irene Kim, and Veronica Lark, whose review of footnotes was exemplary.

Finally, as editors, we offer a very special thanks to our families for giving us the time to make the commitment to bring this Handbook to you.

We hope that you find the Handbook practical and a valuable addition to your collection.

Jill D. Rhodes
Robert S. Litt
Paul Rosenzweig

SECTION I

Cybersecurity Background

Chapter 1

Introduction

Jill Rhodes, Robert S. Litt, and Paul Rosenzweig

Oh, how the world has changed since the publication of our first Handbook in 2013, and even our second Handbook in 2018. Cybersecurity threats and risks for lawyers and law firms during the Covid-19 lockdown of 2020–2021 alone produced enough changes in the way we must think about how to protect ourselves, our law practices, and businesses that it could have been its own handbook. In 2013, few would have understood the depth and extent to which cybersecurity would affect our lives today. Now, as we move into 2022, future threats and risks are as large as our imagination can make them, and larger.

There have been a significant number of "first" or "largest" events since publication of the last handbook, especially during the past year. For example, the SolarWinds breach led to the first case of a chief information security officer (CISO) being sued by shareholders in his personal capacity.[1] Given that one of the editors of this handbook is a CISO, this becomes even more personally alarming. We've also seen members of boards of directors, CEOs, and others sued in their personal capacities.[2] This raises the possibility that we will see attorneys being sued in their personal capacity for risks that become breaches about which they could have or should have warned their

---

1. The SolarWinds breach is discussed throughout this Handbook and involves a supply chain malware that impacted thousands of public and private sector businesses. For a discussion of the lawsuit, see Bruce Sussman, *Suing the CISO: SolarWinds Fires Back*, SECUREWORLD: SECUREWORLD NEWS (Aug. 5, 2021, 9:35 PM), https://www.secureworld.io/industry-news/ciso-lawsuit-solarwinds?hs_amp=true.
2. See Chapter 4 of this Handbook.

clients. Will there become a legal obligation to warn our clients about cyber risks and threats and will we, as attorneys, be held accountable if we do not?[3]

The massive SolarWinds breach has focused more attention on the supply chain threat.[4] Discussed further throughout this Handbook, this breach was revelatory because of the nature of the threat actor (a third party working in Russia), as well as the magnitude of damage that resulted across both public and private sectors. Prior to SolarWinds, the risk posed by third parties that provide supplies, equipment, and software had been known, although the amount of time and consideration that different organizations gave to this threat may have varied. Now, law firms and other practitioners—as well as their clients—must start thinking about all of the organizations that provide hardware, software, and other services to them: how secure are the processes within the vendor companies to ensure that any updates or upgrades received are free from malware? If they are not, what tools and processes are in place to protect the firm if malware is launched?

And . . . just when we thought that supply chain threat couldn't get worse, the Kaseya ransomware breach occurred.[5] This was the first time the world became involved in responding to a ransomware supply chain breach. Kaseya tools are used predominantly by managed service providers, which then leverage those tools to support their customers. The impact of the breach was that organizations using Kaseya management tools and services became infected with ransomware, which was then passed down to their customers. This incident had global impact, and while it was not directly targeted at law firms and practitioners, it easily could have been.

These threats and changes are only enhanced as the bad guys become better organized. Ransomware as a Service (RaaS) organizations are operating openly across the Internet, hiring and firing "employees" based on their productivity in launching effective ransomware against companies. DarkSide, known for ransomware leading to the shutdown of the Colonial

---

3. See Chapter 7 in this Handbook as well as Chapters 4 and 6, which discuss legal and ethical obligations to protect data.

4. See Chapter 2 in this Handbook.

5. This breach is also discussed in detail throughout this Handbook. For a summary, see Charlie Osborne, *Updated Kaseya Ransomware Attack FAQ: What We Know Now*, ZDNet (July 23, 2021, 12:33 PM), https://www.zdnet.com/article/updated-kaseya-ransomware-attack-faq-what-we-know-now/.

Pipeline in May 2021, announced its RaaS offering in August 2020 via a "press release"[6] and also published its own "code of conduct" about what it would and would not tolerate with respect to its ransomware business.[7] On a positive note, the FBI was able to retrieve $2.3 million of the $4.4 million in ransomware payments made during the Colonial Pipeline incident and, due to external pressure, DarkSide closed its business in June 2021.[8] Unfortunately, it's likely that they just reopened their RaaS business under a different name.[9]

There has also been an increase in executive branch responses to these threats. As another first, in October 2020, just prior to the presidential election, the first joint cybersecurity advisory was issued by the Cybersecurity and Infrastructure Security Agency, the Federal Bureau of Investigation, and the Department of Health and Human Services. This advisory was a warning to the health care and public health sectors that there was an imminent ransomware threat against them from malicious cyber actors.[10]

Even the international response to cyberattacks has provided firsts. In July 2021, the United States, NATO, the European Union, the United Kingdom, Japan, Australia, and Canada issued a joint statement condemning China as a major economic and national security threat. The statement blames the Chinese government for ransomware and other cyberattacks, including

---

6. Snir Ben Shimol, *Return of the Darkside: Analysis of a Large-Scale Data Theft Campaign*, VARONIS (July 6, 2021), https://www.varonis.com/blog/darkside-ransomware/.

7. *A Closer Look at the DarkSide Ransomware Gang*, KREBSONSECURITY (May 11, 2021, 12:37 PM), https://krebsonsecurity.com/2021/05/a-closer-look-at-the-darkside-ransomware-gang/.

8. Michael Schwirtz & Nicole Perlroth, *DarkSide, Blamed for Gas Pipeline Attack, Says It Is Shutting Down*, N.Y. TIMES (May 14, 2021), https://www.nytimes.com/2021/05/14/business/darkside-pipeline-hack.html.

9. While Darkside was yielding to public pressure, two other Russian language RaaS providers announced similar "strict new rules governing the use of their products, including bans on targeting government-affiliated entities, hospitals or educational institutions." *See id.*

10. Cybersecurity and Infrastructure Security Agency, *Alert (AA20-302A): Ransomware Activity Targeting the Healthcare and Public Health Sector*, CISA (Nov. 2, 2021), https://us-cert.cisa.gov/ncas/alerts/aa20-302a.

an attack on Microsoft earlier in the year.[11] The United States went further than this announcement, imposing sanctions on China and filing criminal charges against four hackers.[12]

Nationally, the federal government has moved to strengthen security of federal agencies as well as others. In May 2021, immediately following the Colonial Pipeline ransomware, President Biden signed an *Executive Order on Improving the Nation's Cybersecurity*. This executive order focuses on information sharing, protection of federal agencies, public–private partnerships, and the implementation of a zero-trust security architecture across the federal government and potentially the private sector.[13] Numerous cybersecurity bills are pending in the House and the Senate. It is a step in the right direction, but law firms and other practices need to prepare themselves to address these risks.

Law firms and practices have to get cybersecurity right all the time; the bad guys only have to get it right once. Law firms are more prepared than in the past but there is still much to be done. In a recent study of more than 200 small- and medium-sized law firms, LogicForce found that:

- Only 30 percent of law firms use legal specific document management systems that are cloud-based, which offers additional security.
- Only 35 percent of law firms conduct penetration testing of their environments using an external party.
- Only 5 percent of law firms hold cybersecurity training on a monthly basis.[14]

As long as gaps such as these remain, law firms will continue to be vulnerable to threats such as ransomware.

---

11. Press Release, White House, The United States, Joined by Allies and Partners, Attributes Malicious Cyber Activity and Irresponsible State Behavior to the People's Republic of China, WH.Gov (July 19, 2021), https://www.whitehouse.gov/briefing-room /statements-releases/2021/07/19/the-united-states-joined-by-allies-and-partners-attributes -malicious-cyber-activity-and-irresponsible-state-behavior-to-the-peoples-republic-of-china/.

12. *Id.*

13. See Chapter 11 in this Handbook for a full discussion of this Executive Order.

14. 2021 Law Firm IT Scorecard, LogicForce, https://www.logicforce.com/2021/01/13 /lawfirm-it-scorecard-2021/#top (last visited Aug. 25, 2021).

The first edition of this Handbook began with a story about a law firm whose managing partner received a call from the FBI. The agents informed the lawyer that during a separate investigation, the FBI had found many of the law firm's electronic files on computer servers outside the United States, and that it was likely that all of the firm's electronic records had been accessed. When the agents asked the managing partner to give them a heads-up before making the breach public, the managing partner reportedly said, "Go public? I'm not even going to tell my partners!"[15] Today, hopefully, a full response process and plan would be in place. The firm would have cyber insurance to cover the costs of recovery, a forensics firm to help contain the incident and perhaps determine if and how to pay ransom, as well as a public relations firm to help determine what to tell their employees and the public, if anything.

These practices have been discussed in each of this Handbook's prior editions. That said, this third edition is filled with new information, laws, findings, and practical solutions. As editors, we have discussed the efficacy of publishing this third edition. With cyber changing so quickly, publishing a book about it seems a bit outdated and almost ironic. In the time it will take to finalize this publication, thousands of additional cybersecurity stories will post on the Internet and numerous breaches will occur. There will likely be new technology for prevention, detection, response, and recovery; easier ways to identify risks and liabilities; and new legislation. So, the question remains, why a handbook?

First, the Handbook is at your fingertips as a guide to preparing for and responding to cybersecurity threats and incidents. The foundational information is likely to remain relevant even in a changing environment. The recommendations within each chapter, located at the end, provide the reader with an easy guide for developing and implementing an effective cybersecurity program that includes building an understanding of lawyers' legal and ethical obligations to provide effective data security.

---

15. *See* JILL D. RHODES & VINCE I. POLLEY, THE ABA CYBERSECURITY HANDBOOK: A RESOURCE FOR ATTORNEYS, LAW FIRMS, AND BUSINESS PROFESSIONALS 1 (1st ed. 2013). *See generally Eric Savitz, Conversations on Cybersecurity: The Trouble with China, Part I,* FORBES (Jan. 31, 2012, 2:36 PM), http://www.forbes.com/sites/ciocentral/2012/01/3 1/conversations-on-cybersecurity-the-trouble-with-china-part-1/.

Next, the Handbook covers a wide array of topics and provides a comprehensive look not only at the threat developments of the past few years but also at the trends that have been established in cybersecurity. The Handbook addresses concerns and provides recommendations for several different types of legal practices—small firms and large ones, government lawyers and in-house counsel. Overall, best practices are developed and shared throughout the Handbook.

Finally, the authors who have written the chapters are leading experts in the field. The knowledge and insight they bring to these chapters and the overall Handbook makes the Handbook a unique value to the legal community all in one place. Having a handbook gives that value a sense of permanence that is missing from the Internet and digital records.

In addition to updating the chapters from the prior edition, this third edition adds a new chapter (Chapter 14) about disinformation, deepfakes, and the role that lawyers and law firms must play to address these challenges—a problem that was barely on anyone's radar screen a few years ago. This chapter discusses synthetic media and the use of artificial intelligence as a way to quickly spread false information. In 2020, there was an exponential year-over-year growth in disinformation and deepfakes. The chapter discusses legal and business risks that attorneys may need to resolve in the future.

Overall, the structure of this Handbook is similar to the prior editions. It is the work product of nearly 30 authors[16] from across the ABA, and, as just mentioned, they are experts in the field. Most chapters have been substantially updated and rewritten given the pace of change in the cybersecurity space.

Section I provides background and a broader understanding of the cybersecurity threat. In addition to this introduction, Chapter 2 (Understanding Cybersecurity Risks) provides a more detailed explanation of the sources of risk as well as descriptions of recent breaches, ramifications for law firms, and the resulting impact on their clients. The chapter is broad, covering topics from cloud security to mobile device management, and provides a solid overview of much of what is discussed throughout the remainder of the Handbook. The number and types of recent cases and incidents identified

---

16. Biographies of the authors are included at the end of this volume.

throughout the chapter is mind-boggling and demonstrates the risk and gaps firms must address. It concludes by setting out basic principles for how attorneys can protect confidential law firm records and prevent data breaches.

Chapter 3 (Understanding Technology: What Every Lawyer Needs to Know about the Cyber Network) provides an overview of key technology principles in a way that is easily understandable for the nonspecialist. It focuses on three areas: the growth of the web, the nature of cyber threats and vulnerabilities, and how cyber defensive systems and enterprises work. This is a terrific chapter for lawyers whatever the state of their technical knowledge.

The four chapters of Section II focus on lawyers' legal and ethical obligations to their clients, and discuss the need for lawyers to understand data and cybersecurity risks and to inform their clients accordingly.

In Chapter 4 (Legal Obligations to Provide Data Security), the authors discuss applicable laws relating to data security and data breaches. It walks the reader through basic security concepts and the overall duty to provide data security. It also includes a discussion about the duty to notify about security breaches. Appendices A through D provide an extensive list, as of the date of this edition, of current U.S. federal and state laws and regulations related to responsibility to protect data. The information in Chapter 4 is important not only to help lawyers advise their clients but also for them to identify the scope of their own duties.

Chapter 5 (International Norms) takes the work in Chapter 4 one step further to assess global trends. It discusses international standards and doctrine, including the U.S. Cyberspace Solarium Commission, as well as international laws in Europe, Asia/Pacific, Russia, Latin America, and Africa. It continues with a discussion of the source of international norms and the impact on the United States of foreign laws in this area.

Chapter 6 (Lawyers' Obligations to Provide Data Security Arising from Ethics Rules and Other Law) focuses on the ethical requirements placed on attorneys, law firms, and legal practitioners to protect client data, and their applicability in the cyber arena. This chapter discusses in particular the May 2017 ABA Ethics Opinion addressing this topic[17] and follow-on

---

17. ABA Comm. on Ethics & Pro. Resp., Formal Op. 477R (2017) (discussing securing communication of protected client information).

opinions, including the ABA's Formal Opinion 498 on Virtual Practice and a variety of state ethics opinions. Appendices E through I list formal ethics opinions as well as detailed information related to the different types of ethical obligations as mentioned throughout the chapter.

Chapter 7 (Occasions When Counsel Should Consider Initiating a Conversation about Cybersecurity with the Client) explores a variety of scenarios in which counsel should approach clients about cybersecurity matters. These scenarios range from the relatively obvious, such as at the outset of an attorney–client relationship or when a client has suffered a cybersecurity incident, to less obvious situations such as in connection with a possible merger or acquisition, or when clients are adopting new technologies such as artificial intelligence. It provides an invaluable guide to what situations lawyers should be alert to and how they should address cybersecurity issues with their clients.

Section III of the Handbook moves the discussion of threats and legal obligations from a general level to practice-specific arenas. Whether working in a law firm, as in-house counsel, in the public sector, or in the nonprofit world, all lawyers face cybersecurity-related challenges. As we hope is clear, cybersecurity threats do not distinguish between the type and size of a law practices.

Chapter 8 (Large Law Firms) sets out specific challenges confronting global firms. It also sets a general framework for all firms with respect to threats facing the practice and the need to establish an effective cybersecurity risk management program, and thus should be read by all lawyers.

Chapter 9 (Small Firms and Sole Practitioners) is written for smaller firms and sole practitioners. Challenges of resources and capabilities face these types of lawyers, which means that unique solutions must be identified, as the obligation to maintain the security and confidentiality of client data remains the same. This chapter sets out easily understandable controls that small firms and sole practitioners can implement to more effectively protect client data.

Chapter 10 (In-House Counsel) discusses considerations specific to in-house counsel. The realities of the role of in-house counsel increase the obligation to understand specific threats related to an organization's business as well as specific legal and ethical obligations. This chapter includes information about building internal relationships with stakeholders and external relationships with key government officials, and how in-house counsel can be best prepared to address cybersecurity.

Chapter 11 (Considerations for Government Lawyers) addresses key issues facing government attorneys. It provides an extensive review of executive orders and requirements, including the new executive order mentioned earlier, and provides guidance and best practices advice for attorneys working across government agencies. It also serves as a reference guide for all lawyers to the resources available across the government to assist in cybersecurity issues.

Chapter 12 (Why Public Interest Attorneys Should Care about Cybersecurity) discusses the ever-growing cyber threats to nonbusiness, nongovernmental organizations. Malicious cyber actors do not discriminate based on whether an organization turns a profit or not. Indeed, public interest groups may also be targeted politically by nation-states or other threat actors. This chapter touches on the role of the board of directors and its obligation to ensure that nonprofit organizations are effectively protecting data.

Chapter 13 (Get SMART on Data Protection: Training and How to Create a Culture of Awareness) focuses on the human factors that impact cyber risk. It offers recommendations and a program to help build a culture of security for all employees of law firms and other practices. It is only through proper education and training that these risks can be reduced.

Chapter 14 (Disinformation and Deepfakes: The Role for Lawyers and Law Firms), as mentioned earlier, sets out how disinformation has affected society over the past several years, and why this should matter to lawyers. It addresses the role lawyers must play in ensuring clients and firms understand the technology, the practice, and the critical issues relating to disinformation.

Section IV focuses on incident response and cybersecurity insurance coverage. The question, as cyber risk continues to grow, is not *if* law firms will be victims of incidents, as targets or incidentally, but rather *when* and *how* will they respond when they are? These last two chapters address the heart of that question.

Chapter 15 (Achieving Preparedness through Standards and Planning and Best Practices for Incident Response) walks through incident prevention, preparation, and response, including risk management, business continuity planning, third-party risks, and national and international frameworks that can be leveraged to assess risk. It also discusses response planning and how best to prepare an organization to react to a cyber incident. This chapter will support any organization in its development of a business resiliency strategy.

Chapter 16 (Cyber Insurance for Law Firms and Legal Organizations) sets out the ever-changing world of cyber insurance. It discusses different types of insurance offerings as well as the growing challenges both providers and law firms have with insurance against cyber risks. In the three-year period from Q1 2018 to Q4 2020 the number of privacy-compromising events decreased while ransomware events increased dramatically,[18] as cyber actors changed their focus. As a result, cyber insurance premiums are skyrocketing and more organizations are being denied cyber insurance by providers, even without a history of incidents. As ransomware continues to spread, it is critical that lawyers and law firms understand what will be required of them in the future to obtain and maintain their cyber coverage.

Our conclusion looks ahead to the next several years and what we might expect the next cyber challenge to be. Given the speed with which the cyber landscape is changing, it is likely that this will be the last print edition of this Handbook. We believe the time was ripe for this Handbook when the first edition was issued in 2013, and what we've accomplished through its three editions continues to help lawyers and law firms across the country and perhaps around the world. In the future, we expect to work closely with the ABA Cybersecurity Task Force to identify an online means to share up-to-date information on a continuous basis. Finding a way to keep this topic and the areas current is important to all of the authors and editors.

One final, important note: The views expressed throughout this Handbook are those of the authors themselves and not of the ABA, any specific law firm or practice, governmental entity, or any other author or editor affiliation.

We hope that you will learn from this Handbook in a way that helps your practice address the growing challenges presented by cybersecurity and helps you to both protect your own practice and provide competent and important advice to clients.

---

18. *Aon's E&O |Cyber Insurance Snapshot: A Focused View of 2021 Risk & Insurance Challenges* 3 (2021), https://www.aon.com/cyber-solutions/wp-content/uploads/Aon-errors -and-omissions-cyber-insurance-snapshot.pdf.

Chapter 2
Understanding Cybersecurity Risks

Lucy L. Thomson

I. New Technologies Create Unprecedented Challenges for Lawyers

As the frequency and sophistication of cyberattacks have increased in recent years, cybercriminals have targeted lawyers and law firms in the United States and abroad due to the vast amount of confidential client and firm information they collect and store.[1] Firms regularly display their lawyers' work and client lists on their websites, which provides bad actors with the key information they need to orchestrate social engineering attacks. Through these attacks, criminals can trick firms and their clients into revealing valuable data.

In recent years, cybercriminals have shifted away from launching mass attacks designed to steal consumer information to using stolen credentials (logins and passwords) to target businesses and steal their key data and intellectual property (IP).[2] An official of the Federal Bureau of Investigation (FBI) observed that "[m]any scammers have realized it's no longer cost effective

---

1. "Despite excellent standards of cybersecurity, 15% of a global sample of law firms showed signs of compromised networks. These compromises result from an overwhelming attack rate on law firms globally: 100% of law firms analyzed were targeted in attacks by threat actors." *BlueVoyant Launches Its Sector 17-State of Cybersecurity in the Legal Sector Report*, BLUEVOY-ANT (May 27, 2020), https://www.bluevoyant.com/news/bluevoyant-sector-17-press-release/.

2. *Identity Theft Resource Center's 2020 Annual Data Breach Report Reveals 19 Percent Decrease in Breaches*, IDENTITY THEFT RESOURCE CENTER 2020 (Jan. 28, 2021), https://www.idtheftcenter.org/identity-theft-resource-centers-2020-annual-data-breach-report-reveals-19-percent-decrease-in-breaches/. *See* VERIZON, DBIR: 2021 DATA BREACH INVESTIGATIONS REPORT, VERIZON, Professional, Scientific and Technical Services industry sector. "The use of stolen credentials is widespread and employees have a definite tendency to fall for social tactics," 82 Verizon.com/dbir/ (hereinafter VERIZON 2021 DBIR).

to target individuals. Instead, they go after these big companies—real estate firms, law firms, anyone moving huge amounts of money is a target."[3]

Ransomware[4] and phishing attacks,[5] now the most common causes of data breaches, have had particularly devastating consequences for law practices. In numerous breaches, law practices have seen their confidential client data and proprietary information compromised, entire firm computer networks shut down, extortion demands delivered, and client confidences breached when stolen information is published on the dark web.[6] Further, new tactics of criminal groups are becoming more insidious. While in the past, law firms focused on paying ransom to unencrypt their data, now, this is only part of the malicious strategy. Not only are hackers demanding that the victims pay a ransom to reestablish firm access to their encrypted data and networks, they also threaten to publish the firm's stolen data on the dark web or otherwise make it available to the world.

Alerts from law enforcement in the United States and globally have warned of dangerous, sophisticated attacks by state actors and cybercriminals that are endangering law offices and threatening the security of critical infrastructure. Hackers have exploited vulnerabilities in key software products used by law firms to steal personal information, client data, and IP. This generally occurs when malicious actors gain access to the law firm's

---

3. *International Scammer Sentenced: Man Used Phishing Techniques to Steal $11 Million from Company in BEC Scheme*, FBI News (Apr. 26, 2021), https://www.fbi.gov/news/stories /international-scammer-sentenced-for-phishing-bec-scheme-042621.

4. Ransomware is a type of malicious software, or malware, that encrypts data on a computer making it unusable. A malicious cybercriminal holds the data hostage until the ransom is paid. If the ransom is not paid, the victim's data remains unavailable. Cybercriminals may also pressure victims to pay the ransom by threatening to destroy the victim's data or to release it to the public. *See* FBI, Internet Crime Report: 2020, at 14 (2020).

5. Phishing is often used in conjunction with a spoofed e-mail. It is the act of sending an e-mail falsely claiming to be a legitimate business in an attempt to deceive the unsuspecting recipient into divulging personal, sensitive information such as passwords, credit card numbers, and bank account information after directing the user to visit a specified website. The website, however, is not genuine and was set up only as an attempt to steal the user's information. *See* FBI, *Internet Fraud*, FBI: Scams and Safety, https://www.fbi.gov/scams-and-safety /common-scams-and-crimes/internet-fraud (last visited Aug. 25, 2021).

6. Darran Guccione, *What Is the Dark Web? How to Access It and What You'll Find*, CSOonline (July 1, 2021, 2:00 AM), https://www.csoonline.com/article/3249765/what-is -the-dark-web-how-to-access-it-and-what-youll-find.html.

system through phishing or similar means, and then identify software products that are not appropriately patched to exploit.

Attacks resulting in breaches of law firm third-party business partners and vendors have increased, creating significant risks for law firms that outsource important operations. Cybercriminals have targeted vendors who have access to a larger organization's information or a business that holds the valuable information of multiple organizations. These entities may have fewer security measures than the law offices they serve.

The widespread practice of lawyers and staff working remotely, which was intensified by the Covid-19 pandemic, is a trend that is expected to continue, making employees even more vulnerable to many of the most common causes of breaches—particularly theft of credentials, social engineering attacks, and human error.[7] Dark web auctions that sell backdoor access to law firm servers have perhaps become the most unconventional threat to the attorney-client privilege.[8] After gaining administrator privileges through an attack, hackers sell login credentials on the dark web to access law firm networks.[9]

A. Technology of the Law Office

Lawyers and law firms are facing unprecedented challenges from the widespread use of electronic records, mobile devices, and the emerging Internet of Things (IoT). Seeking efficiencies from new technologies, most lawyers and law firms use e-mail extensively, have smartphones, and work on laptops and tablets. Information about a firm and its clients is publicized on the law firm website and on social media. State-of-the-art computer devices

---

7. VERIZON 2021 DBIR, *supra* note 2, figures 20 and 21.

8. Dennis Lawrence, *The Dark Web Secrets of Law Firms*, AON, https://www.aon.com /cyber-solutions/thinking/the-dark-web-secrets-of-law-firms/ (last visited Aug. 25, 2021).

9. Tyler Combs, *Breach of Trust: How Threat Actors Leverage Confidential Information against Law Firms*, ADVINTEL (Feb. 12, 2020), https://www.advanced-intel.com/post/breach -of-trust-how-threat-actors-leverage-confidential-information-against-law-firms. "For example, since November 2020, AdvIntel has identified the RDP credentials of 17 law firms offered for sale in top-tier DarkWeb marketplaces." *See* Paolo Passeri, *The Biggest Data Breaches of 2021*, HACKMAGEDDON (Feb. 17, 2021), https://www.hackmageddon.com/2021/02/17/the -biggest-data-breaches-of-2021/ (The Hackmageddon website is updated frequently, providing a near real-time ongoing summary of events.); Rafia Shaikh, *UK: Top 500 Legal Firms Have Over a Million of Their Credentials Leaked on the Dark Web*, WCCFTECH (Jan. 22, 2018, 9:36 AM), https://wccftech.com/top-500-legal-firms-data-breach/.

are the cornerstones of "electronic courtrooms" around the country. Technology varies extensively, depending upon the firm, but the risks are similar.

IT Operations. Many law firms operate data centers with global networks of computers, servers, mobile devices, websites, and social media. These firms perform the full range of information security, data governance, preservation, and incident response functions. Other firms outsource these responsibilities. Law firms are using cloud computing for storing and processing client and firm records. Many have implemented "bring your own device" (BYOD) or "bring your own technology" (BYOT) for their workforce, which leads to managing the risk of multiple types of devices on the firm's network.

IoT in the Workplace. The convergence of information technology and physical operations in which computers control a broad array of consumer and industrial devices and systems presents new security concerns for law practices. Some experts predict that by 2025, more than 30.9 billion devices will be connected to the Internet and to each other.[10] As law offices modernize, they will likely include IoT devices such as security cameras, wireless locks, motion sensors, automated lighting and window shades, and climate control, such as a smart thermostat that adjusts office temperatures based on changes in the weather. Technologists are creating the "infrastructure of the smart office." Their goal is to create an "intelligent workplace," including smartphones, wearables, and applications that then provide solutions to problems, facilitate decision making, measure performance, and take care of most routine tasks.[11]

Lawyers Working Remotely. The pandemic created an immediate need for lawyers to work remotely, complicating the technology landscape and

---

10. Knud Lasse Lueth, *State of the IoT 2020: 12 Billion IoT Connections, Surpassing Non-IoT for the First Time*, IoT ANALYTICS (Nov. 19, 2020), https://iot-analytics.com /state-of-the-iot-2020-12-billion-iot-connections-surpassing-non-iot-for-the-first-time/.

11. Jason Corsello, *What the Internet of Things Will Bring to the Workplace*, WIRED, https://www.wired.com/insights/2013/11/what-the-internet-of-things-will-bring-to-the-work place/; Sara Angeles, *8 Ways the Internet of Things Will Change the Way We Work*, BUS. NEWS DAILY (Jan. 18, 2019), https://www.businessnewsdaily.com/4858-internet-of-things -will-change-work.html.

introducing numerous cybersecurity risks.[12] The following are examples of some of the challenges law practices must address when lawyers and employees work in remote locations and with devices, such as BYOD, over which the firm has little or no control.[13] Law firms should confirm they have addressed these concerns and are protecting their remote workforces (and themselves) from threats.

- **Phishing and Malware.** Lawyers' computers and smartphones issued by the firm, personal devices used for work, and devices that can be accessed by family members could be the target of phishing scams. Once on a device, malware easily steals legal information. Multitasking and having work and personal e-mail on the same device may increase the risk of someone responding to a phishing e-mail.[14]
- **Authentication.** Stolen or guessed passwords account for a majority of data breaches. Many employees use the same password for personal and work accounts, or across multiple accounts.[15] That, combined with the

---

12. J.R. Raphael, *8 Mobile Security Threats You Should Take Seriously: Mobile Malware? Other Mobile Security Threats Are More Pressing. Every Enterprise Should Have Its Eye on These Eight Issues*, CSO ONLINE (Mar. 1, 2021, 2:00 AM), https://www.csoonline.com/article/3241727/8-mobile-security-threats-you-should-take-seriously.html.

13. *See* Cybersecurity & Infrastructure Security Agency, *CISA Telework Essentials Toolkit, Executive Leaders Drive Cybersecurity Strategy, Investment, Culture*, https://www.cisa.gov/sites/default/files/publications/20-02019b%20-%20Telework_Essentials-08272020-508v2.pdf; CISA, *Telework Reference Materials for the Federal Government*, CISA, https://www.cisa.gov/telework-reference-materials-federal-government (last visited Aug. 25, 2021); *Cybersecurity Experts Provide Remote Work Best Practices*, CIO.GOV (July 8, 2020), https://www.cio.gov/cybersecurity-experts-provide-remote-work-best-practices/; CISA, *Security Tip (ST15-002): Home Network Security*, CISA (Nov. 3, 2020), https://us-cert.cisa.gov/ncas/tips/ST15-002.

14. BITGLASS, 2020 REMOTE WORKFORCE SECURITY REPORT, https://pages.bitglass.com/rs/418-ZAL-815/images/CDFY20Q2RemoteWorkforceReport%282%29.pdf?&utm_source=email&utm_campaign=cd-fy20q2_-_remote_workforce_report&mkt_tok=NDE4LVpBTC04MTUAAAF9bURrFcT47Sw9twye8SKtn5JZiCeLR-9KVBNt8BvMRZplpG52knhEy-wXaaJ2XrDcDvHfxFRpzHN_V4L1Pe1KOA8qg4FbnuGpzeUW9OxFT4z6l7A (65 percent of employers allow their employees to access company applications from unmanaged, personal devices.).

15. For example, in 2018, the MyFitnessPal app suffered a massive breach that compromised user data, including passwords. In 2020, two insurance companies, Independence Blue Cross and AmeriHealth New Jersey, both reported that their member portals had been improperly accessed by hackers reusing the credentials stolen in the 2018 attack. Martin Gontovnikas, *The 9 Worst Recent Data Breaches of 2020*, AUTH0 BLOG (Jan. 14, 2021), https://auth0.com/blog/the-nine-worst-recent-data-breaches-of-2020/#6--Credential-Stuffing-Attacks-Hit-Insurance-Portals.

use of weak passwords, creates attack vectors for criminals seeking to steal law firm data. Many work devices have no mandated measures in place to secure accessible corporate data and have no password, PIN, or biometric security guarding their devices.

- **Mobile Apps.** Privacy statements are often ignored and quickly accepted so the user can access an application. As a result, users regularly grant permission for an app to see and transfer data that should remain private, causing data leakage and potential damage.

- **Software Updates and Patching.** Many smartphones, tablets, and smaller connected IoT devices do not have a process for regular software updates, or a guarantee that updates will be carried out, leaving the devices with known vulnerabilities that hackers can exploit.

- **Insecure Wi-Fi.** Computing devices in home offices or other locations may be connected to Wi-Fi with weak security—improperly configured home networks or public Wi-Fi networks—allowing hackers access to private information. Law firms should confirm how attorneys and staff are connecting to the corporate network to ensure that the connection is secure.

- **Video Conferencing.** The frequent use of videoconferencing, which permits the platforms to access the user's camera, microphone, and shared documents, and often captures the entire array of files stored on the device, puts law firm data at risk.[16] Collaboration software presents serious risks as well.[17] Huge amounts of data flow through platforms such as Teams, Slack, WebEx, and Zoom with video and audio streams, texts, and files. Through targeted attacks, criminals can drop malicious

---

16. *See, e.g.*, Lee Mathews, *500,000 Hacked Zoom Accounts Given Away for Free on the Dark Web*, FORBES (Apr. 13, 2020, 4:59 PM), https://www.forbes.com/sites /leemathews/2020/04/13/500000-hacked-zoom-accounts-given-away-for-free-on-the -dark-web/?sh=28e22ecb58c5. Computer: Preferences: Security and Privacy: "Screen Recording—Allow the apps below to record the contents of your screen, even while using other apps." The credentials of over 500,000 Zoom teleconferencing accounts were found for sale on the dark web and in hacker forums. E-mail addresses, passwords, personal meeting URLs, and host keys are said to have been collected through a credential stuffing attack.

17. Karen Roby, *The Boom in Collaboration Software Creates Extra Security Risks*, TECHREPUBLIC (Apr. 22, 2021, 1:05 PM), https://www.techrepublic.com/article /the-boom-in-collaboration-software-creates-extra-security-risks/.

documents or data into one of these channels. Insider threats, cyber fraud, and sharing of critical information are all present.

Identifying the risks is difficult, because the Chief Information Officer (CIO) and the security team often do not have a full understanding of what is taking place in that massive amount of data.

- **Legal Outsourcing.** It is now common practice for law firms to outsource a variety of services to external vendors and business partners located domestically and overseas. The global legal process outsourcing market was valued at $5.2 billion in 2018 and is expected to grow at a rate of 30 percent through 2025. Law offices that focus on their core businesses and outsource non-core tasks are expected to drive the market.[18]

Legal organizations interconnect their networks electronically for a variety of purposes, ranging from information technology (IT), finance, accounting, and human resources to procurement, contract management, data analytics, and investigations.[19] Legal process outsourcing is a growing trend. Law firms and corporate legal departments are outsourcing legal work such as litigation support for document review, due diligence, legal research, and law libraries.[20] Much of the billions of dollars law firms spend on e-discovery services and forensic investigations is used to hire outside vendors.

This ever-growing paradigm presents heightened risk for law firms and for lawyers, who remain responsible for potentially widespread damage from cyberattacks—especially for systems and services managed externally—and accountable to clients, the courts, and entities with whom they have contracts. Recent breaches suggest that key software products used by law firms must now be considered high-critical, high-severity risk and monitored for new developments risks, vulnerabilities, and exploits. With

---

18. Legal Process Outsourcing Market Size, Share & Trends Analysis Report by Location (Offshore, On-Shore), by Service (e-discovery, Patent Support, Litigation Support), and Segment Forecasts, 2019 2025, at 1 (2019).

19. DELOITTE CONSULTING LLP, *2020 Global Outsourcing Survey*, DELOITTE, https://www2.deloitte.com/global/en/pages/operations/articles/gx-global-outsourcing-survey.html (last visited Aug. 25, 2021).

20. Chambers & Partners, Outsourcing 2020, https://practiceguides.chambers.com/practice-guides/outsourcing-2020 (last visited Aug. 25, 2021).

law firms' core business models centered on discretion and privacy, rigorous security hygiene for key external interfaces and third-party software is critical. The expectation of security is growing, and therefore the responsibility for protecting information, whether held within the firm or outsourced to a third party, is also increasing.

B. Sensitive and Confidential Data at Risk

Lawyers must safeguard client records, as well as their own business records, including IP, attorney work product, and financial and employment records, to name a few. Electronic records are an integral part of every lawyer's business.[21] Throughout the course of representing clients, lawyers receive volumes of sensitive and confidential data—attorney-client privileged information; client trade secrets; all types of personally identifiable information (PII); and financial, health care, law enforcement, and many other types of records.

Law practices also receive sensitive and confidential information through litigation or compulsory process, or as a result of investigations or adversary actions against individuals and organizations. In these cases, not only adversaries but also innocent third parties are often swept up in lawsuits or other legal proceedings. Given that lawyers have access to the most sensitive and secret information in civil and criminal cases—including private investigations, records sealed or under a protective order, classified data, grand jury records, and other information with requirements for secrecy—it is critical that this information is protected from breaches and unlawful exposure.

In addition, law firms acquire a staggering array of sensitive information in e-discovery. It is a sobering fact that much of the data and information obtained by law practices may have been created, used, and maintained in a secure environment, and then transferred, often without the knowledge, agreement, or consent of the individual or organization that created or collected the information, to an environment such as the office of opposing

---

21. See Chapter 4 for an in-depth discussion of the responsibilities of lawyers to protect sensitive and confidential information.

counsel or an e-discovery vendor where the extent of security protections may be unknown or are not assured.[22]

To protect confidential information, lawyers and law firms must know what data they have, where it resides, its level of sensitivity, and how it is secured. In addition to the more obvious places for data, such as computer servers, desktop and laptop computers, mobile devices, and cloud storage, information may reside in other, somewhat less expected locations. For example, computer backups may contain significant amounts of sensitive information. Also, confidential client data may be downloaded from e-mail onto a mobile device and then saved locally. These devices are likely to be linked to the user, not the law firm, which means that the sensitive data could potentially be backed up to the user's personal cloud account, completely outside law firm control, unless specific controls are in place to prevent this.

C.   Protecting the Confidentiality, Integrity, and Availability of Data

Massive data breaches are occurring with alarming frequency. As a result, millions of records have been breached, leading to the compromise of sensitive personal data and IP; critical systems becoming unavailable; and lawyers suffering reputational loss, undermining of trust, and lawsuits. The objectives of hackers and cybercriminals are to undermine the pillars of information security: breach the *confidentiality* of personal records, compromise the *integrity* of the data, and make critical information systems *unavailable*.

Confidentiality. In light of the massive data breaches in recent years, much attention has been given to protecting the *confidentiality* of personal data and sensitive information. The number of records exposed increased to a staggering 36 billion in 2020.[23] The largest data breaches—spanning the financial, health care, retail, technology, and government sectors—illustrate

---

22. *BlueVoyant Launches Its Sector 17-State of Cybersecurity in the Legal Sector Report*, *supra* note 1. Until a law firm has conducted a risk assessment and adopted a comprehensive information security program, it will not be in a position to vouch for an appropriate level of security and its ability to protect sensitive and confidential information, if requested by a client or the court.

23. Maria Henriquez, *The Top 10 Data Breaches of 2020*, Security Mag. (Dec. 3, 2020), https://www.securitymagazine.com/articles/94076-the-top-10-data-breaches-of-2020.

the heightened risk to millions of individuals when large datasets of sensitive personal information are compromised.[24]

Databases such as these are vulnerable to attacks from both insiders and hackers. The vulnerabilities of databases are well documented and include the use of default and weak passwords, failure to patch known vulnerabilities, misconfigurations, and granting excessive privileges to users. Specific security measures must be taken to protect personal data in the databases of legal organizations.[25]

The Intelligence Community's (IC) 2021 Annual Threat Assessment[26] identifies prominent cyber adversaries—nation-states (Russia, China, North Korea, and Iran), terrorist groups, and cybercriminals. In addition, "hacktivists" launch cyberattacks that are politically or ideologically motivated. The IC assessed that cyber threats from nation-states and their surrogates will remain acute. "Foreign states use cyber operations to steal information, influence populations, and damage industry, including physical and

---

24. A website that goes by the name "Information Is Beautiful" provides a visualization of hundreds of the massive data breaches that have affected the private sector and government, http://www.informationisbeautiful.net/visualizations/worlds-biggest-data-breaches-hacks/. The following is a sample of the largest of these breaches: CAM4 (adult live-streaming website), 10.88 billion records/extensive PII (2020); Keepnet Labs (U.K. security company), 5 billion records (2020); Sina Weibo (Chinese social network), 538 million records (2020); Marriott International, 530 million customers (2020); Microsoft, 250 million records (2020); TrueDialog, 1 billion records (2019), highly sensitive data, millions of SMS messages; First American Financial Corporation, 885 million customers (2019); Facebook, 540 million users (2019); Dream Market (data for sale from hacked websites), 620 million records (2019); Canva (graphic design tool), 139 million records (2019); Equifax, 148 million consumers (2017); Anthem Blue Cross, Indiana, 78.8 million health care records (largest health care breach) (2015); U.S. Office of Personnel Management, 21.5 million high-level government employees and judges (2015). *See* Abi Tyas Tunggal, *The 57 Biggest Data Breaches (Updated for 2021)*, UpGuard (Aug. 19, 2021), https://www.upguard.com/blog/biggest-data-breaches.

25. Security measures that should be taken to protect personal data in databases include (1) inventory your databases; (2) classify systems with sensitive data; (3) scan for vulnerabilities and misconfigurations, keep up to date with security patches, enforce strong passwords, and audit configurations and settings; (4) identify privileged users; (5) validate access to sensitive data and assign restricted permissions on tables with sensitive information; (6) prioritize and fix what you can; (7) monitor database activity; and (8) encrypt data in transit and at rest using network-level encryption and column-level encryption; *see* Lucy L. Thomson and Dr. Robert Thibadeau, *Security Challenges of the Big Data Ecosystem Require a Laser-Like Focus on Risk*, 12 SciTech Law 6–11, 19 (2016).

26. Office of the Dir. of Nat'l Intelligence, Annual Threat Assessment of the U.S. Intelligence Community 5–7 (2021).

digital critical infrastructure."[27] Many of these threat actors have significant resources, funded by nation-states or through sophisticated money-laundering operations.

Integrity. As early as 2015, the IC Worldwide Threat Assessment recognized the increasingly critical problem that future cyberattacks will be conducted to compromise the *integrity* of information, with a potentially devastating impact on key information systems that constitute the underpinnings of the economy:

> In the future . . . we might also see more cyber operations that will change or manipulate electronic information in order to compromise its integrity (i.e. accuracy and reliability) instead of deleting it or disrupting access to it. Decision-making by senior government officials (civilian and military), corporate executives, investors, or others will be impaired if they cannot trust the information they are receiving.[28]

Availability. In recent years, cyberattacks designed to restrict the *availability* of websites and services have become more aggressive, primarily with distributed denial of service (DDoS) attacks in which multiple compromised computers, often infected with a Trojan virus,[29] are used to overwhelm a single targeted system; computer viruses that delete user data; or ransomware that encrypts data and demands payment for the encryption key to restore

---

27. *Id.* at 20–21.

28. The Hon. James R. Clapper, Dir. of Nat'l Intelligence, Statement for the Record to the Senate Armed Servs. Comm., Worldwide Threat Assessment of the U.S. Intelligence Community 3–4 (2015).

29. A "Trojan" virus is a type of malware disguised as legitimate software that will enable a cybercriminal to gain access to a user's system and spy on him, steal sensitive data, and gain backdoor access.

access to the data.[30] Law firms have become targets of hackers seeking to profit from ransomware attacks.[31] Doubling down, ransomware groups have used DDoS attacks to take down victims' websites or networks until they negotiate to pay the requested ransoms.[32]

II. Lawyers and Law Firms Are Prime Targets: The Significant Resulting Damage

Due to the huge volume of critical information lawyers collect about companies and individuals, hackers are targeting law firms. Much of the valuable data law firms hold—particularly IP, strategic business data, and knowledge of M&A and international transactions—carries obligations associated with attorney-client privileged data.

Similarly, protective orders imposed by courts to preserve the secrecy of sensitive data may be violated in the event of a data breach. Although Rule 26(b) of the Federal Rules of Civil Procedure allows broad discovery on a variety of issues, Rule 26(c)(7) allows a court to issue an order that "a trade secret or other confidential research, development, or commercial information not be revealed or be revealed only in a designated way." If a data breach were to occur at a firm subject to such an order, arguably that order would be violated and the firm might face serious consequences.

---

30. In the first widespread DDoS attack, the Murai botnet scoured the web for IoT devices protected only by factory-default usernames and passwords. It then enlisted these vulnerable IoT devices such as Internet-connected cameras and DVRs to send junk traffic and temporarily overwhelm popular Internet sites including Twitter, Amazon, Tumblr, Reddit, Spotify, and Netflix; these websites could no longer accommodate legitimate visitors or users. Josh Fruhlinger, *The Mirai Botnet Explained: How Teen Scammers and CCTV Cameras Almost Brought Down the Internet*, CSOONLINE (Mar. 9, 2018, 3:00 AM), https://www.csoonline .com/article/3258748/the-mirai-botnet-explained-how-teen-scammers-and-cctv-cameras -almost-brought-down-the-internet.html; *see* VERIZON 2021 DBIR, *supra* note 2, Denial of Service 35–40 ("this is often one of the easiest threats to mitigate effectively.").

31. *Ransomware Attacks Targeting Attorneys on the Rise*, USI AFFINITY (Jan. 7, 2021), https://insurancefocus.usiaffinity.com/2021/01/ransomware-attacks-targeting-attorneys-on -the-rise.html.

32. Ax Sharma, *Insurer AXA Hit by Ransomware after Dropping Support for Ransom Payments*, BLEEPING COMPUTER (May 16, 2021, 12:24 PM), https://www.bleepingcomputer.com /news/security/insurer-axa-hit-by-ransomware-after-dropping-support-for-ransom-payments/.

From a business perspective, a breach of security or information loss by a law firm can have significant negative effects. The consequences to clients and even innocent third parties of a data breach can be very serious, potentially subjecting them to identity theft, fraud, negative publicity, and even financial ruin. If a firm loses client information, the reputational harm alone may lead a client to take its business elsewhere or potential clients to turn to other firms. For lawyers in the firm, a data breach may result in ethical violations that have serious impacts.[33]

Many different types of attacks have occurred against lawyers and law practices. Millions of files have been compromised, leading not only to data loss but also to reputational loss, lawsuits, and opportunity costs. To prevent data breaches, it is essential to analyze and understand the root causes of the security failures and to develop a specific plan to address them.

The following are examples of the increasingly dangerous threats to sensitive data and the heightened need for lawyers and law firms to address information security risks, build strong information security programs, and utilize necessary security controls. This is not only good business practice, but it will also help firms avoid the high costs associated with responding to data breaches, potential liability, negative press, embarrassment, and ultimately loss of trust of clients, judges, and the public.[34]

A. Largest Law Firm Breach

The law firm Mossack Fonseca, located in Panama, was involved in the largest data breach ever in terms of the volume of records stolen—with irreparable harm. Over 40 years, the firm had set up hundreds of offshore companies, collecting and storing a treasure trove of individuals' confidential

---

33. Chapter 6 provides an in-depth discussion of the ethical requirements lawyers must meet in safeguarding sensitive and confidential data and records.

34. The high costs of responding to data breaches in terms of expenditures for detection, escalation, notification, and response, along with legal, investigative, and administrative expenses, customer defections, opportunity loss, reputation management, and costs associated with customer support such as information hotlines and credit monitoring subscriptions, have been well documented. PONEMON INST. LLC & IBM, COST OF A DATA BREACH REPORT 2020, https://www.ibm.com/security/data-breach. These costs are likely to rise as the notification requirements in the data breach laws become more stringent, increasing the numbers of individuals who must be notified; and the liability imposed by courts and administrative agencies for data breaches increases significantly.

financial information in the process.[35] As a result of the breach and its fall-out, the entire firm of 40 offices closed its doors in March 2018.[36]

The breach (referred to as "leaks" by the media) included publication online of 11.5 million confidential documents dating from the 1970s through late 2015. The 2.6 terabytes of leaked data included 4.8 million e-mails, 3 million database files, 2.2 million PDFs, 1.1 million images, and 320,000 text documents. The compromised data exposed the existence of offshore accounts of world leaders, company executives, celebrities, and others. The firm's leaked internal files contained information on more than 214,000 offshore entities tied to 12 current or former heads of state, 140 politicians, and others.

The source of the breach, using the pseudonym John Doe, sent encrypted files anonymously to the German newspaper *Süddeutsche Zeitung* and shared them with more than 100 other media outlets. The U.S.–based International Consortium of Investigative Journalists (ICIJ) published a searchable database of 214,000 offshore entities uncovered by the "Panama Papers" leak.[37] In an open letter published on the Panama Papers website, Doe announced that he stole the information to expose the use of shell companies to "carry out a wide array of serious crimes that go beyond evading taxes," and said that he believed members of Mossack Fonseca "should have to answer for their roles in these crimes."[38]

International news outlets published articles on the leak, revealing corruption on a massive scale. Repercussions from the leak were felt around

---

35. Aliah D. Wright, *Panama Papers: What Data Breach Means for Law Firms*, SOC'Y FOR HUMAN RES. MGMT. (Apr. 7, 2016), https://www.shrm.org/resourcesandtools/hr-topics/technology/pages/panama-papers-and-what-the-data-breach-means-for-law-firms.aspx; Kirk Semple, Azam Ahmed & Eric Lipton, *Panama Papers Leak Casts Light on a Law Firm Founded on Secrecy*, N.Y. TIMES (Apr. 6, 2016), https://www.nytimes.com/2016/04/07/world/americas/panama-papers-leak-casts-light-on-a-law-firm-founded-on-secrecy.html.

36. Will Fitzgibbon, *Panama Papers Law Firm Mossack Fonseca Closes Its Doors*, INT'L CONSORTIUM OF INVESTIGATIVE JOURNALISTS (ICIJ) (Mar. 14, 2018), https://www.icij.org/investigations/panama-papers/panama-papers-law-firm-mossack-fonseca-closes-doors/.

37. Marina Walker Guevara, *ICIJ Releases Database Panama Papers Offshore Company Datas*, ICIJ (May 9, 2016), https://panamapapers.icij.org/blog/20160509-offshore-database-release.html; Jane McCallion et al., *Panama Papers: Emma Watson Named in Leaked Documents*, ITPRO (Nov. 5, 2016), http://www.itpro.co.uk/data-leakage/26293/panama-papers-emma-watson-named-in-leaked-documents.

38. McCallion et al., *supra* note 37.

the world. The prime ministers of Iceland and Pakistan resigned. Following a U.S. Department of Justice criminal investigation into the leak and the tax avoidance schemes it revealed, an indictment was returned against four individuals who allegedly helped U.S. taxpayer clients of Mossack Fonseca conceal assets and investments, and the income they generated, through a complex trail of offshore shell corporations and bogus foundations used to disguise the beneficial ownership of huge amounts of money.[39] In 2020 a U.S. taxpayer and his accountant pleaded guilty to various fraud and money laundering crimes and received substantial prison sentences.[40] The case continues against two former Mossack Fonseca employees.

The Mossack Fonseca breach that compromised the confidential records of the entire firm was the result of the failure to provide appropriate data security.[41] The firm employed outdated software—older versions of open-source web server software—with critical vulnerabilities that were widely known among hackers, including for its customer portal. Updates to the software were available, but the firm had not updated or properly patched its web server. Security experts suggested that because Mossack Fonseca's web server software was many months out of date, the security failure was particularly egregious, considering the sensitivity of their clients' information. The firm failed to take the most rudimentary steps to protect their confidential client data.[42]

B. Ransomware Attacks: Prominent Legal Organizations Targeted

Ransomware, an insidious type of malware that encrypts, or locks, valuable digital files and demands a ransom to release them, is a massive cyber threat for organizations, particularly small- and medium-size businesses such

---

39. Will Fitzgibbon, *From Front Pages to Prison Time: Behind the Scenes of a Panama Papers Criminal Case*, ICIJ (Apr. 23, 2021), https://www.icij.org/investigations/panama-papers/from-front-pages-to-prison-time-behind-the-scenes-of-a-panama-papers-criminal-case/.

40. Press Release, U.S. Att'ys Office, S. Dist. of N.Y., U.S. Taxpayer in Panama Papers Investigation Sentenced to 4 Years in Prison (Sept. 21, 2020), https://www.justice.gov/usao-sdny/pr/us-taxpayer-panama-papers-investigation-sentenced-4-years-prison.

41. *The Panama Papers: Exposing the Rogue Offshore Finance Industry*, ICIJ, https://panamapapers.icij.org/ (last visited Aug. 25, 2021).

42. Jason Bloomberg, *Cybersecurity Lessons Learned from "Panama Papers" Breach*, FORBES (Apr. 21, 2016), https://www.forbes.com/sites/jasonbloomberg/2016/04/21/cybersecurity-lessons-learned-from-panama-papers-breach/#44829632003f.

as law firms.[43] Twenty-four hundred U.S. companies, local governments, health care facilities, and schools were victims of ransomware in 2020.[44] The FBI warned that "more than just money is at stake" and "ransomware has become a serious national security threat and public health and safety concern." "Ransomware attacks are becoming more targeted, sophisticated, and costly."[45] Lawyers and law firms, as well as bar associations, have been targeted. Also, sophisticated cyber adversaries are increasingly moving downstream from law firms themselves, compromising legal supply chains.[46]

The threat continues to grow more serious.[47] Following the attack that led to the May 2021 shutdown of the Colonial Pipeline,[48] whose 5,500-mile pipeline from Texas to New Jersey provides nearly half of the gasoline and diesel fuel to the U.S. East Coast, Department of Homeland Security (DHS) Secretary Alejandro Mayorkas said "there's no company too

---

43. *FBI Scams and Safety: Ramsomware*, FBI, https://www.fbi.gov/scams-and-safety /common-scams-and-crimes/ransomware (last visited Aug. 25, 2021); *Ransomware: What It Is & What to Do about It*, https://www.ic3.gov/Content/PDF/Ransomware_Fact_Sheet.pdf.

44. *See* FBI, INTERNET CRIME REPORT: 2020, at 14, 19 (2020); Rob Sobers, *81 Ransomware Statistics, Data, Trends and Facts for 2021—Top Ransomware Statistics*, VARONIS (July 6, 2021), https://www.varonis.com/blog/ransomware-statistics-2021/; to view victim organizations, see *Ransomware Attacks BETA*, INFORMATION IS BEAUTIFUL (July 10, 2021), https:// informationisbeautiful.net/visualizations/ransomware-attacks/.

45. *High-Impact Ransomware Attacks Threaten U.S. Businesses and Organizations*, FBI Alert I-100219-PSA (Oct. 2, 2019), https://www.ic3.gov/Media/Y2019 /PSA191002; *see* Mathew J. Schwartz, *Ransomware Gangs' Ruthlessness Leads to Bigger Profits*, BANKINFOSECURITY (May 28, 2020), https://www.bankinfosecurity.com/ ransomware-gangs-ruthlessness-leads-to-bigger-profits-a-14349.

46. *See* Jon Boyens et al., *Cyber Supply Chain Risk Management Practices for Systems and Organizations*, NIST (2021), https://csrc.nist.gov/publications/detail/sp/800-161/rev-1 /draft; Catalin Cimpanu, *Ransomware Incident at Major Cloud Provider Disrupts Real Estate, Title Industry*, THE RECORD (July 19, 2021), https://therecord.media/ransomware-incident-at -major-cloud-provider-disrupts-real-estate-title-industry/. Operating several data centers across the United States, Cloudstar is primarily known in the mortgage, title insurance, real estate, legal, finance, and local government sector, where it provides services like virtual desktop hosting, software-as-a-service offerings, and other managed cloud infrastructure, which underpin many companies' IT infrastructures.

47. The FBI and CISA have issued dozens of alerts warning of the dangers of the various ransomware attacks and providing detailed guidance on how to address them and protect company's infrastructure and critical records and data. FBI *Ransomware*, *supra* note 43; *see also Official Alerts & Statements—CISA*, STOP RANSOMWARE, https://www.cisa.gov/stopran somware/official-alerts-statements-cisa (last visited Aug. 25, 2021).

48. Collin Eaton & Dustin Volz, *Colonial Pipeline CEO Tells Why He Paid Hackers a $4.4 Million Ransom*, WALL ST. J. (May 19, 2021, 4:51 PM), https://www.wsj.com/articles /colonial-pipeline-ceo-tells-why-he-paid-hackers-a-4-4-million-ransom-11621435636.

small to suffer a ransomware attack. We are seeing increasingly small- and medium-sized businesses suffer a ransomware attack."[49] The White House warned American businesses to take urgent security measures to protect against ransomware attacks, as hackers were shifting their tactics from stealing data to disrupting critical infrastructure.[50] Totally disrupting the pipeline, the attackers froze the business records of Colonial Pipeline, not the operational controls over the pipeline. As a result, the company shut down the pipeline because it could not get access to its billing systems or monitor the flow of petroleum to specific locations. With billing systems out of reach, the company had no way to charge customers for deliveries.[51] The FBI confirmed that the DarkSide hacking group based in Eastern Europe was responsible for the ransomware attack.[52] Subsequently, using innovative techniques, law enforcement was able to track the transfers of bitcoin, identify approximately 63.7 bitcoins representing the proceeds of the victim's ransom payment (valued at approximately $2.3 million), and obtain a warrant to seize the ransom payments pursuant to criminal and civil forfeiture statutes.[53]

Shortly thereafter, meat supplier JBS announced that it was the victim of a cyberattack, attributed by the FBI to the REvil (aka Sodinokibi)

---

49. White House, Press Briefing by Press Secretary Jen Psaki, Secretary of Energy Jennifer Granholm, and Secretary of Homeland Security Alejandro Mayorkas, May 11, 2021, WH.GOV (May 11, 2021, 2:13 PM), https://www.whitehouse.gov/briefing-room /press-briefings/2021/05/11/press-briefing-by-press-secretary-jen-psaki-secretary-of-energy -jennifer-granholm-and-secretary-of-homeland-security-alejandro-mayorkas-may-11-2021/ (Statement of DHS Secretary Alejandro Mayorkas).

50. David Sanger & Nicole Perlroth, *White House Warns Companies to Act Now on Ransomware Defenses: An Open Letter Urged Them to Take Many of the Defensive Steps That the Federal Government Requires of Its Agencies and Contractors*, N.Y. TIMES (July 8, 2021), https://www.nytimes.com/2021/06/03/us/politics/ransomware-cybersecurity infrastructure.html.

51. *Id.*

52. *FBI Statement on Compromise of Colonial Pipeline Networks*, FBI NEWS (May 10, 2021), https://www.fbi.gov/news/pressrel/press-releases/fbi-statement-on-compromise-of-colo nial-pipeline-networks. ("The FBI confirms that the Darkside ransomware is responsible for the compromise of the Colonial Pipeline networks. We continue to work with the company and our government partners on the investigation.").

53. Department of Justice: Office of Public Affairs, *Department of Justice Seizes $2.3 Million in Cryptocurrency Paid to the Ransomware Extortionists Darkside*, JUSTICE NEWS (June 7, 2021), https://www.justice.gov/opa/pr/department-justice-seizes -23-million-cryptocurrency-paid-ransomware-extortionists-darkside.

ransomware group.[54] The White House urged businesses to implement the best practices set forth in the Executive Order on Improving the Nation's Cybersecurity, EO 14028 (May 12, 2021):

> The private sector [] has a critical responsibility to protect against these threats. All organizations must recognize that no company is safe from being targeted by ransomware, regardless of size or location. To understand your risk, business executives should immediately convene their leadership teams to discuss the ransomware threat and review corporate security posture and business continuity plans to ensure you have the ability to continue or quickly restore operations.[55]

Escalating Extortion Demands. Ransomware can make information systems unavailable and enable attackers to steal and exfiltrate sensitive personal data and IP. Further, new tactics are even more insidious. Lawyers who are victims of ransomware attacks find themselves at the mercy of hackers pursuing a multipronged attack strategy to the detriment of law offices. Criminals plant malware to embed themselves on the network, steal and exfiltrate huge troves of so-called ace trophy data, then encrypt the network files to make them unavailable. They demand large ransom payments to regain access to the network and the data. The financial extortion may not be limited to getting back access to the files—hackers are also posting stolen firm and client data on the dark web, or leaking it more broadly to the world, and at the same time making extortion demands to both restore access to the data and information system and not publicly release the stolen data, resulting in the breach of client confidences and trust.

Notorious Attacks on Law Firms. Law offices have been swept up in the ransomware attacks. In May 2020, the cybercriminal gang REvil/Sodinokibi stole legal documents from the New York City "law firm of the

---

54. *FBI Statement on JBS Cyberattack*, FBI NEWS (June 2, 2021), https://www.fbi.gov /news/pressrel/press-releases/fbi-statement-on-jbs-cyberattack.

55. Memorandum from Anne Neuberger, Deputy Assistant to the President and Deputy National Security Advisor for Cyber and Emerging Technology to Corporate Executives and Business Leaders, What We Urge You to Do to Protect against the Threat of Ransomware (June 2, 2021).

stars," Grubman Shire Meiselas & Sacks (GSMSLaw). The trove of data allegedly stolen—a total of 756 gigabytes—included contracts, nondisclosure agreements, phone numbers and e-mail addresses, and "personal correspondence" of multiple music and entertainment figures, including Lady Gaga, Madonna, Nicki Minaj, Bruce Springsteen, Christina Aguilera, Mariah Carey, Andrew Lloyd Webber, Luther Vandross, Rod Stewart, Jennifer Lopez, Cam Newton, Bette Midler, Elton John, Tom Cruise, Barbra Streisand, Priyanka Chopra, Robert DeNiro, David Letterman, John Oliver, and Run DMC.[56] The Sodinokibi hackers published a screenshot of the folders they had stolen from the law firm, along with excerpts from legal agreements signed by artists, and threatened to release the confidential documents on the dark web if the law firm refused to pay the demanded ransom of a substantial amount of bitcoins in exchange for the decryption key.[57]

The hackers initially demanded $21 million and published more than 2 gigabytes of Lady Gaga's contracts and other data on the dark web as proof of compromise. After finding files related to then–President Donald Trump, they doubled the ransomware price to $42 million and later published 169 e-mails related to Trump.[58] GSMSLaw had reportedly refused to pay the ransom, as recommended by the FBI. The firm recovered some of the lost data through individuals it hired privately; however, much of the stolen data is still at large and available for purchase online.[59]

Another hacker group, Maze, focused on the legal industry, hacking firms in Texas and Oregon.[60] Active since May 2019, Maze was particularly dangerous because it threatened to leak confidential data if the ransom was not paid. In January 2021, Maze attacked three small law firms in South

---

56. Naveen Goud, *Ransomware Attack on Grubman Shire Meiselas & Sacks Law Firm*, CYBERSECURITY INSIDERS, https://www.cybersecurity-insiders.com/ransomware-attack-on -grubman-shire-meiselas-sacks-law-firm/ (last visited Aug. 25, 2021).

57. Pierluigi Paganini, *Sodinokibi Gang Hacked Law Firm of the Celebrities and Threatens to Release the Docs*, SECURITY AFFAIRS (May 9, 2020), https://securityaffairs.co/word press/102960/cyber-crime/sodinokibi-gang-hacked-stars-law-firm.html.

58. A.J. Shankar, *Ransomware Attackers Take Aim at Law Firms*, FORBES (Mar. 12, 2021, 8:50 AM), https://www.forbes.com/sites/forbestechcouncil/2021/03/12 /ransomware-attackers-take-aim-at-law-firms/?sh=140dc7cca13e.

59. *Grubman Shire Meiselas & Sacks Attack and the Evolution of Ransomware*, EPIC (Oct. 13, 2020), https://epicbrokers.com/insights/grubman-shire-meiselas-sacks-attack/.

60. *Ransomware Attacks Targeting Attorneys on the Rise, supra* note 31.

Dakota in one 24-hour period. Maze published the names of the law firms on websites it used to announce its targets, threatening to reveal their data unless they agreed to pay a steep fee. More recently, Maze exposed the data of Baker Wotring LLP, a Texas law firm, including fee agreements and diaries from personal injury cases.[61]

In an October 2020 breach notification filing, the Seyfarth Shaw law firm of Chicago revealed that "a sophisticated and aggressive malware attack that appears to be ransomware" led to the temporary shutdown of many of the firm's systems.[62] In an update, the firm announced that it had restored all critical systems from the malware attack and none of its client or firm data was accessed or removed.

Earlier in the year, five law firms were targeted in a wave of ransomware attacks that included Texas firm Baker Wotring, whose data was released publicly in a "full dump."[63]

The first prominent ransomware attack on a law firm was against DLA Piper in 2017. The firm was hit with the NotPetya ransomware, which spread rapidly throughout the firm's servers and affected thousands of computers across its network, nearly shutting down the practice and causing enormous damages in direct and indirect costs.[64] This attack put the legal industry on high alert about the potential of breaches to debilitate even large global organizations.[65]

A ransomware attack compromised the network of the Illinois Attorney General's Office in April 2021.[66] It was reported that the ransomware

---

61. Patrick Smith, *Maze Hackers Publish Texas Law Firm's Confidential Data*, LAW.COM (Feb. 11, 2020, 9:44 AM), https://www.law.com/2020/02/11/maze-hackers-delist-texas-law-firm-as-ransom-pressures-mount/.

62. Pierluigi Paganini, *Leading Law Firm Seyfarth Shaw Discloses Ransomware Attack*, SECURITY AFFAIRS (Oct. 13, 2020), https://securityaffairs.co/wordpress/109435/malware/seyfarth-shaw-ransomware-attack.html.

63. Shankar, *supra* note 58.

64. Kim Nash, et al., *One Year after NotPetya Cyberattack, Firms Wrestle with Recovery Costs*, WALL ST. J., (June 27, 2018, 12:03 PM), https://www.wsj.com/articles/one-year-after-notpetya-companies-still-wrestle-with-financial-impacts-1530095906.

65. Jeff John Roberts, *Law Firm DLA Piper Reels under Cyber Attack, Fate of Files Unclear*, FORTUNE (June 29, 2017, 1:46 PM), https://fortune.com/2017/06/29/dla-piper-cyber-attack/.

66. Ill. Att'y Gen., *Illinois Attorney General's Office Issues Public Notification of Network Compromise* (Apr. 29, 2021), https://www.illinoisattorneygeneral.gov/pressroom/2021_04/20210429.html.

group DoppelPaymer posted 68 internal documents labeled "judgments entered," "shakedown cases," and "state prisoners" that were said to be from the state Attorney General's office.[67] According to the Attorney General's notice, the office maintains extensive amounts of sensitive personal information about the public, including names, addresses, e-mail addresses, Social Security numbers and driver's license numbers, and health insurance and medical and tax information.

The New York City Bar Association[68] and the Chicago Bar Association[69] both reported data breaches that involved the potential theft of credit card data. Hackers exploited vulnerabilities with the third-party commerce and management software iMIS on their websites to install malicious code that acted as a credit card skimmer and may have allowed an unauthorized individual to collect credit card data from transactions. "Importantly, the vulnerability, as well as the malicious code, has been removed," reported a Chicago Bar official. Similarly, the Mississippi Center for Legal Services and North Mississippi Rural Legal Services issued a public statement reporting that those organizations were hit by Ryuk ransomware on Christmas Eve.[70]

Other Risks. Ransomware attacks can expose attorneys to third-party liability. For example, a recent lawsuit filed in the District of Columbia alleged that a hacking incident involving a law firm exposed personal information of its former client, a Chinese citizen, to a hacker that had infiltrated

---

67. Rachel Hinton, *Raoul Sets Up Hotline on Computer Breach as "Ransomware" Group Posts Files Claimed Stolen from Attorney General's Office*, CHI. SUN TIMES (Apr. 29, 2021, 7:38 PM), https://chicago.suntimes.com/2021/4/29/22410356/attorney-general-raoul-office-hack -breach-ransomware-network-compromise (Illinois Attorney General Kwame Raoul's office said it "has not yet determined what personal information on its network is impacted," but it could include "names, addresses, email addresses, Social Security numbers, health insurance and medical information, tax information, and driver's license numbers.").

68. N.Y.C. Bar Ass'n, Security Breach Notification to the Maryland Attorney General (June 30, 2020), https://www.marylandattorneygeneral.gov/ID%20Theft%20Breach%20 Notices/2020/ITU-329330.pdf.

69. Chi. Bar Ass'n, Security Breach Notification to the Maryland Attorney General (July 13, 2020), https://www.marylandattorneygeneral.gov/ID%20Theft%20Breach%20Notices/2020 /itu-330787.pdf#search=Chicago%20Bar%20Association.

70. Public Notice, Mississippi Center for Legal Services and North Mississippi Rural Legal Services (Feb. 5, 2020), http://www.mscenterforlegalservices.org/wp-content/uploads/2020/02 /PUBLIC-NOTICE.pdf.

the law firm's servers.[71] Hackers blackmail firms hoping they will pay the ransom to avoid such a scenario.

Malware referred to as HIDDEN COBRA, used by North Korea for ransomware attacks, was identified in a joint alert in May 2020.[72] HIDDEN COBRA has long targeted U.S. industries and is allegedly behind some of the largest hacking incidents, including the global WannaCry ransomware cyberattack in 2017.[73] Throughout the Covid-19 pandemic, nation-state hacking groups continued to target health care providers with coronavirus-related campaigns.

In October 2020, the first of its kind joint alert from the federal Departments of Health and Human Services (HHS), DHS Cybersecurity & Infrastructure Security Agency (CISA), and the FBI warned of an increased and imminent cybercrime threat to U.S. hospitals and health care providers—to infect systems with ransomware for financial gain.[74] While directed to health care organizations, lawyers and their clients should heed its message. The joint cyber advisory warned health care providers to ensure that they take timely and reasonable precautions to protect their networks from these threats.

A CISA alert concluded that "[r]ansomware has rapidly emerged as the most visible cybersecurity risk playing out across our nation's networks. . . . We strongly urge you to consider ransomware infections as destructive attacks, not an event where you can simply pay off the bad guys and regain control of your network (do you really trust a cybercriminal?)."[75]

---

71. *Guo Wengui v. Clark Hill, PLC*, 440 F. Supp. 3d 30 (D.C.C. 2020).

72. CISA, FBI & the Department of Defense, *North Korean Malicious Cyber Activity* (May 20, 2020), https://us-cert.cisa.gov/northkorea.

73. In a ransomware attack in May 2017, hackers unleashed an attack that disabled nearly 230,000 computers globally. Named WannaCry, the ransomware affected tens of thousands of organizations in over 150 countries.

74. Joint cybersecurity advisory by the DHS CISA, the FBI, and the Department of Health and Human Services (HHS). CISA, *Alert (AA20-302A): Ransomware Activity Targeting the Healthcare and Public Health Sector*, CISA (Nov. 2, 2020), https://us-cert.cisa.gov/ncas/alerts /aa20-302a.

75. CISA, *CISA Insights—Ransomware Outbreak*, CISA (Aug. 25, 2021), https://www .cisa.gov/blog/2019/08/21/cisa-insights-ransomware-outbreak.

C. Advanced Persistent Threats and Compromise of the Software Supply Chain

Organizations that collect, process, or store large amounts of PII or IP and strategic business data of high value to criminals have become prime targets of state-sponsored hackers and overseas organized crime.[76] Several of the largest breaches involved sophisticated global organizations of hackers who infiltrated information systems at vulnerable points—where sensitive personal records were unsecured—even though those same records were encrypted in company networks.[77]

Over the past decade, advanced persistent threats (APTs) have been among the most serious types of cyberattacks because their focus is espionage. Often originating in Asia-Pacific countries, APTs employ zero-day exploits (taking advantage of vulnerabilities in software that are known but not yet fixed) and social-engineering techniques (phishing) against company employees to breach networks. The typical intrusion by an APT involves undetected access into a victim computer system (in violation of federal and state law) and then the theft of significant amounts of data. Through the intrusions, hackers establish a foothold into a company's network, sometimes years without discovery, and may even remain after a company has discovered them and attempted to take corrective measures.

Compromise of Software Products. Law firms need to think holistically about the risk of sophisticated cyberattacks and ransomware. Among other things, lawyers should take stock of the software and services they rely on. Sophisticated cyber adversaries are increasingly moving from attacking law firms themselves to compromising legal supply chains.[78]

Several of the most dangerous law firm breaches have involved zero day attacks that exploited significant software vulnerabilities/flaws in technology used by law offices as part of their IT operations—e-mail, transfer of large files, website transactions, and managing their computer networks. Cyber

---

76. Dan McWhorter, *APT1: Exposing One of China's Cyber Espionage Units 20*, MANDIANT (2013), https://www.fireeye.com/content/dam/fireeye-www/services/pdfs/mandiant-apt1-report.pdf.

77. Lucy L. Thomson, *Encrypted Records—Failed Security*, ch. 5 in DATA BREACH AND ENCRYPTION HANDBOOK 57–82 (ABA 2011).

78. *See* Jon Boyens et al., *Cyber Supply Chain Risk Management Practices for Systems and Organizations*, NIST (2021), https://csrc.nist.gov/publications/detail/sp/800-161/rev-1/draft.

exposure is exacerbated when organizations rely on outdated, legacy software that offers little ongoing support and updates—especially upon news of highly visible and well-publicized vulnerabilities and exploits.

1. Malicious Cyber Activity Related to the Coronavirus Pandemic

In a joint alert, law enforcement in the United Kingdom (U.K.) and the United States reported that APT groups and cybercriminals targeted individuals, small and medium businesses, and large organizations with Covid-19-related scams and phishing e-mails.[79] These cyber threat actors often masquerade as trusted entities, using coronavirus-themed phishing messages or malicious applications.

Hackers sponsored by the Russian and North Korean governments targeted seven prominent companies directly involved in researching vaccines and treatments for Covid-19, and in some cases, the attacks succeeded, according to Microsoft corporate vice president Tom Burt.[80] They include vaccine makers with Covid-19 vaccines in various clinical trial stages, a clinical research organization involved in trials, and a developer of a Covid-19 test. Also targeted were organizations with contracts with or investments from governmental agencies around the world for Covid-19-related work. The targets are located in the United States, Canada, France, India, and South Korea.

---

79. *Advisory: APT Groups Target Healthcare and Essential Services*, NAT'L CYBER SECURITY CENTRE (May 5, 2020), https://www.ncsc.gov.uk/news/apt-groups-target-healthcare-essential -services-advisory (Joint U.K. and U.S. advisory highlights ongoing activity by APT groups against organizations involved in the international coronavirus response.).

80. Dan Goodin, *Hackers Sponsored by Russia and North Korea Are Targeting COVID-19 Researchers*, ARS TECHNICA (Nov. 13, 2020, 6:51 PM), https://arstechnica.com /information-technology/2020/11/hackers-sponsored-by-russia-and-north-korea-are-targe ting-covid-19-researchers/ ("Three nation-state-sponsored groups are targeting organizations throughout the world.").

2. *SolarWinds Software Supply Chain Breach—APT*
   Compromise of Critical Infrastructure, Private Sector
   Organizations, and Government Agencies[81]

Exploitation of software flaws is a long-standing attack method. An APT actor (later determined to be based in Russia) was responsible for compromising the SolarWinds Orion software supply chain through phishing and then moving across the company network with sensitive access.[82] The attackers hid malicious code (malware) in a software update for SolarWinds Orion, a product widely used to monitor and manage the operation of computer networks. They also managed to digitally "sign" the updates, which made them look legitimate. The end result was that when SolarWinds sent out the software updates, receiving networks saw the legitimate information but not the hidden malware, and organizations unknowingly accepted both. The malware in these updates gave the nation-state-backed attackers a foothold in computer networks around the globe, including multiple large security companies as well as an extensive number of federal agencies.

In December 2020, DHS CISA reported that the agency was tracking "a significant cyber incident impacting enterprise networks across federal, state, and local governments, as well as critical infrastructure entities and other private sector organizations."[83] The agency advised that 18,000 organizations and governments were at risk; attacks were activated against approximately 50 organizations, including U.S. government agencies. CISA warned that the federal government, state, local, tribal and territorial organizations, as well as critical infrastructure entities and private sector organizations, all

---

81. DHS CISA, *Supply Chain Compromise*, https://www.cisa.gov/supply-chain-compromise (last visited Aug. 25, 2021).

82. DHS, *What Every Leader Needs to Know about the Ongoing APT Cyber Activity*, CISA INSIGHTS (Dec. 2020), https://www.cisa.gov/sites/default/files/publications/CISA%20Insights%20-%20What%20Every%20Leader%20Needs%20to%20Know%20About%20the%20Ongoing%20APT%20Cyber%20Activity%20-%20FINAL_508.pdf; Martin Giles, *The SolarWinds Breach Poses Five Urgent Cybersecurity Challenges for CIOs*, FORBES (Dec. 17, 2020, 5:02 PM), https://www.forbes.com/sites/martingiles/2020/12/17/solarwinds-hackers-five-cybersecurity-challenges-for-cios/?sh=2e82349921b6.

83. DHS CISA, *Supply Chain Compromise*, https://www.cisa.gov/supply-chain-compromise (last visited Aug. 25, 2021).

faced a "grave risk" from the threat.[84] This threat actor has the resources, patience, and expertise to gain access to and privileges over highly sensitive information if left unchecked. The CISA alert urged organizations to prioritize measures to identify and address this threat.[85]

The Justice Department announced in July 2021 that the Russian Solar-Winds supply chain attack compromised the internal network of Microsoft Office 365 e-mail accounts belonging to employees at the offices of 27 state attorneys general.[86]

3. Breach of Accellion Software for Large File Transfers

Law firms manage large volumes of sensitive data as a core part of their businesses. Many firms used software tools like the Accellion File Transfer Appliance (FTA) to help manage those data flows. However, this type of software introduced security risks, both in the form of attacks on software flaws and inadvertent leaks. Major law firms were caught up in the breach of the Accellion FTA software product used to store and share large data files. Attackers leveraged four "zero day" software vulnerabilities to accomplish their attack.[87]

On February 2, 2021, the Boston law firm Goodwin Procter disclosed a data breach that was part of the Accellion FTA compromise.[88] Thereafter, on February 16, 2021, global law firm Jones Day confirmed a data breach involving the Accellion FTA. The following day, open sources reported that Jones Day data appeared on the CL0P LEAKS extortion website. DataBreaches.net published screenshots of stolen Jones Day files that the

---

84. CISA Alert (AA20-352A) *Advanced Persistent Threat Compromise of Government Agencies, Critical Infrastructure, and Private Sector Organizations* (Jan. 7. 2021) update, https://us-cert.cisa.gov/ncas/current-activity/2021/01/06/cisa-updates-emergency-directive-21-01-supplemental-guidance-and.

85. CISA Emergency Directive 21-01 Mitigate SolarWinds Orion Code Compromise (Apr. 15, 2021), https://cyber.dhs.gov/ed/21-01/#supplemental-guidance-v3.

86. U.S. Dep't of Justice, *Department of Justice Statement on SolarWinds Update* (July 30, 2021), https://www.justice.gov/opcl/department-justice-statement-solarwinds-update.

87. Andrew Moore, *Cyber Criminals Exploit Accellion FTA for Data Theft and Extortion*, MANDIANT (Feb. 22, 2021), https://www.fireeye.com/blog/threat-research/2021/02/accellion-fta-exploited-for-data-theft-and-extortion.html.

88. Meghan Tribe, *Goodwin Procter Says It Was Hit by Data Breach of Vendor (1)*, BLOOMBERG LAW (Feb. 2, 2021, 4:57 PM), https://news.bloomberglaw.com/business-and-practice/goodwin-procter-says-it-was-hit-by-data-breach-of-vendor.

CLOP group posted on the dark web as proof it had the stolen records. The group told DataBreaches.net it did not encrypt the files, but only stole copies of the information. The CLOP crew also said Jones Day hasn't responded to its ransom requests.[89]

The Australian law firm Allens also had client data stolen in the attack. It was reported that the breach may have exposed highly sensitive information related to the firm's largest clients, Westpac bank, which the firm defended in an anti-money laundering case, and the Royal Bank of New Zealand and the Australian Securities and Investments Commission (ASIC).[90]

4. Microsoft Exchange Server Compromise[91]

Many law firms use Microsoft's e-mail, calendaring, contact, scheduling, and collaboration platform extensively. In March 2021, it was discovered that organizations using on-premises Exchange Server software (not the cloud-based version) were targets of an aggressive Chinese cyber espionage unit focused on stealing e-mail. This group hacked at least 30,000 organizations across the United States, including law firms, higher education institutions, defense contractors, policy think tanks, and NGOs, as well as small businesses, towns, cities, and local governments.

In a zero day attack, the espionage group exploited four newly discovered flaws in Microsoft Exchange Server e-mail software, and seeded hundreds of thousands of victim organizations worldwide with tools that gave the attackers total, remote control over affected systems, allowing for potential data theft and further compromise.[92] Microsoft released security

---

89. *Threat Actors Claim to Have Stolen Jones Day Files; Law Firm Remains Quiet*, DATABREACHES.NET (Feb. 13, 2021), https://www.databreaches.net/threat-actors-claim-to-have-stolen-jones-day-files-law-firm-remains-quiet/

90. Edward Kost, *Prestigious Australian Law Firm Data at High Risk*, UPGUARD (Jan. 21, 2021), https://www.upguard.com/news/allens-data-breach.

91. *See* Trey Herr, et al., *Breaking Trust: Shades of Crisis across an Insecure Software Supply Chain*, ATLANTIC COUNCIL (July 26, 2020), https://www.atlanticcouncil.org/in-depth-research-reports/report/breaking-trust-shades-of-crisis-across-an-insecure-software-supply-chain/; *Joint Statement by the FBI, CISA, the Office of the Director of National Intelligence (ODNI), and the National Security Agency (NSA)*, CISA.GOV (Jan. 5, 2021), https://www.cisa.gov/news/2021/01/05/joint-statement-federal-bureau-investigation-fbi-cybersecurity-and-infrastructure.

92. Brian Krebs, *At Least 30,000 U.S. Organizations Newly Hacked Via Holes in Microsoft's Email Software*, KREBS ON SEC. (Mar. 5, 2021), https://krebsonsecurity.com/2021/03/at-least-30000-u-s-organizations-newly-hacked-via-holes-in-microsofts-email-software/.

patches for these bugs and urged customers to apply the updates as soon as possible. CISA issued Emergency Directive 21-02 requiring federal civilian departments and agencies running Microsoft Exchange on-premises products to update or disconnect the products from their networks until updated with the Microsoft patch.[93]

The FBI obtained a court order authorizing it to copy and remove malicious web shells—hacking tools that give the attackers total remote control over affected systems—from hundreds of vulnerable computers in the United States. The Justice Department and the FBI announced these and other steps to disrupt the hacking activity "using all of our legal tools, not just prosecutions."[94] In July 2021, the U.K. government, joined by the United States, NATO, and the EU, as well as Microsoft, condemned the "systematic cyber sabotage," claiming the cyberattack was the work of Chinese state-sponsored hackers, namely Hafnium, an APT group.[95]

5. Kaseya VSA Supply-Chain Ransomware Attack[96]

A massive ransomware attack exploited multiple vulnerabilities in a key piece of network management and remote control software developed by U.S. technology firm Kaseya. The software is used to remotely manage a company's IT networks and devices. That software is sold to managed service providers (MSPs)—effectively outsourced IT departments—which then use it to remotely manage the IT networks and devices of their customers,

---

93. *Emergency Directive: 21-02 CISA, Mitigate Microsoft Exchange On-Premises Product Vulnerabilities*, CYBER.GHS.GOV (Mar. 3, 2021), https://cyber.dhs.gov/ed/21-02/.

94. U.S. Dep't of Justice, *Justice Department Announces Court-Authorized Effort to Disrupt Exploitation of Microsoft Exchange Server Vulnerabilities*, JUSTICE NEWS (Apr. 13, 2021), https://www.justice.gov/opa/pr/justice-department-announces-court-authorized-effort-disrupt-exploitation-microsoft-exchange.

95. Foreign Commonwealth & Development Office, et al., *UK and Allies Hold Chinese State Responsible for a Pervasive Pattern of Hacking*, GOV.UK (July 2021), https://www.gov.uk/government/news/uk-and-allies-hold-chinese-state-responsible-for-a-pervasive-pattern-of-hacking.

96. CISA, *CISA-FBI Guidance for MSPs and Their Customers Affected by the Kaseya VSA Supply-Chain Ransomware Attack*, CISA.GOV (July 4, 2021), https://us-cert.cisa.gov/ncas/current-activity/2021/07/04/cisa-fbi-guidance-msps-and-their-customers-affected-kaseya-vsa.

often smaller companies.[97] Kaseya's virtual service administrator (VSA) software tools are used predominantly by small and mid-sized businesses.

Hackers associated with the Russia-linked REvil ransomware-as-a-service group are believed to have used a never-before-seen security vulnerability in the software's update mechanism to push ransomware to Kaseya's MSP customers, which in turn spread downstream to their customers. Many of the companies who were ultimately victims of the attack may not have known that their networks were monitored by Kaseya's software. A notice posted on a dark web site known to be run by REvil claimed responsibility for the attack, and said the ransomware group would publicly release a decryption tool if it was paid $70 million in bitcoin.[98] Ultimately, Kaseya obtained a decryption tool that it provided to its customers. This was the largest supply chain ransomware attack that has been seen to date and opens the door for many similar actions. It's important to also note that the majority of Kaseya customers were small and mid-sized businesses.

Clearly, these many devastating attacks demonstrate that it is no longer enough to simply avoid a data breach; law firms and clients must become proactive and deliberate about network and data security.[99]

D. Social Engineering and Phishing Attacks

Cyber risks have evolved beyond traditional hacking to include sophisticated social engineering scams that rely on unwitting insiders to effectuate the schemes.[100] Criminals use trickery to outwit their victims, creating a sense of urgency combined with fear. In the past several years, organizations around the world have been the victims of multimillion-dollar fraud schemes that were successfully perpetrated online using social engineering. Law firms are especially lucrative targets.

---

97. Zack Whittaker, *Kaseya Hack Floods Hundreds of Companies with Ransomware*, TechCrunch (July 5, 2021, 8:00 PM), https://techcrunch.com/2021/07/05 /kaseya-hack-flood-ransomware.

98. *Id.*

99. Daniel Hudson & Joseph Brunsman, *Cyber-Related Claims without a Breach? They're Coming*, The CPA J. (Apr. 2018), https://www.cpajournal.com/2018/04/06 /cyber-related-claims-without-a-breach-theyre-coming/.

100. *Social Engineering Scams*, Interpol, https://www.interpol.int/en/Crimes/Financial -crime/Social-engineering-scams (last visited Aug. 26, 2021).

Phishing Attacks.   According to the FBI, phishing was the most common type of cybercrime in 2020.[101] It has been a long-standing cyber threat for law firms.[102] $1.8 billion in business losses was directly attributed to phishing. It is among the attack vectors used most often by hackers to launch cyberattacks. Attackers usually masquerade as a trustworthy entity in an electronic communication and target the weakest link in the security chain: the user. "That's probably why it accounts for 90% (that's not a typo) of data breaches."[103]

Although cybercriminals use a variety of techniques to infect victims with ransomware, the most common means of infection are through e-mail phishing campaigns. The criminal sends an e-mail containing a malicious file or link that deploys malware when clicked by a recipient. Cybercriminals historically have used generic, broad-based spamming strategies to deploy their malware, although recent ransomware campaigns have been more targeted and sophisticated. Criminals may also compromise a victim's e-mail account by using precursor malware, which enables the cybercriminal to use a victim's e-mail account to further spread the infection.[104]

The largest health care data breach in history was the result of a phishing e-mail that gave hackers administrative access to the database of Anthem, a major health insurance company. The hackers sent employees phishing e-mails containing links to malware. Once clicked, the malware was installed, giving the hackers a backdoor to the database. They were then able to access it remotely from their command-and-control server. The hackers had administrative access for more than a month. The breach was discovered by a database administrator who noticed a suspicious database query running using his credentials. Then, he found out that other credentials had been compromised. As a result, 78.8 million records of PII were

---

101. FBI INTERNET CRIME REPORT, *supra* note 44, at 6.

102. Law Soc'y of Singapore, *Don't Take the Bait*, LAW GAZETTE (2017), https://v1.lawgazette.com.sg/2017-02/1774.htm.

103. *2021 Cyber Security Threat Trends: Phishing, Crypto Top the List*, CISCO UMBRELLA, https://umbrella.cisco.com/info/2021-cyber-security-threat-trends-phishing-crypto-top-the-list (last visited Aug. 26, 2021).

104. FBI INTERNET CRIME REPORT, *supra* note 44; *see* CISA Security Tip (ST04-014), Avoiding Social Engineering and Phishing Attacks, https://us-cert.cisa.gov/ncas/tips/ST04-014; https://us-cert.cisa.gov/report-phishing.

compromised. The stolen records contained medical IDs, Social Security numbers, addresses, employment history, income data, and so on. They were sold on the dark web. In 2018, Anthem agreed to pay the HHS Office for Civil Rights a record $16 million and take substantial corrective actions to settle potential HIPAA violations. Anthem had previously agreed to pay $115 million in 2017 to settle a class action lawsuit over the data breach.[105]

Business E-mail Compromise. BEC is a sophisticated scam targeting businesses, often working with foreign suppliers or businesses that regularly perform wire transfer payments. The scam, which has targeted businesses of all sizes, is carried out by compromising legitimate e-mail accounts through social engineering or computer intrusion techniques to conduct unauthorized transfers of funds. Account compromise is usually a key part of the scheme, so that an executive or employee's e-mail account is hacked and used to request payments to fraudulent bank accounts. Victims have been identified in all 50 states and 177 countries.[106] In June 2021, five people were arrested in Texas for allegedly laundering nearly $1 million from BEC fraud.[107]

BEC and Phishing Attacks Targeting Lawyers and Law Firms. Lawyers and law practices are frequent targets of BEC schemes. The following are examples of the most serious types of schemes:

- **CEO Fraud and Payroll Phishing Schemes—Data Theft.** According to alerts issued by the Internal Revenue Service (IRS), criminals are now combining CEO fraud and payroll phishing schemes to target a far

---

105. Office for Civil Rights (OCR), *Anthem Pays OCR $16 Million in Record HIPAA Settlement Following Largest Health Data Breach in History*, HHS.gov (Oct. 15, 2018), https:// www.hhs.gov/hipaa/for-professionals/compliance-enforcement/agreements/anthem/index.html.

106. Public Service Announcement, FBI, *Alert No. 1-091019-PSA· Business E-mail Com promise—The 26 Billion Dollar Scam* (Sept. 10, 2019), https:// https://www.ic3.gov/Media /Y2019/PSA190910; FBI, *Business Email Compromise*, FBI: Scams and Safety, https://www .fbi.gov/scams-and-safety/common-scams-and-crimes/business-email-compromise (last visited Aug. 26, 2021). *See* Verizon 2021 DBIR, *supra* note 2, Social Engineering 82.

107. Press Release, U.S. Att'ys Office, W.D. Texas, Five Arrested for Allegedly Laundering Nearly $1 Million from Business Email Compromise Fraud (June 10, 2021), https://www.justice.gov/usao-wdtx/pr/five-arrested-allegedly-laundering-nearly -1-million-business-email-compromise-fraud.

broader range of organizations than ever before.[108] Fraudulent requests are sent utilizing a business executive's compromised e-mail. The targeted recipients are frequently the entities in the business organization responsible for W-2s or maintaining PII, such as the human resources department, bookkeeping, or auditing sections. Some of these incidents are isolated and others occur before a fraudulent wire transfer request. The stolen data can be used for future attacks.

Law firms have been the targets of these payroll phishing attacks. Immigration law firm Fragomen disclosed a data breach that exposed the personal information of current and former Google employees.[109] The accessed file contained information related to the I-9 process used to verify employment eligibility. The I-9 form contains an employee's information, including name, date of birth, phone number, Social Security number, passport number, and mailing and e-mail addresses.

Phishing attacks have been a top security threat for lawyers for years. For example, two of the largest law firms, Jenner & Block and Proskauer Rose, were victimized by phishing attacks. Jenner reported that employees' W-2 forms were "mistakenly transmitted to an unauthorized recipient" in 2017 based on what appeared to be a legitimate management request. The phishing incident may have exposed Social Security numbers, salaries, and other personal information for 859 people.

Proskauer also reported a breach of W-2 information in 2016 when a payroll employee responded to what was believed to be an e-mail request from a senior executive. Proskauer told New York authorities that more than 1,500 people were affected. Three other law firms—Harris Beach, McGlinchey Stafford, and Sanford Heisler Sharp—also reported unauthorized access to e-mail accounts.[110]

---

108. Internal Revenue Service (IRS), *IRS Unveils "Dirty Dozen" List of Tax Scams for 2020; Americans Urged to Be Vigilant to These Threats during the Pandemic and Its Aftermath*, IRS (July 16, 2020), https://www.irs.gov/newsroom/irs-unveils-dirty-dozen-list-of-tax-scams-for -2020-americans-urged-to-be-vigilant-to-these-threats-during-the-pandemic-and-its-aftermath.

109. *Submitted Breach Notification Sample*, Rob Bonta, Att'y Gen., https://oag.ca.gov /ecrime/databreach/reports/sb24-195495/?sb24-10262020/ (last visited Aug. 26, 2021).

110. Debra Cassens Weiss, *More Than 100 Law Firms Have Reported Data Breaches; 2 BigLaw Firms Affected*, ABA J. (Oct. 18, 2019, 9:48 AM), https://www.abajournal.com /news/article/more-than-100-law-firms-have-reported-data-breaches-2-biglaw-firms-affected.

- **Attorney Check Scam.**[111] State bar associations around the country have warned lawyers to be on the lookout for counterfeit check scams. For example, in certain fraud schemes, criminals seek out an attorney, purportedly to accept checks from a fictitious company's customers, deposit the checks into the attorney's bank account, retain a five-figure amount as the attorney's "fee" for providing the service, and then forward the rest of the payment to the fictitious company in a foreign country. These scams usually involve a nonexistent transaction between the company that contacted the attorney hired to collect money for them and a second company that allegedly owes them money in payment of a purchase.[112]

- **CEO Fraud and Business Executive and Attorney Impersonation—Confidential and Time-Sensitive Requests; Receiving or Initiating a Wire Transfer Request.** Attackers pose as the company CEO or any executive and send an e-mail to employees in finance, requesting them to transfer money to the account they control. With respect to lawyers, an attacker may pretend to be a lawyer or someone from the law firm supposedly in charge of crucial and confidential matters. Normally, such bogus requests are done through e-mail or phone, and near the end of the business day.

- **Known Entities.** Attackers pose as legitimate individuals or entities such as IRS agents or bank employees trying to obtain access to sensitive data—including data specifically designed to place attorneys in harm's way.

- **Fake Clients.** Criminals find out about trust accounts or litigation and impersonate a law firm client to change the recipient bank information to a fraudulent account. Alternatively, scammers often pose as prospective clients seeking urgent legal assistance. Lawyers may be asked to provide contact information or even to complete wire transfers. While

---

111. FTC, *How To Spot, Avoid, and Report Fake Check Scams*, Fed. Trade Comm'n: Consumer Info. (Jan. 2020), https://www.consumer.ftc.gov/articles/how -spot-avoid-and-report-fake-check-scams.

112. Don Coker, *Internet Check Scams That Target Attorneys and Law Firms*, HGExperts.com, https://www.hgexperts.com/expert-witness-articles/internet-check-scams-that-target -attorneys-and-law-firms-6673 (last visited Aug. 26, 2021).

these schemes are often easy to spot, scammers have recently grown far more sophisticated, sometimes even stealing the identities of actual professionals to conceal the schemes.

The Florida Bar has warned that attorneys are routinely targeted by cybercriminals, with recent noteworthy examples including the following:[113]

1. The registration of a phony account on the Florida Courts E-Filing Portal under an attorney's name and Bar number, and used to obtain an order disbursing more than $130,000 in surplus foreclosure proceeds from a court registry;
2. Spoofed e-mails purporting to be sent by the executive director or other staff of the Florida Bar, believed to launch malware attacks;
3. Compromise of a paralegal's e-mail account and ensuing attempts to initiate a wire transfer from a law firm's trust account;
4. An e-mail-based cashier's check scam in which a "client" sought an attorney's help collecting a $125,000 discrimination settlement from CVS.

More than ten years ago, the FBI warned that hackers were targeting U.S. law firms to steal confidential information.[114] In 2011, the Washington, D.C., law firm Wiley Rein was a victim of a massive attack by Chinese hackers referred to as Byzantine Candor that encompassed 20 major companies. Security researchers referred to the hackers as the "Comment group" because they infiltrated computers using hidden web page computer code known as "comments."[115] Their attack methodology began with phishing attacks that transmitted malware in e-mails to members of the firm. Audit log files showed that the malware enabled the hackers to access encrypted

---

113. Joshua Feinberg, *Trends, Prevention, and Loss Recovery for Victims of Real Estate Wire Fraud and Other Cybercrimes*, 94 FLA. BAR J. (Nov./Dec. 2020), https://www.floridabar .org/the-florida-bar-journal/trends-prevention-and-loss-recovery-for-victims-of-real-estate -wire-fraud-and-other-cybercrimes/.

114. CISA, *Report Phishing Sites*, CISA.GOV, https://www.us-cert.gov/report-phishing (last visited Aug. 26, 2021).

115. Michael Riley & Dune Lawrence, *Hackers Linked to China's Army Seen from EU to D.C.*, BLOOMBERG MKTS. (July 26, 2012), https://www.bloomberg.com/news /articles/2012-07-26/china-hackers-hit-eu-point-man-and-d-c-with-byzantine-candor.

passwords they were able to crack off-line. The hackers accessed the firm's network and stole sensitive data by acting as network administrators, collecting critical data and exfiltrating it over the course of months. The thousands of pages of e-mails the hackers stole included confidential communications with clients.

On a twist of the law firm phishing attack, hackers sent phishing e-mails from purported, but fake, law firms advising targets that they had been sued and needed to take action immediately.[116] The law firm domain spoofed in one scam—wpslaw.com—now redirects to the website for RWC LLC, a legitimate firm based in Connecticut.

Cybercriminals Insider-Trading Scheme Targeting Law Firms.

This case [United States v. Iat Hong] of cyber meets securities fraud should serve as a wake-up call for law firms around the world: you are and will be targets of cyber hacking, because you have information valuable to would-be criminals.[117]

Hackers have targeted international law firms in insider-trading operations.[118] In 2016, the FBI issued an alert after agents discovered a post on an undisclosed "cybercriminal forum" in which someone was seeking to hire hackers to break into international law firms' computer networks and steal data as part of an insider-trading scheme. According to the *Wall Street Journal*, "a posting appeared on an underground Russian website called DarkMoney.cc, in which the person offered to sell his phishing

---

116. *Legal Threats Make Powerful Phishing Lures*, KREBS ON SECURITY (May 22, 2019, 3:26 PM), https://krebsonsecurity.com/2019/05/legal-threats-make-powerful-phishing-lures/.

117. Press Release, U.S. Att'ys Office, S.D.N.Y., Manhattan U.S. Attorney Announces Arrest of Macau Resident and Unsealing of Charges Against Three Individuals for Insider Trading Based on Information Hacked from Prominent U.S. Law Firms (Dec. 27, 2016), https://www.justice.gov/usao-sdny/pr/manhattan-us-attorney-announces-arrest-macau-resident-and-unsealing-charges-against ("Iat Hong Arrested on December 25 in Hong Kong on U.S. Insider Trading and Hacking Charges; In Addition to Successful Cyber Intrusions into Two Law Firms, Defendants Charged with Attempting to Hack into Total of Seven Law Firms").

118. Gabe Friedman, *FBI Alert Warns of Criminals Seeking Access to Law Firm Networks*, BLOOMBERG LAW (Mar. 11, 2016, 5:40 PM), https://bol.bna.com/fbi-alert-warns-of-criminals-seeking-access-to-law-firm-networks/.

services to other would-be cyber thieves and identified specific law firms as potential targets."[119]

The SEC and the Justice Department separately announced significant cases against three Chinese traders who made nearly $3 million in illegal profits by hacking into the computer networks of two "prominent New York-based law firms." Three Chinese nationals were subsequently indicted for securities and wire fraud for hacking into prominent international law firms with offices in New York City and trading on confidential, nonpublic information they obtained from the e-mail accounts of law firm partners who worked on high-profile mergers and acquisitions (M&A) transactions.[120] According to the indictment, the hackers stole a law firm employee's login credentials to access the firm's e-mail server and plant malware that would allow them to, full access the to server. They then logged into e-mail accounts of partners at the firm to glean details of pending mergers pricing information. They traded on that information before the deals were made public. The hackers targeted seven firms, traded in five public companies, and made profits of nearly $3 million in the process.

E. Third-Party Vendors and Business Partners Can Be a Weak Link—A Two-Edged Sword for Law Firms

Third-party business partners and vendors can provide a pathway into companies of strategic interest to global hackers.[121] Further, from the point of view of hackers, law firms are considered "business partners" of major corporate clients with a trove of proprietary data—a weak link to be exploited. Similarly, it can be said that the security of a law firm is only as strong as that of its weakest business partner. Law firms and corporate legal departments

---

119. Nicole Hong & Robin Sidel, *Hackers Breach Law Firms, Including Cravath and Weil Gotshal*, WALL ST. J. (Mar. 29, 2016, 9:14 PM), https://www.wsj.com/articles/hackers-breach-cra vath-swaine-other-big-law-firms-1459293504; Claire Bushey, *Russian Cyber Criminal Targets Elite Chicago Law Firms*, CHI. BUS. (Mar. 29, 2016, 7:00 AM), http://www.chicagobusiness.com /article/20160329/NEWS04/160329840/russian-cyber-criminal-targets-elite-chicago-law-firms.

120. United States v. Iat Hong, 16 Cr. 360 (S.D.N.Y. 2016). *See* Jeff John Roberts, *Exclusive: China Stole Data from Major U.S. Law Firms*, FORTUNE (Dec. 7, 2016, 10:56 AM), http://fortune.com/2016/12/07/china-law-firms/.

121. Dan McWhorter, APT1, *supra* note 76.

are outsourcing a variety of legal work to outside businesses located domestically and overseas.

Ransomware Attacks on Third Party Vendors. Law firms and court systems can be affected by ransomware indirectly when their managed service providers (MSP) are attacked.[122] The vendors that provide the technology used by law offices as part of their IT operations—e-mail, transfer of large files, website transactions, and managing their computer networks—have been targeted by cybercriminals. The sophisticated cyberattacks that compromised legal supply chains, discussed in Section II.C, are examples of dangerous law firm breaches.

In 2019, Needles and TrialWorks,[123] legal case management firms, were hit with a ransomware attack, shutting down a computer platform for several days and locking some lawyers out of their case files. "The ripples of disruption from this incident made it impossible for lawyers to access the legal documents hosted on TrialWorks' platform."[124] Some customers remained without full access to their documents almost two weeks after the attack began,[125] and one law firm was "forced to request more time to meet a filing deadline in . . . federal court because it could not access its electronic documents."[126]

The 2020 ransomware attack on legal services provider Epiq Global, an e-discovery and web service firm, was designed to put pressure on the lawyer victims by inflicting pain on downstream customers. Epiq took their systems off-line after their devices were encrypted by Ryuk ransomware. Epiq's legal clients were unable to access files and documents through their e-discovery platforms, files needed for court cases and other deadlines.

---

122. Tari Shreider, *Ransomware Attacks in the Legal Profession,* ACEDS (May 27, 2020), https://aceds.org/tari-schreider-ransomware-attacks-in-the-legal-profession/.

123. Both companies were recently purchased by venture capital company Ridge Road Capital Partners d/b/a/Assembly Legal, https://www.needles.com/about/.

124. Ionut Ilascu, *TrialWorks Ransomware Attack Disrupts Court Cases and Deadlines,* BLEEPINGCOMPUTER (Oct. 27, 2019, 10:52 AM), https://www.bleepingcomputer.com/news/security/trialworks-ransomware-attack-disrupts-court-cases-and-deadlines/.

125. Mark Funk, *Ransomware Attack Disrupts Court Cases and Deadlines TrialWorks,* CYBER GUARDS (Oct. 28, 2019), https://cybersguards.com/ransomware-attack-disrupts-court-cases-and-deadlines-trialworks/.

126. Jay Weaver, *"Ransomware Incident" in South Florida Blocked Some Law Firms from Countless Records,* MIAMI HERALD (Oct. 25, 2019), https://www.miamiherald.com/news/local/article236645058.html.

Ryuk is known to go after large enterprises, seeking considerable ransoms, a practice called "big game hunting."[127] Epiq faced a proposed class action lawsuit, originally filed in California state court and removed to federal court, that claimed the legal services provider failed to adequately protect personal information under California's consumer privacy law and that the plaintiffs "face a lifetime risk of identity theft."[128]

In a ransomware attack on TBG West Insurance Services, an insurance vendor of the Cadwalader, Wickersham & Taft LLP (CWT) law firm, hackers encrypted files within their system and stole files that included CWT's current and former employee information (names and Social Security numbers). TBG ultimately paid the ransom to regain access to their data.[129]

Hackers have disrupted the operations of hundreds of businesses by targeting the entities that provide key services to them. For example, Blackbaud of South Carolina was a cloud computing vendor and business associate of hundreds of organizations known to have been affected by a ransomware attack in which hackers gained access to servers housing some of its customers' fundraising databases. Ten million records exfiltrated by the hackers included Social Security numbers and financial information. Blackbaud negotiated a ransom payment and paid to prevent the publication or sale of the stolen data.

In prior years, major law firms were implicated publicly in the breach of the website of HBGary, a cybersecurity firm that investigates data breaches and conducts investigations. The hacker group Anonymous seized control of HBGary's website, defaced its pages, extracted more than 60,000 company

---

127. Zack Whittaker, *Legal Services Giant Epiq Global Offline after Ransomware Attack*, TECHCRUNCH (Mar. 2, 2020, 8:53 PM), https://techcrunch.com/2020/03/02/epiq-global-ransomware/. Typically, this kind of campaign is rolled out in stages, often beginning with a phishing attack, just as this one did. The attackers sought to gain user credentials to get into the organization's network and survey the asset landscape. Follow up stages usually included spying once in the network, data encryption, and eventually the ransom demand and possibly extortion. *See also New Details Emerge on the Ransomware Attack Against Epiq Global*, VIRSEC SYS., https://www.virsec.com/blog/new-details-emerge-on-the-ransomware-attack-against-epiq-global (last visited Nov. 5, 2021).

128. Sara Merken, *After Ransomware Attack, Legal Services Company Epiq Faces California Privacy Lawsuit*, REUTERS (July 30, 2020, 5:08 PM), https://www.reuters.com/article/epiq-dataprivacy-ransomware/after-ransomware-attack-legal-services-company-epiq-faces-california-privacy-lawsuit-idUSL2N2F12Q3.

129. Cadwalader Wickersham & Taft LLP, NYC, Security Breach Notification to Massachusetts Office of Consumer Affairs and Business Regulation (Aug. 31, 2020), https://www.documentcloud.org/documents/20403356-cadwaladerdatabreachreport.

e-mails, and deleted backup files. It then posted those e-mails in a searchable form on the Internet.[130] The released e-mails created a frenzy of media coverage in major publications. News reports indicated that Washington, D.C., law firm Hunton & Williams had hired HBGary as an outsourcing partner to conduct investigations for its clients. The firm suffered embarrassment and its work on behalf of its client the Chamber of Commerce was discussed in extensive media coverage. A fallout of the breach was the filing of an ethics complaint against three Hunton & Williams attorneys.[131]

The confidential e-mails that were stolen from HBGary also revealed extensive details about industrial espionage by hackers in China, Russia, and other countries against law firms and major corporations.[132] The Atlanta-based law firm King and Spalding was mentioned along with Google, which said that in 2010 it had "lost intellectual property assets to hackers based in China," and Adobe, which reported similar hacker attacks. The need for law firms to assess the security practices of their business partners should be clear from the widespread ramifications of this breach.[133]

F. Malicious Insiders

Malicious insider attacks are on the rise and pose a serious threat to the security of sensitive and confidential information.[134] Criminals are using the dark web to recruit employees who have access to corporate networks to become "rogue insiders."[135] The motivation of employees to steal data may range from financial gain (theft of trade secrets and other sensitive

---

130. *Anonymous Hackers Attack US Security Firm HBGary*, BBC Tech. News (Feb. 7, 2011), http://www.bbc.co.uk/news/technology-12380987.

131. *Complaint Accuses Hunton & Williams of Dirty Tricks*, BLT: The Blog of the LegalTimes (Feb. 24, 2011), https://legaltimes.typepad.com/blt/2011/02/complaint-accuses-hunton-williams-of-dirty-tricks.html.

132. Michael Riley & Sarah Forden, *Hacking of DuPont, J&J, GE Were Google-Type Attacks That Weren't Disclosed*, Bloomberg (Mar. 8, 2011), https://www.bloomberg.com/news/articles/2011-03-08/hacking-of-dupont-j-j-ge-were-google-type-attacks-that-weren-t-disclosed.

133. ABA Cybersecurity Legal Task Force, Vendor Contracting Cybersecurity Checklist, 2d ed. (May 11, 2021), https://www.americanbar.org/products/ecd/ebk/411859099/.

134. *DIIS/ALL/PIA-052 Insider Threat Program*, Dep't of Homeland Security, https://www.dhs.gov/publication/dhs-all-pia-052-dhs-insider-threat-program (last visited Aug. 26, 2021).

135. Jeff John Roberts, *Insider Trading on the Dark Web on the Rise*, Fortune (Jan. 31, 2017, 12:10 PM), http://fortune.com/2017/01/31/insiders-dark-web/; Ido Wulkan, Tim Condello & David Pogemiller, *Monetizing the Insider*, RedOwl and Intsights (2017), https://www.nationalinsiderthreatsig.org/itmresources/RedOwl%20Report-Monetizing%20The%20Insider%20Through%20The%20Dark%20Web.pdf.

information for sale) to revenge for perceived wrongs committed against them. Individuals who abused administrative privileges led to a significant number of breaches as did security failures such as not suspending system access for terminated employees.

High-profile criminal cases illustrate the extent of the fraud and theft that can be caused by malicious insiders.[136] In what federal prosecutors called one of the largest data breaches in history with potentially devastating consequences,[137] a single insider hacked a database of Capital One, the third largest issuer of credit cards in the United States, and accessed more than 100 million customer accounts and credit card applications. Paige Thompson, who formerly worked as a software engineer for Amazon Web Services, a cloud hosting company that hosted the Capital One database she breached, exploited a misconfigured web application firewall to compromise one million Canadian social insurance numbers as well.

The hacker was not concerned about hiding her identity. She shared her method of hacking into Capital One with colleagues on the Slack chat service and posted the information on GitHub (using her full name), bragging on social media about it. She was arrested and charged with one count of computer fraud and abuse for hacking Capital One and absconding with the personal information of more than 100 million people in the United States.[138] Seven new charges were filed against Thompson, and the trial is scheduled for March 2022.

In another famous insider threat case, two General Electric (GE) employees stole trade secrets on advanced computer models to expertly calibrate turbines used in power plants.[139] They also stole marketing and pricing

---

136. Jane Grafton, *Famous Insider Threat Cases*, GURUCUL (Sept. 5, 2019), https://gurucul.com/blog/famous-insider-threat-cases.

137. Emily Flitter & Karen Weise, *Capital One Data Breach Compromises Data of Over 100 Million*, N.Y. TIMES (July 29, 2019), https://www.nytimes.com/2019/07/29/business/capital-one-data-breach-hacked.html.

138. Press Release, U.S. Att'ys Office, W.D. Wash., Former Seattle Tech Worker Indicted on Federal Charges for Wire Fraud and Computer Data Theft (Aug. 28, 2019), https://www.justice.gov/usao-wdwa/pr/former-seattle-tech-worker-indicted-federal-charges-wire-fraud-and-computer-data-theft ("Indictment Cites more than 30 Victims of Data Intrusion and Theft").

139. FBI, *Trade Secret Theft*, FBI NEWS (July 29, 2020), https://www.fbi.gov/news/stories/two-guilty-in-theft-of-trade-secrets-from-ge-072920; Press Release, U.S. Att'ys Office, D.C.N.Y., Former GE Engineer Pleads Guilty to Conspiring to Steal Trade Secrets (Dec. 10, 2019), https://www.justice.gov/usao-ndny/pr/former-ge-engineer-pleads-guilty-conspiring-steal-trade-secrets-0.

information for promoting this service. The employees downloaded thousands of files with trade secrets from company servers. They then uploaded the files to the cloud or sent them to private e-mail addresses. In addition, they convinced a system administrator to grant them unauthorized access to sensitive corporate data. With the stolen intellectual property in hand, one started a new company to compete illegally with GE.

After GE lost several bids to this new, lower-priced competitor it discovered that the company had been founded by its prior employee and reported the incident to the FBI. The FBI investigated this crime for several years and in 2020 both malicious insiders were convicted and sent to prison. They were ordered to pay $1.4 million in restitution to GE.

In a widely publicized insider case, a computer technician who worked in Bank of New York Mellon's IT department stole the identities of 2,000 bank employees and opened bank and brokerage accounts. He then used the accounts to steal more than $1.1 million from charities, nonprofit groups, and other entities.[140] The defendant pleaded guilty to grand larceny, money laundering, and computer tampering.

Malicious insiders pose a serious risk for law firms. For example, nonequity partners of the Governo law firm (GLF) in Boston who planned to create a new law firm, CMBG3, stole more than 24 million pages of documents—a "treasure trove" of proprietary materials—from GLF, including material from the research library, databases, and administrative files. The research library, developed over 20 years, contained more than 10,000 documents related to asbestos litigation, including witness interviews and expert and investigative reports. Databases organized the research material into categories sortable by multiple criteria, including by legal theory or client. The stolen material downloaded by the departing attorneys included client files for which they had not received authorization to transfer from the client.

GLF sued the departing attorneys and CMBG3 for a number of claims, including conversion, breach of the duty of loyalty, conspiracy, and, importantly, unfair or deceptive trade practices in violation of the Massachusetts consumer protection law, G.L.c. 93A, section 11.

---

140. Press Release, N.Y. Cnty. Dist. Att'ys Office, District Attorney Vance Announces Guilty Plea in Massive Identity Theft Scam (July 1, 2010).

On April 9, 2021, the Massachusetts Supreme Judicial Court held that the type of activity that occurred in this case could form the basis of a deceptive trade practice claim because the then-employee defendant lawyers misappropriated material for the purpose of competing with their now-former employer.[141]

Insider trading is a motivation for law firm employees to misappropriate confidential data and nonpublic client information.[142] Securities regulators have brought cases charging law firm employees with exploiting the firms' computer systems to access and steal inside information. The misconduct of Matthew Kluger offers a strong cautionary tale for law firms. In what the government described as one of the longest-running insider trading schemes ever investigated and prosecuted in the United States, the SEC charged a law firm associate who had worked at four well-known law firms over a 17-year period with tipping on at least eight deals that generated more than $30 million in profits. The Justice Department filed parallel charges in New Jersey.[143] Between 1994 and 2011, Kluger obtained inside information on more than 30 different corporate transactions and netted more than $32 million in illicit profits from the scheme.

Although the law firm tried to protect corporate information by using code names for the parties involved, Kluger was repeatedly able to figure out the identities of such companies because he knew that the earliest documents would always have the parties' real names and, as the deal got closer, the lawyers would begin to use code names. In June 2012, a federal judge in New Jersey sentenced him to 12 years in prison—a record sentence for an insider-trading defendant.[144]

---

141. *Governo Law Firm v. Kendra Bergeron*, 487 Mass. 188, 166 N.E.3d 416 (2021).

142. Bruce Carton, *Why Law Firms Are a Breeding Ground for Insider Trading*, COMPLIANCE WEEK (Apr. 7, 2014, 8:00 PM), https://www.complianceweek.com/why-law -firms-are-a-breeding-ground-for-insider-trading/13906.article.

143. SEC Litig. Release No. 22,345 (Apr. 25, 2012), https://www.sec.gov/litigatio n/litreleases/2012/lr22345.htm.

144. United States v. Kluger, No. 11-cr-0858, ECF No. 49 (D.N.J. June 4, 2012); Press Release, U.S. A.G.'s Office of New Jersey, Lawyer Gets Record Prison Sentence—12 Years—In Insider Trading Scheme That Used Information Stolen from Preeminent Law Firms (June 4, 2012), https://www.justice.gov/archive/usao/nj/Press/files/Kluger,%20Matthew%20and%20 Bauer,%20Garrett%20Sentencing%20News%20Release.html.

A Florida lawyer, Walter "Chet" Little, former partner at an international law firm, pleaded guilty to engaging in a nearly $1 million insider-trading scheme using information he improperly obtained from his law firm's databases. He was sentenced to 27 months in prison for conspiring to commit insider trading. Canadian lawyer Gil Cornblum was investigated for using the night secretarial staff's temporary passwords when he searched the law firm's document management system for confidential information about transactions. Cornblum allegedly gained inside information about 46 corporate transactions and used this information to generate more than $9 million in illegal profits.[145]

Law firms must look beyond the lawyers and staff working on a specific case or deal to protect clients' information. The SEC charged a law firm network IT manager with using his position to access information about 22 M&A deals, and tipping his brother-in-law.[146]

Defending an organization's perimeter from external attack does not protect against valuable information seeping out because of insider malfeasance, whether that behavior is characterized as malicious, mischievous, or ignorant/accidental.[147] Carnegie Mellon University has published a list of best practices to minimize the risk of insider attacks.[148]

---

145. Press Release, U.S. Att'ys Office, S.D.N.Y., Partner at International Law Firm Sentenced for Insider Trading (Feb. 22, 2018), https://www.justice.gov/usao-sdny/pr/partner-international-law-firm-sentenced-insider-trading. After Cornblum committed suicide in 2009, his accomplice was sentenced to prison for insider trading. *Toronto Lawyer Jailed 39 Months for Insider Trading*, CBC NEWS (Jan. 7, 2010), https://www.cbc.ca/news/business/toronto-lawyer-jailed-39-months-for-insider-trading-1.973790.

146. SEC v. Jeffrey J. Temple and Benedict M. Pastro, Lit. Rel. No. 21765 (Dec. 10, 2010).

147. Tara Seals, *Insider Threats Responsible for 43% of Data Breaches*, INFOSECURITY MAG. (Sept. 25, 2015), https://www.infosecurity-magazine.com/news/insider-threats-reponsible-for-43/; Rutrell Yasin, *Employee Negligence the Cause of Many Data Breaches*, DARK READING (May 24, 2016), http://www.darkreading.com/vulnerabilities---threats/employee-negligence-the-cause-of-many-data-breaches-/d/d-id/1325656.

148. *See* CERT Insider Threat Ctr., Carnegie Mellon Univ., http://www.cert.org/insider_threat/; DHS CISA, *Combating the Insider Threat* (May 6, 2014), https://us-cert.cisa.gov/security-publications/Combating-Insider-Threat.

G. Cloud Computing and Wi-Fi Risks

Because of the increased flexibility and efficiency afforded by computing resources available on demand, law firms are using cloud services for processing and storing confidential client data and records. However, cloud computing introduces IT security and privacy risks related to outsourcing the administration and physical control of sensitive data to a third-party vendor and maintenance of the data on shared computing platforms, risks that will need to be carefully evaluated and addressed by legal entities that intend to put client data in the cloud.[149] Storing documents in a cloud storage service such as Dropbox creates risks.[150] The cloud should be considered a public repository, and sensitive documents should be encrypted before they are placed there.

Given the significant risks with cloud technology, the White House has made the development of a new federal cloud-security strategy a priority. Section 3 of EO 14028 provides that the migration to cloud technology shall adopt Zero Trust Architecture[151] in accordance with NIST standards and guidance and DHS will develop security principles governing Cloud

---

149. *See* Wayne Jansen & Time Grance, *NIST Spec. Pub. 800-144, Guidelines on Security and Privacy in Public Cloud Computing*, CSRC (Dec. 2011), https://csrc.nist.gov/publications /detail/sp/800-144/final.

150. Dave Johnson, *Is Dropbox Secure? Here's How Dropbox Has Improved Its Security Measures, and What You Can Do to Protect Yourself*, BUS. INSIDER (Mar. 4, 2021, 4:19 PM), https://www.businessinsider.com/is-dropbox-secure ("[T]he largest vulnerabilities are often the end users and their security hygiene. To be safe, you should enable two-factor authentication, be wary of public folder sharing, and consider using file-level encryption.").

151. "Zero Trust Architecture is an evolving set of cybersecurity paradigms that move defenses from static, network-based perimeters to focus on users, assets, and resources. Zero trust assumes there is no implicit trust granted to assets or user accounts based solely on their physical or network location (i.e., local area networks versus the internet) or based on asset ownership (enterprise or personally owned). Authentication and authorization (both subject and device) are discrete functions performed before a session to an enterprise resource is established. Zero trust is a response to enterprise network trends that include remote users, bring your own device (BYOD), and cloud-based assets that are not located within an enterprise-owned network boundary. Zero trust focuses on protecting resources (assets, services, workflows, network accounts, etc.), not network segments, as the network location is no longer seen as the prime component to the security posture of the resource." Scott Rose et al., *NIST Spec. Pub. 800-207, Zero Trust Architecture*, CSRC (Aug. 2020), https://csrc.nist.gov /publications/detail/sp/800-207/final.

Service Providers (CSPs).[152] The government will develop a cloud-service governance framework, evaluate the types and sensitivity of unclassified data and identify appropriate protection, adopt multifactor authentication and encryption for data at rest and in transit, and enhance information sharing by establishing a framework to collaborate on cybersecurity and incident response activities related to federal cloud technology. These federal best practices should provide valuable resources for private sector entities, including law practices, and could become new standards of care.

Security required for data stored in the cloud. Cloud providers require their customers who put web applications, databases, and other software in a public or private cloud environment to provide their own security. Many customers don't understand that security offered by a cloud provider is an additional option that must be purchased. While the cloud services may offer some basic tools, they do not require customers to use them, including something as basic as a password. A number of large organizations simply fail to add a password to protect their cloud-based data. Lawyers must be vigilant to ensure that their offices and their clients protect valuable records with appropriate security when they are stored in the cloud or in databases that can be accessed through the web.

Securing wireless devices. Wireless communication creates opportunities for hackers to intercept sensitive data such as passwords for logging in to corporate networks and online banking sites. Public Wi-Fi locations such as airports, hotels, and coffee shops—convenient places to check e-mail— often do not have the security features necessary to protect confidential client data. Hackers can use a proxy server to create a fake Wi-Fi hotspot (an "evil twin") and intercept or redirect confidential communications. The National Security Agency (NSA) issued guidance on securing wireless

---

152. Exec. Order 14028, Improving the Nation's Cybersecurity (May 12, 2021). Sec. 3. Modernizing Federal Government Cybersecurity.

(c) As agencies continue to use cloud technology, they shall do so in a coordinated, deliberate way that allows the Federal Government to prevent, detect, assess, and remediate cyber incidents. To facilitate this approach, the migration to cloud technology shall adopt Zero Trust Architecture, as practicable. The CISA shall modernize its current cybersecurity programs, services, and capabilities to be fully functional with cloud-computing environments with Zero Trust Architecture. The Secretary of Homeland Security . . . . shall develop security principles governing Cloud Service Providers (CSPs) for incorporation into agency modernization efforts.

devices in public settings that will be useful to lawyers working remotely or when traveling.[153]

H.   Unsecured Databases

Sensitive Data from 190 Law Firms Exposed from Vendor Online Database. Lax security practices left 10,000 legal documents and sensitive data from more than 190 law firms exposed in an unsecured online database. The impacted firms included the largest law firms in the world, as well as small boutique practices. Infosec firm TurgenSec, which revealed the breach, said the data was unprotected, "accessible to anyone with a browser and internet connection—if they knew where to look."[154] TurgenSec published a comprehensive list of the affected law firms in its update of the data leak timeline. Some of the notable law firms included Clifford Chance and Slaughter and May, both headquartered in London.[155]

The law firms' breached data "appears to contain information relating to the staff of legal firms, and in some cases, potentially sensitive data relating to authentication on behalf of clients." The information included "primary" data categories such as usernames, IDs, hashed passwords, confidential documents, and even passport numbers and eye colors, as well as "form" data that covered information such as authentication codes, company details, and service charges.

The unsecured database belonged to Advanced Computer Software Group Limited, one of the largest software companies in the United Kingdom. Following the Responsible Disclosure Policy, TurgenSec contacted the affected law firms, who confirmed the data leak came from legal documents hosted by Laserform Hub owned by Advanced. Advanced claimed the details exposed were largely of public records and the discernible data was limited and historic and only partially visible. However, commentators responded that it is unlikely law firms could publish legal documents,

---

153. Nat'l Security Agency, *Securing Devices in Public Spaces* (July 2021), https://media
.defense.gov/2021/Jul/29/2002815141/-1/-1/0/CSI_SECURING_WIRELESS_DEVICES_IN
_PUBLIC.PDF.

154. Public Statement, TurgenSec Limited, 193 Law Firms—Advanced Data Breach Closure
Update (May 4, 2021), https://community.turgensec.com/190-law-firms-data-breach-disclosure/.

155. *Id.*

including hashed passwords or the first three letters of security responses. The first three letters are highly discernable and could give hackers hints about possible names, thus making it easy to perform brute force attacks.[156]

Further, in 2021, TurgenSec reported that 345,000 sensitive legal and court documents from the Office of the Solicitor General of the Philippines related to ongoing legal cases were made publicly available online.[157] The firm warned that

> [t]his data breach is particularly alarming as it is clear that this data is of governmental sensitivity and could impact on-going prosecutions and national security. An unknown third party has this data and it is likely now in the millions of sensitive and personal records have been exposed because the databases in which they are stored were unsecured and accessible without a password.[158]

Exposure of billions of highly sensitive records. Many billions of highly sensitive records have been exposed in databases discovered to be unsecured (without even a password) since 2019, leading to the possibility of the data being stolen, posted on the dark web, and used for identity theft.[159] Researchers found that unsecured databases left exposed on the web were

---

156. Alicia Hope, *Over 190 Law Firms Affected by Advanced Data Leak That Exposed over 10,000 Legal Documents*, CPO MAG. (May 18, 2020), https://www.cpomagazine.com/cyber-security/over-190-law-firms-affected-by-advanced-data-leak-that-exposed-over-10000-legal-documents/.

157. Public Statement, TurgenSec Limited, Security Lapse Exposes 345k Documents from the Philippines Solicitor General (Apr. 30, 2021), https://community.turgensec.com/security-lapse-exposes-345k-documents-from-the-philippines-solicitor-general/.

158. *Id.*

159. Since 2019 a vpnMentor research team has been working to identify unsecured databases. They are currently undertaking a huge web mapping project using port scanning to examine known IP blocks. This reveals open holes in web systems, which they then examine for weaknesses and data leaks; *see* Ariel Hochstadt, *9 Best VPNs in 2021 for PC, Mac, & Phone—100% SECURE*, vpnMentor (Aug. 12, 2021), https://www.vpnmentor.com.

targeted by cybercriminals at least 18 times each day for as long as they remained exposed.[160]

Five billion records of Cognyte, a cyber intelligence service used to alert customers to third-party data exposures, were accessible online without authentication.[161] BlueKai, Oracle's web tracker, exposed two billion sensitive records of users' web browsing activity—from purchases to newsletter unsubscribes.[162] The breaches of sophisticated security systems designed to protect companies are particularly problematic. Security audit logs with two billion records for homes, hotels, and businesses were exposed in an unsecured server connected to a hotel and resort management company, Pyramid Hotel Group.[163] Because the group's clients include some of the largest hotel chains across many countries, and the data that was exposed related to their operating systems, security policies, internal networks, and cybersecurity event information, this was a potentially very serious incident.

In a massive data breach involving Suprema-owned biometric security platform BioStar 2, 27.8 million sensitive biometric records were found exposed. BioStar 2 provides thousands of companies with biometric security in order to restrict access to offices, buildings, and other private areas.[164] The system uses facial recognition and fingerprint scanning as part of its means to identify users. This was a huge leak that endangered both the businesses and organizations involved, as well as their employees. Researchers were

---

160. Comparitech, a security firm that over the past few years has found a large number of unsecured databases owned by large corporations exposed on the web, recently conducted a practical test to check how interested cyber criminals are in discovering exposed databases and stealing data stored in such databases. *See* Jay Jay, *Unsecured Databases Targeted at Least 18 Times Every Day by Hackers*, TEISS (June 10, 2020), https://www.teiss.co.uk /unsecured-databases-targeted-by-hackers/.

161. *Cyber Analytics Database Exposed 5 Billion Records Online*, DARK READING (June 14, 2021, 4:50 PM), https://www.darkreading.com/attacks-breaches/cyber -analytics-database-exposed-5-billion-records-online/d/d-id/1341297.

162. Zack Whittaker, *Oracle's BlueKai Tracks You across the Web. That Data Spilled Online*, TECHCRUNCH (June 19, 2020, 10:30 AM), https://techcrunch.com/2020/06/19 /oracle-bluekai-web-tracking/.

163. Davey Winder, *Confirmed: 2 Billion Records Exposed in Massive Smart Home Device Breach*, FORBES (July 2, 2019, 8:13 AM), https://www.forbes.com/sites/daveywinder/2019/07/02 /confirmed-2-billion-records-exposed-in-massive-smart-home-device-breach/?sh=179327c0411c.

164. *Over 27.8M Records Exposed in BioStar 2 Data Breach*, TRENDMICRO (Aug. 15, 2019), https://www.trendmicro.com/vinfo/us/security/news/online-privacy/over -27-8m-records-exposed-in-biostar-2-data-breach.

able to access more than one million fingerprint records, as well as facial recognition information. Combined with the personal details, usernames, and passwords, the potential for criminal activity and fraud is massive. Once stolen, fingerprint and facial recognition information cannot be retrieved. Individuals will potentially be affected for the rest of their lives. Researchers were also able to easily access the accounts associated with this leak, as many of the accounts had default or easily decipherable passwords. Those with more complex passwords were also accessed because they were all saved as plain text in the database.[165]

One of the largest data breaches in history. Because of a website design error, access to the key First American Financial Corporation online document-sharing system EaglePro failed to require verification of who was viewing links to a webpage and exposed 885 million records, the earliest dating back more than 18 years to 2003.[166] Files stored on the company's website, firstam.com, contained personal and mortgage-related documents, including bank account numbers, bank statements, mortgage records, tax documents, wire transfer receipts, Social Security numbers, and photos of driver's licenses. All of that information was available without any protection and could be accessed without a password—as long as a person knew where to look.[167]

The law enforcement consequences for First American, the largest real estate title insurance company and provider of mortgage settlement services, were serious and far-reaching. The New York State Department of Financial Services (DFS) brought the first enforcement action against First American under cybersecurity rules that went into effect in 2017 and require that all

---

165. *BioStar 2 Breach: Millions of Users Exposed in Huge Breach*, vpnMentor (Aug. 14, 2019), https://www.vpnmentor.com/blog/report-biostar2-leak/

166. *First American Financial Corp. Leaked Hundreds of Millions of Title Insurance Records*, Krebs on Sec. (May 24, 2019), https://krebsonsecurity.com/2019/05/first-american-financial-corp-leaked-hundreds-of-millions-of-title-insurance-records/.

167. A.J. Dellinger, *Understanding The First American Financial Data Leak: How Did It Happen and What Does It Mean?*, Forbes (May 26, 2019), https://www.forbes.com/sites/ajdellinger/2019/05/26/understanding-the-first-american-financial-data-leak-how-did-it-happen-and-what-does-it-mean/?sh=19188a27567f. A link to a webpage with sensitive information was created and intended to be seen only by a specific party, but there was no method to actually verify the identity of who was viewing the link. As a result, anyone who knew the URL for a valid document on the website or discovered a link to one document could view it—and access any of the other documents hosted on the site by simply modifying a single digit in the link.

department-regulated entities have a cybersecurity program that, among other things, protects customer nonpublic information (NPI).[168] DFS found that the weakness that exposed the documents was first introduced during an application software update in May 2014 and went undetected for years until the vulnerability was discovered in a penetration test First American conducted on its own in 2018.[169] The SEC accused First American of violating Exchange Act Rule 13a-15(a), bringing a cease-and-desist action against the company.[170] First American reached a settlement with the SEC and agreed to pay a penalty of $488,000 for this breach.[171]

Significant violations of security best practices are evident in these types of breaches, putting at risk the most sensitive data of billions of individuals and companies. Security research reports provide numerous examples of databases exposed online or in the cloud with no passwords or passwords stored in plaintext, data accessible without authorization, misconfigurations of a popular open source database,[172] website design errors resulting in no

---

168. New York Cybersecurity Regulation, 23 NYCRR Part 500; New York State Department of Financial Services (DFS), *In the Matter of: First American Title Insurance Company*, Respondent, No. 2020-0030-C, Second Amended Statement of Charges and Notice of Hearing, https://www.dfs.ny.gov/system/files/documents/2021/07/ea20200721_first_american_noh_revised.pdf; *New York Regulator Charges First American Unit over 2019 Data Breach: Enforcement Action Is the First under Cybersecurity Rules That Went into Effect in 2017*, WALL ST. J. (JULY 22, 2020), https://www.wsj.com/articles/new-york-regulator-charges-first-american-over-2019-data-breach-11595423988.

169. Jeremy Kirk, *First American Financial's SEC Breach Settlement: $488,000*, BANK INFOSECURITY (June 21, 2021), https://www.bankinfosecurity.com/first-american-settles-sec-over-data-beach-for-488k-a-16912. An eight-page document released by the SEC describes what it discovered during its investigation. Even after Krebs broke news of the breach, senior executives at the company were still unaware that its own staff had discovered the vulnerability on their own months earlier.

170. Securities Exchange Act of 1934, Release No. 92176 / June 14, 2021, Administrative Proceeding File No. 3-20367, Order Instituting Cease-And-Desist Proceedings Pursuant to Section 21c of the Securities Exchange Act of 1934, Making Findings, and Imposing a Cease-and-Desist Order, https://www.sec.gov/litigation/admin/2021/34-92176.pdf.

171. *First American Financial Pays Farcical $500K Fine*, KREBS ON SEC. (June 18, 2021), https://krebsonsecurity.com/2021/06/first-american-financial-pays-farcical-500k-fine/.

172. Breaches of the popular open source ElasticSearch database and servers are at the heart of recent data exposure reports. *See* Ralf Abueg, *Elasticsearch: What It Is, How It Works, and What It's Used For*, KNOWI (Mar. 7, 2020), https://www.knowi.com/blog/what-is-elastic-search/. An unprotected AWS ElasticSearch database for the job site Ladders exposed 13 million user accounts and profiles. Job seeker information such as names, e-mail addresses, phone numbers, geolocation, current and desired salaries, employment history, and US H1-B visa status was exposed. Employers' and recruiters' personal information on the site was exposed as well.

verification of who was viewing links to a webpage with sensitive information, server configuration errors,[173] and cloud databases that included basic security protections—however, the protections were not configured. These breaches were not the result of hacker attacks. They demonstrate inexcusable failures of companies to follow the most basic, well-accepted security standards and principles. Law offices must be vigilant to ensure that client records and their own data are protected from these types of errors, and understand the nature and scope of the protections in place at their vendors and business partners so that sensitive and confidential data are appropriately secured and are never left unprotected.

I. Lost and Stolen Computers and Mobile Devices

As the use of mobile devices explodes around the globe,[174] concerns about the security of data and communications with mobile or BYOT devices are increasing.[175] While mobile devices are an integral part of the legal environment, and smartphones, tablets, and laptops have become essential tools

---

173. *Report: Hotel Reservation Platform Leaves Millions of People Exposed in Massive Data Breach*, WEBSITE PLANET (Nov. 6, 2020), https://www.websiteplanet.com/blog/prestige-soft-breach-report. Prestige Software, based in Spain, a hotel reservation platform for Expedia, Hotels.com, Booking.com, and others, stored hospitality data, including years of credit card data from hotel guests and travel agents, on a misconfigured Amazon Web Services (AWS) S3 bucket, a popular form of cloud-based data storage, without any protection in place, putting millions of people at risk of fraud and online attacks. Amazon S3 buckets are similar to file folders and consist of data and its descriptive metadata. In order to protect data, S3 Block Public Access must be turned on. *Amazon S3*, AWS, https://aws.amazon.com/s3/ (last visited Aug. 26, 2021).

174. Mobile devices are the fastest-growing computing technology. By the end of 2013, the number of mobile-connected devices exceeded the number of people on earth. It is expected that there will be 11.6 billion mobile-connected devices by 2021, nearly 1.5 mobile devices per capita. Cisco, *Cisco Visual Networking Index: Global Mobile Data Traffic Forecast Update, 2016–2021* (updated Mar. 28, 2017), https://s3.amazonaws.com/media.mediapost.com/uploads/CiscoForecast.pdf.

175. Michael Ogata et al., *NIST Spec. Pub. 800-163 Rev. 1, Vetting the Security of Mobile Applications*, CSRC (April 2019), https://csrc.nist.gov/publications/detail/sp/800-163/rev-1/final; Joshua Franklin et al., *NIST Spec. Pub. 800-124 Rev. 2* (draft), *Guidelines for Managing the Security of Mobile Devices in the Enterprise*, CSRC (Mar. 2020), https://csrc.nist.gov/publications/detail/sp/800-124/rev-2/draft; Dr. Robert Thibadeau & Lucy Thomson, *Mobile Device Security*, 9(1) ABA SCITECH LAWYER 24–28 (Summer 2013).

for attorneys and support staff alike, they can be full of confidential client communications and by their design present numerous risks.[176]

Laptops and smartphones are often lost or stolen, and the data on them may be accessed with little difficulty.[177] The contents of mobile devices may be unprotected because many devices have no password or only a weak password that can be broken. From a security perspective, experts have identified three "attack surfaces" associated with mobile devices—the device itself, the operating system (OS) on the device, and the external service providers.[178] The Federal Trade Commission (FTC) has brought a number of cases charging that companies engaged in unfair and deceptive practices for marketing mobile devices and software with security vulnerabilities or that exposed personal data without consumers' knowledge.[179]

In 2017, Horizon Healthcare Services, Inc. agreed to pay $1.1 million and improve its security practices after two laptops containing the personal information of 690,000 New Jersey policyholders were stolen. The data was not encrypted as required by federal law.[180] In 2019, a laptop belonging to GridWorks, the transportation vendor for Oregon's largest Medicaid coordinated care organization, Health Share of Oregon, was stolen, compromising 654,000 patient records, including patient names, contact details, dates of birth, and Medicaid ID numbers.[181]

---

176. The opinion of the Supreme Court in *Riley v. California*, 573 U.S. 373, 134 S. Ct. 2473 (2014), concerning individuals' expectations of privacy in cell phones, underscores the need for protecting the contents of mobile devices. "One of the most notable distinguishing features of modern cell phones is their immense storage capacity." *Id.*, 34 S. Ct. at 2490. "[Cell phones] could just as easily be called cameras, video players, rolodexes, calendars, tape recorders, libraries, diaries, albums, televisions, maps, or newspapers." *Id.*

177. Franklin et al., *supra* note 175; Thibadeau & Thomson, *supra* note 175; *see* VERIZON 2021 DBIR, *supra* note 2, Lost and Stolen Assets 41–42.

178. Thibadeau & Thomson, *supra* note 175.

179. FTC, *Mobile Technology Issues*, FEDERAL TRADE COMMISSION: PROTECTING AMERICA'S CONSUMERS, https://www.ftc.gov/news-events/media-resources/mobile-technology (last visited Aug. 26, 2021).

180. Mark Iandolo, *Horizon Healthcare Services Settles Data Breach Case for $1.1 Million*, LEGAL NEWSLINE (Mar. 1, 2017), https://legalnewsline.com/stories /511085361-horizon-healthcare-services-settles-data-breach-case-for-1-1-million.

181. *Identity Protection*, HEALTH SHARE, https://www.healthshareoregon.org/idprote ction (last visited Aug. 26, 2021); Charlie Osborne, *Health Share of Oregon Discloses Data Breach, Theft of Member PII*, ZDNET (Feb. 6, 2020, 11:21 AM), https://www.zdnet.com /article/health-share-of-oregon-discloses-data-breach-theft-of-member-pii/.

The vulnerabilities are particularly serious if the mobile devices are used to communicate with legal clients by e-mail or through social media, or to view, process, or store confidential client data or information. Data breaches in such cases can be prevented by encrypting the data on the devices, enforcing procedures that do not permit individuals to transport sensitive data on moveable media, keeping careful track of the devices, and having the highest standards and requirements for couriers to move backup tapes and CDs to off-site storage facilities or from one location to the another.

The Identity Theft Resource Center has analyzed the problem this way:

> This is 100% avoidable, either through use of encryption, or other safety measures. Laptops, portable storage devices and briefcases full of files, outside of the workplace, are still "breaches waiting to happen." With tiered permissions, truncation, redaction and other recording tools, PII can be left where it belongs—behind encrypted walls at the workplace.[182]

Requirements for Mobility in a Legal Environment.   Seeking efficiencies from new technologies, many organizations are considering whether to implement BYOD or BYOT policies. BYOD may appear to be a good approach for organizations seeking to reduce costs and accommodate a generation of younger lawyers who are investing in the latest mobile devices, but the practice carries potential risks that are not well understood. Adopting a BYOD program carries with it significant responsibilities from both an information governance and technical perspective.[183] Targeted toward consumers for on-demand personal access to communications, information, and services, mobile devices are not configured by default for business use. To reduce risk to sensitive data and systems, law practices need to adopt appropriate governance policies for the use of mobile devices to access office

---

182. ITRC, *Data Breaches: The Insanity Continues* (2012), http://www.idtheftcenter.org /artman2/publish/lib_survey/Breaches_2009.shtml.

183. For a general overview, see Steven S. Wu, A Legal Guide to Enterprise Mobile Device Management: Managing Bring Your Own Device (BYOD) and Employer-Issued Device Programs (ABA 2013). This book examines the legal and practical implications of BYOD and highlights future challenges for organizations both in the U.S. and internationally. *See also* Franklin et al., *supra* note 175.

resources and client information. As well, offices must create the infrastructure to manage and secure mobile devices, applications, content, and access.

While there are a number of steps a law firm should take to protect confidential data on mobile devices if it chooses to permit personal devices on the network, several are key. Where possible, the law firm should use mobile device management that provides a centralized way to manage mobile devices remotely, including, significantly, the ability to check a lost device's geographic location and lock or erase it remotely. Only known users and devices should be permitted on the network; app providers should be known as well. Phones that have been jailbroken or rooted should not be permitted on the network. Phones and tablets that are used to create, transmit, or store sensitive data, even in e-mail, should have centralized management of passwords with acceptable password policies, and all user data should be encrypted. Such management software is readily available from many vendors.

J.   Improper Disposal of Personal Information

Sensitive personal records in paper, as well as digital formats, must be protected. At least 35 states, D.C., and Puerto Rico have enacted laws that require either private or governmental entities, or both, to destroy, dispose, or otherwise make personal information unreadable or indecipherable.[184]

K.   Physical Security

Physical security is a critical component of information security. In 2018, a medical records maintenance, storage, and delivery services provider, Filefax, Inc., was fined $100,000 by the HHS Office for Civil Rights (OCR). An OCR investigation found that Filefax impermissibly disclosed protected health information (PHI) by leaving the PHI in an unlocked truck in the Filefax parking lot, or by granting permission to an unauthorized person

---

184. *See* Nat'l Conference of State Legislatures, *NCSL Data Disposal Laws*, NCSL (Jan. 4, 2019), https://www.ncsl.org/research/telecommunications-and-information-technology /data-disposal-laws.aspx.

to remove the PHI from Filefax, and leaving the PHI unsecured outside the Filefax facility.[185]

III. Steps to Protect Confidential Law Firm Records and Prevent Data Breaches: Top Considerations

Law firms that collect, use, store, and share sensitive, confidential, and proprietary information must protect the information and ensure that it is not compromised by hackers or malicious insiders, inadvertently accessed, or lost. The following is a list of top considerations for lawyers and law practices when addressing information security and data protection.

1. *Develop a comprehensive information security plan* specifically designed to prevent data breaches. The plan must include appropriate security for all aspects of the computer network, including *technical, operational, and management controls*. For example, spear phishing is currently a common attack methodology used by hackers; address it by creating a culture of security throughout the law firm and enforcing security policies to combat this problem.

2. *Follow security-by-design principles.* To properly support an organization's risk management framework, security must be incorporated into the architecture and design of the organization's information systems and supporting IT assets.

3. *Conduct a risk assessment.* Carefully document how the security controls selected and implemented address all risks identified. Ensure that information security continuous monitoring is a part of organization-wide risk management.

4. *Prioritize the use of scarce resources to address the most serious problems.* Prioritize security resources so that the most critical and

---

185. Resolution Agreement, https://www.hhs.gov/sites/default/files/filefax-receiver-racap .pdf.

vulnerable aspects of the system are addressed first. Consider the recommendations of experts about how to prioritize.[186]

5. *Combat ransomware*[187] by taking the following actions:

- Backup your data, system images, and configurations and keep the backups off-line.
- Update and patch systems.
- Make sure your security solutions are up-to-date.
- Implement multifactor authentication on every single account that is under the control of the organization.
- Implement the principle of least privilege on key network resources admin accounts, limiting access as much as practical.
- Review and exercise your incident response plan.
- Pay attention to ransomware events and apply lessons learned.

   Address the most common threats such as *phishing attacks, ransomware, BEC, stolen credentials,* and *software patching.* Understand key risks and threats and stay informed about new ones as they are discovered.

6. *Do not purchase or implement* devices, software, or systems with known vulnerabilities.

7. *Focus on vendor management.* Use procurements as an opportunity to specify requirements for appropriate security in vendor contracts and business partner agreements.

8. *Secure the law firm's sensitive data using appropriate encryption technology.* Remember that inadequate or inappropriate key management can result in data breaches and/or loss of data; ensure that appropriate encryption is utilized on mobile devices.

---

186. *See, e.g., CIS Controls,* Ctr. for Internet Sec., https://www.cisecurity.org/controls/ (last visited Aug. 26, 2021). The CIS Critical Controls provides guidance on how to maximize the impact of government and private sector security efforts, and identifies 18 critical priority controls, most of which can be continuously monitored. The CIS website provides a wealth of valuable information about the leading information security methodologies and how they relate to each other.

187. MS-ISAC, *Ransomware Guide* (Sept. 2020), https://www.cisa.gov/sites/default/files /publications/CISA_MS-ISAC_Ransomware%20Guide_S508C_.pdf.

9. *Where possible, use mobile device management* to protect confidential data on mobile devices, including the ability to lock or erase a lost device remotely, and check its geographic location.

10. *Allow only known users, devices, and apps* onto the network. App providers should be known as well. Phones that have been jailbroken or rooted should not be permitted on the network. Phones and tablets that are used to create, transmit, or store sensitive data, even in e-mail, should have centralized management of passwords with acceptable password policies, and all user data should be encrypted.

11. *Be prepared if a data breach occurs.* Build internal firm teams of first responders who have been briefed on the security issues and their implications, so they do not have to think through such things for the very first time in the middle of a security incident or data breach.

12. *Understand key risks and threats and stay aware of new ones as they are discovered.* Identify and build bridges with ISPs, law enforcement, and other security resources, so you know who to go to when an incident or breach occurs, and so they know who you are.[188] Work with the Legal Services Information Sharing and Analysis Organization (LS-ISAO) and take advantage of their resources and expertise.[189]

---

188. The FBI has emphasized the importance of law enforcement collaboration and partnerships with the private sector, *see* FBI, *Office of Private Sector*, FBI.GOV, https://www.fbi .gov/about/partnerships/office-of-private-sector (last visited Aug. 26, 2021).

189. *The Legal Services ISAO*, ISAO (LS-ISAO) provides intelligence and information-sharing services to law firms. https://www.isao.org/information-sharing-group/sector /legal-services-isao/ (last visited Aug. 26, 2021).

Chapter 3
Understanding Technology: What Every Lawyer Needs to Know about the Cyber Network

Paul Rosenzweig and Bryson Bort

Lawyers pride themselves on being generalists. We often say that we can learn a topic quickly and well enough to embody it in a contract or present it to a jury. Whether the question is medical malpractice standards or the history of price supports for prunes, lawyers stand ready to dive right in.

Unfortunately, some lawyers seem to have a phobia about technical topics that bear on their own business operations. Countless attorneys look at the Internet and, metaphorically, put their hands over their ears and mumble "nyah, nyah, nyah" in the hopes that someone else (the "IT guy" down the hall) will deal with the problem. That head-in-the-sand approach is no longer acceptable as a matter of professional responsibility. Every lawyer who uses modern cyber technology has an obligation—to clients, to partners, and to himself—to understand how the cyber network[1] works, if only at a rudimentary level.

This short chapter is intended as a basic introduction to the topic. Readers will learn:

- The basic organization of the world-wide cyber network;

---

1. In general, this chapter uses the phrase "computer network" or "cyber network" as a signal that the network is larger and broader than the "Internet" to which we are most accustomed. At its broadest, the network encompasses all chip-enabled technology, including everything from servers that provide communications services to end-user devices like a connected home thermostat.

- The nature of cyber threats and vulnerabilities; and
- How cyber defensive systems and enterprises work.

I. The Growth of the Network

The Internet as we know it is nearly 40 years old. The very first entries on the World Wide Web were made in the early 1980s. More broadly, the technology of the cyber network (the protocols that allow information to be transferred between two servers) is less than 50 years old. Put another way, the oldest partner in your firm probably remembers a time without personal computers and your middle-aged partner can recall a time without the Internet. Yet your newest associates were, in effect, born connected.

This sea change provides us an important context within which to situate our technical understanding. The explosive growth of the network lies at the heart of its penetration of modern economic activity, and also at the heart of our technological vulnerability. Consider that in 1973 the earliest network (exclusively run by educational and governmental institutions) had only 100 nodes on it[2] (that is, only 100 different servers or systems that were connected to the network). Today there are so many nodes globally that we, quite literally, cannot count them.

The growth of the network has also been driven by the technological improvements that make its expansion feasible. Consider again: In the late 1980s, the U.S. government purchased the Cray XMP-1 supercomputer. It was, at the time, the fastest computer in existence. It was unique and the government tasked it with super hard computational problems, such as development of mathematical models to predict climate change, and the modeling of the structure of nuclear weapons. It ran at an unheard of speed of more than 200 mega FLOPS per second (that is, more than 200 million calculations per second).

The iPhone 7 was faster, and today's iPhone 12 is nearly ten times as fast. In other words, if you own an iPhone (or the equivalent Android phone), you have in your hand more computing power than the most powerful computer in the world at the time of the Reagan presidency. That is not just an evolution

---

2. A node is any system or device that is connected to the network.

of capability, it's a revolution. The change lies behind all of the many advantages of the network, like Google searches and Zappos next-day shipping. It is the technology that enabled the near instantaneous transition, in 2020, to at-a-distance learning and meetings in reaction to the pandemic.

But it also lies behind the empowerment of malicious actors. Today the network is a massive world-girding enterprise with more than 64 percent of the world's population connected. It amasses new data at a rate that doubles human data production every three to six months. Put another way, we create more data in a year now than was created in all the time from the pharaohs to 9/11. And, as we said, 40 years ago the technology that powers it didn't exist.

II. The Structure of the Network

So, what makes this system work? How did it grow so quickly? Why is it so readily usable, generally reliable, and, perhaps most importantly, scalable to ever-larger demand? Put simply, how can a system that had fewer than 100 nodes in 1973 work with the tens of billions of nodes that exist today?

The answer lies in a system of Internet addressing and formatting protocols that undergird the network. These protocols have names like HTTP (which stands for Hypertext Transfer Protocol, and governs how web pages are formatted) and IP, or Internet Protocol, which controls addressing functions for data as it transits the network.

These addressing and structure protocols are, in turn, linked to and support a system of domain names (the text-based identifiers that link to particular IP addresses). This domain name system (or DNS) is how an e-mail to @americanbar.org gets translated into an IP address that points to the ABA's servers (the IP address will typically look something like this: 138.118.82.199).

The addressing system itself is managed by an international nonprofit organization, and functions in a highly distributed manner. At the top of the chain are several ur-source address lists,[3] known as the root. But those root address lists are copied many times and distributed in tens of thousands of

---

3. For a definition of ur-source, see *ur-source*, Wiktionary, https://en.wiktionary.org/wiki/ur-source (last visited June 29, 2021).

locations globally. When your web browser wants to look up a new domain IP address it finds the right answer from some nearby server.

The last link in the structural puzzle is the idea of packet switching—the concept that data flowing between two nodes (whether a web page, an e-mail, or some other code) does not need to travel as a unit. Instead, it travels in multiple small packets of data that take different routes across the network to be reassembled for delivery. Thus, unlike a traditional letter or traditional telephone call, there is no single, direct line of communication from originator to recipient. Instead, the message travels in dozens of packets.

One result of this is that interception and disruption of communications is demonstrably harder. Another is that concealment of origin is demonstrably easier since messages are harder to trace. This latter characteristic gives rise to the "attribution problem"—that is, the well-known difficulty of identifying actors in the cyber domain. Data sent from one country may pass through multiple countries and locations before reaching its final destination, thereby making it extremely difficult to trace back to its original departure point, and thus for malicious actors to disguise their nature and origins.

III. Changing Architectures

Layered on top of this basic structure, there is a changing architecture of how people interact with the network. No broad description of the structure of the cyber network would be complete without identifying five broad, overarching trends in structural change that are being driven by technology today: the cloud, the Internet of Things, the BYOD phenomenon, the use of industrial control systems (ICS), and the rise of artificial intelligence.

A. Cloud Computing

In the early 2000s, most computer system architecture revolved around enterprise servers—that is, the private, physical servers owned by each individual or company, also known as "bare metal." Each company, or individual, provided its own data storage and processing capacity (and, as a result, was also solely responsible for its own security).

That old model has increasingly been replaced by what we have come to call the "cloud." The cloud is in physical structure not terribly different from independent enterprise systems—it involves data storage, security, and processing, in much the same way. The critical difference is that the infrastructure, programming, and storage are now provided as a service to the consumer. Multiple factors are driving this trend, including the shift to a more remote workforce and the need for simplified security. The advantages of the cloud architecture are significant in economic efficiency—the convenience to quickly provision computing resources as needed at scale, the flexibility to create and use only the resources you need on a temporary basis, and the access to expertise that maintains and secures these resources.

One cost, however, is that the data "owner" is divested of much of his or her control—which now devolves to the cloud service provider. Another cost is greater jurisdictional uncertainty. When data is stored in the cloud, for example, it may be stored in a different geographic location from the owner, or it may even be broken up and stored in multiple locations, creating all sorts of legal and policy complications. The problem of cloud geographic diversity is one reason that many nations have begun requiring local data storage as a way of ensuring legal control. Companies that use the cloud also have to wrestle with new types of security challenges: the cloud inherently is outside of their perimeter, which has led to multiple examples of real-world data leakage. Many assume that the cloud provider's security expertise transfers to their own use of the cloud, but, in the end, the security burden and obligation still lies with the customer. The cloud should be an extension of the customer's security posture, including technical expertise, access management, and the like. Almost all of the questions it asks about its internal security are equally relevant to the security of its cloud provider.

B.   Internet of Things

Another major macro-trend is the growth of the Internet of Things (IoT)—the increasing presence of Internet-enabled communications in physical devices with embedded computing capabilities. This trend is driven by the accessibility of increasingly cheap computing resources that can be deployed almost anywhere. Where, previously, connectivity had been limited to systems that operated at a wholesale level, today, the IoT is bringing connection to the retail level—refrigerators, thermostats, cars, and insulin pumps, for example.

There are many benefits to this connectivity. Remote access and control of personal devices enable everything from driverless cars to doctors monitoring patients' vital signs at a distance. It increases convenience and also lowers costs.

But the increase in connectivity also has a cost—the number and scale of vulnerabilities is now much larger. Ten years ago, we were concerned with the security of tens or hundreds of thousands of devices. Today, it is hundreds of millions, if not billions of nodes that are potentially vulnerable.

The most common consumer concern around IoT is privacy. We fear the creepy attacker accessing our webcam to watch us step out of the shower. But that is not the only concern—the prevalence of IoT devices also creates new vulnerabilities for the network and potential for malicious misuse. Since many IoT devices are "adjacent" to traditional computer networks in your home, they allow attackers to access IoT systems and then move, laterally, into your home or a work network.

Worse yet, unlike larger server systems, IoT devices often have simple, yet common vulnerabilities that make their misuse easier. Two of note:

- Many IoT devices are deployed with a limited number of default user and password combinations, allowing attackers to easily guess them to gain access—one famous breach, known as Mirai,[4] took down much of the East Coast Internet and used this method of attack.
- IoT devices are more difficult to patch. In larger systems, as vulnerabilities are identified, patches are released. It is up to the user to apply the patch and to understand the implications of using a system that is accessible to others. This could be anything from a voice-enabled microphone (like Alexa) recording and transmitting all of your conversations, to the data your car collects and shares with the manufacturer.

---

4. Josh Fruhlinger, *The Mirai Botnet Explained: How Teen Scammers and CCTV Cameras Almost Brought Down the Internet*, CSO (Mar. 9, 2018, 3:00 AM), https://www.csoonline .com/article/3258748/the-mirai-botnet-explained-how-teen-scammers-and-cctv-cameras -almost-brought-down-the-internet.html.

But many IoT consumers don't patch and some IoT devices cannot be patched. This allows attackers to build a catalog of vulnerabilities and easily gain access to many IoT devices—this was the modus operandi of a famous campaign that went by the name Reaper/IoTRoop.[5]

C. Personal Devices and the BYOD Phenomenon

The third macro-trend to consider in our survey of system architecture is the growth in the independence of actors and devices. In the past, many enterprises would issue computers and personal devices to employees for their use for business purposes. That allowed the enterprise to both provision and control when and how those devices were used. They could, for example, have effective limits on access to gambling websites.

Even before the recent pandemic, it was becoming much more common for each employee to have his or her own device. That device was dual-use—employees intermingled personal and enterprise purposes in a single operating environment. Naturally, each different device comes with its own vulnerabilities—as to the hardware, the software, and the user's own security profile. This trend has only been exacerbated since the start of the Covid-19 pandemic. As employees increasingly "work from home" and use their own in-home systems, the security perimeter of business enterprises has increased exponentially. The commingling of these assets means that corporate safeguards can be easily circumvented by home devices that are not configured to the same levels of protection and that much of the traffic on these devices is not analyzed. The rarity of outside-the-office work has now become the norm. And that brings with it risks: in a large enterprise, security is dependent on the weakest link—and the Bring Your Own Device (BYOD) phenomenon makes maintaining security architecture even harder. BYOD means there are nonstandard devices now on the computer network that often are not being monitored, logged, or analyzed for malicious behaviors.

---

5. Adarsh Verma, *IoTroop/Reaper: A Massive Botnet Cyberstorm Is Coming to Take Down the Internet*, FOSSBYTES (Oct. 26, 2017), https://fossbytes.com/iotroop-reaper-botnet-attack/.

D.   Industrial Control Systems (ICS)

Industrial control systems (ICS) is a group term used to describe the different kinds of systems that control or automate industrial processes. In simple terms, these are the computers that underpin critical infrastructure, building automation systems like HVAC, and manufacturing. The specifics of the systems vary by their industrial/sector application, but are the same in the way they differ from traditional computers like your laptop. ICS are designed to operate in specific physical environments (they may be outside or subject to high temperatures) and for high availability and reliability—these are critical systems that cannot fail. While the worst impact from a breach of a traditional computer is data centered (ransomware or stolen information, for example), ICS vulnerabilities affect the physical world, and in the worst case can lead to the loss of life or limb.

The most famous ICS attack was Stuxnet, a purported U.S./Israel collaboration to constrain Iran's nuclear ambitions by sabotaging its uranium enrichment centrifuges. Though rarely made public, at least a few other ICS attacks have been reported. For example, the TSMC[6] attack disrupted chip manufacturing in Taiwan. A Russian attack, known as CRASHOVERRIDE,[7] on Ukraine's electrical grid in 2015 shut off electricity in that country. More recently, the DarkSide ransomware that affected Colonial Pipeline[8] forced the company to stop its ICS operations, shutting down a pipeline transporting gasoline and affecting customers across the East Coast. In general, ICS issues will not be of direct concern to practicing attorneys—but they should be aware of the issue, both because it may impact them as consumers of ICS services and, of course, because ICS systems may be clients who have legal concerns.

---

6. Jeremy Kirk, *WannaCry Outbreak Hits Chipmaker, Could Cost $170 Million*, BANKINFOSECURITY (Aug. 7, 2018), https://www.bankinfosecurity.com/chipmaker-tsmc -wannacry-attack-could-cost-us170-million-a-11285.

7. Dragos, Inc., *CRASHOVERRIDE: Analyzing the Malware That Attacks Power Grids* (June 12, 2017), https://www.dragos.com/resource/crashoverride-analyzing -the-malware-that-attacks-power-grids/.

8. José Rodriguez Sr., *The Colonial Pipeline Was Fine, But Its Owner Shut It Down to Make Sure They'd Get Paid Correctly*, JALOPNIK (May 17, 2021, 3:22 PM), https://jalopnik .com/the-colonial-pipeline-was-fine-but-it-was-shutdown-to-1846911689.

E. Artificial Intelligence (AI)

Artificial intelligence (AI) is the concept of computer systems that can make decisions and effectively imitate human intelligence and behavior. A subset of AI is machine learning (ML), which is the ability for computer algorithms to adjust themselves based on the data they gain from operation. Much of the future of decision making will be driven by AI to take advantage of increasing speed and complexity. Computers are faster than human thinking; it's only a question of when they will be as smart.

So how do you train a computer to be like a human? It requires very large data sets to train computers in all of the fundamentals that build up to more complex understanding and actions. [As an aside, the value of large data sets is one of the reasons that some are concerned about foreign access to American data sets, as the recent TikTok controversy demonstrates.[9] TikTok, a video application used by many younger Americans, became a national security issue as questions emerged about the plethora of data that Americans generated on TikTok that could be handed over to the Chinese government.] To date, AI has been moderately successful in relatively simple tasks like chatbots and facial recognition. But the ways that humans naturally pattern match and add context turn out to be very complex processes that are difficult to replicate. Today's technology is years from the level of practical intelligence that we are accustomed to seeing in science fiction.

There are two categories of risk in AI: training and operation. Since the data sets are chosen by humans, implicit bias or error can be introduced. In addition, the quality of the data sets is key—the old adage "garbage in, garbage out" applies to AI.

In operation, AI can apply these implicit biases or gaps and wind up with widely differing and sometimes inappropriate impacts. Here's an example of the problem: a YouTube video[10] of a "racist soap dispenser." The video shows a man with dark skin trying unsuccessfully to get an automated device to dispense soap—his skin color is not recognized. When he uses a

---

9. Brian Fung, *TikTok Is a National Security Threat, US Politicians Say. Here's What Experts Think*, CNN Business (July 9, 2020, 6:47 AM), https://www.cnn.com/2020/07/09/tech/tiktok-security-threat/index.html.

10. Futureism, *This "Racist Soap Dispenser" at Facebook Office Does Not Work for Black People*, YouTube (Aug. 18, 2017), https://www.youtube.com/watch?v=YJjv_OeiHmo.

white paper towel, the dispenser works as it should. The engineers did not (we assume) intentionally build a "racist" device, but they failed to consider the proper data sets and use when designing the dispenser.

IV. Threats on the Cyber Network

As we have noted, the explosive growth of the network, its scalable architecture, and its changing nature lie at the core of an immense economic expansion. But they also bring with them an immensely greater prospect of criminality and other malicious activity. As Dan Geer, the chief information security officer (CISO) of In-Q-Tel (the CIA's venture capital company), once put it, we live in a world where "[e]very sociopath is your next-door neighbor."[11]

So, what are the risks? How are they manifested? In other words, how do you describe the threat to your attorneys, your staff, and your family (who may use the same home computer that you use to work remotely)?

Broadly speaking, each threat can be thought of as having three component parts: a propagation method for moving the malware to your system, an exploit that targets a weakness in the system, and a payload that does the damage.

A. Propagation

Malware propagation is, in essence, the vector for attack. It is the first step in the process of gaining access to a system and often involves both technological and social methods of access. Propagation methods are widely known, but despite this, they continue to have frequent success. Once an attacker gains initial access, they begin an iterative process (post-access) of discovery and lateral movement through other computers toward targets of interest. Once an initial breach occurs, the attackers begin to roam inside your system.

---

11. Dan Geer, *Shared Risk at the National Scale* (2004), http://web.stanford.edu/class /msande91si/www-spr04/slides/geer.pdf.

The most common initial access attack is phishing: an e-mail with a bad link inside to click on. (The name "phishing" is intended to evoke the idea of fishing—the link is the bait and, sadly, you are the fish.) Most of the attacks we've seen start with phishing campaigns because, quite simply, they work, and it costs little to scale into a campaign. We've also seen USB stick attacks (where the malware is on a USB that is "given away" for free and plugged into a system) and website auto downloads (where the malware is latent on a dodgy website—like a gambling site or pornography—and automatically runs whenever the site is accessed).

It is fair to say that a large majority of attack methods (like our phishing example) rely on human factors. The link is the technology, but the danger is in the well-crafted message that seduces the reader to make the wrong choice.

B. Exploits

Exploits are the code that manipulates a computer system. According to computer scientists, it is a truism that *every* system has vulnerabilities, that is, flaws in the computer code that can be exploited by outsiders. Given how large some programs are (the operating system for Windows 10 has more than 60 million lines of code), it is impossible for there not to be such flaws—no human enterprise of that size could plausibly be flawless.

Some of these flaws are well known. For example, there is one well-known exploit called a "buffer overflow" that has been around for more than a dozen years, but it still works because the flaw is too difficult to fix.[12]

By far the most dangerous exploits, however, are those that are not well known—new exploits that someone has recently discovered. We call these types of exploits zero-day (or 0-day) exploits because they work on the first day they are tried in the real world (day zero, so to speak). Known exploits can be patched, though sometimes only with great effort. Unknown

---

12. For those who are interested, here is a short, nontechnical description of the problem: A computer program will typically have a buffer in it—that is a place into which to write data. Most buffers are created with a fixed size. In some programs an anomaly exists where, if I write into the buffer a data set that is larger than its fixed size, the data will overrun the buffer's boundary and overwrite adjacent memory location. This lets a malicious actor purposefully write data outside the buffer and, thereby modify how the system operates.

zero-day exploits don't have patches, and may not for some time. That is precisely why they are so valuable, and often sell for tens of thousands of dollars on the black market.

The recent attacks on SolarWinds and the Microsoft Exchange system[13] both used zero-day exploits that had not previously been discovered—which is part of what made them so unexpected and so devastating. Sadly, the reality is that exploits are impossible to eliminate—so we need to deal with a world of persistent vulnerability.

C. Payloads

Payloads are the payoff, so to speak. This is where the true malware danger lies. After gaining entry and manipulating your system to allow the outsider to control it, the payload is what the malicious actor uses to achieve his or her ends. Sometimes it may be a program that wipes out your data or degrades it in some way. One of the relatively newer forms of malware is called ransomware—a program that encrypts your data so that you can't access it and holds you to ransom to get it back. The world witnessed the effects of ransomware in the Colonial Pipeline attack that affected the gasoline supply for much of the East Coast in May 2021.[14]

Another change in payload attack was evidenced by the Solarwinds incident from 2020, where Russian intruders subverted the supply chain/software update system to deliver their payloads.

For lawyers and law firms, the major risks relate to the confidentiality of our work. Lawyers need to worry about access to critical client data (hence, fears of ransomware). And they also need to be particularly concerned about the theft (what hackers call "exfiltration") of sensitive client information from the firm. When even large Wall Street law firms like Cravath, Swaine

---

13. SolarWinds is a commonly used IT Network Management software platform that was initially compromised by Russia forcing an extensive and expensive response by thousands of U.S. companies. *See* Pam Baker, *The SolarWinds Hack Timeline: Who Knew What, and When?*, CSO (June 4, 2021, 2:00 AM), https://www.csoonline.com/article/3613571/the-solarwinds-hack-timeline-who-knew-what-and-when.html. Microsoft Exchange is one of the most common e-mail platforms in use and was compromised with multiple 0-days by a Chinese-related organization. *See* Microsoft, *HAFNIUM Targeting Exchange Servers with 0-Day Exploits* (Mar. 2, 2021), https://www.microsoft.com/security/blog/2021/03/02/hafnium-targeting-exchange-servers/.

14. This is discussed further in Chapter 2 of this Handbook.

& Moore[15] and Jones, Day[16] are subject to attack, one can be certain that no law firm is immune.

D. Attackers

A final thing to consider about cyber risk is not the "how" of it but the "who." Attacker motivations are extremely varied, as are their tactics and their objectives. Thus, one critical component of understanding the threat is what cybersecurity experts call "threat intelligence"—that is, knowing who the attackers are, which gives you an insight into how and why they are acting. For example, "hacktivists" are individuals who hack for political reasons. They may steal data from an enterprise, but they typically will not try to profit from it—rather they will use it to publicly embarrass the law firm or one of its clients (as, for example, with the Panama Papers hack of the Panamanian law firm Mossack Fonseca).[17]

By contrast, "script kiddies" are young hackers who attack just for fun. Criminals steal data for exploitation and profit. More recently, with the SolarWinds and Hafnium/Microsoft attacks,[18] we have seen an increase in the incidence of nation-state attacks targeted at national security or economic security objectives. Each uses different types of exploit and propagation methods and typically uses different payloads—and so the defense against each will also vary. One easy rule of cybersecurity is "know your enemy."

---

15. Matthew Goldstein, *Cravath Law Firm Discloses a Data Attack*, N.Y. TIMES (Mar. 30, 2016), https://www.nytimes.com/2016/03/31/business/dealbook/cravath-law-firm-discloses -a-data-attack.html.

16. Chris Opfer, *Jones Day Hit by Data Breach as Vendor Accellion Hack Widens*, BLOOMBERG LAW (Feb. 16, 2021), https://news.bloomberglaw.com/business-and-practice /jones-day-hit-by-data-breach-as-vendor-accellion-hacks-widen.

17. Grant Gross, *The Massive Panama Papers Data Leak Explained*, COMPUTERWORLD (Apr. 5, 2016, 9:25 AM), https://www.computerworld.com/article/3052218/the-massive-pan ama-papers-data-leak-explained.html.

18. *See supra* note 13.

V. Defensive Systems and Enterprise Challenges

The final piece of the puzzle lies in how one responds to the threat environment. Some of the responses are technological in nature; others involve systematic changes in enterprise management that are necessary to make the technological responses effective—as we said earlier, most threats involve the human factor, so while technology can help, it is no panacea and will not be the entire solution to a law firm's cyber vulnerability problems. And, indeed, there is no "solution"—one can mitigate the risk, but it cannot ever be fully eliminated.

A. Technology and Defense

The number of defensive technologies that are available is as varied as the types of malicious attacks. No brief piece could hope to catalog them all. However, we can offer a typology of the most common systems that are routinely deployed, many of which would be useful in every law firm context.

1. Systems for Detecting and Preventing Intrusions

There are many different types of preventative systems available to an enterprise. The simplest is a "firewall"—a network security system that monitors and regulates traffic into and out of a computer system based on a fixed set of security rules. An "intrusion detection system" (IDS) is typically somewhat more sophisticated in that it attempts to go beyond a fixed set of rules to identify an attack based on some variation that it observes from the "norm," or baseline, of enterprise behavior. So, for example, an IDS might observe traffic from a new IP address located in Russia that had never before attempted to access the law firm's website and flag that anomaly for assessment. To the extent that the detection system takes the follow-on step of trying to prevent the intrusion from happening, it is sometimes called (unsurprisingly) an "intrusion prevention system," or IPS. As you may imagine, the number and variety of IDS/IPS systems are vast and there are innumerable vendors.

Picking the right IDS/IPS for your enterprise is one of the critical decisions for the person responsible for information security in your organization, often a chief information security officer (also known as the CISO). As

Dmitri Alperovitch, co-founder of the cybersecurity firm Crowdstrike has said, the quickness of your detection and response is critical. Your objective can be captured in the 1-10-60 rule—that is how fast the defender must react (in minutes) to detect (1), respond (10), and remediate (60) an attack in order to prevent it from breaking out beyond the initial malicious access, when the scope of the breach becomes exponentially more expansive.

2.   Information Sharing

Of course, intrusion detection works better if you know in advance what intrusions may look like. Recall that previously unobserved exploits are often called zero-days because they work on day zero and nobody has seen them before. Notably, a zero-day for one enterprise may not be a zero-day for another. The second enterprise might have seen the intrusion two weeks ago and fixed the problem—but the first enterprise is still vulnerable unless the latter organization shares its knowledge of the exploit. Hence, one of the most common forms of defense is simply to participate in an information-sharing system with other similarly situated companies, so that everyone in the group can benefit from shared threats and experiences. The industry approach is formalized as an Information Sharing and Analysis Center[19] (ISAC)—a sector-specific (maritime, automotive, finance, etc.) organization of public–private partnerships to facilitate cybersecurity threat intelligence.

In December 2015, Congress passed the Cybersecurity Act of 2015, which was intended to make information sharing even easier and more common.[20] The act set the parameters for how federal, state, local, and tribal government agencies share and receive cybersecurity-related information. It also provides safe harbor to private organizations that share information, shielding them from legal liability. Today, most enterprises are part of an ISAC and routinely share information. As with most government programs, some of the ISACs are better than others.

---

19. National Council of ISACs, https://www.nationalisacs.org/ (last visited June 29, 2021).
20. The bill was Division N of the 2015 Omnibus Appropriations Act. *See* Consolidated Appropriations Act, H.R. 2029, 114th Cong. (2016).

3. Insider Threat Systems

As also noted earlier, most intrusions happen because of fundamental human factors. Often, this is the product of human error (mistakenly clicking on a bad link, for example). But sometimes it is the product of a malicious insider (say, a disgruntled employee who is planning to leave the firm). In either case, another form of defense is to monitor employee conduct with systems that, broadly, go under the name of "insider threat" systems. These systems often use sophisticated algorithms to attempt to identify aberrant behavior in employees. This can include things as simple as "employee A is reusing a password" or as complex as "employee Z has never accessed that database before, why is he doing so now?" Once identified, these anomalies can be flagged for management follow up. These systems differ from purely technical intrusion detection systems in that they focus on human behavior—with all its greater complexities and sensitivities. It should go without saying that law firms considering deploying insider threat systems should proceed with caution and with full transparency to employees.

4. Multifactor Authentication

One subset of threat that has special salience is the threat of unauthorized access—in other words, the intrusion that arises because some malicious actor has abused Internet-accessible authentication in order to access the system in an apparently permitted way. Sadly, today, identity theft is rampant and most users have weak or ineffective passwords—and so fraudulent access of this form is on the rise.

The most effective way to combat unauthorized access is through a process known as "multifactor authentication" (MFA) or "two-factor authentication" (2FA) to establish identity. MFA allows one to prove identity. We often say that you can do so by using something you have (like an application/device linked to the account), providing something you are (like your user ID or, these days, your fingerprint or face), or by demonstrating something you know (like your password). Typical examples of MFA today include a key fob with a rotating random number that needs to be inputted or an independent authorization program that needs to be used through, say, a smart phone device or tablet.

The most common form of authentication is through text messages (SMS), because of its ease of use, where the authentication prompts a user to respond with a keycode texted to the user's registered number. This method is not perfect—it can be defeated by attackers who have developed multiple ways to intercept the text. But it is still better than not using any additional authentication method at all. Whatever the methodology, the underlying thesis is simple—access is restricted to those who both know a password/user name combination *and* can authenticate their identity through some second channel of communication. Any enterprise with multiple users would be wise to consider implementing MFA.

5. Encryption

The final technological defense to consider is the growing use of encryption. Encryption is a way of encoding a message or data so that only people with the authorized decryption code can access the information. Properly implemented, today's encryption programs cannot be broken by attackers. Data that is properly encrypted is akin to money in an unbreakable safe—even if the robber gets into the house, the contents of the safe remain protected. Today, encrypted communications systems are common—most consumers have access to systems like Signal, Telegram, or WhatsApp that provide for end-to-end encrypted conversations.

Encryption often comes, however, with some enterprise costs—it can limit collaboration, for example, and can sometimes result in the loss of data when the encryption passphrase is lost (or, itself, stolen). Encryption may also have broader social costs, as it is sometimes argued that increased use of encryption can protect malicious actors. (Others, of course, make the counterargument that encryption enhances security and privacy at a social scale.) Either way, these costs are likely to be worth incurring for sensitive and high-value data, of which law firms typically possess quite a lot.

B. Enterprise Challenges

Beyond technical systems for defense, there are organizational issues that frequently get in the way of an effective response. Again, the number and variety of such issues is as wide as the number of organizations—each enterprise has its own particular nature. But make no mistake, though we like to think of law firms as "different," in terms of corporate organization and security challenges, they are pretty much like any other enterprise. Here are three challenges that have been common in law firms and may merit special attention:

First and foremost is simply the lack of knowledge of and/or commitment to understanding key cybersecurity issues and then fixing cybersecurity problems within the firm's management committee. The lack of knowledge can be remedied—bar associations have plenty of resources on cybersecurity, and online advice is also available.

Still, good cybersecurity is not free; it always comes with a cost, sometimes quite a significant one. While improved cybersecurity can be readily justified as a necessary expense to avoid even greater potential harm, there is no disguising the fact that it detracts from the bottom line. Especially for firms that have not, themselves, experienced a breach—or are not aware that they have—gaining a firm-wide commitment to reasonable cybersecurity measures is often a challenge.

Second, firms often see cybersecurity as a subset of information technology issues and put their CISO (chief information security officer) in a separate IT/management silo. This is often a mistake; in a large firm the CISO is the firm's first line of cyber defense. Yet often the CISO operates cut off from firm-wide risk-management practices. For larger firms, cyber threat intelligence often benefits from a broader, more holistic picture of what risks the firm is incurring and how they are being managed in other contexts. Firms may want to consider whether their current administrative architecture is effective in developing a firm-wide resistance to cybersecurity threats.

Of course, solo practitioners and smaller firms may not have a dedicated CISO. They may only have a part-time "IT guy" whose job it is to set up and maintain the system. In these cases, the lawyer would be wise to consider some form of audit—the hiring of an outside evaluator to review the firm's practices and make cost-effective suggestions for change. Small firms and solos like to think that they will not be targets (we call this instinct the idea of "security by obscurity"), but increasingly that is not true—and even smaller-sized practitioners have practical obligations to their clients that require some form of precautionary response.[21]

---

21. Issues for solo and small firm practitioners are further described in Chapter 9 of this Handbook.

Finally, one challenge that is not unique to law firms but is perhaps more common in firms than in other organizations is the diversity of employee age and experience. As we noted at the outset, lawyers of different ages have different experiences and expectations from the cyber network. Some older employees were born well before the network existed—they may find passwords and multifactor authentication difficult to implement. (A no-doubt apocryphal story tells of one senior law firm partner who demanded that his password be his first name, so that he could remember it.) By contrast, some younger employees expect to have their own devices for use in the workplace and many grew up in a "sharing" world where Facebook and Instagram predominate. As a result, they may not have fully internalized core legal ethical concepts of client confidentiality and their nonwork practices may pose unique risks to the firm's data integrity. Navigating these different social expectations will require differentiated training and education programs, and will significantly complicate the effort to maintain the firm's security posture.

In today's world, law firm practice is deeply dependent on the vast world cyber network. Having become so dependent on it, lawyers can no longer remain ignorant of or intimidated by the technology. As a matter of best practices (if not ethical obligation) they need to be more proactive and self-educated. This short introduction is, we hope, a useful first step.

VI. Looking Forward—The Next Five Years

Predicting the future is always risky—especially so when we speak of computer networks and the cyber domain. The pace of change in cyberspace is fast, and it will only get faster. Nonetheless, no introduction to cybersecurity would be complete without a brief effort to peer into the mists of the future. Here are a few trends (beyond those already described) that will likely be salient:

- IoT will continue to go macro and global; within the next five years, cars, trucks, and industrial systems of all sorts will be massively interconnected.
- Everything will be automated; as AI improves, tasks as diverse as warfare and surgery will increasingly be done without human intervention, at least at the tactical level.

- Ransomware will move from global enterprise issue to affecting us in our daily lives: Want to start your car? One Bitcoin please.
- Internet balkanization: the fault lines of nation-state conflict will lead to multiple separate Internets that may be almost completely isolated, like North Korea, or very limited for regional control, like China.
- Large data aggregation and enhanced artificial intelligence analytics will continue to erode privacy as legal restrictions struggle to keep up with technological reality.
- Quantum computers (which use quantum physics to do computations) are in active development. If they are ever commercially available, quantum computers will likely increase processing speeds exponentially. We can't know what the effects of this will be, but one example often talked about is that quantum computers may make data encryption nearly impossible.
- Reality itself will be contested; building on the disinformation campaigns of the past few years, the propagation of "deepfake" technologies that can mimic and mutate real-life experiences will make debates about facts and "fake news" ever more prominent.

VII. Top Ten Considerations

Following are key considerations attorneys should keep in mind related to the technology side of cybersecurity:

1. The worldwide computer network is no longer brand new. The Internet is more than 40 years old.
2. The network is growing and speeding up at an ever-increasing rate. Today's iPhone is ten times faster than the supercomputer of 40 years ago.
3. The network is not like the phone network. It runs on distributed addressing and structural protocols without any centralized control.
4. The architecture of the network is changing as we adopt:
   a. Cloud computing;
   b. Internet of Things consumer devices;

    c. Enhanced use of personal devices in enterprise settings;

    d. Reliance on Industrial Control Systems; and

    e. Artificial intelligence.

5. Threats on the network propagate through logical vulnerabilities in code and, more frequently, through exploitation of human factors, such as phishing e-mails.

6. It is impossible to eliminate vulnerabilities in the network. Perfect code cannot be written. It is critical to be able to identify vulnerabilities and address them.

7. Threat intelligence is critical; know who is after you and what they are after.

8. Technological defenses help. An enterprise defense should include systems for:

    a. Detecting and preventing intrusions;

    b. Information sharing; and

    c. Insider threat detection.

9. To protect enterprise systems, one should:

    a. Deploy multifactor authentication; and

    b. Implement encryption, where practicable.

10. Some of the most important defensive steps involve organization-wide responses, like incorporating cyber risk into an enterprise-wide risk assessment. Cyber threats are not isolated, and incidents will quickly spread across an entire enterprise.

SECTION II

LAWYERS' LEGAL AND ETHICAL OBLIGATIONS TO CLIENTS

Chapter 4
Legal Obligations to Provide Data Security

Thomas J. Smedinghoff and Ruth Hill Bro

Recent high-profile and well-publicized security breaches have highlighted our almost total dependence on electronic networks and digital data, as well as the significant risks of harm that can result from a security breach. Virtually all transactions and key records of a business are created, used, communicated, and stored in electronic form using networked computer technology. Although such technology provides organizations with increased flexibility and tremendous economic benefits, including reduced costs and increased productivity, it also creates significant vulnerabilities that can adversely affect the business, its clients and customers, and other entities with which it interacts.

The Covid-19 pandemic further spotlighted these vulnerabilities, as organizations shifted to remote working, which is likely here to stay in many respects. Beyond this, greater security challenges for organizations are coming, including ransomware and attacks by global state actors. Creating, using, communicating, and storing information in electronic form greatly increases the potential for unauthorized access, use, disclosure, alteration, loss, or destruction of the information. Front-page news stories about data security missteps made by companies, government agencies, and other organizations (including law firms) are a testament to the growing significance of this problem and should serve as a wake up call for lawyers in all practice settings. Insert your firm's name, or your client's name, in the most recent ransomware or data breach headline, and the risk of not taking sufficient security steps (especially those that are legally required) becomes all too real. That risk not only affects the organization itself, but also can do serious harm to employees, customers and clients, vendors, shareholders, investors, and, in some cases, the public.

As a consequence, data security has become a legal obligation. Concerns about individual privacy, accountability for financial information, the authenticity and integrity of transaction data, and the need to protect the confidentiality and security of sensitive business and client data are driving the enactment of new laws and regulations designed to ensure that all organizations adequately address the security of the information assets in their possession or under their control. Such concerns and calls for legislative responses have been fueled by the ever-increasing volume and sophistication of cyberattacks (such as phishing, ransomware, and targeting of off-site vendor, client, and employee access, all amplified by the Covid-19 pandemic) and the escalating injury to the public and other stakeholders of all types.

Taken as a group, data security laws and regulations impose two fundamental legal obligations on organizations:

- The duty to provide security for their information assets; and
- The duty to notify others of security breaches that occur.

All organizations (including law firms), whether regulated or not, are generally subject to these legal duties regarding the security of the information assets in their possession or under their control. The following sections begin with an explanation of basic data security concepts, followed by an analysis of the sources and scope of those two legal duties.

I.   Basic Data Security Concepts

A.   What Is Data Security and What Are Its Objectives?

The general concept of "*security*" refers to the steps an entity takes to protect one or more of its *assets* (such as buildings, equipment, cargo, inventory, data, and people) from *threats*. The steps taken to provide such protection are often referred to as *security measures* or *security controls*.

The subset of security known as "*data security*" (also referred to as "cybersecurity" or "information security") involves the implementation of *security controls* to protect an organization's *information assets*. An organization's information assets can generally be divided into the following two categories:

- **Information.** This includes a wide variety of data, such as personal data about employees, customers and clients, prospects, and other individuals; corporate financial information; information regarding corporate business transactions, attorney–client information; trade secrets and other confidential information; electronic transaction records; and information relating to corporate communications, including e-mail,)process control instructions, and a variety of other types of corporate data. Such information can take a variety of digital forms, including databases, e-mail messages, documents, voice recordings, images, video, software, and other content in digital form.
- **Information systems.** This includes the computers, communication networks, mobile phones, storage media, software, firmware, services, and related resources that are used to acquire, store, process, manage, communicate, and transmit information. Such systems may be controlled and managed by the company, its employees or contractors (who use their own mobile phones and home computers), or third-party service providers, such as vendors, cloud providers, and outsource providers.

The objectives of *data security* have generally been defined as "the protection of *information* and *information systems* from unauthorized access, use, disclosure, disruption, modification, or destruction in order to provide confidentiality, integrity, and availability."[1]

These objectives can be viewed both in terms of the negative consequences to be avoided and the positive results to be achieved. The negative consequences to be avoided are unauthorized access, use or processing, disclosure or transfer, disruption, modification or alteration, and loss or destruction. The positive goals to be achieved are *confidentiality*, *integrity*, and *availability*.

---

1. *See* definition of "information security" in *Glossary of Key Information Security Terms*, NAT'L INST. OF STANDARDS & TECH. (NIST), https://csrc.nist.gov/glossary/term/information_security (emphasis added); NIST, SPEC. PUBL'N 800-53, REV. 5, SECURITY AND PRIVACY CONTROLS FOR FEDERAL INFORMATION SYSTEMS AND ORGANIZATIONS 404 (Sept. 2020).

Confidentiality involves ensuring that information is not made available or disclosed to unauthorized persons or processes—that is, that it remains secret, with access limited to appropriate persons and processes only. It requires protecting information assets to ensure that an intruder, attacker, or any other unauthorized party or process cannot access or in any other way compromise the organization's systems or information. In some cases, it also involves protecting information so that, even if unauthorized access is obtained, the information is indecipherable or not usable (e.g., encrypted).

Integrity involves ensuring that information or information systems have not been altered or destroyed in an unauthorized manner. It requires guarding against improper information modification or destruction, including ensuring information nonrepudiation and authenticity. Within the context of data security, integrity can be viewed from two perspectives:

- **System integrity.** This entails ensuring that the computers, other devices, networks, and software that comprise or interact with an organization's information systems operate properly and are correctly configured, and that no changes are made except as authorized.
- **Data integrity.** This entails ensuring that the information itself is accurate and complete, and that no unauthorized alterations are made to the information either intentionally or accidentally.

A compromise affecting either system or data integrity could have a serious impact on the organization, depending on the nature and value of its information assets.

Availability involves ensuring that data or information is accessible and useable upon demand by an authorized person, and ensuring timely and reliable access to and use of information. A loss of availability is the disruption of access to or use of information or an information system.

Availability requires that the computer systems, networks, and data are operational, fully functioning, available for use, and accessible whenever needed. This means that the computing system used to store and process information, the security controls used to protect it, and the communication channels used to access it must be functioning correctly and be able to withstand a variety of possible disruptive threats, such as power failures, natural disasters, accidents, or cyberattacks.

Availability protects against intentional or accidental attempts to deny legitimate users access to information or systems. If an organization's computer system, or its information, is not available, the organization likely will be seriously affected. Consider, for example, the impact of the unavailability of an airline's or hotel's reservations system or of a law firm's network and document database.[2]

B. What Threats and Vulnerabilities Does Data Security Address?

A *security breach* occurs whenever a threat (whether coming from inside or outside the entity) is able to exploit a vulnerability, resulting in a compromise of the confidentiality, integrity, or availability of a company's information assets. Thus, achieving the objectives of data security requires taking steps to protect against threats to an organization's information assets. A *threat* is anything that has the potential to cause harm. The types of threats, where they come from, what is at risk, and the seriousness of the consequences will, of course, vary greatly from one organization to another. Threats can originate inside or outside of an organization; when they materialize, they typically cause damage by exploiting the organization's vulnerabilities.

Threats to the security of information and information systems can be divided into three categories: *physical* and *environmental, technical,* and *people.*[3]

1. Physical and Environmental Threats

Physical and environmental threats involve the theft, damage, destruction, or other interference with the operation of the physical elements comprising the information system (e.g., servers, laptop computers, storage media). They include:

- Natural disasters or so-called acts of God, such as earthquakes, hurricanes, floods, storms, tornadoes, fire, and lightning that physically damage information systems or that interfere with their operation;
- Infrastructure failures that cause problems, such as power failures or fluctuations, hardware failures, water damage, and improper air conditioning, humidity, or heating; and

---

2. *See, e.g., DLA Piper Still Struggling with Petya Cyber Attack,* FIN. TIMES (July 6, 2017), https://www.ft.com/content/1b5f863a-624c-11e7-91a7-502f7ee26895.

3. *See, e.g.,* NIST, SPEC. PUBL'N 800-53, REV. 5, *supra* note 1, at 422.

- **Intentional acts aimed at the physical computer system, network, or storage devices,** such as theft of equipment or storage media, criminal destruction (including vandalism or sabotage), civil disorders, terrorism, and war.

2. Technical Threats

Technical threats are those carried out by the use of computer code or other automated mechanisms. While such threats can sometimes cause physical damage, they most likely result in the inoperability or improper operation of a computer system or network, or the unauthorized access to information and/or disclosure, alteration, or destruction of information. Although frequently the result of human programming activity, technical threats can be (1) *unintentional* or *negligent* or (2) *intentional* and *malicious*.

- **Unintentional or negligent technical threats** include programming errors that occur during the development of a computer system or software program, and system configuration errors, such as the use of improper settings or parameters when software is installed or the failure to change default passwords that come from the vendor when the system is installed.
- **Intentional and malicious technical threats** typically involve the use of computer code or other technical devices designed to cause trouble. Examples include software bugs intentionally added to computer programs, or malicious software that modifies or destroys data, renders systems or data unusable, or engages in other mischief. This can include viruses, worms, Trojan horses, spyware programs designed to copy and transmit communications or other information, ransomware that locks up data and renders it unusable, network spoofing, denial-of-service attacks, password cracking, e-mail hijacking, packet replay, and packet modification.

3. People Threats

People threats come from individuals, both insiders and outsiders. Although press coverage of security breaches focuses primarily on outsiders (such as hackers) who break into an organization's computer system, more often than not the primary people threats come from insiders (such as employees, consultants, or others) who are authorized to have access to an entity's information assets.

- **Insiders.** In some cases, individuals abuse their authorization (e.g., when an employee who has authorized access to customer personal information sells some of that information to a third party). In other cases, however, insider-originated security breaches are the result of simple negligence, inattention, or lack of education (e.g., when an employee who does not understand proper procedures inadvertently clicks on a phishing e-mail or negligently discloses confidential information). Unintentional mistakes or omissions by employees who are not properly trained or who are negligent (such as system administrator errors, operator errors, and programming errors) are common.
- **Outsiders.** Outsiders often are able to breach an organization's security through a variety of means. These include impersonation (e.g., misrepresenting their identity or source), social engineering (e.g., tricking an unsuspecting insider into clicking on a phishing e-mail and releasing password information or otherwise allowing access or disclosing confidential information), hacking (e.g., gaining access through the use of technical tools, such as exploiting weaknesses in software systems) or brute force attacks (e.g., continuing to guess passwords until one is successful).

Threats become a problem when they can exploit a *vulnerability*, which is any flaw or weakness in a company's information systems (including deficiencies in its security controls) that could be accidentally triggered or intentionally exploited by a threat to compromise or cause harm to its information assets.[4] A vulnerability might be an unlocked door, a system with easy-to-guess passwords, unencrypted data on a laptop computer, disgruntled employees, or employees who simply do not understand what steps they need to take to protect the security of the firm's data.

---

4. *Id.* at 423.

Moreover, a vulnerability can also result from any flaw or weakness in the information systems of a third party. Because a web of security interdependencies (e.g., between an entity and its vendors) frequently exists, a failure of data security at one enterprise can be a threat to data security at another. No entity is an island when it comes to considering threats and vulnerabilities.

The likelihood that a threat will exploit a vulnerability to cause harm creates a *risk*. In other words, risk is the likelihood that something bad will happen that causes harm to an information asset. Somewhat more precisely, "[r]isk is a measure of the extent to which an organization is threatened by a potential circumstance or event, and is typically a function of: (i) the adverse impacts that would arise if the circumstance or event occurs; and (ii) the likelihood of occurrence."[5] Risk is present wherever a threat intersects with a vulnerability. For example, if the threat is theft of equipment, and the vulnerability is an unlocked door, risk is the likelihood that a thief will enter the building through the unlocked door and steal equipment or do other damage. Similarly, if the threat is a hacker, and the vulnerability is open Internet access to a server containing sensitive data, risk is the likelihood that a hacker will enter the system and view, copy, alter, or destroy the sensitive data.

C. What Types of Security Controls Are Used to Achieve Those Objectives?

Achieving the foregoing objectives of data security involves implementing *security controls* designed to protect information assets from the various threats they face.

Security controls (sometimes called security measures or safeguards) are the various policies, procedures, organizational structures, devices, hardware, software, and other means implemented by organizations to protect the confidentiality, integrity, and availability of information that is processed, stored, and transmitted by an organization.[6]

---

5. NIST, Spec. Publ'n 800-30, Rev. 1, Guide for Conducting Risk Assessments 8 (Sept. 2012).

6. *See, e.g.*, NIST, Spec. Publ'n 800-53, Rev. 5, Security and Privacy Controls for Federal Information Systems and Organizations (Sept. 2020). This publication provides a list of security controls recommended for consideration by organizations to satisfy their data security requirements. Which of those should be implemented, and how implementation should be addressed, are answered in the context of an organization's risk management process and the threats it faces (discussed *infra*).

Security controls designed to protect information assets from threats generally are grouped into three separate categories based on the nature of the control: *physical, technical,* and *administrative.* Within each of these categories, security controls can be further classified based on their timing with respect to the risks and threats they are designed to address—that is, whether they are designed to prevent the risk from occurring (*preventive*), to detect and identify the risk or breach (*detective*), or to respond to the risk after it has occurred (*reactive*).

- **Physical security controls.** These security measures are designed to protect the tangible items that make up the physical computer systems, networks, and storage devices that process, communicate, and store the data, including servers, devices used to access the systems, storage devices, and the like. Physical security controls are often intended to prevent unauthorized persons from entering that environment, or to help protect against environmental threats or natural disasters. Examples of the three types of physical security controls include the following:
  - **Preventive:** locks, fences, security guards, double door systems, and key-card access controls
  - **Detective:** sensors and alarms, such as motion detectors, smoke and fire detectors, and closed-circuit television monitors
  - **Reactive:** sprinkler systems, locking doors, and systems designed to automatically notify the police and fire departments of a problem
- **Technical security controls.** These security measures typically involve the use of software and data safeguards incorporated into computer hardware, software, and related devices. These measures are designed to ensure system availability, control access to systems and information, authenticate persons seeking access, protect the integrity of information communicated via and stored on the system, and ensure confidentiality where appropriate. Examples of the three types of technical security controls include the following:
  - **Preventive:** firewalls, access-control software and associated passwords, smart cards and biometric tokens, antivirus software, and encryption
  - **Detective:** intrusion detection systems and audit trails

- **Reactive:** cutting off access or shutting a system down
- **Administrative security controls.** Sometimes referred to as "procedural" or "organizational" controls, administrative security controls consist of written policies, procedures, standards, and guidelines to guide conduct, prevent unauthorized access, and provide an acceptable level of protection for computing resources and data. Administrative security measures also inform people about how to conduct day-to-day operations. Examples of the three types of administrative security controls include the following:
    - **Preventive:** procedures for proper screening of personnel before hiring, security awareness education and training for employees, separation of duties so that no one employee can effectively compromise the system, procedures for employee termination, and requirements for appropriate supervision
    - **Detective:** regular employee security reviews and audits, employee reporting, and rotation of duties
    - **Reactive:** appropriate discipline for employees who violate policies

Most security statutes and regulations require addressing each of these three categories of security measures (i.e., physical, technical, and administrative), either expressly or impliedly. For example, federal financial regulations require covered entities to "implement a comprehensive written information security program that includes administrative, technical, and physical safeguards,"[7] and Massachusetts security regulations require all businesses to "develop, implement, and maintain a comprehensive information security program that . . . contains administrative, technical, and physical safeguards."[8]

---

7. GLB Security Regulations, 12 C.F.R. pt. 30, Appendix C.
8. MA Standards for the Protection of Personal Information of Residents of the Commonwealth, 201 Mass. Code Regs. 17.03(1) [hereinafter "Mass. Standards for the Protection of Personal Info." or "Massachusetts Security Regulations"].

II. The Duty to Provide Data Security

The duty to provide data security is imposed on virtually all organizations through a variety of differing laws, regulations, and other legal mechanisms (e.g., contracts). Certain sectors of the U.S. economy are, of course, subject to extensive regulations regarding data security. This typically includes critical infrastructure sectors, such as financial, health care, the power grid, and so on. But nonregulated organizations also are subject to data security obligations from a variety of sources. While the level of detail may vary, virtually all sources of the legal duty to provide security express the obligation in largely the same manner.

A. What Is the Duty?

Defining the scope of an organization's duty to provide security begins with understanding that the law views security as a relative concept. Thus, the basic legal duty to provide data security is often stated as an obligation to implement *"reasonable"* or *"appropriate"* security measures designed to achieve the security objectives noted above (i.e., ensure the *confidentiality*, *integrity*, and *availability* of information). For example, most states generally impose a duty to implement *"reasonable security* procedures and practices" on all organizations that collect or process personal data about their residents.[9] Likewise, numerous FTC enforcement actions since 2001 interpret the failure to provide "reasonable security" as an unfair business practice in violation of section 5 of the Federal Trade Commission Act.[10] Key sector-specific regulations do the same. They include federal health care regulations (which require *"reasonable and appropriate"* security), federal financial sector regulations (which require security *"appropriate* to the size and complexity of the bank and the nature and scope of its activities"),[11]

---

9. For a list of state security laws generally applicable to all organizations, see Appendix B (State Statutes) of this Handbook. The duty to provide security also can be enforced by the various state attorneys general under their unfair trade practice statutes.

10. See FTC security cases at https://www.ftc.gov/datasecurity.

11. For a list of federal security laws and regulations governing various sectors, see Appendix A (Federal Statutes) and Appendix C (Federal Regulations) of this Handbook.

and state insurance laws and regulations (which require implementation of "*appropriate*" security measures).[12]

To meet this standard and achieve these security objectives, organizations must develop and implement a security program that includes appropriate physical, technical, and administrative security measures to protect both information and information systems from the various threats they face. Because laws and regulations recognize that security is a relative concept, they rarely specify or provide detailed guidance regarding what specific security measures or technology an organization should implement to satisfy those legal obligations. Accordingly, determining appropriate and compliant security controls can vary depending on the situation. Some laws, however, do include specific requirements for particular security measures that must be implemented, in addition to the general requirement for reasonable security.[13] A few laws are even starting to provide safe harbors.[14]

B.   What Is the Source of the Duty, and to Whom Does It Apply?

There is no single law, statute, or regulation that governs the obligations of organizations (including law firms) to provide security for the information in their possession or under their control. Instead, legal obligations to implement data security measures are found in an ever-expanding patchwork of state, federal, and international laws, regulations, and enforcement actions, as well as in common-law duties and other express and implied obligations to provide "reasonable" or "appropriate" security for business data. Even cities are starting to impose data security obligations.[15] Thus, although any

---

12. *See, e.g.*, Nat'l Ass'n of Ins. Comm'rs, Insurance Data Security Model Law (2017), adopted in 13 states, https://content.naic.org/sites/default/files/inline-files/MDL-668.pdf.

13. For example, the Massachusetts security regulations require implementation of firewalls, the use of virus software, and, in certain cases, the use of encryption. *See* Mass. Standards for the Protection of Personal Info., 201 Mass. Code Regs. 17.00 *et seq.* (2012), www.mass.gov/ocabr/docs/idtheft/201cmr1700reg.pdf.

14. Security safe harbors are discussed *infra*.

15. For example, New York City's Tenant Data Privacy Act (TDPA), enacted on May 30, 2021, regulates the collection, use, retention, and safeguarding of biometric and other data gathered in "smart access buildings," with required security measures of encryption, password reset capability (where the system uses a password), and regularly updated software to address security vulnerabilities; https://legistar.council.nyc.gov/LegislationDetail.aspx?ID=4196254&GUID=29A4B0E2-4C1F-472B-AE88-AE10B5313AC1&Options=ID%7cText%7c&Search=.

particular law or regulation may not apply to a specific organization, one or more other laws likely will.

Some laws seek to protect the organization and its owners, shareholders, investors, and business partners. Other laws focus on the interests of employees, customers, and prospects. In some cases, governmental regulatory interests or evidentiary requirements are at stake. Many of the requirements are industry specific (e.g., focused on the financial sector or the health care sector) or data specific (e.g., focused on personal information or financial data). Some laws focus only on public companies or on specific critical infrastructure sectors. When viewed as a group, however, such laws and regulations cover virtually all business activity.

The most common sources of obligations to provide data security include the following:

1. Statutes and Regulations

Numerous state, federal, and international statutes and regulations impose obligations to provide data security. Sometimes they use recognizable terms such as "security" or "safeguards," but in many cases they are more subtle by referring to particular attributes of security, such as "authenticate," "integrity," "confidentiality," "availability of data," and the like. Such statutes and regulations include:

- **Privacy laws and regulations,** which typically include provisions imposing an obligation to provide adequate security for personal data collected, used, communicated, or stored by an organization.
- **Security laws and regulations,** such as the state-level security laws that impose a general obligation on businesses to protect the security of certain personal data they maintain about individuals and/or that regulate the communication or destruction of certain data.[16]
- **E-transaction laws,** which are designed to ensure the enforceability and compliance of electronic documents generally; examples include the federal Electronic Signatures in Global and National Commerce Act

---

16. At least half of the states in the United States have such laws. See Appendix B (State Statutes) of this Handbook.

(E-SIGN) and the state Uniform Electronic Transactions Act (UETA, now enacted in all states but New York), which require security for storage of electronic records relating to online transactions.

- **Corporate governance legislation and regulations,** which are designed to protect public companies and their shareholders, investors, and business partners; examples include Sarbanes-Oxley and implementing regulations (which require public companies to ensure that they have implemented appropriate information security controls for their financial information) and Securities and Exchange (SEC) regulations (which impose various requirements for internal controls over information systems).[17]
- **Unfair business practice laws,** at both the federal and state levels, and precedent set by related government enforcement actions, such as FTC enforcement of FTC Act section 5 to compel reasonable security.
- **Sector-specific regulations,** such as the security regulations focused on the health care, financial, insurance, and other critical infrastructure sectors.

Selected federal statutes are provided in Appendix A, state statutes in Appendix B, federal regulations in Appendix C, and state regulations in Appendix D; given the speed at which the legal landscape is changing, counsel should check the applicable jurisdictions for the most recent laws and regulations.

2.   Common Law Obligations

Courts increasingly are accepting the view that there is a common law duty to provide appropriate security for corporate and personal data, the breach of which constitutes a tort. In a 2005 case, for example, the court held that "defendant did owe plaintiffs a duty to protect them from identity theft by providing some safeguards to ensure the security of their most essential confidential identifying information."[18] In a 2007 case of particular significance to lawyers, the court allowed plaintiffs to proceed on a "negligent

---

17. Sarbanes-Oxley Act: Pub. L. No. 107-204, §§ 302, 404; 15 U.S.C. § 7241 (corporate responsibility for financial reports) and § 7262 (management assessment of internal controls).
18. Bell v. Mich. Council, 205 Mich. App. LEXIS 353, at *16 (Mich. App. Feb. 15, 2005).

misrepresentation" claim based on the theory that the defendants made implied representations that they had implemented the security measures required by industry practice to safeguard personal and financial information.[19] In 2014, a federal court recognized the legal duty to "safeguard a consumer's confidential information entrusted to a commercial entity" and noted that failing to use "industry-standard" encryption breached a legal duty of care.[20] In 2018, a state supreme court found that the defendant (which had suffered a data breach) had a legal duty to employees "to use reasonable care to safeguard their sensitive data in collecting and storing it on an Internet-accessible computer system." The employer required employees to provide sensitive data as a condition of employment and chose how to store that data; the employer's data collection and storage could foreseeably expose the employees to "unreasonable risk of harm."[21] The court held that the employer could be liable for data breaches of employee information, and that the economic loss doctrine would not bar such claims.[22]

3. Rules of Evidence

Providing appropriate security to ensure the integrity of electronic records (and the identity of the creator, sender, or signer of the record) can be critical to securing the admission of an electronic record in evidence in a dispute. This conclusion is supported by the form requirement for an "original" in electronic transaction laws,[23] the evidence rules regarding authentication,[24] and case law addressing evidentiary authentication requirements.[25]

---

19. *In re* TJX Cos. Retail Security Breach Litig., 524 F. Supp. 2d 83 (D. Mass. 2007).

20. *In re* Sony Gaming Networks & Customer Data Sec. Breach Litig., 996 F. Supp. 2d 942, 966 (S.D. Cal. 2014).

21. Dittman v. UPMC, 196 A.3d 1036 (Pa. 2018).

22. *Id.* The court noted that ". . . under Pennsylvania's economic loss doctrine, recovery for purely pecuniary damages is permissible under a negligence theory provided that the plaintiff can establish the defendant's breach of a legal duty arising under common law that is independent of any duty assumed pursuant to contract."

23. *See, e.g.*, Unif. Electronic Transactions Act (UETA) § 12(d); Electronic Signatures in Global and National Commerce Act (E-SIGN), 15 U.S.C. § 7001(d)(3).

24. *See, e.g.*, FED. R. EVID. 901(a).

25. *See, e.g.*, Am. Express v. Vinhnee, 336 B.R. 437 (B.A.P. 9th Cir. 2005); Lorraine v. Markel, 241 F.R.D. 534 (D. Md. May 4, 2007).

4. Rules of Professional Responsibility

In addition to the legal obligations discussed here, lawyers also have ethical obligations to protect client data via the rules of professional conduct. State rules generally are patterned after the ABA Model Rules of Professional Conduct, which were amended in August 2012 at the recommendation of the ABA Commission on Ethics 20/20 to include updated guidance regarding a lawyers' use of technology[26] and the lawyer's confidentiality obligations as they relate to information relating to client representation.[27] Thus, any client-related data held by a law firm is likely to be subject to ethical obligations to protect the security of that data.[28]

5. Contractual Obligations

In some cases, data security regulations impose on businesses an obligation to push down certain security requirements to third parties with whom they do business. Examples include the Massachusetts security regulations[29] and the financial sector's Gramm-Leach-Bliley Act (GLB) Safeguards Rule,[30] which requires the business to impose appropriate security obligations on third-party organizations with access to its data. In those cases, businesses frequently try to satisfy (at least in part) their obligation to protect their data by entering into contracts with third-party vendors who will process, or have access to, their data. This approach also is particularly common in outsourcing and cloud agreements and has become a source of data security obligations for law firms that agree to comply with security requirements imposed on them by their clients.

In other cases, businesses must contractually agree to comply with the requirements of certain technical security standards. One example is the

---

26. ABA MODEL RULES OF PRO. CONDUCT r. 1.1 cmt. [8].

27. These rules and other law applicable specifically to lawyers are covered in Chapter 6 of this Handbook.

28. ABA MODEL RULES OF PRO. CONDUCT r. 1.6(c).

29. Mass. Standards for the Protection of Personal Info., 201 MASS. CODE REGS. 17.00 *et seq.* (2012).

30. FTC Standards for Safeguarding Customer Information (Safeguards Rule) (to implement §§ 501 and 505(b) of the Gramm-Leach-Bliley Act, 16 C.F.R. pt. 314 (FTC)).

Payment Card Industry Data Security Standard (PCI Standard),[31] to which merchants must agree as a condition of accepting credit cards.

6. Self-Imposed Obligations

In many cases, security obligations are self-imposed. Through statements in privacy notices, on websites, in advertising materials, or elsewhere, organizations often make representations regarding the level of security they provide for their data (particularly personal data collected from persons to whom the statements are made). By making such statements, organizations impose on themselves an obligation to comply with the standard they have told the public that they meet. If those statements are not true, or are misleading, they may become deceptive trade practices under section 5 of the FTC Act or equivalent state laws.

Thus, the duty of any organization (and any law firm) to provide security can come from several different sources and several different jurisdictions—each perhaps regulating a different aspect of the organization's information—but the net result is a general obligation to provide security for all of the organization's information and information systems.

In some cases, the duty to provide security can be enforced by a private right of action. In most cases, however, it is enforced by the applicable regulatory agency, or by the FTC or the various state attorneys general (AGs). One need look no further than the last 20-plus years of FTC enforcement actions, as well as state AG enforcement actions, to see that numerous nonregulated organizations have been targeted for failing to provide appropriate data security for their own data. Targets of such enforcement actions have included a wide range of organizations, such as consumer electronics companies, data brokers, hardware and software vendors, hotels, ID theft prevention services, mobile app developers, mobile phone makers, property management firms, retailers, restaurants and entertainment establishments, social media and networking sites, technology services, transportation

---

31. *See* PCI Security Standards Council, www.pcisecuritystandards.org.

services, travel emergency services, transcription services, tax preparation services, virtual platforms, website operators, and many others.[32]

C. Requirements for Providing Legally Compliant "Reasonable Security"

Complying with the duty to provide reasonable security requires the development of what is frequently referred to as a "written comprehensive information security program." A *security program* provides a documented set of the organization's cybersecurity processes, policies, procedures, guidelines, and standards. Yet, because the law treats security as a relative concept that will vary from one organization to the next, there is no standard form security program. Instead, implementing a legally compliant "reasonable" or "appropriate" data security program is a fact-specific exercise.

Nonetheless, a legal standard for the process to implement "reasonable" security is emerging. That standard generally rejects one-size-fits-all requirements for specific security measures (such as specific firewall or password requirements) and instead adopts a process-based, fact-specific approach to security obligations. Specifically, it requires engaging in a repetitive "process" to:

- Establish program governance,
- Identify the information assets to be protected,
- Identity and assess the risks to those assets,
- Identify and implement appropriate security measures responsive to those risks,
- Provide training and education,
- Monitor and test the security controls to verify that they are effectively implemented,
- Oversee third-party arrangements, and
- Periodically review and readjust the program to update it in response to new developments, including changes in the law or the threat environment.

---

32. *See, e.g.*, list of FTC data security cases and enforcement actions, https://www.ftc.gov /datasecurity; May 2017 state attorneys general settlement agreement with Target Corp., http:// www.illinoisattorneygeneral.gov/pressroom/2017_05/17-AVC-0008TargetCorporation.pdf.

This "process-oriented" legal standard for information security has been widely adopted in numerous federal, state, and international statutes and regulations.[33] These steps are explained next.

1. Establish Program Governance

Assign Responsibility. Most of the key data security laws and standards recognize that someone in the organization must be responsible for security. Thus, they typically require appointment of a responsible person to oversee the development and maintenance of the security program.

For example, the Massachusetts security regulations require that "every comprehensive information security program shall include . . . [d]esignating one or more employees to maintain the comprehensive information security program."[34] Likewise, the NY Shield Act[35] requires "designat[ion of] one or more employees to coordinate the security program." Consent decrees under section 5 of the FTC Act typically require that the defendant designate "an employee or employees to coordinate and be accountable for the security program."

Ensure Management Oversight. Security laws increasingly recognize that overall responsibility for fulfilling the organization's obligation to provide security falls directly on the board of directors or senior management. Beginning in 2001, the role of the board of directors in the development and implementation of the information security program of financial institutions

---

33. *See, e.g.*, GLB regulations titled *Interagency Guidelines Establishing Standards for Safeguarding Consumer Information* issued on February 1, 2001, at 12 C.F.R. Part 30, Appendix B (OCC), 12 C.F.R. Part 208, Appendix D-2 and 12 C.F.R. Part 25, Appendix F (Federal Reserve System), 12 C.F.R. Part 364, Appendix B (FDIC), 12 C.F.R. Part 568 and 570, and later were adopted by the FTC in its *Safeguards Rule* on May 23, 2002 at 16 C.F.R. Part 314; Federal Information Security Management Act of 2002 (FISMA) at 44 U.S.C. § 3544(b); HIPAA *Security Standards* issued by the Department of Health and Human Services on February 20, 2003, at 45 C.F.R. Part 164; FTC enforcement decisions at www.ftc.gov/datasecurity; Nat'l Ass'n of Ins. Comm'rs, Insurance Data Security Model Law (2017; Mass. Standards for the Protection of Personal Info., 201 MASS. CODE REGS. 17.00 *et seq.*; the NY Shield Act, N.Y. Gen. Bus. Law § 899-BB, and N.Y. Dep't of Fin. Servs., Cybersecurity Requirements for Financial Services Companies, N.Y. Comp. Codes R. & Regs. tit. 23, § 500.02. See also *Small Entity Compliance Guide for the Interagency Guidelines Establishing Information Security Standards*, Dec. 14, 2005, www.federalreserve.gov/boarddocs/press/bcreg/2005/20051214/default.htm.

34. Mass. Standards for the Protection of Personal Info., 201 MASS. CODE REGS. 17.03(2)(a) (2012).

35. N.Y. GEN. BUS. LAW § 899-BB, Section 2(b)(ii)(A)(1).

was explicitly recognized in financial sector regulations. In particular, the GLB regulations required that "the Board of Directors or an appropriate committee of the board" must:

- "Approve the institution's written information security program" and
- "Oversee the development, implementation, and maintenance of the institution's information security program, including assigning specific responsibility for its implementation and reviewing reports from management."[36]

Thereafter, similar requirements have appeared in other data security laws, regulations, standards, and best practice documents. Examples include the regulations issued by the New York Department of Financial Services[37] and the NAIC Insurance Data Security Model Law.[38]

Put It in Writing. Most of the key data security laws expressly require that the security program be in writing. In fact, numerous regulators, including the FTC, take the view that "if the security program is not in writing, it doesn't exist." Thus, virtually all of the FTC consent decrees require that the defendant's security program "must be fully documented in writing."[39] Likewise, financial regulations require covered entities to "implement a comprehensive *written* information security program," health care regulations require that security "policies and procedures implemented to comply with this subpart [be] in *written* (which may be electronic) form,"[40] the Massachusetts security regulations require "a comprehensive information security program that is written,"[41] the New York DFS regulations require that "Each Covered Entity shall implement and maintain a *written* policy or

---

36. 12 C.F.R. Part 364, Appendix B, III.A.

37. N.Y. Dep't of Fin. Servs., Cybersecurity Requirements for Financial Services Companies, N.Y. COMP. CODES R. & REGS. tit. 23, § 500.023

38. Nat'l Ass'n of Ins. Comm'rs, Insurance Data Security Model Law (2017), at Section 4.E; now adopted in 13 states.

39. See list of FTC data security cases and enforcement actions, https://www.ftc.gov /datasecurity.

40. 45 C.F.R. § 164.316(b)(1)(i).

41. Mass. Standards for the Protection of Personal Info., 201 MASS. CODE REGS. 17.03(1).

policies,"[42] and the NAIC insurance model law requires that insurers "shall develop, implement, and maintain a comprehensive *written* Information Security Program."[43] In the EU, the General Data Protection Regulation (GDPR) privacy regulation also requires a written security policy.[44]

2. Identify Information Assets

To protect something, you must know what it is, where it is, how it is used, how valuable it is, and so forth. Thus, when addressing data security, the first step is to identify the organization's information assets to be protected and their location (whether inside or outside of the organization). This involves taking an inventory of the information that the organization creates, collects, receives, uses, processes, stores, and communicates to others. It also requires identifying the systems, networks, and processes by which such data is created, collected, received, used, processed, stored, and communicated.

Data files are often found in a variety of places within an organization. Data also is often found outside of the organization—more specifically, in the possession and control of a third party, such as an outsource service provider or cloud provider. Yet the organization (or law firm) is still responsible for the security of its (and its clients') data in the possession of third parties. Data location analysis also requires identifying in which jurisdictions (country and state or province) they are collected, processed, and stored, as this will affect which laws apply.

Identifying information assets is also key in identifying compliance obligations, as different data security laws and regulations may come into play depending on the specific type of information asset. This includes, for example, protected health information regulated under HIPAA, personally identifiable financial information regulated under GLB, information about children regulated under the Children's Online Privacy Protection

---

42. N.Y. Dep't of Fin. Servs., Cybersecurity Requirements for Financial Services Companies, N.Y. COMP. CODES R. & REGS. tit. 23, § 500.03.

43. Nat'l Ass'n of Ins. Comm'rs, Insurance Data Security Model Law (2017), at Section 4.A; now adopted in 13 states.

44. Regulation (EU) 2016/679 of the European Parliament and of the Council of 27 April 2016 on the protection of natural persons with regard to the processing of personal data and on the free movement of such data, and repealing Directive 95/46/EC [hereinafter GDPR], at Articles 30(1)(g) and 30(2)(d).

Act (COPPA),[45] and other types of personal information regulated under state and local security laws, the Fair Credit Reporting Act (FCRA),[46] and section 5 of the FTC Act.

Good practice and many security laws, regulations, and guidance documents expressly require identification of information assets. Examples can be found in guidance from the FTC,[47] NIST,[48] and the state of California.[49]

3. Identify Risks—Conduct Periodic Risk Assessments

Just as you cannot implement security until you identify what you have that needs to be protected, you also cannot implement security until you know what risks you need to protect against. Thus, implementing reasonable security to protect the information assets of an organization requires a thorough assessment of the potential risks to the entity's information systems and data.

Accordingly, most laws and regulations are risk-based and require that an organization's data security program must be based on a risk assessment. Various federal security statutes and regulations, including GLB[50] and HIPAA,[51] expressly require a risk assessment, as do almost all of the data security consent decrees entered in FTC enforcement actions.[52] Likewise, numerous state data security laws and regulations, such as in

---

45. Children's Online Privacy Protection Act of 1998 (COPPA), 15 U.S.C. §§ 6501 *et seq.*

46. Fair Credit Reporting Act (FCRA), as amended by the Fair and Accurate Credit Transactions Act (FACTA), 15 U.S.C. §§ 1681 *et seq.*

47. FTC, *Protecting Personal Information: A Guide for Business* 2 (Oct. 2016), https://www.ftc.gov/tips-advice/business-center/guidance/protecting-personal-information-guide-business.

48. NIST Framework for Improving Critical Infrastructure Cybersecurity (Feb. 12, 2014) ("Cybersecurity Framework"), Framework Core at Appendix A, at www.nist.gov/cyberframework. The Cybersecurity Framework is discussed throughout this Handbook.

49. *See* Cal. Att'y Gen., *California Data Breach Report 2016*, at 29 (Feb. 2016), https://oag.ca.gov/breachreport2016.

50. 16 C.F.R. 314.4(b).

51. 45 C.F.R. 164.308(a)(1)(ii)(A).

52. See FTC enforcement actions alleging failure to provide reasonable security at www.ftc.gov/datasecurity; resulting consent decrees typically require "the identification of material internal and external risks to the security, confidentiality, and integrity of covered information that could result in the unauthorized disclosure, misuse, loss, alteration, destruction, or other compromise of such information."

Massachusetts,[53] New York,[54] Ohio,[55] and Oregon,[56] as well as state AG guidance documents in California[57] and Illinois[58] expressly require a risk assessment. The EU GDPR also expressly requires a risk assessment.[59]

Most other security laws impliedly require a risk assessment, typically by requiring that the company must provide a level of security "appropriate to the risk." Various security frameworks and standards, such as the NIST Cybersecurity Framework[60] and the ISO 27000 Series,[61] also make clear that risk assessments are essential. In addition, several U.S. courts have held that a risk assessment plays a key role in determining whether a duty will be imposed and liability found. For example, one court held that where injury is foreseeable and preventable, an organization has a duty to provide appropriate security to address the potential harm.[62] On the other hand, another court held that where a proper risk assessment was done,

---

53. Mass. Standards for the Protection of Personal Info., 201 MASS. CODE REGS. 17.03(2)(b).

54. NY Shield Act, N.Y. GEN. BUS. LAW § 899-BB, Section 2(b)(ii)(A)(1); N.Y. Dep't of Fin. Servs., Cybersecurity Requirements for Financial Services Companies, N.Y. COMP. CODES R. & REGS. tit. 23, § 500.02 and 500.09(a).

55. Ohio Data Protection Act, OHIO REV. CODE §§ 1354 et seq.

56. OR REV. STAT. 646A.622(2)(d)(A).

57. Cal. Att'y Gen., *California Data Breach Report*, at 29 (Feb. 2016), (https://oag.ca.gov /sites/all/files/agweb/pdfs/dbr/2016-data-breach-report.pdf), stating that "[i]nformation security laws and regulations generally require a risk management approach. In essence, this means organizations must develop, implement, monitor, and regularly update a comprehensive information security program [under which organizations must] assess risks to the assets and data."

58. Ill. Att'y Gen., *Information Security and Security Breach Notification Guide 5* (Jan. 2012), www.illinoisattorneygeneral.gov/consumers/Security_Breach_Notification_Guidance. pdf, stating that businesses and government agencies should "[i]dentify reasonably foreseeable internal and external risks to the security, confidentiality, and integrity of customer information that could result in the unauthorized disclosure, misuse, alteration, destruction, or other compromise of such information, and assess the sufficiency of any safeguards in place to control these risks."

59. *See* GDPR, at Recital 83 and Article 32.

60. NIST Framework for Improving Critical Infrastructure Cybersecurity, Version 1.1 (April 16, 2018) (hereinafter NIST Cybersecurity Framework), https://www.nist.gov/cyberframework /framework.

61. ISO/IEC 27001 (2018) Information Security Management, https://www.iso.org/isoiec -27001-information-security.html.

62. *See, e.g.*, Wolfe v. MBNA Am. Bank, 485 F. Supp. 2d 874, 882 (W.D. Tenn. 2007); Bell v. Mich. Council, 2005 Mich. App. LEXIS 353 (Mich. App. Feb. 15, 2005).

but a particular harm was not reasonably foreseeable, the defendant would not be liable for failure to defend against it.[63]

A *risk assessment* is the process of identifying vulnerabilities and threats to the information assets used by the organization or firm and assessing the potential impact or harm that would result if a threat materializes. This forms the basis for determining what countermeasures (i.e., security controls), if any, should be implemented to reduce risk to an acceptable level. Thus, a risk assessment requires:

- Conducting a threat assessment to identify all reasonably foreseeable internal and external *threats* to the information assets to be protected;
- Conducting a *vulnerability* assessment to identify the organization's vulnerabilities;
- Assessing the *risk* posed by the threats and vulnerabilities—that is, assessing the *likelihood* that each of the threats will materialize and, if so, the probability that one or more of the vulnerabilities will be exploited to cause harm;
- Evaluating the potential impact or *damage* that will result; and
- Assessing the sufficiency of the security controls in place to guard against each identified threat.

This risk assessment process will be the baseline against which security controls can be selected, implemented, measured, and validated. The goal is to understand the risks that the organization faces and to determine what level of risk is acceptable, in order to identify appropriate and cost-effective safeguards to combat those risks. Thus, such risks should be evaluated in light of the nature of the organization and its clients, its transactional capabilities, the sensitivity and value of the stored information to the organization and its trading partners, and the size and volume of its transactions.[64]

---

63. *See* Guin v. Brazos Higher Educ. Serv., 2006 U.S. Dist. LEXIS 4846, at *13 (D. Minn. Feb. 7, 2006) (finding that where a proper risk assessment was done, the inability to foresee and deter a specific burglary of a laptop was not a breach of a duty of reasonable care).

64. *See, e.g., Authentication in an Electronic Banking Environment*, FED. FIN. INST. EXAM. COUNCIL 3 (July 30, 2001), www.ffiec.gov/pdf/authentication_guidance.pdf.

Although laws typically do not specify how to do a risk assessment, the following publications provide general information and guidance on conducting a risk assessment:

- NIST Special Publication 800-30, Rev. 1, *Guide for Conducting Risk Assessments*[65]
- Commonwealth of Massachusetts, *A Small Business Guide: Formulating A Comprehensive Written Information Security Program*[66]
- Commonwealth of Massachusetts, Executive Office of Technology Services and Security (EOTSS), *Information Security Risk Management Standard*[67]
- Federal Financial Institutions Examination Council (FFIEC), *IT Examination Handbook, Information Security Booklet*[68]
- Cyber Security Agency of Singapore (CSA), *Guide to Conducting Cybersecurity Risk Assessment for Critical Information Infrastructure*[69]

4. Develop and Implement an Appropriate Security Program to Address Identified Risks

Following completion of the risk assessment, security laws generally require an organization to design and implement a security program consisting of reasonable physical, technical, and administrative security measures designed to manage and control the risks identified during the risk assessment—that is, to reduce the risks and vulnerabilities to a reasonable and appropriate level.

---

65. *See* NIST, *Guide for Conducting Risk Assessments*, NIST, Spec. Publ'n No. 800-30, Rev. 1 (Sept. 2012), http://nvlpubs.nist.gov/nistpubs/Legacy/SP/nistspecialpublication800-30r1.pdf.

66. *See* Massachusetts Office of Consumer Affairs, *A Small Business Guide: Formulating a Comprehensive Written Information Security Program*, https://archives.lib.state.ma.us/handle/2452/685875; https://paulohm.com/classes/infopriv13/files/week13/MA%20form%20WISP.pdf.

67. Commonwealth of Massachusetts, Executive Office of Technology Services and Security (EOTSS), *Information Security Risk Management Standard* (2020), https://www.mass.gov/doc/is010-information-security-risk-management-standard/download.

68. FFIEC, *IT Examination Handbook, Information Security Booklet* (Sept. 2016), http://ithandbook.ffiec.gov/it-booklets.aspx.

69. Cyber Security Agency of Singapore (CSA), *Guide to Conducting Cybersecurity Risk Assessment for Critical Information Infrastructure* (2019), https://www.csa.gov.sg/-/media/csa/documents/legislation_supplementary_references/guide_to_conducting_cybersecurity_risk_assessment_for_cii.pdf.

It should be noted, however, that the presence or absence of any specific security measures says little about the status of an organization's compliance with its information security obligations. The security measures implemented by an organization must respond to the particular threats it faces and address its specific vulnerabilities. Posting armed guards around a building sounds impressive as a security measure, but it is of little value if the primary threat the organization faces is unauthorized remote access to its data via the Internet. Likewise, firewalls and intrusion detection software are often effective ways to stop hackers and protect sensitive databases, but if an organization's major vulnerability is careless (or malicious) employees who inadvertently (or intentionally) disclose passwords or protected information, then even those sophisticated and important technical security measures will not adequately address the problem.

Most laws do not require organizations to implement specific security measures or use a particular technology, but instead provide flexibility to use measures reasonably designed to respond to the risks identified in the risk assessment to achieve the security objectives of ensuring confidentiality, integrity, and availability. This focus on flexibility means that, like the obligation to use "reasonable care" under tort law, determining compliance can be somewhat difficult.

Nonetheless, for purposes of developing a security program, most statutes and regulations consistently focus on the need to address the three types of security controls (physical, technical, and administrative). Within those three types, they frequently focus on certain *categories* of security measures that organizations should consider (although how an organization must address each category—that is, which security controls it should implement—is typically not specified). Categories of security controls most often mentioned include:[70]

- **Physical Facility and Device Security Controls.** Measures to safeguard the facility; measures to protect against destruction, loss, or damage of information due to potential environmental hazards (such as fire and water damage or technological failures); procedures that govern the receipt and

---

70. *See supra* note 6.

removal of hardware and electronic media into and out of a facility; and procedures that govern the use and security of physical workstations.

- **Physical Access Controls.** Access restrictions at buildings, computer facilities, and records storage facilities to permit access only to authorized individuals.

- **Technical Access Controls.** Software, policies, and procedures to ensure that authorized persons who need access to the system have appropriate access (and no more), and that those who should not have access are prevented from getting it, including procedures to determine access authorization, grant and control access, verify that a person or entity seeking access is the one claimed (i.e., authentication), and terminate access when it is no longer needed.

- **Remote Access Controls.** Measures to respond to the increased reliance on remote communications and personal devices used by employees, and to address the security of those remote devices and the communications channels being used.

- **Intrusion Detection Procedures.** Software, policies, and procedures to monitor login attempts and report discrepancies; system monitoring and intrusion detection systems and procedures to detect actual and attempted attacks on, or intrusions into, the organization's information systems; and procedures for preventing, detecting, and reporting malicious software (e.g., virus software).

- **Employee Procedures.** Job control procedures, segregation of duties, and background checks for employees with responsibility for or access to protected information, and controls to prevent employees from providing information to unauthorized individuals who may seek to obtain this information through fraudulent means.

- **System Modification Procedures.** Procedures designed to ensure that modifications to system hardware or software are authorized, appropriate, and implemented in a manner consistent with the organization's security program.

- **Data Integrity, Confidentiality, and Storage.** Software and procedures to protect information from unauthorized access, alteration, disclosure, or destruction during storage or transmission, including storage of data in a format that cannot be meaningfully interpreted if accessed (e.g., encrypted), or in a location that is inaccessible to unauthorized persons and/or protected by a firewall.

- **Data Destruction and Hardware and Media Disposal.** Procedures regarding final disposition of information and/or hardware on which it resides, and procedures for removal of data from media before re-use of the media.
- **Audit Controls.** Maintenance of records to document repairs and modifications to the physical components of the facility related to security (e.g., walls, doors, locks, etc.), and hardware, software, and/or procedural audit control mechanisms that record and examine activity in the systems.
- **Contingency Plan.** Procedures designed to ensure the ability to continue operations in an emergency, such as a data backup plan, disaster recovery plan, and emergency mode operation plan.
- **Incident Response Plan.** A plan for taking responsive actions if the organization suspects or detects that a security breach has occurred, including ensuring that appropriate persons are promptly notified of the breach, and that prompt action is taken in responding to the breach (e.g., to stop further information compromise and work with law enforcement) and in notifying appropriate persons who may be injured by the breach.

Which of these (or other) categories of security controls should be addressed, and which types of security controls should be implemented in each relevant category, must be based on the risks identified in the risk assessment. From there, a determination as to which specific security controls will most effectively address those risks will depend on a variety of factors, given that there is no one-size-fits-all approach.

Traditional negligence law suggests that the relevant factors are (1) the probability of the identified harm occurring (i.e., the likelihood that a foreseeable threat will materialize), (2) the gravity of the resulting injury if the threat does materialize, and (3) the burden of implementing adequate precautions.[71] In other words, the standard of care to be exercised in any

---

71. *See, e.g.,* United States v. Carroll Towing, 159 F.2d 169, 173 (2d Cir. 1947) (Judge Learned Hand's BPL formula, where negligence liability depends on whether B (burden) is less than P (probability) multiplied by L (loss/injury)). *See also* DCR Inc. v. Peak Alarm Co., 663 P.2d 433, 435 (Utah 1983); Glatt v. Feist, 156 N.W.2d 819, 829 (N.D. 1968) (the amount or degree of diligence necessary to constitute ordinary care varies with the facts and circumstances of each case).

particular case depends on the circumstances of that case and the extent of foreseeable danger—that is, the risk assessment.

Security laws and regulations take a similar approach and, as a group, indicate that the following factors are relevant in determining what security measures should be implemented:

- The probability and criticality of potential risks—that is, the risk assessment;
- The size, complexity, and capabilities of the organization;
- The nature and scope of the organization's activities;
- The nature and sensitivity of the information to be protected;
- The organization's technical infrastructure, hardware, and software security capabilities;
- The state of the art of technology and security; and
- The cost of the security measures.

The bottom line is that which security controls are necessary to satisfy the duty to provide reasonable security will vary widely from one organization to another, depending both on the results of the risk assessment and on the factors just identified.

5.   Provide Training and Education[72]

Training and education for employees is a critical component of any security program, both practically speaking and as a legal matter. Even the very best physical, technical, and administrative security measures are of little value if employees do not understand their roles and responsibilities regarding security. For example, installing heavy-duty doors with state-of-the-art locks (whether physical or virtual) will not provide the intended protection if the employees authorized to have access leave the doors open or unlocked for unauthorized persons to pass through. Likewise, given the prevalence of phishing attacks, employees must understand the need to become aware of phishing e-mails and not to click on them. With more employees working remotely, it is critical to understand and address (including through

---

72. Training and education are discussed in more detail in Chapter 13 of this Handbook.

training) the additional security issues created by remote access and use of personal devices.

From a legal perspective, training can be required expressly or impliedly in various laws (e.g., for government entities and regulated industries) and also in lawyers' professional rules of responsibility.[73] In a 2018 case, for example, a federal court[74] pointed to unreasonably deficient cybersecurity training (despite known risks) in holding that an employer whose employee was tricked into sharing personal information of employees in response to a phishing e-mail could be committing an intentional disclosure under the North Carolina Identity Theft Protection Act.[75]

Security education begins with communicating applicable security policies, procedures, standards, and guidelines to employees. It also includes implementing a security awareness program, providing periodic security reminders, and developing and maintaining relevant employee training, such as user education on virus protection, password management, ways to detect phishing and other scams, and how and when to report discrepancies or missteps. It also is important to impose appropriate sanctions against employees who fail to comply with security policies and procedures.

6.   Monitor and Test the Security Controls

Merely implementing security measures is not enough. An organization also must ensure that the security measures have been properly put in place and are effective (and continue to be effective). This includes conducting an assessment of the sufficiency of the security measures in place to control the identified risks and conducting regular testing or monitoring of the

---

73. *See, e.g.,* MODEL RULES OF PRO. CONDUCT r. 1.1 (Competence), cmt. [8], noting that lawyers should "keep abreast of changes in the law and its practice, including the benefits and risks associated with relevant technology. . . ". *See* Chapter 6 of this Handbook for further discussion about the types of professional responsibility requirements (which often include education and training) placed on lawyers and law firms.

74. *See* Curry v. Schletter Inc., No. 1:17-CV-0001-MR-DLH, 2018 U.S. Dist. LEXIS 49442, 2018 WL 1472485 (W.D.N.C. Mar. 26, 2018). The court noted that ". . . the Defendant failed to adequately train its employees on even the most basic of cybersecurity protocols. . .".

75. *Id.* The court noted: "As the Plaintiffs cogently set out in their brief, this was not a case of a data *breach*, wherein a hacker infiltrated the Defendant's computer systems and stole the Plaintiffs' information, but rather was a case of data *disclosure*, wherein the Defendant intentionally responded to an email request with an unencrypted file containing highly sensitive information regarding its current and former employees."

effectiveness of those measures. Existing precedent[76] also suggests that an organization must monitor compliance with its security program. To that end, a regular review of records of system activity, such as audit logs, access reports, and security incident tracking reports, is vital.

7. Review and Adjust the Security Program

The legal standard for information security recognizes that security is a moving target. Organizations must continually keep up with ever-changing threats, risks, and vulnerabilities as well as the security measures available to respond to them. This requires conducting periodic internal reviews to evaluate and adjust the information security program in light of:

- The results of the testing and monitoring;
- Any material changes to the business or client arrangements;
- Any changes in technology;
- Any changes in internal or external threats;
- Any environmental or operational changes; and
- Any other circumstances that may have a material impact on the reasonableness of security procedures.

In addition to conducting periodic internal reviews, it also may be appropriate to obtain a periodic review and assessment (audit) by qualified independent third-party professionals. Such professionals use procedures and standards generally accepted in the profession to certify that the security program meets or exceeds applicable requirements and that the program is operating with sufficient effectiveness to provide reasonable assurances that the security, confidentiality, integrity, and availability of information are protected.

The organization should then adjust the security program in light of the findings or recommendations that come from such reviews.

---

76. *See, e.g.,* the following regulations: GLB Security Regulations, 12 C.F.R. Part 364, Appendix B, III.C.3 (FDIC); 16 C.F.R. § 314.4 (FTC); MASS. STANDARDS FOR THE PROTEC-TION OF PERSONAL INFO., 201 MASS. CODE REGS. 17.03(2)(h) and (j); N.Y. Dep't of Fin. Servs., Cybersecurity Requirements for Financial Services Companies, N.Y. COMP. CODES R. & REGS. tit. 23, § 500.5; GDPR, Article 32(1)(d).

8. Oversee Third-Party Service Provider and Remote Worker Arrangements

In today's business environment, companies and law firms often rely on third parties, such as outsource providers and cloud providers, to handle much of their data. Firm or client data that is in the possession or under the control of a third party presents special security challenges. Thus, it is important to address the security of the organization's data in the possession of such third parties.

To that end, laws, regulations, and FTC orders imposing information security obligations on organizations often expressly address requirements regarding the use of third-party outsource providers. Such rules and regulations make clear that regardless of who performs the work, the legal obligation to provide the security itself remains with the organization. As it is often said, "you can outsource the work, but not the responsibility." Thus, third-party relationships should be subject to the same risk management, security, privacy, and other protection policies that would be expected if a company or firm were conducting the activities directly.

Generally, the legal standard for addressing third-party security imposes three basic requirements on organizations that outsource. They must (1) exercise due diligence in selecting service providers, (2) contractually require third-party providers to implement appropriate security measures, and (3) monitor the performance of the third-party providers.[77]

Additionally, the remote working trend fueled by the pandemic has created a series of new data security challenges (such as lack of security on employee remote devices, insecure home Wi-Fi, unencrypted file sharing, weak passwords, and increased susceptibility to phishing) that should be addressed in the security program.

D. Possible Additional Obligations

1. Protecting Sensitive Data

In addition to imposing a general obligation to provide data security, some laws and regulations require protection of specific data elements, such as Social Security numbers, credit card transaction data, and other sensitive data (such as health status, race, religion, sexual orientation, genetic information, etc.).

---

77. *See, e.g.,* Mass. Standards for the Protection of Personal Info., 201 Mass. Code Regs. 17.02(2)(f).

The various security breach notification laws have created a de facto category of sensitive information in the United States. These laws require special action (i.e., notification) upon a breach of security for a subcategory of personal data generally considered to be sensitive because it can facilitate identity theft.

The security of Social Security numbers has been the particular focus of state laws (virtually all states now have them).[78] The scope of these laws ranges from restrictions on the manner in which Social Security numbers can be used to requirements for security when communicating or storing such numbers. For example, several states have enacted laws that prohibit requiring an individual to transmit his or her Social Security number over the Internet unless the connection is secure or the number is encrypted. Some state statutes require provision of credit monitoring for a certain duration where a data breach involves a Social Security number.

A new area of concern is biometric data, which is increasingly being used for security, authentication, and other purposes. Biometric identifiers are biologically unique to the individual and thus highly personal; unlike Social Security numbers, biometric data cannot be changed and therefore poses unique identity theft risks. Given this, the need to secure (including timely destruction) and otherwise protect such data is heightened. Illinois led the way in 2008 by establishing the first biometric privacy law, the Illinois Biometric Information Privacy Act (BIPA);[79] the law gained high visibility years later with the filing of class action lawsuits, starting in 2015 and gaining speed since then.[80] Biometric data currently covered by the Illinois law includes retina and iris scans, fingerprints, voiceprints, and scans of hand or

---

78. *See, e.g.*, Appendix B.5 (State Social Security Number Laws), and Appendix B.6 (State Laws Requiring Social Security Number Policies) of this Handbook.

79. 740 ILCS 14/1 *et seq.*

80. For example, Facebook users in *Patel v. Facebook* filed a class action lawsuit on August 28, 2015, against the social media giant alleging BIPA violations based on its facial recognition tagging feature; Facebook settled these claims for a landmark $650 million (settlement approved in 2021); *see* https://cdn.vox-cdn.com/uploads/chorus_asset/file/22333300/In_re_Facebook_Biometric_Information_Privacy_Litigation_final_order.pdf. Other multimillion dollar lawsuits have followed, including against Walmart, which has faced BIPA lawsuits on behalf of employees alleging required use of a palm-scanning device ($10 million settlement approved in 2021) and improper recording and tracking of voiceprints (pending); *see* https://cookcountyrecord.com/stories/605642967-class-action-walmart-improperly-tracks-warehouse-workers-using-their-voiceprints without consent.

face geometry (the latter is key in facial recognition applications). Texas[81] and Washington[82] now have biometric identifier laws of their own. Other states include biometric data in their definitions of personal data in their various security laws. Pending biometrics-related legislation in numerous states and even cities across the country could also come into play (with corresponding security and destruction obligations), as could the European Commission's proposed artificial intelligence regulations. Watch this space.

For organizations that accept credit card transactions, the PCI standard[83] imposes significant security obligations for credit card data captured as part of any credit card transaction. Organizations that accept credit cards are required to comply with the contractually binding PCI standard, jointly created by the major credit card associations. State law obligations regarding the PCI standard also may apply.[84]

2. Encrypting Data

Some laws and regulations impose obligations to use encryption in certain situations. Initially this included state laws that mandate encryption of Social Security numbers for communication over the Internet.[85] More recently, however, some state laws prohibit the electronic transmission of any personal information to a person outside of the secure system of the organization unless the information is encrypted. Most notable are the Massachusetts security regulations, which require organizations to encrypt personal information if it is stored on "laptops or other portable devices," "will travel across public networks," or will "be transmitted wirelessly."[86]

---

81. Tex. Bus. & Com. Code Ann. § 503.001.

82. Wash. Rev. Code §§ 19.375.010 *et seq.*

83. https://www.pcisecuritystandards.org/document_library.

84. *See, e.g.,* Appendix B.2 (State Laws Imposing Obligations to Provide Security for Credit Card Information) of this Handbook.

85. *See, e.g.,* Ariz. Rev. Stat. § 44-1373, Cal. Civ. Code § 1798.85, Conn. Gen. Stat. § 42-470, Md. Commercial Law Code Ann. § 14-3402(4). *See also* Appendix B.5 (State Social Security Number Laws) of this Handbook; many state SSN laws mandate use of encryption when transmitting Social Security numbers.

86. Mass. Standards for the Protection of Personal Info., 201 Mass. Code Regs. 17.04(3) and (5).

3. Securely Destroying Data

Several laws and regulations impose security requirements regarding the way that data is destroyed.[87] Such statutes and regulations generally require organizations to properly dispose of personal information by taking reasonable measures to protect against unauthorized access to, or use of, the information in connection with its disposal. For information in paper form, this typically requires implementing and monitoring compliance with policies and procedures that require the burning, pulverizing, or shredding of papers containing personal information so that it cannot be read or reconstructed. For information in electronic form, such regulations typically require implementing and monitoring compliance with policies and procedures that require the destruction or erasure of electronic media containing consumer personal information so that it cannot be read or reconstructed.

E. Security Frameworks for Compliance and Potential Safe Harbors

Numerous security frameworks have been developed and recognized as models for developing an organization's security program. As noted later, compliance with several of these frameworks also has been recognized in some recent legislation as providing a safe harbor for legal requirements to implement reasonable security.

One of the most well-known security frameworks is the NIST Cybersecurity Framework. It was developed through a collaboration between industry and government to provide a consensus description of what's needed for a comprehensive cybersecurity program. It "enables organizations—regardless of size, degree of cybersecurity risk, or cybersecurity sophistication—to apply the principles and best practices of risk management to improve the security and resilience of critical infrastructure."[88]

The Cybersecurity Framework references several generally accepted domestic and international security standards that constitute best practice for cybersecurity, and collates such standards into a framework of activities that arguably establishes a set of best practices for the development of

---

87. *See, e.g.*, Appendix B.3 (State Data Disposal/Destruction Laws) and Appendix C.3 (Federal Data Disposal/Destruction Regulations) of this Handbook.

88. NIST Framework for Improving Critical Infrastructure Cybersecurity, Version 1.1, at V (Apr. 16, 2018), https://www.nist.gov/cyberframework.

a "reasonable" security program. Moreover, it carries the weight of being a government-issued framework that was the result of extended collaboration between industry and government to develop a voluntary "how to" guide for organizations to enhance their cybersecurity.

The Cybersecurity Framework is not industry specific, nor is it country specific. Most importantly, the Framework is not a comprehensive information security program, but instead assists in developing such a program. Consistent with existing law, the Cybersecurity Framework adopts a risk-based approach to managing cybersecurity risk. As such, it fits quite well with the approach of existing legal requirements for cybersecurity obligations. It provides general approaches and steps to address cybersecurity for all organizations. The Framework is designed to complement existing business and cybersecurity operations; it can serve as the foundation for a new cybersecurity program or as a mechanism for improving an existing program.

Other security frameworks are often used as a methodology to implement reasonable security in an organization. Two of the more commonly used are (1) the ISO/IEC 27001 framework, which was developed by the International Organization for Standardization (ISO) and the International Electrotechnical Commission (IEC),[89] and (2) the Critical Security Controls for Effective Cyber Defense, which was created by the Center for Internet Security.[90]

Some of the newer state data security laws have also relied on the security frameworks as the basis for a security compliance safe harbor. By recognizing the importance and reliability of the more well-known security frameworks, these statutes provide a navigation map to compliance with corporate cybersecurity obligations by encouraging reliance on generally accepted security frameworks. States taking this approach include Ohio,[91]

---

89. ISO/IEC 27001, Information Technology—Security Techniques—Information Security Management Systems—Requirements (2013), available for purchase at https://www.iso.org /isoiec-27001-information-security.html.

90. Center for Internet Security, Critical Security Controls for Effective Cyber Defense, https://www.cisecurity.org/controls/.

91. Ohio Rev. Code §§ 1354 *et seq.*

Utah,[92] and Connecticut.[93] These laws may provide some guidance to businesses struggling to ensure that they have implemented legally required reasonable security.

As part of their safe harbor approach, these statutes introduce two very important concepts relevant to cybersecurity compliance:

- First, an implicit recognition that compliance with selected industry norms and best practices provides legally compliant "reasonable security" and
- Second, for organizations that follow one of the framework approaches designated in the law, a safe harbor in the form of an affirmative defense to certain actions that are brought against the organization alleging that it failed to implement reasonable information security controls, resulting in a data breach concerning personal information.

To obtain the benefit of the safe harbor under these laws, a business must create, maintain, and comply with a written cybersecurity program appropriate for the business to protect the confidentiality, integrity, and availability of the information, which must "contain administrative, technical, and physical safeguards . . . *that reasonably conform to an industry recognized cybersecurity framework* as described in [the law]."[94] Businesses that meet these requirements are entitled to an affirmative defense to a cause of action sounding in tort that alleges that the failure to implement reasonable information security controls resulted in a data breach concerning personal information or restricted information.[95]

The "industry-recognized cybersecurity frameworks" that qualify for the safe harbor under the these laws (and to which an organization's cybersecurity program must "reasonably conform") include the following:

---

92. Utah Cybersecurity Affirmative Defense Act, UTAH CODE ANN., § 78B-4-701.
93. Connecticut HB 6607, An Act Incentivizing the Adoption of Cybersecurity Standards for Businesses (passed House 7/6/2021); Public Act No. 21-119.
94. OHIO REV. CODE § 1354.02(A) (emphasis added).
95. OHIO REV. CODE § 1354.02(D).

- NIST Cybersecurity Framework[96]
- NIST Special Publication 800-171 ("Protecting Controlled Unclassified Information in Nonfederal Systems and Organizations")[97]
- NIST Special Publications 800-53 ("Security and Privacy Controls for Information Systems and Organizations")[98] and 800-53A ("Assessing Security and Privacy Controls in Federal Information Systems and Organization")[99]
- The Federal Risk and Authorization Management Program (FedRAMP) Security Assessment Framework[100]
- Center for Internet Security (CIS), Critical Security Controls for Effective Cyber Defense[101]
- International Organization for Standardization/International Electrotechnical Commission 27000 Family of Information Security Standards—information security management systems ISO-27000 family[102]

This approach appears to recognize that cybersecurity programs based on any of the foregoing provide "reasonable security" and that providing "reasonable security" is a defense in the case of a breach.

The Ohio statute was the first cybersecurity law providing an express safe harbor for entities that exercise "reasonable security." It should be noted, however, that the California attorney general released a report in

---

96. NIST Framework for Improving Critical Infrastructure Cybersecurity, Version 1.1 (Apr. 16, 2018), https://nvlpubs.nist.gov/nistpubs/CSWP/NIST.CSWP.04162018.pdf.

97. NIST, SPEC. PUBL'N 800-171, REV. 1, PROTECTING CONTROLLED UNCLASSIFIED INFORMATION IN NONFEDERAL SYSTEMS AND ORGANIZATIONS (Dec. 2016), https://nvlpubs.nist.gov /nistpubs/specialpublications/nist.sp.800-171r1.pdf.

98. NIST, SPEC. PUBL'N 800-53, REV. 5, SECURITY AND PRIVACY CONTROLS FOR INFORMATION SYSTEMS AND ORGANIZATIONS (Aug. 2017), https://csrc.nist.gov/CSRC/media// Publications/sp/800-53/rev-5/draft/documents/sp800-53r5-draft.pdf.

99. NIST, SPEC. PUBL'N 800-53A, REV. 4, ASSESSING SECURITY AND PRIVACY CONTROLS IN FEDERAL INFORMATION SYSTEMS AND ORGANIZATION (Dec. 18, 2014), https://nvlpubs.nist .gov/nistpubs/SpecialPublications/NIST.SP.800-53Ar4.pdf.

100. FedRAMP Security Assessment Framework, Ver. 2.4 (Nov. 15, 2017), https://www .fedramp.gov/assets/resources/documents/FedRAMP_Security_Assessment_Framework.pdf.

101. Center for Internet Security, CIS Controls, Ver. 8 (2021), https://www.cisecurity.org /controls/.

102. ISO/IEC 27000 Family of Information Security Standards, https://www.itgovernance .co.uk/iso27000-family.

2016 setting forth what might be described as a reverse safe harbor—that is, if you don't take certain steps, then you will be deemed *not* to have provided legally compliant reasonable security. In the "California Data Breach Report 2016,"[103] the California attorney general referenced the requirement under California law that businesses implement "reasonable" security and further noted that the Critical Security Controls for Effective Cyber Defense from the Center for Internet Security[104] are designed to address this challenge. But then the AG's report went further, stating that failure to implement those controls constitutes a lack of reasonable security. Specifically, the Report stated that:

> The 20 controls in the Center for Internet Security's Critical Security Controls identify a minimum level of information security that all organizations that collect or maintain personal information should meet. *The failure to implement all the Controls that apply to an organization's environment constitutes a lack of reasonable security.*

Although this statement reflected the California AG's view at the time, and is not law, an organization subject to the California security law would be well advised to consider the CIS Critical Security Controls when developing its security program.

Regardless of whether any of the foregoing security frameworks are used for purposes of safe harbor compliance in the selected states, all of these frameworks provide important guidance that can be useful in the development of a comprehensive written information security program.

---

103. Cal. Att'y Gen., *California Data Breach Report 2016*, at 27–34 (Feb. 2016), https://oag.ca.gov/breachreport2016.

104. The CIS Critical Security Controls for Effective Cyber Defense, now known as the CIS Controls, Ver. 8, are available from the Center for Internet Security at www.cisecurity.org/. Formerly known as the SANS Top 20, the Controls are now managed by the Center for Internet Security (CIS), a nonprofit organization that promotes cybersecurity readiness and response by identifying, developing, and validating best practices.

III. The Duty to Notify of Security Breaches

Legal and regulatory requirements are not limited to obligations to *implement* security measures to protect data. All U.S. states, and most other U.S. and international jurisdictions, impose an obligation to *disclose* security breaches of specific types of personal data to (1) the persons affected and (2) applicable regulators or enforcement agencies.

A.   What Is the Source of the Duty?

All U.S. states have enacted security breach notification laws applicable to all businesses, including law firms.[105] Several sector-specific federal regulatory agencies also do the same (e.g., for the health care, banking, energy, and defense sectors).[106] Many international jurisdictions have done so as well.

These laws impose an obligation similar to the common law "duty to warn" of dangers, which is often based on the view that a party who has superior knowledge of a danger of injury or damage to another posed by a specific hazard must warn those who lack such knowledge. By requiring notice to persons who might be adversely affected (e.g., those whose compromised personal information may be used to facilitate financial account takeover or identity theft), such laws seek to warn those persons that their personal information has been compromised and provide an opportunity to take steps to self-protect against the consequences of identity theft.

In addition to applicable federal and state laws, lawyers may have additional notification obligations under the rules of professional responsibility, other laws applicable specifically to lawyers, or contractual obligations to clients.

B.   What Is the Statutory Duty?

The statutory duty, as embodied in the state and federal security breach notification laws, generally requires that any organization that possesses

---

105. See, for example, Appendix B.4 (State Security Breach Notification Laws) of this Handbook.

106. See Appendix C.4 (Federal Security Breach Notification Regulations) of this Handbook.

or controls certain categories of personal information must disclose any breach of such information.

The key elements of the breach notification statutes can be summarized as follows:

Covered information. Breach notification laws generally apply to unencrypted personal information. Many countries apply the notification requirements to all personal data, which generally refers to information related to an identified or identifiable natural person (but the specific definition can vary from jurisdiction to jurisdiction and from law to law). Other breach notification laws, particularly U.S. state breach laws, require notification only if the breach involves certain categories of personal data. Categories commonly included in the state breach laws are information consisting of first name or initial and last name, plus one of the following: Social Security number, driver's license or state ID number, or financial account number or credit or debit card number (along with any PIN or other access code where required to access the account). In some states, this list is longer and may also include, for example, medical information, insurance policy numbers, passwords by themselves, biometric data, professional license or permit numbers, passport numbers, telecommunication access codes, account credentials, mother's maiden name, employer ID number, military identification, student identification number, electronic signatures, private key (used to authenticate or sign electronic record), and descriptions of an individual's personal characteristics.

Triggering event. The event that triggers the obligation to provide notice of a breach involving personal information is typically referred to in the breach statutes as a "breach of the security of the system" or something similar. This term often is defined as: "unauthorized acquisition of unencrypted computerized data that compromises the security, confidentiality or integrity of personal information maintained by the person or business,"[107] or as "a breach of security leading to the accidental or unlawful destruction, loss, alteration, unauthorised disclosure of, or access to, personal data transmitted, stored or otherwise processed."[108] The requirements of this

---

107. *See, e.g.,* CAL. CIVIL CODE § 1798.82(d).
108. *See, e.g., id.*

definition, in combination with certain exclusions available in many states (e.g., an exclusion for security breaches that the custodian of the exposed data determines will not likely cause harm),[109] allow for more than one approach to determining when factors are present that impose an obligation to notify under the breach notification statutes.

Who must be notified. Under the laws in U.S. states, notice must be given to, at a minimum, any residents of the state whose unencrypted personal information was the subject of the breach.[110] Many statutes also require notification to the state attorney general or other regulatory agency responsible for privacy and security enforcement. In some cases, notification requirements also extend to informing credit reporting agencies and the press. In the EU, under GDPR, notice must first be given to the applicable supervisory authority; if the breach is likely to result in a high risk to the rights and freedoms of individuals, notice then must be given to the individuals.

When notice must be provided. Generally, persons must be notified in the most expedient time possible and without unreasonable delay (although some states specify a certain number of days). In most states, the time for notice may be extended:

- For the legitimate needs of law enforcement, if notification would impede a criminal investigation.
- To take necessary measures to determine the scope of the breach and restore reasonable integrity to the system.

Some breach laws, however, require that notice be given within very short time periods—for example, 72 hours.[111]

---

109. For example, Iowa's Breach Notification Statute stipulates that notification is not required if "after an appropriate investigation or after consultation with the relevant federal, state, or local agencies responsible for law enforcement, the person determined that no reasonable likelihood of financial harm to the consumers whose personal information has been acquired has resulted or will result from the breach. Such a determination must be documented in writing and the documentation must be maintained for five years." *See* Iowa Code § 715C.2(6).

110. Exception: Where the business maintains computerized personal information that the business does not own, the laws require the business to notify the owner or licensee of the information, rather than the individuals themselves, of any breach of the security of the system.

111. *See, e.g.,* GDPR Article 33; N.Y. Dep't of Fin. Servs., Cybersecurity Requirements for Financial Services Companies, N.Y. Comp. Codes R. & Regs. tit. 23, § 500.17(a).

Form of notice. Notice may be provided in writing (e.g., on paper and sent by mail), in electronic form (e.g., by e-mail, but only in compliance with E-SIGN[112]), or by substitute notice. If the cost of providing individual notice is greater than a certain amount (e.g., $250,000), or if more than a certain number of people would have to be notified (e.g., 500,000), the organization may use substitute notice as defined in each statute.

Requirements vary from state to state, however, and some requirements have become controversial. One of the biggest issues concerns the nature of the triggering event. In California, for example, notification is required whenever there has been unauthorized access that compromises the security, confidentiality, or integrity of electronic personal data. In other states, unauthorized access does not trigger the notification requirement unless there is a reasonable likelihood of harm to the individuals whose personal information is involved or unless the breach is material.

C. When Does a Contract-Based Duty Arise?

It also is increasingly common for contracts with business partners of all types to require the recipient or processor of an organization's data to notify the organization in the event of a breach. This trend also is being extended to law firms. Clients (particularly in regulated industries such as financial or health care) are requiring that their law firms provide prompt notice of any security breach. For example, breach reporting is a key requirement of the Model Information Protection and Security Controls for Outside Counsel Processing Company Confidential Information ("Model Controls"), released in 2017 by the Association of Corporate Counsel (ACC).[113]

---

112. Electronic Signatures in Global and National Commerce Act (E-SIGN), 15 U.S.C. §§ 7001 *et seq.* This generally requires that entities comply with the requisite consumer consent provisions of E-SIGN at 15 U.S.C. § 7001(c).

113. Association of Corporate Counsel (ACC), *Model Information Protection and Security Controls for Outside Counsel Processing Company Confidential Information* ("*Model Controls*"), www.acc.com/advocacy/upload/Model-Information-Protection-and-Security-Controls-for-Outside-Counsel-Jan2017.pdf.

IV. PRACTICAL CONSIDERATIONS: A TOP 10 LIST

Organizations have many legal obligations to provide data security that arise from generally applicable law. Following is a list of practical tips regarding compliance with those obligations:

1. Identify the data in your possession or control (i.e., the data for which you are responsible), and understand where it is stored, how it can be accessed, and how it is used.
2. Determine which data (yours, client data obtained during due diligence or discovery, etc.) is subject to which laws and regulations (including special sector-specific regulations such as GLB or HIPAA), and be sure you handle that data in accordance with any special requirements in those laws and regulations. Keep in mind that laws and regulations governing data security may apply to the data in your possession or under your control, independent of ethical obligations of confidentiality specifically applicable to attorneys.
3. Conduct a risk assessment to evaluate the risks to the data you have.
4. Develop a security program (documented in writing) to protect that data against the identified risks.
5. If you use third parties (e.g., providers of cloud services or outsourcing services) to store or process the data, take appropriate steps to make sure that they adequately protect the security of the data you entrust to them.
6. On a regular basis, reevaluate the risks you face and the adequacy of your security program, and adjust the program as necessary.
7. Recognize that everyone within the organization can be a weak link, and provide appropriate training and awareness-raising reminders for everyone on an ongoing basis.
8. Develop an incident response plan (including communications strategy) that covers the data you have.
9. Keep in mind that legal compliance is not enough; reputations are easily cracked but not easily mended, and your organization can be tried in the court of public opinion for security missteps, despite compliance with applicable laws.
10. Remember that security is a process and is never complete, so you must remain vigilant for new threats and new laws.

Chapter 5
International Norms
Kevin E. Lunday[1] and Harvey Rishikof[2]

Cybersecurity norms in the international context are in a period of dynamic change with significant implications for legal practitioners, who must not only maintain legal competence but also counsel clients on how to navigate the changing risk landscape.

Today, nearly every major business has significant international connections requiring understanding of and fluency in international laws, regulations, and standards. These connections go beyond firms that focus on delivery of goods and services to overseas markets and customers. Most companies depend on international supply chains, especially for software and information technology, that involve non-U.S. components and manufacturers. Further, the increasing market focus on monetizing data about consumers carries significant risk as cross-border data flows open up firms to foreign jurisdictions and regulations, which can carry significant monetary and business risk.

Increasingly data and privacy issues are overtaking the traditional priorities in cybersecurity of protecting information systems, computers, and networks. Recent high-profile compromises of technology supply chains, such as the 2020 SolarWinds incident, reinforce to the international

---

1. The views expressed herein are those of the author and not to be construed as official or representing the views of the Commandant or of the U.S. Coast Guard.

2. The views expressed herein are those of the author and do not represent the views of the Department of Defense or the American Bar Association.

cybersecurity world that technology supply chains must be understood to adequately gauge the risks they present.[3]

The collection and use of increasing volumes of data, and the growing interconnectedness between the physical and digital domains with the expansion of networked technologies (i.e., the "Internet of Things"), means that data has become a "strategic asset" for every firm, no matter its market or size. The exploitation of data offers firms not only substantial value but also significant legal and business risk. The new emerging legal frameworks have serious consequences for failure to adequately protect data from unauthorized transfer or use or to report data breaches. The traditional emphasis on protecting the confidentiality and availability of information is giving way to the need to safeguard data integrity itself, because assumptions about the veracity and inherent accuracy of data are being challenged.[4]

Privacy—the ability of individuals to control the use of information about themselves by others—is taking on greater significance given the power of major technology and social media companies to monetize and trade information about persons for business value: "data is the new oil."[5] Businesses have developed significant markets for data flows, especially for the aggregation and analysis of data about individuals. At the same time, individuals are demanding greater protection and control over how private firms gather, use, store, protect, and share data about them. These issues concerning privacy continue to fuel the debates about the use of encryption and the ability of states for security needs to pierce different privacy protections under the color of law.

Threats and compromises to technology supply chains have exploded as a major source of risk.[6] Supply chain intrusions mean that malicious actors

---

3. Christopher Nissen et al., *Deliver Uncompromised: A Strategy for Supply Chain Security and Resilience in Response to the Changing Character of War*, MITRE (Aug. 2018), https://www.mitre .org/publications/technical-papers/deliver-uncompromised-a-strategy-for-supply-chain-security.

4. Michael Nieles et al., *An Introduction to Information Security*, NAT'L INST. OF STANDARDS & TECH. (NIST) SPECIAL PUBL'N 800.12, REV. 1 (June 2017), https://nvlpubs.nist .gov/nistpubs/SpecialPublications/NIST.SP.800-12r1.pdf. Section 1.4 describes the purpose of information security is to ensure the confidentiality, integrity, and availability of information.

5. *The World's Most Valuable Resource Is No Longer Oil, but Data*, THE ECONOMIST (May 6, 2017), https://www.economist.com/leaders/2017/05/06/the -worlds-most-valuable-resource-is-no-longer-oil-but-data.

6. *See supra* note 3.

are able to gain access to physical platforms, digital infrastructure, or code early in the development or deployment process, typically well before traditional cybersecurity measures have been applied. This is analogous to a burglar setting up in a house, as the architect, while it is being designed and constructed, well before the family moves in and locks the door. Assumptions that vendors have provided technology that is adequately protected from compromise prior to deployment are now in question. The 2020–2021 SolarWinds, Colonial Pipeline, and Kaseya incidents are striking in scale, scope, and sophistication, and experts judge that the extent of the damage and compromise, and the full cost and timeline for recovery, remain largely unknown.[7]

Because technology does not stand still, the acceleration of access to, and the utility of, the next generation of telecommunications infrastructure,[8] artificial intelligence, and machine learning, all powered by mass volume of digital information, have only increased the focus on data and privacy. International law and norms that have always had a tendency to lag, given the pace of technology change, are again being challenged by these evolving developments.

---

7. Press Briefing by Press Secretary Jen Psaki and Deputy National Security Advisor for Cyber and Emerging Technology Anne Neuberger (Feb. 17, 2021), https://www.whitehouse .gov/briefing-room/press-briefings/2021/02/17/press-briefing-by-press-secretary-jen-psaki-and -deputy-national-security-advisor-for-cyber-and-emerging-technology-anne-neuberger-febru ary-17-2021/; Department of Homeland Security, Cybersecurity and Infrastructure Security Agency, *Emergency Directive 21-01: Mitigate SolarWinds Orion Code Compromise* (Dec. 13, 2020), https://cyber.dhs.gov/ed/21-01/; Laura Hautala, *SolarWinds Products Had Three Serious Security Flaws, Researchers Find*, CNET (Feb. 3, 2021), https://www.cnet.com/tech /services-and-software/solarwinds-products-had-three-serious-security-flaws-researchers-find/; Brian Barrett, *Security News This Week: Russia's SolarWinds Hack is a Historic Mess*, WIRED (Dec. 19, 2020), https://www.wired.com/story/russia-solarwinds-hack-roundup/.

8. Internet service providers are deploying the Fifth Generation (5G) of telecommunications infrastructure that will enable significant increases in bandwidth and the scale and speed of data transfer. *5G Security and Resilience*, U.S. DEP'T OF HOMELAND SECURITY, CYBERSECURITY & INFRASTRUCTURE SECURITY AGENCY, https://www.cisa.gov/5g (last visited Aug. 25, 2021).

I.   Key Laws in Europe, Asia/Pacific, Russia, Latin America, and Africa

In light of the increasing globalization of business, and the growth of cross-border data flows, lawyers need to be familiar with the laws in a variety of jurisdictions. Increasingly, ransomware and cyber intrusions are becoming a global phenomenon cutting across jurisdictions. This section provides only a general overview of the development of laws in several regions. It does not substitute for an in-depth understanding of relevant laws and regulations.

A.   European Union

The European Union has consistently been a global leader in cybersecurity norm development across a range of issues, including privacy and data protection. Article 8 of the European Convention on Human Rights (ECHR), which applies to all signatory states even if they are not EU members, requires states to protect any data collected from their citizens, regardless of the geographical location of that data or whether it is in the hands of a third party.[9]

The EU took an early leadership role in establishing governance for consumer privacy and data protection in 1995—in the early days of the Internet—with the Data Protection Directive (DPD) 95/46EC, which set forth initial standards on protection of personal information and disclosure of use and unauthorized release of consumer information. The DPD also regulated cross-border data flows to other non-EU states and restricted such flows where the privacy and data protection regulations of those states were found inadequate from an EU perspective.[10] To ensure continued data flows between U.S. and EU markets, the United States and EU negotiated a set of International Safe Harbor Privacy Principles ("Safe Harbor") in 2000.[11] The Safe Harbor agreement remained effective until 2015, when the Court

---

9. *Guide on Article 8 of the European Convention on Human Rights*, European Court of Human Rights (Dec. 31, 2020), https://www.echr.coe.int/documents/guide_art_8_eng.pdf.

10. Directive 95/46/EC of the European Parliament and of the Council of 24 October 1995 on the protection of individuals with regard to the processing of personal data and on the free movement of such data, O.J. (L 281), 23/11/1995 P. 0031 – 0050.

11. Ernst-Oliver Wilhelm, *A Brief History of Safe Harbor*, INT'L ASS'N OF PRIVACY PROS, https://iapp.org/resources/article/a-brief-history-of-safe-harbor/ (last visited Aug. 25, 2021).

of Justice of the European Union (CJEU) struck it down as inadequate in the case of *Schrems I*.[12] As a result of that decision, the United States and EU negotiated the Privacy Shield Framework, which increased standards and requirements on EU–U.S. data flows.[13] The Privacy Shield Framework is administered by the U.S. Department of Commerce for U.S. companies. U.S. firms are not required to participate in the Privacy Shield Arrangement, and may employ other mechanisms, such as Standard Contractual Clauses (SCC) and Binding Corporate Rules (BCR), to ensure compliance with General Data Protection Regulation (GDPR) provisions.[14]

At the same time the United States and EU were addressing the impact of the 2015 *Schrems I* case, in 2016, the EU adopted the GDPR, which superseded the original DPD and came into full force in 2018. The GDPR includes broad individual data privacy rights, including (1) the "right to be forgotten," that is, to have data erased by processing entities; (2) the adoption of data use minimization by all data controllers; (3) breach notification within 72 hours to individuals affected; (4) the appointment of a corporate Data Protection Officer, who is required to keep internal records of data use and answer information requests by national data protection agencies; and (5) restrictions on transfer of personal data to countries that do not have privacy standards that are essentially equivalent to those in the EU. The GDPR also includes significant penalty provisions for companies not in compliance, with fines as much as 4 percent of "global turnover" or 20 million euros, whichever is higher.[15]

In July 2020, the CJEU decided in a subsequent case, *Schrems II*, that the EU–U.S. Privacy Shield Framework was invalid because it did not provide adequate protections for personal data as required under the GDPR. In particular, the CJEU invalidated the decision of the European Commission that U.S. law provided adequate rules for access to personal data by

---

12. Case C-362/14, Schrems v. Data Prot. Comm'r (Schrems I), ECLI:EU:C:2015:650 (Oct. 6, 2015) [hereinafter *Schrems I*].

13. *Privacy Shield Overview*, U.S. Dep't of Commerce, https://www.privacyshield.gov /Program-Overview (last visited Aug. 25, 2021).

14. *Standard Contractual Clauses (SCC)*, European Commission, https://ec.europa.eu/info /law/law-topic/data-protection/international-dimension-data-protection/standard-contractual -clauses-scc_en (last visited Aug. 25, 2021).

15. *General Data Protection Regulation*, 2016 O.J. (L 119), https://gdpr-info.eu.

government agencies. Although the CJEU upheld the use by companies of Standard Contractual Clauses (SCC) and Binding Corporate Rules (BCR) to transfer data to third countries, the court specifically noted that the companies are responsible for ensuring that any data shared with the United States (or any other non-EU country, for that matter) is adequately protected to GDPR standards.[16] This means that companies transferring data to the United States under SCCs today are responsible on a case-by-case basis for undertaking their own independent analyses of all relevant and current U.S. law relating to privacy protection and government access to data, as well as the facts and circumstances of data transfers and applicable safeguards, in assessing whether the transfers satisfy EU law. This places an extraordinary burden and risk on U.S. companies to ensure that data transferred to the United States is adequately protected under GDPR requirements. This new regime means that any EU judgment about the adequacy of a specific data transfer or concerns about responsiveness of a company to compliance demands could force an immediate halt to cross-border data flows permissible under SCCs. The ruling has generated uncertainty in the stability and predictability of data transfer arrangements, whether under the Privacy Shield Framework or SCCs.[17] The U.S. Department of Commerce has issued guidance to companies on how to ensure compliance with GDPR adequacy measures using SCCs, but *Schrems II* has "gutted" the established framework for cross-border data flows.[18] Going forward, many expect the United States and EU to establish an enhanced Privacy Shield agreement or similar arrangement to satisfy the *Schrems II* decision. In the interim, the U.S. Department of Commerce has encouraged the more than 3,500

---

16. C-311/18, *Data Protection Commissioner v. Facebook Ireland & Maximillian Schrems* (*Schrems II*), ECLI:EU:C:2020:559 (July 16, 2020).

17. Letter from Deputy Assistant Secretary for Commerce James Sullivan on the *Schrems II* Decision, Sept. 2020, https://www.commerce.gov/about/letter-deputy-assistant-secretary-james-sullivan-schrems-ii-decision; Joshua P. Meltzer, *The Court of Justice of the European Union in Schrems II: The Impact of GDPR on Data Flows and National Security*, Brookings (Aug. 5, 2020), https://www.brookings.edu/research/the-court-of-justice-of-the-european-union-in-schrems-ii-the-impact-of-gdpr-on-data-flows-and-national-security/.

18. *Information on U.S. Privacy Safeguards Relevant to SCCs and Other EU Legal Bases for EU-U.S. Data Transfers after Schrems II*, Dep't of Com. (Sept. 2020), https://www.commerce.gov/sites/default/files/2020-09/SCCsWhitePaperFORMATTEDFINAL508COMPLIANT.PDF.

companies who are enrolled in the EU–U.S. Privacy Shield arrangement to continue under its provisions while negotiations to resolve the requirements of the *Schrems II* decision continue.[19]

Alongside the GDPR and fallout from the CJEU rulings in *Schrems II*, the EU had continued norm development on cybersecurity and in August 2016 issued the Network and Information Security Directive (NIS Directive). The NIS Directive provided regulations and guidance for OESs, who operate critical infrastructure, as well as DSPs, who operate online markets, search engines, and cloud services. Under the NIS Directive, OESs and DSPs are required to take "appropriate measures" to defend their networks from cyberattacks, as well as to create a method for reporting potential breaches to national authorities. The NIS Directive also requires that member states establish a national Computer Security Incident Response Team (CSIRT), promulgate a national cybersecurity strategy, and enforce penalties on OESs and DSPs within their state who do not meet security minimum standards. The NIS Directive does not specify minimums of acceptable security measures for OESs or DSPs, as those security minimums vary depending on the type of critical infrastructure and rapidly changing nature of technology. Rather, the NIS Directive places the responsibility on member states to determine sufficient "best practices" linked to relevant risk to each OES and DSP.[20]

In December 2020, the EU released an EU Cyber Strategy, which sets forth lines of effort to update and enhance existing regulations, better integrate cybersecurity governance with other regulations addressing risks to critical infrastructure, and expand efforts focused on resilience and recovery.[21]

At this writing in 2021, the EU is preparing to issue a major revision to the NIS Directive ("NIS 2 Directive"), which would (1) expand the applicability of cybersecurity requirements to add new sectors based on their

---

19. Privacy Shield Framework, *FAQs – EU–U.S. Privacy Shield Program Update*, INT'L TRADE ADMIN., U.S. DEP'T OF COMMERCE (last updated Mar. 31, 2021), https://www.priv acyshield.gov/article?id=EU-U-S-Privacy-Shield-Program-Update.

20. Directive (EU) 2016/1148 of the European Parliament and of the Council of 6 July 2016 concerning measures for a high common level of security of network and information systems across the Union, 2016 O.J. (L 194).

21. *The Cybersecurity Strategy*, European Commission, https://ec.europa.eu/digital-single -market/en/cybersecurity-strategy (last updated July 1, 2021).

criticality; (2) include all medium and large size firms within the regulation; (3) remove the prior distinction between OESs and DSPs; (4) require covered entities to implement a standard cybersecurity framework and standards; and (5) require covered entities to address cybersecurity risks in supply chains and supplier relationships.[22] In sum, after *Schrems II* there is significant uncertainty to navigate on EU–U.S. cross-border data flows and privacy under the GDPR, and a changing regulatory landscape on cybersecurity requirements with the proposed NIS 2 Directive. Legal counsel would be well advised to closely monitor the evolving legal frameworks.

B. Asia/Pacific

1. China

The People's Republic of China (PRC or China) employs an extensive and intrusive network of state laws, regulations, and enforcement measures to exercise strict sovereignty and regulation over the Internet and other telecommunications within its territory. The so-called Great Firewall of China approach enables the PRC to exercise control over "access" and the "privacy of persons" within China and subject companies seeking to transact business with China to substantial surveillance and inspection measures. For example, China's Cybersecurity Law for the People's Republic of China (PRC) (2017) created a "real name registration" system, requiring Chinese citizens to register for Internet services and to provide identifying information. The law also requires companies to tie user accounts to this identifying information, which can then be used by Chinese national security and other government organizations to prosecute those accused of violating Chinese laws or standards. China restricts access to external Internet sites and controls the manner and volume of cross-border data flows. Companies doing business with China are subject to strict requirements. Data collected from or generated about Chinese citizens must be stored within Chinese territory and must undergo a security review before it can be transferred

---

22. *This Summer, Have Your Say on What Is Important to You in Digital*, European Commission, proposal for directive on measures for high common level of cybersecurity across the Union, https://digital-strategy.ec.europa.eu/en/library/proposal-directive-measures-high -common-level-cybersecurity-across-union (last visited Oct. 28, 2021).

offshore. Companies must also meet strict reporting requirements, such as timely reports of data breaches or loss, and are subject to regular inspections or other demands for information to ensure compliance, with heavy penalties for noncompliance. This regime has created valid concerns about the security of company intellectual property and data within China, and uncertainty over how to manage compliance risk due to uneven or unpredictable application or enforcement of the law.[23]

Additionally, the Chinese National Intelligence Law requires organizations and persons in China to comply with requests from state intelligence authorities for information. This may result in companies being required to turn over data to Chinese authorities that is stored in China, even proprietary data that is not related to Chinese citizens.

In late 2020 and April 2021, China proposed new draft measures in a new Personal Information Protection Law (PIPL).[24] The proposed law would require companies or persons that collect user data in China to gain user consent by providing specific information about how the data will be used, including changes in use of user data, and enable users to withdraw consent. The PIPL would also severely restrict cross-border transfers of Chinese citizen data. The law would apply extraterritorially and carry significant financial penalties for violations (e.g., a fine of up to $7.4 million or 5 percent of operating revenue).[25]

2. Japan

The Basic Act on Cybersecurity, amended in 2018, sets forth the roles and responsibilities of government agencies and departments; establishes

---

23. *Overview of China's Cybersecurity Law*, KPMG IT Advisory (Feb. 2017), https://assets.kpmg/content/dam/kpmg/cn/pdf/en/2017/02/overview-of-cybersecurity-law.pdf; Lauren Maranto, *Who Benefits from China's Cybersecurity Laws?*, CTR. FOR STRATEGIC & INT'L STUDIES (June 25, 2020), https://www.csis.org/blogs/new-perspectives-asia/who-benefits-chinas-cybersecurity-laws.

24. *See* Graham Webster, *Translation: Personal Information Protection Law of the People's Republic of China (Draft) (Second Review Draft)* (Apr. 29, 2021), https://digichina.stanford.edu/news/translation-personal-information-protection-law-peoples-republic-china-draft-second-review.

25. *China Unveils Draft Personal Information Protection Law*, CROWELL MORING (Oct. 30, 2020), https://www.crowell.com/NewsEvents/AlertsNewsletters/International-Trade-Bulletin/China-Unveils-Draft-Personal-Information-Protection-Law.

a national cyber incident response organization; and establishes guidelines for cybersecurity standards, incident response, and reporting.[26]

In 2017, Japan put into effect the Act on the Protection of Personal Information (APPI), which regulates "personal information business operators" and includes requirements to gain consent from individuals whose data is collected (typically through use of a company privacy policy), consent for collection and use of personal information, notice and consent requirements for data flows to other business operators, and notice and consent requirements for cross-border data transfers. In June 2020, Japan's legislature passed an amended APPI, which is scheduled to become fully effective April 1, 2022, although stricter penalties are already in force. The amended APPI will strengthen the rights of individuals to require businesses to electronically disclose how their personal information is being used and to demand that a business cease use of the individual's personal information. It will also place a regulatory burden on the business receiving personal data (not only the distributor of it) to ensure the subject of the personal data transfer has given consent to its use. The amended APPI will also require prompt notification of known or likely data breaches involving sensitive personal information, potential property damage, potential cyberattack or other improper purpose, or involving more than 1,000 data subjects. The amended APPI will allow use of "pseudonymized" personal information, which will provide business with exceptions to certain requirements if the personal information requires association with other data to identify the individual.[27]

---

26. *Japan: Basic Law on Cybersecurity Amended*, LIB. OF CONG. GLOBAL LEGAL MONITOR (2018), https://www.loc.gov/item/global-legal-monitor/2018-12-26/japan-basic-act-on-cybersecurity-amended/.

27. *Laws and Policies*, PERSONAL INFO. PROTECTION COMM'N JAPAN, https://www.ppc.go.jp/en/legal/ (last visited Aug. 25, 2021); Hiroyuki Tanaka & Noboru Kitayama, *Japan Enacts Amendments to the Act on the Protection of Personal Information*, INT'L ASS'N OF PRIVACY PROS. (IAPP) (June 9, 2020), https://iapp.org/news/a/japan-enacts-the-act-on-the-protection-of-personal-information/. *See also* Hiroyuki Tanaka, *Japan Updates Enforcement Rules for Amended APPI*, INT'L ASS'N OF PRIVACY PROS. (IAPP) (Mar. 30, 2021), https://iapp.org/news/a/japan-updates-enforcement-rules-for-amended-appi/.

3. Australia

Australia has a strong body of domestic laws governing cybersecurity and privacy. The federal Privacy Act (1988) and Australian Privacy Principles, as well as a separate body of state and territory privacy laws, provide the framework for data and privacy protection. The Assistance and Access Act of 2018 authorizes law enforcement agencies to access encrypted data for investigations of serious crimes, and requires telecommunications service providers to comply with requests for assistance.[28] In 2020, Australia released a new cyber strategy that sets forth a comprehensive national vision and effort to ensure Australian security in the digital domain.[29] Perhaps most relevant for international norms, Australia has invested substantial effort and funding to advance its International Cyber Engagement Strategy, which focuses on improved governance in the Pacific and Asia as well as support for global norm efforts, such as the 2019–2021 UN GGE.[30]

4. India

India has taken measures to strengthen its legal framework governing cybersecurity and data privacy. The Information Technology Act (2000) and Information Technology Rules (2011) provide the most significant legislation, requiring companies to take adequate measures to protect data, to have a privacy policy, and to obtain consent before processing data on individuals. As of this writing, India is preparing to enact new privacy legislation in the Personal Data Protection Act (PDPA), which appears to be based on the regulatory framework in the EU GDPR. The law would implement a broad framework requiring companies that gather personal information about individuals to obtain consent for collection, use, and transfer of data. It would also enable individuals to demand that companies

---

28. Cat Barker et al., *Cybersecurity, Cybercrime and Cybersafety: A Quick Guide to Key Internet Links*, PARLIAMENT OF AUSTRALIA (Apr. 1, 2019), https://www.aph.gov.au/About_Parliament/Parliamentary_Departments/Parliamentary_Library/pubs/rp/rp1819/Quick_Guides/CybersecurityCybercrimeCybersafety.

29. Australian Government Department of Home Affairs, https://www.homeaffairs.gov.au (last visited Aug. 25, 2021).

30. *Australia's International Cyber and Critical Tech Engagement Strategy*, AUSTRALIAN DEP'T OF FOREIGN AFFAIRS & TRADE (Apr. 2021), https://www.internationalcybertech.gov.au/sites/default/files/2021-04/21045%20DFAT%20Cyber%20Affairs%20Strategy%20Internals_Acc_update_1_0.pdf.

disclose how they are using their information and stop the use or transfer of their information (the so-called right to be forgotten). The law would apply extraterritorially and carry significant penalty provisions, similar to those contained in the EU GDPR.[31]

C. Russia

Russia, like China, has taken a strong sovereignty position to regulate and control the Internet within Russia and data flows impacting Russian citizens. In late 2019, Russia implemented its "Sovereign Internet Law," which provides the government sweeping powers to mandate that companies operating in Russia install software to track, filter, and reroute Internet traffic. It also enables the government to block access and data flows and to shut down access from Russia to the external Internet outside of Russian borders.[32] On data privacy, the Russian Federal Law on Personal Data, amended in 2018, provides the structure for individual privacy protections.[33]

D. Latin America and the Caribbean

Latin America lacks a regional consensus or strong maturity in cybersecurity governance or norms, although states within the region recognize the importance of norms to economic and national security. According to a 2020 Report by the Inter-American Development Bank and the Organization of American States (OAS), more than half of the states in the region have developed cybersecurity strategies and strengthened frameworks to respond to cyber threats, including protection of citizens' personal data.[34] Further, the OAS participated in the UN GGE 2019–2021 on cyber norms, discussed later.

---

31. *Data Protection Framework*, India Ministry of Electronics & Info. Tech., https://www.meity.gov.in/data-protection-framework (last visited Aug. 25, 2021). *See also The Personal Data Protection Bill, 2019*, https://dataprotectionindia.in/act/ (last updated Oct. 15, 2020).

32. Merrit Kennedy, *New Russian Law Gives Government Sweeping Power Over Internet*, NPR (Nov. 1, 2019), https://www.npr.org/2019/11/01/775366588/russian-law-takes-effect-that-gives-government-sweeping-power-over-internet.

33. *Russia Adopts Increased Fines for Data Protection Violations*, Hunton Privacy Blog (Dec. 2, 2019), https://www.huntonprivacyblog.com/2019/12/02/russia-adopts-increased-fines-for-data-protection-violations/.

34. *IDB-OAS: Efforts to Improve Cybersecurity in the Americas Increase, but Work Is Needed*, Inter-Am. Dev. Bank (IDB) (July 28, 2020), https://www.iadb.org/en/news/idb-oas-efforts-improve-cybersecurity-americas-increase-work-needed.

E. Africa

Cybersecurity norms across Africa are nascent. In 2014, the African Union (AU) established the African Union Convention on Cyber Security and Personal Data Protection, which obligates member states to establish legal, policy, and regulatory measures to promote cybersecurity governance, control cybercrime, and protect the personal data of citizens. However, relatively few of the AU member states have issued a national strategy, created a cyber incident response capability, or implemented data and privacy protection laws.[35]

II. Sources of International Norms: A Mosaic of Treaties, Customary International Law, and Nongovernmental Actors

Absent multilateral international agreements that codify formal frameworks and binding obligations for states, international cybersecurity norms are largely being established through customary international law and practice. These practices are aided by informal frameworks and guidelines set forth by nongovernmental organizations (NGO) and ad hoc international working groups. In some cases, NGOs have gained quasi-governmental status given their early involvement in Internet architecture and conventions,[36] and their role to date has largely been accepted by many sovereign states as a matter of necessity and practice. In other cases, NGOs offer more limited influence on norms by advancing positions on specific issues, such as engineering technical standards or the application of certain areas of the law, such as human rights.

The United Nations (UN) and other established international governmental bodies are moving to establish and develop more concrete international norms, and as expected this has proved to be slow, deliberate work. The most progress has been made by regional governmental organizations, such as the EU, which might be best described as more of an exercise of collective

---

35. *African Union Convention on Cyber Security and Personal Data Protection,* AFRICAN UNION (May 11, 2020), https://au.int/en/treaties/african-union-convention-cyber-security-and-personal-data-protection.

36. *See infra* notes 52–54.

state sovereignty than international governance. However, the influence of EU standards has the potential to set the pace and drive behavior of other states that may eventually evolve into customary international law.

In addition to efforts to develop norms through international cooperation, individual states are increasingly exercising sovereign power to control and govern data, information technology, and privacy through domestic laws and regulations, often with extraterritorial effect. This trend is being driven by the necessity to provide rules when international norms prove insufficient to address the economic and security challenges, but may over time lead to a more informal development of norms.

A. United Nations

The UN has made clear that international law applies in cyberspace.[37] It has been active for decades in developing international norms for information and communications technology (ICT), acting through specialized agencies and forums to advance dialogue and standards ranging from engineering to cybersecurity to arms control. UN efforts have expanded since 2004 through a series of five Group of Governmental Experts (GGE) sessions and other efforts focused on establishing standards for the Internet and cyberspace.[38]

GGE working groups in 2013 and 2015 built consensus among select participating states and organizations to create normative principles for the Internet and cyberspace.[39] The GGE work in 2013 and 2015 established a three-part framework: recognizing the application of international law to the Internet, advancing nonbinding norms of state behavior, and confidence-building measures.[40] The 2015 GGE report provided that (1) common international law tenets, such as state sovereignty and non-interventionism, apply to cybersecurity and telecommunications infrastructure;

---

37. Rep. of the Group of Governmental Experts on Developments in the Field of Information and Telecommunications in the Context of International Security (2013), transmitted by the Letter dated 7 June 2013 from the Chair of the Group. Established Pursuant to Resolution 66/24 (2012).

38. *Developments in the Field of Information and Telecommunications in the Context of International Security*, U.N. OFFICE OF DISARMAMENT AFFAIRS, https://www.un.org/disarmament/ict-security/ (last visited Aug. 25, 2021).

39. Net Politics, *The UN GGE on Cybersecurity: What Is the UN's Role?*, COUNCIL ON FOREIGN RELATIONS (Apr. 15, 2015), https://www.cfr.org/blog/un-gge-cybersecurity-what-uns-role.

40. *See infra* note 43.

(2) humanitarian law concepts of proportionality, necessity, and distinction apply in responses to cyberattacks; and (3) states are not necessarily liable for attacks that emanate from within their borders without state involvement, but may be held liable for their own complicity in wrongful acts. Perhaps most notably, the 2015 GGE report advanced 11 voluntary norms of state behavior:

1. States should cooperate in developing and applying measures to increase stability and security in the use of ICTs and to prevent ICT practices that are acknowledged to be harmful or that may pose threats to international peace and security.

2. In case of ICT incidents, states should consider all relevant information, including the larger context of the event, the challenges of attribution in the ICT environment, and the nature and extent of the consequences.

3. States should not knowingly allow their territory to be used for internationally wrongful acts using ICTs.

4. States should consider how best to cooperate to exchange information, assist each other, prosecute terrorist and criminal use of ICTs, and implement other cooperative measures to address such threats.

5. States, in ensuring the secure use of ICTs, should respect applicable UN resolutions on the promotion, protection, and enjoyment of human rights on the Internet, as well as UNGA resolutions on the right to privacy in the digital age and to guarantee full respect for human rights, including the right to freedom of expression.

6. States should not conduct or knowingly support ICT activity contrary to their obligations under international law that intentionally damages critical infrastructure or otherwise impairs the use and operation of critical infrastructure to provide services to the public.

7. States should take appropriate measures to protect their critical infrastructure from ICT threats.

8. States should respond to appropriate requests for assistance by another state whose critical infrastructure is subject to malicious ICT acts. States should also respond to appropriate requests to mitigate malicious ICT activity aimed at the critical infrastructure of another

state emanating from their territory, taking into account due regard for sovereignty.

9. States should take reasonable steps to ensure the integrity of the supply chain so that end users can have confidence in the security of ICT products.

10. States should encourage responsible reporting of ICT vulnerabilities and share associated information on available remedies to such vulnerabilities to limit and possibly eliminate potential threats to ICTs and ICT-dependent infrastructure.

11. States should not conduct or knowingly support activity to harm the information systems of the authorized emergency response teams (e.g., computer emergency response teams or cybersecurity incident response teams) of another state. A state should not use authorized emergency response teams to engage in malicious international activity.[41]

After the 2017 GGE failed to produce a consensus outcome, the UN General Assembly in 2018 created two parallel efforts to continue: a fourth GGE and a separate Open Experts Working Group (OEWG).[42] These parallel efforts created structural challenges because of the leadership and format within each effort and the differences in scope.[43] In the spring of 2021, both the OEWG and GGE independently completed their work.[44]

---

41. Rep. of the Group of Governmental Experts on Developments in the Field of Information and Telecommunications in the Context of International Security (2015), transmitted by the Letter dated 26 June 2015 from the Chair of the Group. Established Pursuant to Resolution 68/243 (2014).

42. Microsoft, *Protecting People in Cyberspace: The Vital Role of the United Nations in 2020*, U.N. OFFICE FOR DISARMAMENT AFFAIRS (Dec. 4, 2019), https://www.un.org/disarmament/wp-content/uploads/2019/12/proteciting-people-in-cyberspace-december-2019.pdf.

43. For example, a GGE is exclusive in membership, typically less than 25 states. The 2012 GGE included only 11 states and the 2015 GGE included 20 states. The 2019 GGE included 25 states and consultations with member organizations, such as ASEAN and the OAS. The GGE, which reports to the UNGA First Committee, focuses principally on disarmament and threats to peace that affect the international community, but not typically on privacy or other relevant issues. Christian Ruhl et al., *Cyberspace and Geopolitics: Assessing Global Cybersecurity Norm Process at a Crossroads*, CARNEGIE ENDOWMENT FOR INT'L PEACE (Feb. 2020), https://carnegieendowment.org/files/cyberspace_and_geopolitics.pdf [hereinafter Carnegie Report].

44. *See supra* note 39.

The OEWG issued its consensus report in March 2021.[45] The OEWG report was most notable in that it represents a broader consensus among 150 state participants and observers than before and that it recognizes the voluntary international norms announced in the 2015 GGE report (which only involved 20 participating states). The OEWG acknowledged the increased risk of harmful ICT against critical infrastructure and critical information infrastructure across sectors, and acknowledged that medical technologies and health facilities could be considered part of critical infrastructure. The OEWG affirmed that the UN Charter applies to ICT and emphasized the importance of capacity building, information sharing, and confidence building measures among states. The OEWG also affirmed states' commitment to the general availability and integrity of the Internet.

The 2019–2021 GGE issued an advance report on its proceedings in May 2021.[46] First, the GGE achieved a consensus among participating states. The GGE built on the work of the 2015 GGE report and emphasized concerns about the growing risk of harmful ICT against critical infrastructure, and acknowledged the growing number of states developing ICT capabilities for military purposes. The GGE affirmed that the UN Charter in its entirety applies to the ICT environment, and that international humanitarian law (IHL) applies to the use of ICT in situations of armed conflict. The 2019–2021 GGE also set forth measures for increased transparency and confidence building, encouraging states to designate points of contact for coordination and information sharing and state participation in regional fora to increase use of confidence building measures. The GGE defined characteristics for attribution of cyberattacks and encouraged direct communication between states affected by a cyberattack and the state which was the origin point of the cyberattack.

---

45. Final Substantive Report by Open-ended working group on developments in the field of information and telecommunications in the context of International security, U.N. Doc. A/AC.290/2021/CRP.2 (Mar. 2021).

46. Rep. of the Group of Governmental Experts on Developments in the Field of Information and Telecommunications in the Context of International Security (2021), transmitted by the Letter dated 28 May 2021 from the Chair of the Group. Established Pursuant to Resolution 73/266 (2018).

The UNGA in December 2020 decided to convene the next OEWG from 2021–2025 to further develop rules and norms for responsible state behavior.[47]

B. Nongovernmental Efforts and Organizations

1. Tallinn Manuals

The Tallinn Manuals were developed in a series of meetings from 2011 to 2017, to create a normative framework of rules for states in cyberspace, focused principally on sovereignty, national security, and the law of armed conflict. The Tallinn Manuals, viewed as early authoritative work on international law governing cyberspace, are a useful resource for understanding the current application of Western international law norms to cybersecurity challenges. The Manuals are a product of a group of international scholars convened by the NATO Cooperative Cyber Defense Centre of Excellence in Tallinn, Estonia. The first Tallinn Manual (2013) was focused on "severe cyber operations, those that violate the prohibition on the use of force in international relations [and/or] entitle states to exercise the right of self-defense."[48] The second Tallinn Manual 2.0 (2017) focused on less damaging events to encompass the "gray space"—"the more common cyber incidents that states encounter on a day-to-day basis and that fall below the thresholds of the use of force or armed conflict."[49] Although the Tallinn Manuals are not NATO policy and do not offer specific solutions to legal issues raised by cyber incidents, the quality of scholarship and international membership of the Tallinn Manuals have made them a widely respected source for the development of Western cyber norms.

2. International Organization for Standardization

The International Organization for Standardization (ISO) is an international nongovernmental organization dedicated to developing standards governing a range of topics, including information technology and information security

---

47. G.A. Res. 75/240 (Dec. 31, 2020).
48. MICHAEL N. SCHMITT, TALLINN MANUAL ON THE INTERNATIONAL LAW APPLICABLE TO CYBER WARFARE (1st ed. 2013).
49. MICHAEL N. SCHMITT, TALLINN MANUAL ON THE INTERNATIONAL LAW APPLICABLE TO CYBER WARFARE (2nd ed. 2017).

management systems. These standards, while nonbinding, are commonly viewed as tools for achieving baselines for business processes, quality, and risk management. The ISO standards provide frameworks and process guides that firms can use as a common reference for cybersecurity and information management policies and activities.[50] Companies may employ recognized third-party auditors to certify demonstrated adherence to ISO standards, which provides assurance to other companies, governance bodies, and risk markets (such as insurers) that certified companies are acting with "due diligence" to protect data and information technology.[51] Although ISO standards have not been adopted by the UN, the close relationship between cybersecurity standards, risk management, and organizational planning make ISO standards a shared comprehensive initial framework. However legal counsel should still plan to calibrate their cybersecurity frameworks to the legal standards of the nation or nations in which their organizations are operating, in addition to the ISO regime.

3. Expert Commissions, Industry Groups, and Stakeholder Forums

Other NGOs, both standing and ad hoc, have employed experts and influential stakeholders to advance dialogues and consensus on international norms. Examples include the Global Commission on the Stability of Cyberspace (2018),[52] the Paris Call for Trust and Security in Cyberspace (2018),[53] and the Microsoft project on International Cybersecurity Norms (2018).[54] Although these groups do not create binding standards, the work of these assembled experts is influencing the efforts of UN forums and informing the practices that help shape customary international law.

---

50. *About Us*, INT'L ORG. FOR STANDARDIZATION, https://www.iso.org/about-us.html (last visited Aug. 25, 2021).

51. *Certification*, INT'L ORG. FOR STANDARDIZATION, https://www.iso.org/certification .html (last visited Aug. 25, 2021).

52. *Global Commission on the Stability of Cyberspace*, https://cyberstability.org (last visited Aug. 25, 2021).

53. *Paris Call*, https://pariscall.international/en/ (last visited Aug. 25, 2021).

54. *International Cybersecurity Norms*, MICROSOFT, https://www.microsoft.com/en-us /cybersecurity/content-hub/international-cybersecurity-norms-overview (last visited Aug. 25, 2021).

III. Notable International Cyber Incidents

Cyber intrusions and incidents, data breaches, and compromises of data and digital infrastructure continue to proliferate and present growing risk to companies. Cyber incidents and data breaches with regional or global impacts have become more prominent, with potentially catastrophic economic and security effects well beyond a state's sovereign borders.

In May 2017, the WannaCry ransomware spread through an estimated 200,000 or more information systems using outdated Microsoft Windows operating systems worldwide, disrupting business systems and in some cases destroying valuable data if Bitcoin ransoms were not paid.[55]

Later, in June 2017, the NotPetya wiperware, a destructive computer code, spread rapidly throughout the Internet and information systems around the world starting in Ukraine. This code proliferated and destroyed data and information systems in multiple business sectors, including maritime transportation critical infrastructure. The global incident disrupted ship and port operations and destroyed valuable data. For many experts, NotPetya represented the first cyberattack with global impact.[56] In 2020, the U.S. Department of Justice charged six officers of the Russian military intelligence service (GRU) with being responsible for the NotPetya incident.[57]

The SolarWinds compromise, which was first publicly reported in November 2020, revealed a highly sophisticated compromise of a widely used technology product that had gone undetected for nearly nine months. Most striking, initial reports indicate that the intrusion into the Solar-Winds software occurred early in the supply chain.[58] In December 2020,

---

55. Matt Reynolds, *Ransomware Attack Hits 200,000 Computers across the Globe*, NewScientist (May 15, 2017), https://www.newscientist.com/article/2130983 -ransomware-attack-hits-200000-computers-across-the-globe/.

56. *Id.*

57. Press Release, Six Russian GRU Officers Charged in Connection with Worldwide Deployment of Destructive Malware and Other Disruptive Actions in Cyberspace, Dep't of Just. (Oct. 19, 2020), https://www.justice.gov/opa/pr/six-russian-gru-officers -charged-connection-worldwide-deployment-destructive-malware-and.

58. Joint Statement by the Federal Bureau of Investigation, the Cybersecurity and Infrastructure Security Agency, The Office of the Director of National Intelligence, and the National Security Agency (Jan. 5, 2021), https://www.cisa.gov/news/2021/01/05 /joint-statement-federal-bureau-investigation-fbi-cybersecurity-and-infrastructure.

in a reportedly related incident, Microsoft announced that cyber actors had gained access to the company's source code for Windows 365, its most important and widely used product by governments and business world-wide. In April 2021, the U.S. government formally named the Russian Foreign Intelligence Service (SVR) as the perpetrator of the SolarWinds cyber-espionage intrusion.[59]

In July 2021, Kaseya, a manage service provider that companies use to administer networks, was compromised. These forms of supply chain attack "are particularly pernicious because the scope of who they affect depends not just on a given company's suppliers but on their suppliers' suppliers."[60]

IV. Key Takeaways

1. *Competence: There's a reason it's first on the list.* Attorneys as always must ensure they meet ethical obligations to provide competent representation to clients.[61] In the field of cybersecurity, this requires that attorneys understand not only the law but also the technologies that clients are employing, as well as how rapidly both are changing. This doesn't require that counsel necessarily hold technical certifications or an engineering degree, but it does demand much more than general or passing knowledge of information technology and cyberspace. There are many sources available for counsel to advance their knowledge beyond this Handbook, including self-study and continuing legal education.[62] In many ways, the changing nature of technology described

---

59. Raphael Satter & Joseph Menn, *SolarWinds Hackers Accessed Microsoft Source Code, the Company Says*, REUTERS (Dec. 31, 2020), https://reuters.com/article/us-global-cyber-microsoft-idUSKBN2951M9; *Fact Sheet: Imposing Costs for Harmful Foreign Activities by the Russian Government*, THE WHITE HOUSE (Apr. 15, 2021), https://www.whitehouse.gov/briefing-room/statements-releases/2021/04/15/fact-sheet-imposing-costs-for-harmful-foreign-activities-by-the-russian-government/.

60. Nicholas Weaver, *What Happened in the Kaseya VSA Incident?*, LAWFARE (July 4, 2021), https://www.lawfareblog.com/what-happened-kaseya-vsa-incident.

61. MODEL RULES OF PRO. CONDUCT r. 1.1 (Am. Bar Ass'n).

62. *See, e.g.*, Jamie Baker, *Beyond the Information Age: The Duty of Technology Competence in an Algorithmic Society*, 69 S.C. L. REV. (2018), https://ssrn.com/abstract=3097250.

in the introduction to the chapter reveal that grasping the facts, not the law, may be the most substantial challenge for counsel.

2.   *Look in the mirror*. Practicing attorneys and law firms are also businesses that depending on practice may themselves be subject to international laws and regulations governing cybersecurity, including data privacy regulations. Further, rules of professional responsibility governing client confidentiality impose special obligations and responsibilities on counsel to protect client information from unauthorized disclosure.[63]

3.   *"Don't touch that, you have no idea where it came from."* Supply chains are a growing area of legal and business risk. Increasingly states are trying to "illuminate" the supply chains so that companies have a greater sense of the provenance of both the software and hardware.[64] This indicates a growing potential for government regulation of businesses to identify and manage risk of software and hardware used in business operations.

4.   *People are more than data.* There is a clear trend in most jurisdictions, with the United States as a notable exception to date, toward state laws that increasingly empower individuals to influence the collection, use, and transfer of information about them by companies. The practice of obtaining a customer's lawful contractual consent to unfettered use of their data through use of click-without-reading "terms of service" provisions, such as in software applications, may be on the wane. How states apply new regulations and, as *Schrems II* proves, how courts apply them in response to legal challenges, could have significant consequences as the legal landscape regarding individual data privacy protections evolves.

5.   *Counsel as crisis manager.* The nature and severity of potential risk for firms means that counsel must be prepared to take an increasingly expanded role in advising clients during a crisis, which may involve training and preparation in incident response and crisis management

---

63. *See, e.g.,* ABA Comm. on Ethics & Pro. Resp., Formal Op. 477R (2017).

64. *See, e.g.,* Exec. Order on America's Supply Chains (Feb. 24, 2021), https://www.whitehouse.gov/briefing-room/presidential-actions/2021/02/24/executive-order-on-americas-supply-chains/.

procedures, including crisis communications.[65] More and more companies are creating "risk management" committees with general counsels as chairs.

6. *Corporate responsibility is evolving.* Attorneys advising corporate clients should press clients for active board of directors' and C-level officers' understanding and participation in matters involving cybersecurity norms and privacy and data protection laws and regulations. Adherence to cybersecurity norms must be an integral part of corporate governance and requires a clear commitment from business leaders to be personally involved in ensuring cybersecurity policies, standards, and compliance are fully integrated into decision making, internal controls, and risk-management frameworks.[66] Because client activities may involve operations in or other connections with multiple jurisdictions, counsel must be familiar with and understand the legal and regulatory requirements within each to appropriate advise on risks of compliance.

7. *Who are you going to call?* Attorneys advising clients should establish and sustain relationships early with competent counsel who are knowledgeable about the laws and regulations of relevant jurisdictions. Attorneys should also establish relationships with non-attorney subject matter experts who can provide understanding on how technology functions or how data is used in practice. As with other international legal practice, this may well involve language fluency competent in technical and legal areas. Further, attorneys need to understand who the competent government authorities for cybersecurity are within relevant jurisdictions, which is frequently complex and changing. Many states vest authority for regulation and enforcement of laws within multiple cabinet departments and agencies with overlapping

---

65. Leonard Wills, *A Brief Guide to Handling a Cyber Incident*, ABA PRACTICE POINTS (Feb. 27, 2019), https://www.americanbar.org/groups/litigation/committees/minority-trial -lawyer/practice/2019/a-brief-guide-to-handling-a-cyber-incident/; *Incident Response Training*, CYBERSECURITY & INFRASTRUCTURE SECURITY AGENCY, https://www.cisa.gov/incident-response -training (last visited Aug. 25, 2021).

66. *See* Harvey Rishikof & Kevin Lunday, *Corporate Responsibility in Cybersecurity: Building International Global Standards*, 12(1) GEORGETOWN J. INT'L AFFAIRS (Winter/Spring 2011), https://www.jstor.org/stable/43133860.

responsibilities. Reporting a cyber intrusion or data breach to one government agency may not fulfill the client's legal reporting obligations in every case.

8.   *Growing State Exercise of Sovereignty*. Despite the progress on establishing international cyber norms from the UN GGE and OWEG in 2021, there is a clear trend toward states independently exercising sovereign authority to govern cybersecurity risk, data collection and transfer, and technology supply chains within and beyond their borders. This "balkanization" of the Internet with regard to the free flow of information will increase the complexity of legal regimes that firms must navigate to compete and conduct business across international borders.

9.   *Artificial intelligence: not just a derogatory term for new associates*. No longer the stuff of science fiction movies and novels, it's here today and increasingly used in business with implications for cybersecurity and data privacy within the United States and across international jurisdictions.[67] Attorneys should understand how AI is increasingly impacting clients' business and legal risks as more firms seek to take advantage of opportunities AI offers.

---

67. *See, e.g.*, JAMES E. BAKER, THE CENTAUR'S DILEMMA: NATIONAL SECURITY LAW FOR THE COMING AI REVOLUTION (Brookings Institution Press 2020).

Chapter 6

Lawyers' Obligations to Provide Data Security Arising from Ethics Rules and Other Laws

Lucian T. Pera and Shelley M. Bethune

The obligation of lawyers to secure their clients' sensitive information is defined and governed by ethics rules, common law, and statutes that traditionally cover the activities of lawyers.

I. The Current ABA Model Rules of Professional Conduct and ABA Formal Opinion 477R

At the center of legal ethics guidance nationally on lawyers' ethical obligations to protect clients' confidential information in our increasingly digital, mobile, cloud-based, technology environment stands the ABA Standing Committee on Ethics and Professional Responsibility's Formal Ethics Opinion 477R (revised May 22, 2017).[1] Issued almost immediately before the publication of the second edition of this Handbook, Opinion 477R has become the seminal opinion on this subject.

Opinion 477R weaves together and expands upon the 2012 "technology amendments" to the ABA Model Rules and their comments into a broad framework for understanding the ethical obligation at the heart of this chapter. It directly informs the more detailed discussion that follows. Any reader of this chapter should also review in detail ABA Formal Opinion 477R.

---

1. *See* ABA Comm. on Ethics & Pro. Resp., Formal Op. 477 (May 11, 2017; rev. May 22, 2017).

This opinion[2] is by no means the final word on lawyer cybersecurity. Many jurisdictions have offered helpful guidance, some of which is detailed here, and more of which is cited in the appendices to this chapter.[3] The ABA has continued to expand its guidance in related areas, including at least three other ethics opinions:

- Formal Opinion 483, Lawyers' Obligations After an Electronic Data Breach or Cyber Attack (October 17, 2018), which addressed not only the subject stated in its title but also lawyers' ethical obligations to prevent, monitor for, and prepare to respond to breaches and cyberattacks.
- Formal Opinion 482, Ethical Obligations Related to Disasters (September 19, 2018), which addressed the obligations of lawyers to prepare for disasters—obligations that overlap considerably with cybersecurity obligations.
- Formal Opinion 498, Virtual Practice (March 10, 2021), which highlights a lawyer's cybersecurity obligations as one of a number of concerns arising when lawyers practice without or away from a traditional brick-and-mortar office.

All of these build upon the guidance of Opinion 477R.

Opinion 477R first reviews the ABA's most prominent earlier opinion in this area, ABA Formal Opinion 99-413 (March 10, 1999), which generally blessed lawyer use of unencrypted Internet e-mail for client confidential information. The new opinion then reviews the 2012 "technology amendments" to the ABA Model Rules of Professional Conduct, discussed in more detail later. These amendments, now adopted in a majority of U.S. jurisdictions,[4] generally confirm, clarify, and remind lawyers of their ethical obligations concerning the use of information technology and the protection of client confidentiality in a rapidly changing environment. The 2012

---

2. *See* ABA, ABA Formal Opinion 477R: Securing Communication of Protected Client Information (June 27, 2017).

3. See also Appendix E, E-mail; Appendix F, Metadata; Appendix G, Outsourcing; Appendix H, Cloud Computing; and Appendix I, Social Media, in this Handbook.

4. For analysis of adoption by individual jurisdictions of particular model rules, see the charts maintained by the ABA Center for Professional Responsibility at http://www.americanbar.org/groups/professional_responsibility/policy/rule_charts.html.

amendments confirm that, in the central tenet of amended Rule 1.6(c), "[a] lawyer shall make *reasonable efforts* to prevent the inadvertent or unauthorized disclosure of, or unauthorized access to, information relating to the representation of a client" (emphasis added).

Nothing in Opinion 477R makes obsolete earlier guidance from the ABA and other authorities. The opinion does, however, reject an overly broad interpretation of earlier ABA Formal Opinion 99-413, which some read to mean that a lawyer was ethically permitted to use unencrypted e-mail for client confidential communications *in every circumstance*. Quoting the first edition of this book, Opinion 477R states that:

> in an environment of increasing cyber threats, the Committee concludes that, adopting the language in the ABA Cybersecurity Handbook, the reasonable efforts standard: . . . rejects requirements for specific security measures (such as firewalls, passwords, and the like) and instead adopts a fact-specific approach to business security obligations that requires a "process" to assess risks, identify and implement appropriate security measures responsive to those risks, verify that they are effectively implemented, and ensure that they are continually updated in response to new developments.[5]

This opinion then reviews in some detail some of the factors that should guide lawyers in making a "reasonable efforts" analysis, including factors set out in revised Comment [18] to Rule 1.6, discussed later. Applying these factors to lawyer use of unencrypted e-mail to communicate client confidential information, the committee concludes that, given today's technology and threat environment, while unencrypted e-mail may well be appropriate for routine communications including information of "normal or low sensitivity," transmitting "highly sensitive information" might require more secure communications technology or even avoiding the use of electronic communications altogether.

---

5. *See* ABA Comm. on Ethics & Pro. Resp., *supra* note 1, at 4 (citing ABA Cybersecurity Handbook 48–49 (1st ed. 2013)).

The opinion then identifies and explores a series of pragmatic considerations that a lawyer may consider in seeking to use "reasonable efforts" to protect client confidential information:

1. Understand the nature of the threat.
2. Understand how client confidential information is transmitted and where it is stored.
3. Understand and use reasonable electronic security measures.
4. Determine how electronic communications about clients' matters should be protected.
5. Label client confidential information.
6. Train lawyers and nonlawyer assistants in technology and information security.
7. Conduct due diligence on vendors providing communication technology.[6]

Finally, Opinion 477R emphasizes the need and duty of a lawyer to communicate with the client about the sensitivity of information concerning the representation and the appropriate means and methods of protecting confidentiality. In many ways, this new opinion distills the ethics guidance of the last 20 years and updates it in light of the current technology environment. Aligned with this opinion, this chapter reviews existing guidance and demonstrates how the broader principles restated and reformulated in Opinion 477R apply to particular circumstances faced by lawyers in their practices.

II. Lawyer Ethics Rules

A. Confidentiality

1. ABA Model Rule 1.6
Lawyers and law firms must adopt safeguards to protect their clients' information because they have an ethical duty to keep that information confidential. ABA Model Rule 1.6(a) states that, with limited exceptions,

---

6. *Id.* at 5–10 (omitting discussion of each consideration).

"[a] lawyer shall not reveal information relating to the representation of a client unless the client gives informed consent." This obligation to maintain confidentiality of all information concerning a client's representation, no matter the source, is paramount. The obligation is no less applicable to electronically stored information than to information contained in paper documents or not reduced to any written or stored form.

So what does this mean? What steps must a lawyer take to protect the client's information? The last major review and revision of the ABA Model Rules of Professional Conduct was led by the ABA Ethics 20/20 Commission.[7] With regard to issues raised by new technology, the signature change made to the Model Rules by the Ethics 20/20 Commission was the addition of a new section to the core rule on client confidentiality. This new Rule 1.6(c) codified the existing understanding of a lawyer's affirmative obligation to protect confidential information: "A lawyer shall make reasonable efforts to prevent the inadvertent or unauthorized disclosure of, or unauthorized access to, information relating to the representation of a client." While this revision merely confirms prior law under the ethics rules of every American jurisdiction, versions of these revisions have been adopted by a majority of U.S. jurisdictions as of this writing. Even in jurisdictions that have not adopted these amendments, there is a strong argument that the substance of the revisions is, in fact, an accurate statement of the law on a lawyer's ethical obligations.

Revised Comments [18] and [19] to Rule 1.6 also now include more detailed guidance—guidance largely consistent with existing rules in virtually every jurisdiction—concerning how to measure the reasonableness of a lawyer's efforts to protect against inadvertent disclosure or unauthorized access. This language forms the core set of principles used throughout virtually all ethics opinions in American jurisdictions that address confidentiality

---

7. Created by then ABA President Carolyn B. Lamm in 2009, the Ethics 20/20 Commission performed a thorough review of the ABA Model Rules of Professional Conduct and the U.S. system of lawyer regulation in the context of advances in technology and global legal practice developments. Further information about the commission is available at ABA Commission on Ethics 20/20, https://www.americanbar.org/groups/professional_responsibility/committees_commissions/aba-commission-on--ethics-20-20/.

concerns in the cybersecurity context. Comment [18] sets out how reasonableness under Rule 1.6(c) should be determined:

> Factors to be considered in determining the reasonableness of the lawyer's efforts include, but are not limited to, the sensitivity of the information, the likelihood of disclosure if additional safeguards are not employed, the cost of employing additional safeguards, the difficulty of implementing the safeguards, and the extent to which the safeguards adversely affect the lawyer's ability to represent clients (e.g., by making a device or important piece of software excessively difficult to use). A client may require the lawyer to implement special security measures not required by this Rule or may give informed consent to forgo security measures that would otherwise be required by this Rule.

The comment goes on to note that "a lawyer may be required to take additional steps to safeguard a client's information in order to comply with other law, such as state and federal laws that govern data privacy or that impose notification requirements upon the loss of, or unauthorized access to, electronic information," but that any such obligations are "beyond the scope of these Rules."

Comment [19] concludes the Model Rules' framing of a lawyer's obligations to maintain the security of client confidential information, including its limits:

> When transmitting a communication that includes information relating to the representation of a client, the lawyer must take reasonable precautions to prevent the information from coming into the hands of unintended recipients. This duty, however, does not require that the lawyer use special security measures if the method of communication affords a reasonable expectation of privacy. Special circumstances, however, may warrant special precautions. Factors to be considered in determining the reasonableness of the lawyer's expectation of confidentiality include the sensitivity of the information and the extent to which the privacy of the communication is protected by law or by a confidentiality agreement. A client may require the lawyer to implement special security measures not required by this Rule or may give

informed consent to the use of a means of communication that would otherwise be prohibited by this Rule.

In effect, this comment envisages a balancing test: the more sensitive the data being transmitted and the lower the legal or technological protection afforded by the method of communication, the more likely it is that special precautions may be reasonably necessary to protect client confidences.

From 2013 through 2015, the ABA, through its House of Delegates, approved a series of resolutions proposed by the ABA's Cybersecurity Task Force that highlighted the threat of cyberattacks on lawyers and law firms. In Revised Report 109 (2014), the Task Force observed:

> The threat of cyber attacks against law firms is growing. Lawyers and law firms are facing unprecedented challenges from the widespread use of electronic records and mobile devices. There are many reasons for hackers to target the information being held by law firms. They collect and store large amounts of critical, highly valuable corporate records, including intellectual property, strategic business data and litigation-related theories and records collected through e-discovery.

As described throughout this book, that threat continues to grow. A number of state bar ethics opinions have addressed a lawyer's obligations to protect client confidential information in this age of electronic communications. The focus of these opinions ranges from suggested security safeguards to an examination of new technologies and the need for lawyers to have a basic understanding of the risks and benefits associated with them.

2. State Bar Opinions: Suggested Safeguards

Some state bar associations have issued ethics opinions that suggest specific measures that a law firm should take to protect their clients' electronically stored information. For example, Arizona State Bar Opinion 09-04 (2009) provides some examples of what lawyers should be doing to secure their clients' electronically stored information: "In satisfying the duty to take reasonable security precautions, lawyers should consider firewalls, password protection schemes, encryption, anti-virus measures, etc."

The client file system that was the subject of this Arizona opinion protected the files by using a method of encryption and also applied several layers of password protection. Additionally, the system used unique and randomly generated folder names and passwords, and converted each document to PDF format that required yet another unique alpha-numeric password to review its contents. Based on these safeguards, this Arizona opinion concluded that the file system met the requirements set forth by Rule 1.6.[8]

3. State Bar Opinions: Technology as Moving Target

Other state bar opinions have recognized, as did ABA Opinion 477R, that the swiftly changing nature of technology makes it very difficult to identify specific security measures that lawyers should take that will invariably ensure that confidential client information will be protected.[9] Their focus is on the scope of the lawyer's obligations to take reasonable precautions under the circumstances to protect client information. For example, Kentucky Bar Opinion E-437 (2014) states:

> Because technology evolves every day, we decline to mandate in this opinion specific practices regarding the protection of confidential client information in the world of the cloud. The reality is that such practices soon would be obsolete—and our opinion would be obsolete as well. Rather, we choose to guide lawyers in the exercise of reasonable judgment regarding the use of cloud technology.[10]

---

8. *See also* N.J. Advisory Comm. on Pro. Ethics, Op. 701 (2006); N.C. State Bar Council, Formal Ethics Op. 5 (2008) ("law firm must enact appropriate measures to ensure that each client only has access to his or her own file [and] that third parties cannot gain access [to] any client file").

9. *See* Ill. State Bar Ass'n, Pro. Conduct Advisory Op. 16-06 (2016).

10. *See* Vt. Eth. Op. 2010-6 (2010) (constantly changing nature of cloud technology makes establishing "specific conditions precedent" to use not appropriate); Ohio Informal Adv. Op. 2013-03 (2013) ("applying existing principles to new technological advances while refraining from mandating specific practices—is a practical [approach]").

4. State Bar Opinions: Security Precautions Need Not Be Infallible; They Must Be Reasonable under the Circumstances

Regardless of whether state bar opinions provide specific guidelines or suggestions as to the appropriate technical safeguards lawyers should take, or instead focus on the scope of a lawyer's obligations to use reasonable care to protect client confidences, it is important to bear in mind that, under the rules of professional conduct, the security measures that lawyers are required to put in place are not required to be invulnerable. As stated in Tennessee Board of Professional Responsibility Formal Ethics Opinion 2015-F-159 (2015):

> The lawyer is not required by the rules to use infallible methods of protection. "When transmitting a communication that includes information relating to the representation of a client, the lawyer must take reasonable precautions to prevent the information from coming into the hands of unintended recipients. This duty, however, does not require that the lawyer use special security measures if the method of communication affords a reasonable expectation of privacy. . . ."[11] ". . . Rather, the lawyer must use reasonable care to select a mode of communication that, in light of the circumstances, will best protect confidential client information and the lawyer must advise affected parties if there is reason to believe that the chosen communications technology presents an unreasonable risk to confidentiality."[12] "Special circumstances, however, may warrant special precautions."[13] What safeguards are appropriate depends upon the nature and sensitivity of the data.[14]

As illustrated in the preceding discussion, lawyers cannot take the "ostrich" approach of hiding their heads in the sand and hoping that their office or firm will not suffer a data breach, compromising client information. Lawyers must implement administrative, technical, and physical

---

11. RPC 1.6 Cmt. [16].
12. Me. Ethics Op. 207 (2013); N.C. 2011 Formal Ethics Op. 6 (2012).
13. RPC 1.6 Cmt. [16].
14. Alaska Ethics Op. 2014-3 (2014).

safeguards to meet their obligation to make reasonable efforts to protect client information.

Furthermore, under ABA Model Rule 1.9(c), this obligation of confidentiality also applies to information about former clients:

> A lawyer who has formerly represented a client in a matter or whose present or former firm has formerly represented a client in a matter shall not thereafter: (1) use information relating to the representation to the disadvantage of the former client except as these Rules would permit or require with respect to a client, or when the information has become generally known; or (2) reveal information relating to the representation except as these Rules would permit or require with respect to a client.

B.   Competence

In addition to the obligation to keep client communications and sensitive information confidential, a lawyer's ethical obligation of competence requires that lawyers become and remain competent about the technology they use so as to be able to protect client confidential information.

ABA Model Rule 1.1 states that "[a] lawyer shall provide competent representation to a client. Competent representation requires the legal knowledge, skill, thoroughness and preparation reasonably necessary for the representation." One recent change to the ABA Model Rules based on an Ethics 20/20 Commission proposal amended Comment [8] to Rule 1.1, so that it now reads: "To maintain the requisite knowledge and skill, a lawyer should keep abreast of changes in the law and its practice, *including the benefits and risks associated with relevant technology*" (added language italicized).

California State Bar Opinion 2015-193 (2015) examined the parameters of a lawyer's obligations to understand the benefits and risks of technology in the context of e-discovery, stating:

> An attorney's obligations under the ethical duty of competence evolve as new technologies develop and become integrated with the practice

of law. Attorney competence related to litigation generally requires, among other things and at a minimum, a basic understanding of, and facility with, issues relating to e-discovery, including the discovery of electronically stored information (ESI). On a case-by-case basis, the duty of competence may require a higher level of technical knowledge and ability, depending on the e-discovery issues involved in a matter, and the nature of the ESI. Competency may require even a highly experienced attorney to seek assistance in some litigation matters involving ESI. An attorney lacking the required competence for e-discovery issues has three options: (1) acquire sufficient learning and skill before performance is required, (2) associate with or consult technical consultants or competent counsel, or (3) decline the client representation.[15]

Note especially the second item in the last sentence: If an attorney is not competent to decide without expert assistance whether use of a particular technology (e.g., e-discovery, cloud storage, public Wi-Fi) allows reasonable measures to protect client confidentiality, the ethics rules require that the lawyer must get help, even if that means hiring an expert information technology consultant to advise the lawyer. The level of technology expertise of many lawyers on many such technologies probably means that expert help is often needed by lawyers in making these decisions, whether that expert help comes from inside or outside the lawyer's own organization.

Getting expert help is a recurring theme (as well as good advice) in ethics opinions on this subject. Arizona Bar Opinion 09-04 (Dec. 2009) reminds lawyers that, if they provide an online file storage and retrieval system for client access of documents, then they must take reasonable precautions to protect the security and confidentiality of client documents and information. With respect to a lawyer's obligation to be competent, the opinion noted that "[i]t is also important that lawyers recognize their own competence limitations regarding computer security measures and take the necessary time and energy to become competent or alternatively consult available experts in the field."

---

15. Cal. State Bar Op. 2015-193 (2015).

Moreover, competence requires continued vigilance and learning, as technology advances, in order to comply with a lawyer's duties under the ethics rules. Again, the Arizona Bar also reminded lawyers that "[a]s technology advances occur, lawyers should periodically review security measures in place to ensure that they still reasonably protect the security and confidentiality of the clients' documents and information." In other words, lawyers may not assume that their ignorance about technology will be a recognized excuse for their failure to learn, and stay up-to-date, about technology related to a client's electronically stored information.[16]

C. Supervision of Lawyers and Nonlawyers

Finally, it is not enough that the lawyer is concerned about his individual use of technology and handling of sensitive client information. The ethics rules in every jurisdiction also obligate lawyers to appropriately supervise those who work for them. So, for example, ABA Model Rule 5.1 provides that "[a] partner in a law firm, and a lawyer who individually or together with other lawyers possesses comparable managerial authority in a law firm, shall make reasonable efforts to ensure that the firm has in effect measures giving reasonable assurance that all lawyers in the firm conform to the Rules of Professional Conduct."

Similarly, with respect to a nonlawyer employed or retained by or associated with a lawyer, Rule 5.3 provides that "a partner, and a lawyer who individually or together with other lawyers possesses comparable managerial authority in a law firm, shall make reasonable efforts to ensure that the firm has in effect measures giving reasonable assurance that the person's conduct is compatible with the professional obligations of the lawyer."

Thus, lawyers in any supervisory role not only are obligated to follow the ethics rules personally in protecting client confidential information, but must also be vigilant and make reasonable efforts to ensure that lawyers and nonlawyers they supervise adhere to them as well.

These obligations were emphasized in the ABA's latest guidance on this subject, in ABA Formal Opinion 477R, discussed earlier.

---

16. For further information on lawyers' ethical obligations of competence when using technology, see ABA Ctr. for Pro. Resp., *Searching for the Mr. Spock in You* (May 13, 2016), https://abaforlawstudents.com/2016/05/13/searching-mr-spock/.

III. The Law of Lawyering

A narrow focus on a lawyer's obligation under the law of legal ethics may well lead lawyers and law firms to ignore other related liability that might result from confidentiality breaches. While a breach that results from a lawyer's failure to comply with her obligations under the ethics rules like ABA Model Rule 1.6 might lead to lawyer discipline, a breach of confidentiality caused by a lawyer's conduct could well lead to liability to clients and others harmed under other related law, such as malpractice law, fiduciary duty law, and the law of contract.

One source of the obligation of lawyers and law firms to protect against disclosure of confidential information entrusted to them is the common law of malpractice liability and fiduciary duty, as well as traditional statutory remedies available in some jurisdictions for some lawyer misconduct, including laws prohibiting unfair and deceptive trade practices. Despite the novelty of all the new technology involved and the new laws covering this technology discussed elsewhere in this chapter and this Handbook, these traditional causes of action and remedies are just as applicable to a breach of security in the latest cloud-based technology as they are to the loss of a box of paper documents containing confidential client information.[17]

It may be instructive to recall that the common law concerning the standard of care and tort liability has evolved over decades specifically to account for dynamic technological developments. Judge Learned Hand's famous 1932 decision in *The T.J. Hooper*,[18] which has been a staple of law school casebooks for generations, offers an example from the days when radio technology was new. In that decision, cargo and barge owners were permitted to recover against the owner of two tugboats when their barges and cargo were lost in an Atlantic storm. The primary theory of recovery concerned the tugboat owners' failure to equip their tugboats with radio receivers on which they could monitor regular weather reports and storm warnings. That lack of equipment caused them to miss radio alerts of the

---

17. For treatment of the insurance coverage of the liability of lawyers and law firms under lawyer professional liability theories, see Chapter 16 of this Handbook.
18. *The T.J. Hooper*, 60 F.2d 737 (2d Cir. 1932), *aff'g* 53 F.2d 107 (S.D.N.Y. 1931).

storm that caused the loss of the barges and cargo. Other tugboats had been equipped with the new technology, had been able to hear the storm warnings, and had made it to safety, protecting their crews and cargo. While the use of radios was not yet standard industry practice, that court found it unreasonable for the tugboats' owner not to use it. Hand observed that in most cases reasonable prudence is in fact common prudence; but strictly it is never its only measure. A whole calling may have unduly lagged in the adoption of new and available devices. While courts must in the end say what is required, there are precautions so imperative that even their universal disregard will not excuse their omission.[19]

On the grounds that the tugboats' owners had not equipped the tugs with radio receivers to hear available storm warnings, the tugs were held unseaworthy, and the injury to the cargo owners "a direct consequence of this unseaworthiness."[20] On the right facts, would the failure of a law firm to avail itself of available cybersecurity techniques or equipment, in the event of a preventable cybersecurity incident that caused injury, lead to the law firm's liability?

There can be no doubt that traditional bodies of law used to hold lawyers and law firms accountable for certain harms resulting from their conduct can be used for data and other cybersecurity breaches. With respect to harms suffered by clients, the law offers an obvious path for malpractice liability to a client predicated on a breach of confidentiality and for liability to a client for breach of the fiduciary duty of confidentiality. Indeed, even inadvertent disclosures, or breaches by malicious third parties, could give rise to claims by those with an interest in confidential information (whether a client or a third party), perhaps on a theory of negligent safeguarding of that information by a lawyer.

In recent years, the prevalence of "outside counsel guidelines," specific and often detailed requirements on various subjects imposed upon lawyers by clients, may well provide another avenue for clients to recoup losses from data breaches and cyberattacks suffered by lawyers and law firms.

---

19. *Id.* at 740.
20. *Id.*

Indeed, many clients, especially in highly regulated industries, have recently begun to impose, and strictly monitor and enforce, specific technology and cybersecurity requirements on their counsel. It seems reasonably clear that, in the right circumstances, a lawyer or law firm's failure to abide by these contractually agreed requirements, where that failure can be shown to have led to injury to the client, could lead to liability.

Under all these theories, however, it is sometimes quite difficult for claimants to prove loss causation to the extent required by law.

IV. Examples of the Emerging Application of Ethics and Lawyering Law to New Technology

In this section, we review the application of the rules to particular technologies as they have arisen, been adopted by lawyers and their clients, and changed over time. One fundamental principle runs through all of these authorities: When a lawyer decides to use any of these new technologies, the lawyer must have a basic understanding of the technology employed and must take reasonable, prudent steps to preserve client confidentiality, balancing the degree of sensitivity of the information with the need to take additional precautions as appropriate.

A. E-mail

1. To Encrypt or Not to Encrypt?

E-mail was one of the first types of new technology to cause widespread concern in the profession because of perceived threats to client confidentiality. Early in the 1990s, a number of ethics committees issued opinions warning against the use of e-mail to transmit confidential client information, and several of these concluded that a lawyer should not transmit client information through e-mail unless it was encrypted.

As the thinking around e-mail developed, later state bar ethics opinions concluded that an e-mail is similar to a telephone call, and that lawyers have a reasonable expectation of privacy when using it, since it is just as illegal to intercept an e-mail as it is to wiretap a phone call. However, these opinions also stated that lawyers should still exercise caution when using e-mail, just as they would with any other form of communication. If the information is so sensitive that a lawyer would not discuss it over the telephone, chances are that he or she should not use e-mail either.

In 1999, the ABA Standing Committee on Ethics and Professional Responsibility weighed in on this issue in Formal Opinion 99-413, Protecting the Confidentiality of Unencrypted Email. In language quite similar to the Ethics 20/20 Commission's later amendments to the comments to Rule 1.6, the committee stated that, if a lawyer has a very sensitive matter to be discussed with a client, he should do it in person. The opinion stated:

> The Committee believes that email communications, including those sent unencrypted over the Internet, pose no greater risk of interception or disclosure than other modes of communication commonly relied upon as having a reasonable expectation of privacy. The level of legal protection accorded email transmissions, like that accorded other modes of electronic communication, also supports the reasonableness of an expectation of privacy for unencrypted email transmissions. The risk of unauthorized interception and disclosure exists in every medium of communication, including email. It is not, however, reasonable to require that a mode of communicating information must be avoided simply because interception is technologically possible, especially when unauthorized interception or dissemination of the information is a violation of law.

The conclusions reached in this opinion do not, however, diminish a lawyer's obligation to consider with her client the sensitivity of the communication, the consequences of its disclosure, and the relative security of the contemplated medium of communication. Particularly strong protective measures are warranted to guard against the disclosure of highly sensitive matters. Those measures might include the avoidance of e-mail, just as they would warrant the avoidance of the telephone, fax, and mail.

The ABA revisited this guidance in Opinion 477R, discussed earlier, and rejected an overly broad interpretation of earlier Opinion 99-413. The Opinion 477R rejected the reading by some of Opinion 99-413 that a lawyer was ethically permitted *in every circumstance* to use unencrypted e-mail for client confidential communications. In retrospect, that reading of Opinion 99-413 was an over-reading of its conclusion; it was, however, a product of its time, when encryption was expensive and technologically and practically impossible for most lawyers and clients. In formulating guidance for when additional security measures might be needed, the committee writing Opinion 477R looked, among other authorities, to Texas Opinion 648 (2015), which identified six situations in which a lawyer should consider whether to encrypt or use some other type of security precaution:

1. Communicating highly sensitive or confidential information via email or unencrypted e-mail connections;

2. Sending an e-mail to or from an account that the e-mail sender or recipient shares with others;

3. Sending an e-mail to a client when it is possible that a third person (such as a spouse in a divorce case) knows the password to the e-mail account, or to an individual client at that client's work e-mail account, especially if the e-mail relates to a client's employment dispute with his employer;

4. Sending an e-mail from a public computer or a borrowed computer or where the lawyer knows that the e-mails the lawyer sends are being read on a public or borrowed computer or on an unsecure network;

5. Sending an e-mail if the lawyer knows that the e-mail recipient is accessing the e-mail on devices that are potentially accessible to third persons or are not protected by a password; or

6. Sending an e-mail if the lawyer is concerned that the National Security Agency or a law enforcement agency may read the lawyer's e-mail communication, with or without a warrant.[21]

In a similar vein, Pennsylvania Bar Association Committee on Legal Ethics and Professional Responsibility Formal Opinion 2011-200 encouraged encryption when using "vulnerable methods of communications":

---

21. Pro. Ethics Comm. for the State Bar of Tex., Op. 648 (2015), https://www.legalethics texas.com/Ethics-Resources/Opinions/Opinion-648.aspx.

Compounding the general security concerns for e-mail is that users increasingly access webmail using unsecure or vulnerable methods such as cell phones or laptops with public wireless internet connections. Reasonable precautions are necessary to minimize the risk of unauthorized access to sensitive client information when using these devices and services, possibly including precautions such as encryption and strong password protection in the event of lost or stolen devices, or hacking.

2. Duty to Warn Client When Third Parties May Have Access to Client's Computer

ABA Formal Opinion 11-459, Duty to Protect the Confidentiality of Email Communications with One's Client (2011), addressed the precautions lawyers should take when they know that their clients are using an employer's computer or other electronic device to communicate with the lawyer. The opinion noted that, under such circumstances, the employer may, as a matter of company policy, have access to the employee's communication and stated that the lawyer should warn the client about the risks of using such devices:

> Given these risks, a lawyer should ordinarily advise the employee-client about the importance of communicating with the lawyer in a manner that protects the confidentiality of email communications, just as a lawyer should avoid speaking face-to-face with a client about sensitive matters if the conversation might be overheard and should warn the client against discussing their communications with others. In particular, as soon as practical after a client-lawyer relationship is established, a lawyer typically should instruct the employee-client to avoid using a workplace device or system for sensitive or substantive communications, and perhaps for any attorney-client communications, because even seemingly ministerial communications involving matters such as scheduling can have substantive ramifications.

State bar opinions have come to similar conclusions.[22]

---

22. For additional information, see Appendix E, E-mail (Ethics Opinions on Lawyer Confidentiality Obligations concerning E-mail) of this Handbook.

B. Portable Devices and Other Devices That Retain Data

Law firms today use many devices that store confidential client information, including desktop computers, laptops, tablets, printers that store data, flash drives or thumb drives, and cell phones and smartphones. The fact that these devices can store vast amounts of confidential client information mandates that lawyers should take adequate precautions to ensure that the information is protected from disclosure. The extreme portability of some of these devices—smartphones and flash drives come to mind immediately—makes it particularly important for lawyers to use them with thought and care.

But, in recent years, lawyers and others have also learned that danger lurks in devices not ordinarily thought of as likely to retain confidential information. Basic security measures have long included efforts to remove all confidential information from devices before they are disposed of or recycled. More recently, however, press reports that some modern copiers and printers include memory technology that retains images of documents, essentially on a permanent basis, have led many users to understand that disposal of even these pieces of equipment must be accompanied by erasure or removal of memory, just as with the disposal of a desktop computer. For example, Alabama Opinion 2010-2 (2010) states that when disposing of electronic devices, lawyers should ensure that confidential information has been removed. This obligation tracks closely the well-understood obligation of a lawyer to dispose of paper client files in a way that avoids the possibility of disclosure of confidential information (for example, by shredding).

In 2010, the Ethics 20/20 Commission's Working Group on the Implications of New Technologies suggested possible precautions lawyers should take when using portable devices, and most of these precautions apply with equal force to any piece of equipment, portable or not, that stores confidential information:

- Providing adequate physical protection or having methods for deleting data remotely in the event that a device is lost or stolen;
- Encouraging the use of strong passwords;
- Purging data from devices before replacement;
- Installing safeguards to combat viruses, malware, and spyware;

- Erecting firewalls;
- Ensuring frequent backups of data;
- Updating computer operating systems to ensure that they contain the latest security protections;
- Configuring software and network settings to minimize security risks;
- Encrypting sensitive information, and identifying (and, when appropriate, eliminating) metadata from electronic documents before sending them; and
- Avoiding public "Wi-Fi hotspots" when transmitting confidential information.[23]

The ubiquity and ease of use of portable devices carries particular problems for lawyers. One common example is the use of laptops and other portable devices away from a lawyer's regular place of work.

California State Bar Opinion 2010-179 (2010) addressed a situation where a lawyer used a law firm laptop both in a local coffee shop, accessing the Internet using the coffee shop's Wi-Fi connection, and at his home, using his personal wireless connection. The opinion listed a number of factors for a lawyer to consider when using different types of technologies that have the capability of storing and disseminating confidential client information. These factors include the lawyer's ability to understand and assess the level of security offered by the particular technology, how the particular technology differs from other media, whether reasonable steps can be taken to increase the level of security of such technology, and the limitations on who has access to it. The opinion stated that lawyers should also assess the legal consequences to third parties, including possible criminal charges or civil claims should they illegally intercept or access the confidential information, as this could affect the extent to which the lawyer using the service or technology could claim a reasonable expectation of privacy. The lawyer should also take into consideration the degree of sensitivity of the information, and the extent to which unauthorized disclosure would adversely affect the client; the greater the sensitivity, the less risk the lawyer should

---

23. Lance J. Rogers, *Model Rules: Ethics 20/20 Commission Invites Comments on Issues Raised by Growing Use of Internet*, 26 LAW. MAN. ON PRO. CONDUCT 586 (ABA/BNA Sept. 29, 2010) (discussing Ethics 20/20 working group's Sept. 20, 2010, memorandum).

take. Finally, if the client has instructed the lawyer not to use a certain type of technology, the lawyer should abide by the client's instructions.

Applying these factors to the scenario described in the opinion, the California committee concluded that the lawyer should not have used the wireless services offered in the coffee shop unless he had in place adequate safeguards such as wireless encryption and firewalls to protect client information. With regard to use at home of the laptop, the committee stated that the lawyer could use it so long as his home system had adequate security features.

C. Metadata Leaks

Many ethics committees have addressed the application of ethics rules to questions involving metadata—that is, electronic information about electronic documents that is often associated with, or a part of, the document, but often not readily visible to the ordinary user. The question most frequently addressed, however, is whether a lawyer who receives a document containing metadata (for example, a Word file containing a document being negotiated between the lawyer's client and someone else) may ethically look for and review that metadata, as the metadata may well contain useful, otherwise confidential, information.

While those opinions reflect varied opinions on whether the receiving lawyer may or may not look for and review metadata, a number of ethics opinions address the related question: What obligation does a lawyer have to protect against the disclosure of metadata that reveals confidential information of his or her client? The authorities that do address this question apply the same analysis for the protection from disclosure of metadata as for ordinary data—a lawyer must take reasonable precautions to avoid disclosure of confidential client information, in whatever form.[24]

D. Outsourcing

Outsourcing is another area where confidential client information is subject to cybersecurity threats. When a lawyer engages an outside service provider

---

24. For additional information, see Appendix F, Metadata (Ethics Opinions Concerning a Lawyer's Obligations to Prevent the Inadvertent Disclosure of Confidential Client Information in Metadata) in this Handbook.

to provide legal or law-related services for his or her clients, and allows the provider access to confidential client information, the lawyer must ensure that the outside entity has in place reasonable safeguards to protect against unauthorized disclosure. If the service provider is a legal professional outside of the United States, the lawyer may well have an obligation to ascertain whether the laws and professional conduct rules of the foreign jurisdiction share the same basic core values of client confidentiality.

Recent developments in technology and legal-services delivery have reshaped these concerns a bit. On the one hand, lawyers and law firms have increasingly—and largely appropriately—outsourced their cybersecurity obligations as key software and storage needs have rapidly migrated to the cloud. Further, new legal-services providers, from providers of temporary or contract lawyers to outsourced receptionist services, have grown in acceptance by lawyers. But all these technology changes have simply increased the need to carefully vet and oversee outsourcing vendors of all types.

The latest revisions to the ABA Model Rules of Professional Conduct, based on 2012 proposals from the Ethics 20/20 Commission, address a lawyer's obligations concerning outsourcing. These amendments codified, to a great extent, a 2008 ABA ethics opinion on this subject in amendments to comments to Rules 1.1 and 5.3.

The commission proposed amendments to the comments to Rules 1.1 and 5.3 on how to supervise and select outside service providers that have in place adequate measures to protect client information. New Comment [6] to Rule 1.1 states:

Retaining or Contracting with Other Lawyers or Professional Support

[6] Before a lawyer retains or contracts with other lawyers outside the lawyer's own firm to provide or assist in the provision of legal services to a client, the lawyer should ordinarily obtain informed consent from the client and must reasonably believe that the other lawyers' services will contribute to the competent and ethical representation of the client. See also Rules 1.2 (allocation of authority), 1.4 (communication with client), 1.5(e) (fee sharing), 1.6 (confidentiality), and 5.5(a) (unauthorized practice of law). The reasonableness of a decision to retain or contract with other lawyers outside the lawyer's own

firm will depend upon the circumstances, including the education, experience and reputation of the nonfirm lawyers; the nature of the services assigned to the nonfirm lawyers; and the legal protections, professional conduct rules, and ethical environments of the jurisdictions in which the services will be performed, particularly relating to confidential information.

In 2008, the ABA Standing Committee on Ethics and Professional Responsibility addressed a number of these issues relating to confidentiality in its Formal Opinion 08-451, Lawyer's Obligations When Outsourcing Legal and Nonlegal Support Services.

The opinion considered outsourcing in a wide variety of contexts, such as the use of contract or temporary lawyers, photocopy shops or information technology vendors, legal research services, or foreign lawyers to draft patent applications. Among the lawyer's duties implicated by the use of such outsourcing, the opinion noted, are the duty of competence (Rule 1.1) and the duty to supervise (Rules 5.1 and 5.3). The committee offered the following suggestions to help the outsourcing lawyer comply with the duties of competence and supervision:

- Conduct background checks of any lawyer, nonlawyer, or placement agency involved;
- Interview the principal lawyers involved, and assess their educational backgrounds;
- When working with an intermediary, inquire into its hiring practices so as to ascertain the character of the employees who are likely to have access to client information;
- Investigate the security measures in effect in the provider's premises, including its computer network and refuse disposal systems;
- Depending on the circumstances, consider conducting an onsite visit in order to get an impression of the professionalism of the lawyers and nonlawyers involved.

The committee stated further that when the work will be outsourced to a foreign country, the outsourcing lawyer should also ascertain whether the legal training received in that country is comparable to that in the United

States, whether legal professionals in that country share the same core ethical principles with lawyers in the United States, and whether there is an effective professional discipline system. If the legal professionals' legal system does not share the same core principles or does not have an effective lawyer discipline system, the outsourcing lawyer would have a heightened duty to scrutinize the work produced, and may have an obligation to disclose to the client the risks associated with having the work outsourced to that country.

The opinion also particularly highlighted an outsourcing lawyer's duty to protect client confidentiality, including by taking reasonable measures to protect confidential information necessarily disclosed in the course of the outsourcing, for example, by using confidentiality agreements to bind vendors contractually to protect client information. Further, the outsourcing lawyer who uses foreign vendors will need to evaluate the protection afforded the client's confidentiality by the foreign jurisdiction.

In a like vein, a much earlier opinion, ABA Formal Opinion 95-398, Access of Nonlawyers to a Lawyer's Data Base (1995), had addressed the ethical implications of allowing a computer maintenance company to have access to a law firm's computer network. The opinion stated that the law firm could allow access so long as it took steps to ensure that it had in place adequate security measures to protect confidential client information.[25]

E.   Cloud Computing

"Cloud computing" can describe any system whereby a lawyer stores digital information on servers or systems that are not under the close control of the lawyer or the lawyer's firm.[26] In the wake of the coronavirus pandemic lockdowns and "stay-at-home" orders in spring 2020 that forced many lawyers to exclusively work remotely, lawyers and law offices of all sizes and types dramatically accelerated their adoption of cloud-based services for their operations. Well before the pandemic, however, lawyers had been

---

25. For additional information, see Appendix G, Outsourcing (Ethics Opinions on Lawyer Confidentiality Obligations Concerning Outsourcing) in this Handbook.

26. Additional discussion about the technical aspects of cloud computing can be found in Chapter 3 of this Handbook.

provided significant guidance on their ethical obligations in using the cloud, both for storage and various services essential to their work.

A lawyer's use of cloud computing can be both economical and beneficial, but as many state bar ethics opinions have noted, lawyers who use "the cloud" must take steps to ensure that confidential client information that is placed there is adequately protected from disclosure. Many opinions suggest a number of factors to use in assessing whether the protections are adequate, but with the proviso that rapidly evolving technology means that these factors cannot provide a "safe harbor." Lawyers should monitor and reassess the protections of the cloud provider as the technology evolves.

As an example, Illinois State Bar Advisory Opinion 16-06 (2016) suggested the following steps lawyers should consider taking when deciding whether to engage the services of a cloud computing provider:

1. Reviewing cloud computing industry standards and familiarizing oneself with the appropriate safeguards that should be employed;
2. Investigating whether the provider has implemented reasonable security precautions to protect client data from inadvertent disclosures, including but not limited to the use of firewalls, password protections, and encryption;
3. Investigating the provider's reputation and history;
4. Inquiring whether the provider has experienced any breaches of security and if so, investigating those breaches;
5. Requiring an agreement to reasonably ensure that the provider will abide by the lawyer's duties of confidentiality and will immediately notify the lawyer of any breaches or outside requests for client information;
6. Requiring that all data is appropriately backed up completely under the lawyer's control so that the lawyer will have a method for retrieval of the data;
7. Requiring provisions for the reasonable retrieval of information if the agreement is terminated or if the provider goes out of business.

Opinions addressing cloud computing also make clear that a lawyer must have a basic understanding of the technical aspects of cloud computing, and should conduct a due diligence evaluation of the provider to ensure that it has adequate security measures. As Washington State Bar Opinion 2215 points out, ignorance of technology is no excuse for the failure to conduct such an investigation. A lawyer who does not understand the technology or whether it is sufficiently secure for use should consult with someone who does.[27]

In order to determine whether a lawyer has made "reasonable efforts" to ensure that outside vendors who provide communications technology have taken appropriate steps to protect client confidences, the ABA's Formal Opinion 477R suggests a number of factors for evaluating technologies and vendors that are very similar to those identified by the many state bar ethics opinions on cloud computing.

F. Social Media

1. Lawyers and Social Media

Social media networks such as Facebook, Twitter, and LinkedIn have grown exponentially in recent years. Though lawyers have been slower than the general public and other businesses to adopt social networks, their use is becoming more and more prevalent among lawyers. While the use of social media networks may pose various risks for lawyers and others, for purposes of cybersecurity for lawyers and law firms, the questions about these networks revolve around confidentiality and lawyers' understanding of the technology that drives them.[28]

The strong tendency on social networks for users, including lawyers, to freely share information, and to do so without considered thought, opens the possibility that client confidential information may be shared by a

---

27. For additional information, see Appendix H, Cloud Computing (Ethics Opinions on Lawyer Confidentiality Obligations Concerning Cloud Computing) in this Handbook.

28. Perhaps the best two sources available to lawyers and others on legal ethics issues associated with social media are JAN L. JACOBOWITZ & JOHN G BROWNING, LEGAL ETHICS AND SOCIAL MEDIA: A PRACTITIONER'S HANDBOOK (ABA 2017), https://www.americanbar.org/products/inv/book/276236835/, and *Social Media Ethics Guidelines* (Com. and Fed. Litig. Section, N.Y. State Bar Ass'n) (updated June 20, 2019), https://nysba.org/app/uploads/2020/02/NYSBA-Social-Media-Ethics-Guidelines-Final-6-20-19.pdf. While the NYSBA publication is focused on New York authority, it nevertheless provides an excellent starting point for research in other jurisdictions.

lawyer, perhaps without careful deliberation. Of course, the lawyer's confidentiality obligations do not stop when the lawyer is logged on to social media. Moreover, the increased sharing of information among a wide range of people (sometimes including people not known to the lawyer using the service) may lead to the disclosure of seemingly innocuous information that may somehow reveal confidential client information (for example, the mergers and acquisition lawyer's plans for travel to a city in which a particular business is located).

Even when social networks are, in fact, used by lawyers for professional purposes—for example, posting a query to other lawyers about a knotty procedural problem in a pending case—the risk of disclosing client confidential information exists. In ABA Formal Opinion 98-411 (1998), Ethical Issues in Lawyer-to-Lawyer Consultation, the ethics committee addressed lawyer-to-lawyer consultations of a similar type:

> The consulting lawyer should not assume, however, that the anonymous or hypothetical consultation eliminates all risk of disclosure of client information. If the hypothetical facts discussed allow the consulted lawyer subsequently to match those facts to a specific individual or entity, the information is not already generally known, and disclosure may prejudice or embarrass the client, the consulting lawyer's discussion of the facts may have violated his duty of confidentiality under Rule 1.6.

The sweeping reach of client confidentiality under ABA Model Rule 1.6—which requires protection of all "information relating to the representation," from whatever source—and under the rules in most jurisdictions counsels great care on the part of lawyers in sharing information that may touch on their professional lives. Further, just as with any other technology, lawyers have an obligation to be knowledgeable enough about any social network they use such that they can appropriately protect client confidential information.

Moreover, a lawyer's duty to supervise other lawyers and nonlawyers may include educating them concerning how their confidentiality obligation applies even among "friends" on Facebook and alerting them that "casual" comments made on LinkedIn after a difficult hearing may be risky. Rules 5.1 and 5.3 on supervision may also require that a lawyer or law firm have in place internal firm policies designed to protect client confidences in this context. These rules do require that lawyers who manage their own practices or their firms must make sure they have in place "measures giving reasonable assurance that" obligations under the ethics rules, including confidentiality obligations, are met.

It is common practice to post the minutiae of daily life on social media sites. However, when lawyers post information about their clients, they confront the broad reach of Rule 1.6 that protects from disclosure all information relating to the representation without client consent, unless impliedly necessary to carry out the representation, or unless another exception listed in Rule 1.6(b) applies. Even a post that refers to a client matter that is redacted to remove any identifying information can be a breach of confidentiality if someone who reads the post could reasonably ascertain to whom the lawyer is referring and what the matter is about.[29]

2.   *Passive Communications with Jurors*
As with all forms of technology, it is vitally important that lawyers understand the consequences of certain technical features of social media. To illustrate, consider the body of ethics opinions and court rules that have arisen over issues involving "passive" communications with jurors on social media.

While it is common practice for trial lawyers preparing for voir dire to search the Internet to acquire information about potential jurors, some jurisdictions have found such investigation to be inappropriate to the extent that the juror becomes aware that he or she is being monitored. Based on some of these opinions, the ethical propriety of the lawyer's conduct may depend on the functionality of the social media network.

On some social media networks, the network alerts a user when someone else views or visits the user's page or profile; on other social media networks, a user may have no idea of the identity of someone (such as a

---

29. *See* Appendix I, Social Media (Ethics Opinions Relating to Lawyers' Passive Communications with Jurors on Social Media) in this Handbook.

lawyer doing investigation for purposes of voir dire) viewing the user's page or profile. Indeed, on some social networks, whether a user is alerted to such viewing or the identity of the viewer may depend on how the viewer accesses the network or even the settings of the user or the viewer. Knowing these details of the functionality of the particular social media network may well be crucial for a lawyer deciding whether and how to ethically investigate potential jurors.

ABA Formal Opinion 466, Lawyer Reviewing Jurors' Internet Presence (2014), addressed this issue and concluded that a juror's becoming aware of a lawyer's investigation was not a communication from the lawyer to the juror since it was the social media platform and not the lawyer that initiated the notification to the juror, analogizing the situation to that of a neighbor who reports to the juror that he saw the lawyer's car driving down the juror's street.

The committee cautioned, however, that lawyers should educate themselves about the features of the different social media platforms sites and that "lawyers who review juror social media should ensure that their review is purposeful and not crafted to embarrass, delay or burden the juror or the proceeding."[30]

Earlier opinions from New York appeared to reach different conclusions, stating that notifications received by jurors from their social media websites that the lawyer had visited their sites had the potential to harass and intimidate jurors and constituted an impermissible communication with a juror in violation of Rule 3.5. In view of this potential to run afoul of Rule 3.5, these opinions cautioned that lawyers have an obligation to familiarize themselves with the features of a particular social media platform so as to avoid any inappropriate communications with a juror.[31] Clearly, trial lawyers interested in investigating potential jurors, or having someone do that for them, must become knowledgeable of the current ethics guidance in their jurisdiction, as well as in the courts in which they appear.

---

30. ABA Standing Comm. on Ethics & Pro. Resp., Formal Op. 477 Lawyer Reviewing Jurors' Internet Presence (Apr. 14, 2014), https://www.americanbar.org/content/dam/aba/administrative/professional_responsibility/formal_opinion_466_final_04_23_14.authcheckdam.pdf.

31. *See* N.Y. City Bar Ass'n Comm. on Pro. Ethics, Formal Op. 2012-2 (2012); N.Y. Cnty. Lawyer Ass'n, Formal Op. 743 (2011).

G. Ransomware

Perhaps the key theme underlying a lawyer's ethical obligations to protect the cybersecurity of client information is the dynamic nature of that obligation, which changes as the technology lawyers use and the threat environment changes. At the time of this writing, the threat most feared by most lawyers, law firms, and others is ransomware—the malicious encryption of lawyer and client data on a lawyer's or law firm's electronic systems and the demand for a ransom from the lawyer or law firm for the data's safe return or decryption. In some instances, even when a ransom is paid, the client and lawyer confidential information may be stolen or even published.

As of this writing, no U.S. authorities have issued ethics guidance specifically addressing what a lawyer is required to do to prevent a ransomware attack or in response to one. That said, there is emerging guidance on what might amount to "reasonable efforts" by a lawyer or law firm either to prevent or remediate a ransomware attack. These include training for firm personnel in recognizing phishing attacks designed to allow access to deploy ransomware in firm systems; good passwords for access to firm systems; multifactor authentication for access to firm systems; and robust and regular backups of firm systems. We have no guidance yet, from court decisions or ethics opinions, on whether the failure to use these basic techniques might lead to the disciplinary or civil liability of a lawyer whose client suffered a loss from a ransomware attack on the lawyer. Still, we are in an era where the next *T.J. Hooper* decision might well answer those questions for some unlucky lawyer or law firm.

V. Conclusion

We lawyers, like our clients, live and practice in a rapidly changing communications and technology environment, and there is no end in sight for these changes. Over the last 20 years, our ethics rules have been interpreted to provide guidance as to how we can discharge our ethical obligations in a time when threats, technology, security vulnerabilities, and protection measures available, as well as their relationships one to another, are also dynamically changing.

Whether it be cloud computing, the newfound perils of remote work, the use of unencrypted or encrypted e-mail, participating in social media, or the use of the latest electronic gadget, lawyers have an obligation to make reasonable efforts to protect their client confidential information. What is found to constitute "reasonable efforts" will depend on a number of factors, including the sensitivity of the information, the likelihood of disclosure if additional safeguards are not employed, and the cost and difficulty of implementing them.

Applying these factors, ABA Formal Opinion 477R informs us that when transmitting client information over the Internet, encryption should be considered as an additional security safeguard when warranted by the circumstances.

Lawyers also have an obligation to understand the benefits and risks associated with these new technologies. If for any reason they are unable to do so, they should consult with someone who does.

Lawyers who supervise other lawyers and nonlawyers also have a duty to make reasonable efforts to ensure that their conduct conforms to the rules of professional conduct and that they follow appropriate security procedures to protect client confidences.

Following are the top ten ethical and other considerations with respect to lawyer obligations to protect client data:

1. A lawyer must acquire a basic understanding of the "benefits and risks associated with relevant technology" used in his or her day-to-day practice. A lawyer who does not have such an understanding should identify and consult with someone who does.

2. Technology is a moving target. Keeping current about changes in technology is an ongoing process. A lawyer must continually reassess and evaluate security measures as new technologies develop and come into use by lawyers and their clients. A lawyer may be able to meet this obligation by "outsourcing" this continuing diligence to a trusted technology expert.

3. Be aware that the scope of the information protected under the ethics rules—ABA Model Rule 1.6—is very broad. It includes all information relating to the representation.

4. Be mindful of obligations to protect a former client's confidential information (under Model Rule 1.9(c)) as well.

5. When using technology to either store or transmit information, lawyers must make reasonable efforts to prevent the inadvertent disclosure of or unauthorized access to confidential client information.

6. Reasonable efforts to prevent the inadvertent disclosure of or unauthorized access to confidential client information include assessing the sensitivity of the information and the likelihood of disclosure if additional safeguards are not employed. Depending on the circumstances, for example, encryption and multifactor authentication may be appropriate additional security safeguards. Lawyers should consult their technology experts.

7. In an office or firm, have in place procedures by which both lawyers and nonlawyers are trained and monitored in their use of technology to ensure that client confidences are protected.

8. When disposing of portable electronic devices, take precautions to ensure that all confidential client information has been removed. If the devices are recycled, verify that the recycler follows appropriate protocols to remove the data.

9. When transmitting electronic documents to third parties, remove metadata that contains confidential client information.

10. When using cloud computing or outsourcing services, verify that the service provider has in place adequate security measures to prevent the inadvertent disclosure of or unauthorized access to confidential client information.

Chapter 7

Occasions When Counsel Should Consider Initiating a Conversation about Cybersecurity with the Client

Roland L. Trope

I. Introduction

A. The Problem: Lawyers and Law Firms Have Become High-Priority Targets for Cyberattacks

Cyber adversaries have evolved into formidable threats to enterprises and their counsel. Sophisticated cyber adversaries have developed capabilities to breach businesses of any size. Their capabilities enable them to operate stealthily and to remain undetected for months or longer. They acquire administrative privileges that give them unfettered access to all corners of an enterprise's digital systems. They misappropriate valuable troves of intellectual property (IP) from IP rich enterprises and collect intelligence ("intel") on targeted enterprises and share it with other cyber adversaries.

For decades, cyber adversaries improved their capabilities incrementally. In recent years, their capability enhancements have accelerated, particularly in the use of advanced persistent threat (APT) attacks and ransomware attacks. Cyber adversaries increasingly combine a ransomware attack with extortion—threats to leak or sell sensitive information exfiltrated through "dwelling," that is, spending "weeks or months embedded in an organization's computer system undetected."[1] And, in each instance, the attackers may be maliciously modifying the target's data.

At the same time, cyber adversaries have leveraged their improved ransomware attacks to extract ever larger amounts of funds from their targets. They have capabilities now to target hundreds of companies in a short span with one attack. They increasingly select as targets major critical infrastructure companies.

- In November 2017, hackers executed a ransomware attack on G&G Oil Co. of Indiana (G&G) and demanded a bitcoin payment to restore G&G's control over its servers. G&G paid the ransom: $34,477.50.[2]
- In May 2021, ransomware attackers caused the shutdown of Colonial Pipeline, which supplies roughly 45 percent of gas and jet fuel for the East Coast. The company paid a much higher ransom—$4.4 million— and did so "because executives were unsure how badly the cyberattack had breached its systems, and consequently, how long it would take to bring the pipeline back."[3]

What cyber adversaries do to client enterprises, they also do to the lawyers and law firms that represent them and possess digital copies of their highly sensitive data and intellectual property.[4] Undetected cyber reconnaissance, attempted intrusions, and successful breaches of law firm computers and digital records have become the norm. So have ransomware attacks.[5]

Disruption of law firm global operations demonstrates that lawyers and law firms are as much the potential targets of cyberattacks as their

---

1. Lynsey Jeffrey & Vignesh Ramachandran, *Why Ransomware Attacks Are on the Rise— And What Can Be Done to Stop Them*, PBS NEWS HOUR (July 8, 2021), https://www.pbs.org /newshour/nation/why-ransomware-attacks-are-on-the-rise-and-what-can-be-done-to-stop -them.

2. G&G Oil Co. of Ind. v. Cont'l W. Ins. Co., No. 19A-PL-1498, slip op. at 3 (Ind. Ct. App. Mar. 31, 2020), https://law.justia.com/cases/indiana/court-of-appeals/2020/19a-pl-1498.html.

3. Collin Eaton & Dustin Volz, *Colonial Pipeline CEO Tells Why He Paid Hackers a $4.4 Million Ransom*, WALL ST. J. (May 19, 2021), https://www.wsj.com/articles /colonial-pipeline-ceo-tells-why-he-paid-hackers-a-4-4-million-ransom-11621435636.

4. *See* ABA Comm. on Ethics & Pro. Resp., Formal Op. 477, at 2 (May 11, 2017; rev. May 22, 2017).

5. FT Reporters, *Global Groups Hit by Fresh Ransomware Cyberattack*, FIN. TIMES, June 28, 2017, at 11.

clients, and perhaps more so, since intruder access to one law firm may give intruders access to all client confidential information residing on and transiting through the firm's servers and storage media. And lawyers and law firms may well have been breached by the APT attacks that in 2020–2021 affected hundreds of enterprise customers of the attackers' initial targets SolarWinds and Microsoft.[6]

In this Handbook's Second Edition we cautioned that it may be prudent for all lawyers and law firms to adopt a working assumption that their computer networks and critical IT systems—as well as those of vendors to whom they may outsource the storage and processing of client confidential information—are vulnerable to cyberattacks. In addition, they are increasingly the targets of cyberattacks, and at this time remain largely indefensible and at high risk of being breached. In light of what we know so far of SolarWinds and the Microsoft Exchange attacks, the earlier caution needs to be enhanced.

Foremost among the initial lessons we should learn from the SolarWinds and Microsoft Exchange incidents is that too much of the impact, persistence, and potential for future compromise and damage remains unknown. It will reportedly "take years to know for certain which networks the Russians control and which ones they just occupy" and may have rendered persistently compromised unless rebuilt with uncontaminated hardware and software.[7] In short, we do not know enough about these APT intrusions to say that they are "over" or even that we have ascertained their full scope, when they began, or what intelligence they gleaned that might be used to stage future attacks.

As a result, lawyers and law firms face the possibility that incidents of such sophistication may create "new abnormal" conditions for cyber networks. The victims might not be able to operate securely in degraded cyber conditions. Instead, they might be left with computer systems so untrustworthy and insecure that digital storage and communications might need to be avoided altogether.

---

6. Jessica Shumaker, *Massive SolarWinds Breach Poses Risk to Law Firms, Courts as Well as Businesses*, LEGALNEWS (Jan. 29, 2021), http://legalnews.com/detroit/1496019/. See discussion of SolarWinds, Microsoft, and Kaseya VSA breaches in Chapter 2.

7. Sue Halpern, *After the SolarWinds Hack, We Have No Idea What Cyber Dangers We Face*, THE NEW YORKER (Jan. 25, 2021), https://www.newyorker.com/news/daily-comment/after-the-solarwinds-hack-we-have-no-idea-what-cyber-dangers-we-face.

This chapter will review the need for counsel to be aware of occasions that warrant initiating a conversation about cybersecurity with a client to avoid unnecessary risk to the client's interests. This chapter identifies ten such occasions. The aim of each such conversation is for counsel and client to explore the ways in which the client's activities may be putting the client at increased exposure to cyber threats and risks and to reduce that exposure by assisting the client in improving its approach to cybersecurity.

We recognize that whether the recommended improvements will be made and prove durable will ultimately depend upon the client's decisions. The client must accept making imperfect decisions after assessing the trade-offs between increased investments in cybersecurity and potential reduced investment in other high-priority objectives. Each client will make its own adjustments in those trade-offs, but if counsel can help improve the client's understanding of the need to protect its data assets from the growing risks of cyber intrusions, then the conversations about cybersecurity will have contributed to counsel's fulfillment of its ethical responsibilities to the client and to a client's protection and pursuit of its interests.

II. Ten Occasions That Warrant Discussion of Cybersecurity

Ten reasonably predictable occasions illustrate typical scenarios that will either trigger a professional obligation to initiate a conversation about cybersecurity with a client, or will make it prudent for counsel to have such conversation:

- First, at the start of a representation;
- Second, when the client enters a regulated field of activity;
- Third, when applicable statutes or regulations are amended or reinterpreted with significant cybersecurity implications, especially if the changes bring lawyers and law firms within reach of the regulations;
- Fourth, when litigation or an enforcement action or investigation is reasonably anticipated;
- Fifth, when the client or its key suppliers, critical infrastructure service providers, or corporate counterparties experience a cyber incident,

particularly if the client has a regulatory or contractual obligation to report an incident promptly or by a specified number of hours after discovery of the incident;

- Sixth, when counsel experiences a cyber incident, or when reports of cyber incidents demonstrate that law firms need to enhance their capabilities to safeguard client confidential information;
- Seventh, when the client anticipates that it will pursue, or become the target of, a merger or acquisition, particularly if counsel anticipates the need for a review of the transaction by the Committee on Foreign Investment in the United States (CFIUS), which has become more likely for a broad range of such transactions as a result of the expansion of CFIUS' jurisdiction by enactment of the Foreign Investment Risk Review Modernization Act of 2018 (FIRRMA) and promulgation of the FIRRMA regulations that took effect on February 13, 2020;
- Eighth, when the client anticipates providing goods or services for new communications technologies in a regulated sector, for example, providing Internet of Things (IoT) devices for use in connected vehicles or adoption of artificial intelligence (AI)–enhanced performance of work or AI-augmented operation of equipment and systems;
- Ninth, when the client embarks on a major transition in its corporate or commercial activities and may be tempted to devise software to circumvent regulatory obstacles or may be tempted to deviate from good software and engineering practices to facilitate a new product's release or to forestall withdrawal of a product from service; and,
- Tenth, when high-impact, low-frequency (HILF) events (like pandemics and advanced persistent threat (APT) cyberattacks) disrupt workplace operations and supply chains, and cause enterprises to adapt by directing personnel to work from home and other locations where cybersecurity may be diminished.

The following considers the cybersecurity features inherent in each occasion and what issues counsel may want to discuss with the client to improve the chances that the client will understand the issues and address them responsibly.

A.   At the Start of a Representation

1.   The Occasion

When a representation starts, the client usually expects its communications with counsel will be kept confidential. The letter of engagement may reinforce that expectation and may put a client on notice that action or inaction by the client may result in a waiver of the attorney-client privilege. As digital technologies proliferate, the risks to attorney-client confidentiality have rapidly grown. As a result, counsel's initial conversations with a client deserve to be far-reaching and probing.

2.   The Reason

Without careful conversation and exploration, the client may be unaware of risks that cybersecurity deficiencies can pose to the attorney-client privilege. The client may be unaware of the enhanced surveillance it needs over its electronic communications to avoid violating export controls and trade sanctions. It may be unaware that increases in cyber threats to critical infrastructure or in cyber vulnerabilities and risks might warrant a review of the client's existing cybersecurity policies (as occurred when the coronavirus (Covid-19) pandemic prompted redeployment of employees to working remotely from home and other sites and thus beyond an employer's existing on-premises security controls, practices, and procedures.

3.   The Joint Exploration

On this occasion, the conversation about cybersecurity could include exploration of the following:

- Business operations: the extent to which the client's business operations and activities use and depend on legacy digital technologies;
- Data processing: where and how the client obtains, creates, processes, stores, backs up, and purges its electronic records, and whether it outsources such activities to a "cloud" vendor or other third party;
- Preservation of the client's IP portfolio: whether the client's IP policies have kept pace with digital technologies and emerging cyber threats;
- Client's contingency and disaster recovery plans: the extent to which the client's data might be damaged, lost, accessed, or modified without

authorization in the event of a damaging cyber incident. The same concerns for data confidentiality, accessibility, and integrity arise when there is widescale disruptions of a nation's social order, economy, or security from non-cyber causes, such as a pandemic. Crises such as these create opportunities for malicious cyber actors to exploit reductions in security and the capability to respond promptly and effectively to sophisticated and stealthy intrusions;

- Preservation of privilege: the need for cybersecurity in order to preserve attorney-client privilege and other confidential communications; such needs increase when personnel work remotely or at home. An enterprise's or law firm's security procedures might not reach or may be found insufficient at remote locations (e.g., home offices in apartments or other dwellings where individuals have the same or overlapping workspaces and engage in telecommunications with little or no means to ensure confidentiality of their respective communications with officers, managers, coworkers, or clients).
- Avoidance of inadvertent violations: the extent to which the client may need to enhance its compliance policies to ensure that electronic transfers of technical data or funds do not violate the Export Administration Regulations, the International Traffic in Arms Regulations, the Economic Sanctions Regulations, the Foreign Corrupt Practices Act, or similar laws.

B. When the Client Enters a Regulated Field of Activity

1. The Occasion
When clients enter a new and regulated area of activity, they may be unaware of applicable regulations or postpone adopting the requisite compliance policies and procedures.

2. The Reason
Clients entering a new regulated field of activity may not be aware of cybersecurity regulations applicable to that new field. As a result, clients making such transitions may be at heightened risks of failing to meet, or of violating, applicable cybersecurity standards and regulations. Ensuring a client's

compliance at the start can avert enforcement actions that may impose fines or limit a client's range of commercial activities (e.g., by debarment or denial of export privileges).

3. The Joint Exploration

On this occasion, the conversation about cybersecurity should explore the regulatory regimes that apply to the client's new business operations and activities, including the extent to which the client's cybersecurity policies and procedures may not have kept pace with changes in the substance, interpretation, or enforcement of regulatory requirements for cybersecurity. The conversation could focus on examples of field-specific cybersecurity statutes, regulations, and rules such as the following:

- Those requiring or imposing data security standards for:
  - Health care companies at the federal level (e.g., the Health Insurance Portability and Accountability Act[8] (HIPAA));
  - financial institutions at the federal level (e.g., Gramm-Leach-Bliley Financial Services Modernization Act of 1999[9]) or state level (e.g., New York State Department of Financial Services' Cybersecurity Requirements for Financial Companies[10]);
  - handling of classified data (e.g., National Industrial Security Program Operating Manual[11]);
  - handling of controlled unclassified information (e.g., Defense Federal Acquisition Regulation Supplement (DFARS): Safeguarding Unclassified Controlled Technical Information[12]);
- Those requiring or imposing data control obligations on "dual use" items and services (e.g., export controls under the Export Administration

---

8. Pub. L. No. 104-191 (1996).

9. 15 U.S.C., subch. I.

10. N.Y. State Dep't of Fin. Servs., *Cybersecurity Requirements for Financial Services Companies*, N.Y. COMP. CODES R. & REGS. tit. 23, pt. 500 (eff. Mar. 2017), https://www.dfs.ny.gov/industry_guidance/cybersecurity.

11. U.S. DEP'T OF DEF. MANUAL 5220.22-M (Feb. 28, 2006), http://www.dss.mil/documents/odaa/nispom2006-5220.pdf.

12. 76 Fed. Reg. 69,273–82 (Nov. 18, 2013), https://www.gpo.gov/fdsys/pkg/FR-2013-11-18/pdf/2013-27313.pdf.

Regulations[13]) and on defense articles and services (e.g., export controls under the International Traffic in Arms Regulations[14]); and

- Those requiring reports of cyber incidents or intrusions (e.g., DFARS: Safeguarding Covered Defense Information and Cyber Incident Reporting[15] or HIPAA[16]).

Companies that are entering fields of business that involve operations in or affecting foreign countries need to be aware of the relevant laws in those jurisdictions as well.[17]

C.   When Cybersecurity Regulations Are Issued, Amended, or Judicially Reinterpreted

1.   The Occasion

In regulated industries, when cybersecurity regulations are issued, amended, or judicially reinterpreted, a client's cybersecurity obligations may change. On such occasions, it is prudent for counsel to initiate a conversation with the client about whether such changes may affect the client's operations and activities and whether the client's regulatory compliance programs may need to be modified. When new cybersecurity regulations bring within their scope the client's third-party service providers, counsel should determine if the client's outside counsel are thereby covered by such regulations. If so, counsel should promptly initiate a conversation with the client about how counsel will ensure its compliance with such regulations.

---

13. 15 C.F.R. §§ 730–774.

14. 22 C.F.R. §§ 120–130.

15. DFARS 252.204-7012(c), https://www.acquisition.gov/dfars/252.204-7012-safe guarding-covered-defense-information-and-cyber incident-reporting.

16. 81 Fed. Reg. 72,986–3001 (Oct. 21, 2016), https://www.gpo.gov/fdsys/pkg/FR-2016 -10-21/pdf/2016-25315.pdf.

17. See, for example, China's enactment in June 2021 of the "Anti-Foreign Sanctions Law," *Law of the PRC on Countering Foreign Sanctions*, CHINA LAW TRANSLATE (June 10, 2021), https://www.chinalawtranslate.com/en/counteringforeignsanctions/; and *China Issues Data Security Law*, NAT'L L. REV. (June 16, 2021), https://www.natlawreview.com/article /china-issues-data-security-law.

2. The Reason

Unless counsel initiates a conversation about the client's cybersecurity policies on such occasions, the client's and counsel's conduct may result in noncompliance and enforcement action.

3. The Joint Exploration

These conversations about cybersecurity could explore recent developments that may warrant changes in the client's cybersecurity policies or may change how counsel and client will fulfill cyber incident reporting requirements. The kinds of developments that would prompt such conversations might include the following:

- When a court decision construes what constitutes "reasonable data security" for institutions in a regulated field (e.g., the decision by the U.S. Court of Appeals for the First Circuit that a bank had failed to provide commercially reasonable security to protect a consumer from fraud[18]);
- When a court finds that a contractor knowingly misrepresented its compliance with federal regulation cybersecurity requirements, contained in an acquisition contract, the misrepresentation may be a violation of the False Claims Act (FCA) and expose the contractor to potential liability for up to treble damages;[19]
- When federal agencies require new or enhanced cybersecurity disclosures to the public or the federal or state governments or set precise time limits by which such disclosures must be made;[20] and

---

18. *See* Patco Constr. Co. v. People's United Bank, 684 F.3d 93 (1st Cir. 2012).

19. *See* United States v. Aerojet Rocketdyne Holdings, Inc., 381 F. Supp. 3d 1240 (E.D. Cal. 2019). For discussion of Rocketdyne, see Roland L. Trope, *To Secure, or Not Secure, Data Integrity—That Is the Question: Cybersecurity Developments*, 75 Bus. Law. 1655, 1660–63 (Winter 2019–2020). Other companies have also been held accountable for cyber security deficiencies in their products. *See* Joseph Marks, *Cisco to Pay $8.6 Million Fine for Selling Government Hackable Surveillance Technology*, Wash. Post (July 31, 2019), https://www.washingtonpost.com/politics/2019/07/31/cisco-pay-million-fine-selling-government-hackable-surveillance-technology/.

20. *See* SEC, CF Disclosure Guidance: Topic No. 2 (Oct. 13, 2011), https://www.sec.gov/divisions/corpfin/guidance/cfguidance-topic2.htm; DoD, Safeguarding Covered Defense Information and Cyber Incident Reporting, DFARS 252.204.7300 *et seq.*; DFARS 252.204-7012(c) (requiring reports of "cyber incidents" to the cognizant contracting officer within "72 hours" of discovery).

- When state agencies promulgate new cybersecurity regulations that apply not only to the regulated "covered entities" but also to their third-party service providers, including outside counsel.[21]

D. When Litigation, Enforcement Action, or Investigation Is Reasonably Anticipated

1. The Occasion

When a client reasonably anticipates litigation, it has a duty to preserve and produce all relevant records—hard copy and electronic. In addition, judges emphasize that counsel "must oversee compliance with the litigation hold, monitoring the party's efforts to retain and produce the relevant documents."[22]

Less well known, and frequently overlooked, is that a duty to preserve and produce all relevant records also attaches when a client reasonably anticipates enforcement action or investigation, such as by the U.S. Department of Justice (DoJ), the Office of Foreign Assets Control (OFAC), the Office of Export Enforcement, or the Directorate of Defense Trade Controls.[23]

Moreover, if no such action or investigation has begun, but client and counsel want the opportunity to make a voluntary self-disclosure, they will need to have a conversation about cybersecurity to ensure the preservation of all relevant records.

---

21. *See* N.Y. State Dep't of Fin. Servs., *Cybersecurity Requirements for Financial Services Companies*, N.Y. COMP. CODES R. & REGS. tit. 23, pt. 500 (eff. Mar. 2017), https://www.dfs.ny.gov/industry_guidance/cybersecurity. Note: the "Cyber Requirements" of the New York statute extend to "third-party service providers," defined as "a person that: is (1) not affiliated with a covered entity, (2) provides services to a covered entity, and (3) maintains, processes or otherwise is permitted access to nonpublic information through its provision of services to the covered entity." 23 CRR-NY 500.1(n) (emphasis added). This arguably extends to a Covered Entity's outside law firm.

22. Zubulake v. UBS Warburg LLC (*Zubulake V*), 229 F.R.D. 422 (S.D.N.Y. 2004).

23. *See* 31 C.F.R. Appendix A to Part 501—Economic Sanctions Enforcement Guidelines, § III(G)(2), (3) (describing factors OFAC may consider in evaluating an investigated company's cooperation, which include providing OFAC "with all relevant information regarding an apparent violation," which may not be possible if the company has not preserved at the outset all potentially relevant records).

2. The Reason

If client and counsel fail to fulfill their e-discovery duties, the court may make a finding of spoliation and impose penalties.[24]

If a client seeks to make a voluntary self-disclosure but fails to preserve all relevant evidence, the result may be disastrous. For example, under OFAC's Enforcement Guidelines, if a "subject person" submits a self-report about apparent violations, its report will not qualify as a voluntary self-disclosure if the report "is materially incomplete." That may be the result if client and counsel have not taken the steps needed to preserve all relevant records. In that event, the client will not receive the substantial reduction in penalties the Enforcement Guidelines authorize for a voluntary self-disclosure. Instead, the client will find it has incriminated itself, has triggered enforcement action, and faces the imposition of large fines.

3. The Joint Exploration

On these occasions, the conversation about cybersecurity should explore recent developments that might warrant changes in the client's cybersecurity policies, procedures, or practices. Such developments would include the following:

- Recent cases addressing e-discovery duties;
- Recent enforcement actions that concern violations through electronic transfers; and
- Steps that the client is going to take to ensure that document preservation obligations are complied with throughout the enterprise.

E. When the Client Experiences a Cyber Incident or Circumstances Put Clients at Significantly Heightened Risk of Cyber Intrusions

1. The Occasion

When a client experiences a cyber intrusion that results in data disclosure, there will probably be conversations and explorations with counsel

---

24. Pension Comm. of Univ. of Montreal v. Banc of Am. Sec., 2010 U.S. Dist. LEXIS 4546, at *2, *109 (S.D.N.Y. Jan. 15, 2010) (amended opinion).

about the client's cybersecurity, incident response, and data breach reporting obligations.

With thousands of cyber incidents occurring globally every hour, every client will eventually experience (and many already have experienced) multiple or repeated cyber intrusions from outside, unauthorized access from inside, or a loss of data through a misplaced or stolen device or misdirected transmission of data (a "cyber incident"). Counsel should plan on having the conversation before the client next experiences a cyber incident and address the risks of APT attacks going undetected for months and rendering the client's networks continuously insecure.

In addition, such conversations may also be timely to a client when circumstances create opportunities for malicious actors to take advantage of enterprises being distracted by external disruptions and of enterprises having to adjust in order to survive such disruptions. A widespread catastrophic disruption of a nation's critical infrastructure—by severe weather,[25] ransomware,[26] or pandemic[27]—can create such opportunities.

2. The Reason

The risk of post-incident liability and efforts to minimize that risk will remain one of the most compelling reasons for counsel and client to have a conversation about improving the resilience of the client's enterprise, that is, its ability to continue operations (even if at a degraded level) despite disruptions by a cyberattack and its preparedness to restore disrupted or damaged operations to pre-attack levels.

---

25. Matt Largey, *Texas' Power Grid Was 4 Minutes and 37 Seconds Away From Collapsing. Here's How It Happened*, HOUSTON PUBLIC MEDIA (Feb. 24, 2021), https://www.houstonpublicmedia.org/articles/news/energy-environment/2021/02/24/392290/texas-power-grid-was-4-minutes-and-37-seconds-away-from-collapsing-heres-how-it-happened/.

26. Allison Quinn, *Ransomware Attackers Stole Heaps of Data Before Gas Pipeline Shutdown*, DAILY BEAST (May 9, 2021), https://www.thedailybeast.com/ransomware-attackers-strike-the-jugular-of-us-gas-with-shut-down-of-colonial-pipeline?ref=topic.

27. Misha Glenny, *Pandemic Accelerates Growth in Cybercrime*, FIN. TIMES, ILLICIT GOODS & SERVS. SPECIAL REPORT (Apr. 27, 2021), https://www.ft.com/content/49b81b4e-367a-4be1-b7d6-166230abc398.

3. The Joint Exploration

On these occasions, the conversation about cybersecurity could explore the client's preparedness for post-incident response and recovery, with specific attention to the following:

- The client's incident response plans and their ability to effectively respond to an incident;
- Emerging industry-specific standards;
- The Cybersecurity Framework authorized by Executive Order 13,636 and developed and issued by the National Institute for Standards in Technology;
- Cybersecurity and data breach regulations at the federal and state levels applicable to the client's operations and business activities;
- The anticipated federal government efforts to enhance cybersecurity through new regulations; and
- The federal government's enhanced guidance for commercial enterprises that might have been targeted by an APT attack (like those spread through intrusions of SolarWinds and Microsoft Exchange Server).[28]

It would be prudent if the conversation also included a check of the client's preparedness for recovery and restoration when subjected to conditions that exceed the imagined worst-case scenario, as occurred in 2012 with Hurricane Sandy and in 2020–2021 with SolarWinds and the Microsoft Exchange Server attacks. If a client's disaster recovery plans cannot pass the "Hurricane Sandy test" and "SolarWinds/Microsoft Exchange tests," they might also fail if cyber incidents caused prolonged, and potentially more severe disruptions.[29]

---

28. Excellent examples of recent guidance by U.S. government agencies include (1) *Remediating Networks Affected by the SolarWinds and Active Directory/M365 Compromise: Risk Decisions for Leaders* (Mar. 9, 2021), https://www.cisa.gov/sites/default/files/publications/CISA_Insights_SolarWinds-and-AD-M365-Compromise-Risk-Decisions-for-Leaders_0.pdf; and (2) *FBI-DHS-CISA Joint Advisory: Russian Foreign Intelligence Service (SVR) Cyber Operations: Trends and Best Practices for Network Defenders* (Apr. 26, 2021), https://us-cert.cisa.gov/ncas/alerts/aa21-116a.

29. See Chapter 15 of this Handbook for further discussion of preparedness and response.

F. When Counsel Experiences a Cyber Incident or When Reports of Cyber Incidents Demonstrate the Law Firm's Need to Enhance Its Safeguards of Client Confidential Information

1. The Occasion

When a counsel experiences a cyber incident, the best course of action will probably be difficult to plot, because the client may view it with much less understanding and much closer scrutiny than its own cyber incident. Moreover, unlike companies that have had a decade of experience with the fairly bright-line requirements of data breach reporting statutes, law firms have no bright-line requirements and may be disinclined to report cyber incidents to a client.

Furthermore, a law firm will be understandably reluctant to disclose a cyber incident unless and until it has determined with reasonable certainty whether the incident compromised the specific client's confidential communications and its other sensitive information.

However, clients increasingly require that law firms disclose and discuss with them the precise cybersecurity policies, procedures, and measures the firms use (and thereby ask clients to rely upon) for protection of client confidential information.[30] Moreover, even apart from requirements that may be imposed by the law or by the Rules of Professional Conduct, clients are equally interested to know whether the law firm will promptly inform them if a cyber incident might have compromised their confidential information, particularly if client trade secrets might have been exfiltrated and could be misused commercially to put the client at a competitive disadvantage.

Counsel may find it difficult to initiate such conversations and may find it even more challenging to navigate them to a satisfactory understanding with a client. But a first step toward reaching an ethically sound outcome is to ensure that client and counsel agree on what each expects of the other in order to minimize the possibility that a cyber incident produces what the client will deem, in hindsight, an unacceptable outcome.

---

30. See Section III of this Handbook for further discussion about law firm practices.

2. *The Reason*

It is common knowledge that cyber incidents that compromise a client's confidential communications and other data might cause a loss of privilege, access to proprietary business plans, or a public release of trade secrets. However, in light of the more recent attacks at the time of this writing, there are additional incentives for this conversation between a lawyer and a client. Cyber actors may corrupt data or make malicious modifications of trade secrets or strategically crucial data. They may also deny access to data by ransomware at a time when counsel needs such access for its representation and guidance of a client. Occurrences like these may strain counsel's relationship with a client and may put counsel at risk of appearing to have committed an inadvertent ethical violation.

These are untested waters for counsel. No one really knows how clients will react and what reputational harm a cyber incident may cause a law firm and its lawyers.

Ransomware, and the demand for payment by the malicious actors, may create layers of risk, both regulatory and ethical:

- **Regulatory Risk.** Lawyers and their law firms may need to do whatever due diligence they can on the actor(s) demanding the ransom (despite the seemingly insurmountable difficulties of gaining such information and assessing it in what may be an imminent deadline). If counsel pays a ransom to parties or entities targeted by U.S. economic sanctions regulations (ESR), the payment may require a license from the U.S. Department of the Treasury, Office of Foreign Assets Control (OFAC); such license may also be required for law firms whose insurance and financial activities may facilitate payment of a ransom. Failure to obtain such licenses may risk violations of the ESR, as cautioned in an OFAC advisory issued on October 1, 2020, which:

  > describes these sanctions risks and provides information for contacting relevant U.S. government agencies, including OFAC, if there is a reason to believe the cyber actors demanding ransomware payment may be sanctioned or otherwise have a sanctions nexus.[31]

---

31. U.S. Dep't of Treasury, Office of Foreign Assets Control, *Advisory on Potential Sanctions Risks for Facilitating Ransomware Payments* 1 (Oct. 1, 2020), https://home.treasury .gov/system/files/126/ofac_ransomware_advisory_10012020_1.pdf.

OFAC's advisory is directed at parties that could become involved in facilitating a ransom payment (usually through digital currency) such as those "providing cyber insurance, digital forensics, incident response, and financial services involved in processing ransom payments (including depository institutions and money services businesses)." The advisory encourages parties to implement a "risk-based compliance program to mitigate exposure to sanctions-related violations."[32] OFAC's advisory emphasizes:

> [T]he sanctions compliance programs of these companies should account for the risk that a ransomware payment may involve an SDN [specially designated national] or blocked person, or a comprehensively embargoed jurisdiction. Companies involved in facilitating ransomware payments on behalf of victims should also consider whether they have regulatory obligations under Financial Crimes Enforcement Network (FinCEN) regulations.[33]

In light of OFAC's advisory, counsel considering its response to a ransomware attack should also address the risks that they might be viewed by OFAC as possibly committing ESR violations. The need is implicit in the advisory's express encouragement that "victims and those involved with addressing ransomware attacks to contact OFAC immediately if they believe a request for a ransomware payment may involves a sanctions nexus."[34]

OFAC's guidance turns on whether the affected law firm "believe[s]" a request for a ransomware payment might involve a "sanctions nexus." However, OFAC's guidance does not authorize the affected law firm to "turn a blind eye" to a "sanctions nexus" risk, or to view the due diligence as so difficult to perform as to excuse a failure to attempt and document it. Contacting OFAC at the outset of a ransomware attack thus has the added benefit of giving the law firm an opportunity to rely on guidance from OFAC and possibly gain protection from being viewed by OFAC as having deliberately or inadvertently violated the ESR.

---

32. *Id.* at 3–4.
33. *Id.* at 4.
34. *Id.* (emphases added).

- **Ethical risk.** What if, after due diligence, counsel determines the ransom demand does not pose a risk of an ESR violation? Is there an ethical risk if the law firm decides to pay the ransom to a party clearly engaging in criminal conduct? As of this writing, there does not yet appear to be an ethics opinion on that issue from a bar association within the United States.

There is, however, thoughtful guidance contained in an ethics opinion issued by the QLS Ethics Centre of Queensland, Australia, entitled Is It Ethical (or Legal) for Law Firms to Pay Cyber-ransom? ("QLS Opinion").

The QLS Opinion addresses the "don't pay" case and case for payment, and then the legality of ransom payments by Australian law firms. Its conclusions, issued in December 2017, resonate when one compares them to OFAC's 2020 advisory. As the QLS Opinion notes:

> Prima facie it is unlawful to pay a ransom to a terrorist organization or an organization proscribed by UN sanction.[35]
> An offence is committed when a person makes funds available to a "terrorist organisation," knowing or reckless to the fact that it is such. . . .

> Where there is any reason to believe than an embargoed or prohibited organization will be the recipient of the payment, a practitioner should seek specialist legal advice prior to making it.[36]

3. The Joint Exploration

On these occasions, the conversation about cybersecurity will probably be guided by concerns the client expresses upon being informed of the cyber incident. Counsel may want to be prepared to answer questions a client might ask at the outset, such as:

---

35. Footnotes that appear in the QLS Opinion are omitted.

36. David Bowles, *Is It Ethical (or Legal) for Law Firms to Pay Cyber-ransom?*, QLS ETHICS CENTRE, QUEENSLAND L. SOC'Y (Dec. 8, 2017), https://www.qls.com.au /getattachment/2ee73b54-fd00-4ad6-882a-54a5b2e88451/doc20171208_is_it_ethical_or _legal_for_law_firms_to_pay_cyber-ransom_final_djb.pdf (emphases added).

- How could you let this happen to our confidential information?
- What did you do to avert it?
- How much did you invest financially in cybersecurity?
- Did the compromise result from a security lapse by a lawyer employed by the firm? By someone supervised by the firm? From a lack of sufficient resources and training?
- From what you know in hindsight from the cyber incident, could the firm have taken measures that would have protected our confidential information from such an attack?
- If so, should you have known about such measure from reported cyber incidents affecting other law firms or enterprises without having to learn the lesson at our expense and at the compromise of our confidential information?

As the client considers counsel's answers, the client may ask additional questions, such as:

- What has happened to our data?
- Who might have our data?
- What changes might cyber actors have made to our data that render it no longer accurate and reliable?
- What malware might cyber actors have secreted in counsel's computers, servers, and networks that could be triggered at a later date?
- In light of what may have been learned about the cyber incident, how secure, reliable, and trustworthy are counsel's computers, servers, and networks, especially for ensuring confidentiality, accessibility, and integrity of a client's sensitive data?
- Who might be able to obtain it?
- What legal risks do we have that we did not have before?
- Did this happen because of a deficiency in the firm's cybersecurity?
- What additional steps are you prepared to take to protect our company's confidential information?
- Are you going to compensate us if our company's data has been damaged or destroyed, or if IP we entrusted to you has been misappropriated?
- Do you have cyber incident insurance that covers losses resulting from what may turn out to have been a deficiency in the firm's cybersecurity?

As these questions suggest, the issues are delicate and potentially dicey.

G. When the Client Anticipates Being the Buyer or Target in a Merger or Acquisition, Particularly If Counsel Anticipates the Need for a Review of the Transaction by CFIUS

1. The Occasion

When an enterprise plans to pursue a merger or acquisition (M&A), its officers and directors will want to understand the condition and value of the target's key assets. Due diligence reviews have been an acquirer's customary means of gaining and verifying that knowledge. Until recently, however, an acquirer's due diligence review team did not give much attention to the cyber preparedness of its target or whether the target's key assets (which are often digital assets) have been misappropriated, modified, or in other ways diminished in value as the result of a cyber breach.

As a consequence, the due diligence in an M&A deal should be designed to include identifying salient cybersecurity issues that counsel to the acquirer and target need to consider addressing with their respective clients before the parties negotiate the definitive terms of the deal. Such concerns can no longer be limited to M&A transactions. Enactment of FIRRMA expanded the aperture of CFIUS' authority to review certain noncontrolling direct foreign investments to address national security concerns.[37]

When counsel learns that a client may be embarking on an M&A transaction, or any foreign direct investment subject to CFIUS' review, counsel should immediately initiate a conversation with the client about enhancing the due diligence review to include, as a priority, a cybersecurity review of the investing party and of the target company. And if the transaction appears to come within CFIUS' review authority, counsel should include in the conversation a discussion of CFIUS' concerns for the U.S. target company's data and the need for a "cyber security plan" that "will be used to

---

37. *See* CFIUS, *Summary of the Foreign Investment Risk Review Modernization Act of 2018*, https://www.treasury.gov/resource-center/international/Documents/Summary-of -FIRRMA.pdf.

protect against cyberattacks on the operation, design, and development of the U.S. business's services, networks, systems, data storage and facilities."[38]

2. The Reason

Two M&A transactions—the acquisition of Neiman Marcus in 2013 and Verizon's acquisition of Yahoo that began in 2016 (and closed shortly before publication of the second edition of this Handbook)—demonstrate good reasons for counsel to initiate pre-transaction conversations that address cybersecurity due diligence questions. The following brief description of those two transactions is not intended to suggest that acquirer's counsel in either instance did not have such conversations, but rather that counsel in future transactions may find what happened in these two deals useful in initiating and continuing discussion of cybersecurity due diligence.

a. Occurrence of Undetected Cyber Incidents during the Acquisition of Neiman Marcus

In 2013, Neiman Marcus agreed to be acquired by a group led by Ares Management and a Canadian pension plan for approximately $6 billion. At least six weeks before the parties signed the acquisition agreement, a cyber-attack breached and compromised the Neiman Marcus customer payment processing system, eventually exfiltrating information from about 350,000 customer payment cards. The intruders operated undetected within Neiman Marcus' networks until five days after the acquisition of Neiman Marcus closed. Thus at the time of acquisition, neither the target nor the acquirers knew of the cyber incident. The intruders used the customer data to commit identity theft, which finally brought the cyber incident to the attention of Neiman Marcus under its new owners.

One of the consequences of the cyber incident for the new owners of Neiman Marcus was a consolidated class action by customers for damages from fraudulent use of customer payment cards and for future potential harm to other customers of Neiman Marcus whose card data had been compromised by the hackers. In September 2014, the District Court dismissed the suit for lack of standing. However, in July 2015, the Seventh

---

38. 31 C.F.R. § 800.402(c)(3)(viii).

Circuit reversed, holding that plaintiffs had shown sufficient risk of harm to have standing to sue. In March 2017, Neiman Marcus entered into a settlement with the class action plaintiffs and agreed to create a settlement fund in the amount of $1.6 million to cover claims, legal fees, and other litigation-related expenses.[39]

The settlement costs, the legal fees to defend the class action suit, and the distraction costs for the target and the acquirers were far exceeded by the approximately $6 billion price the acquirers paid for Neiman Marcus. However, the cyber incident and ensuing litigation provide lessons for counsel and client that may be useful when addressing cybersecurity due diligence questions:

- Cyber intruders can successfully attack and operate within a target for months or years without detection;
- M&A transactions can start and close without detection of ongoing cyber incidents involving the target and/or the acquirer;
- Parties to an M&A transaction should therefore factor in the risk of cyber incidents that may have occurred months or years before the transaction, or occurred during it, and that could create exposure to post-closing liability and/or substantial reduction in the value of the target's digital assets.

b. Occurrence of Detected (But Undisclosed) Cyber Incidents Years Before Verizon's Agreement to Acquire Yahoo

On July 23, 2016, Yahoo agreed to be acquired by Verizon for $4.83 billion in cash. On about September 9, 2016, Yahoo represented to the SEC that Yahoo had no knowledge of any incidents of "'security breaches, unauthorized access or unauthorized use' of its IT systems."[40] However, on September 20, 2016, Yahoo informed Verizon that, in late 2014, Yahoo

---

39. Hilary Remijas et al. v. The Neiman Marcus Grp. LLC, Case No. 1:14-cv-01735 (N.D. Ill. July 20, 2015).

40. Nic Fildes, Madhumita Murgia & Tim Bradshaw, *Yahoo Faces Questions over Delay in Data Breach Revelation*, FIN. TIMES (Sept. 25, 2016), https://www.ft.com/content/54ec6bd8-818e-11e6-8e50-8ec15fb462f4.

experienced—and detected—a cyber incident involving compromise of 500 million user accounts.

On November 9, 2016, Yahoo disclosed that, as a result of the 2014 cyber incident, Verizon "may seek to terminate the Stock Purchase Agreement or renegotiate the terms of the Sale transaction."[41]

In December 2016, Yahoo determined that a cyber incident, "likely distinct" from the earlier reported incident, had occurred in August 2013.[42] In the 2013 cyber incident, "an unauthorized party . . . stole data associated with more than one billion user accounts."[43]

In February 2017, as a result of the two cyber incidents, Yahoo agreed with Verizon to amend the acquisition agreement by reducing the purchase price by $350 million and by providing that Yahoo would be responsible for certain liabilities associated with the cyber incidents.[44]

The investigation by an independent committee of Yahoo's board of directors found that what was known in 2014 about the 2014 cyber incident by Yahoo personnel (including senior executives and legal staff) had not been reported to the board until after Yahoo and Verizon signed the acquisition agreement.

Yahoo's handling of its cyber incidents suggests the following lessons:

- A target's board might not be reasonably well-informed of its company's recent experience of serious cyber incidents, notwithstanding the size of the company and its reputation for expertise in digital and Internet businesses;
- A target's cybersecurity personnel might know of serious cyber incidents, and have alerted senior executives and the general counsel, but they may nonetheless fail to report it promptly (or at all) to the

---

41. *Id.* at 69.

42. Thus, Yahoo's second reported cyber incident occurred a year before its first reported cyber incident.

43. YAHOO INC., FORM 8-K FOR THE PERIOD ENDING 12/14/16, exh. 99.1 (Dec. 14, 2016). *See also* Bob Lord, CISO, *Important Security Information for Yahoo Users*, YAHOO! WEBSITE PRESS CTR. (Dec. 14, 2016), https://yahoo.tumblr.com/post/154479236569/important-security-information-for-yahoo-users.

44. YAHOO! INC., FORM 10-K FOR THE FISCAL YEAR ENDED DECEMBER 31, 2016, at 5, https://www.sec.gov/Archives/edgar/data/1011006/000119312517065791/d293630d10k.htm.

target's board, even when it is clear that such cyber incidents will be significant to the negotiations of an anticipated merger or acquisition; and

- The corporate officer of a target who should be in a good position to know of serious cyber incidents and to appreciate their significance to an anticipated merger or acquisition is the general counsel. For those reasons, a target's outside counsel should consider initiating a discussion about cybersecurity with the target's general counsel, its chief information officer, and/or its chief information security officer when M&A activity appears probable.

3. The Joint Exploration

If outside counsel or a general counsel has a conversation with the client about cybersecurity issues that may arise in an anticipated M&A transaction, the focus should be on ensuring that the client—acquirer or target—appreciates that risks to its deal objectives can be generated by unknown or belatedly discovered or untimely revealed cyber incidents.[45] Addressing the following issues may help structure the conversation if the client will be the acquirer:

- How important is it to the client that the target may have recently experienced cyber incidents that resulted in exfiltration, modification, damage, or destruction of the target's most valuable digital assets?
- If the target's valuable digital assets include a portfolio of trade secrets that are important to the acquirer and those may have been stolen in a cyber incident, how might the client want to address that in the acquisition agreement and in post-closing remediation?
- If the target's and the acquirer's computer networks and servers will be interconnected after the closing, what precautions does the client want to take to minimize the risks that any malware and ongoing

---

45. For discussion of cybersecurity due diligence in M&A transactions, see GUIDE TO CYBERSECURITY DUE DILIGENCE IN M&A TRANSACTIONS (Thomas J. Smedinghoff & Roland L. Trope eds., ABA 2017), including chapter 10 therein, "Special Issues in Cybersecurity Due Diligence: Resilience and Reviews by CFIUS."

cyber incidents could be extended into the acquirer's computer networks and servers?

- Does the target follow any cybersecurity model or framework, and does it have a program to address cybersecurity issues including staff focused on solely cybersecurity?
- Approximately how much of the target's valuable assets (or the assets that will be most valuable to the acquirer) are in digital form?
- How vulnerable to cyberattack are the target's key digital assets?
- Has the target experienced cyber incidents that modified, damaged, or exfiltrated copies of the target's key digital assets and substantially diminished their value?
- How probable is it that the target's key IT staff and general counsel would know if the target has experienced a serious cyber incident that may have substantially diminished the value of its digital assets?
- How long could a serious cyber incident continue without the target's key IT staff and general counsel learning of it, or of the extent of harm it caused the target?
- How probable is it that the target's board, senior executive officers, and general counsel may not know or be fully informed of the target's experience of serious cyber incidents over the past five years?
- How probable is it that the target's board, senior executive officers, and general counsel may have incentives for postponing until late in the transaction any disclosure or access to any information concerning the target's recent experience of serious cyber incidents?

Addressing each of those questions may contribute to the acquirer's risk assessment of the transaction. The answers may contribute to the acquirer's determination, in consultation with its general counsel and outside counsel, whether counsel—or a third party in tandem with counsel—will conduct a well-defined cybersecurity due diligence review of the target, and if so, the scope, time, resources, and budget that will need to be allocated to do the review thoroughly.

Counsel for the target will need to address the same issues with its client in order for the target and its counsel to be prepared to negotiate with the acquirer and its counsel the timing, scope, access, and procedures that will govern a cybersecurity due diligence review.

If the acquirer or potential investor is a foreign-owned or controlled company and the target is a U.S. company, it would be prudent for acquirer's counsel to raise early the possible need for a review of the proposed transaction by CFIUS. In that event, counsel may want the conversation to explore the following issues:

- Will the contemplated transaction be a transaction that is subject to a CFIUS review under CFIUS's post-FIRRMA jurisdiction, and, if so, how will the cybersecurity issues be handled (including preparation of a cybersecurity plan to protect against cyberattacks on the target U.S. company's services, networks, systems, data storage, and facilities)?[46]
- Does the contemplated transaction raise data security issues that may prompt CFIUS concerns about a foreign acquirer's access to what the new CFIUS regulations term "material non-public technical information" or "sensitive personal data?"

  Data security concerns may well have been among the reasons for certain compulsorily blocked or unwound transactions, including the following:

  - The proposed hostile takeover of U.S.–based Qualcomm Inc. by Singaporean chipmaker, Broadcom Ltd. (blocked in 2018 by order of the president);[47]
  - Acquisition of data app developer Grindr by Beijing Kunlun Tech (unwound in 2019 at CFIUS' request);[48] and
  - Acquisition of hotel property management software company StayNTouch Inc. by Beijing Shiji Information Technology Co. (unwound in 2020 by order of the president).[49]

---

46. U.S. Dep't of Treasury, Regs., 31 C.F.R. § 800.402(c)(3)(viii).

47. *See* Kate O'Keeffe, *Trump Orders Broadcom to Cease Attempt to Buy Qualcomm*, WALL ST. J. (Mar. 13, 2018), https://www.wsj.com/articles/in-letter-cfius-suggests-it-may-soon-recommend-against-broadcom-bid-for-qualcomm-1520869867.

48. *See* Echo Wang, *China's Kunlun Tech Agrees to U.S. Demand to Sell Grindr Gay Dating App*, REUTERS (May 13, 2019), https://www.reuters.com/article/us-grindr-m-a-beijingkunlun/chinas-kunlun-tech-agrees-to-u-s-demand-to-sell-grindr-gay-dating-app-idUSKCN1SJ28N.

49. *See* David McLaughlin, *Trump Blocks Chinese Deal for U.S. Software Firm StayN-Touch*, BLOOMBERG (Mar. 6, 2020), https://www.bloomberg.com/news/articles/2020-03-06/trump-blocks-chinese-deal-for-hotel-management-software-company.

- Should that cybersecurity plan address the possibility that the acquirer may only belatedly learn of recent or ongoing cyber incidents involving the target, and if so, how should it address such possibilities?
- What risks to the U.S. target's "services, networks, systems, data storage, and facilities" may result not from vulnerabilities and cyber incidents involving the target but from those involving the acquirer?

H.   When the Client Anticipates Providing Goods or Services for New Communications Technologies in a Regulated Sector

1.   The Occasion

Deployment and adoption of new digital communications technologies tend to proceed on the touted advantages they provide to the end user. Assessment, if any, of the cybersecurity risks that the new technology may introduce tends to be insufficient and understated. Security risks of new technologies are often treated as something that can be remedied with retrofits or software updates when, and if, the risks have proved so serious that fixing becomes an imperative. This section focuses, however, on a significant subset of "new" digital technologies, namely "emerging and foundational technologies" (which, for convenience, will be referred to as "emergent technologies").[50]

Emergent technologies often pose serious risks to enterprises, especially if adoption proceeds without verifying their cyber-worthiness against the risks that their use will introduce into the client enterprise a range of unknown enhanced vulnerabilities to cyber intrusions, APTs, ransomware, as well as new forms of malicious intrusions that attackers may develop and utilize.

Thus, when a client starts to design, develop, manufacture, or rely upon the use of an emergent technology, counsel should recognize that the time is ripe to initiate a conversation with the client on the subject of adjusting its

---

50. The Export Control Reform Act of 2018 (ECRA) uses the term "emerging and foundational technologies," and under ECRA such technologies are those that are essential to the national security of the United States and are not critical technologies described in Section 721(a)(6)(A)(i)–(v) of the Defense Production Act of 1950 as amended (DPA). ECRA notes the national security importance of U.S. leadership in science, technology, engineering, and manufacturing, including foundational technology that is essential to innovation. *Identification and Review of Controls for Certain Foundational Technologies*, BUREAU OF INDUS. & SEC. 52934 (Aug. 27, 2020), https://www.govinfo.gov/content/pkg/FR-2020-08-27/pdf/2020-18910.pdf.

cybersecurity to address the emergent technology and its attendant threats and risks to the enterprise.

The occasion will be particularly urgent when the client's enterprise, industry, or market are regulated (or start to be), or when the emergent technology begins to be regulated. Not infrequently, those occasions will arise concurrently. As a result, the sooner counsel initiates the conversation, the greater the chances that counsel can help its client find the best ways for it to comply with such regulations and improve the client's chances of averting severe disruptions when targeted by sophisticated cyberattacks.

2. The Reason

At present, several emergent technologies appear poised to cause widespread transformative changes to regulated industries, the enterprises within them, and to the cybersecurity of the enterprises' operations, communications, and IP: AI augmented machines and systems, including robotics ("AI systems"); quantum computing; position, navigation, and timing (PNT) technology; 3D printing; and IoT[51] and other "smart" devices.[52]

In regulated sectors, counsel may be better positioned than the client to discern where adoption and deployment of emergent technologies may intersect unexpectedly with existing or new cybersecurity regulations and the cyber risks that, if not properly addressed by the enterprise, may bring it into potential violations of those regulations or put it at heightened risk of a severe cyber incident and its adverse consequences.

If emergent technologies would likely have little or no influence on critical infrastructure or national security, then the reason prompting counsel's conversation with the client could be limited to compliance with cybersecurity regulations and to enhancing the enterprise's cybersecurity both to ensure such compliance and to reduce the risks that a serious cyber incident

---

51. See Chapters 2 and 3 of this Handbook for a description of risks posed by the emergent IoT technologies.

52. *See* BIS, *Review of Controls for Certain Emerging Technologies*, 83 Fed. Reg. 223, 58201–58202 (Nov. 19, 2018), https://www.govinfo.gov/content/pkg/FR-2018-11-19/pdf/2018 -25221.pdf, for what the BIS proposed as representative technical categories and examples of "foundational and emergent technologies."

could cause severe harm to the enterprise (by disruption, loss of IP and other assets, and degraded competitiveness).

Emergent technologies, however, are not usually so limited in their impact. Conversations with a client on cybersecurity implications of its development or use of emergent technologies will benefit from including as priority topics the role that the emergent technology plays (or may soon play) in national security and in encouraging the client to recognize that the cybersecurity of its enterprise has national security implications. Many clients may resist such suggestions and find them unwelcome. But as the cyberattacks on Colonial Pipeline highlight, U.S. critical infrastructure has increasingly become a priority target for cyberattacks. And those attacks increasingly appear aimed at disrupting for prolonged periods the country's critical infrastructure.

Although many enterprise owners and operators might prefer to remain "neutral" to competition, disagreements, and possible conflicts among nation states, the APT attacks and ransomware attacks experienced during the Covid-19 pandemic show that nation-states and their sponsored cyber actors do not respect such "neutrality." Once targeted, a critical infrastructure enterprise needs to view its cybersecurity as a national security priority—and it's reasonable for such enterprises to assume they have long been targeted and that the cybersecurity of any emergent technology they make or use has national security implications—not only for the U.S. but for the adversary supporting the attack(s). It's therefore important for client and counsel to prepare the enterprise and its emergent technologies as already targeted and to prepare accordingly for the day when (not if) the enterprise will experience a severe cyber incident.[53]

To clarify this intersection of emergent technology, cybersecurity, and national security, this section will focus on one emergent technology—AI—and review the reasons for initiating the conversation with a client on the client's development or use of AI systems, both in regulated industrial sectors and when AI itself is what the government intends to regulate.

Counsel for clients awarded commercial or governmental research and development grants, or acquisition contracts, will need to prepare clients to identify contractual and security risks that arise from inherent limitations

---

53. See Section J in this chapter on High Impact, Low Frequency events.

and security deficiencies in AI and that will probably remain limitations and security risks to AI for the foreseeable future.

First, AI systems cannot explain how they generate their predictions. Their designers cannot interrogate or question them nor trace their complex connecting of data "dots" that generate some of their most surprising, inexplicable, but not infrequently accurate predictions.

Second, AI systems develop predictions by noticing patterns, and thus work by correlation. AI cannot, as yet, search through multiple correlations and sift out and verify causation (or doubt such results and determine when an inferred causation is incorrect). Those boundary conditions to AI are quite important to a client's business. It may be trying to determine what specifications for AI it can sign up to meet. Or it may need to determine what warranty, if any, if can offer on the results its AI device will and will not generate. Or it may need to know how to recognize when an AI system is at risk of being exposed to cyber threats that can contaminate or maliciously modify its training data sets.

Third, AI systems are not self-critical and cannot base predictions on common sense. As a result, AI systems (if based on machine learning) cannot, as yet, escape the confines of the data from which they learn. AI cannot, as yet, "think outside the box" of its data set(s); it cannot recognize the boundaries of its data-delimited box and search for other data as humans can.

Fourth, unlike humans, AI systems do not, as yet, fail gracefully. Humans have a capacity to fail gracefully, doing so in ways other humans view as intelligent. When we err, make mistakes, or fail at tasks, we use "common sense to recognize the error and go about trying, in reasonable ways (including trial and error) to get it right."[54] An AI system, by contrast, may fail to recognize the misfit between its output and a desired solution or that it has encountered data not included in its training data. AI also cannot tell when the training data contains serious bias. As a result, a malicious actor may modify the AI machine's data sets to train into it degraded performance and erroneous predictions. Yet the AI system may generate those flawed

---

54. Roland L. Trope & Charles Palmer, *AI-Controlled Vehicles: How Will We Frame Thy Fearful Symmetry*, in THE LAW OF ARTIFICIAL INTELLIGENCE AND SMART MACHINES 134 (Theodore F. Claypoole ed., ABA Section of Business Law, 2019).

predictions, and humans may accept them with a high degree of confidence. An enterprise developing AI needs to address such risks.

And fifth, AI does not, as yet, appear any more within the control of its designers and developers than its antecedent technologies of algorithms implemented in software programs. Getting software to produce intended, desired results is an achievable, though often difficult, task; preventing software from generating unintended, undesired results remains next to impossible. Moreover, it is often commercially impracticable to test sufficiently to discover the full range of a software program's potential for generating unintended, undesired results. AI, to date, suffers the same limitations, but with an additional layer of serious risks. Humans may be tempted to rely on an AI system more than its capabilities can justify and more than its cyber defenses can reliably secure.

Clients will need to anticipate these limitations and security deficiencies in AI systems, whether they are developers or end users. Counsel therefore may want to initiate a discussion about the security that AI needs in order to safeguard its design and development as well as its operation and users.

Equally important, counsel may want to initiate a discussion to check with the client that its representations of its collection and use of data for its AI development complies with applicable federal and state laws and regulations. A client that lacks guidance of that scope and depth, or disregards it, can find itself at significant risk. The client risks an expensive regulatory enforcement action, potential fines, and, possibly, an order requiring destruction of its core AI algorithms, models, and software. The net effect of those actions can be the loss of the intellectual property rights to those intangible assets.[55]

3. The Joint Exploration
In the conversations about cybersecurity and AI systems, counsel will need to anticipate being asked by directors, officers, and general counsels: What

---

55. *See, e.g.*, In the Matter of Everalbum, Consent Order (approved May 6, 2021), https://www.ftc.gov/system/files/documents/cases/1923172_-_everalbum_decision_final.pdf. The Consent Order required defendant company to destroy all the algorithms, models, and software derived from data the defendant company obtained in violation of applicable regulations.

are the questions we should be asking? The questions might include the following:

- How will involvement of the company's businesses in the new technology change the nature of cyber incidents that the client needs to be prepared to manage?
- If the new technology will require quicker responses by directors, officers, and general counsels, what changes should the board and management be considering to ensure that they can take and implement decisions in the reduced timeframes?
- What aspects of the new technologies should directors, officers, and general counsels ensure they understand in order to fulfill their respective duties in a company that will become dependent on new technologies?
- Are there new kinds of security vulnerabilities and new kinds of cyber threats and risks that have emerged during the development and deployment of the new technologies (especially with AI)?
- Are there any emerging regulatory standards or ethical codes (as in the case of AI systems) that might set unrealistic requirements for the client's products or services and which the board may need to be apprised of to avoid being "blind-sided" by the issue?[56]
- Are there any aspects of the use of the new technologies that might adversely affect the company's culture and its commitment to doing the "right thing" in pursuit of its corporate mission?

That last question is the least obvious one, but perhaps the most important one. Adoption of emergent technologies tends to be evaluated by directors and officers for the benefits the technologies promise. Their drawbacks and disadvantages tend to be deemphasized by their proponents, their

---

56. Consider, for example, DoD's adoption, in February 2020, of a series of AI Ethical Principles that apply to both combat and noncombat functions. *See* C. Todd Lopez, *DOD Adopts 5 Principles of Artificial Intelligence Ethics*, DoD News (Feb. 25, 2020), https://www.defense .gov/Explore/News/Article/Article/2094085/dod-adopts-5-principles-of-artificial-intelligence -ethics/. See FTC Comm'r Rebecca Kelly Slaughter, *Algorithms and Economic Justice* (Jan. 24, 2020), https://www.ftc.gov/system/files/documents/public_statements/1564883/remarks_of _commissioner_rebecca_kelly_slaughter_on_algorithmic_and_economic_justice_01-24-2020 .pdf, for a discussion of "problematic algorithmic outcomes" in the design and development of AI that counsel might need to be aware of and to alert its clients to.

makers, and by their early adopters. Even when they are considered, the assessment of the drawbacks of a new technology seldom extends to the impact it may have on a company's culture and its commitment to doing the "right thing" when attempting to achieve a challenging mission.[57]

Consider, for example, hypothetical enterprise Ruritania, Inc., which plans to adopt two AI systems: one to sort through and predict which prospective applicants for entry-level positions should be rated high enough to be invited for interview, and one to evaluate the video recorded interviews and forecast from the applicants' facial expressions which individuals will "thrive at the company" and should thus be offered employment. But will Ruritania include in the AI procurement agreement any requirements for verifying and validating that the AI systems are not "subject to the biases of their human creators" as may occur if they were trained "on biased data or with 'rules' created by experts with implicit biases"?[58] After acquiring the AI systems, will *Ruritania* audit them to determine whether any algorithm updates (purportedly to improve the AI systems) have introduced bias? And, will Ruritania's management and board give serious consideration to whether the AI systems might perpetuate employment biases the company unwittingly practices? Without addressing those questions with an open and critical mind, Ruritania's management and board might find that Ruritania's culture resists any ethically motivated improvements because the persons hired share the biases that the AI system forecasts leads to a "successful" career at *Ruritania*. And to be fair to Ruritania, in many instances, it's unlikely that a company's executives or human resource officers will recognize certain biases because those biases are so ingrained in the predominant business culture.

Failing to address such questions can leave a company vulnerable to serious unintended and unanticipated consequences, including bias and other ethical lapses by personnel who may narrowly focus on utilizing the new technology and lose sight of the concomitant need to conduct themselves

---

57. See discussion in Section I of this chapter of ethical and engineering lapses at VW in "dieselgate" and at Boeing in development of its 737 MAX aircraft.

58. Brian Uzzi, *A Simple Tactic That Could Help Reduce Bias in AI*, 4 Harv. Bus. Rev. (2020), https://hbr.org/2020/11/a-simple-tactic-that-could-help-reduce-bias-in-ai.

ethically. That is the focus of the ninth suggested occasion to initiate a conversation with a client about cybersecurity.

I. For In-House Counsel, When the Client/Organization Embarks on a Major Transition in Its Corporate or Commercial Activities and May Be Tempted to Devise Software to Circumvent Regulatory Obstacles

1. Occasion

When an enterprise embarks on a major transition in product line, there may not be a good alignment of the objective, the engineering challenges to achieve it, and the limits that management may have imposed on cost and schedule. When that happens, the company engineers may face an infeasible task—and management may know it.

In such circumstances, management may leave it to company engineers to try to struggle to do the impossible (within schedule and cost constraints) and to come to the realization that if they are to meet management demands they have no choice but to depart from regulatory requirements, contractual obligations, and good engineering practices (which, if not adhered to, may create risks in safety-critical software or AI systems, or both).

If counsel discerns or learns of engineers believing that they have no choice but to depart from engineering standards of security and safety in digital-based or AI systems, that is a "red flag" that general counsel and outside counsel must not refrain from addressing.

Similarly, if senior officers appear to be directing or giving company engineers no choice but to develop AI and other digital systems contrary to good engineering practices and in ways that appear headed toward circumvention of regulatory and safety requirements, counsel should initiate a conversation with the client promptly and with diplomatic firmness.[59]

---

59. Note: counsel should be alert to the risks that may arise if an "AI" project gets redefined or recharacterized as a "software" program. Counsel may be more alert to the risks that novel AI projects pose, and may be inclined to view software programs as more routine and less risky. However, throughout the decades of AI's gradual emergence, enterprises refer to a project as "AI" when it's new to the public, and as "software" when the novelty and "magic" of a specific use of AI has worn off. Whether called AI or software, the risks from underestimated project objectives or infeasible goals remain and warrant a serious conversation by counsel with the client.

2. The Reason

When good companies and management change direction and start doing bad things, it's lamentable in hindsight to see the ways it could have been avoided, if someone with sound judgment had intervened before it was too late or brought the matter to the board's attention when the things ill-done and done to others' harm were apparent and board action could halt them and prevent the worst from happening. It's not so much a case of one or two "missed opportunities," but tends instead to be repeated unwillingness to speak up. The corporate culture at some enterprises has ceased to encourage, let alone tolerate, someone "speaking up" and pointing to an engineering, legal, or ethical obligation that the company seems willing to violate, whether by indifference, disregard, or circumvention.

The following brief case studies illustrate that the more safety-critical the product and the more safety-consequential the software and AI systems they utilize, the more important it is for counsel to be prepared to initiate a conversation if the client enterprise appears to be subverting its engineering practices and cybersecurity procedures.

a. VW's Defeat Device Software

In 2006, VW was designing a diesel engine for vehicles intended for the U.S. market. VW's engineers "realized that VW could not design a diesel engine that would meet stricter U.S. [nitrogen oxides] emission standards . . . and attract sufficient customer demand in the U.S. market."[60] VW's supervisor of engine development directed VW's engineers to design, create, and implement a software function to detect, evade, and defeat U.S. emission standards.[61] The subsequent "defeat device" ensured apparent compliance with applicable U.S. and California emission standards, but at the same time allowed vehicles to discharge up to 40 times the permitted NOx exhaust. As a result, VW deliberately misrepresented to the Environmental Protection Agency (EPA) that its diesel vehicles complied with U.S. emission standards. Due to this misrepresentation, VW received legal permission to import hundreds

---

60. United States v. Volkswagen AG, Rule 11 Plea Agreement, exh. 2, Statement of Facts, at 2-12 (E.D. Mich. Jan. 2017), https://www.justice.gov/opa/press-release/file/924436/download.
61. *Id.*

of thousands of vehicles equipped with defeat devices into the United States from 2009 to 2015.

When questioned by the EPA, VW denied that its vehicles contained defeat device software. In August/September 2015, when the EPA threatened to withhold permission for VW to import the next year's models of its diesel vehicles into the United States, VW admitted that indeed its vehicles contained defeat device software.[62]

In January 2017, VW pled guilty to three counts of criminal wrongdoing. VW's reckoning has been costly. By May 2020, VW had been assessed fines and entered into settlements in the amount of approximately $34.69 billion (not including the costs of internal investigations and legal fees to defend lawsuits).[63] VW had also seen criminal charges filed in the United States against certain mid-level managers and senior executives,[64] and charges in Germany against the cognizant CEO for knowing of the practice and failing to inform regulators and consumers.[65]

b.   Boeing's Departure from Good Engineering
     Judgment in Development of the 737 MAX

The in-flight cause of the two crashes of Boeing 737 MAX's (and deaths of 346 people onboard) was the autonomous operation of the Maneuvering Characteristics Augmentation System (MCAS) anti-stall system. As noted in a Congressional Final Committee Report,

> The new [MCAS] . . . had the ability to trigger non-pilot-commanded flight control movements that could place the airplane into a dangerous

---

62. *See* Roland L. Trope & Eugene K. Ressler, *Mettle Fatigue: VW's Single-Point-of-Failure Ethics*, 14(1) IEEE SECURITY & PRIVACY 12–30 (Jan./Feb. 2016), https://ieeexplore.ieee.org /document/7397718.

63. Reuters Staff, *Volkswagen Says Diesel Scandal Has Cost It 31.3 Billion Euros*, REUTERS (Mar. 17, 2020), https://www.reuters.com/article/us-volkswagen-results-diesel /volkswagen-says-diesel-scandal-has-cost-it-31-3-billion-euros-idUSKBN2141JB.

64. Jack Ewing, *Former VW Executive Is Arrested in Croatia in Emissions Case*, N.Y. TIMES (June 17, 2020), https://www.nytimes.com/2020/06/17/business/VW-dieselgate-arrest -croatia.html.

65. *See* Jon Porter, *Ex-VW CEO Charged over Dieselgate, Faces Millions in Fines and 10 Years in Prison*, THE VERGE (Apr. 16, 2019), https://www.theverge.com/2019/4/16/18369528 /vw-ceo-martin-winterkorn-dieselgate-germany-volkswagen-emissions-scandal.

nose-down attitude that challenged the pilots' ability to control the aircraft. . . . [T]he MCAS software operated on input from one of the two angle-of-attack (AOA) sensors externally mounted on the fuselage on either side of the airplane.[66]

On October 29, 2018, during Lion Air flight 610 from Jakarta, the 737 MAX aircraft's MCAS activated based on an erroneous reading from the newly installed AOA sensor (i.e., indicating inaccurately a steeper than actual angle of attack of the wings, and one that, were it happening, would risk causing the aircraft to "stall"). To avert that hazardous condition (that the AOA erroneously registered and transmitted to the MCAS) the MCAS "commanded" the airplane's horizontal stabilizer to push the nose down. And each time the pilots struggled against it to stabilize the airplane, MCAS overpowered their efforts and pushed the nose down.[67]

This occurred more than 20 times as the pilots fought MCAS while struggling to maintain control of the aircraft. . . . Amid a cacophony of confusing warnings and alerts on the flight deck, the horizontal stabilizer ultimately forced the airplane into a nose-down attitude from which the pilots were unable to recover.[68]

Regrettably, Boeing did not recommend that airlines cease flying all 737 MAX aircraft until Boeing could determine the cause. Boeing declined the opportunity to diagnose and fix the problems with all aircraft on the ground.

About five months later, on March 10, 2019, a faulty AOA sensor on a Boeing 757 MAX similarly triggered the MCAS, causing the downing of Ethiopian Airlines flight 302.[69]

It appears that, in development of the aircraft's software-operated AOA and MCAS, Boeing departed from good engineering judgment. For example,

---

66. Majority Staff of the House Comm. on Transp. & Infrastructure, *Final Committee Report: The Design, Development & Certification of the Boeing 737 MAX 8* (Sept. 2020), https://transportation.house.gov/imo/media/doc/2020.09.15%20FINAL%20737%20MAX%20Report%20for%20Public%20Release.pdf.

67. *Id.*

68. *Id.* at 9.

69. *Id.*

it violated good engineering practice by introducing a single point of failure in the MCAS system, designing it to rely on a single sensor's input, which whether accurate or erroneous, would trigger the MCAS.[70]

As the Congressional Report put it:

> The MAX crashes were not the result of a singular failure, technical mistake, or mismanaged event. They were the horrific culmination of a series of faulty technical assumptions by Boeing's engineers, a lack of transparency on the part of Boeing's management, and grossly insufficient oversight by the FAA.[71]

In January 2021, Boeing entered into a deferred prosecution agreement with DoJ to pay more than $2.5 billion and to implement remediations (including to "meet with the DoJ Fraud Section at least quarterly and to submit yearly reports to the Fraud Section regarding the status of its remediation efforts") to resolve "a criminal charge related to a conspiracy to defraud" the FAA Aircraft Evaluation Group "in connection with its evaluation of Boeing's 737 MAX airplane."[72]

The misuse of software at these companies (VW's defeat device and Boeing's single-point-of-failure MCAS) proceeded not from a "one-off" decision but from a succession of decisions. Many of those decisions amounted to a reconfirmation that crucial decisions should continue to be implemented, remain concealed, and, in VW's case, if questioned by regulators, should be disingenuously denied.

---

70. In the 737 MAX, Boeing "designed an automated safety system that abandoned the principles of component redundancy, ultimately entrusting the automated-decision making to just one sensor—a type of sensor that was known to fail. Boeing's rival, Airbus, has typically depended on three such sensors. 'A single point of failure is an absolute no-no,' said one former Boeing engineer who worked on the MAX . . . ." Mike Baker & Domilnic Gates, *Lack of Redundancies on Boeing 737 MAX System Baffles Some Involved in Developing the Jet*, SEATTLE TIMES (Mar. 26, 2019), https://www.seattletimes.com/business/boeing-aerospace/a-lack-of-redundancies-on-737-max-system-has-baffled-even-those-who-worked-on-the-jet/.

71. *Final Committee Report*, *supra* note 66, at 6–7.

72. DoJ, Office of Public Affairs, *Boeing Charged with 737 Max Fraud Conspiracy and Agrees to Pay over $2.5 Billion*, JUSTICE NEWS (Jan. 7, 2021), https://www.justice.gov/opa/pr/boeing-charged-737-max-fraud-conspiracy-and-agrees-pay-over-25-billion.

When counsel observes a client company apparently intent on achieving an infeasible objective, counsel should be alert to signs that management will not accept failures to achieve its declared objectives and to signs that the corporate culture has become one in which "speaking up" is neither encouraged nor tolerated.

If counsel discerns such developments, counsel should consider that the engineers and other personnel may be under substantial pressure to depart from good engineering practices, legal obligations, and ethical standards. Counsel should then give serious consideration to finding ways to look into the matter, and to do so by initiating a conversation with management, and if necessary, with the board.

3. The Joint Exploration

When an illicit practice or departure from good engineering judgment comes to light, as often happens, the discovery tends to prompt questions about how the company could ever have decided to subvert its own brand. The questions often include why key personnel did not intervene to halt the practice before it started: Where was the board? And where were their lawyers—that is, where was the general counsel and legal staff?

These questions suggest that there is an expectation that the general counsel should be responsible for averting misguided, ill-considered business practices that may subvert the enterprise's interests, because general counsel is in the best position to do so. This is a heavy burden to place on general counsel. But, as Ben W. Heineman Jr., the vice president-general counsel of General Electric from 1987 to 2003, observes:

> Ignorance is no defense . . . for the General Counsel when the legal function is right at the core of the problem—with responsibility to determine if there is real liability due to design or manufacturing defects. . . ."[73]

What happened at VW and Boeing illustrate risks not limited to the automotive and aerospace industries.

---

73. *Id.* at 98.

The challenges of entry into a new market, of launching a new product line, or of seeking rapid preeminence in a market not infrequently tempt a company's senior executives to direct company personnel to achieve the objective through the design and development of software that circumvents regulatory obstacles or fails to adhere to good engineering judgment. This misdirection of software development for company objectives is difficult for customers and regulators to detect. The practice will seldom be reported to the company's board of directors. Company executives will rarely, if ever, ask outside counsel to opine on the legality and advisability of setting aside good engineering judgment in a major software or AI development project—probably because they know that outside counsel would strongly advise against it.

In high-tech companies, officers and project managers are supposed to exercise good engineering judgment to set limits on acceptable risks and then keep within those limits. Major high-tech enterprises (like automotive or aerospace enterprises) or agencies (like NASA, with respect to the Challenger space shuttle) might disregard those limits when developing safety or mission-critical systems. If so, they might proceed on the assumption that they can manage risks they have relaxed control over. And then, the result could be a catastrophic outcome: customers harmed, enterprise value depressed, reputations damaged. And corporate reckoning with regulators is an expensive drain on personnel.

In hindsight, whether officers and managers deliberately engage in misconduct (which at VW resulted in "dieselgate") or seemingly lose sight of the imperative to adhere to good engineering judgment (which appears to have happened at Boeing in development of the 737 MAX), the root causes usually include managerial and engineering "hubris"[74] and ethical "mettle fatigue."[75] Once that begins, it's difficult for those who see it happening to

---

74. John Gapper, *Boeing's Hubris Brought Failure to the 737 Max*, FIN. TIMES (Apr. 10, 2019), https://www.ft.com/content/2de01914-5ac5-11e9-9dde-7aedca0a081a.

75. "For people who work in situations in which no one questions ethically dubious activities, including outright subterfuge like the defeat device, there can be a corrosion of character. Long exposure can only worsen the effect, preventing those who succumb from recognizing reality, accepting facts, and responding with integrity [footnotes omitted]. We refer to this as 'mettle fatigue.'" Trope & Ressler, *supra* note 62, at 28.

persuade decision makers to reconsider or to bring the issue to the attention of the company's board of directors.

In the instance of VW, the VW brand development department engineers were ordered to design and install the defeat device, and did so reluctantly.[76] Lower-level engineers, with the support of their supervisors, objected to the defeat device. However, the supervisor in charge of the department "decided that VW should continue . . . with the defeat device, and instructed those in attendance, in sum and substance, not to get caught."[77]

If VW's in-house counsel had regular face-to-face interactions with the department engineers and the supervisors who supported their objections, counsel may have learned from those conversations of the engineers' ethical misgivings and objections to the defeat device and been in a position to alert VW's board.

In Boeing's case, the infeasible objective was making unrealistic assumptions about a pilot's ability to sort through the chaotic warnings and alarms that co-occur when the MCAS "commanded" maneuvers of the aircraft that the pilots were unaware of and could not "overcome" unless they had been trained to shut off the MCAS in the midst of loud alarms of an imminent stall. As the NTSB noted:

> [N]either Boeing's system safety assessment nor its simulator tests evaluated how the combined effect of alerts and indications might impact pilots' recognition of which procedure(s) to prioritize in responding to an unintended MCAS operation caused by an erroneous AOA input.[78]

When a company like Boeing departs from good engineering and managerial judgment, it will be difficult for in-house counsel to be aware of it, unless personnel bring it to their attention. This will probably happen only if counsel has developed an understanding with personnel so that they will come to counsel with their concerns.

---

76. United States v. Volkswagen AG, Rule 11 Plea Agreement, exh. 2, Statement of Facts, at 2 13 (E.D. Mich. Jan. 2017), https://www.justice.gov/opa/press-release/file/924436/download.
77. *Id.* at exh. 2-14.
78. *Id.* at 8 (emphasis added).

And, counsel probably would have authority and leverage to raise concerns when the company appears intent on circumventing regulations or concealing information from regulators.

What is uncertain is whether and how counsel might learn of when a company has deviated from good engineering judgment by setting infeasible objectives—but that may be among the most important issues for counsel to find a way to influence and reverse.

One of the values of reviewing Boeing's judgmental errors on the development of the 737 MAX and VW's in "dieselgate" is to alert counsel to the symptoms of when a company may be departing from its own well-established best practices and adherence to good engineering judgment.

In each instance, the company's senior executives made a sharp departure from previous, well-established engineering practices in order to expedite development of a new (and thus untested) software-intensive and software-dependent technology. When that happens in the context of production and competition pressures, counsel should be extra vigilant. Counsel may then find it possible to notice signs that disclosures to regulators might be unwisely and incautiously edited and trimmed to fit commercial objectives. Counsel may also start to notice if pursuit of commercial objectives appears infeasible except through the circumvention of regulatory requirements, which in turn (as at VW and Boeing) were symptomatic of departures from good engineering judgment in the design and development process.

Learning key features of successful software development and the symptoms of unsuccessful or subversive software development will be even more important for counsel advising clients engaged in the development of emergent technologies like AI that are based on algorithms, models, and software, but are far more complex than previous software projects. And with AI, the cybersecurity needed to prevent insiders and outsiders from making unauthorized, adverse changes to the training data could jeopardize the secure and reliable development of the AI algorithms and software.

Thus, the general counsel and others in the legal department may need to initiate proactive conversations with engineers and supervisors about new algorithms and software and designs to ensure potential threats of misuse and other departures from good engineering judgment are minimized. Moreover, it is critical for lawyers to ask questions and explore potential ethical crises with their clients. And, for the general counsel and other in-house counsel, the client is not the CEO, but the company, including its board of directors.

To protect the "client," the general counsel and other in-house counsel need to circulate and engage with personnel. By doing that, they can acquire a more reliable understanding of activity and decision making within the enterprise. The general counsel and other in-house counsel can then leverage their understanding and proactively address and oversee certain high-risk situations.

If the company plans to introduce a product or service that requires extensive software development, and no problems were reported in the development or integration phases (which is an unrealistic achievement), counsel might encourage officers or directors to ask the engineers and supervisors of the project, "How did you do it?" "How did you do it without any reported problems?" and "If there were reported problems that posed serious threats to the project, how did you solve those problems?" If the company plans to pursue seemingly unrealistic objectives, counsel might encourage officers or directors to ask, "How are we going to do that, when no one else can?"

Given the difficulty boards may face in learning of corporate decisions to circumvent legal requirements by a systematic misuse of software, there is a need and opportunity for a well-placed counsel to bring the issue tactfully to the board's attention.

A well-placed lawyer, in this instance, will seldom be outside counsel. This is a task best handled by the general counsel, who will also be in the best position to observe and perceive the symptoms of a misuse of software. The challenge will be not only how to initiate the conversation on this kind of cybersecurity threat where the practice may have already begun, but how to bring up the topic when the decision may not yet have been taken and when the general counsel may have sufficient leverage to dissuade officers from proceeding without a formal legal review. Outside counsel can be leveraged to support in-house counsel in these discussions, determining the risk and possible repercussions to the client.

For example, the nature of "corrupt software"—and the fact that its use depends on it being a corporate decision and part of a company's culture—makes it a topic for the kind of conversation a general counsel and her legal department will increasingly find is necessary to initiate if they are to protect the company, the brand, and the officers and directors. The subject, if it is to be raised, should likely be broached by the general counsel. The question, of course, is, when might these occasions arise?

The clearest instances will be when and if the general counsel is informed that the use of "corrupt software" or potentially biased AI is being considered by the client. The chances that the general counsel will learn that the client has authorized, or might authorize, creation and installation of "corrupt software" or biased AI in its products will be far greater if she interacts regularly with engineering teams and personnel in their workspace, rather than waiting for someone to have the courage to report (directly or anonymously) to the legal department. Having learned that a potentially subversive decision may have been taken or is being considered, the general counsel has the ethical duty to advise against the practice and to pursue the matter to ensure that the company does not adopt and begin to use "corrupt software" or biased AI or continue the practice if it has already begun. There is an improved chance that the general counsel will learn of its company's consideration or adoption of "corrupt software" or biased AI if the company has effective anonymous whistleblower procedures in place and encourages employees to use them.

The more challenging instances will be when the general counsel has reason to believe, or should reasonably suspect, that the client is accomplishing an objective by means that appear *too good to be true*, or where there are *too few reported problems* in the development of a new and important product, or where entry into new markets overcomes challenging legal impediments *too easily and without the usual struggles to achieve compliance.*

In these instances, the general counsel's best way to initiate the necessary conversation about the possible use of "corrupt software" or biased AI will be to approach the issue obliquely, by inquiring about projects and activities that must comply with demanding legal requirements. Counsel should tactfully, but with commonsense curiosity, ask "How did we do it?" and follow up with additional questions if the answers are less than direct, complete, or convincing. Any discovery of a use of "corrupt software," biased AI, or other deviations from good engineering and managerial judgment will then need to be addressed with executive management and potentially the organization's board of directors.

As counsel contemplates those risks, it may need to keep abreast of the impact on security vulnerabilities that increased reliance on AI and its underlying algorithms, training data, and software may introduce. AI products may be "honey-combed with vulnerabilities to remotely executed hacks."[79] Moreover, advances in AI may create opportunities for bad actors to develop novel, more sophisticated kinds of cyberattacks that may be more difficult to detect, contain, and eradicate:

> Progress in AI will enable new varieties of attacks. These attacks may use AI systems to complete certain tasks more successfully than any human could, or take advantage of vulnerabilities that AI systems have but humans do not.[80]

Any company engaged in development of software or of AI systems, not only those in automotive and aerospace industries, can be put at risk if management allows or authorizes teams of engineers and their overseeing managers to depart significantly from good engineering practice. These sanctioned deviations may create security and safety threats to software that will be utilized in, and can exert control over, safety-critical systems in vehicles and aircraft. That risk would not appear to be an outlier, but one that officers of such companies may be tempted to take.

It would therefore be prudent for in-house counsel to give serious consideration to an important possibility: Insiders (and outsiders) may heighten the risks of maliciously introduced faulty data in AI systems, and such data may already exist in designs of new vehicles, aircraft, and any other AI-augmented products. As a *Fortune* article recently cautioned regarding the cybersecurity of software and AI systems in aircraft:

---

79. Trope & Palmer, *supra* note 54, at 164.

80. *The Malicious Use of Artificial Intelligence: Forecasting, Prevention, and Mitigation, Future of Humanity Institute*, UNIV. OF OXFORD, AND CTR. FOR THE STUDY OF EXISTENTIAL RISK, UNIV. OF CAMBRIDGE 17 (Feb. 2018), https://arxiv.org/pdf/1802.07228.pdf; *Artificial Intelligence and National Security*, CONG. RSCH. SERV. 19–20 (Nov. 10, 2020), https://fas .org/sgp/crs/natsec/R45178.pdf.

Boeing's 737 Max is being publicly scrutinized in many ways. . . . But what about the cyber security implications? If an aircraft's safety software can cause pilots to lose control—what prevents malicious hackers from taking advantage of the same flaw? It may be time for the aerospace industry to take a close look at the state of software security. Security researchers have already shown . . . that commercial jets are vulnerable to hacking.[81]

J. When High-Impact, Low-Frequency (HILF) Events (Like Pandemics and Advanced Persistent Threat (APT) Cyberattacks) Disrupt Workplace Operations and Supply Chains, and Cause Enterprises to Adapt by Directing Personnel to Work from Home and Other Locations Where Cybersecurity May Be Diminished

1. The Occasion

Among owners, operators, and regulators of critical infrastructure, there is a class of risks called high-impact, low-frequency (HILF) events. They rarely occur. They elude efforts to predict them. They occur with random distribution in human timescales. And they may have catastrophic consequences. As Professor Lucy Jones observes, "we humans don't like" random events. As she explains:

Random means every moment presents a risk, leaving us anxious. Psychologists describe a "normalization bias," the human inability to see beyond ourselves, so that what we experience now or in our recent memory becomes our definition of what is possible. We think the common smaller events are all that we have to face, and that, because the biggest one isn't in anyone's memory, it isn't real.[82]

---

81. George Avetisov, *Malware at 30,000 Feet—What The 737 Max Says about the State of Airplane Software Security*, FORBES (Mar. 19, 2019, 4:25 PM), https://www.forbes.com /sites/georgeavetisov/2019/03/19/malware-at-30000-feet-what-the-737-max-says-about-the -state-of-airplane-software-security/#32e310c052a9.

82. Dr. Lucy Jones, *Big Ones: How Natural Disasters Have Shaped Us (and What We Can Do About Them)*, DOUBLEDAY 10–11 (2018) (the quoted passages can be accessed at https:// www.amazon.com/Big-Ones-Natural-Disasters-Shaped-Us/dp/0385542704?asin=0385542704 &revisionId=&format=4&depth=1).

These features of our perception of HILF events tend to persuade officers and directors to treat them as "too remote to consider." They and their enterprises seldom, if ever, include HILF events in their contingency plans.

HILF events during 2020–2021 made headlines (e.g., the Covid-19 pandemic, disruption of the Texas electricity grid by subfreezing temperatures, disruption of the Colonial Pipeline fuel pipeline by a ransomware attack, and the APT attacks on SolarWinds and Microsoft). The extraordinary concurrence of multiple HILF events suggests it would be prudent for counsel to initiate a conversation with clients concerning the extent to which the client has upgraded its contingency plans to address HILF events.

Such plans may need to be modified to address adjustments that enterprises tend to make to survive and recover from HILF events (that degrade enterprise cybersecurity) and the risks that cyber adversaries may seize the opportunities thus presented.

2. The Reason

The current Covid-19 pandemic eclipses the HILF events of the past half century (e.g., Fukushima earthquake, hurricanes, the 2003 bulk power outage, and 9/11). For many of us, it may be the defining non-bellicose HILF event in our lifetimes. Few, if any, enterprises appear to have planned for extended or indefinite shutdowns of societies round the world. Few enterprises seemed prepared for the additional disruptions caused by second and third waves or surges of the pandemic in countries whose governments treated the pandemic as defeated and "in the rear view mirror."

Society-wide or jurisdiction-wide shutdowns forced enterprises to survive by adapting. Enterprises that relied on office space to conduct business tended to close the offices, and encourage or direct personnel to work remotely. As the pandemic disrupted supply chains and parties conferred with counsel about whether to declare an event(s) of force majeure or how to respond to it, enterprises appear to have addressed those immediate concerns. They tended to postpone or lose sight of the change in their enterprise's security and cyber risk profile.[83]

---

83. For review of such risks, see Sara Brown, *How to Think about Cybersecurity in the Era of COVID-19*, MIT MGMT. SLOAN SCH. (Aug. 20, 2020), https://mitsloan.mit.edu /ideas-made-to-matter/how-to-think-about-cybersecurity-era-covid-19.

Working from home has opened multiple vectors for cyberattacks through the heightened dependency on personal devices and home networks. . . . Critical business assets and functions are significantly more exposed to opportunistic and targeted cyberattacks by criminal organizations and nation states seeking to exploit vulnerabilities and plant seeds for future attacks.[84]

Cyber actors appear to have grasped the attack opportunities created by the pandemic-induced disruptions and enterprises' efforts to adapt. Cyber actors also appear to have exploited those opportunities more quickly than governments and enterprises recognized the risks. And cyber actors appear to have exploited those opportunities in ways that seem designed to take advantage of the widespread reductions in cybersecurity, alertness to cyber-attacks, and capabilities to detect and respond to APTs.

Most businesses do not appear to have had to account for their cyber vulnerabilities and cyber incidents during the pandemic. If post-pandemic assessments verify that to have been the case, one reason may be that existential adaptations to the pandemic may have had so high a priority in everyone's minds that no one will readily fault companies for belatedly addressing the cyber risks created by those efforts.

Another related reason may be the pandemic mindset that has affected many, including probably many officers and directors. For communities hardest hit around the United States, the peak surges of the pandemic exerted a persistent hold on the minds of most citizens. The combination of anxiety, apprehension, and raw fear of the contagion created a pandemic mindset that affected many. Depending on one's nature and imagination, they may have experienced the pandemic as an exile from the familiar continuity of

---

84. Charles Blauner, *5 Principles for Effective Cybersecurity Leadership in a Post-COVID World*, WORLD ECON. FORUM (May 26, 2020), https://www.weforum.org/agenda/2020/05 /principles-for-effective-cybersecurity-leadership-covid-19-coronavirus-pandemic-cyberattacks -cyber-risk-security-cloud-technology/.

the past to the future,[85] or a siege with an accompanying "siege mentality."[86] Prevailing against the pandemic and its disruptions has mattered most. So much so that the widespread reports of surges of cyber actor attacks have not been accompanied by the usual reportage or commentaries criticizing enterprises' lack of cyber preparedness.

Outside and in-house counsel, however, should consider the risks that the relaxation of cyber preparedness (resulting from working remotely with poorly secured digital devices) may have created. Counsel should also consider whether the pandemic mindset (e.g., "siege mentality") might have encouraged a relaxation of accountability for failure to avert, detect, and promptly remediate cyber intrusions.

As an HILF's impacts lengthen and deepen, they may encourage a view that at such times existential efforts to preserve the enterprise will suffice. Attention solely focused on that may cause officers and directors to overlook that cyberattacks, if they cause severe disruption, can themselves amount to an HILF. Cyber actors may perceive that view to be widespread and persistent. If it is, bad actors may base future attacks on the failure of enterprises to learn crucial lessons from the surge in cyberattacks during the pandemic.

It would be prudent for counsel to observe if a client appears to be adopting those views of immunity from accountability for diminished or neglected cyber preparedness. If so, counsel may find it appropriate to initiate a conversation with the client concerning the failures or deficiencies in cyber preparedness that occurred at different stages of the unfolding of the HILF event. If adaptations to remote working occurred, then as the crisis ebbs, it will be important to know what risks the enterprise took with security. It will also be important to examine the extent to which the

---

85. As described by Camus: "It was undoubtedly the feeling of exile—that sensation of a void within which never left us, that irrational longing to hark back to the past or else to speed up the march of time, . . . Still, if it was an exile, it was, for most of us, exile in one's own home." ALBERT CAMUS, THE PLAGUE 71, 73 (Vintage 1948).

86. In a "siege mentality," persons experienced the pandemic as potential, multiple levels of loss (deaths, threats to loved ones, loss of physical contact with family and social networks, loss of jobs and financial security, and of precrisis way of life and one's sense of normalcy); those levels of loss "generate ongoing fears to individual's and families' hopes and dreams of the future." Joshua M. Gold, *Siege Mentality in the 2020 Pandemic: Building Family Resilience*, 29(2) FAMILY J.: COUNSELING & THERAPY FOR COUPLES & FAMILIES 143 (2021), https://journals.sagepub.com/doi/pdf/10.1177/1066480720977515.

enterprise's expanded digital domain may have been attacked, breached, and had data modified or otherwise compromised.

3. The Joint Exploration

It will be important to address these issues at the earliest practicable time. The longer after the crisis the discussion occurs, the greater the probability that the client will be satisfied with its cyber preparedness and the more reluctant it will be to have a serious, searching conversation. Clients may have been lucky to get through the pandemic without a major cyber breach or having their data rendered inaccessible by ransomware. But counsel needs to find ways to bring real and likely possibilities to a client's attention. What may appear to be a lack of a cyber intrusion may, in fact, be a compromised state that the client has not yet detected, and cyber actors may be active in its networks. And even if a client has not been breached this time, it should not assume it would be so lucky the next time.

In preparation for these conversations, counsel should learn how enterprises missed opportunities to follow up on anomalies that would have led to a much earlier detection of SolarWinds and other attacks. Cyber actors do make mistakes; counsel needs to recognize when an apparent anomaly or peculiar occurrence needs to be investigated and not dismissed or underestimated.

Counsel may also want to discuss adjusting contingency plans to address future co-occurrences of pandemics, degraded cybersecurity, and state-sponsored APTs. Those adjustments are best made before "normalization bias" sets in and causes officers and directors to define the "worst case" scenario as what we experienced during the pandemic. The next pandemic will probably co-occur with more damaging cyber events; the use of AI in cyber weaponry will probably bring about exponential increases in cyber-attacks' sophistication, stealth, speed, duration, and severity.

Counsel needs to anticipate that cyber actors will endeavor to launch attacks that outwit "worst case" scenario security plans. In particular, cyber actors may be able to cause a target enterprise to lose "situational awareness," without knowing it. That is what happens when a stealthy attack remains undetected for months. It's also what happens when an HILF event deprives an enterprise of its critical infrastructure and on-site support. Relocating personnel to remote work sites or home offices seems, initially, a success. Work goes on. Customers receive goods and services. But the enterprise's cyber terrain, its data depositories and processing units when relocated to home offices may be more vulnerable than any "worst case" scenario planning has contemplated. And as seen during the Covid-19 pandemic, cyber actors know it. They have seized opportunities that vulnerabilities and lack of incident detection and response mechanisms have created.

The focus throughout these conversations with the client should be on how much of a "paradigm shift" has occurred in cyberattacks as a result of two facts. First, vulnerabilities were opened by the pandemic's disruptions of enterprises and by enterprises' existential adaptations to survive. Second, state actors and their proxies have made extraordinary enhancements to ATPs and ransomware attacks. Any enterprise that has not taken, at a minimum, certain remediation steps as the pandemic ebbs (or continues) is losing a crucial opportunity. It needs to enhance its cyber preparedness in order to have the requisite resilience to survive the next HILF event that disrupts it, its supply-chain vendors, and its service providers. Counsel may want to discuss with the client taking the following steps:

- Assess the extent to which the enterprise's adaptation to the pandemic's disruptions led the enterprise to reduce its security and cyber preparedness;
- Identify specifically the added risks the enterprise thereby took and implement remediations to reduce them before they become embedded long-term practices;
- Assess the extent to which the enterprise may need to revise its cybersecurity plans to address;
- Security deficiencies in the event that the enterprise continues to have personnel work from home or other remote locations outside the enterprise's security perimeter;
- Intrusion detection and incident response procedures for intrusions that may initially target off-site computers and digital storage media, or may seek to leverage intrusions at those locations to penetrate the enterprise's main servers and networks;

- The reduced cyber awareness that personnel may have when working at home, and the need for precautions to avert breaches of confidentiality when spouses share adjacent workspaces or even computers at home for their respective work tasks;
- The possibility that the enterprise might be among those affected by APTs and will have an indefinitely long period of degraded capabilities. Computer systems may be unreliable, insecure, and compromised; if so, the enterprise might want to consider alternatives to cyber storage of its "crown jewel" trade secrets, including its cybersecurity plans.

Counsel should anticipate that the client may think that if it and its supply chain have no knowledge of any cyber intrusions, then nothing happened. The enterprise is safe and sound. On that premise, the client may resist any review of the security risks its pandemic adaptations may have introduced. The premise of "we've seen nothing—so nothing happened" is, however, unsound. As the corollary: "nothing happened—so whatever security risks we took by pandemic adaptations, we can safely continue to take."

Cyber actors may well be inside the client's enterprise. The client may be unaware of it because of the stealth and sophistication of the attack. The client may be blind to it because of the security deficiencies the client introduced by its adaptations to the pandemic. Each day the client permits those security deficiencies to remain unidentified and unremediated puts the enterprise at heightened risks of cyber intrusions that might cause it catastrophic damage.

Counsel will also need to find ways to initiate conversations on cybersecurity to help its client avoid being misled by the belief that the success of its commercial survival of the pandemic involved no trade-offs in cybersecurity. Counsel will also need to help its client avoid being misled by the belief that having no awareness of an attack on its enterprise, it must have escaped the HILF cyberattacks that co-occurred with the pandemic. The client may not have been that lucky. And, if so, its luck may soon run out.

Reducing cybersecurity safeguards during a period of exponential growth in cyberattacks would seem an imprudent risk for an enterprise to take. Most enterprises had to take that risk initially as they adapted commercially to the pandemic. The sooner counsel can bring those risks to its client's attention, the greater the client's chances of remediating its security profile before it's too late. Counsel should also alert the client that mid-course in the remediation, the client may discover bad actors active in its computer systems. Thus, the incident response and recovery plans will almost certainly need to be improved at the outset, with close attention to the security risks the client took to ensure its commercial survival during the pandemic.

III. Practical Considerations

The following practice considerations may help counsel to prepare for and initiate conversations about cybersecurity:

1. Cybersecurity deserves to be among the issues discussed in depth between counsel and client at the time that the attorney-client relationship is formed.
2. At a minimum, the conversation at the start of the attorney-client relationship should explore the cybersecurity safeguards that the company relies upon, whether they qualify as reasonable precautions in light of existing cyber threats and risks, and cybersecurity deficiencies in the client's business operations that could result in compromise of attorney-client communications and the irrevocable loss of the client's high-value digital assets.
3. Whenever the client or counsel is considering adopting and deploying a new communications technology, it would be prudent to have a conversation about the potential vulnerabilities that may be inherent in the technology and the improvements in cybersecurity that may be necessary to manage the resulting cyber risks is critical.
4. When companies anticipate embarking on an M&A transaction, outside counsel and the general counsels of the acquirer and the target should initiate a succession of conversations about the cybersecurity issues that could adversely affect the transaction, including the expanded set of such issues under FIRRMA and its implementation in the January 2020 CFIUS regulations.

5. Alert the client to the possibility that cybersecurity deficiencies in the enterprise may enable or facilitate intruder access to, and compromise of, its design and development processes and products. In that event, the client may be at risk of failing to fulfill contractual or regulatory obligations.

6. As clients extend their businesses into the use of AI systems and other emergent technologies that distance the user from an easily accessible understanding of what makes their digital tools work, they are ever more likely to subject themselves to regulations whose potential applicability may not be known by the client's management, board, or general counsel. Outside counsel and the general counsel may find that they need to team up to initiate conversations with the client to address such risks.

7. As general counsels become increasingly responsible and accountable for corporate decisions to misuse software to circumvent regulatory requirements, they may find it a prudent precaution to initiate timely conversations with senior officers and directors about those risks, especially when something the client is attempting to accomplish seems "too good to be true" and may be pressuring its engineers to achieve infeasible objectives. A general counsel who has regular interactions with supervisors and engineering teams will be in a far better position to perceive, from her own observations, when an achievement of an enterprise objective strains credulity, asks the impossible, or raises a red flag. General counsels should work with outside counsel to bring the misguided practices to light while there is still time to halt, contain, and correct them.

8. HILFs and APTs should alert counsel and its clients to the need for HILF-level security plans.[87] In some instances, that may require

---

87. For excellent discussions of HILF risks and events and the need to adjust response, recovery, and security plans to address them, see N. Am. Elec. Reliability Corp., High-Impact, Low-Frequency Event Risk to the North American Bulk Power System (2010), https://www.energy.gov/sites/default/files/High-Impact%20Low-Frequency%20Event%20Risk%20to%20the%20North%20American%20Bulk%20Power%20System%20-%202010 .pdf; Bernice Lee & Felix Preston, Preparing for High-Impact, Low-Probability Events: Lessons from Eyjafjallajökull (Chatham House 2012), https://www.chathamhouse .org/sites/default/files/public/Research/Energy,%20Environment%20and%20Development /r0112_highimpact.pdf.

reversion to predigital technologies for indefinitely long periods of time. In the meantime, degraded operations can only continue for non-sensitive communications. Trade secrets and sensitive communications should not be introduced into any digital devices that may be of doubtful security, especially if they are subject to a "new abnormal."

Counsel and clients may need to assume the presence of cyber actors in the enterprise until it can be verified reliably that intruders have, indeed, been eradicated. But at this time, the possibility of verification that "all's clear" in a digital system remains uncertain. Verification with a high level of confidence may only be achievable with systems rebuilt from uncompromised components and software. If the data on which AI has been trained has been compromised, the rebuild will need to be extended to the AI's underlying algorithms, models, and software—a daunting but necessary task when a "new abnormal" is the state of the enterprise's cybersecurity profile.

9. Before APT intrusions and other HILF events become a more frequent occurrence, lawyers and law firms should initiate a series of conversations with their clients to recalibrate their shared understanding of the universe of "worst-case" scenarios and how they may affect the attorney-client relationship.

Once counsel and clients accept the possibility of HILF events, they can discuss what each will rely on the other to do if such events disrupt and degrade for an indefinite time counsel's ability to serve its clients or their respective abilities to communicate privileged and confidential information securely.

SECTION III

UNDERSTANDING DIFFERENT LEGAL PRACTICE SETTINGS

Chapter 8
Large Law Firms
Alan Charles Raul and Michaelene E. Hanley

I. Introduction to Cybersecurity for Large Law Firms

Attorneys at law firms understand that the transactions and litigation that drive their practices are of significant interest not only to their clients but also to their clients' competitors, government regulators, the press, criminals, and others in the outside world. Accordingly, attorneys are attuned to the confidentiality needs of their clients, and must be readily able and willing to adjust their practices to protect client confidentiality. Clients entrust law firms with their most important business and legal information, and firms must take appropriate steps to safeguard that data. Failure to do so not only risks a firm's reputation—if a firm loses its clients' trust, it is also likely to lose its clients—but also entails risk to the ability of the firm's lawyers to meet their professional responsibilities.

Safeguarding data has become increasingly critical and difficult. In 2021, cyberattacks and data breaches can come at a great cost for commercial enterprises. For example, the attack against one global media and entertainment company in April 2011 caused an estimated $1.24 billion loss for the company, and is heralded as serving as a wake up call for large companies to improve their information security practices.[1] Today companies are reminded regularly that cybersecurity risks should be top of mind; a flood of recent ransomware attacks have publicly, temporarily crippled companies

---

1. *See Law Firms Prime Targets of Cyber Attacks*, ABA, Div. for Comm. & Media Rel. (Feb. 5, 2012), https://abanow.org/2012/02/law-firms-prime-targets-of-cyber-attacks/.

across industries, from the energy sector[2] to meatpacking facilities.[3] Cyberse-curity has become the most pressing concern for CEOs while costs continue to increase for companies,[4] particularly when considering recent heavy fines related to data breaches. A major airline was fined more than $26 million in 2020 by the U.K.'s Information Commission's Office (ICO) under the GDPR, and in 2019 a credit reporting agency agreed to pay between $575 million and $700 million in a regulatory settlement with the Federal Trade Commission, Consumer Financial Protection Bureau, and 50 U.S. states and territories.[5]

Companies of all sizes are now targets—as are courts and government agencies,[6] celebrities, political organizations, and law firms—and costs are rising; analysts estimate that as of 2020 cybercrime costs have exceeded $1 trillion globally.[7] The Federal Bureau of Investigation's Internet Crime Complaint Center reported that it "received a record number of complaints from the American public in 2020, with reported losses exceeding $4.1 bil-lion, a 69% increase in total complaints from 2019."[8]

But while companies increasingly have been taking protective and proac-tive measures to defend against cyberattacks,[9] not all attorneys who provide

---

2. Brian Fung & Geneva Sands, *Ransomware Attackers Used Compromised Password in Colonial Pipeline Network*, CNN (June 4, 2021), https://www.cnn.com/2021/06/04/politics/colonial-pipeline-ransomware-attack-password/index.html.

3. Dee-Ann Durbin & Frank Bajak, *JBS, World's Biggest Meat Supplier, Says Its Systems Are Coming Back Online after Cyberattack Shut Down Plants in U.S.*, Wash. Post (June 1, 2021), https://www.washingtonpost.com/business/2021/06/01/jbs-cyberattack-meat-supply-chain/.

4. Alwyn Scott, *Cybersecurity Is Top Business Worry in 'Age of Risk'*—Marsh & Mclen-nan CEO, Reuters (Nov. 16, 2020), https://www.reuters.com/article/events-insurance-cyber/cybersecurity-is-top-business-worry-in-age-of-risk-marsh-mclennan-ceo-idUSL1N2I21WO.

5. Dan Swinhoe, *The Biggest Data Breach Fines, Penalties, and Settlements So Far*, CSO Online (Mar. 5, 2021), https://www.csoonline.com/article/3410278/the-biggest-data-breach-fines-penalties-and-settlements-so-far.html.

6. Debra Cassens Weiss, *Federal Court Documents and DOJ Emails Compromised in Cybersecurity Breach*, A.B.A. J. (Jan. 7, 2021), https://www.abajournal.com/news/article/federal-court-documents-and-justice-department-emails-apparently-compromised-in-data-breach.

7. *See* Zhanna Malekos Smith & Eugenia Lostri, *The Hidden Costs of Cybercrime*, McAfee (Dec. 7, 2020), https://www.mcafee.com/enterprise/en-us/assets/reports/rp-hidden-costs-of-cybercrime.pdf; Lily Hay Newman, *The Year's Biggest Hacks, from Yahoo to the DNC*, Wired (Dec. 31, 2016), https://www.wired.com/2016/12/years-biggest-hacks-yahoo-dnc/.

8. FBI Internet Crime Complaint Center, *Internet Crime Report 2020* (Mar. 17, 2021), https://www.ic3.gov/Media/PDF/AnnualReport/2020_IC3Report.pdf.

9. *See* PWC, 2021 CEO Survey: US Findings, https://www.pwc.com/us/en/library/ceo-agenda/ceo-survey.html (last visited Aug. 19, 2021) (noting that almost half of U.S. CEOs

them with services and advice have implemented adequate cybersecurity measures.[10] According to the 2020 ABA Legal Technology Survey, only 29 percent of lawyers in firms report that their firm has cyber intrusion prevention and detection systems, which is only a 2 percent increase from the 2016 ABA Legal Technology Survey.[11] Unfortunately, failures by lawyers to take reasonable measures to secure their data and networks can put both law firms and law firm clients at risk from harmful cyberattacks and espionage.

The past decade has shown that hackers are plainly aware of the important role large law firms play in business and have increasingly targeted these firms.[12] Attorneys routinely advise on regulatory matters, conduct due diligence, negotiate matters, engage in discovery, and litigate disputes for the world's largest companies. These attorneys, as a result, often have access to a diverse array of clients' most sensitive information, including trade secrets, intellectual property,[13] financial data, corporate strategies, evidence from internal investigations into possible malfeasance, and internal research. A large law firm's computer system may represent a honeypot of useful data for hackers bent on industrial espionage, trade secret or intellectual property theft, public embarrassment, or other activities targeting multiple firm clients. And for the most part, the law firm "treasure chest" is easily opened. Some of the biggest New York law firms have acknowledged

---

planned to increase investments in cybersecurity and data privacy and 71 percent of U.S. CEOs are "extremely concerned" about cyber threats).

10. *See* JOHN LOUGHNANE, ABA TECHREPORT 2020: CYBERSECURITY (Oct. 19, 2020), https://www.americanbar.org/groups/law_practice/publications/techreport/2020/cybersecurity/ (noting that the use of certain security tools—such as encryption, two factor authentication, and intrusion detection—remains at less than half of survey respondents, even amid the heightened cybersecurity risks related to today's threat actors and increased remote work due to the pandemic).

11. *Id.*; *cf.* DAVE RIES, ABA TECHREPORT 2016 SECURITY (Dec. 1, 2016), http://www .americanbar.org/publications/techreport/2016/security.html.

12. *See* Julie Sobowale, *6 Major Law Firm Hacks in Recent History*, A.B.A. J. (Mar. 1, 2017), http://www.abajournal.com/magazine/article/law_firm_hacking_history; Victoria Hudgins, *Meet the Hacker Groups Snatching Law Firms' Client Data*, LAW.COM (May 21, 2020), https://www.law.com/legaltechnews/2020/05/21/meet-the-hacker-groups-snatching -law-firms-client-data/ (noting in a span of nearly six months, at least seven law firms have been infiltrated by ransomware).

13. Some sources suggest that U.S. companies have lost billions of dollars in intellectual property alone as a result of cyberattacks and espionage. *See* Ed Finkel, *Cyberspace under Siege*, A.B.A. J. (Nov. 1, 2010), https://www.abajournal.com/magazine/article/cyberspace_under_siege.

direct attacks as part of insider-trading schemes targeting merger information, a Panama-based law firm suffered 2.6 terabytes of leaked data that disclosed client names and their alleged efforts to evade taxes, and recently several large law firms' private data was exposed as a result of a breached vendor's file transfer system.[14] Breaches like these can continue undetected for weeks and sometimes even months, at a time.[15] Criminals may target the firm or specific attorneys because they believe that the attorney will access highly sensitive information, rather than seek that information from the client. But criminals may forgo targeting specific information, instead deploying all-encompassing ransomware. Both scenarios may cause significant disruption or lead to a breach of a lawyer's high standards and obligations to protect information.[16]

Large law firms are therefore a target-rich environment with sometimes significantly less cybersecurity protection than their clients.[17] As more firms move to the cloud and use other new technologies, and particularly as many quickly moved to fully remote work during the pandemic, they create a greater risk of experiencing a breach unless they conduct relevant diligence and implement proper safeguards. During the pandemic, law firms saw ransomware attacks increase. Although several attacks did not expose client data, others did, including an attack on one of Hollywood's top talent firms that led to leaked contracts and other documents containing information about famous clients.[18] The increased use of technologies

---

14. *See* Sobowale, *supra* note 12; Chris Opfer, *Jones Day Hit by Data Breach as Vendor Accellion Hack Widens*, BLOOMBERG LAW (Feb. 16, 2021), https://news.bloomberglaw.com /business-and-practice/jones-day-hit-by-data-breach-as-vendor-accellion-hacks-widen.

15. Robert McMillan, *Hackers Lurked in SolarWinds Email System for at Least 9 Months*, WALL ST. J. (Feb. 2, 2021), https://www.wsj.com/articles/hackers -lurked-in-solarwinds-email-system-for-at-least-9-months-ceo-says-11612317963.

16. VERIZON COMMC'NS, 2020 DATA BREACH INVESTIGATIONS REPORT, https://enterprise .verizon.com/resources/reports/2020-data-breach-investigations-report.pdf [hereinafter VERI-ZON 2020 REPORT].

17. *See* Xiumei Dong, *Law Firms' Reported Cyberattacks Are "Tip of the Iceberg"*, LAW360 (Nov. 4, 2020), https://www.law360.com/articles/1326001; John Reed, *The New Cyber Vulnerability: Your Law Firm*, FOREIGN POL'Y (Nov. 7, 2012), http://foreignpolicy.com/2012/11/07 /the-new-cyber-vulnerability-your-law-firm/.

18. Dong, *supra* note 17; *cf.* Ashley Cullins, *Why High-Profile Hacks Could Increase Amid Pandemic-Prompted Remote Work*, HOLLYWOOD REPORTER (May 18, 2020), https://www.hollywoodreporter.com/business/business-news/how-pandemic-related -remote-work-could-lead-an-increase-high-profile-hacks-1294980/.

also increases the risk that a firm will be collateral damage from attacks on service providers or potentially unintended collateral from nation-state activities (e.g., Stuxnet, SolarWinds). Like government agencies and companies, law firms can continue to do a better job of combating rampant cyberattacks and espionage.

Beyond a lawyer's professional responsibility to protect client data,[19] affected firms face immediate and long-term costs from breach investigation and notification, resulting lawsuits, and a potential loss of client and public trust.[20] And, if a firm does not have sufficient data security measures in place, clients may leave. The Association of Corporate Counsel (ACC) released its first set of model cybersecurity practices in 2017, drafted as a contract between the company and its outside counsel that requires measures such as the encryption of all confidential information and notification of a breach within 24 hours.[21] Although the ACC recommends that in-house counsel use the model as a guide to meet a company's needs and not as a one-size-fits-all industry standard, one can imagine that a firm that fails to implement such protections may lose opportunities to represent clients in matters. Cautious in-house counsel may choose firms they believe appear more secure as they worry their decisions may face increased scrutiny in the event of a breach.[22] These costs can be somewhat minimized by reacting quickly and appropriately in line with an incident response policy and

---

19. On May 22, 2017, the American Bar Association issued revised Formal Opinion 477R to address "how a lawyer should comply with the core duty of confidentiality in an ever-changing technological world." The opinion concludes that lawyers should, inter alia, take "reasonable efforts to prevent inadvertent or unauthorized access" when transmitting information over the Internet and stay "abreast of the benefits and risks associated with rel evant technology." ABA Comm. on Ethics & Pro. Resp., Formal Op. 477R, at 2–3 (2017).

20. Roy Strom, *Chicago's Johnson & Bell First US Firm Publicly Named in Data Security Class Action*, AM. LAW. DAILY (Dec. 9, 2016), http://www.americanlawyer.com/id=1202774361560 /Chicagos-Johnson—Bell-First-US Firm Publicly-Named-in-Data-Security-Class-Action.

21. Ass'n of Corporate Counsel, *Model Information Protection and Security Controls for Outside Counsel Possessing Company Confidential Information* (Mar. 10, 2017), https:// www.acc.com/sites/default/files/resources/advocacy/1454057_1.pdf [hereinafter ACC *Model Security Guidelines*].

22. Jennifer Williams-Alvarez, *After Yahoo, Are In-House Counsel Jobs at Risk over Cybersecurity?*, CORP. COUNSEL (Mar. 2, 2017), http://www.corpcounsel.com/id=1202780379239 /After-Yahoo-Are-InHouse-Counsel-Jobs-at-Risk-Over-Cybersecurity?

having a strong cybersecurity framework in place.[23] But the best defense is preventing as many incidents as possible and addressing the threats and challenges facing firms today while being prepared to handle an incident when it occurs.

Law enforcement is well aware of efforts by hackers to infiltrate computers and networks of America's largest law firms. As far back as November 17, 2009, the FBI issued an alert to law firms and other professional services organizations warning about the proliferation of "spear phishing" attacks.[24] Two years later, in late 2011, the FBI met with representatives from major law firms to discuss the rising number of cyberattacks on the firms, and to warn them that hackers perceive large firms as a relatively unprotected backdoor into corporate America. The ABA Journal reported on the lawyers' meeting with the FBI in an article entitled, "Some NY Law Firm Reps Said to Be Clueless as FBI Warned of Hackers Seeking Corporate Data."[25]

Over a decade later, law firms and the FBI continue to work together. The FBI publishes notifications when it becomes aware of various schemes[26] and can be an active partner during cyberattack investigations.[27] And while law firms might not be described as "clueless" about hackers anymore, many firms still have "less-than-optimal information security practices and pro-

---

23. *See, e.g.,* Debra Cassens Weiss, *Seyfarth Shaw Is in 'Restoration Phase' after Malware Attack,* A.B.A. J. (Oct 16, 2020), https://www.abajournal.com/news/article /seyfarth-shaw-is-in-restoration-phas-after-malware-attack.

24. In this type of attack, hackers send spoofed messages—which appear to be genuine e-mails from trusted sources—to employees of the target organization with the intent of having the employees click on links that lead to the installation of malware, and hacker backdoors, onto the network. Given that lawyers typically maintain many historical messages in their e-mail, access to attorney in-boxes can have serious data security consequences.

25. Debra Cassens Weiss, *Some NY Law Firm Reps Said to Be Clueless as FBI Warned of Hackers Seeking Corporate Data,* ABA J. (Jan. 31, 2012), http://www.abajournal.com/news /article/some_ny_law_firm_reps_said_to_be_clueless_as_fbi_warned_of_hackers_seeking_/.

26. *See, e.g.,* Gabe Friedman, *FBI Alert Warns of Criminals Seeking Access to Law Firm Networks,* BLOOMBERG BNA (Mar. 11, 2016), https://bol.bna.com/fbi-alert-warns-of-criminals -seeking-access-to-law-firm-networks/. The FBI continues to issue alerts, but recent warnings have been less tailored to specific industries. An increase in attacks, particularly ransomware, that can be leveraged to attack a wide range of industries and agencies has led to warnings that all industries should consider. *See, e.g.,* Federal Bureau of Investigation and Dep't of Homeland Sec./Cybersecurity Infrastructure and Security Agency (CISA), *Mamba Ransomware Weaponizing DiskCryptor* (Mar. 23, 2021), https://www.ic3.gov/Media/News/2021/210323.pdf.

27. *See* Xiumei Dong, *Seyfarth Shaw Hit By Ransomware Attack,* LAW360 (Oct. 12, 2020), https://www.law360.com/articles/1319008/seyfarth-shaw-hit-by-ransomware-attack.

cedures," and malicious actors target these cybersecurity vulnerabilities.[28] In 2020 and 2021, ransomware and malware attacks continued to plague law firms and their service providers as firms increased their reliance on remote capabilities and technology during the pandemic.[29] The security vulnerabilities and high-target status of law firms are commonly acknowledged in the press.[30] The difference in levels of protection between law firms and the clients they represent will expand unless law firms take proactive measures to shore up their security programs.

II. Cybersecurity Issues and Challenges for Large Firms

Firms face many cybersecurity issues and challenges today. All companies face an increased cybersecurity risk, but law firms are prime, high visibility targets with large amounts of sensitive information that present special risk. Similarly, all large global companies face additional challenges from a dispersed network, which law firms must address in addition to considering law firm security culture challenges. A law firm must navigate the current threat landscape and a combination of internal considerations to help defend itself against cybersecurity threats.

A. Today's Threat Landscape

Hackers use an ever-evolving arsenal of techniques to exploit law firms' systems. Many attacks, such as distributed denial of service attacks, take advantage of well-known network and system vulnerabilities.[31] However,

---

28. Dong, *supra* note 17.

29. *Id.*; Debra Cassens Weiss, *BigLaw Firm and Bar Groups Report Data Breaches*, A.B.A. J. (Nov. 13, 2020), https://www.abajournal.com/news/article /biglaw-firm-and-bar-groups-report-data-breaches.

30. *See, e.g.*, Dong, *supra* note 17 (noting "two recent high-profile data security incidents at BigLaw firms have once more drawn attention to law firms' cybersecurity vulnerabilities, and with the coronavirus pandemic forcing lawyers to adapt to a remote work environment, experts warn that the disclosed events are just the 'tip of the iceberg' of such attacks"); Reed, *supra* note 17; Hudgins, *supra* note 12; Blake Edwards, *Verizon GC: Law Firms Are Prime Targets for Hackers*, BLOOMBERG BNA (Feb. 4, 2016), https://bol.bna.com /verizon-gc-law-firms-are-prime-targets-for-hackers/.

31. While distributed denial of service (DDoS) attacks are primarily used to cause system downtime, often to cause embarrassment or as a form of hacktivism, they may be used as a

hackers often take the path of least resistance and attack the human element. The use of social engineering techniques to gain access to firms' data is often a hacker's weapon of choice. Many notorious hacking exploits in recent years have occurred as a result of spear phishing. The social engineering component of a spear phishing attack leads an organization insider to unwittingly install malware that the network's security system might otherwise prevent the hacker from installing.

For instance, when an organized group of hackers targeted firms involved in pending major mergers and acquisitions to gain insider information for use in stock trades, the hackers sent lawyers at the firms e-mails that purported to be from a well-known British publication announcing that it was honoring the attorney for his or her achievements.[32] When the links or e-mail attachments were opened, the hackers were able to gain access to the firms' networks and gather information relating to non-public transactions. The U.S. Attorney for the Southern District of New York noted that the case "should serve as a wake-up call for law firms around the world: you are and will be targets of cyber hacking, because you have information valuable to would-be criminals."[33]

Further complicating matters, fraudulent e-mails continue to become more difficult to distinguish from valid e-mails. Law firms can enable some technical controls to help users, like flagging of external e-mail addresses. But phishing e-mails and social engineering attacks are successful because they rely on humans making mistakes.[34] Phishing awareness training can drastically reduce the number of employees who fall victim to a phishing

---

diversionary tactic for hackers seeking to exploit a system. For instance, a DDoS attack may force IT staff to pay attention to the attack on one system resource, rendering it more difficult for them to monitor exploits occurring elsewhere on a system. *See* Office of the Comptroller of the Currency, *Information Security: Distributed Denial of Service Attacks and Customer Account Fraud, Alert 2012-16* (Dec. 21, 2012), https://www.occ.gov/news-issuances/alerts/2012 /alert-2012-16.html ("Fraudsters also use DDoS attacks to distract . . . personnel and technical resources while they gain unauthorized remote access.").

32. Ed Beeson, *Anatomy of a Hack*, LAW360 (Mar. 27, 2017), https://www.law360.com /privacy/articles/905062/how-cybercriminals-are-breaching-biglaw-s-defenses.

33. Press Release, Dep't of Justice, Manhattan U.S. Attorney Announces Arrest of Macau Resident and Unsealing of Charges against Three Individuals for Insider Trading Based on Information Hacked from Prominent U.S. Law Firms (Dec. 27, 2016), https://www.justice.gov/usao-sdny /pr/manhattan-us-attorney-announces-arrest-macau-resident-and-unsealing-of-charges-against.

34. *See, e.g.*, VERIZON 2020 REPORT, *supra* note 16.

attempt: a recent benchmarking survey suggests the number of employees in the legal industry who click on a suspicious link or obey a fraudulent request drops from 39.2 percent down to 5.4 percent after a year of ongoing awareness training.[35] Law firms should therefore focus training on other cornerstones to consider, such as whether the request is odd or oddly timed, requires urgent action such as passwords expiring or security alerts, or contains unexpected DocuSign requests or shipping delivery notices. And careful attention should always be paid to wiring instructions, including verbally providing passwords and ensuring wiring information is not in the body of settlement agreements.

Law firms representing clients conducting business in markets where hacking is endemic—for example, China or Russia—or in market sectors of critical interest to those countries also face a significant risk of government-backed cyber espionage. FireEye and other cybersecurity firms continue to discover advanced persistent threats (APTs) that target both public and private entities in the United States.[36] Indeed, the FBI warned law firms representing companies in business dealings or litigation with Chinese state-owned enterprises of their increased likelihood of cyberattack.[37]

The number of nation-states increasing these APT capabilities continues to rise, and their reach continues to widen.[38] Even as far back as 2010, law firms were already reporting that they experienced significant cyberattacks originating abroad that could reasonably be tied to their representation of a party adverse to a foreign state.[39] Today firms are increasingly facing

---

35. KnowBe4, Phishing by Industry 2020 Benchmarking Report (Mar. 24, 2020), https://www.knowbe4.com/hubfs/2020PhishingByIndustryBenchmarkingReport.pdf.

36. An advanced persistent threat is a prolonged, targeted attack that aims to compromise a specific system and gain information. *See* FireEye, *Advanced Persistent Threat Groups: Who's Who of Cyber Threat Actors*, https://www.fireeye.com/current-threats/apt-groups.html (last visited Aug. 19, 2021) (various APT reports available).

37. Matthew Huisman, *Online Attacks*, Nat'l L.J. 1–2 (Apr. 23, 2012).

38. Dep't of Homeland Sec., Commodification of Cyber Capabilities: A Grand Cyber Arms Bazaar (2019), https://www.dhs.gov/sites/default/files/publications/ia/ia_geo political-impact-cyber-threats-nation-state-actors.pdf (noting increasingly sophisticated and persistent campaigns targeting various sectors originating from more countries, including North Korea, Vietnam, and Ukraine).

39. *See* Jennifer Smith, *Lawyers Get Vigilant on Cybersecurity*, Wall St. J. (June 26, 2012), https://www.wsj.com/articles/SB10001424052702304458604577486761101726748 (citing the 2010 experience of Los Angeles firm Gipson Hoffman & Pancione, which represented

both direct targeting and incidental breaches, particularly as nation-state actors like Russia and China improve tradecraft and gain access to numerous industries with a single exploit via common upstream service providers underscored by the increasing frequency of Cybersecurity and Infrastructure Security Agency alerts for vulnerabilities.[40] Several of these vulnerabilities have been active for months, allowing time and access for the malicious actors to not only obtain information but also the opportunity to alter or destroy information.[41] Meanwhile, the Department of Justice "underscores the value of early, proactive engagement and cooperation between the private sector and the government" to help it pursue charges against individuals supporting these nation-state efforts.[42] These types of attacks may target American law firms representing any number of global clients.[43]

B.   A Large Law Firm's Additional Challenges and Considerations

Firms with multiple offices, domestic or abroad, face additional risks due to their numerous locations, which increase potential hacking targets, access points, culture and communication challenges, and perhaps expedited notification deadlines (such as 72 hours for personal data breaches in the EU). The experience of dealing with local law enforcement, and computer emergency

---

a software company in a suit against the Chinese government and other defendants, only to receive a significant number of e-mails containing malware immediately following the filing of the lawsuit); Thomas Claburn, *Law Firm Suing China Hit by Cyber Attack*, INFORMATIONWEEK (Jan. 14, 2010), https://www.darkreading.com/attacks-breaches/law-firm-suing-china-hit-by-cyber-attack (same).

40. *See, e.g.*, Dina Temple-Raston, *A 'Worst Nightmare' Cyberattack: The Untold Story of the SolarWinds Hack*, NPR (Apr. 16, 2021), https://www.npr.org/2021/04/16/985439655/a-worst-nightmare-cyberattack-the-untold-story-of-the-solarwinds-hack; *see also* CISA, 2021 NATIONAL CYBER AWARENESS SYSTEM ALERTS, https://us-cert.cisa.gov/ncas/alerts/2021 (containing alerts for Microsoft Cloud and Microsoft Exchange Servers, Accellion File Transfer, and Pulse Connect Secure, and following closely on the heels of the December 2020 Solar-Winds alert).

41. *Id.*

42. *See, e.g.*, Press Release, Dep't of Justice, Manhattan U.S. Attorney Announces Charges Against Seven Iranians for Conducting Coordinated Campaign of Cyber Attacks Against U.S. Financial Sector on Behalf of Islamic Revolutionary Guard Corp-Sponsored Entities (Mar. 24, 2016), https://www.justice.gov/usao-sdny/pr/manhattan-us-attorney-announces-charges-against-seven-iranians-conducting-coordinated.

43. *See* Alan Charles Raul, *Cybersecurity—It's Not Just about "National Security" Anymore: "Directors Desk" and Other Incidents Sound Wake-Up Call for the Executive Suite and Board Room*, BNA PRIVACY & SEC. LAW, 10 PVLR 347 (Feb. 28, 2011).

readiness teams (or government agencies), is also likely to vary considerably by country and jurisdiction. Firms with a distributed presence should be sure to create a cohesive cybersecurity policy and program to help prevent gaps in the network, while balancing local data protection and transfer requirements. Similarly, law firms should be sure that their vendors and cloud providers, including outsourced hosting sites and data rooms, offer adequate cybersecurity as well. Regulators in many industries are increasingly focused on vendor management and oversight because of the large risk these service providers create. This risk holds true for firms. Large-scale hacks like those targeting SolarWinds' network monitoring software used by thousands of institutions, from Fortune 500 companies to federal agencies alike, are successful because they are supply chain attacks that grant access to such a wide-ranging type and number of institutions.[44] Numerous law firms have been affected by incidents that stemmed from vendor-based vulnerabilities, from attacks on file share systems like the Accellion breach to the ransomware attack on a vendor that exposed some law firm employee information, including Social Security numbers.[45]

As law firms take advantage of new technologies that make working easier and more efficient, including the staggering and sudden increase of fully remote work due to the pandemic, the potential access points to firm data significantly increase. Providing firm devices to remote lawyers and staff with forced security settings can help address some concerns related to remote work, but law firms of all sizes still face increased risks from potential vulnerabilities at employees' homes, for instance with poorly set up routers and printers.[46] Remote employees should also be aware of their surroundings to protect information and privilege, including disabling

---

44. *See* Temple-Raston, *supra* note 40.

45. *See* Opfer, *supra* note 14; Cassens Weiss, *supra* note 29.

46. *See, e.g.,* Jane Wakefield, *Millions at Security Risk from Old Routers, Which? Warns,* BBC (May 6, 2021), https://www.bbc.com/news/technology-56996717; Nitzan Daube, *One of the Greatest Threats Facing the IoT: Router Security,* CYBER DEFENSE MAG. (Aug. 3, 2019), https://www.cyberdefensemagazine.com/router-security/ (noting a 2018 report found a 539 percent increase in attacks targeting routers since 2017 and that 83 percent of WiFi routers in US homes and offices leave their users at risk of cyberattacks due to inadequately updated firmware for security vulnerabilities); *see also* Lee Mathews, *Nearly a Million Printers at Risk of Attack, Thousands Hacked to Prove It,* WALL ST. J. (Aug. 31, 2020), https://www.forbes .com/sites/leemathews/2020/08/31/800000-printers-vulnerable-28000-hacked/.

personal digital assistants such as Amazon's Echo and Alexa, Google Home, and Apple devices with Siri, as these devices could overhear calls with confidential client information. Data security risks are not limited to cyber and technological risks in the remote environment; for example, there is an increased risk for breaches resulting from improper document destruction for items printed at home.

Lawyers at law firms need to confront the fact that the "bring your own device" or "BYOD" problems that exist at other workplaces are equally present in the context of a law firm. Many employers now face the growing question of how to treat employees' portable devices (e.g., personal laptops, iPads, smartphones), which are frequently used to transport data or to supplement devices provided to the employees by their employers. A liberal BYOD policy may result in employees or attorneys unknowingly or unwittingly introducing malware or viruses into a firm's network through the use of a compromised device. However, law firms do need to consider the benefits many attorneys and staff derive from the use of such devices in a world where clients expect 24/7 availability: They make the remote conduct of business manageable, and allow for the transfer of large volumes of data that could otherwise hamper network administration.

Law firms may routinely obtain data related to clients that are regulated entities subject to specific statutory data security requirements, even though the firms and attorneys may not themselves be covered entities. This means that they process legally protected information while perhaps lacking commensurate infrastructure and relationships with government and private sector resources to detect and report threats. For instance, in the course of transactions or litigation, law firms may handle sensitive data regulated under the Health Insurance Portability and Accountability Act (HIPAA),[47] the Gramm-Leach-Bliley Act (GLBA),[48] or other similar statutes that mandate significant—and potentially specific—safeguards and levels of data privacy and security. While the covered entities providing the data to the law firms may have adopted appropriate security regimes, it is not always

---

47. Health Insurance Portability and Accountability Act, Pub. L. No. 104-191, 110 Stat. 1936 (1996). For example, law firms that are "business associates" of their "covered entity" clients may be obligated to conduct specific HIPAA risk assessments.

48. Gramm-Leach-Bliley Act, Pub. L. No. 106-102, 113 Stat. 1338 (1999).

the case that the covered entities' lawyers have achieved these security levels. And although covered entities should validate a law firm's controls prior to sharing such data to ensure both parties maintain compliance, it would be prudent for firms to proactively establish expected controls through engagement agreements or other documents or interactions with clients. Additionally, in light of President Obama's February 2013 executive order on cybersecurity,[49] President Trump's 2017 follow-on executive order,[50] and President Biden's 2021 executive order on cybersecurity,[51] law firms working with critical infrastructure entities, or that serve themselves as government contractors or subcontractors, must also be mindful of the security obligations in this sector. The Department of Homeland Security (DHS), the Department of Defense, and the National Institute for Standards and Technology (NIST) are involved in the development of cybersecurity standards for critical infrastructure entities. For instance, DHS expanded the Enhanced Cybersecurity Services (ECS) initiative, developed to protect defense industrial base companies, to support all critical infrastructure sectors. The ECS initiative involves a cooperative arrangement between the critical infrastructure entity, the entity's commercial service provider (i.e., its ISP), and the National Security Agency. DHS further expanded the program to all interested U.S.-based public and private organizations in 2015.

Anecdotal evidence suggests that attorneys at law firms are believed by some to have displayed reluctance to prioritize information security. Indeed, some busy attorneys would argue that concrete legal or business objectives, especially where they involve actual deadlines or quantifiable metrics, take precedence over never-ending background concerns over data security, even where the risk of harm has become more visible and less remote in recent years. Lawyers may even wrongly assume that they fly more under the hacker radar screen than their more famous or well-resourced clients. Information security can be seen as a hindrance, as law firms have become accustomed to the use of "open architecture" systems where access is quick and relatively free of intrusions. Security systems that slow down or

---

49. Exec. Order No. 13,636, 78 Fed. Reg. 11,739 (Feb. 12, 2013).
50. Exec. Order No. 13,800, 82 Fed. Reg. 22,391 (May 11, 2017).
51. Exec. Order No. 14,028, 86 Fed. Reg. 26,633 (May 12, 2021).

complicate the attorneys' ability to work remotely, to share or access documents, or to use personal devices (such as personal computers, smartphones, or USB drives) may be viewed or treated as unwarranted and unwanted impositions. The common refrain seems to be that "security comes at the price of convenience."[52] And too often to date there is a perception that attorneys and other professionals emphasize convenience over security, in part because clients expect their lawyers to be available (and working) 24/7, and from any location in which they may happen to be.

The culture of confidentiality and privacy that exists at most law firms also complicates the ability of firms to deploy cutting-edge cybersecurity strategies. For example, network and computer monitoring can detect the installation of malware or the exfiltration of data to an unknown server, but many lawyers may chafe at the concept of having their data flows monitored on a continual basis. However, a risk-benefit analysis, illustrating the damage to the firm's clients and reputation, accompanied by an illustration of how the data tools work in practice, could serve to change perceptions of these practices. For instance, if software causes only minor interference with the speed at which an attorney reboots his or her computer, this cost, even in aggregate, may pale in comparison to possible liability or lost business following a potentially preventable cyberattack that compromises client data. Articulation of risk to the business or reputation of the firm, as opposed to the individual lawyer, will play an important part in changing this culture. As a law firm's security posture matures, improved information risk management will allow the firm to manage and mitigate risks by balancing the probability of an incident against the magnitude of the resulting loss.

The dynamic of partnerships at law firms may also lend itself to frustrating a firm's efforts toward data security and protection. Law firms' partners are owners of the firms, and often have expectations that they will enjoy broad access rights to systems and data. While it may be reasonable for a smaller firm with a handful of partners to grant system-administrator-level rights to each partner, large firms have too many partners for this to be a prudent approach. Instead, large-firm partners must be willing to

---

52. *See* Natalie Posgate, *Legal Experts: Cyber Security Growing Issue for Lawyers*, Tex. L. Book (June 29, 2012).

sacrifice total control over management of the computer system to permit the firm's IT department and experts to provide adequate security execution, employee training, data protection, and cybersecurity to protect client data. The partners should of course set cybersecurity governance strategy and policies and conduct ongoing oversight.

Finally, cybersecurity at a law firm may be impaired by reluctance on the part of the firm's partners to spend on "overhead." This reluctance, which exists in firms of all sizes, is exacerbated in the large firm setting because the cost of providing security commensurate with the sensitivity of the data is so high. This is particularly the case where a firm has not conducted a thorough risk assessment. Without weighing the risks of an attack, or how a security failure could negatively affect the firm, it may be difficult for a firm's management to see the importance of maintaining a well-rounded information security program. It can be difficult, without an impartial assessment by a third-party expert, for a firm to ascertain the degree of risk it faces from cyber incidents, and this upfront cost to conduct an assessment and implement security may also cause additional sticker shock.

III. How Large Law Firms May Address Cyber Risk

Law firms have legal and ethical obligations relating to data protection, as discussed in Chapters 4 and 6 of this Handbook.[53] Fortunately, among professional service firms, law firms should be particularly well equipped to address cybersecurity challenges. Law firm cultures inculcate confidentiality, and are generally accustomed to the sort of top-down procedures that would be necessary to improve data security. These cultural norms make law firms well suited to take appropriate measures to protect their systems and data. In other words, the culture of confidentiality that may cause some attorneys to chafe at the idea of network and computer monitoring

---

53. For example, in May 2017, the American Bar Association issued Formal Opinion 477R, updating a 1999 ethics opinion on confidentiality obligations to account for "the 'technology amendments' made to the Model Rules in 2012, identify some of the technology risks lawyers' face, and discuss factors other than the Model Rules of Professional Conduct that lawyers should consider when using electronic means to communicate regarding client matters." *See* ABA Comm. on Ethics & Pro. Resp., *supra* note 19.

can also be used to encourage more robust data protection as a method of protecting clients' interests.

A failure to safeguard client's most sensitive business and privileged information risks a firm's reputation and the ability of the firm's lawyers to meet their professional responsibilities. To mitigate these risks, firms should know their obligations to their clients and take reasonable steps to identify and defend against their exposure to cyberattack and data breach. Aside from defining and implementing a standardized, auditable, risk-based information security program, law firms must monitor and address new and immediate threats. The following multifaceted, seven-part plan is a practical approach to ensure that a law firm covers all of its bases: (1) strong governance and strategy; (2) cyber preparedness, including training and education; (3) administrative, technical, and physical measures, including insider threat preparedness; (4) vendor management; (5) incident response and threat intelligence; (6) recovery and continuity; and (7) ongoing process improvements and consideration of lessons learned from their own and others' mistakes.

A.   Governance and Strategy

First, law firms should bolster their overall information security programs by creating systems that minimize the likelihood and impact of a breach and implement security programs based on risk. Programs should be created with "reasonable" security requirements in mind based on the firm's size and maturity.[54] In evaluating potential safeguards, firms should consider (1) the sensitivity of information; (2) the likelihood of disclosure if additional safeguards are not deployed; (3) the cost of deploying additional safeguards; (4) the difficulty of implementing the safeguards; and (5) the extent to which the safeguards adversely affect the lawyers' ability to represent clients.[55] Law firms should evaluate the client information and data they store, and develop additional controls to safeguard the most valuable

---

54. As a starting place, firms may consider reviewing New York's Stop Hacks and Improve Electronic Data Security Act ("SHIELD Act"), 2019 N.Y. Ch. 117, or CIS Controls—available at https://www.cisecurity.org/controls/cis-controls-list/—as sources for benchmarking possible administrative, technical, and physical safeguards.

55. *See* ABA MODEL RULES OF PRO. CONDUCT r. 1.6, cmt. [18].

and sensitive data.[56] A law firm's risk assessment may evaluate system and network vulnerabilities for "persistent" threats, review exposure of valuable information and communication assets, evaluate exposure to third parties and service providers (including cloud and file-share hosting providers), and consider possible countermeasures to disrupt or divert attacks on the firm's systems and networks. This process will involve large firms engaging with IT and audit experts to evaluate and test the firms' systems. In the course of this assessment, law firms should evaluate areas in which they can improve data hygiene. By applying principles—including data minimization (limiting data collection), purpose specification (specifying a purpose at collection and limiting use to the specified purpose), and retention limitations (deleting data regularly and limiting the length of time data is maintained)—law firms can help further mitigate the potential damage in a successful attack and enhance the firm's cyber strategy.[57]

Strengthening an information security program can help significantly reduce the amount of time that elapses between a breach in security and its discovery—faster discovery and response will limit the damage to firm systems and the amount of data available to an attacker.[58] At a minimum, a firm's security program should include mandated software patch installation, robust use of antivirus and anti-malware programs, well-maintained spam filters, installation and use of system intrusion detection systems, continuous network monitoring for threats (both internal and external), incident response, and information security awareness.

Just as privacy and data security practitioners advise their clients to establish information governance systems that identify cyber risks and assign organizational accountability for managing and mitigating those risks, law firms should take similar steps. For a large firm, this will likely

---

56. To evaluate risk, law firms should obtain a basic understanding of the NIST Cybersecurity Framework, which approaches cyber risks through the following parameters: identify, protect, detect, respond, and recover, as discussed in more detail in Chapter 2.

57. *See, e.g.*, Falon Fatemi, *Best Practices for Data Hygiene*, FORBES (Jan. 30, 2019), https://www.forbes.com/sites/falonfatemi/2019/01/30/best-practices-for-data-hygiene/?sh=363556422395; *see also Guidelines on the Protection of Privacy and Transborder Flows of Personal Data*, O.E.C.D. Doc. C(80)58(Final) (Sept. 23, 1980).

58. *See* NAT'L INST. OF STANDARDS & TECH., COMPUTER SECURITY INCIDENT HANDLING GUIDE, NIST SPECIAL PUBLICATION 800-61 Revision 2, at 6 (Aug. 2012), https://nvlpubs.nist.gov/nistpubs/SpecialPublications/NIST.SP.800-61r2.pdf.

involve several components. As a first step, firms should review and refine their information governance structure and perform asset mapping. This could involve the creation of a committee within the firm that is responsible for cybersecurity, data protection, and information privacy that will establish expectations for the firm management, provide ongoing reporting regarding information risks and controls, and review top-level policies. This committee should be enabled to develop accountability and reporting obligations within the firm, and should be provided with adequate resources for the completion of its tasks. Each firm should also consider, if it has not done so already, appointing a chief information security officer and chief privacy officer to assist in managing and mitigating risks. A firm should also consider cybersecurity insurance and understand what is and is not covered by the policy. The firm committee should also actively monitor legislative, policy, industry, contractual, litigation, marketplace, consumer, and employee developments and expectations with implications for managing and mitigating cyber risk.

Law firms should also consider discussing clients' expectations regarding data security with them. Many large companies, as part of their own efforts to improve cybersecurity, are developing protocols for managing outside access to their data. For instance, some companies engaging in high-stakes financial transactions or litigation will require lawyers or bankers to go on-site to the company's offices to review documents in order to reduce the risk that files are hacked or otherwise accessed while in the care of third parties.[59] Clients are beginning to require certain data security measures and audit the computer and network security policies of their law firms, quickly making the potential business costs of inadequate data security very real and tangible to law firms.[60] It is also increasingly common for sophisticated clients, particularly in the financial sector, to require their outside law firms to respond to detailed information security questionnaires to provide assurance that satisfactory safeguards are in place to protect those clients' data. And as all lawyers know, there is nothing like client expectations to get (or

---

59. *See* Michael A. Riley & Sophia Pearson, *China-Based Hackers Target Law Firms to Get Secret Deal Data*, BLOOMBERG (Jan. 31, 2012), http://www.bloomberg.com/news/2012 -01-31/china-based-hackers-target-law-firms.html.

60. *See, e.g.*, ACC *Model Security Guidelines*, *supra* note 21.

keep) more legal business and motivate law firm behavior. Once there is a risk-based compliance regime in place, the firm should ensure there are robust firm-wide compliance and training programs that disseminate this information to create a cyber-savvy workforce.

B. Cyber Preparedness

Second, law firms should increase their cyber preparedness. Firms should consider ways to protect shared information, including using encryption and other secure tools. Such considerations should encompass encryption for all internal e-mails, for sensitive or confidential e-mails and documents, and for storage of client files and other sensitive firm files. Law firms should also focus on security management for video and audio conference calls, particularly as more audio calls are placed using Voice Over Internet Protocol (VoIP).

As the phishing technique highlights, personnel education is critical to any effort to ensure adequate network security.[61] Each professional at a law firm, and every administrative staff member, must be impressed with the personal responsibility that he or she owes to the firm's clients and partners with regard to information security. Many aspects of employee education are relatively self-evident. Attorneys and staff should be informed of the common threats faced by law firms, and how those threats will appear to them (e.g., an e-mail from an unknown address—or even an unanticipated e-mail from a known address—requesting that the attorney click a link to review a request for counsel).[62] The education should also inform attorneys and staff of firm policies, the rationale supporting those policies, and the availability of firm support staff to address any questions regarding the implementation of policies. Law firms can educate using periodic security awareness alerts, implementing an annual CLE requirement that covers security and privacy issues, actively testing phishing awareness, and conducting data breach table top exercises for those at the firm who would be involved in incident response. And while a law firm may have a high-level

---

61. KnowBe4, *supra* note 35.

62. *See* Reece Guida, *How Law Firms Can Prevent Phishing and Malware*, 10(35) Nat. L. Rev. (Feb. 4, 2020), https://www.natlawreview.com/article/how-law-firms-can-prevent-phishing-and-malware.

cybersecurity plan, it is critical to also develop and implement plans to cover business continuity, incident response, and recovery for an inevitable incident. More information on training and education is available in Chapter 13, and incident response is further discussed in Chapter 15.

C.   Administrative, Technical, and Physical Measures

Third, the firm should implement administrative, technical, and physical measures and insider threat programs as an additional layer of protection to counterbalance human error. Firms should automatically deploy patches and upgrades to network computers to prevent hackers from using known exploits against the system. The importance of deploying vendor-provided patches in a timely manner to maintain a secure and reliable environment cannot be overstated; some studies suggest that as many as one in three incidents occur as a result of an unpatched vulnerability.[63] Although the downtime required to install patches can create friction with lawyers' work demands, prompt updates are a necessity.

Firms should also log and monitor network access and deploy data loss prevention tools to monitor where data is going and to flag or block unusual file transfers. Law firms may set policies backed by technological restrictions that prohibit use of certain technologies and require encrypted connections or devices when conducting work for the firm. These policies could, for instance, (1) mandate strong password requirements; (2) proscribe the use of public Wi-Fi with firm computers; (3) prohibit the use of unsanctioned cloud storage for client files; (4) block the download of executable files or certain forms of scripts from non-white-listed websites; or (5) block private e-mail, instant messaging, unauthorized downloads, and unsanctioned file transfer mechanisms.[64] If these or similar policies have not already been implemented, they may cause initial grumblings because of the limitations they impose on attorneys' use of computers. However, explaining the cost-benefit analysis of these policies and their ability to greatly reduce the risk that human error creates for cyberattack can lead to greater acceptance.

---

63. Steve Ranger, *Cybersecurity: One in Three Breaches Are Caused by Unpatched Vulnerabilities*, ZDNet.com (June 4, 2019), https://www.zdnet.com/article/cybersecurity-one-in-three-breaches-are-caused-by-unpatched-vulnerabilities/.

64. *See* Posgate, *supra* note 52, at 2.

Firm-sanctioned policies lay the groundwork for a mature, enforceable information security program. These policies will allow a firm to measure security posture and subsequently mature over time.

D.   Vendor Management

Fourth, proper vendor management can further support a law firm's cybersecurity, but it is not enough merely to include in the contract a provision that the vendor will follow best practices and indemnify the firm. A firm should review prospective vendors' security plans and question service providers about cybersecurity, as well as recovery and continuity plans. Law firms may request third-party audits and certifications as part of ongoing due diligence and efforts to protect client and personnel data. Firms should not overlook their vendor's management of service providers as well (e.g., fourth-party providers). It is critical to know which vendors or subvendors have which types of information, whether they can access it, what privacy and security measures they have in place, and how they monitor their service providers for privacy and security.

E.   Incident Response and Threat Intelligence

Fifth, law firms should acknowledge reality; no security system is impenetrable. Because breaches in security will occur, it is important not only to lessen their likelihood but also to mitigate their impact. Firms should take steps to plan for responding to data security incidents by drafting an incident response plan that details who has ownership of key decisions and the processes to follow in the event of an incident. The firm's incident response plan should include a ransomware protocol, as payment demands continue to increase and attacks increasingly involve exfiltration of data.[65] If a firm determines it would consider making a payment, it should create a plan for ensuring OFAC compliance[66] and, for global firms, also confirm that such payment is not a violation of foreign law prohibitions. A firm that handles

---

65. Sophos 2021 Threat Report (Nov. 2020), https://www.sophos.com/en-us/media library/PDFs/technical-papers/sophos-2021-threat-report.pdf.

66. Office of Foreign Assets Control, *Advisory on Potential Sanctions Risks for Facilitating Ransomware Payments*, U.S. Dep't of Treasury (Oct. 1, 2020), https://home.treasury .gov/system/files/126/ofac_ransomware_advisory_10012020_1.pdf.

data incidents for clients should also keep in mind that facilitating ransomware payments on behalf of a victim may also violate OFAC regulations.[67]

A firm should identify applicable notification and reporting standards or requirements, from state- or sector-specific data breach notification laws to contractual provisions. Firms should carefully consider when to consult proactively with law enforcement to investigate an incident, and should be prepared to inform, where necessary or appropriate, any potentially affected client of what occurred. The last step may be a tough pill to swallow, particularly given the premium that law firms place on their brand reputation. Required notification timelines are quickly becoming shorter, with 72-hour notice required under the EU's General Data Protection Regulation, effective May 2018, and some U.S. jurisdictions requiring regulator notification within 10 to 14 days.[68] Firms should create template documents that include required content in a workable framework and prompt the drafter to enter key information to help the firm meet these regulatory requirements, from notifying individuals to credit reporting agencies.[69] Developing critical contact points with law enforcement and regulators and retaining incident response vendors in advance will further help lawyers know whom to call when faced with a breach.[70] Table-top simulation exercises allow key law firm actors, and external contacts if desired, to practice responding to a breach to work out any kinks in a response plan before the stakes are real.

Firms should also identify and remediate the data security shortfalls that lead to a breach of security. Threat intelligence may possibly prevent a breach, and firm leadership should discuss how to obtain and integrate threat intelligence into the firm's program. Will the firm hire a third party

---

67. *Id.*

68. Some clients may be subject to shorter reporting timelines, such as the 72-hour notification period for entities subject to N.Y. Dep't of Financial Serv. 23 NYCRR 500.17.

69. Templates might include communication with regulators (including U.S., state, and international), communication to law enforcement, "risk of harm" assessment framework, affected individual notification letter, state attorney general and other state regulator reporting letter(s), credit reporting agency reporting letter, information sharing letter for law enforcement/DHS, notification letter to business customers, demand letter to vendors, notification letter to insurance carrier(s), and HIPAA business associate model documents.

70. A list of external resources and points of contact may include law enforcement and national security points of contact, pre-vetted forensics and credit monitoring service providers, and pre-vetted public relations and communication firms skilled in handling cyber incident responses.

to monitor and analyze the dark web and social media and provide early detection alerts of potential data leaks, breaches, and sale of data? Will the firm participate in threat sharing under the Cybersecurity Information Sharing Act and share threat data with the government?[71] How will the firm receive and respond to threat information from sector-specific threat-sharing platforms like the legal Information Sharing and Analysis Center or Information Sharing and Analysis Organization? Participating in these organizations can improve threat intelligence awareness, and perhaps prevent an incident in the first place.[72] Once aware of shortfalls in its security, especially if a firm is made aware as a result of an attack on its own system, it is important to swiftly and adequately remediate the issues to help mitigate further attacks and potential liability claims.

F. Data Recovery and Business Continuity

Sixth, a firm must protect itself through contingency planning for recovery and continuity in the event of a breach or ransomware attack. It is key to establish business continuity and resiliency plans in the event of material cyber risks or disruptions, including ransomware attacks. A law firm's reputation depends on its ability to meet court, regulator, and client deadlines, despite an incident.[73]

G. Continual Process Improvements from Lessons Learned

Finally, law firms should continually monitor and improve the preceding processes as hackers' methods evolve and technology changes. Firms should also adjust their cybersecurity plans as they learn lessons from others' public

---

71. Cyber threat indicators can potentially be shared with the U.S. government and private sector firms without waiving privilege. 6 U.S.C. § 1504(d)(1); Dep't of Homeland Sec. & Dep't of Just., *Guidance to Assist Non-Federal Entities to Share Cyber Threat Indicators and Defensive Measures with Federal Entities under the Cybersecurity Information Sharing Act of 2015*, at 18 (Oct. 2020), https://www.cisa.gov/sites/default/files/publications/Non-Federal%20Entity%20Sharing%20Guidance%20under%20the%20Cybersecurity%20Information%20Sharing%20Act%20of%202015_1.pdf.

72. Organizations offering legal services-specific threat intelligence include the Legal Services Information Sharing and Analysis Organization (LS-ISAO), https://www.fsisac.com/ls-isao; the Legal Vendor Network, https://www.prevalent.net/legal-vendor-network/; and the International Legal Technology Association LegalSEC (ILTA LegalSEC), http://www.iltanet.org/resources/legalsec.

73. See Chapters 15 and 16 of this Handbook for further discussion.

breaches, at law firms and companies alike. A data security incident may reflect poorly upon a firm if the firm has not taken reasonable and appropriate steps to ensure the security of client data and practice that security. Having an effective data security program will ultimately reduce the number and scope of data security incidents affecting the firm, and will reduce the likelihood that a firm is in a position where it has to report breaches to government authorities and/or clients. Ultimately, "cybersecurity is a team sport that [all parties] need to play effectively together."[74]

IV. Top Ten Considerations for Large Law Firm Lawyers

As a starting point for addressing cybersecurity, lawyers practicing in a firm should consider taking the following ten steps to evaluate and mitigate risk. Of course, in the event of a breach, lawyers should also consider crisis management, public relations, and relationships with forensics firms. If a firm does not have its own cyber practice, consider consulting with a firm that does!

1. Evaluate the firm's current cybersecurity risk profile, taking into account the current data and device controls in place, the nature of data and information accessed by the firm, ethical obligations, and other relevant factors.

2. Evaluate client-specific data security considerations (e.g., for covered entities under GLBA or HIPAA, or for clients entrusting particularly sensitive corporate or personal data) that may require additional steps by the firm's lawyers.

3. Organize and empower an information security and data governance committee within the firm to obtain a basic understanding of the NIST Cybersecurity Framework that approaches cyber risks, manage information security and cybersecurity risks, and report regularly to the firm's most senior management.

---

74. *See* Finkel, *supra* note 13 (citing Philip Reitinger, U.S. Dep't of Homeland Sec.).

4. Appoint an individual within the firm (or hire an individual from outside of the firm) to serve as a chief information security officer responsible for managing the firm's day-to-day cybersecurity risks and stay up-to-date on new technology and threats.

5. Define and implement a standardized, auditable, risk-based information security program addressing cybersecurity, including vendor management and insider threats. This program should include establishing business continuity and resiliency plans in the event material cyber risks or disruptions occur, including ransomware attacks.

6. Establish stringent requirements for data security in software installations, cloud or other data services, and vendor contracts.

7. Develop, as part of the information security program, a data security incident response protocol or playbook that addresses notification to clients, government authorities, or individuals affected by breaches. Expect administrative personnel to escalate significant cyber incidents involving, for example, data breaches requiring notice to individuals, regulators, or clients, or significant impact to critical firm systems or confidential information. As part of this process, consider consulting with law enforcement, if and when appropriate, about cybersecurity risks.

8. Develop controls on Internet access and the use of personal devices by members and employees of the firm.

9. Conduct training and educate lawyers and staff within the firm of their obligations relating to cybersecurity and of their roles within the firm's information security program—and warn about the risk of falling prey to phishing attacks!

10. Conduct routine audits of the firm's information security risks and vulnerabilities.

Chapter 9
Small Firms and Sole Practitioners
Melissa Ventrone

I can hear some lawyers saying it now: "I'm just a solo. I don't need a complicated computer security system. I'm not at risk of a cyberattack. Besides, I don't have an IT department to handle it or a big budget to spend on computer security. I'm not as important as a large firm; no one would want to attack me."

Wrong. Solo practitioners and small firms are, in some instances, at higher risk of suffering a catastrophic cyberattack. These types of firms have smaller IT budgets and fewer resources to identify and address cybersecurity risks, meaning that a cyberattack can cause more damage to a small firm than it would a larger firm. Most attacks are not targeted at a particular company or individual. Instead, attackers conduct automated scans and attacks that search for and identify vulnerabilities in systems, which they then use to access the victim's system and perpetrate an attack.

First, while there is no guarantee that any cybersecurity system will be bulletproof, confidential client information can be lost if a casual approach to security is employed. Firms must take the appropriate steps to protect their systems and client information.

Second, the traditional requirement to protect the confidentiality of client information and work product[1] has been updated. State bar authorities

---

1. MODEL RULES OF PRO. CONDUCT r. 1.6(c): "A lawyer shall make reasonable efforts to prevent the inadvertent or unauthorized disclosure of, or unauthorized access to, information relating to the representation of a client." Comment [18]. "The unauthorized access to, or the inadvertent or unauthorized disclosure of, information relating to the representation of a client does not constitute a violation of paragraph (c) if the lawyer has made reasonable efforts to prevent the access or disclosure. Factors to be considered in determining the reasonableness of the lawyer's efforts include, but are not limited to, the sensitivity of the information, the likelihood of disclosure if additional safeguards are not employed, the cost of employing additional safeguards, the difficulty of implementing the safeguards, and the extent to which the safeguards adversely affect the lawyer's ability to represent clients (e.g., by making a device

in many states now require attorneys to be familiar with technology,[2] and employ reasonable technological safeguards as part of any attorney's commitment to be competent in the practice of law.[3]

Third, while you may think your firm is too small to be of interest to anybody, that is certainly not the case. Your client information may be significant to a competitor, a foreign government, a personal enemy, or a cybercriminal looking for a chance to make some money. Is there technology that might be cutting edge? Do you have clients with public profiles that might generate someone who wants to get revenge? Are your clients involved in negotiations to buy or sell a business where having inside information may be useful in stock trading? Someone might want to learn private information just for "doxing"—publishing private information on the Internet.

Fourth, if an attacker is able to disrupt your systems and prevent you from accessing data or programs, this will have a significant impact on your ability to provide services to your clients or meet key deadlines. If you cannot access e-mail, your document management system, or data on your laptop because an attacker has blocked access or encrypted all of your systems, your ability to provide services to your clients will be significantly impacted and may cause you to lose clients. It will certainly have a significant financial impact on your firm.

Fifth, and perhaps most importantly for solos and small firms, the failure to provide adequate security for the electronic aspects of your practice goes to the heart of your practice model. Technology allows solos and small firms to compete with bigger firms. Whether it is the ability to work from any location, to access huge stores of information, or to operate without

---

or important piece of software excessively difficult to use)." Any client whose data is lost due to a cybersecurity incident should be notified, but in most cases (e.g., not involving public companies or consumer personally identifiable information) small firms or solos probably will not be required to make public announcements of a security breach.

2. As of Feb. 1, 2021, 35 states had adopted this requirement.

3. MODEL RULES OF PRO. CONDUCT r. 1.1: "A lawyer shall provide competent representation to a client. Competent representation requires the legal knowledge, skill, thoroughness and preparation reasonably necessary for the representation." Comment [8]: "To maintain the requisite knowledge and skill, a lawyer should keep abreast of changes in the law and its practice, *including the benefits and risks associated with relevant technology*, engage in continuing study and education and comply with all continuing legal education requirements to which the lawyer is subject" (emphasis added).

a big dedicated office server and staff, modern tools allow for the practice of law at the highest level of quality. You can compete with the big guys in many areas, and perhaps surpass their service levels with individual attention to clients, responsiveness, and transparent billing practices. But in order to compete you need to be able to provide your clients with the assurance that they will not be putting their data, their business, or even their lives, at risk. Some clients, particularly large companies, may well require a security audit before retaining your firm.

Cyberattacks are becoming more pervasive and destructive. As fast as we develop new ways to protect our systems, the cybercriminals find ways to bypass the protections and perpetrate the attack. For instance, ransomware attacks originally involved the attacker deploying malware that encrypted the data in the system. For a "fee" or "ransom," the attackers would provide a decryption key that the company could use to decrypt and recover its data. More companies started to use backups so they could quickly restore their systems if they suffered a ransomware attack. Now, an attacker steals data from its victim and will release the data publicly if the company does not pay the ransom. The cost to a small firm from the type of system interruption a ransomware attack would cause, coupled with the impact to its reputation if data is released, could be catastrophic.

It isn't a question of if you will experience a cyberattack; the appropriate questions are when, and are you ready? In addition to taking steps to protect your systems, you should also ensure you have implemented the following controls to enable you to recover quickly should an attack occur. They don't necessarily need to be done in the order they are listed here, but they should be done sooner or later—preferably sooner.

1. **Multifactor authentication.** Multifactor authentication (MFA) is one of the most important security controls small firms should implement for remote access to any system. MFA is the process of using two or more credentials to authenticate to a system. If a vendor or business partner needs access to your systems, you should require that they use MFA to do so. If you have services that are hosted, such as bank accounts, human resources, or cloud-hosted backup services, you should make sure access to any of these services is also protected by MFA. Access

to e-mail via online portals or remotely should have MFA as well. If a hacker attempts to log into an account that is protect by MFA, you will notice the attempt via the request for the second factor and be able to quickly take steps to protect your systems.

2. **Supported Systems.** Review your systems and identify any that are not fully patched or may be currently end-of-life. End-of-life equipment is that which is no longer supported by the manufacturer. In other words, the manufacturer does not provide any updates or security patches for the equipment and vulnerabilities are often exploited by attackers. In addition, if an attack occurs, data may be corrupted and unrecoverable, complicating efforts to restore systems. Also, ensure you have a process for identifying and applying critical security patches. Vulnerabilities are often made public through the Critical Vulnerability and Exposures (CVE[4]) program. This list is monitored by attackers, who then conduct automated scans to identify companies that have not patched the vulnerabilities. The attackers will then exploit the vulnerability to gain access to the system and perpetrate a cyberattack.

3. **Vendor Due Diligence.** Because small firms have limited resources, many outsource various cybersecurity requirements to vendors. Vendors include not just those who may provide services to help you protect your systems but also cloud and other hosted platforms. But vendors are at just as much risk of a cyberattack as are small law firms, and it is important that you conduct a thorough review of their security controls. Do they have a written information security program, and require their vendors to comply with the program? Do they have a security certification, such as ISO 27001[5] or a SOC2 certification?[6] Do they conduct regular internal and external vulnerability scans and penetration testing and address any issues? Are their systems up-

---

4. *See* CVE, cve.mitre.org/index.html; the CVE Program is intended to "identify, define, and catalog publicly disclosed cybersecurity vulnerabilities." CVE is sponsored by the U.S. Department of Homeland Security Cybersecurity and Infrastructure Agency.

5. *ISO/IEC 27001 Information Security Management,* ISO, https://www.iso.org/isoiec -27001-information-security.html (last visited Nov. 19, 2021).

6. *SOC 2®—SOC for Service Organizations: Trust Services Criteria,* AICPA, https:// www.aicpa.org/interestareas/frc/assuranceadvisoryservices/aicpasoc2report.html (last visited Nov. 19, 2021).

to-date and regularly patched? Do they conduct routine training for employees? Do they have backups in place that are segmented from their network, and have they tested the restoration process? Do they have cyber insurance in the event they experience an attack? There are other questions you may want to consider, but these are some of the most important to ask your vendors.[7]

4. **Vendor Contracts.** Once you have identified a vendor that meets your qualifications, carefully review the contract to ensure it has the appropriate protections in place. Many vendor contracts contain clauses that limit recovery of any damages to fees paid over a certain period of time. If your vendor suffers an attack that causes its systems to be unavailable for a significant period of time, or suffers a breach of your data, or an attack that causes you to lose all data, consider whether the contractual recovery will be sufficient. The contract should also require the vendor to have cyber insurance, include security controls, and require the vendor to provide information to you and cooperate with you should they suffer a cyberattack.

5. **Training.** You can spend as much money as you would like on security tools and programs, but if you don't include training, the best protections will be for naught.[8] Often, security controls are bypassed or defeated because of human error, or a lack of recognition or understanding of the risk. For example, one company had implemented MFA on its e-mail environment to protect access through the online portal. For the second "factor," the employee would receive a phone call requesting access to the account. An attacker compromised an employee's credentials and tried to log into the account. As a result, the employee started receiving a number of phone calls requesting they authorize access. The employee got tired of receiving the phone calls, and instead of contacting IT, authorized access bypassing MFA.[9]

---

7. The American Bar Association Cybersecurity Task Force recently published a book to support small businesses with third-party risks. *See* VENDOR CONTRACTING PROJECT: CYBERSECURITY CHECKLIST (2d ed. 2021), https://www.americanbar.org/products/ecd/ebk/411859099/.

8. See Chapter 13 *infra* for a more complete discussion of education and training.

9. *Cybersecurity*, CISA, https://www.cisa.gov/cybersecurity-training-exercises (last visited Nov. 19, 2021).

Training is key and needs to be up-to-date and relevant. Regularly training employees on recognizing and responding to suspicious cyber activity will help you protect your network. Your employees are the first ones who may see that an attack is occurring and let you know so you can take steps to mitigate damage and protect your systems and your clients.

Training should touch on topics like social engineering, vishing,[10] smishing,[11] and phishing.[12] Employees should also be instructed not to open attachments in e-mails from unfamiliar senders. Even if an e-mail is from a familiar name, but it seems peculiar or unexpected, don't open any attachment or click on a link in the e-mail; contact the sender and ask if they sent the e-mail. The attachment or the link may release malware onto the computer. If anyone receives a pop-up that their computer is "infected with a virus," they should know that this is an actual attempt to infect their computer, and it should be ignored or deleted.

6. **Written Information Security Program.** Establish a written information security program (often called a WISP) that outlines the security controls for your systems. The WISP should contain policies that direct employees what they can and cannot do with their firm computer, or while they are in the office (or, if you are a solo practitioner, what you should or shouldn't do). The WISP should also outline the security controls for your security systems and those that vendors are required to follow. Clients often require firms to provide information about

---

10. Vishing is a combination of voice and phishing, and is the attempt to obtain personal information through telephone systems. *See* Genevieve Bookwalter, *What Is Vishing? Tips for Spotting and Avoiding Voice Scams*, Norton, https://us.norton.com/internetsecurity-online -scams-vishing.html (last visited Nov. 19, 2021).

11. Smishing is the attempt by an attacker to obtain personal information via text messages. *See Avoid the Temptation of Smishing Scams*, Fed. Commc'ns Comm'n (Nov. 9, 2018), https://www.fcc.gov/avoid-temptation-smishing-scams.

12. Phishing is an attempt by an attacker to obtain your personal information via email or text messages to gain access to your accounts. *See How to Recognize and Avoid Phishing Scams*, Fed. Trade Comm'n: Consumer Info. (May 2019), https://www.consumer.ftc.gov /articles/how-recognize-and-avoid-phishing-scams.

their security programs, and may request that you provide proof that you have written policies and procedures.

There are a variety of security controls the WISP should address. For instance, you should include a password management policy that requires complex passwords,[13] which are changed on a rolling basis. Part of your password management policy should include immediate cancellation of a password of any employee (including attorneys) who leaves the firm. If any vendors have a password that allows access to your systems, these should be rotated on a routine basis and be terminated if the relationship ends. Set passwords to "lock out" after a set number of failed attempts. And as noted earlier, MFA should be enabled on any remote access.

7. **Backups.** Backups are critical for the resiliency of your system. Establish backups so that you can recover quickly in the event of a physical or security disaster. Attackers frequently gain access to a system and, if they can access it, delete backups. Review your backup configuration to make sure the backups are segmented from your network. If you rely on cloud services or other vendors, make sure they also have a robust backup protocol. Ensure access to the cloud backup is protected by MFA. Attackers will gain access to your system and monitor your activity. One company discovered that during this process, the attackers learned how the backups were set up, obtained the password to its cloud backup, deleted the backups, and then encrypted its systems. Also, make sure that you and your colleagues actually store data on the cloud provider's site, and don't just save items to the local drive. A device may fail due to a mechanical problem, such as a crashed hard drive. Or, a criminal may penetrate your workstation, take your data hostage, and demand a large ransom. Occasionally test the restoration process as well; make sure it works and the restoration process takes hours, not days.

---

13. *See* Whitney Merrill, *Advanced Password Tips and Tricks*, Fed. Trade Comm'n: Consumer Info. (July 30, 2015), https://www.consumer.ftc.gov/blog/2015/07/advanced-password-tips-and-tricks.

8. **Security Incident or Data Breach Preparation.** As mentioned at the beginning of this chapter, it isn't "if" you will experience a cyberattack, but rather "when." Preparation is key, and helps mitigate damages and protect your brand. You should have an incident response plan (IRP) that outlines the steps to take in the event you experience a cyberattack. The IRP should also include key points of contact, such as your cyber insurer. Print the plan out and practice it—if your systems are encrypted, you won't be able to access the plan and having a printed copy is key.[14]

9. **Cyber Insurance.** You've done all of this to enhance your cybersecurity, but you still should have insurance to cover you in the event of a disaster. The terms of cyber insurance policies tend to vary from company to company, and, like any other contract you review, you should make sure that you have a clear understanding of all the provisions.[15] For example, precisely when will coverage start? In some cases, insurance companies may take the position that a loss was due to a breach that occurred prior to the effective date of the policy. Make sure that there is agreement on what constitutes "unauthorized access" to your system. Does it include lost laptops? Does it include someone being tricked into providing a password? Make sure that there is agreement on the level of security that the insurance company considers the minimum acceptable level. Will the policy provide the type of services needed to help you recover from a security incident? Will it help you restore data and establish new (and presumable more robust) security protocols? Will the amount of coverage be sufficient for remediation, or for paying a ransom demand?

10. **Cybersecurity and Data Compliance.** Every year, more laws are enacted or amended that include cybersecurity or privacy requirements for organizations that either do business in that state or in a particular industry. Your clients may have to comply with these requirements if they operate in certain states or industries, and through contract you may be required to do so as well. Although the default requirement

---

14. See Chapter 15 of this Handbook for further discussion of incident preparation.
15. See Chapter 16 of this Handbook for further discussion of cyber insurance.

is that all client communications or attorney work product should be maintained in confidence,[16] other data that may require additional protections or controls (e.g., Intellectual Property, International Traffic in Arms Regulations, information related to acquisitions, or personally identifiable information) should be identified and appropriately protected (e.g., as per Health Information Portability and Accountability Act, Payment Card Industry Data Security Standards, Gramm-Leach-Bliley Act, Family Educational Rights and Privacy Act, or state law).

11. **Other Security Controls.** There are a number of other security controls you should consider implementing. For instance, encryption technology is much less expensive today than it was years ago, and in many instances is included on new devices at no additional cost. Make sure your laptops or workstations are encrypted and ensure any smartphones or other mobile devices connecting to your network are encrypted. Determine whether it is feasible for databases containing sensitive information to be encrypted as well. If you frequently handle highly sensitive information, set up secure file transfer methods for sharing documents with clients or others who may need access. An up-to-date antivirus or endpoint threat detection program should be installed on all devices, including servers, that can be connected to the firm network. You should have a spam filter enabled for e-mails, and employees should be instructed not to install programs on firm computers without approval. Talk to your IT provider about remote methods of connecting to your systems. The most common way systems are compromised is through insecure remote connection protocols.

12. **Document Retention Policy.** If you don't need it, don't keep it. Most document retention policies refer only to how long you may be required to keep information, they generally don't include a require ment to delete data. But the less data you have on your systems, the

---

16. MODEL RULES OF PRO. CONDUCT r. 1.6, Confidentiality of Information: "(a) A lawyer shall not reveal information relating to the representation of a client unless the client gives informed consent, the disclosure is impliedly authorized in order to carry out the representation or the disclosure is permitted by paragraph (b)."

less information you have to protect. Remove data (and paper files) that no longer need to be saved (with consent of clients if it is client information). The less information you have, the smaller the footprint that you need to protect.

Small firms must recognize that they are just as much of a target as larger firms for a cyberattack, and the impact could be even more devastating because small firms lack the IT resources and overall funding of larger firms. Although the preceding list might feel overwhelming, many of the suggestions can be implemented at little to no cost. And overall, the cost of a cyberattack is much more expensive than taking the steps now to protect your systems, your data, and your clients.

Chapter 10
In-House Counsel
Angeline G. Chen

I. The Cyber Threat Landscape for In-House Counsel

> Nothing in life is to be feared, it is only to be understood. Now is the
> time to understand more, so that we may fear less.
>
> — Marie Curie

Over the last three decades and more, greater scrutiny has been placed on
the changing role of general counsel along with, by extension, all in-house
counsel.[1] In addition to being formal stewards of legal and compliance
matters for their respective companies, in-house counsel are regularly now
called upon to serve in a much broader role as executive leaders, fully
integrated business partners, risk managers, participants in creating the
company's strategies, and "key members of the corporate decision-making
team."[2] At the same time, larger macro-level developments and technological advancements are transforming the corporate environments in which
these lawyers operate.

---

1. See, e.g., Wendy King, 5 New Roles the General Counsel Is Expected to Fill
in 2021, JDSupra (Feb. 3, 2021), https:/www.jdsupra.com/legalnews/5-new-roles
-the-general-counsel-is-8546725/; Angus Haig, The Evolving Role of In-House Counsel, Ctr. for Legal Leadership, https://www.legalleadership.co.uk/knowledge
/progressing-my-career/enhancing-your-role/the-evolving-role-of-in-house-counsel/ (last
visited Aug. 26, 2021); Elaine McArdle, In the Driver's Seat: The Changing Role of the
General Counsel, Harv. Law Today (July 1, 2012), https://today.law.harvard.edu/feature
/in-the-drivers-seat-the-changing-role-of-the-general-counsel/.
2. See McArdle, supra note 1.

In his book *Thank You for Being Late*,[3] author and columnist Thomas Friedman notes the "Age of Acceleration" is upon us as a result of the convergence of several global and interdependent trends in the economic, environmental, and societal domains. As the corporate world is swept into and competes in this Age of Acceleration, digitalizing[4] and transforming at an accelerated rate of organizational convergence and expansion, the legal profession adapts.

Meanwhile, global drivers ranging from the growing focus on ESG and CSR principles, shifting political philosophies, social unrest such as "Occupy Wall Street" and worldwide protests on issues of social justice and racial inequality, and the coronavirus pandemic highlight the imperative for general counsel to also be positioned to provide insights and guidance on how companies must traverse increasingly complex environments.[5] As the environments in which the general counsel's entity operates change and evolve, and become more fluid and subject to different external factors, the general counsel must adapt and learn and gather sufficient information, skills, and resources to best advise and influence the entity.

It is against this backdrop that in-house counsel, whose core responsibility remains advising and counseling their companies on how to navigate the legal parameters of their organizational existence, must be prepared to

---

3. THOMAS L. FRIEDMAN, THANK YOU FOR BEING LATE: AN OPTIMIST'S GUIDE TO THRIVING IN THE AGE OF ACCELERATION (Farrar, Straus & Giroux, Nov. 2016).

4. It is important to recognize the difference between "digitization," which refers to the act of converting physical or analog things such as paper documents, photographs, sounds, etc., into digital form, i.e. bits and bytes and "digitalization," which refers to a transformation of the workplace through the integration of digital technologies and *digitized* information in order to create revenue, increase business optimization and efficiencies, transform processes, and otherwise create a work environment that leverages full and deliberate engagement of business systems and processes.

5. *See, e.g.*, Matthew K. Fawcett, *Insight: GCs Must Balance ESG in an Age of Activism*, BLOOMBERG LAW (Mar. 4, 2020), https://news.bloomberglaw.com/us-law-week/insight-gcs -must-balance-esg-in-an-age-of-activism; Michael W. Peregrine, *The General Counsel as Key Corporate Social Responsibility Advisor*, HARV. LAW SCH. FORUM ON CORP. GOVERNANCE (June 24, 2018), https://corpgov.law.harvard.edu/2018/06/24/the-general-counsel-as-key -corporate-social-responsibility-advisor/; John Amer, *The General Counsel as Senior Leader: More Than "Just a Lawyer,"* KORN FERRY, https://www.kornferry.com/insights/articles/gen eral-counsel-senior-leader-more-just-lawyer (last visited Aug. 26, 2021); Lauren Boehmke & Matt Hurd, *How Covid-19 Is Changing the General Counsel's Leadership Role*, CORP. SEC'Y (Jan. 5, 2021), https://www.corporatesecretary.com/articles/covid-19/32411 /how-covid-19-changing-general-counsel%E2%80%99s-leadership-role.

understand and advise their clientele on how to address the legal aspects of cyber security requirements and threats.

A. Role Differentiation

The role of in-house counsel is materially distinct from that of outside counsel in several ways. While it is beyond the scope of this chapter to address all of these differences in depth, it is worth noting some of the core aspects of being in-house that make addressing cybersecurity issues all the more challenging.

In Chapters 8 and 9, this Handbook discusses factors relevant for consideration by law firms in dealing with cybersecurity. The examination of cyber issues set forth in those chapters is equally and directly applicable to corporate law departments, and so we encourage you to review those chapters closely. Law firms, however, independent of size or practice area(s), share core commonalities. They predominantly adopt a hierarchical model for operations to meet the singular purpose of providing legal services as a business. Presumably, the firm takes those client representations whose needs align with the firm's specific areas of expertise, but the services offered are the same: legal advice. Both parties to the transaction understand the parameters of the work product to be provided by the law firm, viz., professionally sound legal advice addressing the specific issue or question articulated by the client(s).

In-house attorneys work for the sole benefit of a single client: the corporation.[6] Companies have different DNA than law firms, (1) having a broader, complex charter addressing the full scope of needs arising from a wider and often varied scope and nature of products, services, or solutions offered to the marketplace; and (2) encompassing the interdependencies of the functions and entire workforce devoted to the company charter. In-house attorneys are integrated into the business on a sustained basis, not just for specific projects bounded by time or on a negotiated retainer, or even for designated topical areas. And while in-house counsel have one,

---

6. While we reference the "corporation" throughout this chapter, the gist of the discussion and analysis set forth herein are also relevant to nonprofit organizations and associations, and government attorneys the key focus here being that the general counsel's client is the entity by which he or she is employed. For more specifically focused discussion, see Chapters 11 and 12.

and only one, client—the corporation[7]—this carries with it the affirmative obligation to advance the needs of the corporation over that of any individual employee (even corporate officers and directors) if the latter conflicts with the corporation's best interest.[8] Thus, in addition to being required to act in a professional capacity as an attorney, in-house counsel's fiduciary duty is to serve and advance the needs of the business above all else.[9] This deceptively simple statement may seem to bear no distinction from the role of a law firm until one considers the fact that a corporation—as a juridical entity—is more than the sum of its parts (e.g., the industry in which the company operates, the full breadth of its business and operational activity, its management, its workforce, its governance structure, its shareholders, the geographical locations in which it does business, and the like), to which the in-house attorney must serve as a constant legal counselor and business partner. Outside counsel, no matter how skilled or client focused, are by definition always outsiders to the business; outside counsel can only see what is parceled to them and thus can understand and advise solely on selected windows into the corporate organism.[10]

Today's in-house attorney must develop a broad range of competencies beyond expertise in a specific area(s) of the law; they must learn to think and act operationally.[11] The successful in-house attorney must develop a broader business understanding, deeper expertise in compliance and risk management, and the ability to manage the legal function and execute legal tasks independently and collaboratively as a critical part of the company, to serve as leaders and influential advisors, and to be fully engaged in the

---

7. *See* MODEL RULES OF PRO. CONDUCT r 1.13(a) (2021) [hereinafter "MRPC"], which provides "A lawyer employed or retained by an organization represents the organization acting through its duly authorized constituents."

8. MRPC 1.13(b).

9. ACC, *Becoming In-House Counsel: A Guide for Law Students and Recent Graduates*, ASS'N OF CORP. COUNSEL 1 (Dec. 3, 2013), https://www.acc.com/resource-library /becoming-house-counsel-guide-law-students-and-recent-graduates.

10. This is not to discount the effectiveness and value of outside counsel who establish committed relationships with their clients to better understand the company's needs, or who ably service smaller companies who do not have in-house attorneys.

11. *See* McArdle, *supra* note 1; Harish Suryavanshi, *Today's In-House Counsel: Evolving Roles as Business Enablers*, ASS'N OF CORP. COUNSEL 61 (Jan. 1, 2014), https://www.acc.com /resource-library/todays-house-counsel-evolving-roles-business-enablers.

company's strategic activities.[12] In today's accelerated business environment, in-house counsel cannot wait for their advice to be sought, but instead must now be on the frontlines with—and even ahead of—the business. These skills are precisely aligned with how the in-house attorney must prepare to tackle the unique and distinctive legal challenges presented by cybersecurity.

B.   The In-House Perspective

Legal analysis of cybersecurity issues in the corporate environment must take into account corporate strategy and enterprise risk management plans, environmental variables of the relevant workplace, workforce and system considerations, actual and potential interdependencies, and operational impacts.

Everything explored and discussed in this Handbook becomes amplified. In-house counsel is tasked with understanding the laws, regulations, and policies relevant to cybersecurity—ongoing, emergent, and proactive. In-house counsel is also charged with determining the applicability and implementation of such legal requirements to the company's operations, business activities, and strategies. The in-house attorney must execute this task in a manner that appropriately balances adherence to the law and attendant risks, while still facilitating the company's business objectives and positioning the company to achieve same in a compliant and sustainable manner. This can only be accomplished through supporting, relying upon, and coordinating closely with other interdependent functions and personnel, many of whom may be outside or independent of the decision-making chain involved in executing any legal advice given. While some of these responsibilities can be outsourced, ultimately in-house counsel bears the responsibility for identifying the issue and determining what resources are needed, including budget allocation and competent management of same, if outside counsel is deemed appropriate.

---

12. *See* Elizabeth Benegas, *Be Proactive: 5 Ways for In-House Legal Teams to Build a Better Relationship with the Business*, ACC DOCKET (Dec. 23, 2020), https://www.accdocket.com/be -proactive-5-ways-house-legal-teams-build-better-relationship-business; *Summary of In-house Legal Teams: Identifying and Nurturing Value*, LEXISNEXIS UK REPORT (2013), http://www .lexisnexis.co.uk/pdf/0413-017_In-house_legal_teams-Identifying_and_nurturing_value.pdf.

Moreover, outside counsel cannot replicate the internal day-to-day relationships integral to effective execution of legal guidance on a corporation's operational activities. There is a reason why so many in-house counsel tout variety and constant intellectual challenge as one of the most significant reasons they love their jobs, and why general counsel ultimately must become a Jack (or Jill) of all trades while a master of some.[13]

Key aspects of the cyber threat are clear: (1) the cyber threat is real—every company is a target;[14] (2) the types and avenues for attack continue to grow and become more sophisticated; (3) the attackers come from different sources—both external and internal—and have different motivations; (4) each attack or cyber incident creates a myriad of situation-specific issues requiring legal review and advice; (5) while certain risks can be articulated, the distinction between legal and business risks is likely to be blurred or more inherently interdependent in the cyber domain than in other areas; (6) there is less certainty of the outcome from the trade-offs of these interdependent risks; and (7) it is often not intuitive what laws and regulations may be implicated (or may be in potential conflict with each other) for any given issue or situation, or even if such laws and regulations exist. As a result, it is indisputable that companies can no longer ignore the threat, and shareholders are increasingly holding corporations accountable for their cybersecurity postures.[15] As former FBI Director Robert S. Mueller III

---

13. *See* McArdle, *supra* note 1.

14. *See* Jason Remilard, *50 Things You Need to Know to Optimize Your Company's Approach to Data Privacy and Cybersecurity*, ENTREPRENEUR (June 22, 2021), https://www.entrepreneur.com/slideshow/365902; Steve Ursillo, Jr. & Christopher Arnold, *Cybersecurity Is Critical for All Organizations – Large and Small*, IFAC (Nov. 4, 2019), https://www.ifac.org/knowledge-gateway/preparing-future-ready-professionals/discussion/cybersecurity-critical-all-organizations-large-and-small; Andrew Martins, *Cyberthreats Named the Most Concerning Issue for Businesses*, BUS. NEWS DAILY (Sept. 30, 2019), https://www.businessnewsdaily.com/15295-cyberthreats-biggest-business-concern.html; Daniel Lohrmann, *The Top 17 Security Predictions for 2017*, GOV'T TECH. (Jan. 8, 2017), http://www.govtech.com/blogs/lohrmann-on-cybersecurity/the-top-17-security- predictions-for-2017.html.

15. *See* Eric B. Stern & Andrew A. Lipkowitz, *Shareholder Lawsuits Arising from Cyber Incidents and Implications for Potential Insurance Coverage*, LAW.COM (Aug. 19, 2020), https://www.law.com/insurance-coverage-law-center/2020/08/19/shareholder-lawsuits-arising-from-cyber-incidents-and-implications-for-potential-insurance-coverage/?slret urn=20210128160923.

stated in 2012, "[t]here are only two types of companies: those that have been hacked and those that will be hacked."[16]

In-house lawyers are uniquely positioned to provide critical insights and recommendations on the development of mitigation and defensive steps that work for their company that stay within the parameters of the evolving legal and regulatory landscape. The influence and role of in-house counsel in supporting, and sometimes leading, the entity's corporate governance efforts with respect to cybersecurity, is increasing, especially where there are conflicts of interest between or amongst stakeholders that carry legal ramifications. The company's legal department must weigh in when this occurs, and ultimately arbitrate if such conflicts cannot be resolved.[17]

C. Duties and Responsibilities

The in-house attorney's specific duties and responsibilities will influence the level and scope of cybersecurity law competencies required. A quick assessment of what these might look like can be divided into two areas: those pertinent to the specific attorney's role, and those pertinent to the corporation as an organization.

Any attorney presumably understands the basic aspects of his or her role, and perhaps the associated technical responsibilities. For example, an in-house M&A attorney will know that steps will need to be taken to protect proprietary information regarding deals. An employment attorney will know that personally identifiable information will need to be properly managed and secured. Positionally, a general counsel (GC) or chief legal officer (CLO) has a broader base of competencies and interface with executive and upper management as peers, as well as possibly with the board of

---

16. Robert S. Mueller, III, Remarks at RSA Cyber Security Conference, San Francisco, CA (Mar. 1, 2012), https://archives.fbi.gov/archives/news/speeches/combating-threats-in-the -cyber-world-outsmarting-terrorists-hackers-and-spies. *See also* Richard Bejtlich, *The Origin of the Quote "There Are Two Types of Companies,"* TaoSecurity Blog (Dec. 18, 2018), https://taosecurity.blogspot.com/2018/12/the-origin-of-quote-there-are-two-types.html [https:// perma.cc/48V7-3L87] (exploring the history of the commonly used phrase "There are two Types of Companies").

17. *See, e.g.,* H. Jeff Smith, *The Shareholders vs Stakeholders Debate,* MITSloan Mgmt. Rev. (July 15, 2003), http://sloanreview.mit.edu/article/the-shareholders-vs-stakeholders -debate/ (noting such conflicts are addressed through legal application of the existing duties of care and loyalty).

directors. In addition, being in charge of managing the legal function and activities of the corporation places the GC or CLO in the ultimate position of responsibility for, at a minimum, addressing the legal aspects of cyber threats or a cyber incident either directly or through staff and/or additional resources. Next-tier attorneys leading business units or groups of specialists may also have a similar scope as the GC, whereas specialists will need to and should focus on cybersecurity developments pertinent to their area and internal client base. In-house counsel also often play a key role in drafting or reviewing company policies and procedures.

A key competency is of particular relevance in the cyber domain: emotional intelligence and the ability to collaborate on a 360-degree basis. The ability to interact with others in an effective and empathetic manner is already important for any in-house attorney, drawing directly on the capabilities to not only recognize, understand, and manage one's own emotions but also to do the same and influence the emotions of others.[18] When dealing with understanding both the impact and defensive strategies relating to cybersecurity, understanding workforce motivations and behaviors is key. People are at the center of the effort to secure data and establishing a culture of cybersecurity awareness and vigilance; human error remains one of the highest risk factors in the cause of cyber incidents.[19] Understanding the different motivations of hackers assists in identifying the potential attack vectors and designing optimized mitigations against phishing attacks and other types of social engineering.[20] This competency is thus critical in

---

18. Ronda Muir, *Emotional Intelligence for Lawyers*, AM. BAR ASS'N (Sept. 30, 2015), https://www.americanbar.org/careercenter/blog/emotional-intelligence-for-lawyers/. *See also* DANIEL GOLEMAN, EMOTIONAL INTELLIGENCE: WHY IT CAN MATTER MORE THAN IQ (New York: Bantam Books 1995). For the importance of emotional intelligence in business leaders, see Jeff Moss, *Emotional Intelligence in Business and Leadership*, FORBES (Nov. 13, 2018), https://www.forbes.com/sites/forbesnycouncil/2018/11/13/emotional-intelligence-in-business -and-leadership/?sh=603cfc2459eb; Joe Makhluf, *The Importance of Emotional Intelligence in Business*, THE BUS. J. (Aug. 11, 2017), https://www.bizjournals.com/bizjournals/how-to /human-resources/2017/08/the-importance-of-emotional-intelligence-in.html.

19. Nadja El Fertasi, *Three Ways to Leverage Emotional Intelligence and Minimize Cyber Risk through Human Vulnerability*, GLOBAL CYBERALLIANCE ORG. (Nov. 10, 2020), https:// www.globalcyberalliance.org/three-ways-to-leverage-emotional-intelligence-and-minimize -cyber-risk-through-human-vulnerability/.

20. Phishing remains one of the top attack vectors in cybersecurity breaches. *See* VERIZON COMMC'NS, 2020 DATA BREACH INVESTIGATIONS REPORT, https://www.cisecurity.org/wp -content/uploads/2020/07/The-2020-Verizon-Data-Breach-Investigations-Report-DBIR.pdf.

enabling a company to successfully prepare and execute a sound strategy and plan to address cyber incidents in a manner that is legally compliant, and also navigates the company through the competitive business environment, to the most optimal outcome.

II. Fundamentals of What In-House Counsel Needs to Know

A. The Basics

Statistical data regarding the vulnerability of companies to cyber threats and highly visible examples of breached companies are available and covered in the news almost daily. In-house counsel may be tempted to defer tackling the challenges of cybersecurity, electing instead to operate under the assumption that the responsibility lies with some other part of the company; to wait until they are directed to review the issues; or perhaps to decide that the easier path would be to take the chance that they will not be confronted with a cyber incident. As the continuing trend of high-visibility cyber incidents and their impacts continue such as the SolarWinds breach in 2020 and the Colonial Pipeline and JBS cyber breaches in 2021,[21] as well as cases such as the Yahoo breach (and the subsequent departure of Yahoo's executive management, including the general counsel) illustrate, however, such assumptions may prove to be a fallacy, where not only the attorney might suffer misfortune but others, including both the company and its customer base, as well.[22]

From a more positive aspect, this area also provides in-house counsel with an opportunity to develop new expertise and key competencies, and to potentially gain visibility for recognition or advancement. Having at least a rudimentary grasp of cybersecurity issues is arguably now a requirement

---

21. See list of significant cyber incidents by year as tracked by the Center for Strategic & International Studies, found at https://www.csls.org/programs/strategic-technologies-program /significant-cyber-incidents.

22. *See, e.g.*, Jennifer Williams-Alvarez, *After Yahoo, Are In-House Counsel Jobs At Risk Over Cybersecurity?* CORP. COUNSEL (Mar. 2, 2017), http://www.corpcounsel.com/printer friendly/id=1202780379239; William Vogeler, *Why Your In-House Job Is At Risk Over Cybersecurity*, FINDLAW (Mar. 7, 2017), http://blogs.findlaw.com/in_house/2017/03/why -your-in-house-job-is-at-risk-over-cybersecurity.html.

for in-house counsel, certainly the general counsel or CLO, as well as for executive management and the board.[23]

In-house counsel may wonder where to start. As with other legal risks, the risks of cyber must be articulated in a manner relevant to the context of the business. This is necessary to establish common understanding with other functions, and to garner necessary resources (internal and external talent and budget). In order to initiate this discussion *in advance* of a risk being realized, the attorney must be armed with facts and speak from the position of risk management. There are ample resources available to assist in this endeavor. As but one example, in April 2018, the National Institute of Standards and Technology (NIST) issued an updated Cybersecurity Framework, which utilizes a risk management approach to lay out processes that can help enable companies to become informed about cybersecurity and better prioritize decisions.[24]

B.   The Amorphous and Unusual Nature of the Threat Compared to Traditional Risks

Cyber threats are equal opportunity. In this area, size truly does not matter, nor does industry sector. No one is safe. It is clear that large corporations are targets, especially in certain industry sectors such as health care, defense, and financial, due to the core nature of the data in which those industries traffic. Small companies in particular, however, should also be aware. Verizon's 2016 Data Breach Report provided sobering confirmation that nearly 60 percent of cyber breaches resulting in data loss occurred in small companies (defined as having fewer than 1,000 employees).[25] And while Verizon's 2020 Data Breach Report indicates that only 28 percent of breaches for that year involved small business victims, even assuming this number isn't impacted by underreporting, this percentage can be deceiving as it does not

---

23. *See* Christopher Skroupa, *Legalities of a Cyber Breach—Heed Your In-House Counsel*, Company Resilience (Sept. 7, 2016), https://skytopstrategies.com /legalities-cyber-breach-heed-house-counsel/.

24. Nat'l Inst. of Standards & Tech., Framework for Improving Critical Infrastructure Cybersecurity Ver. 1.1 (Apr. 16, 2018), https://nvlpubs.nist.gov/nistpubs/CSWP /NIST.CSWP.04162018.pdf.

25. Verizon Commc'ns, 2016 Verizon Data Breach Report, http://www.verizon enterprise.com/resources/reports/rp_DBIR_2016_Report_en_xg.pdf.

contradict the disproportionate impact and consequences a breach can have for small businesses with fewer resources and capabilities to rebound and for which cyber breaches can be catastrophic.[26]

The threat emanates from a number of places external and internal, from different actors with different motivations ranging from nation-states to organized crime syndicates to cyber-savvy criminals to hacktivists to employees with malicious intent or who are simply careless.[27] Any one or more of these threats could be directed at any or all facets of the business: from the systems (to disrupt or halt operations) to the data (corporate espionage, corruption of information) to the personnel (identity theft, access, blackmail) to the end customer or end use (counterfeit parts). Attacks do not need to be sequential or coordinated. The price and barriers to entry are low, with hacking tools and codes easily available on the Internet and dark nets, often for free. Last, the nature of the cyber domain is that it is literally "on" 24/7/365.

C.   Identifying Interdependencies and Establishing Essential Relationships

In-house counsel must work with other departments that form the organizational framework of the company in a manner that mitigates the risks created by the threat. Cyber risks include a combination of external attacks, insider threats, company information system and device vulnerabilities, and operational risks. Consideration should be given to how each of these threats might manifest itself in the corporate environment, and appropriate mitigation options identified and analyzed for effectiveness in addressing each of the risks. An established relationship between the legal and IT team is essential, especially in the period preparing for a breach and reacting to one.[28] Of equal importance is a strong working relationship with human resources, as a critical element of being able to educate the workforce and build a cyber-savvy culture. In addition to ensuring clear communication

---

26. *See supra* note 20.

27. *See Inside the FBI: Director Comey Addresses Cybersecurity Experts*, INSIDE THE FBI (Sept. 2, 2016), https://www.fbi.gov/audio-repository/inside-podcast-comey-cyber-speech-090216.mp3/view.

28. *See* GUERRERO HOWE, THE GENERAL COUNSEL'S GUIDE TO DIGITAL DEFENSE (Sept. 20, 2016).

and strong relationships are built with other key functions, so too must the relationships with senior management and the shareholders be considered as essential to implementing effective cybersecurity practices and corresponding legal advice.

Relationships should also be established with certain governmental agencies such as the FBI that have cybersecurity resources and knowledge, in order to establish an open dialogue of cooperation. The government is playing an increasing role in the notification of companies of cyber breaches, often when the companies themselves are unaware of the ongoing attack.[29] Companies are better served if they are able to draw upon an existing communication channel and partnership in the event the government must be notified or assistance is being requested in the event of a breach. Traditional views that argue against sharing information regarding a cyber breach with the government, especially law enforcement, typically arise out of fear of retributive enforcement actions or loss of competitive data. The more persuasive argument, however, in the face of the increasing cyber threat is that the private sector is far better served by sharing information and drawing upon the considerable expertise and knowledge of the U.S. government to the greatest extent possible.[30]

Governmental agencies and relationships are likewise goldmines for information useful to the company, enabling companies to have a more global view and understanding of how the cyber threat landscape is evolving. As

---

29. While exact numbers are not available, a recent report released by the Office of the Inspector General (OIG) of the U.S. Department of Justice (DoJ) indicated that as of 2017, more than 20,000 notifications had been issued by the Federal Bureau of Investigation (FBI) to companies impacted by cyberbreaches through the FBI's Cyber Guardian program. DoJ OIG audit report of the FBI's cyber victim notification process. Off. of the Inspector Gen., *Audit of the Federal Bureau of Investigation's Cyber Victim Notification Process*, Dep't of Justice (Mar. 2019), https://oig.justice.gov/reports/2019/a1923.pdf. *See also* Ellen Nakashima, *U.S. Notified 3,000 Companies in 2013 about Cyberattacks*, Wash. Post (Mar. 24, 2014), https://www.washingtonpost.com/world/national-security/2014/03/24/74aff686-aed9-11e3 -96dc-d6ea14c099f9_story.html.

30. *See* James B. Comey, Privacy, Public Safety, and Security: How We Can Confront the Cyber Threat Together, Remarks at the International Conference on Cyber Engagement at Georgetown University, Washington, D.C. (Apr. 26, 2016). *See also* Kimberly Peretti & Lou Dennig, *What In-House Counsel Should Know About Cybersecurity Information Sharing*, Corp. Counsel (July 7, 2016), http://www.corpcounsel.com/id=1202761997713/What -InHouse-Counsel-Should-Know-About- Cybersecurity-Information-Sharing (positing that the benefits outweigh any perceived risks).

the government itself is constantly under cyberattack, industry benefits from the government's "lessons learned" and a more informed understanding of where to focus limited resources, such as on the "insider threat."[31] Other data available from the government provides insight into the types of attacks (e.g., nation-state versus organized crime) and new types of threat vectors.[32] Such data is useful in helping to better tailor company policies and practices, and in developing more effective mitigation measures and controls.

Legal should also develop a strong and open relationship with the Communications Department, which can be drawn upon when needed. In the aftermath of a cyber incident, Communications should be briefed and prepared to answer questions from the media and customers, following an appropriately crafted cyber incident/cyber response plan (which should incorporate a communication plan). This is a key element in how the company can mitigate the potential for extensive reputational damage, or at least avoid exacerbating a bad situation through an ill-advised remark or (in today's news- and rumor-hungry climate) a failure to make a public statement, and share the company's perspective openly.

Other key relationships should be tended in a manner prioritized in accordance with the company's business and internal infrastructure, but which reasonably would include finance, supply chain, as well as certain consultants, key business partners, along with the board of directors.

---

31. In Verizon's 2020 Data Breach Incident Report, data confirmed that the majority of cybersecurity incidents arose from either accidental or negligent cyber hygiene on the part of employees. *See supra* note 20. *See also* SentinelOne, *Insider Threats in Cyber Security—More Than Just Human Error*, SENTINELONE (Dec. 9, 2016), https://www.sentinelone.com/blog/insider-threats-in-cyber-security-more-than just-human-error/.

32. New technologies introduce new vulnerabilities, especially when combined with increased dependence on Internet-of-Things devices and cloud-based content management systems. Attacks are increasing in number (e.g., ransomware attacks increased by nearly 500 percent in 2020, BITDEFENDER, 2020 CONSUMER THREAT LANDSCAPE REPORT, https://www.bitdefender.com/files/News/CaseStudies/study/395/Bitdefender-2020-Consumer-Threat Landscape-Report.pdf), and sophistication, as evidenced by the zero day exploits used to attack on-premises versions of Microsoft Exchange Server (the "HAFNIUM" attack).

D. Distinguishing Advice for Operational Matter Compliance from Legal and Regulatory Compliance

Finally, the in-house attorney must keep in mind the differences in providing advice for operational business activities, such as how to ensure business data remains available in a manner that allows the business to continue operating; for litigation or matters in formal legal dispute fora; and for legal and regulatory purposes, such as appropriately defining and protecting specific categories of data such as personally identifiable information or health information, and disclosures required by SEC or other governmental requirements.[33]

Operational compliance addresses the identification and mitigation of the risk of loss or failure of controls that result from inadequate or failed internal processes, people, and systems or from external events.[34] Operational risks include legal risks, but exclude strategic and reputational risks. Market-based considerations address customer relations and communications, industry coalitions, interactions with business partners or competitors, and public relations, all of which may implicate legal or regulatory considerations. In contrast, legal and regulatory compliance addresses the consequences of failure to comply with specific laws, regulations, rules, codes of conduct or duties, or other standards monitored or enforced by agencies or organizations that are applicable to the entity or industry.

Examples of operational compliance might include ensuring a company maintains an ISO certification, follows a sound strategic sourcing process, or advising on the establishment of disciplined supply chain security. Market-based considerations might involve advising on a new branding campaign, working with a trade association on new provisions of the Federal Acquisition Regulations, or establishing or revising new standards.

---

33. For publicly traded companies the lawyer can be expected to play a key role in ascertaining what needs to be publicly disclosed under SEC regulations versus potentially disclosing excessive information.

34. *See, e.g.,* Off. of the Comptroller of the Currency, Comptroller's Handbook: Corporate and Risk Governance (ver. 2.0, July 2019), https://www.occ.gov/publications-and-resources/publications/comptrollers-handbook/files/corporate-risk-governance/pub-ch-corporate-risk.pdf; Basel Comm. on Banking Supervision, *Principles for the Sound Management of Operational Risk* (June 2011), https://www.bis.org/publ/bcbs195.htm.

III. Be Prepared

In-house counsel should be proactive in ensuring the company is positioned as best as possible—within the parameters of available resources and maturity of the entity's corporate governance framework—to handle a cyber incident. How to best prepare? Certain fundamentals can be identified and prioritized in a tailored manner, taking into account existing resources (e.g., if there is an IT group or if IT is outsourced), corporate structure, existing command media, and so on, and starting with a basic plan of attack that incorporates the following elements.

A. Understand as Much as You Can about the Risks

1. Read, Absorb, Translate, and Stay Current
Bad actors in the cyber domain are getting better and smarter. Cyber-related issues are relevant to virtually all aspects of in-house practice (e.g., handling of electronically stored HIPAA-protected or personally identifiable information, digitized trade secrets or M&A documentation, company-sensitive and market competitive information, or embedded software being sold to an end consumer). In-house counsel must do what attorneys always must do: seek and obtain as much information as you can about the risks associated with cybersecurity, focused on your company's particular industry and your specific role (e.g., a general counsel versus a specialty area such as ERISA or labor and employment) and the organizational infrastructure in which you sit.

The dynamic and evolving nature of cybersecurity demands that in-house counsel stay abreast of new developments as much as possible. New methods of attack and compromise are developed every day, and originate from multiple sources and means. As technology evolves, so does the attack surface area of your company. Regular refreshes of what you know and assumptions that might be relied on in establishing your company's cybersecurity posture are a sound practice.

Determine the most efficient way to get to the information most relevant to you and your company. Sign up for alerts on proposed regulations, developments, and industry trends. Follow blogs focused on legal issues associated with cybersecurity. Many law firms provide cybersecurity news feeds, webinars, and panel presentations that lay out high-level overviews and preliminary analysis in the area. This information can be distilled and communicated to stakeholders.

2. Don't Reinvent the Wheel

Due to the incredibly amorphous nature of cybersecurity, it is impossible for one attorney to know everything (which underscores the imperative for creating a team to address cyber threats and a network to stay current on developments and trends in the law concerning cybersecurity). The good news is that a sufficient number of experts, organizations, and institutions have been tackling the issue for decades. Even if from different perspectives, there is a wealth of information available through the Internet and other channels, often at little or no cost. Find credible information and facts from reputable sources such as this Handbook; the 2020 ACC Foundation Report on the State of Cybersecurity; and governmental agencies such as the FBI, National Institute of Standards and Technology, and the Department of Commerce, which post significant amounts of information and practical tips regarding cybersecurity. In many instances, governmental entities will issue guidance documents in an effort to educate specific industries.[35] Certain sectors, such as aerospace and defense, have been driven by the national security imperative, to develop cybersecurity frameworks (such as the Department of Defense's Cybersecurity Maturity Model) and best practices (such as those captured in standards like NIST 800-171) that can be leveraged and used for benchmarking and gap assessments.

3. Know Your Client

In-house counsel must apply the knowledge gathered to a specific corporation. This requires understanding the company's industry, business model, products and services, workforce composition, governance framework, and the like. Does your company operate globally? Does your industry carry specific regulations (such as health care, financial, or defense)? Is it publicly

---

35. *See, e.g., Cybersecurity*, U.S. Food & Drug Admin., https://www.fda.gov/medical
-devices/digital-health-center-excellence/cybersecurity (last visited Aug. 26, 2021).

traded? Do you have represented employees or employees with diverse citizenships or locations? Are you in manufacturing? Do you engage in research and development? Are there certain products, services, or strategies that expose the company to specific types or greater levels of cyber threats than others? Are the laws most relevant to your company's industry or market sector being expanded to now include cybersecurity or other relevant data management or recordkeeping requirements (which would apply to digitized information or to your company's systems and networks)?

4. Know What and Where Your Crown Jewels Are

Any digitized data or physical facility (accessible through electronic controls such as badges, etc.) of value is a target. Information of your customers and of your workforce are also attractive targets (sometimes indirectly, for instance, as a means of finding an entry point to compromising your company's systems). Effective policies and procedures and a sound incident response plan requires knowing where the most important information and data of the company are stored. Being able to create data maps and data inventories is necessary for creating an effective breach response plan. Creation of such data maps and inventories can be labor intensive, and must take into account the constantly changing type, amount, and state of data managed by the corporation.[36] Without them, however, there is no way to otherwise determine what has been lost or compromised in the event of a cyber breach (a necessary step to determining the extent and nature of a breach and thereby what legal obligations may apply and next steps must be taken).[37]

---

36. David Zetoony, *Data Privacy and Security: A Practical Guide for In-House Counsel*, 77 WASH. LEGAL FOUND.: CONTEMPORARY LEGAL NOTE SERIES 1–2 (May 2016), https://iapp.org/media/pdf/resource_center/WLFDataPrivacyandSecurityHandbook.pdf (hereinafter "Data Privacy and Security Guide") (provides excellent roadmap to setting up a data security plan).

37. Brad Brian & Grant Davis-Denny, *Data Breaches and the Role of the In-House Attorney*, U.S. NEWS—BEST LAWYERS 36–37 (2016).

B. Ensure That the Company's Governance Framework Encompasses Cybersecurity, and Develop Cyber Incident and Cyber-Breach Plans That Align with That Framework

Cyber incidents and company response planning should be considered from an enterprise-wide level. This should entail development of a cyber breach and cyber incident response plan that takes into account all functions and incorporates a communications plan. It should also include periodic reassessments of the company's cyber response plan, command media (policies and procedures), and organizational resources, in order to identify any potential competency gaps in personnel or functional responsibilities.

1. Cyber Incident / Cyber Breach Response Plan

Many companies have crisis management plans. Cyber incident response plans can leverage such plans, but should also lay out particular steps to be taken in the event of a cyber event, in order to ensure specific elements of responding to a cyber event are addressed. The plan must be actionable and *practical*—in drafting the plan, it is advisable to obtain inputs from those functions and key personnel who will be involved in different roles during execution. It is helpful to follow the risk management process approach known as the RACI model, where the plan clearly identifies what departments or individuals are *Responsible* for the specific issue or action; to whom each such individual is *Accountable* and who must *Approve* decisions or actions to be taken; what department or individuals are in a *Supporting* role; who must be *Consulted* in order to complete the task(s); and who must be *Informed* of status or results, but may not necessarily need to be consulted.[38]

The key elements of the response plan[39] should include:

- Identification of the response team, including the team lead. All team members should also have identified backups;

---

38. *See RACI Model Summary*, VALUEBASEDMANAGEMENT.NET, http://www.valuebased management.net/methods_raci.html (last visited Aug. 26, 2021).

39. Certain industries, such as the health care sector, have industry-specific requirements, such as compliance with the Health Insurance Portability and Accountability Act of 1996 (HIPAA). Any such applicable industry-specific legal or regulatory requirements should be incorporated into the response plan and communication plans.

- Provision for training on execution of the plan, in addition to substantive training on relevant policies and procedures. Active drills should be held on a periodic basis as if the company was responding to an actual cyber event;
- Checklists identifying what should be done, by whom, and what needs to be documented, during and throughout various stages of the cyber event;
- Provision for identifying and fixing the cause of the breach, while continuing to conduct forensics to determine the extent and cause of the damage;
- Identification of all legal obligations and conflicting requirements or initiatives;
- A communications plan that provides for status reports to executive management, the board of directors, as well as a public affairs and customer relations component to address any messaging to clients and the public;[40]
- Contact information for any third-party consultants and service providers, such as identity theft and data breach resolution vendors.

Form notifications and responses to queries can be drafted in advance, to save time and effort in the midst of responding to a cyber event. This can prove especially helpful for small companies with limited resources.

2. Policies and Procedures

The company should review its policies and procedures to ensure they align with the incident response plan and vice versa, as well as to ensure there are no gaps in the policies and procedures relating to cybersecurity concerns. As an example, if employees are permitted to use personal devices for work, the company should have well-crafted bring your own device policies, in addition to password and other standard information security policies. Due to the quick cycle of upgrades to technology and developing law, the company should review its command media pertinent to cyber issues on an annual or more frequent basis.

---

40. Consideration can also be given to engaging a public relations firm specializing in crisis management in the event of a significant or large enough breach.

3. Checklist for Assessing the Company Governance Framework and Response Plan and Evaluating the Company's Cybersecurity Posture on a Periodic Basis

A general checklist can be useful in assessing the company's governance framework. The following questions can help identify potential gaps:

- Are cybersecurity policies and procedures in place?
- Does the company conduct regular assessments of its cybersecurity risks?
- Does the company have training and education programs in place to ensure cybersecurity protocols are understood and being followed?
- Have all legally binding agreements been reviewed, especially with respect to any indemnity or warranty provisions, to understand the company's rights, liabilities, and obligations with respect to cybersecurity?
- Is there a cyber incident response plan in place? Does it include a communications plan?
- Has an insurance assessment for cyber incidents been conducted? Is coverage sufficient?
- Have potential disclosure duties been identified, as well as triggering events?

Given the speed and vectors by which cyber threats evolve, the framework and response plan should be reevaluated on a regular basis to ensure it remains current, understood insofar as its implementation requirements within the company, and identifies any new or previously missed gaps and vulnerabilities.

C. Identify and Establish Key Internal and External Relationships

1. Within the Corporation

As discussed in Section I.C, ensuring you are part of the internal team is critical for success. There are ample resources available for companies on how to build teams to manage cybersecurity.[41] All point to the need for

---

41. *See, e.g.,* Tim McIntyre, *Insider Trips for Building Your Cybersecurity Team,* Security (Mar. 1, 2017), http://www.securitymagazine.com/articles/87844-insider-tips-for-building -your-cybersecurity-team; Amber Corrin, *7 Ways to Build Your Cybersecurity Team,* FCW. com (Sept. 16, 2013), https://fcw.com/articles/2013/09/16/cybersecurity-workforce-tips.aspx.

companies to have appropriate cybersecurity talent, and to recognize the interdisciplinary nature of strong cybersecurity teams and need for executive support.[42] Because of its established expertise, Legal is uniquely positioned to help articulate the risk parameters in the legal and regulatory arenas but can also provide valuable and relevant input for operational and market-based domains. If a team has already been established, and Legal is not a member, in-house counsel should reach out and get involved. The issue of cybersecurity should be suggested for regular inclusion at board meetings or board committee proceedings as appropriate.

2. External Third Parties

In-house counsel are especially important when engaging with external third parties. Relationships with cyber-knowledgeable law firms and consultants enable the in-house attorney to more quickly retain outside service providers with the requisite expertise. Having such relationships established *before* a breach occurs helps ensure selection of competent external partners who can get up to speed much more quickly, and who are more familiar with the company's culture and governance framework. The same principles apply to potential technical subject matter experts that may be needed depending on the type of cyber incident that occurs. Other external parties that might be considered could also include public relations firms specializing in crisis communications, key business partners, and lobbyists.

3. Governmental Entities and Officials

Multiple government agencies at all levels (federal, state, and local) and with different missions are examining and devoting resources to cyber issues. These resources range from reports, trends, and metrics to services for the general public or industry segments. Relationships should be formed with these governmental agencies. Many cyberattacks originate from nation-states and international crime syndicates. Defending against such attacks requires close coordination and interaction with relevant U.S. government agencies.

---

42. *See* Alejandra Quevedo, *How Cybersecurity Teams Can Convince the C-Suite of Their Value*, Harv. Bus. Rev. (Sept. 21, 2016), https://hbr.org/2016/09/how-cybersecurity-teams-can-convince-the-c-suite-of-their-value; Security for Bus. Innovation Council, *Transforming Information Security: Designing a State-of-the-Art Extended Team* (Sept. 2016), https://www.scribd.com/document/242060926/h12227-isa-designing-state-of-the-art-extended-team-pdf.

D.   Identify Legal Issues Associated with a Cyber Incident

Cyber threats are now sufficiently common that one can identify in advance what legal issues and risks might arise in an advance of a cyber incident. For example, in-house counsel can proactively consider the impact to the company (and the legal or regulatory risks that would arise) in the event there was a:

- Distributed denial of service attack or other disruption of Internet-based service;
- Theft or other compromise of personally identifiable information (generally defined as information that identifies—directly or indirectly—a person, including information that can be attributed to that person) or other confidential data owned or entrusted to the company; and/or
- Interrupted or suspended processing of payments, and so on.

In addition, in-house counsel would do well to familiarize themselves with the following:

- What technology and services (including outside service providers) the company has in place that would be impacted by or utilized during a cyber incident or breach;
- The appropriate authorizations that legally should be in place to permit network monitoring;
- The cyber incident and breach plans, in addition to relevant company policies and procedures; and
- Any legal areas and questions that might arise in the cybersecurity area. In this respect, in-house counsel should become familiar with potentially relevant technology laws such as the Computer Fraud and Abuse Act, laws relating to electronic surveillance in the workplace, privacy laws, and so on.

Legal requirements arising from a cyber event can also be identified in advance for different scenarios, such as:

- The need for an investigation, remediation measures, or incident notification;

- The need to (identify and) comply with specific domestic and foreign laws and regulations regarding data or information security, as well as breach notification;
- The need for SEC or foreign exchange disclosures, and potential or actual impact to share prices in the event of a public disclosure of an incident;
- Governmental notifications or inquiries regarding cyber incidents, or investigations into the company's security posture;
- Class actions, shareholder derivative lawsuits, or other legal action taken by parties with standing;
- Placement of (or claim placement against) a cyber insurance policy;
- The need or desire to place or flow down information security requirements to the company's suppliers or partners; and
- Contractual disputes relating to cybersecurity controls.

Throughout, in-house counsel will also need to consider the applicability and reach and possible waiver of the attorney-client privilege and attorney work product doctrines to (1) information that has been breached; (2) information that is generated in preparation for, during, or after, a cyber incident or breach; (3) any related investigations; (4) any disclosure made to governmental agencies; (5) governmental inquiries; and (6) information that may be potentially relevant to actual or anticipated litigation associated with the cyber incident or breach.[43]

---

43. The issues attendant to the attorney-client privilege are further complicated in light of the ongoing debate regarding the appropriate scope of the privilege as applied in the corporate context. Although *Upjohn Co. v. United States*, 449 U.S. 383 (1981), established that the privilege attached to corporations, within the company itself there can often still be confusion as to who, exactly, holds the privilege (the corporation), who speaks for the corporation with respect to the privilege; and who can waive the privilege. Logistical challenges arise in certain circumstances, most notably in internal investigations, where *Upjohn* warnings should be provided to employees being interviewed in order to ensure that the corporate privilege is retained and an attorney-client privilege is not inadvertently created with the employee. Decisions must be made in the context of governmental investigations and potential corporate misconduct, where federal sentencing guidelines and agency guidance can take a company's cooperation—especially in sharing investigative information—into account. Further complications in this sometimes difficult analysis on the part of in-house counsel arise from the issuance by the U.S. Department of Justice of a memorandum commonly referred to as the "Yates Memo." Memorandum from Sally Yates on Individual Accountability for Corporate Wrongdoing, Dep't of Justice (Sept. 9, 2015). The Yates Memo updated the Justice Department's

E. Cultivate a Cyber-Aware Culture and Community

In-house counsel should initiate and support efforts to ensure that the company's workforce and business partners are at least aware of cyber issues. All employees should be trained on cybersecurity, proper cyber hygiene, and the company's policies and procedural requirements with respect to cyber matters. Such training can be incorporated into the company's normal training program on managing proprietary information, use of company information assets and systems, and the like. Educational efforts should be combined with checks on employee understanding and absorption, through simulations such as periodic send-outs of mock phishing e-mails.[44]

Executive leaders—as well as in-house counsel—should model behavior, and create opportunities to develop a culture of awareness regarding the significant adverse impact that could be created by cyber incidents, and how such events and their aftermath might impact not just the corporation but also the employee.

Principles of Federal Prosecution of Business Organization, intending to provide more insight into the government's treatment of the privilege in the corporate context which, pursuant to numerous intervening memos issued by various prior Deputy Attorney Generals, had already been made subject to convoluted analysis, if not considerably eroded. For a discussion on treatment of the privilege in the context of a cyber breach, see Bart W. Huffman & Charles M. Salmon, *Privilege Considerations in Cyber Incident Response*, LAW360.COM (Aug. 29, 2016), https://www.law360.com/articles/833807/privilege-considerations-in-cyber-incident-response. The Yates Memo was updated by the Department of Justice in November 2018, to scale back the level of disclosure demanded of companies who are the target of a criminal investigation. Specifically, pursuant to the revisions, rather than provide the U.S. government with "*all* relevant facts about the individuals involved in corporate misconduct" in order to be eligible to receive cooperation credit in resolving investigations, the revision now requires that information regarding only those individuals who are "substantially involved in or responsible for the criminal conduct" be disclosed. *See* Peter Baldwin and & Antonio M. Pozos, *Department of Justice Announces Important Revisions to the Yates Memo*, NAT'L L. REV. (Dec. 12, 2018), https://www.faegredrinker.com/en/insights/publications/2018/12/doj-announces-important-revisions-to-yates-memo. Corporations and individuals having responsibilities for cybersecurity should not interpret the revisions to relieve them of their duties, however, as the revised policy is likely to have little practical impact in criminal investigations which still require that corporations "identify every individual who was substantially involved in or responsible for the criminal conduct" to receive the corporation credit, just not those who were substantially involved in or responsible for the conduct at issue. Nonetheless, the revisions does allow corporations some comfort in knowing that they might still be able to obtain cooperation credit even if they are unable to provide evidence on *all* potentially relevant individual wrongdoers for whatever reason.

44. Further discussion of organizational culture can be found in Chapter 13 of this Handbook.

IV. Responding to a Cyber Incident

No attorney is ever as fully prepared as he or she would wish when confronted with the realization that the company is under active attack. When the call is received, however, and the in-house attorney has no plan in place (or what plans that do exist do not fit the situation), there are guiding principles on what to do and how to prioritize.[45] Templates are also available which can serve as a helpful starting point.[46]

A. Identify the Attack and Damage

First, attempt to assess the type of attack, how much and what kind of damage is being or has been caused, who the attacker is, and the source of the vulnerability that has been exploited. If you do not know where to start, reach out to your IT resources. As soon as a basic understanding can be reasonably articulated, notify executive management (and your insurers if you are carrying cyber insurance) and the board of directors. Ensure that appropriate steps are taken to maintain confidentiality of the investigation. Depending on the situation, consider when and how you might reach out to law enforcement. Consult outside counsel if you are unsure of the legal implications or issues presented.

B. Limit the Damage

Next, enlist whatever resources you have or can get to limit any further damage. At this step, again, IT is a critical partner. IT should be able to monitor or filter traffic, take steps to insulate the affected systems, and begin gathering data and information regarding the cyber incident. Likewise, the sophistication and complexity of cyberattacks nowadays also warrant enlisting the assistance of external resources with expertise in managing and responding to cyber incidents.

---

45. *See supra* note 28.

46. *See, e.g., FTC Data Breach Response: A Guide for Business* (Feb. 2021), https://www.ftc.gov/tips-advice/business-center/guidance/data-breach-response-guide-business.

C. Record and Document

Begin compiling records on the extent of the damage, scope, and impact of the cyber incident. As it is unlikely you will be able to rule out potential criminal or legal action, records should be kept in a disciplined and ordered manner that ensures evidence is maintained and can be accounted for.

> The U.S. Justice Department recommends retention of: (a) a description of all events relating to the incident, including dates and times; (b) information relating to phone calls, e-mails, and other communications regarding the incident; (c) the identity of all individuals working on aspects of the cyber-incident, including a description of their specific roles, tasks, or responsibilities, amount of time spent, and approximate hourly rates for each; (d) identification of the systems, accounts, networks, databases, etc. affected by the cyber-incident; (e) information relating to the type and amount of damage sustained; (f) information regarding the company's network topology; (g) identification of software and applications being run on affected networks and devices; and (h) any unique aspects of the company's network architecture.[47]

D. Engage and Notify

If needed (and not already done), engage outside counsel to assist. As appropriate, inform law enforcement (DHS, FBI, district attorney), and other pertinent government agencies requiring notification. Identify and notify affected parties if any. Engage relevant third-party service providers (e.g., identity theft protection services if Personally Identifiable Information (PII) has been compromised).

E. Correct and Close

Ensure that vulnerabilities have been identified and patched, documentation is complete, and necessary parties have been provided ongoing status and closure reports. Develop and establish policies and other mitigation and

---

47. U.S. Dep't of Justice, Comput. Crime & Intell. Prop. Div., *Best Practices for Victim Response and Reporting of Cyber Incidents* (Version 2.0, Sept. 2018), https://www.justice .gov/criminal-ccips/file/1096971/download.

control measures to avoid being caught by surprise again, or repeating the same missteps that led to the cyber incident. Ensure that a lessons-learned session is held, and followed by additional self-assessments (and possibly external reviews), to ensure that a sustainable and "learning" framework is established for the company's cybersecurity posture.

F. Follow-Up

When and as appropriate, but certainly after the incident has been dealt with and remedied, ensure that any reporting requirements (e.g., to relevant government agencies, customers, or in SEC disclosures) have been identified and craft appropriate language reporting the incident that meets the applicable legal or regulatory disclosure requirements.

V. In the Aftermath

There are already a number of examples of highly publicized breaches of corporations in the past few years, and certainly more to come. Companies should keep in mind the variety of methods of attack and motivations that underpin such attacks and prioritize ensuring they are better prepared to defend themselves. While much remains unknown to the public at large regarding even the more publicized breaches, conclusions can still be drawn from what *is* known. For example, pleadings made in the lawsuit filed against Sony following its embarrassing breach in 2014 allege that the breach was caused by the company's alleged failure to properly secure its computer systems in a manner that could have prevented its systems from being hacked.[48] More recently, toward the end of 2018, Marriott International Hotel joined the ranks of numerous other companies in having to notify its customers that a breach of its systems resulted in the loss of personal information of nearly 500 million of its guests globally—a notification made all the more painful for the company as it also had to confirm that encrypted payment card numbers had also been stolen. Similarly, more than

---

48. *See* Steven Rubin & A. Jonathan Trafimow, *Cyber Wars and the Legal Lessons from the Sony Hack (op-ed)*, LIVESCIENCE.COM (Jan. 5, 2015), https://news.yahoo.com/cyber-wars-legal-lessons-sony-hack-op-ed-192143521.html.

380,000 customers of British Airways had personal information, including payment card information, hacked from its website as well as its online app in 2018. Meanwhile, while lawsuits based upon cyber breaches continue to find limited success prevailing, the saga of the 2014 Anthem breach serves as a sober reminder of the need for hypervigilance and preparedness. Anthem paid nearly $180 million to settle legal proceedings with the Department of Health and Human Services Office of Civil Rights, a class action lawsuit, and litigation brought by multiple state attorneys general. The underlying breach resulted from a phishing e-mail opened by a user within one of Anthem's subsidiaries that gave the hackers remote access and, ultimately, access to the company's enterprise data warehouse. Any company decision to "accept the risk" of not reviewing and addressing cybersecurity risks is now officially subject to challenge and, in the event of a breach, legal action.[49]

The in-house legal community can point to concrete examples on how to shape and develop standards and defensible cybersecurity practices, as we attempt to set forth in this chapter.[50] In-house counsel must consider aspects specific to the company's business. For instance, the Yahoo and Target breaches illustrate the additional legal complications (and impact to reputation and brand) attached to consumer data, as the Anthem breach does for health care data, and the SolarWinds and the Colonial Pipeline breaches do for utility and critical infrastructure consumers and users.[51] These cases likewise are helpful in better highlighting the risks to a company's reputation and other tangible consequences, such as an effect on stock prices and

---

49. *Id.*

50. David Fontaine & John Reed Stark, *Guest Post: Three Cybersecurity Lessons from Yahoo's Legal Department Woes*, THE D&O DIARY (Mar. 30, 2017), https://www.dandodiary.com/2017/03 /articles/cyber-liability/guest-post-three-cybersecurity-lessons-yahoos-legal-department-woes/.

51. *See* William Turton & Kartikay Mehrota, *Hackers Breached Colonial Pipeline Using Compromised Password*, BLOOMBERG (June 4, 2021), https://www.bloomberg.com/news /articles/2021-06-04/hackers-breached-colonial-pipeline-using-compromised-password; Isabella Jibilian, *The US Is Readying Sanctions Against Russia Over the SolarWinds Cyber Attack*, BUS. INSIDER (Apr. 15, 2021), https://www.businessinsider.com/solarwinds-hack-explained -government-agencies-cyber-security-2020-12; Marianne Kolbasuk McGee, *A New In-Depth Analysis of Anthem Breach*, BANK INFOSECURITY (Jan. 10, 2017), https://www.bankinfosecurity. com/new-in-depth-analysis-anthem-breach-a-9627; Stephen Rossi, *Lessons from the Target Data Breach Settlement*, LAW360 (May 4, 2015), https://www.law360.com/articles/649450 /lessons-from-the-target-data-breach-settlement.

the need to think holistically regarding the types of operational risks that can arise from a company's business activities in unforeseen ways.

Social media and nontraditional media outlets make recovery and crisis management of a cyber incident even more difficult. Where once the so-called Washington Post rule might have been used to caution against unwise behavior, today the admonition is to avoid becoming a viral meme on Facebook, Instagram, Snapchat, or Twitter.

All companies can learn from each other. Publicized breaches underscore the need to constantly reassess a company's fundamental cybersecurity posture. Companies often rally to address bad situations and exert Herculean efforts to fix the problem. But after implementing new policies and training, some believe those measures are sufficient to forestall a repeat event. This is a particularly unsound assumption in the cyber domain, where threats continue to evolve and actors continue to multiply.[52] In-house counsel must become the watchmen against complacency.

VI. Special Considerations

This chapter focuses primarily on cyber threats to corporate assets and organizational activities. This is not intended to ignore other areas of the law that carry significant cyber considerations such as consumer protection laws, privacy, and e-discovery. With respect to those other legal areas with direct, indirect, and overlapping relevance to cybersecurity considerations as discussed elsewhere in this Handbook, our suggestion to in-house counsel is to be sufficiently familiar with what the company must do to comply with these concurrent obligations or mitigate attendant risks. This way, the team addressing cybersecurity can align cyber threat mitigation strategies and planning with these other areas.

---

52. Perhaps this explains why even though Heartland was the victim of one of the earlier high-profile instances of corporate cyber breaches in 2009, it found itself suffering through a hellish version of "Groundhog Day" five years later as it once again found itself in the cyber breach spotlight. Tony Martin-Vegue, *Lessons from the Heartland Payment Systems Data Breach, Redux*, CSO (June 15, 2015), http://www.csoonline.com/article/2935814/data-breach/lessons-from-the-heartland-payment-systems-data-breach-redux.html.

Mention should likewise be made of the impact of other economic, technological, and sociological trends affecting the workplace, such as the increasing percentage of the workforce reaching retirement age and increased multigenerational workforce considerations. These trends, and associated lessons learned or resulting new or adjusted modes of operations, must be taken into account when drafting social media policies and procedures, and when assessing the impact of social engineering attacks on company personnel and representatives or other considerations implicating the company's cybersecurity posture. This includes the aftermath of influential external events such as natural disasters (such as the severe California wildfires or unexpected drop in temperature in Texas in 2020 and 2021) or the Covid-19 pandemic, which forced companies to implement or otherwise accommodate wholesale work-from-home arrangements.

In sum, in-house counsel are uniquely positioned to assume a leadership and influential role in better preparing their companies to deal with the cyber threat. In addition, they are presented the rare opportunity to provide input into the ongoing dialogue regarding the balance market autonomy and governmental regulation of industry in this constantly evolving and complex area. Given the vast array of actors and threats in the cyber domain, and the growing dependence of the world on Internet-driven commerce and communication, managing the risks requires all hands on deck.

VII. Summary and Tips

In closing, in-house counsel should apply the following commonsense steps:

1. Be proactive;
2. Stay current on cybersecurity law developments;
3. Broaden your risk management measures;
    - Ensure the company has a cyber incident and breach response plan, including a communications plan;
    - Consider obtaining cybersecurity insurance;

4. Build your partnerships (internal and external)
   - Functional partners: Stay close with HR, Finance, and particularly IT. The rapid evolution of technologies and complex task of maintaining information systems will continue changing your work environment. Having an IT partner willing to work with you is an absolute priority;
   - Identify third-party entities that can be engaged if and where needed;
   - Select law firms that are knowledgeable regarding cyber threats and that practice sound cybersecurity measures;
5. Manage and provide input to your policies and procedures;
6. Build a credible case for budget and resources;
7. Expand your network and list of resources and references so that you cannot just establish a baseline understanding of cybersecurity basics but also keep current on developments and emergent trends; and
8. Take to heart the now entrenched understanding that it is not a question of if a cyber incident will occur, but when. Be ready and prepared for a crisis so that your response will be measured and thoughtful.

In addition to being helpful to in-house counsel, we hope this chapter is helpful to outside counsel in better understanding the perspectives of their clients. Having a stronger sense of the environment in which in-house counsel must operate, beyond the specific issue or project brought to outside counsel, will help law firms better shape their opinions in a manner that assists in-house counsel to support *their* client in a practical manner.

Chapter 11
Considerations for Government Lawyers

Sandra Hodgkinson

Like their private sector counterparts, government lawyers remain on the frontline of cybersecurity concerns. In fact, law firms, business professionals, and other attorneys can and should learn from the experiences of the government and its attorneys. Private sector lawyers should also understand the functions of the government entities with cyber authorities. Government entities offer many resources and services to private entities and their lawyers that may help to facilitate improvements to their cybersecurity postures. These government entities also may be able to assist when private entities experience a cyber incident.

At the end of 2020, when so much focus was placed on election security, the discovery of the SolarWinds breach brought to light the cyber risks faced by government employees and the attorneys responsible for protecting them and upholding the law.[1] Indeed, the Department of Justice announced that the e-mail accounts of prosecutors in many U.S. attorney's offices had been compromised in that breach.[2] In fact, more than 250 organizations, including government agencies such as the National Security Agency (NSA), State

---

1. For a thorough discussion of the SolarWinds breach, see Chapter 2, Understanding Cybersecurity Risks.

2. In early January 2021, DoJ announced that the SolarWinds incident had resulted in a significant intrusion into its Microsoft O365 e-mail environment. Press Release, DoJ, Office of Public Affairs, Department of Justice Statement on Solarwinds Update (Jan. 6, 2021), https://www.justice.gov/opa/pr/department-justice-statement-solarwinds-update. In a follow-up statement issued on July 30, 2021, DoJ provided more details, acknowledging that the unauthorized Advanced Persistent Threat actors had access to compromised e-mail accounts at 27 different U.S. Attorney General offices from approximately May through December 2020, including the e-mail accounts of "at least 80 percent of employees working in the U.S. Attorneys' offices located in the Eastern, Northern, Southern, and Western Districts of New York." Id.

Department, Treasury Department, and Department of Homeland Security, were affected.[3] The SolarWinds cyber event has increased awareness of the vulnerability of government organizations, as well as the private sector, to supply chain and other unlawful attacks, and was the driving force behind heightened attention to these issues in the first half of 2021.

The SolarWinds incident reinforces the view that government lawyers and their clients continue to face many of the same problems as lawyers in private practice and industry, including data breaches, phishing attempts, exfiltration of data, insecure software and systems, and malicious insiders. Indeed, the risk may also be greater, given the information the government stores, manages, and protects and the issues government organizations address. As we have seen, government lawyers are often on the front line protecting their clients against ideologically and politically motivated attacks. These attacks against the government and critical infrastructure companies can emerge from a broad spectrum of actors and can be designed to affect national security, collect intelligence, steal data and intellectual property, commit espionage, or seek revenge for perceived wrongs. And, as is true for the private sector, these attacks can be launched from anywhere with very little attribution. Moreover, threats may come from nation-states themselves, as well as from organizations operating independently that are tolerated within those nation-states.[4]

Federal, state, and local governments store vast amounts of valuable and vulnerable data. In addition to sensitive national security information, they store data on citizens and residents for tax purposes, including financial data and institutions, Social Security numbers, medical information, and immigration status. They also collect and store information on individuals for use in criminal law enforcement and many other purposes. In the wrong

---

3. Deeba Ahmed, *SolarWinds Supply Chain Attack Affected 250 Organizations*, HACKREAD (Jan. 5, 2021), https://www.hackread.com/solarwinds-supply-chain-attack-affected-organizations/.

4. The Biden administration specifically alleges a Russian SVR role in the compromise of the SolarWinds software supply chain as a way "to spy on or potentially disrupt more than 16,000 computer systems worldwide." Press Release, White House, FACT SHEET: Imposing Costs for Harmful Foreign Activities by the Russian Government (Apr. 15, 2021), https://www.whitehouse.gov/briefing-room/statements-releases/2021/04/15/fact-sheet-imposing-costs-for-harmful-foreign-activities-by-the-russian-government/.

hands, any of this information could be used for a variety of improper purposes, including identity theft, theft using personal data for online services, blackmail, illegal immigration, and other criminal acts.

There are also cyberattacks that are not related to data theft at all but which aim to destroy, disrupt, or otherwise alter our military or domestic computer systems, radars, communications systems, weapons systems, borders, and critical infrastructure that provide the essential services we rely on every day. Many of these malicious actors focus on ransomware and disruption of services, more than data theft. The ransomware that hit Atlanta in 2018 and then Baltimore in 2019 wreaked such havoc on the cities' operations that Atlanta alone spent $2.6 million to recover from a ransomware attack in which the payment request was about $50,000.[5] Charges in this case were filed against Iranian nationals.[6] Whether these increasing cyber threats and attacks are aimed directly at government agencies or at critical infrastructure companies, government lawyers increasingly play a key role, ranging from the development of cyber standards or requirements for incident response to post-incidents activities such as mitigation, enforcement, and potential cyber response.

In addition, government lawyers who focus on national security must be able to identify when a cyber intrusion or attack may rise to the level of an "armed attack" that could justify a military response, as opposed to a law enforcement one. These determinations can be extremely difficult and often require consensus and approvals at the highest levels of our government due to the sensitivity and possible risks of involving the military in physical responses to cyberattacks. In cases that do amount to an "armed attack," the cyberattackers most often come from outside of our borders, and attribution can be particularly challenging. In contrast with a traditional military enemy that wears uniforms and travels in military equipment, an enemy that travels through cyberspace incognito at the blink of a second is difficult to identify, respond to, and deter from future attacks. Use of the

---

5. Lily Hay Newman, *Atlanta Spent $2.6M to Recover from a $52,000 Ransomware Scare*, WIRED (Apr. 23, 2018, 8:55 PM), https://www.wired.com/story/atlanta-spent-26m-recover-from-ransomware-scare/.

6. https://www.justice.gov/usao-ndga/pr/atlanta-us-attorney-charges-iranian-nationals-city-atlanta-ransomware-attack.

military to respond to attack will necessarily invoke a higher level of scrutiny from the public, international community, and the press.

This chapter of the Handbook provides guidance for government lawyers who require familiarity with the evolving laws related to cybersecurity, and also serves as a reference for attorneys outside of the government who may be seeking government support for a potential cyber incident. The chapter begins with an overview on leadership from the White House on cybersecurity and the roles and missions of the government cybersecurity lawyers. It then discusses significant data breaches and cyberattacks against the government and what cyber lawyers should know about them. Next, it briefly summarizes some of the key cyber laws the government has put in place to protect data. It concludes with a summary of key lessons learned and best practices applicable to both government lawyers who specialize in cybersecurity, and also the vast majority who do not but still require a basic understanding of the government's role in cybersecurity protection.

I. Leadership from the Oval Office

Each of the last three presidents, just as their recent predecessors, has taken significant steps in an effort to improve the cybersecurity posture of the federal government and critical infrastructure response. While these will be addressed beginning with the most recent president, it should be noted that each successive administration has built on the hard work of the prior administration. Most recently, following the SolarWinds breach and shortly after entering office, President Biden outlined his administration's cybersecurity priorities as follows:

> As we bolster our scientific and technological base, we will make cybersecurity a top priority, strengthening our capability, readiness, and resilience in cyberspace. We will elevate cybersecurity as an imperative across the government. We will work together to manage and share risk, and we will encourage collaboration between the private sector and the government at all levels in order to build a safe and secure online environment for all Americans. We will expand our investments in the infrastructure and people we need to effectively

defend the nation against malicious cyber activity, providing opportunities to Americans of diverse backgrounds as we build an unmatched talent base. We will renew our commitment to international engagement on cyber issues, working alongside our allies and partners to uphold existing and shape new global norms in cyberspace. And we will hold actors accountable for destructive, disruptive, or otherwise destabilizing malicious cyber activity, and respond swiftly and proportionately to cyberattacks by imposing substantial costs through cyber and noncyber means.[7]

In May 2021, in the face of a marked increase in ransomware and other serious cyberattacks on government, critical infrastructure, and other private entities, President Biden began to implement his cybersecurity priorities by issuing Executive Order (EO) No. 14028,[8] kicking off a series of organizational initiatives aimed at not only modernizing and enhancing the federal government's cybersecurity defenses and incident response capabilities, including through uniform implementation of security best practices, moving toward adoption of zero trust architecture[9] and acceleration of the movement to secure cloud services, but also enhancing private–public cyber information sharing, enhancing software supply chain security,[10] and establishing a Cybersecurity Safety Review Board[11] modeled on the National Transportation Safety Board, with government and private participants,[12] to ensure that lessons learned from significant cybersecurity events are both

---

7. INTERIM NATIONAL SECURITY STRATEGIC GUIDANCE 18 (Mar. 2021), https://www.whitehouse.gov/wp-content/uploads/2021/03/NSC-1v2.pdf.

8. Exec. Order No. 14028, Improving the Nation's Cybersecurity, https://www.govinfo.gov/content/pkg/FR-2021-05-17/pdf/2021-10460.pdf. The fact sheet for that EO 14028 can be found at https://www.whitehouse.gov/briefing-room/statements-releases/2021/05/12/fact-sheet-president-signs-executive-order-charting-new-course-to-improve-the-nations-cyber security-and-protect-federal-government-networks/.

9. To learn more about Zero Trust Architecture, see National Security Agency/Cybersecurity Information, *Embracing a Zero Trust Security Model* (Feb. 2021), https://media.defense.gov/2021/Feb/25/2002588/9/-1/-1/0/CSI_EMBRACING_ZT_SECURITY_MODEL_UOO115131-21.PDF.

10. Exec. Order No. 14028 at Section 4.

11. *Id.* at Section 5.

12. *See* https://www.whitehouse.gov/briefing-room/statements-releases/2021/05/12/fact-sheet-president-signs-executive-order-charting-new-course-to-improve-the-nations-cyber security-and-protect-federal-government-networks/.

identified and implemented. The combined impact of this EO and enhanced legislative activity focused on cybersecurity will continue to increase the cyber roles and responsibilities of various agencies and, thus, the need for federal lawyers well versed in all aspects of cyber legal issues.

Four years previously, in May 2017, President Trump issued an EO similarly focused on improving both the federal government's and critical infrastructure entities' cybersecurity posture. EO 13800, Strengthening the Cybersecurity of Federal Networks and Critical Infrastructure,[13] aimed to make federal agency heads accountable for managing cybersecurity risk at their organizations using the NIST's *Framework for Improving Critical Infrastructure Cybersecurity*[14] and provide a report to the president. The EO also called on DHS and other agencies to provide the president a report on their existing authorities to assist critical infrastructure entities on cyber-related activities, and after engaging with such critical infrastructure companies, to provide a report to the president detailing their recommendations.

President Obama also dedicated significant attention to cyber security. Consistent with his National Security Strategy, on October 16, 2012, President Barack Obama signed a classified presidential policy directive related to cyber operations, PPD-20,[15] which recognized the growth in cyber incidents and threats against the U.S. government. PPD-20 established principles and processes for the use of cyber operations to enable more effective planning, development, and use of our capabilities. The policy promoted a whole-of-government approach and sought to undertake the least action necessary to mitigate threats, while prioritizing network defense and law enforcement as preferred courses of action.[16] The White House had also previously issued an International Strategy for Cyberspace in May 2011 that focused efforts

---

13. Strengthening the Cybersecurity of Federal Networks and Critical Infrastructure, 82 Fed. Reg. 22391 (May 11, 2017).

14. NIST developed the first version of this Framework (i.e., 1.0) under President Obama's Executive Order 13636, "Improving Critical Infrastructure Cybersecurity" (Feb. 2013), and, as contemplated by the Cybersecurity Enhancement Act of 2014 (15 U.S.C. § 272(e)(1)(A)(i)), continues to responsible for updating the document. Version 1.1 of the Framework, which was issued in April 2018, can be found at Framework for Improving Critical Infrastructure Cybersecurity, Version 1.1 (nist.gov).

15. Presidential Pol'y Directive 20 (PPD-20), unclassified release, Fact Sheet on PPD-20 (Jan. 2003 [superseding NSPD-38]).

16. *Id.*

on working with allies to address the growing cyber threat through the establishment of international norms.[17]

In July 2016, President Obama issued a second cybersecurity-related presidential policy directive—PPD-21[18]—designed to ensure a coordinated U.S. cyber incident response across the government for incidents involving both government agencies and private entities. The PPD identified principles to inform government incident response and, along with its annex,[19] detailed various federal agencies' responsibilities in responding to "significant cyber incidents."[20] Notably, PPD-21 authorized NSA to stand-up a cyber unified coordination committee to ensure an effective "whole-of-government response" in response to such significant incidents. The NSA exercised this authority several times in Obama's second term. The Trump administration invoked this process once in response to the SolarWinds cyber incident in December 2020.[21]

II. Government Cyber Lawyers and Their Mission

Given the nation's cybersecurity priorities, federal lawyers are increasingly required to engage on cybersecurity issues. While lawyers at every federal organization face some cyber legal issues in today's threat environment, including addressing and reporting cyber incidents, lawyers at certain federal agencies play a larger role in providing the critical cyber advice on which the agencies rely to protect and secure our nation and critical infrastructure from cybersecurity threats.

---

17. International Strategy for Operating in Cyberspace (May 2011). See also Chapter 5 of this Handbook for a discussion of international norms.

18. Presidential Pol'y Directive 41 (PPD-41), United States Cyber Incident Coordination.

19. PPD-41 Annex, "Federal Government Coordination Architecture for Significant Cyber Incidents," https://irp.fas.org/offdocs/ppd/ppd-41.html.

20. PPD-41 defined significant cyber incidents as "a cyber incident that is (or group of related cyber incidents that together are) likely to result in demonstrable harm to the national security interests, foreign relations, or economy of the United States or to the public confidence, civil liberties, or public health and safety of the American people."

21. See, e.g., https://www.cyberscoop.com/solarwinds-white-house national-security-council-emergency-meetings/; https://thehill.com/policy/cybersecurity/530357-pentagon-state-department-among-agencies-hacked-report.

A. Department of Defense (DoD)/U.S. Cyber Command

DoD is at the core of the nation's efforts to defend cyberspace. The most recent DoD cybersecurity strategy was published in 2018.[22] It identifies DoD's key cyber objectives as (1) ensuring DoD can achieve its missions in a contested cyberspace; (2) conducting cyberspace operations to enhance U.S. military advantages; (3) defending U.S. critical infrastructure from malicious cyber activity; (4) securing DoD information and assets against such activity; and (5) expanding DoD's cyber cooperation with other organizations, industry, and international partners.[23] Many of DoD's cybersecurity efforts are led by the U.S. Cyber Command, which is headquartered with the National Security Agency.[24] Cyber Command identifies its core focus as defending DoD infrastructure, providing support to military leaders in execution of their missions, and strengthening our nation's resilience and ability to respond to cyberattacks.[25]

Throughout the DoD, there are a host of civilian and military lawyers working to support the following critical cyber missions: cyber intelligence collection, which is the use of cyber warfare to conduct espionage; offensive cyber operations, which are full-spectrum cyber operations that project power through the use of force in cyberspace; and defensive cyber operations, which are passive and active cyberspace operations intended to preserve the ability to use friendly cyberspace capabilities and protect data, systems, and networks.[26] The legal and policy issues associated with offensive and defensive cyber operations are certainly of the utmost importance. At U.S. Cyber Command, at each of the services' cyber commands, on the Joint Staff, and in the Office of the Secretary of Defense, there are lawyers at several levels performing these critical functions. Since 2012, the U.S. Cyber Command has hosted an annual unclassified legal conference

---

22. 2018 DoD Cybersecurity Strategy Summary, https://media.defense.gov/2018/Sep/18/2002041658/-1/-1/1/CYBER_STRATEGY_SUMMARY_FINAL.PDF.

23. *Id.* at 3.

24. To learn more about the U.S. Cyber Command, see https://www.cybercom.mil/About/History/.

25. *See* https://www.cybercom.mil/About/Mission-and-Vision/.

26. *See* SECDEF Memorandum, Establishment of a Subordinate Unified U.S. Cyber Command under U.S. Strategic Command for Military Cyberspace Operations (June 23, 2009); Defense Strategy for Operating in Cyberspace (July 2011); 2018 DoD Cyber Strategy, *supra* note 22.

addressing the latest developments with respect to these critical issues.[27] For those interested in learning more about these issues, a recording of the 2021 legal conference can be viewed online.[28]

B. Department of Homeland Security (DHS)/Cybersecurity and Infrastructure Security Agency

DHS has longed played a significant role in protecting the homeland from cyberattack, and through its National Protection and Programs Directorate (NPPD) in working with the private sector to ensure that there are public–private partnerships exploring ways to address the cyber threat with private entities, including critical infrastructure. More recently, in November 2018, the Cybersecurity and Infrastructure Security Agency (CISA) was established as a separate agency within DHS,[29] continuing the NPPD's important mission. The cyber mission of CISA, which characterizes itself as the "Nation's Risk Advisor," includes (1) leading the efforts to secure federal civilian executive organization networks; (2) working with public agencies and private entities to improve the security and resilience of critical infrastructure; and (3) responding to significant cyber incidents. Notably, CISA has played an integral role in working with state governments to ensure election security.

Given the central role CISA plays in our nation's cybersecurity, its lawyers expend significant efforts on its cybersecurity mission. In a recent article on the practice of cybersecurity law,[30] CISA's chief counsel summarized the breadth of responsibilities of the cyber-focused lawyers on his staff:

Our team of lawyers has a broad portfolio, including supporting responses to the most complex cyber incidents facing the country, negotiating

---

27. https://www.cybercom.mil/Media/News/Article/2526508/us-cyber-command-holds-2021-legal-conference/.

28. https://www.dvidshub.net/tags/video/uscybercomlegalconference2021 A speech by the then-DoD General Counsel, Hon. Paul C. Ney, Jr., given at the 2020 conference provides an overview of the domestic and international law considerations that DoD lawyers use in reviewing potential military cyber operations is also available online. *See* https://www.defense.gov/Newsroom/Speeches/Speech/Article/2099378/dod-general-counsel-remarks-at-us-cyber-command-legal-conference/.

29. The Cybersecurity and Infrastructure Organization Act, Pub. L. No. 115–278 (Nov. 16, 2018), https://www.congress.gov/115/plaws/publ278/PLAW-115publ278.pdf.

30. Daniel Sutherland, *What Is a Cybersecurity Legal Practice?*, LAWFARE (Apr. 2, 2021, 11:10 AM), https://www.lawfareblog.com/what-cybersecurity-legal-practice.

complex technology agreements, developing legal and governance frameworks to address threats of emerging technologies and nation-states intent on compromising them, drafting legislation, and responding to audits and investigations.[31]

C. Department of Justice (DoJ)/Federal Bureau of Investigations (FBI)

DoJ's cyber resources are predominantly housed within its National Security Division, which focuses attention on a variety of national security issues, including the development of law in the cybersecurity arena, and the Computer Crime and Intellectual Property Section in the Criminal Division, which investigates computer crime activity worldwide. In the first six months of 2021, DoJ announced it both had formed a new Ransomware and Digital Extortion Task Force[32] and was launching a 120-day internal review to update its strategy for defending and deterring emerging cyber threats, to include supply chain attacks such as SolarWinds.[33]

DoJ works closely with the FBI, the lead federal organization investigating cyber incidents. The FBI cyber strategy is to discourage cyberattacks by "impos[ing] risk and consequences on cyber adversaries."[34] Partnering within the federal government, private entities, and global counterparts is a core part of the FBI's strategy. The FBI is responsible for developing and leading the National Cyber Investigation Joint Task Force (NCIJTF), which includes representatives of over 30 agencies from law enforcement, the intelligence community, and DoD working together. The NCIJTF is

---

31. *Id.*

32. *See* https://dd80b675424c132b90b3-e48385e382d2e5d17821a5e1d8e4c86b.ssl .cf1.rackcdn.com/external/dojransomwarememo.pdf. In June, it was reported that DoJ has instructed U.S. attorney offices that ransomware investigations should be coordinated with the newly formed task force. *See* Christopher Bing, *Exclusive: U.S. to Give Ransomware Hacks Similar Priority as Terrorism*, REUTERS (June 3, 2021), https://www.reuters.com/technology /exclusive-us-give-ransomware-hacks-similar-priority-terrorism-official-says-2021-06-03/

33. *See* Maggie Miller, *Justice Department to Undertake 120 Day Review of Cybersecurity Challenges*, THE HILL (Apr. 30, 2021), https://thehill.com/policy/cyber security/551195-justice-department-to-undertake-120-day-review-of-cybersecurity.

34. *See* https://www.fbi.gov/video-repository/wray-cisa-091620.mp4/view.

responsible for coordinating, integrating, and sharing information in support of cyber threat investigations and developing and supporting cyber intelligence analysis.[35]

DoJ and the FBI, working together, are increasingly implementing more innovative steps to combat cybercrime and mitigate risks associated with specific incidents, in addition to continuing its efforts to indict cybercriminals. For example, in April 2021, DoJ announced it had obtained authorization from a federal court to allow the FBI to remove malicious web shells from privately owned compromised Microsoft Exchange servers.[36] DoJ was also able to recover much of the ransom paid by Colonial Pipelines after it suffered a ransomware attack.[37]

D. Department of Treasury

On April 1, 2015, the White House provided the Treasury Department with a significant tool for addressing cyber threats in Executive Order 13,694, Blocking the Property of Certain Persons Engaging in Significant Malicious Cyber-Enabled Activities.[38] This order allows the U.S. government to block the assets of individuals who, from outside of the country, have attacked our critical infrastructure and prevented a service; caused significant damage to the availability of our computer network; or caused a significant misappropriation of funds, trade secrets, personal data, or financial information for commercial or private gain.[39] This gives an enforcement tool short of the use of force (or cyberattack) to deter or respond to the acts of hackers and cybercriminals.

In October 2020, in the wake of an unprecedented increase in the number of ransomware attacks and amounts of ransomware being paid, the Treasury Department issued guidance to discourage ransomware payments. The

---

35. *See* https://www.fbi.gov/investigate/cyber/national-cyber-investigative-joint-task-force.

36. U.S. DoJ, *Justice Department Announces Court-Authorized Effort to Disrupt Exploitation of Microsoft Exchange Server Vulnerabilities* (Apr. 13, 2021), https://www.justice.gov/usao-sdtx/pr/justice-department-announces-court-authorized-effort-disrupt-exploitation-microsoft.

37. *Department of Justice Seizes $2.3 Million in Cryptocurrency Paid to the Ransomware Extortionists Darkside* (June 7, 2021), https://www.justice.gov/opa/pr/department-justice-seizes-23-million-cryptocurrency-paid-ransomware-extortionists-darkside.

38. Exec. Order No. 13,694, Blocking the Property of Certain Persons Engaging in Significant Malicious Cyber-Enabled Activities, 80 Fed. Reg. 18,077 (Apr. 1, 2015).

39. *Id.*

Office of Foreign Assets Control (OFAC) advisory warns private entities that facilitate payment of ransomware (e.g., victim companies, cyber insurers, and financial institutions) that such payments may risk violating U.S. laws that prohibit U.S. persons or entities from engaging in direct or indirect transactions with certain specifically identified individuals or entities sanctioned by OFAC.[40] That same month, the Treasury Department's Financial Crimes Enforcement Network (FinCEN) issued a ransomware advisory to alert financial institutions to the trends, typologies, and potential red flag indicators of ransomware and associated money laundering activities, and reminded entities involved in the facilitating of such payments that they could be subject to potential registrations and reporting requirements.[41]

E.   Other Government Enforcement Activities

In addition to government efforts just identified, many government lawyers are actively engaged in cybersecurity and privacy enforcement-related activities at federal agencies such as the Federal Trade Commission and Securities & Exchange Commission as well as at state attorneys general offices.

1.   Federal Trade Commission (FTC)

Although the United States has not enacted a comprehensive federal cybersecurity or privacy law, the FTC has leveraged its authority under Section 5 of the Federal Trade Commission Act[42] to prohibit unfair or deceptive practices in the marketplace to regulate inadequate cybersecurity and privacy practices of consumer-facing companies, or misleading statements about those practices.[43] Companies that are found to have engaged in such practices as

---

40. *See* U.S. Dep't of the Treasury, Advisory on Potential Sanctions Risks for Facilitating Ransomware Payments (Oct. 1, 2020), https://home.treasury.gov/system/files/126/ofac_ransomware_advisory_10012020_1.pdf.

41. *See* FIN-2020-A006, Advisory on Ransomware and the use of Financial System to Facilitate Ransom Payments, https://www.fincen.gov/sites/default/files/advisory/2020-10-01/Advisory%20Ransomware%20FINAL%20508.pdf.

42. 15 U.S.C. § 45(a).

43. For an overview of recent FTC cybersecurity cases, see recent annual FTC 2019 and 2020 Privacy & Security Updates for 2020 and 2021, https://www.ftc.gov/system/files/documents/reports/federal-trade-commission-2020-privacy-data-security-update/20210524_privacy_and_data_security_annual_update.pdf and https://www.ftc.gov/system/files/documents/reports/privacy-data-security-update-2019/2019-privacy-data-security-report-508.pdf/.

a result of an FTC investigation enter into twenty-year consent orders that require the companies to implement and maintain comprehensive security programs, obtain external biennial assessments of their programs, report incidents to the FTC, and have a senior officer submit annual certifications attesting to the company's compliance with the order. In recent years, after facing several court challenges to its authority in privacy and data security matters,[44] the FTC has strengthened consent orders it enters into with companies to impose more specific security requirements, to require certain evidence be maintained to support the required third-party assessment of the company's security or privacy practices, and to require senior executive oversight and certification of the company's security program.[45]

2. Securities and Exchange Commission (SEC)

In addition to issuing guidance, the SEC has become increasingly active with respect to examinations and enforcement.[46] In June 2021, the SEC entered into a settlement order with First American Financial Corporation for failure to maintain proper disclosure controls related to a cyber vulnerability that led to the improper exposure of customers' sensitive personal information.[47]

The SEC also uses its enforcement authorities to address cybersecurity-related matters of the entities it regulates. In September 2017, the SEC established a Cyber Unit within its Division of Enforcement that focuses on such issues as cyber controls at regulated entities, disclosures of cyber risks and incidents, trading based on hacked non-public information, and cryptocurrencies.[48] In 2018, the SEC issued interpretative guidance to assist public companies in determining what cyber risks and incidents should be

---

44. *See* Randy Milch & Sam Bieler, *A New Decade and New Cybersecurity Orders at the FTC,* LAWFARE (Jan. 29, 2020), https://www.lawfareblog.com/new-decade-and -new-cybersecurity-orders-ftc.

45. *See* https://www.ftc.gov/news-events/blogs/business-blog/2020/01 /new-improved-ftc-data-security-orders-better-guidance.

46. *See* SEC 2021 Examination Priorities at 2–3, 24–25, https://www.sec.gov /files/2021 exam priorities.pdf.

47. Press Release, SEC, SEC Charges Issuer with Cybersecurity Disclosure Controls Failures (June 15, 2021), https://www.sec.gov/news/press-release/2021-102.

48. *See* Press Release, SEC, SEC Announces Enforcement Initiatives to Combat Cyber-Based Threats and Protect Retail Investors (Sept. 25, 2017), https://www.sec.gov/news /press-release/2017-176.

disclosed.[49] More recently, in the aftermath of the SolarWinds incident, the SEC Division of Enforcement has sent letters to public companies that it believes, based on its investigation, may have been impacted by the breach but have not made a SolarWinds-related cyber disclosure, seeking information about the impact of this incident and "other compromises" on their companies.[50]

3. State Attorneys General

State Attorneys General (AGs) have also stepped up their cybersecurity and privacy enforcement efforts. Unlike the federal government, all 50 states have privacy laws and many now also specifically require security controls, in addition to existing consumer protection laws. In recent years, many State AGs often work together and sometimes independently to pursue and enter multi-state settlements in particular consumer privacy matters, including those involving cybersecurity.[51] Indeed, sometimes State AGs will join forces with federal enforcers such as the FTC. A notable example of this was in 2019, when a settlement of at least $575 million was reached in connection with the 2017 Equifax breach, which was attributed, in part, to a failure to timely patch vulnerabilities.[52]

III. Government Data: An Increasing Problem of Data Insecurity

Government systems suffer from an array of vulnerabilities and are subject to a variety of threats that range from accidental data loss to advanced persistent threats, often state-sponsored, dangerous, and highly sophisticated. While classified government computers have their own specialized

---

49. https://www.sec.gov/rules/interp/2018/33-10459.pdf.

50. https://www.sec.gov/enforce/certain-cybersecurity-related-events-faqs.

51. Ashley Taylor, Christopher Carlson & Miranda Dore, *State AGs' 2020 Actions Offer Hints at 2021 Priorities*, Law360 (Jan. 12, 2021, 5:51 PM), https://www.law360.com /articles/1343782/state-ags-2020-actions-offer-hints-at-2021-priorities.

52. https://www.huntonprivacyblog.com/2019/07/22/equifax-agrees-to-pay-up-to-700-mil lion-to-resolve-2017-breach-the-largest-data-breach-settlement-in-u-s-history/. For the FTC order in this manner, see https://www.ftc.gov/enforcement/cases-proceedings/172-3203 /equifax-inc.

networks and are generally not connected to the Internet at all, even such "air-gapped" systems have suffered major security breaches. Among the best known breaches in the classified environment are the massive disclosure by Chelsea Manning to WikiLeaks of classified State Department cables and other classified information, the release to the media of thousands of classified documents by Edward Snowden, the theft from the Office of Personnel Management (OPM) of personnel records affecting 21.5 million individuals, the compromise of federal tax information that was subsequently used in filing fraudulent claims, and the compromise of computers at multiple government agencies (and commercial entities) in incidents such as SolarWinds. Other parts of the government that maintain data that contains significant personal information, such as tax information,[53] medical records,[54] immigration status,[55] and information protected by court order,[56] that are also potential targets.

As mentioned earlier, perhaps the most cross-cutting organization breach for the government was the SolarWinds supply chain compromise, which also heavily impacted private industry and the public as well. Cybersecurity threats, including data breaches of all kinds, are clearly not a problem limited to the DoD, State Department, or intelligence agencies handling national security matters and foreign affairs. However, these incidents do provide a series of lessons that can be learned and applied to government and nongovernment cybersecurity programs:

The SolarWinds Supply Chain Compromise. In December 2020, it was discovered that hackers had been able to infiltrate the code development environment of SolarWinds, a supplier of network management software, and successfully insert backdoors into the code of its Orion network management software. The malicious code was then downloaded via routine software updates in March 2020 into 18,000 SolarWinds customers'

---

53. *See* I.R.C. §§ 6103 (prohibiting disclosure of tax return information by federal employees and officers), 7216 (prohibiting disclosure by persons involved in tax return preparation).

54. 45 C.F.R. §§ 160, 164(a), (c) (the Health Information Portability and Accountability Act "Privacy Rule").

55. *See, e.g.,* 8 C.F.R. § 208.6 (asylum and credible fear determinations); 8 U.S.C. § 1367(a)(2), (b) (claims for relief under the Violence against Women Act).

56. *See, e.g.,* 31 U.S.C. § 3730(b)(2), (3) (seal provisions of the Federal False Claims Act).

network environments, including many government agencies and commercial entities. The U.S. government has characterized the attack as "an intelligence gathering effort" and identified the actor as an Advanced Persistent Threat (APT), likely Russia.[57] While many customers were able to remediate the tainted software without further damage, the hackers were able to successfully compromise at least nine federal agencies and 100 companies' computing environments,[58] including the Department of Justice and Department of State.[59] While this sophisticated supply chain attack continues to be investigated and assessed, some key lessons learned are already apparent, including the need both for better software security practices by software vendors and effective third party risk management protocols by customers, particularly for critical vendors.

WikiLeaks/Manning and Snowden. The Manning[60] and Snowden[61] events taught the government that the insider threat can be every bit as dangerous as a threat emanating from outside. One of the crucial lessons to be drawn from these two cases is the need to be able to monitor and detect an insider who is downloading large amounts of data, particularly of a highly classified nature.[62] Additionally, considering that Manning was able to download highly classified information onto a USB and CDs to carry it out of his work environment, many parts of the DoD and the government

---

57. Press Release, Office of the Director of National Intelligence, Joint Statement by the Federal Bureau of Investigation (FBI), the Cybersecurity and Infrastructure Security Agency (CISA), the Office of the Director of National Intelligence (ODNI), and the National Security Agency (NSA) (Jan. 5, 2021), https://www.dni.gov/index.php/newsroom/press-releases /press-releases-2021/item/2176-joint-statement-by-the-federal-bureau-of-investigation-fbi -the-cybersecurity-and-infrastructure-security-organization-cisa-the-office-of-the-director-of -national-intelligence-odni-and-the-national-security-organization-nsa.

58. *See* Press Briefing by Press Sec'y Jen Psaki and Deputy Nat'l Security Advisor for Cyber and Emerging Tech. Anne Neuberger (Feb. 17, 2021), https://www.whitehouse.gov/briefing-room /press-briefings/2021/02/17/press-briefing-by-press-secretary-jen-psaki-and-deputy-national -security-advisor-for-cyber-and-emerging-technology-anne-neuberger-february-17-2021/.

59. Press Release, DOJ, Department of Justice Statement on Solarwinds Update (Jan. 6, 2021), https://www.justice.gov/opa/pr/department-justice-statement-solarwinds-update.

60. https://www.justiceinitiative.org/litigation/united-states-v-private-first-class -chelsea-manning.

61. *Edward Snowden: Leaks That Exposed US Spy Programme*, BBC NEWS (Jan. 17, 2014), https://www.bbc.com/news/world-us-canada-23123964.

62. Vijay Basani, *Edward Snowden and the NSA: A Lesson about Insider Threats*, BLOOMBERG (July 3, 2013).

began to prohibit or more tightly control the use of removable media.[63] They also began to require multifactor identification or a "dual-key" system where more than one person was required to be present in order to access or download particularly sensitive information. To best prevent the large-scale theft of information, government agencies should ensure that they have a multifactor identification process, strong data encryption, and hardened operating systems.[64]

The OPM Breach. Until two years prior to this attack,[65] OPM did not have an internal IT security staff, which may have hindered its ability to inventory its own IT systems.[66] An OPM Inspector General report just prior to the attack identified many deficiencies in IT security, and noted it was uncertain whether there was a vulnerability scanning program at all.[67] OPM had also relied on a new technology, the EINSTEIN intrusion and detection system, developed by US-CERT,[68] which did not allow OPM to discover the December 2014 breach until new threat signatures were added to the system in April 2015.[69]

The IRS Hack. The Internal Revenue Service (IRS) hack involved the use of stolen Social Security numbers, birth dates, and other personal data to allow cybercriminals to answer personal identity verification questions in order to enter the Get Transcript database, which stores personal tax information.[70] This permitted the hackers to file false tax returns and collect

---

63. Raf Sanchez, *WikiLeaks: Five Things We Learned from the Bradley Manning Case,* TELEGRAPH (July 30, 2013).

64. Simon Aspinall, *One Year Later: Lessons Learned from the Snowden-NSA Scandal,* VENTURE BEAT (May 21, 2014), https://venturebeat.com/2014/05/21/one-year-later-lessons-learned-from-the-snowden-nsa-scandal/.

65. https://www.opm.gov/cybersecurity/cybersecurity-incidents/.

66. Joseph Abrenio, *Law Firms Can Learn from Government Data Breaches,* BLOOMBERG BIG LAW BUS. (June 12, 2015).

67. *Id.*

68. US-CERT is the U.S. Computer Emergency Readiness Team, operated by the Department of Homeland Security, which responds to major cybersecurity incidents, analyzes threats, and exchanges cybersecurity information with our partners worldwide. See US-CERT homepage, https://www.us-cert.gov/about-us, for more information.

69. Abrenio, *supra* note 66.

70. Kevin McCoy, *Cyber Hack Got Access to over 700,000 IRS Accounts,* USA TODAY (Feb. 26, 2016), https://www.usatoday.com/story/money/2016/02/26/cyber-hack-gained-access-more-than-700000-irs-accounts/80992822/.

refunds.[71] The fact that this incident occurred was viewed as a culmination of "back-to-back" failures, including failure to screen and conduct background checks on personnel with access to sensitive data, and that the IRS computer system lacked the "minimum requirements" to protect its data.[72] The IRS was, in 2015, still using a 13-year-old operating system, with 19-year-old antifraud software.[73] The IRS Get Transcript program only had single-factor identification, and allowed multiple IRS accounts to be linked to one e-mail address.[74] One critical lesson to be learned for all government lawyers from this event is the importance of maintaining the highest levels of data protection available, including making sure that multiple accounts of any kind containing personal data cannot be accessed through a single e-mail address. As stated in the previous section, the use of multifactor identification is a basic and critical security control.

IV. Government Centric Attacks: National Security and Critical Infrastructure

A. Data Exfiltration

Beyond these known attacks, there are almost certainly compromises of many government systems that neither users nor systems administrators are aware of until it is too late. In today's world, the exfiltration of data is the province not merely of individual hackers or criminals, but increasingly of both foreign governments and hacking collectives such as Anonymous and LulzSec. President Biden's recent attribution to Russia of the Solar Winds incident and decision to retaliate against them on April 15, 2021, marks a turning point in directly calling out a nation-state for an attack.[75] China has long been viewed as another nation-state that engages in cyber breaches, and on July 21, 2021, the Biden administration officially accused China of breaching Microsoft e-mail systems used by government and military

---

71. *Id.*
72. *Id.*; Abrenio, *supra* note 66.
73. McCoy, *supra* note 70.
74. *Id.*
75. *Id.* at 2.

contractors, as well as companies as part of its official policy.[76] Secretary of State Blinken stated that China's Ministry of State Security "fostered an ecosystem of criminal contract hackers who carry out both state-sponsored activities and cybercrime for their own financial gain."[77]

Russia and China have long been viewed as state actors engaging in cybersecurity espionage and activity.

James Clapper, the Director of National Intelligence in 2012, asserted that the prior decade had seen an "increased breadth and sophistication of computer network operations . . . by both state and non-state actors,"[78] citing both China and Russia as state actors of particular concern.[79] The intelligence community also assessed that "Chinese actors are among the most active and persistent perpetrators of economic espionage," and that intelligence services in Russia are also engaging in collection.[80] These include, of course, the well-publicized efforts to interfere with the 2016 presidential election. In 2021, the cybersecurity company Crowdstrike released a report that identified cyber threats by nation-state by industry, including North Korea, China, Iran, and Russia.[81]

B. "Armed" Attacks

Beyond data exfiltration, what happens when a foreign government uses cyberspace to carry out a direct attack on another country? President Joe Biden told U.S. intelligence officials in July 2021 that "if we end up in a

---

76. Zolan Kanno-Youngs & David E. Sanger, *U.S. Accuses China of Hacking Microsoft*, N.Y. TIMES (updated July 20, 2021), https://www.nytimes.com/2021/07/19/us/politics/micro soft-hacking-china-biden.html.

77. *Id.*

78. James R. Clapper, Dir. of Nat'l Intelligence, Unclassified Statement for the Record on the Worldwide Threat Assessment of the US Intelligence Community for the Senate Committee on Armed Services (Feb. 16, 2012), http://www.dni.gov/files/documents/Newsroom /Testimonies/20120216_SASC%20Final%20Unclassified%20-%202012%20ATA%20SFR.pdf.

79. *Id. See also Dozens of Cyber Attacks Target Heart of Government Every Month, GCHQ Chief Warns*, TELEGRAPH, Feb. 12, 2017 (The United Kingdom government also lists China and Russia as the primary culprits.).

80. Office of the Nat'l Counterintelligence Exec., Foreign Spies Stealing US Economic Secrets in Cyberspace: Report to Congress on Foreign Economic Collection and Indus. Espionage, 2009–2011 (Oct. 2011), cited in USTR Special Report (2013), https://ustr.gov/sites /default/files/05012013%202013%20Special%20301%20Report.pdf.

81. *See* Crowdstrike 2021 Global Threat Report, https://www.crowdstrike.com/resources /reports/global-threat-report/.

war, a real shooting war, with a major power—it's going to be as a consequence of a cyber breach of great consequence."[82] On July 28, 2021, President Biden signed a National Security Memorandum on Improving Cybersecurity for Critical Infrastructure Control Systems, designed to prevent attacks against America's critical infrastructure.[83] This was in response to recent ransomware attacks against the United States reportedly by Russia, including an attack against Colonial Pipeline, which provides gasoline to the East Coast of the United States, and JBS which is the world's largest beef producer.[84] The new National Security memorandum creates an Industrial Control Systems Cybersecurity Initiative, which is a collaborative effort between the government and the critical infrastructure community designed to encourage and facilitate the development of new technologies and systems that better detect, warn, and respond against potential critical infrastructure attacks.[85] It also requires relevant agencies to develop and issue cybersecurity performance goals for critical infrastructure in order to better understand baseline security practices that critical infrastructure owners and operators need to follow.[86] Government attorneys will need to follow up on these recent developments and be aware of the new changes and additional legislation that follow them.

The first significant "armed cyberattack" from one country to another, however, was the 2007 attack on Estonia, a country heavily reliant on the Internet, allegedly carried out by the Russian government. Estonia's newspapers were attacked first; then botnets attacked banks, police, and the national government, overwhelming the government systems and emergency response

---

82. Shannon Vavra, *Biden Warns a "Real Shooting War" Could Come from a Cyber Breach "of Great Consequence,"* DAILY BEAST (July 28, 2021), https://www.thedailybeast .com/biden-warns-a-real-shooting-war-could-come-from-cyber-breach.

83. National Security Memorandum on Improving Cybersecurity for Critical Infrastructure Control Systems (July 28, 2021), https://www.whitehouse.gov/briefing-room /statements-releases/2021/07/28/national-security-memorandum-on-improving-cybersecurity -for-critical-infrastructure-control-systems/; David E. Sanger, *Biden Signs an Executive Order Aimed at Protecting Critical American Infrastructure from Cyberattacks,* N.Y. TIMES, July 28, 2021.

84. National Security Memorandum, *supra* note 83.

85. *Id.*

86. *Id.*

systems.[87] As NATO and the EU debated whether and how to respond to this "attack"—whether it was an armed attack that would trigger collective self-defense under article 5 of the NATO Charter, or something else—Tallinn, the capital of Estonia, quickly became the epicenter for the study of cyberattacks. Between 2009 and 2012, a group of 20 international experts at the NATO Cooperative Cyber Defense Center of Excellence prepared the Tallinn Manual, which focused on the complex issue of how to apply international law to cyber operations and cyber warfare.[88] Specifically, the Tallinn Manual assessed when states could respond to cyberattacks as "armed attacks," triggering the right of self-defense under international law.[89] Although it is not a binding legal document, the Tallinn Manual has become an important source on this subject, and is an essential reference for any government attorney who is charged with analysis of these issues.[90]

Consistent with the Tallinn Manual, the U.S. government was the first to publicly state that a cyber operation resulting in death, injury, or significant destruction would likely be considered an illegal use of force against the United States, potentially triggering the right of self-defense under article 51 of the U.N. Charter.[91] NATO followed in September 2014, indicating that such an attack could justify invocation of article 5 of the NATO treaty (the provision for collective self-defense), and shortly thereafter, the U.N. Group of Governmental Experts on Developments in the Field of Information and Telecommunications in the Context of International Security also affirmed the right of self-defense under article 51 of the U.N. Charter.[92] At this point, there is sufficiently broad-based international consensus that cyberattacks can be considered acts of war in appropriate circumstances.

---

87. Patrick Howell O'Neill, *The Cyberattack That Changed the World*, DAILY DOT (last updated Feb. 24, 2017).

88. TALLINN MANUAL ON THE INTERNATIONAL LAW APPLICABLE TO CYBER WARFARE (Michael N. Schmitt gen. ed., 2013).

89. *Id.*

90. For more thorough discussion, see *infra* Chapter 5 on International Law and Norms.

91. Ellen Nakashima, *Cyberattacks Could Trigger Self-Defense Rule, U.S. Official Says*, WASH. POST, Sept. 18, 2012 (referencing U.S. State Department Legal Advisor Harold Koh in a speech at U.S. Cyber Command).

92. UN Gen. Assembly, Group of Governmental Experts on Developments in the Field of Information and Telecommunications in the Context of International Security, A/68/98 (June 24, 2013).

While determination of what constitutes an act of cyber war is not the concern of most government attorneys, it does occupy the time of government cyber attorneys in the national security field.

In March 2016, the U.S. Justice Department announced that members of Iran's Islamic Revolutionary Guards Corps had launched an online attack against critical U.S. infrastructure in 2013, by entering the computerized command and controls of a dam in New York City.[93] Attorney General Lynch stated that this type of attack was particularly alarming because an attack on critical infrastructure can have a large impact on the safety and welfare of our citizens.[94] This event demonstrated the importance of ensuring that all of our government's assets are protected from cyberattacks. What about future attacks on larger dams, the water supply, transportation infrastructure, or hospitals? Harold Koh, then the U.S. State Department Legal Advisor, warned in an earlier speech that a cyberattack on a nuclear plant or a dam above a populated areas, or against the air-traffic control system causing plane crashes, could trigger a response in self-defense.[95] In the same incident, the Iranians also attacked the New York Stock Exchange, AT&T, and several financial institutions,[96] demonstrating the widespread capabilities of their reach and the vulnerability of all of our institutions to cyberattacks from foreign governments. On February 5, 2021, a water treatment facility in Oldsmar, Florida, suffered a cyberattack from a hacker, which adjusted the levels of sodium hydroxide in the water, which could have been dangerous if not addressed immediately.[97] Just a few months later, in May 2021, a Russian hacker group DarkSide initiated the Colonial Pipeline ransomware attack, which resulted in gas shortages and lines, and a spike in gas prices, demonstrating the potential widespread effects of an

---

93. Mark Thompson, *Iranian Cyber Attack on New York Dam Shows Future of War*, TIME (Mar. 24, 2016); Dustin Volz & Jim Finkle, *U.S. Indicts Iranians for Hacking Dozens of Banks, New York Dam*, REUTERS (Mar. 25, 2016).

94. Volz & Finkle, *supra* note 93.

95. Nakashima, *supra* note 91 (referencing U.S. State Department Legal Advisor Harold Koh in a speech at U.S. Cyber Command).

96. Thompson, *supra* note 93.

97. Steve Kardon, *Florida Water Treatment Plant Hit with Cyber Attack*, INDUSTRIAL DEFENDER (Feb. 9, 2021), https://www.industrialdefender.com/florida-water-treatment-plant-cyber-attack/.

attack on critical infrastructure.[98] These incidences highlight the increasing need to ensure that there is clear and applicable legal framework in place for nations to address attacks on their country that could impact national security.

The February 2017 Tallinn Manual 2.0 looks more closely at the legal framework applicable to attacks that do not rise to the level of "armed attack,"[99] making this version much more broadly applicable to lawyers in this field than the original Tallinn Manual. The NATO Cyber Cooperative Center of Excellence has committed to publish a Tallinn Manual 3.0 following the same process as the prior two publications.[100] The Tallinn Manual 3.0 project was launched in 2021 and is expected to last for five years, and will serve as a revision of the existing editions to comply with State practice and statements made by governments and other organizations on international law.[101] The Tallinn Manual 3.0 project will capture evolving State positions on the legal framework applicable to cyber operations, and is expected to address specific evolving legal analysis on the subject of sovereignty and the qualification of cyber operations as "attacks" under the law of armed conflict. Government attorneys who specialize in cybersecurity issues should be familiar with both the Tallinn Manual and Tallinn Manual 2.0, and keep abreast of legal developments coming out of the Tallinn Manual 3.0 process.

V. Significant U.S. Cyber-Related Legislation

Despite multiple attempts at achieving comprehensive federal cybersecurity legislation, Congress has been more successful at passing more focused

---

98. Sean Michael Kerner, *Colonial Pipeline Hack Explained: Everything You Need to Know*, WHATIs.COM (July 7, 2021), https://whatis.techtarget.com/feature Colonial-Pipeline-hack-explained-Everything-you-need-to-know.

99. TALLINN MANUAL 2.0 ON THE INTERNATIONAL LAW APPLICABLE TO CYBER OPERATIONS (Michael N. Schmitt gen. ed., 2d ed. 2017).

100. *CCDOE to Host the Tallinn Manual 3.0 Process*, https://ccdcoe.org/news/2020 /ccdcoe-to-host-the-tallinn-manual-3-0-process.

101. *The CCDOE Invites Experts to Contribute to the Tallinn Manual 3.0*, https://ccdcoe .org/news/2021/the-ccdcoe-invites-experts-to-contribute-to-the-tallinn-manual-3-0/.

legislation than a comprehensive bill. States have generally not passed comprehensive bills either, however, the State legislatures have been active, and at least 38 states plus Washington, DC, and Puerto Rico have all passed significant measures on cybersecurity.[102] These state laws cover topics ranging from training requirements, incident response, and mandating insurance to the establishment of task forces, councils, or commissions.[103]

The two main federal cybersecurity laws that are currently in place are (1) the Federal Information Security Management Act of 2002 (FISMA), as amended by the Federal Information Security Modernization Act of 2014 (FISMA Reform); and (2) the Cybersecurity Information Sharing Act of 2015 (CISA), described in detail later. Together, these two statutes mandate that federal government agencies protect information and systems.

At the time of this third edition of the Handbook, the Cyber Incident Notification Act of 2021, sponsored by Senators Warner, Rubio, and Collins, is reportedly soon to become part of the National Defense Authorization Act.[104] This bill aims to impose mandatory reporting within 24 hours of confirmation of a cyber intrusion or potential intrusion, and subsequent updates within 72 hours of new threat information until the intrusion is mitigated or the investigation is closed.[105] The new legislation will also impose an annual reporting requirement with detailed numbers and types of cybersecurity intrusions that have been reported during the year.[106]

A.   FISMA

In the case of cybersecurity and data breaches at the federal level, attorneys must ensure that their federal government clients have addressed laws requiring the safeguarding of federal systems and the protection of personally identifiable information. FISMA sets forth a comprehensive regime for ensuring the security of information in the federal government. Consistent

---

102. Cybersecurity Legislation 2020, National Conference of State Legislatures (Apr. 1, 2021), https://www.ncsl.org/research/telecommunications-and-information-technology /cybersecurity-legislation-2020.aspx.

103. *Id.*

104. *Bipartisan Group of Senators Introduce Draft Federal Data Breach Notification Bill*, HIPAA J. (June 22, 2021), https://www.hipaajournal.com/bipartisan-group-of -senators-introduce-federal-data-breach-notification-bill/.

105. *Id.*

106. *Id.*

with basic principles of computer security, information security is defined as systems that ensure confidentiality, integrity, and availability of data.[107] FISMA requires departments and agencies to inventory their systems and adopt appropriate security controls "commensurate with the risk and magnitude of the harm resulting from unauthorized access, use, disclosure, disruption, modification or destruction."[108] Lawyers should work closely with the organization's chief information officer (CIO) and chief information security officer (CISO) established under FISMA to administer the organization's responsibilities in reporting its information security posture to the Office of Management and Budget (OMB).

In coordination with their organization's chief privacy officer, government lawyers must also address a series of privacy rules, which include information security provisions. With respect to information about individuals contained in a Privacy Act[109] systems of records, agencies must "establish appropriate administrative, technical, and physical safeguards to insure the security and confidentiality of records and to protect against any anticipated threats or hazards to their security or integrity which could result in substantial harm, embarrassment, inconvenience, or unfairness to any individual on whom the information is maintained."[110] In the case of new technology systems, agencies may be required by the E-Government Act of 2002[111] to perform a privacy impact assessment (PIA). The E-Government Act requires PIAs for new technology systems that include information in an "identifiable form." Among other things, PIAs must include a statement addressing "how the information will be secured."[112]

In addressing these issues, lawyers should consult closely with OMB and should familiarize themselves with OMB guidance with respect to FISMA, the E-Government Act, and the Privacy Act. OMB has issued specific guidance with respect to FISMA to ensure information security. National security

---

107. 44 U.S.C. § 3542(b)(1). *Confidentiality*, *integrity*, and *availability* are information security terms that define the characteristics of secure systems. *See* MICHAEL T. GOODRICH & ROBERTO TAMASSIA, INTRODUCTION TO COMPUTER SECURITY 3–8 (2011).

108. 44 U.S.C. § 3544(a)(1)(A).

109. Privacy Act of 1974, 5 U.S.C. § 552a.

110. *Id.* § 552a(e)(10).

111. Pub. L. No. 107-347, as amended, set out at 44 U.S.C. § 3501 note.

112. *Id.* § 208.

systems are treated separately, with responsibilities shared between the Secretary of Defense and the Director of National Intelligence.[113]

Where data breaches involve classified information, a number of special considerations come into play. Executive Order 13,587 of October 2011, which was issued in the wake of the WikiLeaks disclosures, lays out structural reforms to improve the security of computer networks that contain classified information.[114] It reinforces the responsibilities of agencies to safeguard classified information on computer networks, and to share such information responsibly, addressing the misperception that information-sharing mandates following the September 11 attacks had tipped the balance decisively in favor of sharing such information at all costs.

Executive Order 13,587 established several new interagency bodies to coordinate safeguarding efforts.[115] It also references a number of legal authorities and requirements with which government attorneys in national security agencies should be familiar. For example, attorneys in intelligence agencies must be satisfied that the security of national security information is sufficient to protect intelligence sources and methods;[116] attorneys in DoJ must be concerned with the security of information collected under the Foreign Intelligence Surveillance Act and the orders of the court authorizing such collection.[117] The executive order recognizes the need for greater sharing of cybersecurity-related information across federal agencies. Today, attorneys throughout multiple agencies—not only agencies within the intelligence community—must be concerned with the statutory and other legal protections that apply to information that may have originated within

---

113. Memorandum from Jeffrey D. Zients, Deputy Dir. for Mgmt., and Vivek Kundra, U.S. Chief Info. Officer, Office of Mgmt. and Budget, to Heads of Exec. Dep'ts and Agencies, M-09-29, FY 2009 Reporting Instructions for the Federal Information Security Management Act and Organization Privacy Management (Aug. 20, 2009), https://www.whitehouse.gov/sites/whitehouse.gov/files/omb/memoranda/2009/m09-29.pdf.

114. Exec. Order No. 13,587, Structural Reforms to Improve the Security of Classified Networks and the Responsible Sharing and Safeguarding of Classified Information, 76 Fed. Reg. 198, 3 C.F.R. 276 (Oct. 7, 2011).

115. *Id.*

116. 50 U.S.C. § 403-1(i)(1) ("The Director of National Intelligence shall protect sources and methods from unauthorized disclosure.").

117. *See* 50 U.S.C. § 1802(c)(2) (An order for electronic surveillance must be implemented "in such a manner as will protect its secrecy," and records must be maintained "under security procedures approved by the Attorney General and the Director of National Intelligence.").

another organization. The best thing to do is to spell out such responsibilities in a written information-sharing agreement.

B. CISA

As discussed earlier, in 2015, Congress passed CISA to "improve cybersecurity in the United States through enhanced sharing of information about cybersecurity threats, and for other purposes."[118] This law was designed to improve information sharing between the U.S. government and the private sector on cybersecurity threats that appear in Internet traffic, and permits private companies to share with the government information that is otherwise personal and protected if it poses a cybersecurity threat.[119] There are provisions in CISA to protect personally identifiable information that is not relevant to the potential cyber threat.[120]

Throughout the federal government, issues of data breach and information security can arise in unexpected ways. For example, the Department of Veterans Affairs mistakenly released information on more than 4,000 living veterans to ancestry.com as part of a massive Freedom of Information Act (FOIA) request for the records of over 14.7 million deceased veterans.[121] While attorneys cannot prevent every mistake by their clients, prudence may require treating FOIA requests for large volumes of electronic data differently from those involving paper files. Even a database with a relatively small error rate may result in a large number of mistaken disclosures if the database is large enough.

Beyond the protection of information, Congress passed the National Cybersecurity and Critical Infrastructure Protection Act in 2014, requiring the DHS Secretary to conduct cybersecurity activities to protect against, prevent, mitigate, respond to, and recover from cyber incidents. Along with this mandate, the legislation established the NCCIC (referenced earlier), and directed the DHS to create a cyber workforce.[122]

---

118. Cybersecurity Information Sharing Act of 2015, Pub. L. No. 114-113, div. N, tit. I, 129 Stat. 2936 (Dec. 18, 2015).

119. *Id.*

120. *Id.*

121. Nicole Blake Johnson, *More Than 4,000 Vets Potentially Affected by VA Data Breach*, FED. TIMES (Jan. 25, 2012).

122. H.R. 3696, National Cybersecurity and Critical Infrastructure Protection Act of 2014, 113th Cong. (July 28, 2014), https://www.congress.gov/bill/113th congress/house-bill/3696,

VI. Best Practices for the Government Lawyer for Cybersecurity

The government lawyer needs to know the basics of how to best protect government systems, which store critical personal information on our citizens and which protect the safety and security of our country as a whole. These systems are increasingly under attack from individual actors, cyber hackers, and other nation-states for a variety of purposes as discussed in this chapter. To navigate these challenges, government lawyers should consider the following Top 11 Best Practices.

1. Ensure that you are familiar with all major cybersecurity laws in place and evolving legislation.
   - Be aware of the existing cybersecurity laws, starting with President Biden's 2021 Executive Order 14028 on Improving the Nation's Cybersecurity, as well as FISMA, FISMA Reform, CISA, E-Government Act of 2002, and the Privacy Act, and check regularly for updates to these laws. If the Cyber Incident Notification Act of 2021 is enacted as well, be aware of its new requirements. Review OMB guidance on implementation of these regulations, and their specific guidance on information security. If you work in a national security organization, recognize that there are additional responsibilities managed by the Secretary of Defense and the Director of National Intelligence, and familiarize yourself with these.
   - Consistent with current legislation, there are a series of actions that you should take to ensure that you are compliant with the law and taking those steps necessary to protect sensitive data. Ensure your organization has familiarized itself with the new Cybersecurity Safety Review Board provisions, and is prepared to support its efforts as needed. Similarly, if the Cyber Incident Notification Act of 2021 is enacted, develop a plan for your organization to put it into effect.
2. Assess and make sure that your organization's systems have in place appropriate security controls to protect information from being accessed or altered by unauthorized users. A series of software

options to augment protection where needed can help you to protect against emerging threats. Because the threat continues to develop, you need to remain vigilant about understanding new challenges and vulnerabilities.

3. Ensure that you have in place a program to protect any personally identifiable information (PII) of your employees or of other individuals if your organization collects such information.

4. Establish a strong working relationship with your organization's CIO and CISO, so that you know all of the steps they have put in place to ensure the best cyber hygiene. Verify that they are meeting regular information security reporting requirements to OMB and Congress (where required) and review their reporting to make sure that all legal obligations are being met. Ensure that your organization has in place a cybersecurity protection policy and review it. Engage the CISO in a discussion of areas where you think it may not be strong enough. Engage your CIO and CISO on steps taken to prevent insiders from accessing or altering sensitive data, PII, or classified data if your organization maintains it. Are removable media, such as thumb drives or CDs allowed, and, if so, who is authorized to use them or approve them? Do you have a dual-key authentication requirement in order to download particularly sensitive information?

5. Consult with your organization's chief privacy officer to learn about what policies your organization has in place to protect privacy, and how your organization assesses when you are required to perform a PIA for new technology systems.

6. Examine whether existing training programs are adequate to ensure compliance with all applicable cyber laws. Learn from other agencies what their best practices are for enhancing training opportunities.

7. Verify that your organization's records management policy ensures the protection of sensitive information that may be contained in computer files, databases, or e-mails.

8. Ensure proper handling of sensitive information.
    - If your organization handles classified information, review Executive Order 13,587 to ensure that your organization is compliant and is handling and sharing information responsibly.

- If your organization is involved in intelligence, also verify that any information related to intelligence sources and methods are sufficiently protected.
- If you are handling foreign intelligence issues at the DoJ, ensure that all of the information collected under the Foreign Intelligence Surveillance Act and any court orders are protected on your computer systems.

9. Know how to identify and respond to a cyber event, and when it is necessary to treat a cyber event as an armed attack.

- In the event of a cyber incident, whenever it may occur, ensure that your organization immediately takes every step possible to identify the nature of the threat and counteract it. Timeliness is critical in minimizing damage to a system, protecting information that a third party could be accessing, and taking remedial steps to repair the system. Cyber hackers and intruders may well act when they think the fewest people are watching or are available to respond—late at night, over the weekends, or on holidays.

10. If the cyberattack involves any type of damage or critical infrastructure, ensure that your organization immediately puts in place its highest level of emergency response and engages the DHS.

- For the much smaller number of government lawyers who specialize in national security cyber issues, read the Tallinn Manual and Tallinn 2.0 to be familiar with what types of attacks may be considered armed attacks and know who in your organization you should alert to these issues. Keep abreast of developments on the development of Tallinn 3.0, which will be the most recent international perspective on the application of the law of armed conflict to cyber security. Familiarize yourself with the U.S. policy on cyberattacks that could constitute an armed attack, and what the reporting chain in your department is for such incidents.

11. State AGs need to remain abreast of state-specific privacy laws that may require additional security controls, as well as the state specific consumer protection laws. They should seek opportunities to work with other state AGs on potential multi-state and privacy-related cybersecurity matters that may be of mutual interest. They should also seek opportunities to work with federal organizations such as the FTC.

Chapter 12
Why Public Interest Attorneys Should Care about Cybersecurity

Edward Marchewka and Ozoda Usmanova

I.   What Makes Public Interest Organizations Unique

Public interest organizations (PIOs), nongovernmental organizations (NGOs), and nonprofit organizations (NPOs) are not necessarily different from other organizations. In fact, these organizations are allowed to make a profit. There is a saying in this space, "No margin, no mission." They must generate positive value; otherwise, they cannot continue their good work. The names NGO or NPO are misnomers; in actuality, these names are simply tax designations. These organizations should be called nontaxable entities because the successful ones generate a profit that allows their mission-driven work to continue.

However, due to their nature of being highly mission-driven, information security often takes a backseat to the good work that these organizations complete. A failure in information security will inevitably affect revenue and thus the mission. The strong drive for mission exacerbates the already strained information security relationship between boards and management, often due to knowledge gaps where one party may have more interest and knowledge about information security risks than the other. This gap is called information asymmetry.[1] Information asymmetry between information security professionals and executive leadership or the Board of Directors can

---

1. Donald D. Bergh et al., *Information Asymmetry in Management Research: Past Accomplishments and Future Opportunities*, 45(1) J. MGMT. 122–58 (2019), https://doi.org/10.1177/0149206318798026.

be hard to overcome. This challenge may be due to the immediate negative feelings that most people experience at the mention of cybersecurity[2] due to misunderstanding or perhaps fear of technology, and the lack of direct connection between cybersecurity and the organization's direct mission. Failure to close the information asymmetry gap leads to a poor understanding of true cyber risk and may often lead to emotional decision making, rather than data-based decision making. The result is a lack of focus and attention on information security and the increased risk of a cyber event, incident, or breach, which can have devastating effects. Board members and executives must be informed of risks and how they apply to the organization for the board and executive leadership to overcome these issues and to serve the organization so it can continue its mission. As counsel, being aware of cybersecurity threats and the impact on the organization is paramount given they are mission-focused with potentially significant positive social impact.

II. Impact of Cyber Breaches

It's a widespread misconception that nonprofit organizations engaged in social good are less likely to be targeted by cybercriminals. In fact, 43 percent of cyberattacks target small businesses, with nonprofits being as much of a target as for-profit organizations.[3] Ethical norms do not bind malicious perpetrators. An organization's size does not matter either; organizations of all sizes, regardless of their mission, possess something of value—personal information. Bad actors, therefore, will not shy away from stealing data from charity organizations, just like they would exfiltrate data from for-profit businesses and major corporations.

For example, a small homeless shelter was targeted in April 2019. The nonprofit Father Bill's and Mainspring that runs a downtown homeless

---

2. Karen Renaud et al., *Exploring Cybersecurity-Related Emotions and Finding That They Are Challenging to Measure*, 8(1) HUMANITIES & SOC. SCIS. COMMC'NS (2021), https://doi .org/10.1057/s41599-021-00746-5.

3. Maddie Shepherd, *30 Surprising Small Business Cyber Security Statistics 2021*, FUN-DERA BY NERDWALLET (Dec. 16, 2020), www.fundera.com/resources/small-business-cyber-secu rity-statistics#:%7E:text=Overview%3A%2030%20Small%20Business%20Cyber,than%20 %242.2%20million%20a%20year.

shelter in Massachusetts announced that it was a target in a ransomware attack.[4] However, this Brockton-based nonprofit doesn't believe that anyone's personal information was accessed or stolen.[5] The CEO of Father Bill's stated that an antivirus software used by the nonprofit was able to stop the ransomware attack in its tracks without locking up any of the office computers.[6] Significant credit should be given to this organization that, despite its small size, was prepared and able to thwart an attack.

In February 2021, Midwest Transplant Network (MTN), an organ procurement organization of Kansas City, suffered a ransomware attack that compromised the records of more than 17,000 individuals. Protected health information about deceased donors and transplant recipients, including names, dates of birth, organs donated, and transplant procedures, was stolen. MTN was also locked out of its systems for a brief time.[7]

The impact of these breaches is not only the theft of sensitive and valuable information, as in the case of MTN, but these attacks can also impact an organization's ability to serve its constituents, as was the case with MTN and Father Bill's. MTN and Father Bill's needed to put focus into the investigations. Additionally, with the remediation at MTN, resources were not focused on their mission. In another example, a third-party provider of network services to several nonprofits was hit with a ransomware attack in 2019, which caused one organization to lose all of its data and another nonprofit to cancel a performance.[8] In both cases, operations were impacted, which affected these organizations' ability to meet their mission.

Another event occurred with the breach of a third party in May 2020. Blackbaud, a cloud computing provider that serves the social-good

4. Marc Larocque, *Massachusetts Nonprofit Shelter Targeted by Ransomware*, GovTech (June 28, 2019), www.govtech.com/security/massachusetts-nonprofit-shelter-targeted-by-ransomware.html.

5. *Id.*

6. *Id.*

7. Dan Margolies, *Ransomware Attack on Midwest Transplant Network Affects More Than 17,000*, Kan. Public Radio (May 3, 2021), kansaspublicradio.org/kpr-news/ransomware-attack-midwest-transplant-network-affects-more-17000.

8. Kevin Coughlin, *"It Was Like a Tornado": Cyber Thieves Demand $500K Ransom in Attack Targeting Contractor Serving Greater Morristown Nonprofits*, Morristown Green (Dec. 9, 2019), morristowngreen.com/2019/12/09/it-was-like-a-tornado-cyber-thieves-demand-500k-ransom-in-attack-targeting-contractor-serving-greater-morristown-nonprofits.

community,[9] fell victim to a ransomware attack. The names, addresses, bank account information, records of individual donations, and usernames and passwords of these companies were compromised by hackers, who were then paid an undisclosed ransom to return the data and delete any copies.[10] World Vision, Planned Parenthood, Save the Children, and Human Rights Watch were among the large nonprofits impacted by the breach, and media reports suggest that at least 200 organizations were compromised.[11]

In this case, the attack appeared to come from Nobelium, a known malicious organization based in Russia. While organizations in the United States received the largest share of attacks, targeted victims spanned at least 24 countries. At least a quarter of the targeted organizations were involved in international development, humanitarian, and human rights work.[12] When trying to break down the origin of the attack, it became clear that the same malicious actors that attacked larger organizations were also eager to attack NGOs and others. It was the same actor behind the attacks on SolarWinds customers in 2020.[13] This wave of attacks targeted approximately 3,000 e-mail accounts at more than 150 different organizations.[14]

That said, these attacks appeared to be a continuation of multiple efforts by Nobelium to target government and NGOs involved in foreign policy as part of intelligence-gathering efforts.[15] In May 2021, Microsoft reported cyberattacks by the threat actor Nobelium, targeting government and NGOs, think tanks, and consultants.[16] Nobelium launched these attacks by gaining access to the Constant Contact account, a service used for e-mail marketing

---

9. Members of the social-good community promote practices that are better for the environment and overall society and include nonprofits, foundations, corporations, education institutions, health care organizations, religious organizations, and individual change agents.

10. Coughlin, *supra* note 8.

11. Ben Parker, *Dozens of NGOs Hit by Hack on US Fundraising Database*, THE NEW HUMANITARIAN (Aug. 4, 2020), www.thenewhumanitarian.org/news/2020/08/04/NGO-fundraising-database-hack.

12. The SolarWinds incident is discussed throughout this Handbook. Please see Chapter 2 *infra* for reference.

13. *Id.*

14. *Id.*

15. Tom Burt, *Another Nobelium Cyberattack*, MICROSOFT ON THE ISSUES (May 27, 2021), blogs.microsoft.com/on-the-issues/2021/05/27/nobelium-cyberattack-nativezone-solarwinds.

16. *Id.*

of USAID.[17] From there, the actor was able to distribute phishing e-mails that looked authentic.[18] However, it included a link that downloaded a malicious file that was used to distribute a backdoor to enable a wide range of activities from stealing data to infecting other computers on a network.[19]

Despite the increase of ransomware attacks in the past couple of years, most nonprofits do not have the dedicated staff to deal with cybersecurity incidents. Microsoft surveyed 50 nonprofits through its partners TechSoup and NTEN.[20] Most of the respondents reported that their organizations had modern IT infrastructure;[21] however, Microsoft's survey identified that most respondents did not use essential cybersecurity controls, which would include:

- Inventory and control of enterprise hardware and software assets
- Protecting data
- Secure configuration of enterprise assets and software
- Identity, access control, and account management
- Vulnerability management
- Audit log management
- E-mail web browser and protections
- Malware defenses
- Back-ups and data recovery
- Network infrastructure management, monitoring, and defense
- End-user security awareness and skills training
- Third-party provider management
- Application software security
- Incident response management and penetration testing[22]

---

17. *Id.*

18. *Id.*

19. *Id.*

20. Microsoft Philanthropies, Nonprofit Guidelines for Cybersecurity and Privacy (2017), www.microsoftalumni.com/s/1769/images/gid2/editor_documents/giving/microsoft_nonprofit _cybersecurity_and_data_privacy_best_practices_white_paper.pdf?gid=2&pgid=61&session id=4e57db08-0f9f-47df-a502-f29e03b19036&cc=1.

21. *Id.*

22. CIS (Center for Internet Security), *The 18 Controls* (June 3, 2021), www.cisecurity .org/controls/cis-controls-list.

This data was drawn from a survey of 50 nonprofit organizations: 14 small (1–50 employees), 6 medium (51–250 employees), and 30 large organizations (with more than 250 employees).[23]

Furthermore, the Microsoft survey identified the following deficiencies in many organizations:

1. Sixty percent stated that they did not have or know of an organizational digital policy that would determine how their organization handles cybersecurity risk, equipment usage, and data privacy.
2. Seventy-four percent reported that they did not use multifactor authentication (MFA) to access agency e-mail and other business accounts. MFA is a critical security step in ensuring accounts are not compromised even if passwords are stolen.
3. Forty-six percent reported that they regularly used wireless printers, webcams, and other Bluetooth and wireless devices. Unsecured wireless devices on a network provide an entry for attackers; these devices must be actively managed and regularly updated with required software patches to ensure security.
4. Ninety-two percent stated their staff could access organizational e-mail and files using their personal devices. The remaining 8 percent that did not permit staff to use personal devices for work reported that staff did it regardless.

This survey is another example of how many nonprofits struggle to manage their IT infrastructure and data, which is a critical step in ensuring organizational assets are secured and monitored.

With the increased frequency of adverse events, it is imperative that public interest and nonprofit organization board members and executives understand and embrace their increased responsibility to be stewards of the information under their control. From an optics perspective, protecting sensitive information under their guard is essential to maintaining a positive image and receiving donor and grant funding. Failure to do this could result in significant reputational and financial impact. Beyond the optics are the

---

23. Microsoft Philanthropies, *supra* note 20.

requirements from *Caremark*[24] and *Stone*[25]—landmark cases with respect to risk management. *Caremark* states, generally, that boards need to know about the risks in their organizations.[26] The *Stone* decision said that boards need to take action on those risks to limit personal liability. These two cases have been the benchmark for cases brought against boards and executives whereby the courts have used *Caremark* and *Stone* to decide whether the executives or board were negligent as illustrated in *Marchand v. Barnhill.*[27]

To further illustrate the application of the *Caremark* precedent, Veasey and Holland[28] discuss the duty of care needed from boards by analyzing the 2019 Delaware Supreme Court case of *Marchand v. Barnhill*. In *Marchand*, a derivative suit was brought against the CEO and VP of operations as well as against Blue Bell's directors claiming breaches of their fiduciary duties, in which a listeria outbreak caused a massive recall of ice cream, the sole product produced by Blue Bell Creameries USA, Inc. The listeria outbreak resulted in injury to and death of consumers along with layoffs, fines, reputation damages, and production shutdowns. The court allowed the case to proceed under the *Caremark* standard.

In overcoming the *Caremark* standard, the court permitted Marchand to proceed due to the limited board involvement in vital organizational

---

24. *In re* Caremark Int'l, 698 A.2d 959 (Del. Ch. 1996). In *Caremark*, the shareholders brought derivative action against the board of directors for breaching their duty of care. From this case, the court defined a multifactor test to determine if the board had failed in its duty of oversight.

25. Stone v. Ritter, 911 A.2d 362 (Del. 2006). In *Stone*, the shareholder sued the board members in their personal capacity alleging that the board of directors were derelict in their duties as prescribed in *Caremark*. The court found that while fraud did occur, the board did not breach their duties of care, loyalty, or fiduciary duties. The court held that despite the fact that the employees were able to bypass them, the board had attempted to put measures in place to detect and prevent fraud.

26. Risks include, but are not limited to, cybersecurity, financial, customer impacting, etc.

27. Marchand v. Barnhill, 212 A.3d 805 (Del. 2019). In *Marchand*, a derivative suit was brought against the CEO and VP of operations as well as against Blue Bell's directors claiming breaches of their fiduciary duties, in which a listeria outbreak caused a massive recall of ice cream, the sole product, produced by Blue Bell Creameries USA, Inc. The court ruled in favor of the plaintiffs because despite the fact the board should have known and taken steps, no affirmative action was taken by the board to prevent the listeria deaths.

28. E. Norman Veasey & Randy J. Holland, Caremark *at the Quarter-Century Watershed: Modern-Day Compliance Realities Frame Corporate Directors' Duty of Good Faith Oversight, Providing New Dynamics for Respecting Chancellor Allen's 1996* Caremark *Landmark*, 76(1) BUS. LAW. 1–29 (2021).

operations and a committee's lack of oversight to oversee food safety. Furthermore, there was not a requirement for management to report food safety issues to the board. One can assess the responsibility placed on the board of directors and draw similarities to cybersecurity in this context. This case was a matter of life and death, and while cybersecurity may not seem like it is a matter of life and death, it can be. Consider the case of a woman who died due to a ransomware attack against a hospital.[29]

We live in a more connected world than ever with virtually all businesses online and dependent upon technology for information transfer, ranging from complete e-commerce operations to simple e-mail services. Thus, all organizations need a board committee to receive information regarding cybersecurity risks, a means to discuss the risks, and management reporting risks to the board. This will ensure NGOs and PIOs can remain focused on their mission and meet the requirements of *Caremark* and *Stone*.

III. Current Challenges and Solutions

A.   Sensitive versus Protected Data

One of the challenges that PIOs and NGOs have is the delineation between sensitive and protected data. A complete understanding of the laws and regulations affecting a PIO and NGO is essential. For example, take a child's immunization record. In the hands of a doctor, the record is protected health information (PHI) covered by the Health Insurance Portability and Accountability Act of 1996 (HIPAA).[30] When the doctor passes that exact same piece of paper to the parent, it is no longer protected. In fact, the parent could take out an ad in the paper and publish it (of course, this is not advisable). The parent now passes the same immunization record to the child's school. The document is now covered by Family Educational Rights

---

29. Robert Hackett, *Ransomware Attack on a Hospital May Be the First Ever to Cause a Death. Here's What Happened*, FORTUNE (Sept. 18, 2020), fortune.com/2020/09/18 /ransomware-police-investigating-hospital-cyber-attack-death.

30. Health Insurance Portability and Accountability Act of 1996, 1996 Enacted H.R. 3103, 104 Enacted H.R. 3103, 110 Stat. 1936

and Privacy Act (FERPA)[31]—a federal privacy law that gives students and parents certain protections regarding their children's education records, such as report cards, transcripts, disciplinary records, contact information, family information, and class schedules. However, FERPA does not define PHI. FERPA simply defines their information as student information; thus, the immunization record is protected, but as sensitive health information not subject to HIPAA requirements. Every PIO and NGO must understand its legal obligations. Failure to do so could result in significant penalties and legal challenges.[32]

B. Budget Constraints

A concern of many PIOs and NGOs is the issue of budget. Depending upon the funding source, funds can be restricted per the donor's direction, preventing the organization from spending on administrative services like information security. There is also the general issue of cash flow for grant-funded PIOs and NGOs. Grant-funded or donor-funded organizations tend to focus their funds on mission-related activities. On the other hand, operationally funded organizations, which actively increase revenue through operations versus donations or grants tend to have more capacity or flexibility in this space. But even these PIOs and NGOs need to be mindful of their operating ratios.

As a result of these budget constraints, nonprofits often have to utilize outdated hardware and software, making them more vulnerable to cyberattacks. Additionally, nonprofits cannot afford expensive IT subscriptions and services and often work with free and open-source applications, which may not have necessary protections and may store confidential information, such as donor information, insecurely. Furthermore, small nonprofits often lack a designated security administrator. Despite the increase of ransomware attacks in the past years, surveys[33] show that less than half of

---

31. Family Educational and Privacy Rights Act of 1974 (20 U.S.C. § 1232g).

32. *See* Byrne v. Avery Ctr. for Obstetrics & Gynecology, P.C., 327 Conn. 540, 175 A.3d 1 (2018).

33. *How to Protect Your Non-Profit from Cyber Attacks*, CoverWallet, www.coverwallet.com/business-tips/cyber-attacks-nonprofits (last visited June 17, 2021).

NGOs have dedicated staff members that focus on cybersecurity.[34] Again, this is likely due to budget constraints as many of these NGOs are struggling with staffing for their mission. IT and cybersecurity are farther down the list of priorities.

C. Personnel: Interns, Volunteers, Temp Workers

A significant source of "free" labor for many PIOs and NGOs is volunteers and interns. When working with interns and volunteers, public interest attorneys need to ensure that Human Resources conducts cyber awareness training during the onboarding process to educate new staff on basic cyber practices.[35] This will emphasize the need for information integrity and confidentiality of their clients' and donors' information. While training all employees is critical, often, the expectations and commitments with volunteers differ from those of employees, which makes regular training even more important. Volunteers tend to have less impactful consequences for violating cybersecurity policies than that of an employee. For example, failure to take simple precautions may be viewed as unreasonable and could be considered negligent by employees. Volunteers are seen to have altruistic intentions; they are, as humans, prone to human error when dealing with sensitive information. Ideally, volunteers would be treated equally to employees in this regard, but either way, it is a good idea for volunteers to acknowledge their access or potential access to sensitive or protected information with confidentiality and nondisclosure agreements. The trust of the individuals is not sufficient and will not be enough to lean on when having to explain data loss or data leakage.

Ongoing cyber awareness training with a phishing simulation component serves as an effective tool to keep employee cyber awareness up to date. A further point of review with interns, volunteers, and temporary workers is a review of all relevant cyber policies. Failing to train staff on these cyber-related policies, procedures, standards, and guidelines can open an

---

34. Stan Mierzwa & James Scott, *Cybersecurity in Non-Profit and Non-Governmental Organizations Results of a Self-Report Web-Based Cyber Security Survey with Non-Profit and Non-Government Organizations* (Feb. 2017), icitech.org/wp-content/uploads/2017/02/ICIT-Brif-Cybersecurity-and-NGOs.pdf.

35. Please see Chapter 13 *infra*.

organization to liability if employee duties are not clearly articulated. In the New York case, *Sackin v. TransPerfect Global*,[36] $23 million was lost in a class action settlement due to a phishing campaign because TransPerfect failed to protect current and former employees' PII. By conducting regular training and documenting it the company could have reduced its liability. With the Pennsylvania case, *Enslin v. The Coca-Cola Company*,[37] Coca-Cola had a code of conduct with clear direction regarding the company's responsibilities regarding employee data that protected Coca-Cola. This example is the opposite of *Sackin* where Coca-Cola was able to protect itself because it had the policies, procedures, standards, and guidelines in place. NPOs and PIOs can remain focused on their missions by ensuring that policies, procedures, standards, and guidelines are in place to ensure employees, volunteers, and interns are aware of and trained regarding information security.

D. Available Resources

Most PIOs and NGOs are eligible for discounts for cybersecurity products and services due to their nonprofit status. Following are some recommendations to help PIO and NGOs find this support. A first step to taking advantage of these discounts would be to sign-up for Tech Soup. Tech Soup is an organization that partners with technology and affiliated service providers to provide discounted services to PIOs and NGOs. There are eligibility criteria that must be satisfied for all donations or discounts. The grants and discounts are not limited to hardware and software. There are managed IT and security services available through this platform. Other organizations such as Google and Microsoft offer steep discounts on their products, which include security functions. Microsoft also provides setup assistance for NPOs either directly or through partners. For example, Microsoft offers

---

36. Sackin v. Transperfect Glob., Inc., 278 F. Supp. 3d 739 (S.D.N.Y. 2017). A class action suit was brought again Transperfect Global for failing to protect current and former employees' personal information. The settlement provided claimants Experian's Credit Plus 3-Bureau Plan and up to $4,000 reimbursement.

37. Enslin v. Coca-Cola Co., 136 F. Supp. 3d 654 (E.D. Pa. 2015). Enslin filed a putative class action against Coca-Cola. The court found the employment forms completed by the plaintiff did not create a general duty to protect his personal information.

nonprofit digital skills training and courses[38] covering topics such as security, compliance, and information protection.

Here is a nonexhaustive list of companies in the cyber industry with additional benefits for NPOs and PIOs. The following list is not an endorsement of products or services:

- CHICAGO Metrics®: Metrics and reporting, www.chicagometrics.com
- Okta: Identity and access management, www.okta.com
- Cofense: Anti-phishing solution, www.cofense.com
- Qlik: Data analytics platform, www.qlik.com
- Elevate security: Human attack surface management platform, www.elevatesecurity.com
- Pluralsight: Technology and security training, www.pluralsight.com
- Splunk: SIEM platform, www.splunk.com
- Cisco: Networking and security equipment, www.cisco.com
- Relativity: eDiscovery, www.relativity.com

IV. Conclusion

A. Top Recommendations

Here are several steps that PIOs and NGOs can take to bolster their programs and protect the sensitive data that they house.

1. Locate and Understand Your Data

Take inventory of all the data your nonprofit collects and identify where it is stored, including knowing how sensitive data travels through and in and out of your organization. The inventory will include hardware assets and the software used to store and process the data. Nonprofits store and transfer personally identifiable information such as medical information, employee records, drivers' licenses, addresses, social security numbers, and

---

38. *Nonprofit Training, Courses & Resources*, MICROSOFT FOR NONPROFITS, www.microsoft.com/en-us/nonprofits/resources?rtc=1&activetab=pivot1%3aprimaryr3 (last visited May 1, 2021).

credit card information. This is especially critical when stored in conjunction with contact information like phone numbers and e-mail addresses. Additionally, they collect and store personal preference information such as donation habits, areas of interest, and newsletter subscriptions. Know whether the data your nonprofit collects and maintains is covered by federal or state regulations as "personally identifiable information." If so, 48 states' laws require nonprofits to inform persons whose "personally identifiable information" is disclosed in a security breach, and 31 states have laws that require the disposal of such data in specific ways. Be sure to back up systems regularly, keep a copy off-site, and test your backups periodically. Establish a document retention policy to reduce storage costs and minimize the risk of storing archived data that is no longer needed.

2. Effectively Review and Communicate Risk

Risk communications need to be done regularly in terms the board and executives will understand, which include both financial metrics and security metrics.[39] Speaking in terms the business understands means avoiding jargon, overly technical terms, and acronyms such that a layperson can understand the material and the impact on the organization. Aggregating risks into larger buckets is not uncommon and has been shown to be an effective means to assess risks, such as a credit score. Marchewka suggests using aggregate scores in cybersecurity evaluation, such as confidentiality, integrity, availability, human resources (people), finance, and reputation, to connect information security risks to the organization.[40] In these aggregated buckets, a nontechnical person can assess how risk may impact their area of responsibility in context to the other risks. Receiving and acting on these risks will help ensure board members and executives meet their duties of care, loyalty, obedience, and fiduciary responsibilities while serving their organization's missions. Boards and executives can partner with organizations that work with PIOs and NGOs to meet these requirements to understand and address their risks.

---

39. Randall S. Wright, *Should Accounting Be the Language of Business?*, 62(4) Rsch. Tech. Mgmt. 53–55 (2019), https://www.tandfonline.com/doi/full/10.1080/08956308.2019.1613121.

40. Todd Fitzgerald, CISO Compass: Navigating Cybersecurity Leadership Challenges with Insights from Pioneers (CRC Press 2019).

Some particular risks to consider, which are not necessarily unique to NGOs and PIOs, are employees working from home during a pandemic, use of personal devices to access the organization's database or e-mails, and lack of awareness and education among staff and volunteers. NGOs need to periodically review their third-party risks as well: how likely will your vendor's vulnerability compromise your nonprofit's data security? Many nonprofits don't have permanent staff on payroll and often utilize contractors such as accounting firms, IT tech support, and cloud storage services. If any of these third-party vendors do not employ adequate data security protection, the nonprofit's data security will be at risk.

3. Website Security

Hackers can access a nonprofit's site through a security breach, deface a website, or transform it into something unrecognizable. The hackers may create additional content that can damage a nonprofit's reputation. To improve the website's security, nonprofits should utilize the OWASP's (Open Web Application Security Project®) resources. OWASP is a nonprofit foundation that works to improve software security.[41] OWASP offers complimentary guidelines, standards, articles, tools, and methodologies[42] and aims to raise awareness about application security by identifying some of the most critical risks facing organizations.[43]

OWASP Top 10 provides a ranking of and remediation guidance for the top ten most critical web application security risks.[44] The report is based on a consensus among security experts from around the world.[45] The risks are ranked and based on the frequency of discovered security defects, the severity of the vulnerabilities, and the magnitude of their potential impacts.[46] NGOs can use the direction from the OWASP Top 10 regarding the most prevalent security risks and leverage the report's findings and recommen-

---

41. OWASP Foundation, Open Source Foundation for Application Security, www.owasp .org (last visited June 10, 2021.
42. *Id.*
43. *OWASP*, WIKIPEDIA, en.wikipedia.org/wiki/OWASP (last visited May 26, 2021).
44. *What Is the OWASP Top 10 and How Does It Work?*, SYNOPSYS, https://www.synop sys.com/glossary/what-is-owasp-top-10.html (last visited July 30, 2021).
45. *Id.*
46. *Id.*

dations into their security practices, thereby reducing known risks in their web applications.

4. Treat Your Passwords Like a Toothbrush

- Like a toothbrush, change your password periodically.
- Like a toothbrush, don't allow someone else to use your password; train users not to share their passwords.
- Like a toothbrush that can be hard, soft, electric, and so on, make sure your password meets security requirements such as having sufficient length for its lifespan.

You can use password managers (off-line versions recommended) to remember passwords, which allows users to have different passwords for different applications and websites. Use passphrases (for example, Il0v3S@turdays!). Do not reuse old passwords and do not use the same password to access different systems or databases. Lastly, remember that length trumps complexity.

5. Policies, Procedures, and Guidelines

Every PIO and NGO should maintain a solid set of policies, procedures, and guidelines in compliance with the nonprofit sector's regulatory requirements. The regulatory environment requires the PIO and NGO to understand their legal obligations regarding privacy and security and then transfer those into policy. The policies, procedures, and guidelines should be clear and comprehensive to provide users throughout the organization direction on handling data and responding to incidents.

There are many recognized security frameworks such as ISO 27001 and the National Institute for Science and Technology (NIST) Cybersecurity Framework that a PIO/NGO might choose to leverage to build their program and policies. NIST offers extensive cybersecurity research that is freely available. Staff should be trained on these policies, procedures, and guidelines. Training staff on best security practices will help to reduce the likelihood of an incident. Some of the critical training priorities to consider include reminders: not to click on links without verifying source legitimacy, not to leave sensitive information visible on the desk or monitor, to lock the screen when away, to shred documents containing PII before recycling, and to never share sensitive information over the phone. Nonprofits should create and regularly update a cybersecurity awareness program that allows staff to be continually educated on steps they can take to secure their access to systems. A well-written Incident Response Plan (IRP) must be readily available. It should cover all the essential details such as incident response team contact information and step-by-step incident response actions.

6. Patch Systems

If a dam has a hole in it, the engineers work to fill it. This concept should not be different for computer systems. Too many holes in a system—vulnerabilities—allow threats to exploit these weaknesses. PIOs and NGOs should understand their systems and determine how best to patch them regularly and timely to reduce the likelihood of vulnerabilities from being exploited significantly. In addition, the designated IT person or IT solution partner (e.g., Managed Service Provider) should continually maintain technology to keep it updated. They must ensure that IT systems are routinely patched for firmware updates, ensure end-point protection software is regularly updated, and that updates are applied to all end-points.

7. Use Multi-Factor Authentication (MFA)

MFA adds an extra step to verify the user is, in fact, who they say they are by using a combination of something they know, like a password, something they have, like a token or SMS code, or something they are, like a fingerprint or face recognition. Many people use multifactor authentication when logging onto their bank or even their google or Facebook accounts. Multifactor authentication adds an additional layer of protection and will help reduce the likelihood of compromised credentials from being used negatively against an organization. Multi factor authentication is commonplace today, is considered a reasonable practice for any organization, is a requirement of many regulators, and is recommended by many more.

8. Encryption and Identity Management

Encryption and identity management are needed to ensure the right people have access to organizational data. The reason these two topics are tied together is that encryption protects against physical theft and eavesdropping. However, if a malicious actor compromises identity credentials they will be able to bypass the encryption and retrieve the data. Nonetheless, encryption is important because it is one way to reduce the risk of data being stolen by encrypting or scrambling it in such a way that should it be stolen, it would be useless. Data should also be protected through encryption when at rest and when in transit. In both states, at rest or in transit, only those with the decryption methods can access the data. NGOs and PIOs can implement encryption in transit by adding TLS certificates to their webpages, using secure file sharing links in OneDrive and Google Drive, and encrypting messages sent via e-mail. There are many ways to provide encryption within an enterprise, and a managed service provider can assist with that if in-house IT cannot.

In line with this is the need for strong identity management. Identity management is the process that ensures that only authorized people have access to the technology resources they are intended to have to perform their job functions. For example, setting permission on files and data for the right groups of people. Through solid identity management, the right users with the correct access will be able to access the data at the right time.

9. Cyber Insurance

Nonprofits should add cybersecurity coverage to their existing insurance policy. Attorneys need to review the amount of coverage to ensure it is adequate to mitigate the costs of potential cyber incidents. Many policies can include coverage for incident response, forensics, and ransom payments. Be careful of the exceptions to these policies, as some have exclusions for social engineering.[47]

10. Don't Do It Alone

Cybersecurity is a complicated space that is constantly evolving. Just as there are lawyers to provide legal advice about almost every topic under the sun, cybersecurity professionals can provide guidance in this space. Many are

---

47. Please see Chapter 16 of this Handbook for more detailed information about cyber insurance.

willing to give back and assist NGOs and PIOs. These professionals can be found through various trade organizations such as Information Systems Audit and Control Association (ISACA), Association of Information Technology Professionals (AITP), and InfraGard.[48] Seeking the advice of others that are experts can provide the needed background to allow attorneys to evaluate the legal risks and effectively execute their duties fully. Having experts weigh in on the technical aspects and risks, and how they impact the business is critical in helping attorneys provide advice to the NGOs and PIOs they are intended to protect.

B. Wrap Up

NGOs and PIOs are not that different from other businesses when it comes to cybersecurity. NGOs and PIOs have computers and they have data that is valued from either a content perspective—it can be sold on the black market—or it is valued by the NGO as it is critical to operations. Disruptions of access that data can disrupt business operations. As in for-profit businesses, if operations are disrupted so are the means to generate revenue, and as mentioned at the beginning of this chapter, "No margin, no mission." In the NGO and PIO sector, that lack of business operations and generating revenue, either through grants or operations, means that the social good delivery is not occurring.

Continuing the mission is the imperative of the NGO and PIO and steps to ensure the continued operation are essential. This means understanding the risks in the environment by working with internal resources or partner organizations to determine the risks. Then presenting the risks to executives and the board for a decision on appropriate action and taking steps to avoid, transfer, reduce, or accept the risks. This will ensure reasonable steps are taken to understand risks in the environment at the highest level and that some action, even if the action is acceptance of a risk, is taken. This will meet the requirements of *Caremark* and *Stone* and help to ensure the NGO or PIO can remain focused on their mission.

---

48. InfraGard is a partnership between the Federal Bureau of Investigation (FBI) and members of the private sector for the protection of U.S. Critical Infrastructure.

V. References

- Alexander Bilus, *Higher Education Institutions and Nonprofit Organizations Face Potential Wave of Lawsuits Over Blackbaud Data Breach*, JD SUPRA (Sept. 23, 2020), www.jdsupra.com/legalnews /higher-education-institutions-and-84328.
- Kevin Coughlin, *"It Was Like a Tornado": Cyber Thieves Demand $500K Ransom in Attack Targeting Contractor Serving Greater Morristown Nonprofits*, MORRISTOWN GREEN (Dec. 9, 2019), morristowngreen.com/2019/12/09/it-was-like-a-tornado-cyber-thieves -demand-500k-ransom-in-attack-targeting-contractor-serving-greater -morristown-nonprofits.
- *Cybersecurity for Nonprofits*, NAT'L COUNCIL OF NONPROFITS, www .councilofnonprofits.org/tools-resources/cybersecurity-nonprofits.
- Jill Disis & Zahid Mahmood, *Microsoft Says SolarWinds Hackers Have Struck Again in the US and Other Countries*, CNN (May 28, 2021), edition.cnn.com/2021/05/28/tech/microsoft-solarwinds-russia -hack-intl-hnk/index.html.
- Julie Euber, *Nonprofits Can Protect Their Data by Planning for the Worst*, NON PROFIT NEWS | NONPROFIT Q. (Jan. 8, 2020), nonprofitquar terly.org/nonprofits-can-protect-their-data-by-planning-for-the-worst.
- Fidelity Charitable, *Four Things You Can Do to Protect against Cyber Threats* (Apr. 2020), www.nten.org/wp-content/uploads/2020/04 /Four-Things-You-Can-Do-To-Protect-Against-Cyber-Threats_Fidelity -Charitable.pdf.
- Jacob Fox, *Cybersecurity Statistics for 2021*, COBALT (Mar. 1, 2021), cobalt.io/blog/cybersecurity-statistics-2021.
- Tal Frankfurt, *How to Avoid Security Breaches in the Nonprofit Sector*, FORBES (Mar. 31, 2021), www.forbes.com/sites/forbestech council/2021/03/31/how-to-avoid-security-breaches-in-the-nonprofit -sector/?sh=43e911f55ce0.
- Alex Hamilton, *Blackbaud Data Breach Leaves Lasting Impact on U.S. and International Nonprofits*, IDENTITY THEFT RESOURCE CTR. (Mar. 2, 2021), www.idtheftcenter.org/blackbaud -data-breach-leaves-lasting-impact-on-u-s-and-international-nonprofits.

- Johan Hammerstrom, *Nonprofit Cybersecurity Stats: 10 Numbers to Know in 2020*, CMTY. IT INNOVATORS (Mar. 31, 2020), communityit.com/nonprofit-cybersecurity-stats-10-numbers-to-know-in-2020.
- *How to Protect Your Nonprofit from Cyber Attacks*, COVERWALLET, www.coverwallet.com/business-tips/cyber-attacks-nonprofits (last visited June 17, 2021).
- Ryan Jones, *CyberSecurity for Nonprofits: How to Protect Your Donor Data*, NONPROFIT SOFTWARE | KEELA (May 11, 2021), www.keela.co/blog/nonprofit-resources/cyber-security-for-nonprofits#gref
- Shira Landau, *$650,000 Stolen from Nonprofit and Hackers Got Away*, CYBERTALK (June 7, 2021), www.cybertalk.org/2021/06/07/650000-stolen-from-nonprofit-and-hackers-got-away.
- Marc Larocque, *Massachusetts Nonprofit Shelter Targeted by Ransomware*, GOVTECH (June 28, 2019), www.govtech.com/security/massachusetts-nonprofit-shelter-targeted-by-ransomware.html.
- Ric Opal, *Is Your Nonprofit Prepared for a Cyberattack?*, BDO (Mar. 11, 2021), www.bdo.com/blogs/nonprofit-standard/march-2021/is-your-nonprofit-prepared-for-a-cyberattack.
- *Two U.S. Representatives Lead an Effort to Double Security Grant Funding for Nonprofits*, SECURITY MAG. (May 3, 2021), www.securitymagazine.com/articles/95125-two-us-representatives-lead-an-effort-to-double-security-grant-funding-for-nonprofits.
- Herb Weisbaum, *Data Breach Impacts Donors at Hundreds of Nonprofits*, CONSUMERS' CHECKBOOK MAG. (Oct. 1, 2020), www.checkbook.org/washington-area/consumers-notebook/articles/Data-Breach-Impacts-Donors-at-Hundreds-of-Nonprofits-7409.
- Zach Whittaker, *Education Nonprofit Edraak Ignored a Student Data Leak for Two Months*, TECHCRUNCH (Apr. 8, 2021), techcrunch.com/2021/04/08/edraak-security-exposed-student-data.

Chapter 13

Get SMART on Data Protection Training and How to Create a Culture of Awareness

Ruth Hill Bro and Jill D. Rhodes

I. Data Protection Training Basics and Core Principles

Most cybersecurity incidents are caused by human error.[1] Whether it is a technology that has not been patched or (more likely) an employee clicking on a phishing e-mail, our employees are both our greatest strength and greatest weakness. As a result, it is imperative that cybersecurity risk and threat prevention training occurs on a continuous basis for all employees.

Anyone who has access to the organization's sensitive information can become a conduit for data loss and disaster:

- The senior partner who unleashes ransomware by clicking on a link that looks like it came from a colleague or board member, or the administrative assistant who provides extensive client or firm information after

---

1. See, for example, Verizon 2021 Data Breach Investigation Report (Verizon DBIR), in which the human factor is discussed at length, https://www.verizon.com/business /solutions/secure-your-business/business-security tips/?cmp-knc.ggl:ac:ent:security:80 03162844&utm_term=verizon%20dbir&utm_medium=knc&utm_source=ggl&utm _campaign=security&utm_content-ac.ent.8003162844&utm_term=verizon%20 dbir&gclid-CjwKCAjw3_KIBhA2EiwAaAAlirUBgu7EN3NDQBmv_uCL_JHVHDic 5gHZQqDLK7yr8DexBjtr2QG22RoCYpgQAvD_BwE&gclsrc=aw.ds. See also "Psychology of Human Error," a 2020 joint study by Stanford University Professor Jeff Hancock and security firm Tessian, that found that 88 percent of data breach incidents are caused by employee mistakes, at https://www.tessian.com/research/the-psychology-of-human-error/.

receiving a fraudulent e-mail that was supposedly sent by a supervisor or firm client.

- The remote worker who conducts business on unvetted personal devices (laptop, tablet, smartphone) with public or unsecured home Wi-Fi, enabling hackers to steal confidential data and capture log-in credentials.
- The IT professional who leaves networks vulnerable by failing to protect against known threats on an ongoing basis, or who doesn't adhere to protocols for immediately terminating system access for a disgruntled or downsized employee on the last day of employment.
- The human resources employee who takes sensitive employee records home or leaves them in electronic files with inadequate access restrictions.
- The ever-mobile attorney who compromises the firm's client relationships through a lost laptop, phone, or unencrypted flash drive left on an airplane, in a taxi or rental car, or in a coffee shop or restaurant.
- The technology-loving employee who overshares on social media or fails to realize that digital assistants and smart home technology create new means of eavesdropping that can sabotage the organization's confidential data.
- The third-party vendor who stores data without appropriate security controls.

A patchwork of continually emerging laws at the state and federal levels requires that businesses working with personal and sensitive data must protect that data.[2] Moreover, organizational promises about data protection can lurk in contracts, on websites, and elsewhere. Yet, loss of an organization's data that does not fall within a regulatory requirement or contractual obligation could still wreak havoc, including loss of not only reputation but also potential clients. Law firms and other organizations must develop strategies for protecting their data. When assessing how to do so, organizations often mistakenly rely on technology as the solution. In fact, as discussed throughout this Handbook, four factors are key to

---

2. See Chapter 4 of this Handbook.

implementing a proper information security and data protection program in any setting:

- Establishing the appropriate *governance* for the data, such as policies and the oversight of an executive level committee tasked with reducing data protection risk;
- Ensuring that the *people* working with the data know how best to protect it;
- Assessing data protection and usage *processes*; and
- Employing appropriate *technology* to protect the network.

Each of these factors contributes to a broader level of maturity for an organization while also reducing its risk. This chapter focuses on the people aspect of that equation, but other factors (e.g., governance and processes) also come into play. Most data missteps in law firms and other businesses are directly linked to something an employee or contractor did, whether intentionally or unintentionally. The easiest way to address this risk is to educate employees and others on an ongoing basis about the risks and their role in protecting personal and sensitive data (including serving as an early alert system when something does go wrong).

Education and training can be provided by many components of the organization, whether human resources (HR), the chief privacy officer (CPO), the chief information security officer (CISO), or others. Regardless of which groups do the training (or choose the training, where it involves use of outside resources), it is critical that they work together to produce a common vision and message that is then disseminated across the organization.

A.   Training Is Not a One-Time Action—It's a Cultural Shift

All organizations, including law firms, are increasingly recognizing that data underpins virtually everything that they do and—like other valuable business assets—should be protected. The easiest way to increase this understanding overall is to focus on creating a culture of security around data. To do this, organizations must adopt a comprehensive strategy that makes data protection a part of the culture and the job of every individual working for the business (partners, associates, paralegals, interns/law students, information technology (IT), HR, executives, administrators, administrative assistants, and other staff).[3] Such an approach is designed to:

- Minimize the risk due to employee missteps that can affect the bottom line (inability to access or use data and conduct business; costly litigation; time and resources consumed in responding to government, press, or attorney disciplinary commission inquiries or investigations; adverse media coverage; damage to client or customer relationships; and so on), and
- Help businesses achieve a competitive advantage, enhance their profiles and images, and enrich their relationships with clients and customers.

Yet making data protection a part of the organization's culture is easier said than done:

- Properly addressing data protection issues can require a comprehensive understanding of rapidly changing applicable law in all U.S. states and territories, at the federal level, and globally (where client or customer data might originate, where third parties might be providing U.S.-based businesses with 24/7 services, etc.). Many laws (particularly for government entities and regulated industries) and lawyers' professional rules of responsibility expressly or by implication require appropriate data protection training for employees and sometimes contractors as well. And failure can be costly. For example, a federal court[4] held that an

---

3. This trend is in keeping with the "Privacy by Design" (PbD) and "Security by Design" (SbD) movements that are transforming the way that businesses protect data in an information-driven age. See, for example, *Privacy by Design: The 7 Foundational Principles,* by Ann Cavoukian, PhD, Distinguished Expert-in-Residence, Privacy by Design Centre of Excellence, Ryerson University and former Ontario Privacy Commissioner, at http://www.ryerson.ca/pbdce; see also *Start with Security: A Guide for Business,* FTC, https://www.ftc.gov/tips-advice/business-center/guidance/start-security-guide-business, for insights and guidance on SbD gleaned from over 50 FTC data security settlements.

4. *See* Curry v. Schletter Inc., 2018 U.S. Dist. LEXIS 49442. The court noted that ". . . the Defendant failed to adequately train its employees on even the most basic of cybersecurity protocols, including: (a) how to detect phishing and spoofing emails and other scams including providing employees examples of these scams and guidance on how to verify if emails are legitimate; (b) effective password management and encryption protocols for internal and

employee who was tricked into sharing personal information of employees in response to a phishing e-mail could be committing an intentional disclosure under the North Carolina Identity Theft Protection Act and thereby subject the employer to treble damages; the court pointed to unreasonably deficient cybersecurity training despite known risks.[5]

- Command of the law is not enough, as businesses are often tried in the court of public opinion or are challenged by third-party watchdog groups, regardless of the current legality of the entity's practices.
- Likewise, technological innovation is occurring at a startling and accelerating pace. The Internet, mobile devices, artificial intelligence, and ever-more-sophisticated computer technology (all connected to each other and always on) make it easy to collect, analyze, combine, reproduce, and disseminate data, thereby enhancing efficiency and cost-effectiveness but also escalating the risk of making catastrophic mistakes at the speed of light. Yet employees often do not really understand that the latest "smart" technology at work or home (TVs, appliances, toys or gadgets, automated fish tanks, security cameras, digital assistants, voice-controlled smart home hubs, etc.) could be invisibly eavesdropping on confidential discussions using connected microphones, spying via built-in cameras, or providing a new attack vector for accessing the organization's digital assets.

With all of the responsibilities each employee has within an organization, it's easy to push responsibility for protecting data onto individuals located in the information security office, the privacy office, HR, or IT. It is much more difficult to learn to integrate security and to think about data protection for all employees, all the time. While some factors (such as rapidly

---

external emails; (c) avoidance of responding to emails that are suspicious or from unknown sources; (d) locking, encrypting and limiting access to computers and files containing sensitive information; (e) implementing guidelines for maintaining and communicating sensitive data; and (f) protecting sensitive employee information, including personal and financial information, by implementing protocols on how to request and respond to requests for . . . the transfer of such information and how to securely send such information through a secure file transfer system to only known recipients."

5. See Chapters 4 and 6 of this Handbook for further discussion about the types of legal and professional responsibility requirements (including education and training) placed on lawyers and law firms.

changing applicable laws and regulations) might be overwhelming for all employees to understand, basic principles of information security can be embedded in everything an employee does.

1.   **Security is everyone's responsibility.** While some of the governance, process, and technology aligned with protecting data may be led and managed by an information security team or IT as a whole, everyone in the organization must be aware of the basics about how to protect information. Education and training can help these employees understand the risk, learn not to click on links in suspicious e-mails or text messages, and report anything that doesn't seem right. Everyone in the organization needs to become the eyes and ears of the firm.

2.   **No one is immune from the threat—everyone is at risk of becoming a victim.** Anyone—from the organization's most senior officer to the lowest-level employee—can become a victim of phishing or vishing (phone phishing) attacks. It may be a receptionist, junior associate, senior partner, paralegal, or law clerk. Bad actors are looking for weak links to exploit to enter the firm's network. At times, they may go after a senior attorney; at others, they will go after a paralegal who has access to multiple cases for multiple clients or perhaps someone in IT who may have comprehensive administrative access to the firm's IT systems. Education efforts need to occur at all levels and must assume that everyone is at risk of falling victim.

3.   **Education shouldn't be limited to what employees are doing in the office.** The best way to change the way that employees within the organization think about securing data is to move their thinking from their work environment to all facets of their life. Taking a broad-based approach by educating about factors that also include protecting their family members and friends leads back to greater consideration for protecting data in the office.

4.   **Additional training to expand thinking about security and securing data should be provided for employees who are working from home.** Building on the expanded educational focus, we can provide more specific work-at-home training. With our new work-from-home environment also comes new risks. Even as organizations reopen their

doors and employees return to work, the model of working from an office versus working from home will remain shifted. Although employees may have been required to work in the office before, law firms are showing more flexibility with this. With that flexibility also comes greater risk. New policies may be needed that limit the type of data an employee may access from home, or whether the employee can print from home. Having employees at home provides a prime opportunity to educate them about the many areas where risks may occur, and to encourage them to become more vigilant in their understanding and daily practices regarding protection of law firm data.

Unfortunately, business leaders often breathe a sigh of relief once a state-of-the-art security system is installed and comprehensive data protection policies and procedures have been established. Yet, notwithstanding adoption of the latest technology and sound data protection principles, businesses are only as strong as their weakest link, which is generally human. Countless studies, audit trails, and surveys over the years[6] have repeatedly confirmed that the biggest data protection threats come from within one's own organization. Most missteps are unintentional. Many mistakes can be avoided and risks can be minimized with appropriate training and awareness-raising. Yet this is often an overlooked component of data protection initiatives—the missing link when it comes to security. SMART training, set out next, includes key steps that will help to build a culture of security across an organization's employee base.

B.   What Does SMART Training Look Like?
What does training actually mean, and what are businesses doing to address data protection's weakest link? Over the past years, numerous types of cybersecurity training have emerged through different organizations. In recent years, numerous types of cybersecurity training (including the increasingly popular gamification of cyber awareness) have emerged. At the core of

---

6. *See supra* note 1.

such innovation, however, a consistent methodology for training remains. In short, when conducting training, businesses should be SMART:[7]

> Start training on hiring.
> Measure what you do.
> Always train.
> Raise awareness and provide updates continually.
> Tailor training by role.

In considering these SMART training steps and what they mean for one's business, keep in mind that the particular data protection training that is right for one entity is not necessarily right for another, even if they are in the same industry or are law firms of similar size. Businesses differ in many ways—for example, the degree of centralization, their cultures, the jurisdictions in which they operate, their objectives, their resources and budget, their existing data protection infrastructure, their buy-in from senior management, and so on. That said, even the smallest organizations have become victims of malware attacks and ransomware. As a result, it is important to train no matter the size of the organization.

1.   S—Start Training on Hiring

Given the fundamental role of data in everything a business does, training on how to protect that data should start on day one. Data protection training should be provided to all new employees and, increasingly, to contractors as well. In cases where it is not feasible to do training for all employees initially (due to bandwidth, budget, or other constraints), businesses might choose to focus training on selected employees (e.g., HR personnel and

---

7. The concept of SMART training was distilled in March 2011 by Ruth Hill Bro (co-author of this chapter) from her interviews since 2005 with a wide range of CPOs drawn from various industries, locations, and corporate cultures for her recurring column called *CPO Corner: Interviews with Leading Chief Privacy Officers* (using 17 questions designed to identify trends and best practices and capture key benchmarking and practical implementation information regarding data protection issues). On the question of training, a consistent pattern of answers emerged: businesses need to be SMART, a concept as true today as it was over a decade ago.

those in key business roles or units). At a minimum, new employees should receive and review relevant policies and procedures, which themselves are a component of training and awareness-raising.

In the employee context, training is provided as a part of employee orientation and can take different forms, using a variety of media:

- An initial in-person, instructor-led session (large group, small group, or one-on-one, as appropriate), which can encourage interaction (but may not always be scalable or practical for some organizations in all situations);
- Live or recorded instructor-led video conferences; and
- An intranet- or computer-based training module or series of modules.

Coverage can include a wide range of topics:

- High-level overviews applicable to all employees and contractors;
- Instruction on relevant data protection laws and regulations (and rules of professional responsibility, where applicable), internal policies and procedures (regarding mobile technology, social media, etc.), fundamentals of the relevant technology, and industry best practices;
- Guidelines for protecting confidentiality and security of data;
- Tips regarding hidden data protection hazards when working away from the office, whether at home or elsewhere;
- Updates on practicing daily information security hygiene, such as monitoring for phishing e-mails, using VPN to log in to a network, and how to report something that doesn't appear to be legitimate, and
- Steps to take when addressing a suspected data breach or reporting a security misstep.

The training should be coordinated with other training, especially other privacy training, and should be reviewed to avoid contradictions and conflicts in approach and message. Consideration should be given to whether the time, format, and content are suitable across different parts of the organization. Issues of translation, local law, and local customs can come into play here as well.

2.   M—Measure What You Do

Measurement and assessment are core components of many of these initial training sessions as well as in follow-up training. Administering tests (e.g., a graded online quiz) can help to confirm understanding and gauge the overall effectiveness of the training; it also can help to ensure that the work has actually been done. In addition, other types of measurement, such as the number of employees who have clicked on a "fake" phishing message or the number of times phishing has been prevented due to employee action, may be used. Broader measurements—such as comparisons of incidents and types of missteps before and after training—can help businesses to make training more effective while demonstrating return on investment (which can be important in making the case for budget).

3.   A—Always Train

While law firms sometimes focus on new-hire or annual training, in line with applicable law, rules, or policies, continuous training and education will advance the shift to a culture of security and data protection. More formalized training such as certification or continuing legal education (CLE) or professional responsibility credit could be provided on an annual basis, to build a culture of data protection, but a broader training campaign may be needed. Training of some type should occur as frequently as possible, perhaps monthly, or weekly, depending upon the type of instruction. Training can occur through blog posts, newsletters, spotlights on the law firm's internal website, or through phishing campaigns (which will be discussed further). The more that employees can see information about risks, threats, and response, the more quickly they will be able to integrate awareness into their daily practices.

4.   R—Raise Awareness and Provide Updates Continually

Similar to "A," it is impossible to integrate appropriate data security practices into a culture by using just introductory training on hiring and mandatory annual training. Building a training campaign that raises awareness about risks on a daily basis and addresses risks both within the office and at home will help to change the mindset of employees. As demonstrated in examples throughout this Handbook, incidents occur regularly (one need only open morning news highlights online to see any number of incidents impacting businesses globally). The more that an organization can discuss and highlight an employee's role in prevention of these, the more effective the training becomes.

5. T—Tailor Training by Role

Going beyond high-level, one-size-fits-all training allows for training to be tailored to focus on specific roles and needs of individuals, different generational challenges, and specific requirements for contractors and third parties. Tailoring of data protection training can take various forms, depending on the organization:

- Start with a Data Protection 101 online course that is available on demand (successfully completing it results in a certificate). The basic module can then be supplemented by training and awareness-raising specific to a role, business unit, geographic location, and the like.
- Determine who should receive more direct training from specialized leaders such as the CPO, CISO, CIO or IT director, legal counsel, or other qualified trainers. It can be helpful for such trainers to meet with selected employees to learn about their data practices and then tailor training efforts accordingly. For example, some CPOs or CISOs meet regularly with the company's engineering, product design, and sales teams to raise important issues in planning meetings and gain insights to develop appropriate training.
- Build a training culture that reaches beyond business into other facets of an employee's life. Training about keeping kids safe online or protecting household technology from hacking creates a mindset in which employees are continuously thinking about how best to protect data.
- Hire specialists, internally or externally, to refine and enhance training efforts.
- Leverage external expertise and training companies. Over the past few years, many companies have emerged whose sole purpose is to train an organization's employees about data protection and cybersecurity risk. In addition, there are many resources for small firms or solo practitioners, such as online training modules, training publications, relevant

CLE courses and conferences, resources offered by bar associations and the like (such as the American Bar Association (and its Cybersecurity Legal Task Force[8]) and the ABA's Sections, Divisions, and Forums; state and local bar associations; specialty bar associations; and government entities). Some of these resources are specifically geared to small organizations.[9]

- As noted earlier, training for some roles (e.g., lawyers) may be accompanied by certification or CLE or professional responsibility credit.

Businesses that use SMART training can provide the missing link that will help make data protection a part of the culture and turn their employees into one of their strongest links when it comes to an organization's invaluable data. Employees are the most critical asset of any organization but they also pose the greatest risk. Training is at the core of mitigating this risk.

II. SMART Training in Action

Implementing a SMART training program does not have to be complicated nor require a significant budget. The program pays for itself by reducing the risk of data loss and increasing awareness about data protection.

A. Understanding the Basics of Employees: Role, Generational, and Other Differences

First, any training program should assess and understand the recipients of the training. As mentioned earlier, the role of the employee in the organization will make a difference in the type of training received. An associate working with e-discovery matters and technology every day will have

---

8. See the ABA Cybersecurity Legal Task Force's resources at ambar.org/cyber.

9. See, for example, *Cybersecurity for Small Business*, which contains modules (including videos, quizzes, and employer guides) on various topics (Cybersecurity Basics, Ransomware, Phishing, Secure Remote Access, Physical Security, Tech Support Scams, Vendor Security, etc.), developed by the FTC in partnership with the National Institute of Standards and Technology (NIST), U.S. Small Business Administration (SBA), and Department of Homeland Security (DHS). See also the ABA Cybersecurity Legal Task Force's small firm resources (ABA, government, and other) at ambar.org/cyberforsmall.

different considerations than a mail clerk or even other associates and partners in the firm.

In addition, generational differences can play a role in how training should be developed, the type of training and communication that a person prefers to receive, how best to provide the training, and what types of incentives are offered. Many have examined how various generations might differ in their approach to learning[10] (e.g., each generation grew up with vastly different technology), but it also is important not to assume that all Baby Boomers or Gen Xers are the same. A 2020 report found that younger workers were five times more likely to admit to making cybersecurity errors than were workers over the age of 51.[11] The report noted some factors that made older employees less likely to click on a phishing link, for example, but also cited other characteristics that cut the other way (older employees were less likely to recognize phishing or other cyber missteps in the first place and were less likely to report mistakes because of concerns about their respected position in the workplace).

Other factors can play a role in employee cybersecurity missteps and thus training. Stress, fatigue, distractions (which can occur more frequently in a remote work setting), pressure to work quickly or multitask, and so on can all increase the likelihood of mistakes.[12] Workplace programs aimed at stress management, while not technically cybersecurity training, might help to decrease the likelihood of data protection missteps.

When considering a training program, organizations should consider how best to approach each generation and develop a program that supports them all. One example would be building a reverse mentoring program, in which the more experienced attorneys and staff mentor the more junior staff about law firm practices, while the more junior staff members mentor their

---

10. *See, e.g.,* Cam Marston, Generational Insights: Practical Solutions for Understanding and Engaging a Generationally Disconnected Workforce (2010); Rebecca Knight, *Managing People from Five Generations*, Harv. Bus. Rev. (Sept. 25, 2014), citing Peter Cappelli, Professor of Management at the Wharton School and coauthor of *Managing the Older Worker (2010)* and others.

11. See "Psychology of Human Error," a 2020 joint study by Stanford University Professor Jeff Hancock and security firm Tessian, at https://www.tessian.com/research/the-psychology-of-human-error/.

12. *Id.*

more senior colleagues about topics such as technology advances, leveraging social media, and using gaming as a tactic for training.

As part of this multigenerational environment, it is important to respect the values of each generation.[13] At a speaking engagement several years ago about cybersecurity, one lawyer asked why law firms just don't prevent cell phone and mobile device usage altogether as a solution for potential data loss and cyber threats.[14] While this solution can be appropriate in highly secure and classified environments, it is impractical in a day-to-day legal environment (especially in the age of COVID-19) and negates the experience and values of much of the current workforce.

To address such generational gaps, law firms can involve all generations in the development of training programs. This will create opportunities for each generation to provide input on what is important to them in both the content and the delivery of the training.

B.   Building an Effective and Diverse Program

Leveraging the **SMART** principles just described, any organization can quickly and easily build an ongoing training and education campaign.

First, make the campaign fun, creative, and easy to remember. While the message of data protection is serious, the delivery need not be. People of all generations tend to learn more through consistent messaging that has a direct impact on their lives. Those working on the data protection training should develop easy, fun, and catchy slogans that employees will remember.

One example is the SAFE program,[15] an information security awareness program that was developed for Option Care Health as a way to help employees remember how best to protect and secure sensitive information:

---

13. *See* Bob Weinstein, *How Five Generations Can Effectively Work Together*, RELIABLEPLANT, https://www.reliableplant.com/Read/26581/Five-generations-work-together (last visited Jan. 26, 2022).

14. ABA Standing Committee on Law and National Security Annual Meeting 2018.

15. The SAFE program was developed by Option Care Health CISO Jill Rhodes (co-author of this chapter and co-editor of this Handbook). For further information on the program, contact Ms. Rhodes at jill.rhodes@optioncare.com. © 2016 Option Care Enterprises, Inc. All Rights Reserved.

Secure the organization's data: Where are you storing client data? How
are you deleting it?

Asset protection: Do you know where your laptop, tablet, and phone
are?

Friend or Foe: Who is sending you an e-mail? Is it something you
expected or phishing?

Encrypt: Are you encrypting sensitive e-mails before sending them out?

A program such as SAFE can be used throughout the year to educate staff;
different themes within each of the four SAFE categories can be featured.

Second, identify something, such as a mascot, that represents the organization and symbolizes data protection to help lighten the delivery of a
serious message. For example, Option Care Health, which provides infusion
services to patients in their homes, uses a mascot named "The Infuser." The
Infuser's motto is "Infusing Security into Everything We Do." Every time
employees see this mascot and message they are reminded about protecting
sensitive information. It is a fun, easy, and quick cue that costs very little
to the organization to develop and implement.

Third, ensure that training is continuous, and use various methods to
implement it. In addition to mandatory training at specific times (when
employees join the organization and subsequent annual training), continuous education is key to any successful cultural transformation. At the
same time, people can become numb to messaging that seems repetitive.
"Don't click on the phishing e-mail" is one reminder that needs to be frequently conveyed (as it is one of the top ways for cyberattacks to enter a
network),[16] but this message can easily start to sound like background noise
if it is not updated and kept "fresh." One law firm has taken a "Phish of the
Day" approach to such training; the security department circulates to all
personnel an e-mail in a recognizable format, showing a redacted phishing
e-mail that an employee has just shared and highlighting red flags in that
e-mail (e.g., unexpected, unknown sender, poor or unusual grammar, link
destination unknown, etc.).

The following are some other ideas to keep the momentum going:

---

16. *See supra* note 1.

- Leverage current newsletters, and place brief articles within them that discuss data protection.
- Create short videos with data protection messages.
- Conduct e-mail campaigns (monthly or as needed) with data protection guidelines, relevant media coverage, and so on to remind everyone (or otherwise make them aware) of relevant policies and practices.
- Conduct competitions across the firm related to security awareness; provide incentives for creative ways to address the issue.
- Offer periodic "Data Protection Awareness Weeks" or "Security Awareness Drives" with guest speakers and other special events.
- Strategically place wall posters and other communications that promote data protection.
- Publish monthly articles on the company and line-of-business intranet home pages to raise data protection awareness.
- Send periodic e-mails to highlight ongoing opportunities for online training and in-person sessions conducted by members of the data protection team, other in-house trainers, or outside speakers.
- Provide periodic continuing legal education (CLE) sessions focused on data protection, including sessions that explore the topic from the perspective of rules of professional responsibility and ethics rules (thereby not only raising awareness but also helping attorneys meet their CLE requirements).
- Develop white papers and other material related to relevant data protection topics (aiming for greater frequency and detail over time).
- Remind employees that data protection training is an important part of their job by including it as a factor in their annual performance evaluation; celebrate successes and reward those who meet the objectives (and, if needed, identify opportunities for growth and improvement).

Fourth, involve employees directly. Hold data protection competitions between groups (e.g., divisions, offices, or floors in a building) with the goal of identifying an employee or group activity that protected the organization's information in a noteworthy way. Recognize the individual or group winners, name them in the monthly newsletter or blog, and provide a pizza lunch for the winner—the more recognition, the better.

Fifth, build an ambassador (liaison) or similar program across the organization. Whether it is by office, region, subject matter expertise, or business unit, identify a way to have a data protection representative in each. Although senior leadership is important, the representative should be a mid-level employee who still has influence with peers, subordinates, and leadership. Meet with the data protection ambassadors regularly to discuss data protection issues and ensure that they are a part of the solution by having them serve as the leaders who will train and educate the employees with whom they work on a regular basis. To help the message and enthusiasm stay fresh, and bring new perspectives to the program, swap out ambassadors every two years or so.

Finally, as mentioned previously, educate employees about how to protect data at home as well as in the workplace. Data protection does not start when people log into the network or end when they shut down for the evening. Everyone's family members and friends are constantly touching sensitive or personal digital data. Whether it is through social media or new mobile apps, data is being collected. By educating employees to protect data in all facets of their lives, they will approach data protection more holistically in their daily work life.

All of these methods are easy, cheap, fun, and effective ways to communicate with employees and educate them about enhancing data protection in the organization.

C. Measuring Success

As noted earlier, it is critical to find ways to measure the success of these campaigns (the "M" in "SMART" training). One of the easiest ways to measure the success of a campaign is to test employees by phishing them directly. Phishing normally occurs when a malicious e-mail is sent either directly to an individual (spear phishing) or to many in the hope that the target will click on a link within the e-mail and then spread a virus that could infect the individual's computer, at a minimum, or the entire enterprise network. Ransomware, discussed throughout this Handbook, is often spread by phishing. But malicious actors are becoming ever-more savvy. They now spoof e-mails with names of HR employees or others in the organization and ask employees to e-mail copies of driver's licenses or other information. Tracking these incidents and also the notifications provided by employees about the incidents is one way to measure the effectiveness of training programs.

In addition, as part of a SAFE campaign (the Friend or Foe component), organizations can implement their own company-wide phishing campaign, sending "malicious" e-mails to employees just as someone trying to harm the organization would do. When an employee clicks on the e-mail, instead of infecting the system, the employee receives an educational message about the phishing e-mail and the fact that had it been real, harm could have come to the organization. This type of campaign measures the click rate and, when conducted regularly, can be used to monitor those who are clicking regularly. As a result, specific training can be developed for those individuals or groups. Phishing programs provide a quantitative measurement related to security awareness.

Reporting numbers also can provide both quantitative and qualitative opportunities for measuring success. As more training and education occurs, the number of incidents reported to appropriate leadership also will increase. Increased reporting could be anything from the reporting of a specific data breach or loss incident to reporting of phishing e-mails. As these incidents are tracked, greater information becomes available about employee knowledge and understanding of data protection.

In the end, a data breach or loss most likely will occur as a result of something an employee did or did not do. The best way to prevent such missteps is to educate the people in the organization about how they can better protect the information around them.

III. Ten Key Points

1. Recognize that the biggest risks to data come from the people working for the organization and that training and raising awareness are essential to reducing those risks.
2. Build a corporate culture that focuses on data protection, and make it the job of every individual.

3. Be SMART in training: Start training on hiring. Measure what you do. Always train. Raise awareness and provide updates continually. Tailor training by role.

4. Recognize that one size doesn't fit all; training should fit an organization's own needs.

5. Build a program that represents the organization's employees not only from a role perspective but also reflecting other considerations (e.g., generational) as well.

6. Make any training campaign fun and interesting (let the employees lead it through ambassador (liaison) programs and in other ways), and keep message delivery mechanisms light and easy to understand for all who work for the organization.

7. Train employees on how to protect information in all facets of their lives, not just in the workplace. By helping them protect their family and friends at home, they will further integrate these practices at work.

8. Reward! Reward! Reward! Use competitions with prizes to further induce employees to become more aware and supportive of data protection across the organization.

9. Measure success through phishing programs and tracking reporting of incidents and responses.

10. Know that training and awareness-raising is a never-ending journey (not a destination) that can require changes in direction in response to changes in the law, technology, media coverage, and one's own experiences and new business initiatives. Adapt accordingly.

Chapter 14

Disinformation and Deepfakes: The Role for Lawyers and Law Firms

Matthew F. Ferraro
Contributing Author Suzanne E. Spaulding

I. Introduction

Every day brings fresh evidence that contemporary public discourse is increasingly saturated by disinformation.[1] Lies about the efficacy of coronavirus vaccines, phantom voter fraud, and secretive pedophilic cabals spread like wildfire across the Internet and convince tens of millions of people either that the untruths are true or that there is no way to tell the difference.[2]

Of course, disinformation—lies, gossip, and bearing false witness—is as ancient as human history. But while the vice is old, the vehicles are new. What is different now is the speed with which false information can spread—especially online—its scale, the seeming veracity of forged images and audio, and the credulity of some who become deluded by lies. The result is what has been called "the rise of mainstream conspiracism."[3]

---

1. *See* Thomas Rid, Active Measures: The Secret History of Disinformation and Political Warfare 6 (2020) ("We live in an age of disinformation.").

2. *See generally* Reid J. Epstein & Nick Corasaniti, *Long After Trump's Loss, a Push to Inspect Ballots Persists*, N.Y. Times (May 24, 2021), https://www.nytimes.com/2021/05/24/us/politics/georgia-election-recount.html; Jane Lytvynenko, *In 2020, Disinformation Broke the U.S.*, Buzzfeed News (Dec. 6, 2020, 11:19 AM), https://www.buzzfeednews.com/article/janelytvynenko/disinformation-broke-us.

3. Shadowland, The Atlantic, https://www.theatlantic.com/shadowland/ (last visited May 25, 2021).

It should be obvious, especially after the January 6, 2021, siege of the U.S. Capitol by a mob that was driven to delusion by disinformation,[4] that public falsehoods have grown from petty annoyances into dangerous threats to public health, civic peace, economic security, and, ultimately, our democracy.[5]

This is not solely a political or social problem. Indeed, disinformation poses growing risks to businesses and the private sector. Already, many have weaponized disinformation to harm brands, move markets, conduct fraud, and undermine trust in companies and industries.[6] One 2019 study estimated that firms lose $78 billion each year due to disinformation, including $9 billion that companies and individuals spend every year trying to repair reputations damaged by falsehoods and $17 billion lost due to financial disinformation.[7] According to a 2019 survey by the Brunswick Group, 88 percent of investors consider disinformation attacks on corporations a serious issue.[8] In a more recent survey, 53 percent of American respondents agreed that "CEOs and business leaders should do whatever they can to stop the spread of misinformation, even if it comes from public officials." Only 25% of respondents thought business leaders were currently doing enough.[9]

---

4. *See* Rosalind S. Helderman, Spencer S. Hsu & Rachel Weiner, *"Trump Said to Do So": Accounts of Rioters Who Say the President Spurred Them to Rush the Capitol Could Be Pivotal Testimony*, WASH. POST (Jan. 16, 2021, 2:48 PM), https://www.washingtonpost.com/politics /trump-rioters-testimony/2021/01/16/01b3d5c6-575b-11eb-a931-5b162d0d033d_story.html; Jeffrey Goldberg, *Mass Delusion in America*, THE ATLANTIC (Jan. 6, 2021), https://www.the atlantic.com/politics/archive/2021/01/among-insurrectionists/617580/.

5. *See* Suzanne E. Spaulding et al., *Countering Adversary Threats to Democratic Institutions: An Expert Report*, CTR. FOR STRATEGIC AND INT'L STUDIES (Feb. 2018), https:// csis-website-prod.s3.amazonaws.com/s3fs-public/publication/180214_Spaulding_Counter ingAdversaryThreats_Web2.pdf.

6. Matthew F. Ferraro, Jason C. Chipman & Stephen W. Preston, *Identifying the Legal and Business Risks of Disinformation and Deepfakes: What Every Business Needs to Know*, 6 PRATT'S PRIV. & CYBERSECURITY L. REP. 142, 142 (2020) [hereinafter Ferraro et al., *Identifying Legal and Business Risks*].

7. Michelle Castillo, *Exclusive: Fake News Is Costing the World $78 Billion a Year*, CHEDDAR (Nov. 18, 2019, 11:53 AM), https://cheddar.com/media/exclusive-fake-news -is-costing-the-world-billion-a-year.

8. Robert Moran, Preston Golson & Antonio Ortolani, *Enter the Imposter*, BRUNSWICK REV. (Sept. 18, 2019), https://www.brunswickgroup.com/disinformation -attacks-insight-research-integrity-i12018/.

9. Preston Golson, *The Disinformation Wildfire*, BRUNSWICK REV. (May 5, 2021), https:// www.brunswickgroup.com/disinformation-wildfire-i18810/.

These problems will get much worse as "deepfakes"—media created or manipulated by artificial intelligence (AI)—become more believable and more widely produced. Synthetic media can supercharge viral conspiracies that can be used to harm corporate reputations and move stock prices, to target companies for fraud, to steal business credentials, and much else.

Lawyers and law firms will play critical roles as businesses confront this corrupted information environment. Attorneys can expect to be called upon to counsel clients on preparatory and mitigatory actions in the face of disinformation about businesses and deepfakes targeting private-sector interests. As businesses, law firms themselves are also targets of disinformation and will need to prepare for the same threats.

By the same token, as deepfakes and synthetic media become more common, companies will want to leverage that technology for positive uses, like artistic expression, advertising, and accessibility, among others. These businesses will look to attorneys to help them utilize deepfakes in ways that are ethical and legal, particularly in the face of growing state and federal regulation of synthetic media. Already, seven states outlaw some forms of deepfakes and many more are considering legislation to do so.[10] Attorneys may also be called upon to help shape the regulations of this field. Finally, deepfakes pose novel challenges in the courtroom where there is both the danger that manipulated media will be submitted as unadulterated evidence, or that juries will come to assume that no digital media can be trusted, because it is all just "fake." Attorneys should not baselessly stoke that skepticism for advantage, claiming without good reason that evidence is manipulated or that jurors cannot believe their eyes or their ears. In the face of these new challenges, lawyers have unique ethical obligations to

---

10. The relevant state laws are CAL. CIV. CODE § 1708.86 (West 2020); CAL. ELEC. CODE § 20010 (West 2020); HAW. REV. STAT. ANN. § 711-1110.9 (West 2021); MD. CODE ANN., CRIM. LAW § 11-208 (West 2019); N.Y. CIV. RIGHTS LAW §§ 50-f, 52-c (McKinney 2021); TEX. ELEC. CODE ANN. § 255.004 (West 2019); VA. CODE ANN. § 18.2-386.2 (West 2019); WYO. STAT. ANN. § 6-4-306 (West 2021). *See also* Matthew F. Ferraro & Louis W. Tompros, *New York's Right to Publicity and Deepfakes Law Breaks New Ground*, 38 COMPUT. & INTERNET L. 1, 3 (2021) (summarizing state of deepfakes laws); Matthew F. Ferraro, *Hawaii Outlaws Some Deepfakes*, THE SCIF (July 13, 2021), https://thescif.org/hawaii-outlaws-some-deepfakes-d9feaff05b30.

serve society by acting in ways that buttress the public's confidence in the rule of law and the administration of justice.[11]

II. Defining Disinformation and Deepfakes

A. Disinformation

When we talk about disinformation in this context, we mean "[t]he *deliberate* creation and distribution of information that is false and deceptive in order to mislead an audience."[12] We include in this definition information that may have a kernel of truth but is deliberately presented in a misleading manner.[13] Notably, this definition focuses on the knowing pushing of falsehoods with a specific intent, to influence others' perceptions. This definition is distinct from "misinformation," which is often used interchangeably with disinformation, but which captures "[i]information that is false, though not deliberately; that is created inadvertently or by mistake."[14]

Disinformation as used here can, in some instances, be a subset of "active measures," from the Russian *aktivnye meropriyatiya*, which is generally understood as "covert political operations ranging from disinformation campaigns to staging insurrections"—the kind of information operations engaged in by the Soviet Union, among others, in the 20th century or today by Russia and China.[15] Active measures are "not spontaneous lies by politicians, but the methodical output of large bureaucracies"; the pushed information need not be entirely false, and some of the information operations may be targeting audiences other than the general public, as Professor

---

11. *See* MODEL RULES OF PRO. CONDUCT preamble ¶¶ 6, 13 (Am. Bar Ass'n 2021).

12. RICHARD STENGEL, INFORMATION WARS: HOW WE LOST THE GLOBAL BATTLE AGAINST DISINFORMATION AND WHAT WE CAN DO ABOUT IT 290 (2019) (emphasis added).

13. *See* RID, *supra* note 1, at 10 ("[D]isinformation is not simply fake information—at least, not necessarily.").

14. STENGEL, *supra* note 12, at 290. *See also "Misinformation" vs. "Disinformation": Get Informed on the Difference*, DICTIONARY.COM, https://www.dictionary.com/e/misinformation-vs-disinformation-get-informed-on-the-difference/ (last visited May 25, 2021).

15. Mark Galeotti, *Active Measures: Russia's Covert Geopolitical Operations*, SECURITY INSIGHTS (June 2019), https://www.marshallcenter.org/en/publications/security-insights/active-measures-russias-covert-geopolitical-operations-0.

Thomas Rid wrote.[16] Some of the disinformation discussed in this chapter may qualify as active measures, particularly where nation-states seek to harm private companies through disinformation campaigns designed to bolster favored businesses or national champions,[17] but not all.

B. Deepfakes

The word "deepfake" is a portmanteau of two words, "deep learning" and "fake."[18] Deep learning is a branch of AI that attempts to mimic the workings of the human brain in processing data.[19]

Deepfakes are synthetic media (text, images, audio, or video) that are "either manipulated or *wholly generated* by AI."[20] This technology is seminal because it provides the ability not just to manipulate but to create from whole cloth entirely false, believable media quickly and at scale. These features differentiate deepfakes from the standard, small-scale alterations one encounters with Photoshop editing and Instagram filters, for instance.[21]

Deepfakes are produced through advanced computer systems called "generative adversarial networks" (GANs). GANs involve two computer networks that compete against one another to create false-yet-realistic media.

For example, assume someone wants to create a deepfake image of a human face. To do so, one network would rely on an available data set of images of actual faces to generate an accurate, although entirely new, image of a person's face. In this example, the computer building the fake face is called the generator. It creates content modeled on source data (a collection of real human faces), while a second algorithm (the discriminator) tries to

---

16. RID, *supra* note 1, at 9–10.

17. *See generally* Matthew F. Ferraro & Preston B. Golson, *The Next Gray Zone Conflict: State-Based Disinformation Attacks on the Private Sector*, LAWFARE (Mar. 24, 2020, 10:30 AM), https://www.lawfareblog.com/next-gray-zone-conflict-state-based-disinformation-attacks-private-sector.

18. Jeffery DelViscio, *A Nixon Deepfake, a 'Moon Disaster' Speech and an Information Ecosystem at Risk*, SCI. AM. (July 20, 2020), https://www.scientificamerican.com/article/a-nixon-deepfake-a-moon-disaster-speech-and-an-information-ecosystem-at-risk1/.

19. Marshall Hargrave, *Deep Learning*, INVESTOPEDIA (May 17, 2021), https://www.investopedia.com/terms/d/deep-learning.asp.

20. NINA SCHICK, DEEPFAKES: THE COMING INFOCALYPSE 8 (2020) (emphasis in original). Schick uses the term "deepfakes" to refer only to AI synthesized content used for malicious purposes, not positive-use cases. *Id.* at 8–9. This chapter draws no such distinction.

21. *Id.* at 8.

spot the artificial content.[22] The competition between the two networks produces a better-and-better fake until the discriminator can no longer identify the forgery.[23] The same technology can be used to generate other forms of media, like text that is written by an AI system but reads like it came from a human, and audio, most often through a process called voice cloning, where AI and machine learning algorithms replicate someone's voice based on a series of audio samples.[24]

For our purposes, a deepfake can be understood as a particularly realistic fake piece of media manipulated or created by computers. In this chapter, "deepfake" is used synonymously with "synthetic media" and "manipulated media."

Recent examples of deepfakes include a 2020 video of President Richard Nixon seeming to announce that the Apollo 11 moon landing had failed. The video's creators manipulated film from a different Nixon speech with deepfake technology to alter Nixon's voice and facial movements to make it appear as though he gave a speech he never did.[25] And, beginning in February 2021, Belgian visual effects artist Chris Umé began publishing startlingly realistic deepfake videos through a TikTok account (@deeptomcruise) that seemed to show the actor Tom Cruise walking in a store, swinging a golf club, and doing a magic trick. But it wasn't Cruise at all. Umé had spent weeks training a neural network on publicly available images of Cruise and used the open-source DeepFaceLab deepfake algorithm and common video editing tools to place Cruise's face onto the head of an actor with Cruise's general build who had filmed the scenes.[26] The results were nearly flawless forgeries.

---

22. Sarah Basford, *What Deepfakes Actually Are*, GIZMODO (July 31, 2020, 11:00 AM), https://www.gizmodo.com.au/2020/07/what-are-deepfakes/; Meredith Somers, *Deepfakes, Explained*, MIT (July 21, 2020), https://mitsloan.mit.edu/ideas-made-to-matter/deepfakes-explained.

23. *See* Bobby Chesney & Danielle Citron, *Deep Fakes: A Looming Challenge for Privacy, Democracy, and National Security*, 107 CAL. L. REV. 1753, 1760 (2019) ("Growing sophistication of the GAN approach is sure to lead to the production of increasingly convincing deep fakes.").

24. *See* SCHICK, *supra* note 20, at 141–45.

25. DelViscio, *supra* note 18.

26. James Vincent, *Tom Cruise Deepfake Creator Says Public Shouldn't Be Worried about "One-Click Fakes"*, THE VERGE (Mar. 5, 2021, 10:00 AM), https://www.theverge.com/2021/3/5/22314980/tom-cruise-deepfake-tiktok-videos-ai-impersonator-chris-ume-miles-fisher.

The technology used to make deepfakes is getting better and more accessible. Already, there are apps any user can download on their phones to place a celebrity's face into the user's video selfies.[27] Deepfake technology is being applied to all kinds of imagery, including aerial photography to create fake digital maps, which could have substantial commercial impacts.[28] For example, overhead imagery is regularly used by businesses to track traffic at retail establishments, commodity inventories, real estate growth patterns, and to create maps for traffic apps[29]—all businesses that could be negatively impacted by falsified images.

The number of deepfakes online is increasing rapidly. According to an analysis by the AI company Sentinel, as of 2020, there were more than 100 million deepfake videos online, which represented a year-over-year growth rate of 6,820 percent.[30] A separate study using different methodology by the group Sensity AI estimated in July 2019 that the number of deepfake videos on the Internet was doubling every six months.[31] Soon, the ability to create ever-more convincing fake media showing people doing and saying things that did not occur in reality will be widespread.[32]

Technologists are working on deepfake countermeasures that fall into two general categories.[33] The first method attempts to detect phony media *after* it is created. For example, an Israeli technology firm used deepfake-detection algorithms in July 2020 to reveal that the headshot employed by an author of op-eds in prominent Israeli newspapers was manipulated by AI and that the author himself was a "mirage."[34] Similarly, in September 2020,

---

27. Ferraro et al., *Identifying Legal and Business Risks, supra* note 6, at 152 (describing "Impressions.app").

28. Will Knight, *Deepfake Maps Could Really Mess with Your Sense of the World,* WIRED (May 28, 2021, 7:00 AM), https://www.wired.com/story/deepfake-maps-mess-sense-world/ (describing research of University of Washington Professor Bo Zhao).

29. *See generally* RS METRICS, https://rsmetrics.com/ (last visited June 26, 2021).

30. SENTINEL, DEEPFAKES 2020: THE TIPPING POINT 7 (2020), https://thesentinel.ai/media /Deepfakes%202020:%20The%20Tipping%20Point,%20Sentinel.pdf.

31. Henry Ajder, *The State of Deepfakes 2019: Landscape, Threats, and Impact,* SENSITY AI (Sept. 2019), https://sensity.ai/reports/#.

32. Chesney & Citron, *supra* note 23, at 1762–63.

33. *See generally* Matthew F. Ferraro, *Decoding Deepfakes,* NAT'L SECURITY INST. BACK-GROUNDER (Dec. 2020), https://nationalsecurity.gmu.edu/ddf/.

34. Raphael Satter, *Deepfake Used to Attack Activist Couple Shows New Disinformation Frontier,* REUTERS (July 15, 2020, 8:44 AM), https://www.reuters.com/article/us -cyber-deepfake-activist/deepfake-used-to-attack-activist-couple-shows-new-disinformation -frontier-idUSKCN24G15E.

Microsoft launched a program that assesses media and provides a confidence score about whether that media has been manufactured artificially.[35] The second method verifies photographs and other media at the "point of capture" in such a way that they cannot be altered or modified after the fact without leaving evidence of the manipulation.[36] Efforts to improve and deploy these technologies, like efforts to improve and distribute deepfake technology itself, are ongoing.

A side of effect of the propagation of deepfakes deserves special mention. The mere growth of believable synthetic media can foster what law professors Bobby Chesney and Danielle Citron have called the "liar's dividend,"[37] wherein individuals successfully deny the authenticity of genuine media by claiming that the content is a deepfake. Thus, by leveraging skepticism about the authenticity of media to cast doubt on real evidence of their wrongdoing, liars will accrue a benefit or a dividend. This is already happening. In one prominent example, former President Trump now reportedly claims that the infamous *Access Hollywood* tape in which he can be heard bragging about sexually assaulting women may be "fake."[38]

We are also witnessing the rise of a kind of "zealot's dividend," where partisans who are not even the subjects of the media in question reject inconvenient media evidence that does not fit with their chosen narratives, claiming it is manipulated or synthetic. We saw this with supporters of former President Trump dismissing as a "deepfake" a video of him conceding the 2020 election,[39] and with political partisans claiming falsely that videos of President Joe Biden are deepfakes.[40] The value of the liar's and

---

35. Leo Kelion, *Deepfake Detection Tool Unveiled by Microsoft*, BBC (Sept. 1, 2020), https://www.bbc.com/news/technology-53984114.

36. Mounir Ibrahim & Ashish Jaiman, Opinion, *To Defend Democracy, We Must Protect Truth Online*, THE HILL (Apr. 25, 2021, 5:00 PM), https://thehill.com/opinion /cybersecurity/550191-to-defend-democracy-we-must-protect-truth-online (describing provenance technology).

37. Chesney & Citron, *supra* note 3, at 1785–86.

38. Emma Stefansky, *Trump Now Says the Access Hollywood Tape May Be Fake*, VANITY FAIR (Nov. 26, 2017), https://www.vanityfair.com/news/2017/11/trump-access-hollywood-tape-fake.

39. Amelia Mavis Christnot, *Trump Supporters Are Convinced Trump's Concession Video Is a Deepfake and the Delusion Is Real*, SECOND NEXUS (Jan. 8, 2021), https://secondnexus .com/trump-parler-concession-deep-fake.

40. Reuters Fact Check, *Fact Check-Biden's Skin Tone 'Mismatch' in Video Is Not Evidence of a Deepfake*, REUTERS (May 25, 2021, 12:08 PM), https://www.reuters.com/article

zealot's dividends will grow dearer as more people learn about the quality and availability of this technology.

III. Disinformation and Its Discontents: Business Risks Requiring Legal Counsel

Attorneys will need to help resolve many legal and business risks that arise from disinformation and manipulated media. These risks include, among others:

1. Reputational risk;
2. Personal harassment;
3. Social engineering and fraud;
4. Market manipulation;
5. Insurance fraud; and
6. Labor and employment issues.

Next, we address these issues in turn.

A. Reputational Risk

Litigators, regulatory lawyers, and crisis management attorneys are often called upon to help clients deal with reputational risk. Viral disinformation and deepfakes act as accelerants to those ambient business dangers.

For example, in August 2017, a user on the anonymous website 4Chan wrote that he wanted to inflict pain on a "liberal place" and decided to target Starbucks for a kind of brand assassination by launching a social media campaign to make it appear that the coffee seller was giving free drinks to undocumented immigrants during a so-called Dreamer Day. To spread the disinformation, someone forged realistic-looking graphics using the Starbucks font and logo and promoted a hashtag for the campaign (#border-freecoffee). When the tweets started to trend, the company's communications

/factcheck-biden-notdeepfake/fact-check-bidens-skin-tone-mismatch-in-video-is-not-evidence-of-a-deepfake-idUSL2N2NC1U8.

team went into action and directly responded to individuals who were retweeting false information.[41]

More recently, the furniture seller Wayfair became embroiled in the QAnon conspiracy, a wide-ranging tall tale that claims, in part, that a global ring of satanic pedophiles lurks just beyond sight. The theory spread in the summer of 2020 that Wayfair was connected with child sex trafficking because of the coincidental overlap of the names of some of its furniture pieces and those of missing children.[42] As a result, users on places like 4Chan and Twitter tried to coordinate a campaign to short the company's stock. On Twitter, an account posted the address and Google Map images of Wayfair's office building in Boston. Other users posted the LinkedIn profiles of Wayfair employees. QAnon adherents have also targeted the company's CEO, drawing negative implications from his philanthropic work with nonprofit organizations supporting children, increasing mentions of him on social media tens of thousands of times in a few weeks.[43]

In another example, during the coronavirus pandemic in 2020, online conspiracists spread the bizarre theory that 5G cell towers were responsible for the virus' spread, leading to significant real-world harm, including dozens of arson attacks on cell towers and cases of harassment against telecommunications maintenance workers across Europe and New Zealand.[44] The

---

41. Will Yakowicz, *Fake Starbucks Ad Tries to Lure the Undocumented with Discounted Coffee*, INC. (Aug. 8, 2017), https://www.inc.com/will-yakowicz/fake-starbucks-dreamer-day-4chan -meme.html. *See also* Ferraro et al., *Identifying Legal and Business Risks, supra* note 6, at 144.

42. For example, one social media post suggested that a report about an allegedly missing Ohio teenager named Samiyah Mumin was linked to a Wayfair cabinet called "Samiyah," with a listed price of almost $13,000. *See* Reuters Staff, *Fact Check: No Evidence Linking Wayfair to Human Trafficking Operation*, REUTERS (July 13, 2020, 2:45 PM), https://www .reuters.com/article/uk-factcheck-wayfair-human-trafficking/fact-check-no-evidence-linking -wayfair-to-human-trafficking-operation-idUSKCN24E2M2?fbclid=IwAR3WNOLt9DsNrM dwLO13mylatPo3CB-X3y7gsC1_H5GJ6yNC4Tj5kmgrFBE.

43. *See id. See also* Cindy L. Otis, Opinion, *Conspiracy Theorists Targeted Wayfair. Who Will QAnon Hit Next?*, BARRON'S (July 27, 2020, 6:00 AM), https://www.barrons.com/articles /after-conspiracy-theorists-hit-wayfair-companies-should-ask-will-i-be-next-51595787339.

44. Chris Keall, *After Two More Cell Towers Set Ablaze, Telcos Warn Phone, Internet Could Be Interrupted*, NEW ZEALAND HERALD (May 14, 2020, 9:47 PM), https:// www.nzherald.co.nz/business/after-two-more-cell-towers-set-ablaze-telcos-warn-phone -internet-could-be-interrupted/Y6D7CK24QCDMKTTCIJG5T2OOJQ/; James Rogers, *Telecom Masts in Continental Europe Attacked in Wake of Bizarre 5G Coronavirus Conspiracy Theory*, FOX NEWS (Apr. 28, 2020), https://www.foxnews.com /science/telecom-masts-continental-europe-attacked-bizarre-5g-coronavirus-conspiracy-theory.

U.S. Department of Homeland Security warned the U.S. telecommunications industry at the time that the dangers that coronavirus conspiracists will "incit[e] attacks against communications infrastructure . . . will probably increase as the disease continues to spread."[45]

Foreign governments and organizations may also engage in disinformation campaigns against private business to bolster foreign companies or harm competitors. For example, for the past few years, the Russian backed TV and Internet channel RT America has aired a series of deceptive reports on the dangers of 5G technology. These reports have linked 5G signals to brain cancer, infertility, and Alzheimer's disease, among others, all "claims that lack scientific support," according to the *New York Times*.[46] Russia's goal appears to be to sow doubt about a technology that the United States believes is part of its future high-tech dominance. The reputational harms of this geostrategic competition fall on private parties.

Imagine how much more devastating such disinformation campaigns will be if they involve realistic deepfake media. Here's a thought experiment: What if the Tom Cruise deepfakes that went viral on TikTok showed Cruise not just swinging a golf club and performing a magic trick but announcing to the camera that he was cancelling the next *Mission: Impossible* movie because he discovered that the movie studio producing the film was corrupt. "I've uncovered evidence that they're all crooks," he may have said to the camera, adding: "I promise you I will never work with that studio again. And I call on all my actor friends in Hollywood to do the same—let's boycott them until they fire their dishonest leadership." How might that have impacted the reputation, stock price, and marketability of the studio, to have one of the world's biggest celebrities (seemingly) foreswear them?

Likewise, consider the impact on consumer confidence of a phony yet believable video showing a pricy autonomous vehicle involved in a

---

45. Josh Margolin, *Feds Warn of Attacks Related to Bogus COVID-19 Conspiracy Theory*, ABC NEWS (May 16, 2020, 12:04 PM), https://abcnews.go.com/US/feds-warn-attacks-related-bogus-covid-19-conspiracy/story?id=70721145.

46. William J. Broad, *Your 5G Phone Won't Hurt You. But Russia Wants You to Think Otherwise*, N.Y. TIMES (May 12, 2019), https://www.nytimes.com/2019/05/12/science/5g-phone-safety-health-russia.html.

spectacular accident.[47] Businesses will look to their legal counsel to help remedy the reputational injuries inflicted by such efforts—beginning with helping to retain experts to prove that the imagery was forged.[48]

Law firms, like any other business with reputational concerns, may also be victims of disinformation attacks. Consider the impact on a multinational firm of a manipulated audio clip that makes it sound like the managing partner made disparaging comments about a female associate or used a racial epithet. Thus, firms should prepare accordingly. (On how, see Part IV, *infra*.) Traditional cyber activities can also be part of a disinformation effort. Hacks of a business' network have always included, as a collateral impact, damage to the company's reputation. In fact, business leaders have long seen the loss of customer confidence as a primary concern of cybersecurity.[49] Lawyers and others responding to cyber incidents must now consider that reputational damage may be a primary objective.

B. Personal Harassment

Disinformation and deepfakes pose a substantial risk of personal harassment and extortion. Deepfakes targeting women are already prevalent online. According to a 2019 study, more than 95 percent of all deepfake videos available on the Internet are of nonconsensual pornography—that is, a nonconsenting person's face (whether of a celebrity or an average person) placed on a nude body to create a realistic pornographic image.[50] Most of those images today are of famous female actors, but the technology harms

---

47. Ferraro & Golson, *supra* note 17 (describing how a Russian company recently designed a fake electric car accident to garner attention, and several media outlets treated the bogus video as if it were real); Cat Zakrzewski with Tonya Riley, *Businesses Should Be Watching Out for Deepfakes Too, Experts Warn*, WASH. POST (Dec. 13, 2019, 9:15 AM), https://www.washingtonpost.com/news/powerpost/paloma/the-technology-202/2019/12/13/the-technology-202-businesses-should-be-watching-out-for-deepfakes-too-experts-warn/5df279f1602ff125ce5b2fe7/.

48. *See* Ferraro et al., *Identifying Legal and Business Risks*, *supra* note 6, at 145.

49. *See Protecting the Brand—Cyber-Attacks and the Reputation of the Enterprise*, ECONOMIST INTEL. UNIT (Mar. 24, 2016), https://eiuperspectives.economist.com/technology-innovation/cyber-chasm-how-disconnect-between-c-suite-and-security-endangers-enterprise-0/article/protecting-brand%E2%80%94cyber-attacks-and-reputation-enterprise/.

50. Giorgio Patrini, *Mapping the Deepfake Landscape*, SENSITY AI (Oct. 7, 2019), https://sensity.ai/mapping-the-deepfake-landscape/.

everyone's privacy and has been used to victimize hundreds of thousands of everyday women.[51]

In one notorious example, Indian investigative journalist Rana Ayyub was targeted by a fake pornographic video of her that circulated online, probably produced and spread in response to her reporting on human rights violations by Indian authorities.[52] Ayyub was hospitalized for heart ailments following the harassment and humiliation, and she withdrew from the online public square.[53]

Bad actors could use such deepfakes either to extort concessions from business leaders or to embarrass them. Lawyers will be needed to work with private clients, law enforcement agencies, and prosecutors to counsel on the propriety of paying ransom, and to litigate after the fact against malefactors.

C. Social Engineering and Fraud

Disinformation and synthetic media have been used to impersonate identities and defraud businesses. For example, in March 2019, according to press reports, the CEO of a British energy firm thought he was speaking on the telephone with his boss, the CEO of the firm's German parent company. The German CEO asked the British official to send roughly $250,000 to a Hungarian supplier, and the British CEO complied. Later, the British CEO learned that he had been duped. He had been speaking to someone using AI-based software to impersonate the German CEO's voice, according to the energy firm's insurance carrier, Euler Hermes Group SA.[54]

---

51. *See* Jane Lytvynenko & Scott Lucas, *Thousands of Women Have No Idea a Telegram Network Is Sharing Fake Nude Images of Them*, BuzzFeed News (Oct. 20, 2020), https://www.buzzfeednews.com/article/janelytvynenko/telegram-deepfake-nude-women-images-bot (deepfake technology allowed users to create photo-realistic simulated nude images of 680,000 women without their knowledge or consent, according to tech researchers).

52. Schick, *supra* note 20, at 125–28.

53. *I Was Vomiting: Journalist Rana Ayyub Reveals Horrifying Account of Deepfake Porn Plot*, India Today (Nov. 21, 2018, 7:20 PM), https://www.indiatoday.in/trending-news/story/journalist-rana-ayyub-deepfake-porn-1393423-2018-11-21.

54. Catherine Stupp, *Fraudsters Used AI to Mimic CEO's Voice in Unusual Cybercrime Case*, Wall St. J. (Aug. 30, 2019, 12:51 PM), https://www.wsj.com/articles/fraudsters-use-ai-to-mimic-ceos-voice-in-unusual-cybercrime-case-11567157402. *See also* Ferraro et al., *Identifying Legal and Business Risks*, *supra* note 6, at 145–46. The name of the victim company has not been disclosed.

Similarly, in July 2019, cybersecurity firm Symantec reported that three companies had fallen victim to deepfake audio attacks purportedly from scammers who used AI programs to mimic the voices of the firms' CEOs. Symantec said millions of dollars were stolen, but it did not name the victimized businesses.[55]

Fraudsters do not lack for imagination when it comes to applying new technologies to hoary offenses. We can expect deepfakes to be used to impersonate deceased individuals to collect pension benefits after the pensioner has died, to open new, illegitimate financial accounts, and to synthesize entirely new people for fraudulent purposes.[56] The press reports that such a scheme has already led to the arrest of two individuals in China. They were accused of using AI-created facial images purchased on the black market to create false identities and establish a shell company that issued fake tax invoices, worth about $76 million.[57]

American law enforcement recognizes that the danger of synthetic media-enabled social engineering and fraud is growing. In March 2021, the Federal Bureau of Investigation (FBI) issued a private industry notification (PIN) advising companies that "[m]alicious actors almost certainly will leverage synthetic content for cyber and foreign influence operations in the next 12–18 months."[58] The FBI wrote that it anticipates that synthetic media will be "increasingly used by foreign and criminal cyber actors for spearphishing and social engineering in an evolution of cyber operational tradecraft."[59]

---

55. Bob Keaveney, *RSA 2020: Is Voice Fraud the Next Frontier for Scam Artists?*, Biz Tech Mag. (Feb. 26, 2020), https://biztechmagazine.com/article/2020/02/rsa-2020-voice-fraud-next-frontier-scam-artists; Kaveh Waddell & Jennifer A. Kingson, *The Coming Deepfakes Threat to Businesses*, Axios (July 19, 2019), https://www.axios.com/the-coming-deepfakes-threat-to-businesses-308432e8-f1d8-465e-b628-07498a7c1e2a.html. *See also* Ferraro et al., *Identifying Legal and Business Risks*, *supra* note 6, at 146.

56. *See Deepfakes of the Dead: Could They Be a Threat to the Financial Services Sector?*, IPROOV Blog (Mar. 18, 2021), https://www.iproov.com/blog/deepfakes-dead-threaten-financial-services.

57. Eric Weiss, *Fraudsters Use Deepfake Biometrics to Hack China's Taxation System*, Find Biometrics (Apr. 1, 2021), https://findbiometrics.com/fraudsters-use-deepfake-biometrics-hack-chinas-taxation-system-040103/ (citing news reports).

58. *Malicious Actors Almost Certainly Will Leverage Synthetic Content for Cyber and Foreign Influence Operations*, Fed. Bureau of Investigation i (Mar. 10, 2021), https://www.documentcloud.org/documents/20509703-fbipin-3102021 [hereinafter FBI PIN].

59. *Id.* Spear phishing "is the act of sending and emails to specific and well-researched targets while purporting to be a trusted sender. The aim is to either infect devices with malware

The PIN warned that malicious cyber actors will not just push propaganda on behalf of foreign actors but also leverage deepfake technology to attack the private sector. In particular, the FBI warned that synthetic content may be used in a "newly defined cyber attack vector" called "business identity compromise" (BIC), where deepfake tools will be employed to create "synthetic corporate personas" or imitate existing employees and will likely cause "very significant financial and reputational impacts to victim businesses and organizations."[60]

A month after the FBI issued this PIN, the threat intelligence company Recorded Future reported on a flourishing underground market for "customized services and tutorials that incorporate visual and audio deepfake technologies designed to bypass and defeat security measures."[61] Threat actors are focusing on evading security measures and facilitating fraudulent activities through "fake voices and facial recognition," Recorded Future wrote.[62] The outlook is grim. The report noted that deepfakes have "migrated away from the creation of pornographic-related content to more sophisticated targeting that incorporates security bypassing and releasing misinformation and disinformation."[63] Publicly known examples of the successful use of visual and audio deepfakes highlight "the potential for all types of fraud or crime, including blackmail, identity theft, and social engineering."[64]

These threats represent an evolution in business e-mail compromise (BEC) schemes, which occur when a hacker compromises a corporate e-mail account to facilitate fraudulent financial transactions. Because of the threats

---

or convince victims to hand over information or money." *See* Dan Swinhoe, *What Is Spear Phishing? Why Targeted Email Attacks Are So Difficult to Stop*, CSO (Jan. 21, 2019, 3:00 AM), https://www.csoonline.com/article/3334617/what-is-spear-phishing-why-targeted-email-attacks-are-so-difficult-to-stop.html.

60. *See* FBI PIN, *supra* note 58, at 3. *See also* Matthew F. Ferraro, Jason C. Chipman & Benjamin A. Powell, *FBI Warns Companies of "Almost Certain" Threats from Deepfakes*, 4 J. Robotics A.I. & L. 267, 267–68 (2021).

61. Recorded Future, The Business of Fraud: Deepfakes, Fraud's Next Frontier 1 (Apr. 29, 2021), https://go.recordedfuture.com/hubfs/reports/cta-2021-0429.pdf.

62. *Id.* at 3.

63. *Id.* at 1.

64. *Id. See also* Tim Starks, *Deepfakes Advertised on Underground Markets, Signaling Possible Shift, Recorded Future Says*, Cyber Scoop (Apr. 29, 2021), https://www.cyberscoop.com/deepfakes-doctored-video-audio-future/.

posed by BEC intrusions, many organizations over the past several years have sought to protect their treasury and accounts payable functions from manipulation. The potential for deepfake technology to create a new category of BIC activities threatens to complicate authentication protocols, and cybersecurity and privacy attorneys will likely need to work with clients to revisit their security practices in the face of these intensifying challenges to information security.[65]

Deepfake- or disinformation-enabled social engineering frauds pose many different risks to the private sector. Companies can lose the defrauded funds, be subject to litigation by shareholders, be investigated by regulators, and—if auditors refuse to approve financial statements following such a fraud—face loss of access to capital markets.[66]

D. Market Manipulation

Fraudsters have long used regular disinformation—fake text and simple graphics—to move the financial markets and reap windfalls.

For example, in October 2018, after Broadcom announced its intention to acquire CA Technologies for $19 billion, a phony memo circulated online supposedly from the Defense Department saying the U.S. Government's Committee on Foreign Investment in the United States would scrutinize the acquisition for national security threats. Shares of both companies dropped when the memo was released, and while no charges were filed in that case, short sellers who were prepared for the hiccup could have netted a bonanza from the hoax—what one writer called "a new phase of short-seller espionage."[67]

Similar deceptions have been used to prop up stock prices, too. For example, in December 2020, the Securities and Exchange Commission (SEC) charged a Georgia man and several others with securities fraud violations for allegedly creating false rumors about material business events of public companies, such as corporate mergers or acquisitions, and posting those

---

65. Ferraro et al., *supra* note 60, at 269.
66. *See* Ferraro et al., *Identifying Legal and Business Risks*, *supra* note 6, at 147.
67. Ed Targett, *Fake Memo Hits Broadcom, CA Technologies Shares*, COMPUT. BUS. REV. (Oct. 12, 2018), https://www.cbronline.com/news/broadcom-cfius-ca. *See also* Ferraro et al., *Identifying Legal and Business Risks*, *supra* note 6, at 148.

falsehoods to financial chat rooms, message boards, and real-time financial news services, temporarily pushing up the companies' stocks. The market bumps allowed the defendants to reap tens of thousands of dollars in illicit profits, the SEC said.[68]

And in April 2017, the SEC filed enforcement actions against more than two dozen individuals and entities behind various alleged stock promotion schemes where the defendants penned supposedly independent market analyses on investing websites to hype companies while being secretly compensated for goosing the stock prices. In one example, the SEC alleged a defendant placed dozens of articles in reputable online news outlets about a small pharmaceutical company, driving the shares up by 925 percent.[69]

A 2018 report by JP Morgan Chase suggested there is a systemic risk of disinformation manipulation for those traders who use algorithms based on social media posts and headlines to make trades.[70] The SEC has also issued a public alert for investors to warn them of fraudsters who may try to move share prices by using social media to circulate false or misleading information about stocks.[71]

The dangers of these scams will only grow as believable manipulated media can be easily made and deployed. Imagine the impact of not just an

---

68. Complaint, SEC v. Barton S. Ross, No. 20-cv-05140, ¶¶ 1–5 (N.D. Ga. Dec. 18, 2020), https://www.sec.gov/litigation/complaints/2020/comp24989.pdf; *SEC Charges Former Day Trader with Market Manipulation Scheme*, SEC. & EXCH. COMM'N (Dec. 18, 2020), https://www.sec.gov/litigation/litreleases/2020/lr24989.htm. *See also* Ferraro et al., *Identifying Legal and Business Risks, supra* note 6, at 147–48 (listing examples of disinformation-enabled marked manipulation); Matthew F. Ferraro & Jason C. Chipman, Opinion, *Fake News Threatens Our Businesses, Not Just Our Politics*, WASH. POST (Feb. 8, 2019, 1:33 PM), https://www.washingtonpost.com/outlook/fake-news-threatens-our-businesses-not-just-our-politics/2019/02/08/f669b62c-2b1f-11e9-984d-9b8fba003e81_story.html (same).

69. Complaint, SEC v. Lidingo Holdings, LLC et al., No. 17-cv-02540, ¶¶ 1–5, 89 (S.D.N.Y. Apr. 10, 2017), https://www.sec.gov/litigation/complaints/2017/comp23802-lidingo.pdf; *27 Firms and Individuals Charged with Fraudulent Promotion of Stocks*, SEC. & EXCH. COMM'N (Apr. 10, 2017), https://www.sec.gov/litigation/litreleases/2017/lr23802.htm; *see* Renae Merle, *Schome Created Fake News Stories to Manipulate Stock Prices, SEC Alleges*, L.A. TIMES (July 5, 2017, 2:50 PM), https://www.latimes.com/business/la-fi-sec-fake-news-20170705-story.html.

70. *Fake News and Bad News Are Depressing the Market, JPMorgan Strategists Say*, FORTUNE (Dec. 8, 2018), https://fortune.com/2018/12/08/fake-news-jpmorgan-kolanovic/.

71. *Updated Investor Alert: Social Media and Investing—Stock Rumors*, SEC. & EXCH. COMM'N (Nov. 5, 2015), https://www.sec.gov/oiea/investor-alerts-bulletins/ia_rumors.html.

article touting a phony acquisition but a credible video of what appears to be the companies' CEOs shaking hands to commemorate the transaction.

The experience of the past informs concerns for the future. In September 2018, Tesla CEO Elon Musk smoked marijuana on Joe Rogan's video podcast. The next day, in light of that episode and shake-ups at the company, Tesla stock closed down 6 percent.[72] If short sellers knew that was going to happen, they could have turned a tidy profit. Perhaps next time, enterprising market manipulators will seek to create a similar short by manufacturing a deepfake video of a different, irreverent CEO doing something similar. It will be difficult to correct misperceptions and for the market to recover if the images are convincing.[73]

Attorneys will be needed to help clients mitigate market-manipulation risks at the front end, advocate with regulatory bodies if their clients' valuations are harmed, and bring civil actions to recover damages from market manipulators, if necessary.

E. Insurance Fraud

The insurance industry often relies on the veracity of digital media to adjudicate claims, increasing its exposure to deepfake manipulations. For instance, auto insurers use photographs of cars to validate insurance reports. Particularly because of the Covid-19 pandemic, the insurance industry has moved toward self-service, where insureds rather than adjusters take the photographs that accompany claims. The greater availability of simple-to-use media manipulation technology will raise questions about the authenticity of such photographs, which insurers and their lawyers will need to address.[74]

Likewise, health care companies often rely on medical imagery to verify diagnoses. That imagery will become easier to fake with AI technology. For

---

72. Sara Salinas, *Tesla Stock Closes Down 6% after Top Executives Resign and Elon Musk Smokes Weed on Video*, CNBC (Sept. 7, 2018, 7:32 PM), https://www.cnbc.com/2018/09/07/tesla-sinks-8percent-after-bizarre-musk-podcast-appearance-cao-exit.html.

73. *See* Ferraro et al., *Identifying Legal and Business Risks*, *supra* note 6, at 148. I thank Nina Schick for first suggesting during a webinar that Musk's behavior on the Rogan podcast may be a template for future, similar deepfake scams.

74. Elizabeth Blosfield, *How a Social Media Fad Is Turning into a Cyber Fraud Risk for Insurers*, INS. J. (Mar. 3, 2021), https://www.insurancejournal.com/news/2021/03/03/603345.htm.

example, Israeli researchers have warned about the likely spread of deepfake-manipulated radiology scans that have been altered to show false results, including fake cancerous nodes.[75] Altered scans could be used to defraud insurance companies, who will need to rely on counsel to help alter their trainings, practices, compliance programs, and loss-mitigation litigation strategies as a result.

F. Labor and Employment Issues

Believable yet falsified video or audio could pose potent labor and employment risks. Employees have long used legitimate recordings of harassment or other workplace malfeasance to support wrongful termination or harassment claims. These recordings are usually admissible in court as the most reliable evidence.[76] With this history in mind, the public may automatically assume the validity of future video and audio recordings purporting to substantiate claims of employer wrongdoing, regardless of concerns that the media has been manipulated. Perhaps after someone's employment has been terminated, a video pops up on a social media account that purports to show that the employee was sexually harassed, and it quickly goes viral, even if the employer doubts its authenticity. Legal counsel will need to manage the employment law and reputational risks of inculpatory media and assess the underlying allegations.[77]

---

75. Jane Anderson, *Addressing "Deep Fake" Scans Is Critical Amid Tech Advances*, REP. ON PATIENT PRIV. (Nov. 11, 2019), https.//compliancecosmos.org/addressing-deep-fake-scans-critical-amid-tech-advances (citing Yisroel Mirsky).

76. *See, e.g.*, Byrd v. Reno, 1998 WL 429767, at *1 (D.D.C., 1998) ("[T]here is not and cannot be anything that is the substantial equivalent of the tape recording of a conversation. . . . There is literally no substitute for the tape recordings."); Rauh v. Coyne, 744 F. Supp. 1181, 1183–84 (D.D.C. 1990) (admitting discrimination plaintiff's tape recording as an admission of a party-defendant). *See also* FED. R. EVID. 901(a).

77. *See* Ferraro et al., *Identifying Legal and Business Risks*, *supra* note 6, at 149–50.

IV. The Elite Eight: Best Practices for Managing Disinformation Risk

Businesses should work with counsel to develop strategies to protect their brands and valuations from disinformation and deepfakes, both before and after companies are victimized by them. Companies will need to tailor their responses to their specific circumstances, but here are eight general practices lawyers and their clients will want to consider:

1. **Proactively Communicate an Accurate Positive Message.** Research shows that proactive messaging can establish strong defenses to disinformation. An April 2020 paper in the *HKS Misinformation Review* about Covid-19 disinformation makes this point. It reported that 87 percent of the public believed that handwashing and social distancing inhibit the spread of the coronavirus. The public accepted this truth because people had already absorbed messages about the efficacy of handwashing and social distancing in preventing the spread of the seasonal flu, the article argued. By contrast, it said that more than one in five people surveyed believed that Vitamin C was a remedy for the coronavirus in part because of long-standing misperceptions that Vitamin C cures the common cold.[78] These findings suggest that, in the business context, a company should take steps to build brand resilience[79]—to establish its messages in the public's mind early on, before disinformation starts spreading. If a company can construct stable public perceptions, it will be less likely to lose control of the narrative about its business to a barrage of bogus blogs and tendentious tweets.[80]

2. **Engage in Social Listening.** Companies need to understand how their brands are perceived on social media to get advance warning of any effort to spread disinformation. Law firms, cybersecurity consultancies, or public

---

78. Kathleen Hall Jamieson & Dolores Albarracín, *The Relation between Media Consumption and Misinformation at the Outset of the SARS-CoV-2 Pandemic in the US*, Harv. Kennedy Sch. (HKS) Misinformation Rev. (2020), https://doi.org/10.37016/mr-2020-012.

79. *See* Golson, *supra* note 9 ("Organizations that take the time to learn how to address and mobilize these audiences can build resilience against false information.").

80. Matthew F. Ferraro, *What Corporate America Can Do to Protect Itself from Conspiracy Theories*, Real Clear World (July 22, 2020), https://www.realclearworld.com /articles/2020/07/21/what_corporate_america_can_do_to_protect_itself_from_conspiracy _theories_499674.html.

relations firms can be retained to do this work. Outside counsel can also consider retaining the third-party service providers directly; depending on the circumstances, their work may be entitled to legal privilege.

3. Conduct a Self-assessment. Disinformation risk varies by company and circumstance. Businesses need to look in the mirror and ask, "What upcoming events carry the greatest risk? What aspects of the business are most vulnerable to attack? What messages would have the most resonance?"[81] Preston Golson, a former CIA officer and now a director at the Brunswick Group, has called this "an audit of vulnerabilities." "In a world of complex tensions, organizations that take a position on a controversial issue, criticize the policies of a foreign government, or simply are on one side of a domestic political dispute, can end up being the subject of disinformation," he wrote.[82] It is important that entities understand these pressure points early. Furthermore, because, as noted earlier, disinformation and deepfakes pose special dangers of social engineering and impersonation, businesses should also assess their vulnerabilities to fraud and spear phishing.

4. Register Trademarks and Copyrights. Because of the strong federal protection provided to intellectual property (IP),[83] companies should work with counsel to register preemptively their trademarks, trade dress, and copyrights before they are manipulated by bad actors.[84] If their IP is misused, copyright or trademark owners can bring lawsuits.

Social media platforms also usually remove IP-infringing content if they receive a request from the IP's owner.[85] For example, in 2019, anti-advertising activists uploaded to a social media platform a manipulated deepfake video of Kim Kardashian West appearing to say things she never did. *Vogue* magazine had posted the original video on which the deepfake was based a few weeks earlier, and because the copyright for that video

---

81. *See* Ferraro et al., *Identifying Legal and Business Risks, supra* note 6, at 154.

82. Golson, *supra* note 9.

83. *See, e.g.,* 15 U.S.C. § 1114(1)(a) (Lanham Act); 17 U.S.C. §§ 101–810 (Copyright Act).

84. *See* Ferraro et al., *Identifying Legal and Business Risks, supra* note 6, at 154.

85. *See, e.g.,* Brook Zimmatore, *How to File a DMCA Takedown and Protect Your Reputation,* ENTREPRENEUR (Dec. 3, 2020), https://www.entrepreneur.com/article/359772.

belonged to *Vogue*, the magazine's publisher Condé Nast was able to lodge a copyright complaint against the manipulated video and have it taken down.[86]

5. Make a Plan. Many companies today work with attorneys to develop cybersecurity plans that anticipate cyber hacks and similar crises. Businesses need to expand their crisis planning to anticipate that reputational harm and disinformation may be a key objective of malicious actors. They need to prepare for fraud and social engineering by increasing training for team members (and expanding those who are educated on these threats, to include professionals from communications, public relations, finance, and IT) and updating compliance and internal security protocols.

With regard to corporate reputations, entities cannot hope to design an effective response strategy after canards start to circulate. They need to prepare for such events the same way they should plan for cybersecurity breaches: by assigning specific responsibilities to members of an incident response team and running drills. Companies should also consider using technology to make videos of c-suite executives harder to manipulate.[87]

6. Engage with Social Media Platforms. If a company or its counsel see disinformation spreading online, it should contact the social media platforms being used to spread it and see if the information violates the platforms' Terms of Service. If so, the platforms may remove it.[88]

7. Speak. It can be a challenge to know when to directly address disinformation as opposed to ignoring it. There is a risk of amplifying false information that might otherwise fail to get traction.[89] On the other hand, lies can travel remarkably fast and waiting too long can be costly. As part of their advance planning, companies should consider thresholds for tak-

---

86. Matthew Katz, *Kim Kardashian Can Get a Deepfake Taken Off YouTube. It's Much Harder for You*, DIGITAL TRENDS (June 17, 2019), https://www.digitaltrends.com/social-media /kim-kardashian-deepfake-removed-from-youtube/. *See also* Matthew F. Ferraro & Louis W. Tompros, *Celebrity Disinformation Victims Have Panoply of Remedies*, LAW360 (Sept. 29, 2020, 4:05 PM).

87. *See* Ferraro et al., *Identifying Legal and Business Risks, supra* note 6, at 154; Ferraro, *supra* note 60; Golson, *supra* note 9.

88. *See* Ferraro et al., *Identifying Legal and Business Risks, supra* note 6, at 154.

89. This is referred to as the "Streisand Effect," after an incident involving the famous singer. *See* Mario Cacciottolo, *The Streisand Effect: When Censorship Backfires*, BBC (June 15, 2012), https://www.bbc.com/news/uk-18458567 (after Streisand sued a photographer displaying an image online of Streisand's home, news coverage drove an exponential increase in the online views of the photograph).

ing specific steps, including when to speak directly to their customers, the media, and the public, as well as to third-party validators (who should be identified and contacted in advance as part of crisis planning).[90] They should work with counsel to engage proactively with regulators and file disclosures, as circumstances warrant.[91]

8. If Necessary, Go to Court. Free speech rights protect most opinions, but businesses are not defenseless when their brands are defamed or markets manipulated. For example, in early 2021, lies about fraud in the 2020 election led to high-profile civil actions against purveyors of disinformation. In one case, in February 2021, the voting software machine maker Smartmatic sued Rudy Giuliani and Sydney Powell, *Fox News*, and individual *Fox* hosts for their comments linking unfounded election fraud claims to Smartmatic.[92] In March 2021, Dominion Voting Systems also sued *Fox News*, alleging similar claims.[93] While the defendants maintain their innocence, and no court at this writing has ruled on the viability of these claims, the plaintiffs have already secured several favorable settlements and retractions in response to filing complaints.[94]

V. The Deepfakes Economy: Positive-Use Cases of Deepfakes Requiring Legal Counsel

Thus far, this chapter has addressed the business *risks* of disinformation and deepfakes and what roles lawyers have in assisting clients to address them. This section focuses on how businesses may leverage deepfakes for

---

90. *See* Jamieson & Albarracín, *supra* note 78 (describing research suggesting that a company can wait until disinformation reaches at least 10 percent of the population before correcting it).

91. *See* Ferraro et al., *Identifying Legal and Business Risks*, *supra* note 6, at 154.

92. *See* Complaint, Smartmatic USA Corp. et al. v. Fox Corp. et al., (N.Y. Sup. Ct. Feb. 4, 2021), https://www.smartmatic.com/uploads/Smartmatic_Complaint_Against_Fox_Corporation.pdf.

93. *See* Bente Birkeland, *Election Defamation Lawsuits Open New Front in Fight against Disinformation*, NPR (Mar. 27, 2021, 7.00 AM), https://www.npr.org/2021/03/27/981683224/election-defamation-lawsuits-open-new-front-in-fight-against-disinformation.

94. *Id.*; Bente Birkeland, *Newsmax Issues Retraction and Apology to Dominion Employee over Election Stories*, NPR (Apr. 30, 2021, 5:37 PM), https://www.npr.org/2021/04/30/992534968/newsmax-issues-retraction-and-apology-to-dominion-employee-over-election-stories.

positive uses and what roles attorneys have in counseling clients to ensure this technology is used legally and ethically.

A. Licensing and Ownership of Manipulated Media

In May 2021, an AI company called Veritone launched a platform to enable content creators, celebrities, and others to generate audio deepfakes of their voices to license as they wish.[95] "With complete control over their voice and its usage, any influencer, personality, or celebrity can quite literally be in multiple places at once," the company said in a press release, "This would open the door to a new level of scale that was not humanly possible before, allowing them to increase the number of projects, sponsorships, and endorsements they can do in any given year."[96]

What is true for audio clones is true for visual avatars of famous faces. Recall the verisimilitude of the Tom Cruise TikTok deepfakes. It is only a matter of time until a Hollywood star uses that technology to license his or her likeness for commercial advertisements or small movie roles that he or she does not want to be bothered to record in person.

Indeed, in June 2021, Chris Umé, the artist behind the Cruise deepfakes, co-founded a start-up called Metaphysic that promises in a press release to use "deep learning and artificial intelligence to help brands, creators and the entertainment industry create hyper[-]realistic content without the expense or time required to shoot in-person."[97] The Metaphysic website trumpets the benefits of its technology to fabricate "synthetic performances without the celebrity or actor ever being on set."[98] Metaphysic also goes out of its way to emphasize that it is committed to the "ethical development of

---

95. Alyse Stanley, *Now There's a Deepfake Audio Platform Where Celebrities Can License AI-Generated Voice Clips*, GIZMODO (May 16, 2021, 3:20 PM), https://gizmodo .com/veritone-launches-deepfake-audio-platform-for-celebriti-1846905864.

96. *Announcing the Launch of Marvel.AI, a New Voice as a Service Solution*, VER-ITONE BLOG (May 14, 2021), https://www.veritone.com/blog/announcing-the-launch -of-marvel-ai-a-new-voice-as-a-service-solution/.

97. Press Release, New AI Video Technology Company Metaphysic Launches for Brands and Business to Create Industry Leading Hyperreal Content, AI J. (June 23, 2021), https:// aijourn.com/press_release/new-ai-video-technology-company-metaphysic-launches-for-brands -and-business-to-create-industry-leading-hyperreal-content/.

98. METAPHYSIC, https://metaphysic.ai/ (last visited July 11, 2021).

synthetic media technologies" and to working to create "standards and ethical baselines . . . for fair and productive public policies around synthetic media."[99] It says it will prohibit the use of its technology to create content that it knows is "designed to mislead or deceive."[100]

Veritone's and Metaphysic's new platforms and the products they offer—which we can think of as amounting to providing "Deepfakes as a Service" (DFaaS)—point to the important role lawyers will have in adjusting contracts and licenses where talent can essentially rent their likenesses to third parties. In both the audio and video context, attorneys will need to counsel clients on the proper licensing of their faces or voices, draft contracts for that use, structure royalty arrangements, and help ensure that a client's likeness is not employed for malicious purposes—to defraud or defame a third party, for instance. Veritone, Metaphysic, and companies like them will also need to structure their services to minimize their own liability for impermissible uses.

A lawyer's job may also extend beyond the grave, so to speak. In 2021, New York became the first state to establish a statutory, postmortem right of publicity to protect performers' likenesses—including digitally manipulated likenesses—from unauthorized commercial exploitation for 40 years after death. This right is not enforceable until a successor in interest to the decedent's likeness registers a claim with the New York Secretary of State (a "registration prior to enforcement" requirement similar to federal copyright law). Accordingly, New York artists and their representatives will need to prepare appropriate testamentary documents to register their interests with the Secretary of State to take advantage of the postmortem protections.[101] Other states may soon follow New York's lead in establishing similar regulatory regimes for postmortem digital likenesses.[102]

---

99. Ethics and Synthetic Media, Metaphysic, https://metaphysic.ai/ethics-and-synthetic-media/ (last visited July 11, 2021).

100 Press Release, *supra* note 97.

101. *See* Ferraro & Tompros, *supra* note 10, at 3.

102. For example, Louisiana came within one vote of passing a similar law in 2019. *See id.* *See also* H.B. 377 (Louisiana), http://www.legis.la.gov/legis/ViewDocument.aspx?d=1121437; LA HB 377, Bill Track 50 (May 8, 2019), https://www.billtrack50.com/BillDetail/1111393.

Producers, not just talent, will rely on lawyers for direction in this evolving field. One expects that producers of movies and records will want to include provisions in their contracts with talent that protect the producer's rights to use AI technology to manipulate an artist's performance after the fact. For example, one start-up announced in May 2021 its "deepfake dubs" technology, which can be used to manipulate the mouths of actors on screen to match the lip movements of translated speech, creating much more realistic dubbed movies in every language, at scale.[103] All parties will want to make sure contracts and licenses protect their respective interests in this new technology.

Beyond contracts and licensing, before long, lawyers will need to help determine who owns deepfakes themselves, particularly because they are often created by melding source material together that is copyrighted by numerous different rights holders (such as frames from many movies).[104] It is also an open question when a deepfake constitutes either fair use or represents transformational use such that copyright protections no longer apply.[105] The World Intellectual Property Organization (WIPO) and the U.S. Patent and Trademark Office (USPTO) are both exploring this issue and assessing whether there should be systems of equitable remuneration for individuals whose likenesses are used in manipulated media.[106]

B. Addressing Ethical and Legal Risks of Deepfakes

New consumer products are putting deepfake technology at users' fingertips, literally. As these products and services come to market, businesses and their lawyers need to consider the bounds they should put on their products to minimize business and legal risks.

For example, in February 2021, a genealogy website introduced a tool that uses deepfake technology to animate the faces in old photographs

---

103. James Vincent, *Deepfake Dubs Could Help Translate Film and TV without Losing an Actor's Original Performance*, THE VERGE (May 18, 2021, 10:13 AM), https://www.theverge.com/2021/5/18/22430340/deepfake-dubs-dubbing-film-tv-flawless-startup.

104. *See* Ferraro et al., *Identifying Legal and Business Risks*, *supra* note 6, at 150.

105. *See* Neeraja Seshadri, *Implications of Deepfakes on Copyright Law*, WIPO (July 22, 2020), https://www.wipo.int/export/sites/www/about-ip/en/artificial_intelligence/conversation_ip_ai/pdf/ind_seshadri.pdf.

106. *See* Ferraro et al., *Identifying Legal and Business Risks*, *supra* note 6, at 150–51.

of deceased relatives. The images turn their heads, smile, nod, and blink. Notably, the company deliberately chose not to include a speech feature, which would have allowed adding voice to the old photographs, "in order to prevent abuse, such as the creation of deepfake videos of living people," it said.[107]

Similarly, in March 2021, the snack maker Lay's created an advertising campaign on its website using deepfake technology from the AI company Synthesia. The website allows fans to generate a personalized video of soccer star Lionel Messi.[108] With a few clicks, a user can customize what Messi says. The website alters the movements of Messi's lips and syncs them to a voiceover to make it appear that Messi is inviting a friend (whose name the user supplies) to watch a game with the user, whose name Messi also says. The program can process thousands of names and is available in ten languages.[109]

The Messi website contains lengthy Terms of Use provisions, disclaiming any liability for potentially "fraudulent, libelous, defamatory" threatening or other malicious material and establishing that any user grants Lay's parent company unrestricted, royalty-free, and "perpetual" use of that material.[110] Attorneys will need to consider how to craft such terms in the best interests of clients without unduly burdening the user experience or raising regulatory risks as this technology becomes more common in advertising campaigns.

C.   Counseling Social Media Platforms on Disinformation and Deepfake Policies

As this chapter has shown, disinformation is not an issue associated entirely with social media. Realistic forgeries can be and are being used in many contexts for social engineering, fraud, identity theft, and the rest. But social

---

107. Jane Wakefield, *MyHeritage Offers 'Creepy' Deepfake Tool to Reanimate Dead*, BBC (Feb. 26, 2021), https://www.bbc.com/news/technology-56210053.

108. LAY'S MESSI MESSAGES, https://www.messimessages.com/us/index.html (last visited May 25, 2021).

109. Peter Adams, *Lay's Sends Soccer Fans Personalized Messages from Star Messi Using AI*, MKTG. DIVE (Mar. 18, 2021), https://www.marketingdive.com/news/lays-sends-soccer-fans-personalized-messages-from-star-messi-using-ai/596910/.

110. TERMS OF USE, https://www.pepsico.com/legal/terms-of-use (last visited May 25, 2021).

media companies have been at the forefront of developing policies around manipulated media.[111] Different platforms have adopted different policies, some banning all deepfakes, others only some, or none.[112] Attorneys can play an important role helping social media companies design their deep-fake policies, particularly in light of changing legislative environments.

D.   Legislative Counseling and Public Policy Advocacy

Manipulated media is quickly becoming a government-regulated field. At this writing, seven states (California, Hawaii, Maryland, New York, Texas, Virginia, and Wyoming) have already adopted laws prohibiting certain kinds of deepfakes—related either to nonconsensual deepfake pornography, deepfakes targeting elections, or, in New York, establishing property rights in a deceased performer's digital likeness.[113] Roughly 30 bills have been recently or are currently pending or passed in state houses across the country and in the U.S. Congress.[114] At the federal level, the Congress has passed and the president has signed at least four bills that do not prohibit deepfakes per se but require government research and reports on the dangers the technology poses; these reports and research may serve as predicates for greater congressional action.[115]

---

111. *See, e.g.*, *Building Rules in Public: Our Approach to Synthetic & Manipulated Media*, TWITTER BLOG (Feb. 4, 2020),https://blog.twitter.com/en_us/topics/company /2020/new-approach-to-synthetic-and-manipulated-media; *Enforcing against Manipulated Media*, FACEBOOK NEWS (Jan. 6, 2020), https://about.fb.com/news/2020/01 /enforcing-against-manipulated-media/. *See also* Ferraro et al., *Identifying Legal and Business Risks*, *supra* note 6, at 142–43.

112. *See* Kaveh Waddell, *On Social Media, Only Some Lies Are Against the Rules*, CONSUMER REPS. (Aug. 13, 2020), https://www.consumerreports.org/social-media/social -media-misinformation-policies/ (including chart on what platforms allow manipulated media and deepfakes).

113. *See* Ferraro & Tompros, *supra* note 10, at 1. Not all these laws ban "deepfakes" explicitly, referring instead to "computer-generated" imagery or the like. See *supra* note 10 for citations to these laws.

114. *See id.* at 3; Matthew F. Ferraro, *Deepfake Legislation: A Nationwide Survey*, WILMERHALE CLIENT ALERT (Sept. 25, 2019), https://www.wilmerhale.com/en/insights /client-alerts/20190925-deepfake-legislation-a-nationwide-survey.

115. *See* Matthew F. Ferraro, Opinion, *Congress's Deepening Interest in Deepfakes*, THE HILL (Dec. 29, 2020, 12:00 PM), https://thehill.com/opinion/cybersecurity/531911-congresss -deepening-interest-in-deepfakes (describing federal legislation adopted in December 2020); Matthew F. Ferraro, Jason C. Chipman & Stephen W. Preston, *The Federal "Deepfakes" Law*, 3 J. ROBOTICS A.I. & L. 229, 229–33 (2020).

Attorneys can help companies seeking to leverage deepfake technology comport with these burgeoning legal strictures. Public policy attorneys may also be called upon to advocate for their clients in the shaping of new laws. Like any new technology, the regulation of, and litigation around, deepfakes will likely proceed in fits and starts.

E. Updating Cybersecurity Insurance

Cyber insurance policies have not historically covered the damage wrought by disinformation and deepfakes that target corporate brands, enable fraud, or otherwise cause harm.[116] Nor have they provided liability coverage for businesses that utilize manipulated media technology to increase customer engagement. As these trends continue, businesses will want to consider how to modify or supplement their current insurance policies to address all of their business risks and liabilities.[117] For more on cybersecurity insurance, please see Chapter 16 of this book.

VI. Deepfakes, Disinformation, and Democracy at the Bar

Highly realistic manipulated media poses unique challenges to litigators and courts.[118] Riana Pfefferkorn of the Stanford Internet Observatory, who has written one of the most comprehensive treatments of the issues surrounding deepfakes in court, observed:

> In pre-trial and trial practice, deepfakes will touch every role in the courtroom: lawyers attempting to introduce or exclude videos as evidence; judges determining whether a video is admissible; expert and

---

116. Marianne Bonner, *What Does Cyber Liability Insurance Cover?*, THE BALANCE SMALL BUS. (Mar. 12, 2021), https://www.thebalancesmb.com/what-is-covered-under-a-cyber-liability-policy-462459.

117. *See id. See also* Ferraro et al., *Identifying Legal and Business Risks, supra* note 6, at 151.

118. *See* Ferraro et al., *Identifying Legal and Business Risks, supra* note 6, at 151.

lay witnesses asked to testify about the video, and, finally: jurors weighing the evidence in order to reach a verdict.[119]

The Federal Rules of Evidence impose authentication standards and requirements that will need to be leveraged to keep deepfakes from masquerading as unadulterated media.[120] The rules allow for the authentication of records "generated by an electronic process or system that produces an accurate result," if "shown by a certification of a qualified person" in a manner set forth by the rules.[121] The rules also require advance notice to the other side and the opportunity to challenge the records.[122] If the certification requirements are met, a party need not call a testifying witness at trial to establish authenticity.[123]

Attorneys have obligations to verify the authenticity of media on their own before submitting it to court.[124] Under the Model Rules of Professional Conduct, an attorney may not knowingly offer "evidence that the lawyer knows to be false," like a deepfake.[125] If he or she comes to know that evidence offered by a client or witness is false, the lawyer "shall take reasonable remedial measures," including, if necessary, disclosing that fact to the court.[126] And an attorney "may refuse to offer evidence . . . that the lawyer *reasonably believes* is false," such as a video he or she reasonably believes to be manipulated.[127] At the same time, attorneys should not insincerely challenge the opposing party's evidence as a "deepfake" merely as a litigation tactic where the attorney does not reasonably believe the evidence to be manipulated. Doing so may violate professional rules against making frivolous arguments; baselessly denying factual contentions; or engaging

---

119. Riana Pfefferkorn, *"Deepfakes" in the Courtroom*, 29 B.U. Pub. Int. L.J. 245, 254 (2020).
120. *Id.* at 246.
121. Fed. R. Evid. 902(13); *see also* Fed. R. Evid. 902(14).
122. Fed. R. Evid. 902(11), 902(12).
123. *See* Fed. R. Evid. 902.
124. *See* David Dorfman, *Decoding Deepfakes: How Do Lawyers Adapt When Seeing Isn't Always Believing?*, 80 Or. State Bar Bull., 18, 18, 22 (Apr. 2020).
125. Model Rules of Pro. Conduct r. 3.3(a)(3).
126. *Id. See* Comments [10] and [11] to Rule 3.3 for guidance on remedial measures.
127. *Id.* (emphasis added). *See* Pfefferkorn, *supra* note 119, at 272–74.

in harassing, delaying, or costly motion practice.[128] Doing so could well undermine the public's confidence in the rule of law, which is contrary to an attorney's duty.[129] For their part, judges should prepare for competing expert testimony over the authenticity of videos and audio recordings.[130]

Finally, merely the publicized existence of deepfakes may make jurors skeptical of the veracity of media evidence, even after it has been deemed admissible by a court. This will amount to a kind of "liar's dividend" accruing in the jury box that the court system will need to address.[131]

Beyond the direct implications for the practice of law, disinformation and deepfakes can threaten democracy in ways that lawyers may be uniquely suited to address. For example, the public skepticism generated by the "liar's dividend" can lead Americans to give up on trying to find the truth, or on the idea of truth altogether. And disinformation designed to undermine trust in institutions, including the courts,[132] can accelerate disengagement from vital public institutions. Democracy cannot long function without an informed and engaged citizenry.

Chief Justice of the United States Roberts' *Year-End Report on the Federal Judiciary* for 2019 focused on the dangers of disinformation. He concluded that "we have come to take democracy for granted, and civic education has fallen by the wayside. In our age, when social media can instantly spread rumor and false information on a grand scale, the public's need to understand our government, and the protections it provides, is ever more vital."[133] Chief Justice Roberts highlighted the important work that judges

---

128. MODEL RULES OF PRO. CONDUCT r. 3.1, 3.3(a)(3); FED. R. CIV. P. 11(b)(1), (2), (4); Pfefferkorn, *supra* note 119, at 274.

129. MODEL RULES OF PRO. CONDUCT preamble ¶ 6; Pfefferkorn, *supra* note 119, at 274.

130. Ferraro et al., *Identifying Legal and Business Risks, supra* note 6, at 151; Theodore F. Claypoole, *AI and Evidence: Let's Start to Worry*, NAT'L L. REV. (Nov. 14, 2019), https://www.natlawreview.com/article/ai-and-evidence-let-s-start-to-worry; Riana Pfefferkorn, *Too Good to Be True?*, 73 NW LAW. 22, 24 (Sept. 2019).

131. *See* Pfefferkorn, *supra* note 119, at 255 (describing "reverse *CSI* effect"); Pfefferkorn, *supra* note 130, at 24.

132. *See* Suzanne Spaulding, Devi Nair & Arthur Nelson, *Beyond the Ballot: How the Kremlin Works to Undermine the U.S. Justice System*, CTR. FOR STRATEGIC AND INT'L STUDIES (May 2019), https://csis-website-prod.s3.amazonaws.com/s3fs-public/publication/190430_Rus siaUSJusticeSystem_v3_WEB_FULL.pdf; Spaulding et al., *supra* note 5.

133. JOHN G. ROBERTS, THE 2019 YEAR-END REPORT ON THE FEDERAL JUDICIARY 2 (2019), https://www.supremecourt.gov/publicinfo/year-end/2019year-endreport.pdf.

must do, and are doing, to educate the public about the work of the courts and to live up to the aspirations of an impartial and independent judiciary. But members of the bar can also play an essential role in educating their communities and in helping to put out facts to dispel disinformation about specific cases or judges, or about the justice system as a whole. Attorneys have a vital responsibility, as recognized by the Model Rules of Professional Conduct, to serve as "public citizen[s]" with "special responsibility for the quality of justice" and to "further the public's understanding of and confidence in the rule of law and the justice system because legal institutions in a constitutional democracy depend on popular participation and support to maintain their authority."[134]

VII. Top Ten Highlights

This chapter introduced the role of lawyers in dealing with the evolving issues of disinformation and deepfakes. The top ten takeaways are:

1. We live in an age of intensifying disinformation that poses significant, if often underappreciated, business and legal risks that attorneys need to address.
2. Realistic manipulated media called deepfakes act as an accelerant to the negative trends of disinformation.
3. Disinformation and deepfakes can cause significant private-sector harms, including hurting corporate reputations, facilitating fraud, enabling social engineering, manipulating markets, and causing personal harassment.
4. Law firms, like any other business, are at risk from these dangers, too.
5. Businesses should prepare now for the downsides of disinformation and deepfakes. While every company and situation is different, companies should consider several general principles around preparation, raising awareness, and communication.

---

134. MODEL RULES OF PRO. CONDUCT preamble ¶¶ 1, 6.

6. Lawyers have many important roles to play in dealing with these threats for themselves and their clients. Lawyers can help companies develop disinformation mitigation plans ahead of time, counsel clients when they are the subject to a viral conspiracy or a disinformation-enabled cyber hack, work with regulators, and go to court to vindicate a client's rights.

7. Deepfake technology is not all bad, and the adoption of this technology for positive-use cases by more businesses, particularly in the entertainment and advertising sectors, is assured.

8. Attorneys will be needed to help companies take advantage of these opportunities, from drafting contracts and licenses, to counseling on ethical uses, to advising on regulatory risk and helping to shape the legislative landscape, among others.

9. Deepfakes pose unique challenges to litigators and courts. The rules of evidence require authentication standards that should, in theory, screen out manipulated media, but judges should prepare for dueling experts on the veracity of video and audio exhibits.

10. Attorneys have professional, ethical, and legal obligations to serve the cause of justice by acting in a way that buttresses the public's confidence in the rule of law and the administration of justice, as well as the expertise and opportunity to counter the disinformation that threatens our democracy.

SECTION IV

INCIDENT RESPONSE AND CYBER INSURANCE COVERAGE

Chapter 15

Achieving Preparedness through Standards and Planning and Best Practices for Incident Response

John DiMaria and Claudia Rast

Much has changed in the incident response landscape in the last several years. Threat actors have organized into global crime gangs—often with dotted-line connections to a short list of nation-states. Malware is packaged in kits for easy download on the dark web,[1] and the organized crime syndicates on the dark web maintain "help desks" to facilitate ransom payments from their victims. Compared to prior years, ransomware has seen a huge rise, as have the dollar-amounts demanded, reaching $40 million in early 2021. Four cybersecurity incidents spanning 2020 through the first months of 2021 have accelerated government action and response: (1) SolarWinds, (2) the Hafnium exploit of on-premises Microsoft Exchange servers,[2] (3) the Colonial Pipeline Ransomware attack, and (4) the attack on JSB SA, the world's largest meat processing company.[3] The public and private

---

1. The dark web "is a collection of websites that are publicly visible, yet hide the IP addresses of the servers that run them. That means anyone can visit a Dark Web site, but it can be very difficult to figure out where they're hosted—or by whom"; https://web.archive .org/web/20150607062159/http://www.wired.com/2014/11/hacker-lexicon-whats-dark web/ (last visited Sept. 12, 2021).

2. Affidavit in Support of an Application under Rule 41(b)(6)(B) paragraph 16, filed under seal Apr. 9, 2021. In support of the government's "Application for Warrant to Search Certain Microsoft Exchange Servers Infected with Web Shells," the affiant described the plight of many small companies when stating that "most of these victims [of the Hafnium exploit] are unlikely to remove the remaining web shells because the web shells are difficult to find due to their unique file names and paths or because these victims lack the technical ability to remove them on their own."

3. *Cyber Attack Hits JBS Meat Works in Australia, North America*, REUTERS (June 1, 2021, 10:26 AM), https://www.reuters.com/technology/cyber-attack hits-jbs-meat -works-australia-north-america-2021-05-31/.

sectors have made some strides in deploying data security protections, but when a cyber incident occurs, there are still too many hapless victims without functioning backups or insurance that have little recourse but to pay the ransom, ignoring the standard government advice to not pay.

This chapter covers the importance of business continuity planning and risk management; the current landscape of best practices as reflected in international and U.S. standards, such as ISO and NIST; the elements and implementation process for cyber incident response plans; and certain lessons learned and best practices from the "trenches" of cyber incident response experiences.

I. Business Continuity and Management of the Law Firm's Business Risks

Over the last few years alone, business continuity has been evolving like never before. The upsurge in threats like ransomware has forced organizations to rethink their strategies and deploy new technologies. Of course, the pandemic caught everyone by surprise. Even though a "pandemic" has been an area of concern preached by many business continuity and management (BCM) experts for years, many companies still had the "it won't happen to us" attitude, until last year of course. In the years ahead, even more new risks will come along that will force businesses to shift their continuity resources once again. Law firms, like many industries, implemented defensive practices based on a "whack-a-mole" strategy with the hacker community and tried to respond to various state statutes that arose with new and more demanding requirements for incident responders.

But whereas the continuity landscape is evolving, the main objective is and should always be to instill a culture of resiliency within your organization to ensure your business will keep running in the face of an unfortunate tumultuous event.

The stakes could not be higher. Cyber threat exposure for a company is an everyday concern. Organizations frequently fear cyber danger to their IT infrastructure or information breaches. There is a real threat that lack of due diligence can quickly disrupt an operation and cause loss of clients, revenue, and competitive edge. Additionally, loss of confidential records through unintended disclosures could lead to claims for damages due to negligent acts. While some studies indicate that the root cause of most breaches is misconfiguration,[4] malicious assaults or even discontented staff must be considered in your risk assessment. All law firms want to be prepared for a cyber catastrophe with the aim of having all employees involved by teaching them how to recognize threats and enforcing best practice policies and procedures. In today's connected era, a complete commercial enterprise continuity control system and incident response system is a quintessential goal of any business enterprise aiming to manage and decrease its hazard profile.[5] To further help law firms meet the challenges of maintaining a good robust and tested business continuity process, this section describes the unique opportunities for lawyers, law firms, and law associations to achieve preparedness using national and international best practices that are supported by and aligned with voluntary, consensus standards that ultimately drive industry best practices.

A. Risk Management at the Core of Business Continuity

Business continuity planning for law firms is crucial as most companies never recover after a disaster. Studies have shown that more than 40 percent of businesses never reopen after a disaster, 25 percent fail within one year, and more than 90 percent fail within two years.[6]

The complexity of business and the increase in the frequency and sophistication of incidents have created the need for a simplified, straightforward approach that addresses all hazards, including natural disasters as well as man-made events and, yes, pandemics. Constant cyber disruptions and their secondary impacts on business downtime reveal, in many instances, the lack of information and communications technology preparedness or an effective recovery plan. Law firms and mobile law practitioners cannot

---

4. Filip Turta, *Misconfiguration Remains the #1 Cause of Data Breaches in the Cloud*, SECURITY BOULEVARD (Apr. 16, 2020), https://securityboulevard.com/2020/04/misconfiguration-remains-the-1-cause-of-data-breaches-in-the-cloud/.

5. http://maruyama-mitsuhiko.cocolog-nifty.com/security/files/cloudincidentresponse framework.pdf.

6. https://www.accesscorp.com/press-coverage/study-40-percent-businesses-fail -reopen-disaster/.

afford remote access downtimes, information and communications technology systems breaches or failures, or power outages. Recent major incidents, such as SolarWinds and the Colonial Pipeline and JSB ransomware attacks, prove that any company can be collateral damage due to another's lack of resiliency, explaining why a thorough risk and business impact analysis is critical. By conducting such an analysis, an organization can identify the context and interested parties that comprise its business environment and thus better understand how to respond to threats and attacks.

For example, the Covid-19 pandemic caused most organizations to disperse their workforces to work from home. This resulted in an abrupt change from the relatively controlled office environment to whatever the employee could bring from the office and assemble at home. Such a DIY workplace led to an increase in cyber interferences with information and communications technology (ICT) and created a greater need for information technology (IT) personnel guidance. IT staff were required to identify requirements for at-home ICT, implement controls to mitigate or reduce the risk of disruption, and respond to and recover from disruptions in locations beyond their usual reach. In short, there was a critical need to achieve greater organizational resilience. Organizations like the Cloud Security Alliance that provides security guidance for the cloud globally had to rethink guidance, based on customer demand and the changing environment:

- **Malicious attackers love a crisis.** "From a cloud and cybersecurity perspective, organizations were/are being challenged by a barrage of new cyberattacks and malware, while completely shifting significant portions of their compute infrastructure."
- **Traditional security systems are not designed for the cloud.** "On-premises legacy solutions simply don't have the application awareness needed regarding activities happening in the cloud."
- **A lack of visibility over apps, users, and data.** "Unmanaged Bring Your Own devices used to access emails or data often create security blind spots, increasing the risk of data loss and compliance breaches."
- **An increased attack surface.** "Cloud assets, which have been largely restricted for access through enterprise networks and security controls, were opened up for access from any location and any device."

- **The threat of accidental disclosure.** "Remote collaboration has obviously risen to previously unseen levels, creating greater opportunity for mistakes that increase the risk of unintended data leakage."
- **Traditional VPNs are insufficient.** "Many VPN Gateways were getting overwhelmed and were not designed for the entire workforce to be using them."
- **Smart home threat vector.** "In the old days, a person's home-based work computer might literally be the only computer in a house. In today's smart home, the work-from-home system is coexisting with dozens and even hundreds of devices. Most of these devices are poorly maintained, unpatched and full of vulnerabilities. Home networks do not offer the level of security and scrutiny associated with enterprise networks, with many configured to default security settings."
- **Better updated security awareness.** "With such a drastic change in the work environment it is critical to provide education related to the new risks."[7]

Executives worldwide in public and private companies, government agencies, educational institutions, and nonprofits reported that some business continuity programs lack strong integration with other business functions and robust practices for developing and measuring program performance and are not positioned to address cyberterrorism.[8]

B. Third-Party Risks and Continuity

A law firm's relationships with its critical suppliers and vendors, particularly cloud service providers, should entail periodic review of shared responsibilities, continuity program activities, disaster recovery system details,

---

7. Jim Reavis, *Coronavirus Today and Cybersecurity Tomorrow*, CLOUD SECURITY ALLIANCE (Apr. 8, 2020), https://cloudsecurityalliance.org/blog/2020/04/08/coronavirus -today-and-cybersecurity-tomorrow/; Matt Hines et al., *A Better Than Remote Chance—More People Work from Home in Post COVID World*, CLOUD SECURITY ALLIANCE (Aug. 5, 2020), https://cloudsecurityalliance.org/blog/2020/08/05/a-better-than-remote-chance-more-people -work-from-home-in-post-covid-world/.

8. Punit Renjen, *The Heart of Resilient Leadership: Responding to COVID-19*, DELOITTE (Mar. 16, 2020), https://www2.deloitte.com/us/en/insights/economy/covid-19/heart-of-resilient -leadership-responding-to-covid-19.html.

business continuity procedures, and communication practices.[9] So many of us rely upon third parties for our services (Microsoft, Amazon Web Services, Workday, etc.); thus, it is critical to identify, prepare for, and manage risk if they go down. In the last few years, the global community has responded through the development of voluntary, consensus international management systems standards that enable adopting organizations to conform to requirements and, where appropriate, seek accredited third-party certifications. The standards development process has, in turn, fostered the identification by associations of simplified frameworks and best practices that can help law firms of all sizes to identify, assess, and control the risks that endanger the assets and earning capacity of a law firm.[10] For small- and medium-size law firms, planning and preparing for identified business risks is a "must do" task. While cyberattack is the top threat globally, law firms should consider cybersecurity as a part of their business continuity management (BCM) programs that identify and reduce risks, make the right decisions quickly, cut downtime and financial losses, and, perhaps, save the law firm. Using voluntary, consensus standards that are developed internationally not only provides a road map using best practices but shows the proper due diligence and the all-important "standard of care" that will be challenged in the unfortunate scenario where the firm is called to testify in court.

The importance of supply chain continuity is a strategic component of a BCM program. So much so that it was addressed by the introduction of ISO/TS 22318,[11] Guidelines for Supply Chain Continuity, to the global community. The value of efficient supply chains is well recognized in the business world, but law firms have been slow to recognize the trend and are catching up with their clients by viewing their work as a piece of the whole and altering their legal service models to become value-added partners to their clients for whom supply chain management is a key profitability component. A law firm should concentrate its efforts on suppliers and interested parties whose failure to be in a state of resiliency would most quickly

---

9. A great resource for assessing cybersecurity risks with vendors is the 2021 ABA publication Cybersecurity Checklist (2d ed. 2021), https://www.americanbar.org/products/ecd/ebk/411859099/.

10. https://www.iso.org/developing-standards.html.

11. https://www.iso.org/standard/65336.html.

interrupt prioritized activities, and on clients that specify in contracts and mutual agreements the law firm's demonstrated compliance with supply chain continuity, cyber resilience, periodic audits, and business continuity exercises showing that a firm has the knowledge and understanding of "shared responsibility."

If a control applies to a platform or infrastructure aspect that is outsourced to a third party, it falls under "supplier relationships." You must show evidence that you have done your due diligence and, in fact, validated that your supplier(s) has met your minimum requirements to protect your service and your customers. So, it is important to apply this evidence gathering exercise for controls that were outsourced. Third-party suppliers, such as AWS and Azure, have already submitted information posted to the Cloud Security Alliances' STAR Registry database for cloud service providers, so that may weigh heavily on documenting your due diligence, because meeting the CSA Cloud Control Matrix (CCM) controls would in most cases provide sufficient evidence of compliance.[12]

II. The Cybersecurity Framework

Leading global organizations have robust BCMS and Information Security Management System (ISMS) in place that are designed to ensure that their organizations are prepared to survive a catastrophic event. In addition, since 2012, ISO and ANSI-accredited standards developers have published voluntary consensus standards that focus on BCMS and ISMS.[13] However, the quality of BCM/ISM programs varies widely, and repeated cyber intrusions into critical infrastructures demonstrate the need for improved cybersecurity. This condition has not gone unnoticed by officials charged with safeguarding the U.S. economy and critical infrastructure in the event of a cyber breach.

---

12. *Id.*

13. The Switzerland-based International Organization for Standardization (English acronym is ISO) develops management systems standards for a number of global certifications.

On February 12, 2013, President Obama issued an executive order titled "Improving Critical Infrastructure Cybersecurity."[14] The executive order states: "The cyber threat to critical infrastructure continues to grow and represents one of the most serious national security challenges we must confront. The national and economic security of the United States depends on the reliable functioning of the Nation's critical infrastructure in the face of such threats."[15] In 2014, the NIST Cybersecurity Framework was developed in answer to the president's executive order.

NIST developed and issued standards, such as NIST Special Publication 800-53, Security Controls and Assessment Procedures for Federal Information Systems and Organizations, and more recently NIST Special Publication 800-160, Systems Security Engineering, but none have had the impact of NIST's Framework for Improving Critical Infrastructure Cybersecurity (2014, updated to current version 1.1 in 2018).[16] The Framework is arguably one of the most significant documents released by NIST in the recent past, maybe ever. It has had a definite impact on the private sector and the supply chain that currently services the nation's critical infrastructure. To date, the Framework has had a significant effect on the Department of Homeland Security-defined critical infrastructure industries[17] along with their supply chains. It has now reached a level of international harmonization as it maps to the internationally accepted standard, ISO/IEC 27001, and is being referenced in many of the new guidance documents issued in a wide range of industries, in both public and private sectors. In fact, in 2018, the NIST CSF reached international recognition when ISO/IEC TR 27103:2018 (Information technology—Security techniques—Cybersecurity and ISO and IEC standards) was published using the same nomenclature as the NIST CSF.

---

14. Exec. Order No. 13,636, Improving Critical Infrastructure Cybersecurity, 78 Fed. Reg. 11,739 (Feb. 12, 2013).

15. Press Release, The White House, Executive Order—Improving Critical Infrastructure Cybersecurity (Feb. 12, 2013), https://obamawhitehouse.archives.gov /the-press-office/2013/02/12/executive-order-improving-critical-infrastructure-cybersecurity.

16. https://www.nist.gov/cyberframework/framework.

17. Dep't of Homeland Sec., *Critical Infrastructure Sectors*, https://www.cisa.gov /critical-infrastructure-sectors.

The Framework is designed with the intent that businesses and organizations use an assessment of the risks they face to guide their use of the Framework in a cost-effective way. As per the NIST description of the CSF,

Each of the Framework components (Framework Core, Tiers, and Profiles) reinforces the connection between business drivers and cybersecurity activities. The Framework also offers guidance regarding privacy and civil liberties considerations that may result from cybersecurity activities.

The Framework Core is a set of cybersecurity activities and informative references that are common across critical infrastructure sectors. The cybersecurity activities are grouped by five functions—Identify, Protect, Detect, Respond, and Recover—that provide a high-level view of an organization's management of cyber risks. The Profiles can help organizations align their cybersecurity activities with business requirements, risk tolerances, and resources. Companies can use the Profiles to understand their current cybersecurity state, support prioritization, and measure progress toward a target state. The Tiers provide a mechanism for organizations to view their approach and processes for managing cyber risk. The Tiers range from Partial (Tier 1) to Adaptive (Tier 4) and describe an increasing degree of rigor in risk management practices, the extent to which cybersecurity risk management is informed by business needs, and its integration into an organization's overall risk management practices.[18]

The Framework is a "living document," touted as being not a technical standard or set of security controls, but rather a more holistic risk management tool. In addition, the Framework provides a common language for communicating an organization's cybersecurity posture to external stakeholders such as auditors, insurance underwriters, customers, and regulators. It overlays standards like the ISO/IEC 27001 and NIST Special Publication 800-53, noting it is not a stand-alone standard but meant to be employed

---

18. *Supra* note 16.

as an added tool without the expenses typically incurred when adding, or transitioning to, a new standard.

Finally, and of greatest interest, the Framework aligns with many core cybersecurity practices that can arise in consumer lawsuits and government enforcement actions, such as incident response, due diligence, and negligence, thereby facilitating an organization's ability to mitigate its legal exposure. Organizations using the Framework can point to an accepted government-related framework that has public-sector recognition as evidence that their security program meets an acceptable standard of care, often the fundamental question in litigation. "The development of cybersecurity performance metrics is evolving. Organizations should be thoughtful, creative, and careful about the ways in which they employ measurements to optimize use, while avoiding reliance on artificial indicators of current state and progress in improving cybersecurity risk management."[19]

To further increase emphasis on cybersecurity, on May 12, 2021, President Joe Biden issued "Executive Order on Improving the Nation's Cybersecurity"[20] seeking to improve the state of national cybersecurity in the United States and to increase protection of government networks following the incident involving SolarWinds[21] and more recently the Colonial Pipeline hack.[22] The executive order outlines the requirement to modernize cybersecurity defenses within the country, and to eliminate the road blocks to sharing information regarding cybersecurity threats and breach information. This can without doubt induce considerations for several organizations whose written agreement obligations or Service Level Agreements (SLA) usually make these incidents troublesome to report; however, it additionally highlights the importance of organizations making certain that they

---

19. https://www.nist.gov/cyberframework.

20. Executive Order on Improving the Nation's Cybersecurity (May 12, 2021), https://www.whitehouse.gov/briefing-room/presidential-actions/2021/05/12/executive-order-on-improving-the-nations-cybersecurity/.

21. *Supra* note 15.

22. *The Pipeline Hack: What You Need to Know*, ONETRUST (May 12, 2021), https://www.onetrust.com/blog/colonial-pipeline-hack/?utm_source=publications&utm_medium=csa&utm_campaign=tprmfundamentals&utm_term=executiveorderblogshare.

provide a secure supply-chain where their vendors meet the mandatory cybersecurity necessities.[23]

The White House also published a factsheet[24] that highlights the seven key points that the executive order looked to address:

- Remove barriers to threat information sharing between government and the private sector
- Modernize and implement stronger cybersecurity standards in the federal government
- Improve software supply chain security
- Establish a cybersecurity safety review board
- Create a standard playbook for responding to cyber incidents
- Improve detection of cybersecurity incidents on federal government networks
- Improve investigative and remediation capabilities.

Organizations need to define the information security foundation to use when planning, preparing, managing, and terminating the procurement of a product or service. The supplier relationship must be based on a strategy that includes a measurement of risk assessment and tolerance.

It is critical that organizations put in place proper SLAs and contracts that allow for the transparent sharing of threat and breach information.[25] As previously stated in this chapter, a culture of resilience must be instilled in an organization so that the entire organization is involved not just IT.

---

23. *President Biden's Cybersecurity Executive Order: What Will It Mean for You?*, ONETRUST (May 14, 2021), https://www.onetrust.com/blog/president-bidens -cybersecurity-executive-order-what-will-it-mean-for-you/.

24. Press Release, The White House, FACT SHEET: President Signs Executive Order Charting New Course to Improve the Nation's Cybersecurity and Protect Federal Government Networks (May 12, 2021), https://www.whitehouse.gov/briefing-room/statements-releases/2021/05/12 /fact-sheet-president-signs-executive-order-charting-new-course-to-improve-the-nations-cyber security-and-protect-federal-government-networks/.

25. *Supra* note 23.

III. International Standards as a Benchmark for Best Practices

A. ISO 22301, the International Standard for Business Continuity Management Systems and a Global Benchmark for BCMS Requirements

More organizations, nonprofits, business owners, law firms, and practitioners are thinking seriously about resilience. The 2021 BCI/BSI Horizon Scan Report[26] showed:

- The Covid-19 pandemic was more disruptive to organizations than any incident noted previously in the Horizon Scan reports.
- The secondary impacts of Covid-19: risk ratings for health incidents, safety incidents, IT/telecom outages, and cyberattack all increased significantly on previous years.
- The biggest consequence of previous disruptions was staff morale and well-being.
- Covid-19's legacy has meant practitioners are considering new risks in 2021.
- Climate risk is now the primary medium- to long-term risk for many organizations.
- The number of organizations performing longer-term trend analysis has risen to an all-time high of 81.3 percent—with over half now carrying it out on a centralized basis.

Thus, information security remains a priority for planned information and communications technology (ICT) investments by businesses and legal services providers. Today's lawyers work more and more from home, client offices, hotel rooms, on the road, and in court. You must make reasonable efforts to protect your law firm's data. It must be considered as a part of any organization's protection of ICT systems, especially for lawyers who need to protect privileged attorney-client communication and their clients' secrets. Fortunately, efforts to define standards and best practices to guide

---

26. BCI Horizon Scan Report 2021, https://www.thebci.org/resource/bci-horizon-scan -report-2021.html.

organizations in this challenging work have made great progress and should be considered as authoritative documents and used (at minimum) as guidance documents to support the rationale behind the BCMS strategy.

The 2012 release and 2019 update of ISO 22301 (Security and resilience—Business continuity management systems—Requirements) provides a unifying standard that crosses international boundaries. ISO standards are built by "consensus," using subject matter experts and professionals from a network of 164 national standards bodies. These experts are organized into a technical committee (i.e., ISO Technical Committee 292, Security and Resilience) to negotiate all aspects of the Societal Security standards, including their scope, definitions, and content. ISO 22301 provides the requirements for a BCMS.[27]

ISO 22301 "specifies requirements to plan, establish, implement, operate, monitor, review, maintain and continually improve a documented management system to protect against, reduce the likelihood of occurrence, prepare for, respond to, and recover from disruptive incidents when they arise." If the requirements are implemented correctly, the law firm will assess risk in terms of the inability to recover activities and resources that deliver the firm's most important products and services, a powerful presentation to an executive management audience. [28]

A BCMS is a holistic management system that identifies potential impacts and threats to an organization and provides a framework for building and establishing resilience and capability for an effective response to safeguard the interests of its key stakeholders, its reputation, and its brand and value-creating activities. ISO 22301 has quickly established itself as the global benchmark for BCMS.

The global demand for BCMS is amplified by the vulnerability of information communications and technology networks. According to PricewaterhouseCoopers, hacking has become so prevalent that major organizations, including law firms, should assume that their systems have been

---

27. https://www.iso.org/sites/ConsumersStandards/1_standards.html.
28. A diagram of this process is available at https://info.advisera.com/27001academy/free-download/diagram-of-iso-22301-implementation-process.

compromised and proceed from that assumption in testing and improving their defenses.[29]

B.   ISO 27001: Challenges for Law Firms of All Types and Sizes

It is important that any organization, and particularly law firms of any size, recognize that voluntary consensus standards, conformity assessment systems, and business tools, such as ISO/IEC 27001 and ISO 22301, are currently in place and available, and that their value to organizations has been proven. Any law firm or association, in-house counsel, or governmental entity is able to objectively measure preparedness through the selection of a management systems standard that is designed to stay aligned continuously with the organization's strategic goals. For ICT security, small, medium, and large law firms are choosing to align with ISO/IEC 27001, and achieving accredited certification to the standard.[30] The changes in the 2013 version update ISO/IEC 27001 to conform to new ISO directives on management systems requirements, namely by allowing law firms to have an integrated management system, rather than distinct separate ones. Several law firms are choosing alignment and certification to both ISO 22301 and ISO/IEC 27001, to ensure the continuity of their business activities and the security of their ICT systems.

The opportunities for law firms and associations that adopt industry best practices go well beyond providing a strong emergency response plan or following disaster management strategies that were previously used. Resilience for organizations has evolved from emergency preparedness centered on protection of data and information systems to the more comprehensive and standardized mitigation of risks for the continuity of business products and services. Today's cyber threats require the creation of an ongoing, managed response that ensures the survival and sustainability of a law firm's or association's core activities before, during, and after a disruption. Law firms of all types and sizes must now decide for themselves whether they

---

29. *See also How to Protect Your Companies from Rising Cyber Attacks and Fraud amid the COVID-19 Outbreak*, PWC, https://www.pwc.com/us/en/library/covid-19/cyber-attacks.html.

30. https://www.ironmountain.com/resources/whitepapers/l/leveraging-information-security-standards-in-law-firms.

should implement the minimum requirements for effective business continuity and ICT security, including whether or not they should purchase cyber liability insurance to augment the coverage that the law firms may already have in place.

C. Law Firms: Using International Standards to Contribute to Your Success

Lawyers, law firms, and small business owners want to know how standards contribute to implementing a successful BCMS. Organizations must achieve measurable resiliency, since frequent disruptions are now constant threats to their survival.

Basically, the business continuity management lifecycle has six phases to it: program management, understanding the organization, determining the BCM strategy, developing and implementing a BCM response, exercising the response, and maintaining, reviewing, and embedding BCM in the organization's culture.

Breaking this down, the ABA's pioneering experience with using standards itself offers a simple, four-step process of actions to develop your firm's business continuity plans. The process helps document procedures for responding to disruptive events, including how the firm will continue or recover its activities within predetermined time frames.

1. Establish Your Firm's Core Planning Team or Steering Committee

The size of the team will depend on business operations, requirements, and resources. The team members are typically appointed in writing by senior management and their job descriptions modified to reflect the additional responsibility. From the start, senior management must be supportive and proactive in promoting the success of the program. Commitment is demonstrated by issuing a clear policy statement to the firm that:

- Sets out the purpose of the plan and how it will involve the entire firm.
- Establishes a high priority for the program.
- Details the authority, reporting, and structure of the team.
- Empowers the team to take steps necessary to develop a plan, establish work schedules, plan deliverables/deadlines, and establish budget parameters.

Project management, diplomacy, and common sense are skills needed as the team will be dealing with the whole firm, asking awkward questions, and in some instances changing work practices. Explaining the purpose and selling the changes to those affected will need to be done firmly, but with sensitivity and understanding.

2. Understand Your Capabilities and the Risks You Face

Conduct an initial business impact analysis and threat assessment to determine your firm's vulnerability to possible hazards, emergencies, and disruptions. Try to understand what the current policies and procedures were created for and why.

Review internal plans and policies that have been established by your firm already. Look for documents covering evacuation, fire, occupational safety and health, environmental policies, equipment maintenance guides, security procedures, insurance, office closing plans, staff manuals, and hazardous material plans.

Meet with local government advisors, community organizations, and local utility providers to determine their disaster recovery plans and resources available to respond to any incident. Identify applicable local regulations, such as fire plans, flood tables, environmental regulations, and evacuation plans.

Identify the critical products, services, activities, and operations within your firm and network that enable you to operate your law firm. Review the firm's products and services and the facilities and equipment needed to produce them. Evaluate products and services provided by suppliers, especially sole-source vendors. These can include critical services, such as electrical power, water, sewage, gas, and telecommunications and data connections, or vital equipment and personnel for the continued functioning of the facility.

Identify your firm's internal resources and capabilities that may be needed in the event of an emergency or business disruption.

Identify external resources that may be needed and determine if formal agreements may be required to define a relationship with these resources.

Perform an insurance review of all polices and identify costs/benefits of coverage.

3. Develop a Plan to Control What Happens

When something does happen, a clear plan will be needed to guide you. You may not have time to decide what to do and how to do it, and so the plan will be there to help you provide the fundamental tasks, processes, and guidance.

The plan should have basic components:

- Executive summary, purpose, emergency policy of the firm and of each department, if different
- Roles, responsibilities, and authorization for each group of employees, and identification of potential emergencies
- Location of response and recovery sites
- Emergency response procedures

Write the plan: This activity is a shared event drawing on the particular skills and understanding of the team members. The plan needs to be finally and publicly approved by senior management and distributed within the firm.

4. Implement and Test the Plan

This step is more than putting the plan away until something happens, such as an emergency or business disruption. Your firm should be acting on the strategy or recommendations made during the business impact analysis and risk assessment and reducing risks wherever possible.

Integrating the plan into everyday firm operations is an important function; as your firm changes, so should your business continuity plan. By continually improving and testing your plan, your ability to recover will improve.

Conduct training for all employees at periodic intervals. The training should include the procedures set out in the plan for individual employees. After implementation, test how well the plan has been integrated by asking questions of senior management as well as general staff members. Determine what has been left out, and what needs to be improved or changed.[31]

---

31. *Business Continuity and Risk—A User Guide from BSI*, https://www.bsigroup.com /LocalFiles/en-US/Brochures/Business%20Continuity/BSI-ISO-22301-business-continuity -and-risk-user-guide.pdf.

This process will not only create greater cohesiveness among those responsible for the business processes and their supporting ICT systems, but also define the standard of care. Having a formal process based on international standards could in fact enhance the firm's insurability and creditworthiness as well as it reassures your employees and your clients that you have the ability to recover from even a severe business interruption and continue to serve your customer's needs.

Having said that, law firms cannot take a one-size-fits-all approach when it comes to solutions. You must balance the risk you want to accept (risk appetite) with the costs of being down and what your clients will tolerate. Of course, when you look at the loss in potential revenues by performing a Business Impact Analysis for instance, will most certainly justify a Business Continuity plan covering data protection for firm members, and clients.

Law firms collect and store large amounts of non-public information that is desirable for insider-trading schemes. A recent report issued by PurpleSec indicated that cybercrime was up 600 percent due to the Covid-19 pandemic.[32] That thought should make anyone shudder, but for law firms, it should be of special significance as law firm data is considered the new gold in the circles of cyber hacktivists. Some firms have elaborate security policies, but they are not enforced.

One significant trend that should make law firms sit up and take notice is in how organizations are viewing law departments. To hackers and criminals, law firms are key targets. Valuable information that may include trade secrets, intellectual property, merger and acquisition details, personally identifiable information (PII), and confidential attorney-client-privileged data will draw hackers to your firm. Despite these risks, law firms are obligated to protect their clients' information. If criminals penetrate your firm's security, the consequences can be extensive ranging from minor embarrassments to serious legal issues.

The risks are getting to the point that the simple vendor questionnaire is no longer sufficient. Organizations are seeking independent, data-driven corroboration from cybersecurity rating companies that "score" law firms

---

32. 2021 *Cyber Security Statistics, The Ultimate List of Stats, Data & Trends*, https://purplesec.us/resources/cyber-security-statistics/.

(and other industries) based on their risk exposure.[33] When it comes to seeking inside information on mergers and acquisitions, cybercriminals consider law firms the weakest link.

In order to remain competitive, law firms need to offer correctly priced services and keep non-billable expenses, including IT and security, down. The American Bar Association's 2019 Cybersecurity Tech Report[34] found that 35 percent of respondents whose firms had suffered a security incident had suffered downtime or loss of billable hours as a result.

D. What to Do If You Cannot Meet These Standards

The objective of this section was to describe the opportunities for lawyers, law firms, or law associations to achieve preparedness through alignment with voluntary consensus standards; in particular, through alignment with the international BCMS and ISMS standards, the ISO Guidelines on Information and Communications Readiness for Business Continuity, and NIST's Cybersecurity Framework. It has identified the challenges to the profession of law: loss of client communication; loss of clients, revenue, and competitiveness; loss of data and unintentional disclosures; and claims for damages due to negligent acts and omissions. It was not the objective to infer that a firm must "meet the standard" or get certified but align with the standards that are internationally accepted as a "Standard of Care." To sum things up, consider the following:

The management of business risk is vital; risk is the effect of uncertainty on the law firm's objectives and risk management is the identification, assessment, and economic control of those risks that endanger the assets and earning capacity of a business. Attorneys should make informed decisions about business risk based on business impact analysis and risk assessment. It is important to meet with a business continuity professional to develop a business continuity plan of documented procedures for responding to a disruptive incident, including how the law firm will continue or recover its core activities within a predetermined time frame.

---

33. *See* BITSIGHT TECHS., http://www.bitsighttech.com.
34. John G. Loughnane, *2019 Cybersecurity Tech Report*, ABA (Oct. 16, 2019), https://www.americanbar.org/groups/law_practice/publications/techreport/abatechreport2019/cybersecurity2019/.

Regardless of current capabilities, the international voluntary standards together offer a path for continuous improvement of an organization's BCMS and ISMS, and an effective system for information and communications readiness for business continuity and ultimately organizational resilience. They represent many years of lessons learned and proven best practices. All organizations have responsibilities to clients and stakeholders to deliver on commitments regardless of disruptions that can and will occur. Whether these standards are used as references for alignment, a framework for improvement, or requirements for certification, they will provide value to all organizations and drive performance and continuous improvement.

Top five considerations:

1. Establish a core planning team with the direct support of senior management to develop a comprehensive business continuity plan that will change work practices.
2. Understand your organization's core capabilities and the risks you face by reviewing internal and external dependencies, critical activities, equipment and personnel; focus on products, services, and operations, including a comprehensive insurance review.
3. Develop a plan to control what happens that includes fundamental tasks, processes, and guidance for a disruptive situation.
4. Implement the plan into the everyday operations of your organization, including periodic training and testing of all employees.
5. Create an organizational environment of continual improvement.

IV. Implementing the Cyber Incident Response Plan

A. The First Steps after a Cyber Incident Occurs

Proper notification within the entity suffering the cyber incident is frequently the first stumbling block. Does the employee who first discovers the incident know whom to call? Has a cyber incident contact been named by the company and is that person's contact information available in written form (because the online call sheet may be encrypted and unavailable)? Finally, does the employee know where to find the hard copy of the incident response plan? (A plan that is inaccessible because it is encrypted is useless.) Are several methods of communication outlined for the employee, because company phones and e-mail servers may be down? These questions are all answered in the cyber incident response plan.

Once the incident commander is informed, activities happen quickly. The internal team is notified, and steps are taken to isolate—if possible—other company systems from the spreading virus. The next contact in this scenario is legal counsel. All too often, cyber counsel is not among the first to be called, and this can be a dangerous omission. As with any expert in a crisis situation, cyber counsel can quickly deploy a licensed forensic team whose activities and reports can be subject to attorney-client and work-product privilege. In addition—and this can be critical when it comes to costs— cyber counsel and forensic experts that have been vetted and preapproved by the company's insurance carrier will avoid needless delays in deploying an effective incident response. One element in the incident response plan that helps avoid unnecessary delay after a cyber incident is a pre-negotiated basic terms of engagement template with cyber counsel.

Without knowing either the origins of the incident or the full range of consequences, it is critical to preserve as much evidence as possible. The biggest mistake companies can make is attempting to "fix" the problem using internal IT staff or calling untrained third-party IT companies to help. This is no different from allowing the public to trample across a crime scene, taking what they want and leaving their trash behind. Unwitting IT staff may want to "clean" servers and workstations, but with the harm already done, they are just destroying valuable evidence that might reveal the type and source of the intrusion. Thus, a negotiated preservation policy that anticipates a cyber incident is an important element of the incident response plan.

Occasionally the preferred forensic consultant may not be available; thus, it is best to vet and list two or more licensed forensic teams. Some states require these individuals to be licensed personal investigators, so it is best to check your applicable state laws.

The insurance carrier is another important initial contact point. Cyber liability coverage is widely available and can be invaluable.[35] More often than not, the carrier will require both cyber counsel and the forensic team to be drawn from the carrier's own approved list.

Once the forensic team is deployed on-site, it works quickly to:

- Interview individuals with knowledge of the incident
- Acquire electronic evidence from compromised system(s) and hosts, including ancillary systems and hosts;
- Confirm the scope, type, and impact of the cyber incident (forensic examination of collected and preserved electronic evidence to identify whether confidential, sensitive, or proprietary information has been accessed or compromised); and
- Implement emergency communications (e-mail, phone, etc.).

One response to a bitcoin demand from a ransomware hacker may be to respond, "get lost," and access the company's backups. Often, however, the backups may be unavailable, encrypted as well, or corrupted for some other reason. While experts in this area will warn companies not to pay the bitcoin ransom, companies are often without any other viable choice.

Conducting a bitcoin transaction while working against a countdown clock and communicating with an anonymous hacker who revels in the idea of creating mayhem can be unnerving. The first bitcoin transaction may be only the first of several transactions, as the hacker will hold back some encryption keys for more bitcoins and the company must test the decrypt keys to make sure that they are decrypting properly and without additional embedded malware.[36]

B. Follow Up to a Cyber Incident

One of the more tedious, time-consuming, and vitally necessary activities in the wake of any cyber incident is the inventory and assessment of all devices that may have been connected to the infected network. Of course, it does not help if the network diagrams and device inventories have been

---

35. See Chapter 16 of this Handbook for additional information about cyber insurance.

36. See Sections VI.A and VI.B *infra* for a detailed discussion of the potential pitfalls with regard to payments to threat actors.

encrypted and no hard copy exists. Thus, the incident response plan should include all these diagrams and inventories, be updated periodically, and be available in hard copy form.

As equipment and software are scanned for malware, cleaned, rebuilt, and tested, it is obvious that they should be deployed only into a clean and tested environment. The process of testing for internal and external vulnerabilities is ongoing throughout the response.

1. Assessing Notification Responsibilities

The incident commander and the executive team should consult with cyber counsel about whether there are sufficient indicators to notify external authorities. Certain industries have regulatory control and notification requirements depending on the nature and type of digital records that may have been compromised. Calling the state police or FBI before it is known what records are involved or before the forensic team has a chance to collect and preserve relevant data makes it difficult, if not impossible, to correctly identify "patient zero"[37] or to determine which digital records are involved.[38] Only when sufficient information has been gathered to determine what records have been accessed, compromised, or exfiltrated should the process of external notification begin, but in all instances this decision should be made only in consultation with experience cyber counsel. The incident commander, cyber counsel, and forensic team must carefully assess what enforcement entity should be notified and what notice to provide to the applicable information sharing and analysis center or information sharing and analysis organization. Assistance with messaging from a public relations team is often useful, depending on the nature and extent of the incident.

---

37. "Patient zero" commonly refers to the source individual within a company that the hacker successfully targeted. Finding "patient zero" is a priority that can lead to better understanding of how the hacker gained entry.

38. In one instance, a company assumed that electronic personal health information (ePHI) had been exfiltrated and notified the FBI prior to engaging cyber counsel. When forensic evaluation later determined that ePHI was not exfiltrated but, by an amazing coincidence, an iTunes library was backing up on the company server that was the same size as the medical records file and that the backup occurred within the time window of the hack, the FBI was notified to close its investigation. It bears repeating: do not notify external authorities without first seeking experienced counsel. Gather facts quickly and carefully and know the underlying laws implicated by the results of the hacker's activities.

A natural and critical pause-point occurs once the forensic team has determined the nature and extent of the cyber intrusion. Initial on-scene staff and executive team members have had little sleep and maintaining calm in the face of operational shutdown has an impact on everyone. Simple steps such as contacting carry-out vendors to bring in food and beverages helps fuel employees over long shifts. Managing staff and scheduling to address critical functions is high on the list. With the encryption of many internal and administrative systems, employees that normally work in these areas do not need to be present. Companies need to address how to pay employees if their payroll system is not functioning. Of course, having the company's IT staff available to assist the forensic team is a natural need and additional third-party IT staffing may be necessary as well.

Finally, depending on the nature of the incident, the FBI may want the company to go public as a demonstration or example of a cautionary tale. Going down this road requires careful analysis with the company's management team, inside and outside counsel, and internal and/or external public affairs personnel.

2.   Reviewing the Initial Forensic Indicators

Often the initial forensic indicators can be misleading, sending the forensic team down any number of "rabbit holes" in search of "patient zero" and at the same time determining what data might have been compromised. Typical questions are:

- What servers and devices were infiltrated?
- How and when did the infiltration occur?
- How did the hacker gain entry? Was it an existing vulnerability in hardware or software, or the result of an employee mistake responding to social engineering?
- What are the impacts of the infiltration?

For those companies with cyber liability coverage, it will save much time later if the impacts and consequences of the incident are sorted early on according to the carrier's coverage requirements. This is where consulting with the company's insurance broker can provide a huge advantage to the later filing with the carrier. In addition, keeping track of impacts—and resulting damages—may be important to later claims in litigation if the hacker is identified and subject to U.S. jurisdiction. Sadly, this is infrequently the case.

When the picture of the infiltration becomes clear, then the forensic team's attention turns to the motive:

- What data was accessed on the servers and/or connected devices?
- Was the data exfiltrated?
- Was a company employee the target of a spear-phishing campaign where the employee e-mailed the data to the hacker?
- What reporting obligations are implicated?
- Did the hacker leave any "backdoors" hidden for future access?

In cases involving data breaches, state statutes generally allow for investigative time, with an average requirement of 30 days or so from the date when the breach was discovered, but keep in mind, if you must comply with the General Data Protection Regulation (GDPR), you must report the incident within 72 hours.[39] States will vary widely with their notice triggers and filing requirements, so it is vital to determine early on what types of records might have been compromised, where the owners of these records reside, and how many of these owners reside in each implicated state.

Determining the origin of the cyber intrusion can be painstaking and time-consuming. The task is even more difficult if untrained IT staff have attempted to mitigate the damage and unwittingly destroyed evidence. The identification of "patient zero" will be critical for purposes of insurance coverage questions as well as for traditional liability analysis. In addition, with the recent legislative interest[40] in public–private sector information sharing in the aftermath of a cyber incident, there are benefits to sharing such information with law enforcement.

---

39. https://ec.europa.eu/info/law/law-topic/data-protection/reform/rules-business-and-organisations/obligations/what-data-breach-and-what-do-we-have-do-case-data-breach_en. See the discussion in Section V.A.1.

40. *See generally* Maggie Miller, *Industry Lobbies Congress to Extend Notification Timeline after Cybersecurity Incidents*, THE HILL (Sept. 1, 2021, 6:31 PM), https://thehill.com/policy/cybersecurity/570460-industry-lobbies-congress-to-extend-notification-timeline-after.

3. The Aftermath

In the aftermath of cyber incidents, there is often the question of who did what or who failed to do what. Questions will be raised about what policies were in place, what training occurred, and, if a company employee is identified and implicated, what the consequences may be for that employee. The company's Employee Manual should address the consequences when an employee's act or omission results in a cyber incident.

In the aftermath of a cyber incident, a company can be especially vulnerable, particularly if the incident was reported in public media. Thus, among the post-incident activities are the periodic external and internal vulnerability scans to confirm the integrity of the company's network systems. The message here is that it is never over, you are never "all set," and diligence after a cyber incident must be maintained. It is especially important in the ransomware context: it is not a good thing when word gets out in the dark web that a company both is vulnerable and has paid a ransom.

V. Foreign, Federal, and State Laws

A. Common Foreign Data Protection Laws and Incident Response

It is beyond the scope of this chapter to describe the full list of foreign data breach statutes. There are tools and resources freely available to download;[41] we will highlight the two with the greatest impact to U.S. practitioners here.

1. The General Data Protection Regulation and the Data Protection Act 2018

The General Data Protection Regulation (GDPR EU 2016/679) became effective on May 25, 2018, and it applies to all member states in the European Union. With Brexit on the horizon in 2016, the UK passed a data privacy act called "Data Protection Act 2018" shortly before the effective date of the GDPR that largely mirrors the GDPR.

The GDPR applies:

---

41. See the IAPP RADAR tool available for download here: https://www.radarfirst.com/breach-law-library/.

- When one or both of either a controller (the entity that controls the collection and transmittal of personal data) or a processor (the entity that processes the personal data it receives from the controller) are located in the Union, regardless of whether the processing takes place in the Union; or
- When the data subjects are "in the Union"[42] and they are either being
  - Offered goods or service (irrespective of any payment requirement) or
  - Monitored for their behavior (when their behavior takes place in the Union).

Thus, the territorial scope of the GDPR is vastly greater than any of its predecessors and can easily catch domestic U.S. companies unawares, for it can be applicable to the U.S. company (the controller) using a cloud-based platform (the processor) with U.S.-based servers if the company offers goods or services to data subjects (natural persons) in the EU, or the company in some way monitors the behavior of the data subject while in the EU.[43] Not only is the territoriality aspect a surprising hook for many, but also "personal data" is more broadly defined than U.S. lawyers may be accustomed to seeing.[44]

The breach notification requirements under the GDPR are:

- In the case of a personal data breach, the controller shall without undue delay and, where feasible, not later than 72 hours after having become aware of it, notify the personal data breach to the supervisory authority competent in accordance with Article 55, unless the personal data breach is unlikely to result in a risk to the rights and freedoms of natural

---

42. Many writers miss this point. The language of the Regulation states "in" the Union (EU). There is no requirement to be a resident of the Union or a citizen of the Union.

43. GDPR, Article 4, (1).

44. Personal Data is "any information relating to an identified or identifiable natural person ('data subject'); an identifiable natural person is one who can be identified, directly or indirectly, in particular by reference to an identifier such as a name, an identification number, location data, an online identifier or to one or more factors specific to the physical, physiological, genetic, mental, economic, cultural or social identity of that natural person."

persons. Where the notification to the supervisory authority is not made within 72 hours, it shall be accompanied by reasons for the delay.

- The processor shall notify the controller without undue delay after becoming aware of a personal data breach.

Thus, when an incident does occur that cyber counsel may think is a simple domestic breach, it is imperative to ask whether any impacted servers or cloud providers are located in the EU or whether any of the affected individuals show any indication of being "in the Union" and the controller was either targeting these individuals in some way to offer them goods or services or monitoring their behavior. If it is the processor that suffers the data breach, then notice is required to the controller—unless the agreement between the controller and processor states otherwise.

2. Canada and the Personal Information Protection and Electronic Documents Act

The Personal Information Protection and Electronic Documents Act (PIPEDA)[45] sets national standards for privacy practices in the private sector. PIPEDA applies to federal works, undertakings, or businesses (FWUBs).[46] FWUBs include:

- Banks
- Radio and television stations
- Inter-provincial trucking
- Airports and airlines
- Navigation and shipping by water
- Telecommunication companies such as Internet service providers, phone (cellular or land line companies), cable companies
- Railways, canals, pipelines, ferries, and so on, that cross borders

If an organization is a FWUB, PIPEDA applies to all commercial personal information flows and to employee personal information. If the organization

---

45. S.C. 2000, c. 5, https://laws-lois.justice.gc.ca/eng/acts/P-8.6/.
46. S.C. 2000, c. 5, Part 1, 2(1).

in question operates in a province not subject to substantially similar provincial legislation (Alberta and British Columbia) and is not a FWUB, PIPEDA applies to all commercial activities; however, it does not apply to employee information.

Organizations subject to the (PIPEDA are required to:

- Report to the Privacy Commissioner of Canada breaches of security safeguards involving personal information that pose a real risk of significant harm to individuals,
- Notify affected individuals about those breaches, and
- Keep records of all breaches.

Significant harm includes bodily harm, humiliation, damage to reputation or relationships, loss of employment, business or professional opportunities, financial loss, identity theft, negative effects on the credit record, and damage to or loss of property. Factors that are relevant to determining whether a breach of security safeguards creates a real risk of significant harm include the sensitivity of the personal information involved in the breach of security safeguards and the probability the personal information has been, is being, or will be misused.[47]

B. U.S. Federal Laws and Regulations

Determining which federal agencies require notification post cyber incident naturally depends upon the type of data that may have been subject to unauthorized access or exfiltration and, in some instances, the number of affected individuals:

1. HHS/OCR for Personal Health Information (PHI)

The Department of Health and Human Services is the regulator for a cyber incident involving PHI, and the reporting of such events—and any subsequent investigation—is left to its Office of Civil Rights (OCR). Once a cyber incident involving PHI is reported on the HHS portal, an OCR investigator

---

47. *See also* https://www.priv.gc.ca/en/privacy-topics/business-privacy/safeguards-and-breaches /privacy-breaches/respond-to-a-privacy-breach-at-your-business/gd_pb_201810/.

is assigned. If multiple Covered Entities (CE) and different notification dates are involved in the same cyber incident, the investigator may ask the targeted entity with the reporting obligation to consolidate its later-filed reports as one or more supplements to the original report. In all instances, if a CE decides that it wants to report on its own and not through the targeted entity, OCR will request that the CE should use the same tracking number as the original OCR report so that all reports stemming from the same cyber incident are consolidated.

The pre-breach security requirements that may have been in place during the cyber incident will be subject to particular scrutiny during any post-mortem discussion. Whatever security measures might have been in place will also be included in any OCR investigation if the data breach involved PHI in reportable quantities.

For example, in any cyber incident involving PHI, the report to OCR will require a fairly detailed description of the measures and policies that were in place prior to the incident. The OCR reporting form asks what safeguards were in place prior to the breach, and the typical response would be something like:

- Privacy Rule Safeguards (Training, Policies and Procedures, etc.)
- Security Rule Administrative Safeguards (Risk Analysis, Risk Management, etc.)
- Security Rule Physical Safeguards (Facility Access Controls, Workstation Security, etc.)
- Security Rule Technical Safeguards (Access Controls, Transmission Security, etc.)

Of course, OCR will be looking for these policies and procedures when it begins its investigation.

2. FINCen

The Financial Crimes Enforcement Network (FINCen) assists financial institutions when reporting cyber incidents through reports known as SARs or Suspicious Activity Reports.[48] SAR reports are filed online and primarily cover entities regulated by the Federal Reserve Board, the Federal Deposit Insurance Corporation, the Internal Revenue Service, the National Credit Union Administration, or the Office of the Comptroller of the Currency. The online reporting portal is set up as a series of six tabbed folders with each tab having a separate heading and information requirement.

3. Credit Unions (State and Federal)

Credit unions will also report cyber incidents to the online portal at FIN-Cen, but because of the nature of credit union organizations, a different series of notifications may be necessary. In the first instance, credit unions are member-owned cooperatives, and those who have accounts in credit unions are both members and owners. In addition, individual credit unions often will form cooperatives among themselves, called Credit Union Service Organizations (CUSO), to expand and diversify the services they can offer their members. This can be particularly relevant in any kind of cyber incident because the "owners" in an incident involving a CUSO can be many different credit unions. Quick decision making can be logistically challenging if the targeted credit union is without a current and practiced incident response plan. State, federal, and/or foreign notification follows suit in the same way as any other cyber incident, but the credit union will also report the event to the National Credit Union Administration[49] and, depending on the state where the credit union is organized, the state agency that regulates the credit union.

C. State Statutes and Notification Requirements

Notification requirements in the aftermath of a cyber incident can be overwhelming. Cyber counsel must determine not only whether and what type of personally identifiable information (PII) or personal data might have been accessed and/or acquired without authorization, but also the territorial

---

48. https://www.fincen.gov/frequently-asked-questions-faqs-regarding-reporting-cyber-events-cyber-enabled-crime-and-cyber.

49. https://www.ecfr.gov/cgi-bin/text-idx?SID=6bad163a87/acc23df9cf412.84e8c174f&cmc=true&node=ap12.7.748_12.b&rgn=div9.

reach of the affected individuals, which will determine what reporting jurisdictions are implicated. Most nationally based companies that experience a cyber incident must immediately address the applicability of the notice deadlines and requirements for the 50 U.S. states, Washington, DC, and three U.S. territories.

1. Notice to Affected Individuals

Before the dust settles on the chaotic landscape of a cyber incident and critical in the assessment of a targeted entity's notification obligations is both determining what TYPE of data may have been accessed without authorization and defining the entire universe of potentially affected individuals. The definition of PII will vary across all U.S. state, district, and territorial jurisdictions; thus, the relevant inquiry must focus not only on what types of data may have been accessed but also on which jurisdiction the owner of that data is located at the time of the potential unauthorized access. In addition, while personal health information (PHI) may have a uniform federal definition under the Health Insurance Portability and Accountability Act of 1996 (HIPAA), some states include PHI in their definition of PII so that a targeted entity may not have a reportable incident under HIPAA, if the incident involves the PHI of less than 500 affected individuals, but may nonetheless have to report a data breach under applicable state law.[50]

Other things to consider include:

- What information can be forensically confirmed to have been accessed or exfiltrated without authorization?
- What information can be forensically confirmed NOT to have been accessed or exfiltrated without authorization, which is a critical defense

---

50. A covered entity's reporting obligations under HIPAA will vary depending on whether the data breach of PHI affects 500 or more individuals or fewer than 500 individuals. If the number is 500 or more, the CE must report through the online portal within 60 days of the discovery of the breach. If the number of affected individuals is less than 500, the CE must submit its report within 60 days of the end of the calendar year in which the breach was discovered. *See* https://www.hhs.gov/hipaa/for-professionals/breach-notification/breach-reporting/index.html.

under HIPAA and the Health Information Technology for Economic and Clinical Health (HITECH) Act (HITECH).[51]

For example, only if the relevant log files were both "on" and preserved at the initial phase of the forensic investigation can the practitioner attempt to glean the necessary evidence to assert the "low probability" defense required under HHS current guidance (issued in 2016) for ransomware incidents when PHI is present. The four risk assessment factors that HHS identifies to "demonstrate that there is a low probability that that PHI has been compromised" are:

1. "the nature and extent of the PHI involved, including the types of identifiers and the likelihood of re-identification";
2. "the unauthorized person who used the PHI or to whom the disclosure was made";
3. "whether the PHI was actually acquired or viewed"; and
4. "the extent to which the risk to the PHI has been mitigated."

From the universe of "potentially affected individuals," if you can NOT assert the "low probability" defense required under current HHS guidance, then the next steps are to determine what type of information may have been subjected to the potential unauthorized access or exfiltration:

*   Personally Identifiable Information—PII (Under U.S. State, District/Territorial laws, this requires a 50-state, DC, Puerto Rico, U.S. Virgin Islands, Guam review, since each of these jurisdictions has its own governing law based on the "affected individuals" residing in that jurisdiction).
*   Personal Health Information—PHI (as defined under HIPAA/HITECH). This can be tricky, since some states define PHI under their state data breach laws more stringently than the federal legislation (e.g., Florida).

---

51. HITECH was enacted as part of the American Recovery and Reinvestment Act of 2009 and is designed to promote the adoption and meaningful use of health information technology. It is commonly referenced in tandem with HIPAA.

- Personal Data—as defined under both the General Data Protection Act and the UK's Data Protection Act as "any information relating to an identified or identifiable natural person."
- Personal Information—(broadly defined to mean "information about an identifiable individual" under Canada's Personal Information and Protection of Electronic Documents Act (PIPEDA)).

The type of notice that an individual receives depends on the nature of the affected data and the medium with which the individual interacted with the breach source. For example, if the individual's sole interaction (and sharing of his/her personal data) was via the Internet and the only contact information available for that person is an e-mail address, then e-mail notice may suffice. If the interaction was via regular mail, then print letters, via U.S. Mail delivery is the method of notice. If there is no good contact information, then "substitute notice" in the form of a website notice on the breach source's website may be the only way to reach those individuals.

2. Notice to Attorneys General

States vary about whether they require notification of a data breach to their attorneys general (and what type of information they want). Some states (e.g., Indiana[52]) want notice within 30 days of the incident, even though you may not have been able to determine the nature of the cyberattack or, indeed, whether PII or PHI was subject to unauthorized access or exfiltration. Other states provide notice forms that you can submit electronically (e.g., California, Massachusetts, Nebraska, North Carolina) and others have forms that you can fax or e-mail (e.g., New York). In addition to these requirements, some states also require that you provide a sample of the individual notice that was sent to affected individuals to the attorney general of the state where the affected individuals reside.

Increasingly, states and those agencies designated to respond to breach notifications under their pertinent data breach statutes are becoming more engaged once notified. Typically, these agencies will want more details about the data breach—not only the number of affected individuals in their respective state but also the number of total affected individuals across other

---

52. IND. CODE §§ 4-1-11 *et seq.*, 24-4.9 *et seq.*

jurisdictions, both state and foreign. For a breach involving PHI and requiring OCR notification, the state agencies will seek a copy of the OCR Report filed online at the HHS portal. In addition, depending on the state jurisdiction, the number of affected individuals in the state, and whether the state is a "notice" jurisdiction (i.e., notice to a state agency such as the office of the Attorney General, Insurance Commission, or Consumer Protection Agency), the state's attorney general may seek both to receive all relevant documentation about the cyber incident and to be included in any ultimate OCR investigation.

Some states (Tennessee) have turned the long-time defense of encryption on its head and required notification even if the data subjected to the unauthorized access was encrypted at rest in the target entity's IT environment. Tennessee also requires notification to the state no later than 45 days from the date of discovery.[53] As experienced practitioners know, focusing efforts on notification so early in the forensic process may be laudable from a transparency standpoint, but it also diverts critical resources in the early days of determining what happened, preserving evidence, identifying what types of data may have been accessed, and confirming the pertinent jurisdictions, both domestic and foreign, of the affected population. It is doubtful that state legislators had other state and foreign jurisdictions in mind when they drafted data breach legislation. Assessing and juggling the timing required in multiple state and foreign jurisdictions is a common and nightmarish reality. Once the accessed date, affected population, and jurisdictions are more clearly identified, a second round of notifications may be required.

3. Notice to Insurance Commissioners

Some states require notice by regulated insurance businesses to the applicable regulator in the event of a breach (e.g., Connecticut, Maine, Michigan, Montana, New Hampshire, Ohio, Washington, Wisconsin). For example, in Ohio, all persons or entities holding a license or certificate of authority from the Superintendent of Insurance to conduct business within the state are required to report any "Loss of Control" of policyholder information within their possession to the Superintendent of Insurance. This reporting

---

53. Tenn. Code Ann. § 47-18-2107.

requirement applies in situations involving the loss of personal information of more than 250 Ohio residents.[54]

In Connecticut, regulated entities must provide notice to the Insurance Department in the event of a breach. In addition, for non-insurance regulated entities, Connecticut's data breach law also requires at least 24 months of free identity theft prevention services.[55] Providing identity theft prevention services is generally a best practice, not a statutory requirement. This requirement can prove challenging when the cyber liability coverage under an insurance policy covers only 12 months of reporting, which is a common policy limitation. In those instances where a breach covers jurisdictions with no identity theft prevention services and those that do have such requirements, prior consultation with underwriters' counsel is important. Generally, underwriters will approve a different requirement—for example, Connecticut's 24-month term for theft preventions services—when it is a statutory requirement.

In South Carolina, Michigan, and Ohio, there are special notification obligations in certain circumstances.

- Under South Carolina's Insurance Data Security Act, a licensee, as defined, is required to notify the Director of the Department of Insurance "no later than seventy-two hours after determining that a cybersecurity event has occurred" when certain criteria are met.[56]
- Similarly, under Michigan's Data Security Act, which took effect in January 2021, each licensee, as defined, is required to notify the director "as promptly as possible but not later than 10 business days after a determination that a cybersecurity event involving nonpublic information that is in the possession of a licensee has occurred" when certain criteria are met.[57]
- Ohio's Insurance Data Security Law, which became effective on March 20, 2019, requires notification to the Superintendent of Insurance within three business days.[58]

---

54. OHIO REV. CODE § 3901.07 Bull. 2009-12.
55. CONN. GEN. STAT. § 36a-701b.
56. S.C. CODE § 38-99-40(A).
57. MICH. COMP. LAWS § 500.559(1).
58. OHIO REV. CODE § 3965.11.

4. Notice to Consumer Protection Agencies

As with other specific requirements under state data breach laws, whether or not notice is required to a particular state's consumer protection agency is a state-by-state determination. Whereas some states, such as Massachusetts, New York, and South Carolina, require notification, others do not. For example, Michigan is not a notice state, but when individuals in an affected population begin to contact the Consumer Protection Division with questions about a data breach notification, the Attorney General's office is likely to request information from the targeted entity. This can be a judgment call for cyber counsel: whether or not to provide a courtesy notification to state agencies concurrent with notification to the affected population when that particular state does not require notice.

- In Massachusetts, notice to the Director of Consumer Affairs and Business Regulation of the breach is required "as soon as practicable and without unreasonable delay" following the breach.[59]
- Additionally, Massachusetts requires 18 months of free credit monitoring.[60]
- In New York, notice to the Department of State's Division of Consumer Protection is required in addition to notice to two other offices (the New York Attorney General and the NYS Division of State Police) for any breaches of computerized data that includes private information.[61]
- Notification to New York may also yield an inquiry from the Bureau of Internet and Technology requesting further information.
- In South Carolina, notice to the Consumer Protection Division of the Department of Consumer Affairs is required "if a business provides notice to more than one thousand persons at one time."[62]

5. Notice to Credit Reporting Agencies

With their focus on consumer protection, some states require reporting to credit reporting agencies. For example, Florida requires the reporting entity

---

59. Mass. Gen. Laws 93H §§ 1 *et seq.*
60. Mass. House Bill 4806.
61. N.Y. Gen. Bus. Law § 899-aa.
62. S.C. Code Ann. § 39-1-90(K).

to provide the "timing, distribution, and content of the notices" to "consumer reporting agencies that compile and maintain files on consumers on a nationwide basis" for breaches involving notice of "more than 1,000 individuals at a single time."[63] There is a similar requirement in Maine.[64] Notification to a credit reporting agency may yield a response from one or more of them (Equifax, TransUnion, Experian), requesting additional information, such as a sample notice letter.

6. Notice to Law Enforcement

Whether or not notification of local/state/federal law enforcement is required must be carefully and immediately assessed. For the targeted entity, typical notification would be to local law enforcement, where, in cases such as fraudulent wire transfer, a police report would be useful when trying to get the fraudulent account's recipient's information from the receiving bank. In addition, the affected individuals in a data breach are commonly advised to file police reports, which will prove helpful when taking steps to protect themselves from identity theft. For years, these steps have been part of the FTC website's ID Theft advice page.[65] The timing for such local enforcement notification and the procedures that an enforcement agency uses to communicate within its jurisdiction must be assessed carefully. For example, some local law enforcement agencies use e-blast notices to their constituents, which, if a targeted entity provides immediate notice to its local police, can result in that notice being disseminated throughout the community before all the facts are known. This is not the case when filing an online complaint through the FBI's Internet Crime Complaint Center, as described later in this chapter.

For Internet-based data breaches involving incidents such as ransomware and wire fraud, cyber counsel should file an online complaint on the FBI's Internet Crime Complaint Center, IC3.[66] Often, there is little that the FBI (or local law enforcement) can do besides document the incident, collect the indicators of compromise (if available), and warn the public of new

---

63. Fla. Stat. Ann. § 501.171(5).
64. Me. Rev. Stat. Ann. tit. 10, § 1348(4).
65. https://www.ftc.gov/faq/consumer-protection/report-identity-theft.
66. https://www.ic3.gov/complaint/splash.aspx.

trends or dangerous activities.[67] Recently, the FBI has increased its focus on these Internet crime syndicates, whose threats to lives, property, and critical infrastructure have outstripped our efforts to thwart them. The sharing of information can be valuable to both the public and private sector, but keep in mind that it is generally best to notify law enforcement through experienced cyber counsel.

7. Notice to Parties under Contract

In addition to the legal requirements under federal, state, or foreign laws, an entity must also look to its contractual obligations. The task of reviewing contracts for notification obligations is often overlooked in the flurry of trying to address the immediate forensic issues of what happened, notifying the internal cyber response team, and the external parties—the forensic team, cyber counsel, and the insurance carrier. Then, too, in the effort to go paperless, these documents may exist only in electronic form and very possibly could be inaccessible for a time if they had been encrypted as a result of a ransomware attack. Not only might these documents be inaccessible, but the response team may be unaware that breach notification obligations were added to an agreement with a customer, vendor, or supplier. Entities are generally aware of their notification obligations under their business associate agreements with covered entities but may not realize these additional notice requirements that have been added to contracts in the last five years or so and more recently with the advent of GDPR similar data privacy regulations.

Contractual obligations have real impacts, particularly with the recent and heightened awareness of the potential for cyber incidents of all kinds. From business associate agreements, to data protection agreements under GDPR, to standard IT platforms, SaaS, or other types of agreements in which the contracting parties focus on the security of sensitive data—and thus the need for notice if there is any unauthorized access to that data—there are often notification and shifting burden obligations in these contracts that

---

67. And occasionally the FBI can both raid the threat actor's bitcoin wallet to retrieve more than half the ransom paid in the Colonial Pipeline attack in May 2021, or remediate the vulnerability posed by the Microsoft hafnium exploit in March 2021 via its FRCP Rule 41 Search Warrant.

must be reviewed in the early days of a breach. Of course, identifying and listing these notice obligations in the Incident Response Plan would be an ideal best practice.

8. The Cyber Insurance Carrier

If the targeted entity has cyber liability coverage, notice to its insurance broker should be made as soon as it is evident that a cyber incident of some kind has occurred (noting what kind of coverage the entity has). The broker is an extremely helpful intermediary in helping to assess the nature of the incident, the coverage under the policy and the necessary phrasing and details to send to the carrier. Cyber counsel should be aware that cyber liability policies cover all types of cyber claims and the legal fees associated with assisting the targeted entity with these claims, but typically do NOT cover legal fees for assisting the entity with filing a claim or interpreting the policy, which is a further reason for notifying the broker that assisted the entity in placing the coverage. In addition, unless the targeted entity has experienced internal or outside cyber counsel and forensic experts "pre-vetted" with the insurance carrier, the carrier will assign both cyber counsel and a forensic team from among its paneled experts. These individuals are certainly qualified and capable but often are not local ("boots on the ground" can be critical in the early hours of a breach) and will not have the insight and institutional knowledge of the targeted entity that can be critical with speedy decision making in the early hours of a cyberattack. Thus, if an entity already has cyber counsel and forensic experts incorporated into its Incident Response Plan, it is a best practice to get this team pre-vetted by the insurance carrier and/or its underwriter.

VI. The Rise of Trench-Tested Best Practices

A. Paying Ransom (or Not)

Typically, there is not a lot of time for a targeted entity to evaluate whether to pay a ransom or not and, if so, to negotiate the type of currency. Cybercriminals provide a time deadline—24 or 48 hours—and provide instructions for payment of the ransom. Occasionally, negotiation with the cybercriminal will work to lower the payment demand. In recent years, the average ransom demands have gone from hundreds of thousands of dollars to multiple millions.[68] That's a long way from the early days, when the common demand was $500.

To pay or not to pay is an analysis that begins with the integrity of the targeted entity's backup. More often than not, the backup has also been encrypted or the backup is restored into the environment before all traces of the malware have been eradicated and the backup becomes cross-contaminated. Other factors are whether the time and effort to restore systems using the backup will take longer (and perhaps be just as costly given the downtime to the business) than paying the ransom and starting the decryption process. These are difficult decisions, and often there is little time to evaluate the best solution. The process of decryption can take weeks or months in a large IT environment. Occasionally, the cybercriminal will withhold some decryption keys in an to extort addition ransom. In addition, and more often than not, decryption keys cannot be trusted to be "clean"—these keys will arrive with their own form of mischief; for example, launching additional malware or manipulating the Windows registry files. The best practice in this instance is to run the decryption program in a secure "sandbox," which can be forensically examined prior to introducing the decrypted programs back into the IT environment of the targeted entity.

The most popular cryptocurrency in the ransomware world is bitcoin, although its star is not shining quite as brightly lately. One reason is that bitcoin transactions can be traced back to users, which is not good if you are the cybercriminal trying to hide your tracks. Another reason is the marketing volatility of bitcoin: a demand for 20 bitcoin on day 1 of a ransomware demand could be worth much less on day 2 or 3. Other cryptocurrencies are monero (useful for its privacy features, which stop transactions from being traced back to users) and ethereum (the second largest cryptocurrency by market capitalization).

---

68. Danny Palmer, *Largest Ransomware Demand Now Stands at $30 Million as Crooks Get Bolder*, ZDNet (Mar. 17, 2021), https://www.zdnet.com/article/largest-ransomware-demand-now-stands-at-30-million-as-crooks-get-bolder/.

B. OFAC Issues

The Office of Foreign Assets and Control (OFAC) is part of the Department of Treasury and administers and enforces economic sanctions programs against countries and individuals. If the cybercriminal behind a ransomware attack is on the Specially Designated Nationals (SDN) list, the target entity could be breaking U.S. law by paying a ransomware demand to any cybercriminal identified in a Sanctions List Search application. The OFAC website maintains a lookup for the Sanctions List Search.[69] It's not a good day when the bitcoin payment you make to the cybercriminal will also subject you to OFAC enforcement; thus, a best practice—depending on whether the currency transaction is traceable back to the criminal—is to perform a quick look-up at OFAC. The dilemma, of course, is what if the criminal is on the SDN list? At this point, the targeted entity should have filed a complaint describing the incident on the FBI's Internet Crime Complaint Center (IC3) and would be advised to consult with a special agent versed in this issue.

On October 1, 2020, OFAC released official guidance[70] on this issue in which it warned against making payments to individuals or entities on the "Specially Designated Nationals and Blocked Persons" list or others who may also be covered by country or region embargoes. This guidance was update on September 21, 2021.[71] The critical and noteworthy part of this advisory is the notice to companies that engage with victims of ransomware attacks of the potential sanctions risks for facilitating ransomware payments. The practical result is that if the threat actor is an individual or entity on the "list," then all involved—cyber counsel, forensic consultant, insurance company and the victim entity itself—could be subjected to penalties if a ransom payment is facilitated. In practice, it can be extremely helpful to reach out to Private Sector Coordinators or Cyber Squad Special Agents at nearby FBI field offices for assistance in identifying and addressing payment demands by the threat actors.

---

69. https://sanctionssearch.ofac.treas.gov/.
70. https://home.treasury.gov/policy-issues/financial-sanctions/recent-actions/20201001.
71. https://home.treasury.gov/news/press-releases/jy0364.

C. Managing the Message

Most cyber liability insurance policies will offer coverage for public relations experts. Even if it is not covered, proper messaging is important. Templates covering the typical range of incidents should be part of the incident response plan. As more fully described later, messaging is an ongoing task, beginning with internal notices to company leadership, general employees, customers, suppliers, the public, and responding to media.

1. Entity Leadership

There are numerous examples of how NOT to manage the message when a company becomes the target of a data breach. Examples from the last few years from Uber and Equifax come to mind.

In the Uber data breach, Uber leadership paid $100,000 to the hackers in an effort to keep the breach of 57 million accounts from becoming public information. When the story did break (as disclosed in a blog post by Uber CEO Dara Khosrowshahi, who had not known of the incident that had taken place ten months prior to his arrival at Uber), the chief security officer and his deputy were fired.[72] The data breach occurred in October 2016 and the prior Uber CEO, Mr. Kalanick learned of the hack in November 2016. Mr. Khosrowshahi replaced Mr. Kalanick in September 2017 and subsequently learned of the breach and the payment to the hackers.

Equifax managed its communications a bit differently than Uber, but the results were equally misguided. The allegations are that Equifax officers' sale of company stock preceded public disclosure of the breach. In a statement to the media, Equifax stated that "it found out about the security incident on July 29, 2017, and immediately took action."[73] Presumably, that action would have included notification to its executive team, which should have

---

72. Greg Bensinger & Robert McMillan, *Uber Reveals Data Breach and Cover-up Leading to Two Firings*, WALL ST. J. (Nov. 21, 2017, 11:38 PM), https://www.wsj.com/articles/uber-reveals-data-breach-and-cover-up-leading-to-two-firings-1511305453.

73. Paul R. LaMonica, *Equifax Execs Sold Stock before Hack Was Disclosed*, CNN BUS. (Sept. 8, 2017, 12.35 PM), https://money.cnn.com/2017/09/08/investing/equifax-stock-insider-sales-hack-data-breach/index.html. The breach actually occurred on May 13, 2017, when hackers exploited a known vulnerability in a software platform hosting Equifax's dispute resolution portal. Carole Piovesan, *Cyber Breach Planning: Lessons from the Equifax Breach*, FORBES (Apr. 15, 2019, 12:36 PM), https://www.forbes.com/sites/cognitiveworld/2019/04/15/cyber-breach-planning-lessons-from-the-equifax-breach/, citing the Office of the Privacy Commissioner of Canada's Investigation into Equifax posted on April 9, 2019: https://www

included its general counsel, and its board of directors. Knowing of a potential cyber incident that goes to the heart of what the company's mission entails—protecting the sensitive financial data of millions of Americans—how could the general counsel's approval of the sale of millions of dollars of company stock by three Equifax executives be seen as escaping SEC scrutiny? Reporting indicated that the general counsel knew at the time of his approval that the IT department "had detected suspicious activity."[74] According to news reports and SEC filings at the time:

- Equifax Chief Financial Officer John Gamble sold shares worth nearly $950,000 on August 1;
- Equifax's president for U.S. information solutions, Joseph Loughran, sold shares worth about $685,000 on August 1; and
- Equifax's president of workforce solutions, Rodolfo Ploder, sold stock for just more than $250,000 on August 2.[75]

Yet, when called to appear before the U.S. House Energy and Commerce Committee in the fall of 2017, the CEO blamed the incident on the failure of one employee who failed to implement a critical software patch. This claimed defense failed to hold water with House Committee members, one of whom notably commented "'How does this happen when so much is at stake?' . . . I don't think we can pass a law that, excuse me for saying this, fixes stupid. I can't fix stupid."[76]

Not long after the public notice of the breach, the SEC investigated the activities of Jun Ying, who had been in line to take over the position of Equifax's global CIO. Apparently, soon after the breach and before notice to the public, Ying exercised all of his company stock options and then sold the shares, yielding proceeds of nearly $1 million. As reported by the SEC

.priv.gc.ca/en/opc-actions-and-decisions/investigations/investigations-into-businesses/2019/pipeda-2019-001/.

74. Tara Siegal Bernard & Stacy Cowley, *Equifax Breach Caused by Lone Employee's Error, Former C.E.O. Says*, N.Y. TIMES (Oct. 3, 2017), https://www.nytimes.com/2017/10/03/business/equifax-congress-data-breach.html.

75. https://money.cnn.com/2017/09/08/investing/equifax-stock-insider-sales-hack-data-breach/index.html (last visited Dec. 14, 2021).

76. https://www.nytimes.com/2017/10/03/business/equifax-congress-data-breach.html (last visited Dec. 14, 2021).

in its press release, Ying avoided "more than $117,000 in losses" by selling his stock prior to public notice.[77] On June 30, 2019, Ying was sentenced to four months in prison after which he will be released under supervision for one year. He also has been ordered to pay restitution of the $117,000 in losses he tried to avoid as well as a $55,000 fine.[78]

Later that year, the U.S. government announced a $700 million settlement with Equifax that included more than $425 million for consumers. Affected consumers are eligible for free credit monitoring for ten years, identity restoration services for at least seven years, and, beginning in 2020, free copies of their credit report each year for seven years. Money has also been set aside for consumers with certain other eligible expenses if they can prove their identity theft related expense stemmed from the Equifax breach.[79]

The lessons learned in the Equifax example are many, but two stand out: The first is to get the internal message out immediately to company leadership and all staff to ensure a consistent and clear external message. The second is to deploy a pre-vetted and practiced internal and external team to manage the incident. The time to assemble a media response team and incident response team is not after an incident occurs. As cybersecurity experts will agree, when faced with the heat of a volatile cyber incident, a company is better served when it has a plan in place and funnels all public statements through a company spokesperson.[80] Of course, it also helps when "known vulnerabilities" are patched within days, and not after months have passed.

The SEC also monitors public disclosure of risk, and in recent years, those risks include the use—and misuse—of the data companies collect and claim to protect. In the widely reported Cambridge Analytica matter, in which Cambridge Analytica used Facebook user data the SEC's complaint announced on July 24, 2019, alleged that Facebook discovered the misuse of its data in 2015 but did not correct its original disclosure to investors. The

---

77. Press Release, U.S. SEC, *Former Equifax Executive Charged with Insider Trading* (Mar. 14, 2018), https://www.sec.gov/news/press-release/2018-40.

78. Thomson Reuters NewsRoom 6/30/19 TechSpot (page unavailable online).

79. Mae Anderson & Sarah Skidmore Sell, *Equifax $700M Settlement: What Consumers Should Know*, DENVER POST (July 22, 2019, 4:26 PM), https://www.denverpost.com/2019/07/22/equifax-700m-settlement-faq/.

80. Ben DiPietro, *Regulatory Compliance Is Only Part of Cybersecurity*, WALL ST. J. (Dec. 13, 2017, 11:52 AM), https://blogs.wsj.com/cio/2017/12/13/compliance-is-not-the-goal-of-cybersecurity/?guid=BL-CIOB-13198&mod=searchresults&page=2&pos=5&dsk=y.

original disclosure stated that the Facebook users' data "may be improperly accessed, used or disclosed." Facebook finally made an accurate disclosure of the matter in March 2018, which, in the opinion of the SEC, was not soon enough. The SEC's 2019 response was to criticize Facebook's failure in taking so long to implement the requisite policies and procedures to assess the results of its initial internal investigation into the Cambridge Analytica matter. Facebook knew that Cambridge Analytica had actually misused the user date. The clear take-away message from the SEC press release states: "Public companies must identify and consider the material risks to their business and have procedures designed to make disclosures that are accurate in all material respects, including not continuing to describe a risk as hypothetical when it has in fact happened."[81]

2. Employees, Contractors

Swift and transparent communication to all staff is critical in any cyber incident. Again, having the outline of the message—with only the relevant details to fill in—and the person tasked with its communication at the ready serve several important missions in the early chaotic days of a data breach. A company's employees and contractors are members of a community outside the workplace. Providing them with a clear message that contains as much detail as is both known and safe to convey is the right thing to do. In the face of a cyber incident, there are real concerns about job security, and rightly so. In the past several years, it has been widely reported that around 50 percent of small business would have to shut down in the face of a major data breach.[82] Added to the concern about job future is the real issue of the day-to-day operation of the company facing a major breach. If critical systems are down, so too, is productivity and the ability of the company to produce its goods and/or provide its services. With ransomware

---

81. Press Release, U.S. SEC, Facebook to Pay $100 Million for Misleading Investors about the Risks It Faced from Misuse of User Data (July 24, 2019), https://www.sec.gov/news/press-release/2019-140.

82. In a 2019 report, survey data indicated that 71 percent of small- and mid-sized businesses in the financial and insurance sectors reported that "a major breach would be fatal to their businesses." The percentage was 62 percent in health care and 60 percent in business consulting. Jeff Goldman, *Almost Half of SMBs Would Be Shut Down Permanently by a Major Data Breach*, SMALL BUS. COMPUTING (Feb. 26, 2019), https://www.smallbusinesscomputing.com/news/almost-half-of-smbs-would-be-shut-down-permanently-by-a-major-data-breach.html.

attacks, it can take multiple weeks for operations to resume on a somewhat normal basis. Throughout this period, companies must keep employees, contractors, customers, vendors, and supplies informed as best they can. Such messaging must be done carefully, however, and in consultation with counsel and the PR team.

Even so, such pre-planning does not prevent employees from taking their own message to the media. Witness the recent ransomware incident at Arizona Beverage where "a person familiar with the incident" described the impact of the incident as "effectively shutting down sales operations for days" noting with "surprise" that "an attack hadn't come sooner given the age of their systems," and "'[o]nce the backups didn't work, they started throwing money at the problem.'" The final quote from this unofficial company spokesperson was: "'We were losing millions of dollars a day in sales, . . . [i]t was a complete shitshow.'"[83] The reporter attempted to reach the company spokesperson, but that individual did not respond to the reporter's e-mail requesting comment.[84] This was a missed opportunity by the company to manage the message and the incident. Cyber incidents are by their very nature chaotic and disruptive. That is why having a plan and the right people is place is critical.

3.   Investors

For public companies, their investors should learn about a data breach no sooner than the rest of the public. That certainly is the lesson for those Equifax insiders who knew about the breach and sold their stock prior to the public announcement. For private companies, the concern is a bit different. Here it may be more about resource allocation and assistance as private investors scramble to protect the company. Then there is the example of the Yahoo! data breach. In April 2018, Yahoo! paid a fine of $35 million in a settlement with the SEC for failing to disclose the full impact of its

---

83. Zach Whittaker, *Arizona Beverages Knocked Offline by Ransomware Attack*, TECHCRUNCH (Apr. 2, 2019, 1:25 PM), https://techcrunch.com/2019/04/02/arizona-beverages-ransomware/.

84. *Id.*

2013 data breach until details came out as part of Verizon's due diligence in acquiring Yahoo! in 2016.[85]

4. Business Partners and Vendors

Not only is it smart from a basic business practice perspective to keep business partners, suppliers, and vendors informed, but it also may be contractually required. Among the early tasks in any cyber incident playbook is the discovery and confirmation of contractual as well as statutory reporting obligations. Many are familiar with notification requirements in Business Associate Agreements but may not be as aware of the notice obligations in data protection agreements, commonly part of contracts with global partners. As noted above under the General Data Protection Regulation[86] (GDPR), a "processor" must notify its "controller" without undue delay after becoming aware of a data breach, and that controller—when feasible—has 72 hours to notify the supervisory authority. Three days is not a lot of time to sort through contracts (that may have been encrypted) to determine what to do and whom to notify under the contract.

D. Notable Mistakes

It is easy to second-guess actions taken in the midst of a crisis, but there are a few notable examples in recent years that should not be repeated.

1. Hush Money to Hackers

Perhaps the most headline-grabbing mistake made with regard to dealing with cybercriminals was Uber's attempt to pay $100,000 as hush money to its attackers.[87] It was not a mistake by counsel—an internal board committee later investigated and concluded that neither CEO Travis Kalanick nor Uber's general counsel at the time were involved in the cover-up. The

---

85. *Yahoo Reaches $117.5 Million Settlement in Huge Data Breach*, CBS News (Apr. 9, 2019, 4:45 PM), https://www.cbsnews.com/news/yahoo-data-breach-117-5 -million-settlement-reached/.

86. Regulation EU 2016/679.

87. Jim Finkle & Heather Somerville, *Regulators to Press Uber after It Admits Covering Up Data Breach*, Reuters (Nov. 21, 2017, 5:37 PM), https://uk.reuters.com/article/us-uber-cyber attack/regulators-to-press-uber-after-it-admits-covering-up-data-breach-idUKKBN1DL2UQ; Bensinger & McMillan, *supra* note 72.

apparent source of the hush-money payment were Uber's chief security officer and his deputy, who were fired in the aftermath.

The events unfolded in October 2016, when two hackers gained access to proprietary information that Uber engineers had stored on GitHub (a collaborative web-based service that software developers use). When the breach was announced nearly a year later, a GitHub spokesperson stated that the access to the GitHub site was not a failure of GitHub security. With their GitHub access, the hackers found and lifted Uber's access credentials to Uber's portal on Amazon's Web Service (AWS), the storage location for 57 million individuals' data. The stored data included drivers' license numbers for 600,000 Uber drivers and the e-mail addresses and cell phone numbers of ride-hailing users around the world.[88]

Reports indicated that the co-founder and then CEO Travis Kalanick learned of the incident about one month after it occurred, but never mentioned it to his replacement CEO, Dara Khosrowshahi, when Mr. Khosrowshahi took over in August 2017. At the same time that Kalanick learned of the hack and breach, Uber was negotiating with the FTC as part of the FTC's inquiry over how Uber stored consumer data.

It is difficult to imagine any realistic scenario in which payment of any amount of money could keep hidden a massive breach impacting the personal data of 57 million individuals worldwide. While the CEO (Kalanick) and the then-current general counsel were not implicated in the cover-up, standard best-practice incident response planning procedures would have included notice of the payment (at minimum) to both the CEO and the general counsel. The fact that the chief security officer and his deputy not only had ready access to $100,000 for payment to the cybercriminals, but also believed it possible to keep an incident of this magnitude contained within the Uber IT Department, is extraordinary.

2. Walking Away

Another example that is increasingly common is when the company decides that either the costs of system restoration or the requisite reporting and notification are just too great, and the company owners decide to walk

---

88. Finkle & Somerville, *supra* note 87.

away. An online health industry trade journal reported that a two-doctor ENT and hearing services practice in Battle Creek, Michigan, planned to close permanently and the practice's doctors retire instead of paying the $6,500 ransom demand to restore patient data.[89] While this may be the only economic choice the two doctors had, "walking away" does not relieve them from their legal obligations under applicable state and/or federal law. And this is not an uncommon result for small businesses faced with legal and forensic costs and no cyber liability coverage. In the case of the ENT doctors, it was reported that the FBI was alerted and that "there is not believed to be any risk to patients" because "[n]o patient data appeared to have been viewed or accessed prior to files being deleted."[90] There are a number of questions raised by this statement: Who made the determination that no patient data was viewed prior to being deleted? If this had been a forensic determination, the cost of retaining a qualified forensic expert for this evaluation likely would have exceeded the demanded ransomware payment. Given that the patient data would have been PHI,[91] the guidance under HIPAA/HITECH states that any ransomware breach is a reportable event, unless the targeted entity can assert the "low probability" defense necessary in certain data breaches involving PHI. Missing from this brief news report are critical facts, thus it is difficult to assess the basis for the decision to walk away. Such a decision should not be made, however, without the advice of experienced forensic and legal experts.

3.   A Failure to Communicate

The Equifax data breach just noted highlights the backlash both in public sentiment and federal regulatory interest from a breach impacting at least 145 million individuals in the United States and approximately one million consumers outside of the United States. The U.S. Government Accountability Office (GAO) published a report in August 2018 and identified Equifax's

---

89. *Michigan Practice Forced to Close Following Ransomware Attack*, HIPAA J. (Apr. 2, 2019), https://www.hipaajournal.com/michigan-practice-forced-to-close-following-ransomware-attack/.

90. *Id.*

91. *Id.* Patients interviewed for this story stated that their information included recent test results.

missteps, including its failure to implement industry standard best practices and a lack of internal controls and routine security reviews.[92] What seems remarkable in the early actions after the breach was discovered on July 29, 2017 (a Saturday), was that the Equifax general counsel was either not apprised of the breach, or thought it irrelevant to his approval of the sale of millions of dollars of Equifax stock by three executives on August 1st and 2nd, well in advance of the public announcement of the data breach on September 7, 2017. The approval and timing may have been innocent, but it seems that the general counsel should have been among the first to receive notice of the data breach, and with that notice should have been more circumspect about approving insider stock sales.

Another more common scenario is when an entity is the victim of a business e-mail compromise in which the victim's e-mail credentials are stolen, thus leading to the theft of the victim's mailbox. With the victim's e-mail credentials and contact information, the hackers then start sending phishing e-mails to these contacts in the name of the victim. Some cyber counsel may advise the targeted entity not to warn these contacts, which generally include clients and customers, while the event is still evolving, thinking that this is some type of admission of liability. Yet, the better practice—if the event is still new and unfolding—is to inform these contacts with a brief warning about the phishing attempt and the danger of clicking on a malicious link.

VII. Ten Key Ways to Mitigate Risk

1. Implement multifactor authentication (threat actors thrive when MFA is not deployed).
2. Mandate Virtual Private Networks (VPNs) for remote access to company networks (critical for a dispersed and/or work-from-home workforce).
3. Deploy endpoint detection and response (EDRs will detect and prevent most incidents automatically and do so 24/7/365) and turn on

---

92. *Data Protection: Actions Taken by Equifax and Federal Agencies in Response to the 2017 Breach*, GAO@100 (Aug. 30, 2018), https://www.gao.gov/products/GAO-18-559.

logging to capture events at least as far back as six months or more (you can't find what you can't see).

4. Implement an Incident Response Plan (without a plan, it can be chaos) and update it periodically.

5. Encrypt confidential and sensitive data both at rest and in transit (encrypted data is useless to threat actors and a non-event under most data breach laws).

6. Back up data (encrypted) to an immutable storage device (one that can be written to only once) and secure that backup off-site (with a good backup available, no ransom payment is necessary).

7. Segment data across IT networks (don't make it easy for threat actors to crawl across your network).

8. Conduct periodic external and internal vulnerability scans (security is not a one-and-done effort and requires constant vigilance).

9. Digital and Physical Controls. Control access credentials to need-to-have individuals (threat actors target IT managers with the "keys" to the network); maintain physical security controls (lock your doors and lock up your sensitive equipment).

10. Implement periodic training for all (training works and it's simple to do).

11. Bonus Point: Purchase a comprehensive cyber insurance policy (and pre-vet your cyber counsel and forensic team), but be prepared for rising premiums and decreasing coverages in the wake of increasing claims.

The point is this: if the preceding practices are implemented company-wide, the rate and impact of cyberattacks will be reduced markedly. There may be costs associated with their implementation, but the costs of non-implementation are much higher.

Chapter 16

Cyber Insurance for Law Firms and Legal Organizations

Kevin P. Kalinich and Tom Ricketts

I. Insurance as a Cyber Risk Management Tool Hit a "Hard" Market in 2021

Insurance can provide a financial transfer backstop for the cyber risks set forth in this Handbook. Insurance is a contract, represented by a policy, in which the attorney, law firm, or other entity with lawyers receives financial protection or reimbursement against cyber-related losses from an insurance company. Unfortunately, we are facing a "hard" insurance market with average cyber insurance premiums increasing by 20 percent to 50 percent.[1] A "hard" insurance market is a period of time when insurance demand is high, but there is a lower supply of coverage available. 2021 saw cyber insurers demand higher premiums, higher deductibles, reduced coverage (e.g. exclusions, co-insurance, sublimits, etc.), lower limits offered, and less insurance carrier competition.[2] What caused the hard market and what can insureds do about it?

Cyber insurance models were built on the shifting sands of too many legacy property, plant, and equipment historical loss assumptions, many of which do not map to cyber risk. A big and flawed assumption with respect

---

1. Aon's E&O |Cyber Insurance Snapshot: A Focused View of 2021 Risk & Insurance Challenges 1 (2021), https://www.aon.com/cyber-solutions/wp-content/uploads/Aon-errors-and-omissions-cyber-insurance-snapshot.pdf [hereinafter Cyber Insurance Snapshot].

2. Cyber insurance premiums skyrocketing, which means firms not being able to procure sufficient coverage without paying 30 percent to 50 percent+ premium increases—even if the insured has no claims.

to cyber risks is that past loss activity is a reasonable analogue of future loss activity. Over the past few years, the frequency of privacy breach incidents decreased by double digits, while ransomware events increased by triple digits[3] as cybercriminals changed tactics. Personally identifiable information (PII) has been decreasing in value and harder to monetize as more of it becomes available for sale on the dark web, while ransomware operators have been realizing increasingly substantial rewards as they have refined their operating tactics. The trend has continued in 2021.

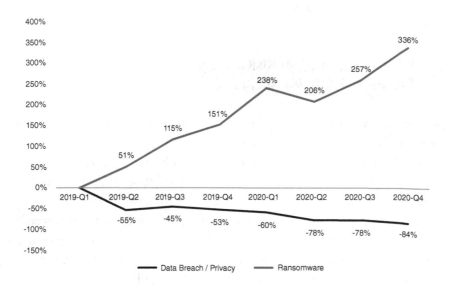

Figure 16.1   Cyber Inident Rate Trends: Ransomware versus Data Breaches

As a result, some cyber insurers suffered loss ratios of more than 100 percent in 2020 and law firms show loss ratios higher than many other industries.[4] 2020 witnessed a 100 percent year-on-year increase in cyber events and saw three new matters per business day, with the majority being ransomware attacks, and the trend has continued into 2021. There was also

---

3. *Cyber Insurance Snapshot, supra* note 1, at 3.
4. The loss ratio formula is insurance claims paid plus adjustment expenses divided by total earned premiums.

growth in the average loss severity for claims.[5] As insurance premium rates decreased and coverage broadened from 2015 to 2019, insurers underestimated the following perils that are causing massive losses, each of which will be explained in detail later:

- Systemic/correlated/aggregated cyber risks (e.g., BlackBaud,[6] Solarwinds Orion,[7] Microsoft Exchange Server,[8] Accellion,[9] Work from home IoT[10]);
- Increase in frequency and severity of ransomware and data theft extortion (several major law firms were named in the press as having been victims of ransomware attacks from the Accellion hack, and in 2021 three high-profile ransomware payments became public knowledge: Colonial Pipeline's $4.4 million payment, meat company JBS paid $11 million to hackers, and CNA Insurance's $40 million payment);[11]
- Criticality of supply chains/vendors;[12]

---

5. *E & O Cyber Matters Jumped 100% in 2020: Aon*, Bus. Ins. (Mar. 11, 2021), https://www.businessinsurance.com/article/20210311/STORY/912340375/E&O-cyber-matters-jumped-100-in-2020-Aon; Mark Hollmer, *E&O-Cyber Incidents Worsened in 2020: Aon*, Ins. J. (Mar. 10, 2021), https://www.insurancejournal.com/news/national/2021/03/10/604607.htm.

6. Blackbaud, cloud software provider, has been sued in 23 proposed consumer class action cases in the United States and Canada related to the ransomware attack and data breach that the company suffered in May 2020. Maria Henriquez, *Blackbaud Sued after Ransomware Attack*, Security (Nov. 6, 2020), https://www.securitymagazine.com/articles/93857-blackbaud-sued-after-ransomware-attack.

7. SolarWinds hack was "the largest and most sophisticated attack the world has ever seen," Microsoft president Brad Smith.

8. Charlie Osborne, *Microsoft Exchange Server Hacks "Doubling" Every Two Hours*, Zero Day Net (Mar. 12, 2021, 8:35 AM), https://www.zdnet.com/article/microsoft-exchange-server-hacks-doubling-every-two-hours/.

9. A third-party file sharing system provided by Accellion called FTA was illegally accessed through a previously unknown zero-day vulnerability. Ben Carr, *Qualys Update on Accellion FTA Security Incident*, Qualys Cmty. (Apr. 2, 2021), https://blog.qualys.com/vulnerabilities-research/2021/03/11/qualys-update-on-accellion-fta-security-incident. The two-stage mega-hack in December 2020 and January 2021 highlights a threat that security experts fear might be getting out of hand: intrusions by top-flight criminal and state-backed hackers into software supply chains and third-party services.

10. Security camera hack at Verkada exposed hospitals, workplaces, schools, factories, jails, and corporate offices. Maria Henriquez, *Verkada Breach Exposed Live Feeds of 150,000 Surveillance Cameras inside Schools, Hospitals and More*, Security (Mar. 10, 2021), https://www.securitymagazine.com/articles/94789-verkada-breach-exposed-live-feeds-of-150000-surveillance-cameras-inside-schools-hospitals-and-more.

11. All of these breaches are discussed in detail in other chapters throughout this Handbook.

12. Supply chain is the weakest security link for 92 percent of U.S. companies. The devastating Target breach—the result of an earlier attack on the retail giant's HVAC

- Necessity of in-depth and breadth IT security scrutiny;[13] and
- Non-correlated losses in the professional services sector that negatively affected the insurers' books[14]

Ransomware is up 486 percent from Q1 2018 to Q4 2020.[15] Data and privacy breaches did not disappear, and in 2020 several law firms and bar groups (New York City Bar Association, the Chicago Bar Association, Washington State Bar Association) were among legal organizations to report data breach incidents, contributing to cyber insurers' losses for this sector.[16]

The cyber insurance marketplace has been building up to major shifts in pricing and underwriting as the industry attempts to stem the tide of ransomware, but vendor management and aggregation issues remain a worry for the future and can't be solved by increased premium rates alone.[17] This chapter will advise how to respond to the hard market by reviewing cyber insurance developments over the past five years and predicting our direction for the next five years, including attorneys' increasing use of new

---

vendor—wasn't an anomaly. Research from BlueVoyant found that 92 percent of U.S. organizations suffered a breach in 2020 as a result of weakness in their supply chain. *Managing Cyber Risk*, BLUEVOYANT (Oct. 12, 2021), https://www.bluevoyant.com/resources /managing-cyber-risk-across-the-extended-vendor-ecosystem/.

13. Cyber insurance carriers should have read The ABA Cybersecurity Handbook (2d ed.), which recommended enhanced underwriting of these cyber resilience issues.

14. Attorneys and law firms might expect to pay higher cyber insurance rates if they suffer malpractice-type losses, but they also suffer the "hard" insurance market because of non-legal -related losses in the professional services arena, such as a $600 million settlement by a major consulting firm that had provided advice to Purdue Pharma in connection with the marketing of opioids. While it seems unfair, most professional services firms are often lumped together by insurance companies when they calculate their loss ratios.

15. *Cyber Insurance Snapshot, supra* note 1, at 3.

16. Christine Simmons, Xiumei Dong & Ben Hancock, *More Than 100 Law Firms Have Reported Data Breaches. And the Problem Is Getting Worse*, LAW.COM (Oct. 15, 2019, 1:10 PM), https://www.law.com/2019/10/15/more-than-100-law-firms-have-reported -data-breaches-and-the-picture-is-getting-worse/; Andrew Maloney, *Cadwalader and Bar Groups among Latest to Report Data Breach Incidents*, LAW.COM (Nov. 9, 2020, 8:00 PM), https://www.law.com/americanlawyer/2020/11/09/cadwalader-and-bar-groups-among -latest-to-report-data-breach-incidents.

17. For example, one firm was surprised to find out that they were scanned by a potential insurer, without notice, without consent. While legally having the right to do so, the insurer then used such information (valid or not) as a data point when pricing the insurance. In fact, some insurers have commenced scanning their insureds on a monthly basis to look for additional risk. Other insurers utilize multiple third party IT security assessment scores.

technologies such as Artificial Intelligence (AI), Internet of Things (IoT) (from working remote due to Covid-19), biometrics, and 5G.

In order to examine the *supply* of insurance coverage, we first look at the frequency and types of cyber incidents that motivate the growing *demand* for such insurance. According to the 2020 American Bar Association Legal Technology Survey Report:[18]

- Twenty-nine percent of respondents experienced a security breach compared to 26 percent in 2019 (such as a lost/stolen computer or smartphone, hacker, break-in, website exploit) (21 percent report that they do not know whether their firm has ever experienced a security breach).
- Thirty-six percent report having their systems infected with viruses, spyware, and malware (26 percent were not aware whether any such infection has ever occurred).
- Costs associated with cybersecurity incidents include:
  - Consulting fees for repair,
  - Downtime/loss of billable hours,
  - Temporary loss of network and Internet access,
  - Expense for replacing hardware or software,
  - Repair for destruction or loss of files,
  - Notifying clients of the breach.
- Thirty-six percent of law firms purchased cyber liability insurance policies (compared to 33 percent in 2019, and 26 percent in 2017).

What coverage is available to address such cyber-related losses?

Buyers of insurance complain, rightly, that cyber policies are confusing, with multiple sections and insuring agreements, difficult language, and complex definitions; they also struggle with the lack of consistency between

---

18. John G. Loughnane, *2020 Cybersecurity Tech Report*, ABA (Oct. 19, 2020), https://www.americanbar.org/groups/law_practice/publications/techreport/2020/cybersecurity/. Responses came from attorneys practicing in a wide range of settings: solos (26%); firms of 2–9 attorneys (30%); firms of 10–49 attorneys (17%); firms of 50–99 attorneys (5%); firms of 100–499 attorneys (10%), and firms of 500+ attorneys (12%).

policies that makes it difficult, if not impossible, to determine which policy is best suited to the client's needs. Some of these issues are endemic to the coverage, which puts together First Party insurance with Third Party Liability, covers regulatory investigations, extortion payments and many other risks, which by their nature involve complexity. Construction and general layout of policies can vary enormously between insurers as they seek clarity of coverage, using as few as two and in some policies eight or more insuring agreements. The problem of language differences persists as insurers seek to be clear about what they will and will not cover when dealing with a rapidly changing technological environment and even more dynamic threat landscape. On the other hand, a lot of the complexity is due to each insurer having designed their own approach to cyber insurance and trying to differentiate themselves from the rest.

Cyber insurance is still going through a process of convergent evolution that will eventually produce a policy with more consistent structure and language across insurers (as it has with property, general liability, and professional indemnity, etc.).

Despite the differences between policies offered by each insurer, cyber insurance coverage (as distinct from wording) has undergone considerable convergence in recent times. The categories of coverage are not always described the same way and components within these coverages are not always allocated to the same category between different insurers' policies, but the following is a guide to components that are typically available.

Cyber policies are unusual in that they cover both First Party Losses (i.e., damage that the firm has suffered, such as the cost to rehabilitate systems and loss of revenue) and Third Party Liabilities (i.e., the cost of defending a lawsuit and paying compensation to someone who has been harmed by the loss or publication of their data).

There are five core coverage segments (three First Party and two Third Party) common to nearly all stand-alone cyber insurance policies:

1. First Party
    a. Breach response / event management
    b. Network interruption (loss of revenue)
    c. Extortion (ransomware)

2. Third Party
   a. Privacy and network security liability
   b. Media liability

II. FIRST PARTY COVERAGE

A. Breach Response and Event Management

Breach response/event management covers:

- Breach counsel (legal advice to assist the insured in negotiating the event, liaising with attorneys general and law enforcement, advising on statutory notification requirements, and providing client-attorney privilege)
- Forensic consulting (expert cybersecurity consulting to investigate whether or not there was an incursion and then to establish how the threat actors got into the system, what they did and how, what data they accessed, etc.)
- Security consulting (remediation of systems, ejecting threat actors / malware / "backdoors")
- Crisis communications consulting (expert advice on messaging to clients, staff, press, and public)
- Data remediation (reconstruction of systems and restoration of data from backups)
- Cost of voluntary or statutorily required notifications to individuals whose personally identifiable information (PII) or protected health information (PHI) has been compromised, plus cost of providing identity theft insurance, credit monitoring, and a 1-800 call center service for victims
- Cost of responding to a regulatory investigation, including fines and penalties

The essence of "Event Management" coverage is to pay for the resources needed for an immediate and comprehensive response to a cyber event (including the cost of investigating to establish whether detected "Indicators of Compromise" are a real event).

In some, particularly older policies "Digital Asset Restoration" (also known as Data Remediation) may not be covered. In the era of ransomware, restoration of systems and the data on those systems (including the programs and operating systems) is a major cost item in recovering from a cyberattack and it is therefore important to check that this element of coverage is present and to the full limit of the policy.

There is rarely public information made available on the breakdown of costs for a substantial Event Management incident; however, in 2013 one of the largest school districts in the country suffered a breach that exposed the PII of some two million individuals. The published breakdown of costs for this event (totaling $26 million[19]) included:

- Breach counsel and legal advice: $9.3 million
- Cybersecurity consulting and remediation of data and systems: $7.5 million
- Notifications and credit monitoring: $7 million
- Public relations, records management, and miscellaneous administration: $2.2 million

This same Community College District was hit with another cyberattack in March 2021 that caused its systems to be taken off-line for two weeks.[20]

*Limitations on Use of Consultants and Vendors
to Respond to a Cyber Event*

Insurers usually have a list of approved vendors (Breach Counsel, Forensic Incident Response, Extortion Consultants, Crisis Communications Consultants) that can be used in response to an event and whose cost will typically be fully reimbursed to the insured (so-called panel vendors). Insurers would normally agree to use of a non-panel vendor if the insured had a particular association or preference for a vendor not on the insurer's pre-approved panel.

---

19. Mary Beth Faller, *Maricopa County Colleges Computer Hack Cost Tops $26M*, The Republic | AZCentral.com (Dec. 17, 2014, 11:15 AM), https://www.azcentral.com/story/news/local/phoenix/2014/12/17/costs-repair-massive-mcccd-computer-hack-top-million/20539491/.

20. Emily Wilder, *Maricopa Community College Classes Resume, Systems Restored after Cyberattack Causes District-Wide Outage*, Ariz. Republic (Mar. 30, 2021, 6:07 PM), https://www.azcentral.com/story/news/local/arizona-education/2021/03/30/maricopa-community-college-classes-resume-after-cyberattack/4812791001/.

As loss ratios deteriorate and as complexity (and therefore cost) of responding to incidents increases due to the prevalence of Covid-induced remote working, insurers are closely reviewing third-party vendor costs incurred in responding to and investigating cyber incidents. To reduce (or at least combat the increase in) these costs, insurers are demonstrating less flexibility in the use of non-panel or pre-agreed vendors. In addition to more challenges related to the use of non-panel vendors—particularly if there was no discussion/vetting of the vendor before the vendor's engagement for an incident—insurers are making fewer exceptions related to vendor rates. It is becoming increasingly common for insurers to only reimburse non-panel vendors at a capped rate that is equal to (or even below) what the insurer would have paid a panel vendor.

B. Interruption and Extra Expense

Interruption and extra expense cover:

- Loss of revenue and extra expense incurred due to the firm's systems being impaired or shut down by a covered event
- Loss of revenue and extra expense due to a failure of the firm's systems (i.e., an unexpected failure or unplanned outage that causes an extended interruption)
- Loss of revenue and extra expense incurred due to a vendor's systems on which you depend being impaired or shut down by a covered event (e.g., a cloud provider, data host, software platform provider, etc.)
- Loss of revenue and extra expense incurred due to failure/outage of a vendor's systems on which you depend

This coverage grant provides reimbursement coverage to the insured for actual lost net income caused by a network security failure, as well as associated extra expense. The greater of a dollar amount retention or waiting period retention of between 6 to 24 hours applies (i.e., business interruption coverage applies after the firm's computer system is down for 6 to 24 hours).

The most frequent events giving rise to these claims in 2021 are ransomware events. Several large law firms have been reported in the press as having suffered a ransomware event causing them to shut down all of their systems. Two very recent examples of the devastating and long-lasting impact of this type of event are the CNA Insurance event and the Colonial Pipeline event. In both cases the corporations involved were obliged to shut down all of their systems. In both cases the shutdown lasted two weeks or more, and full restoration of systems took more time beyond the immediate shutdown. Possibly the largest event of this type would be the NotPetya cyberattack of June 2017 that shut down a large number of public corporations and these reported substantial loss of revenue as a direct result of that attack, "Maersk lost between $250 and $300 million, Mondelez $188 million, and Merck a staggering $870 million."[21]

An extension to this coverage that continues to be available (often for an additional premium) is System Failure coverage. This provides coverage for any systems interruption arising from any unintended, unplanned, and unexpected cause. This could be an outage caused by a system upgrade or patch installation that goes bad and takes down the entire system, or simple human error. Revenue loss from a planned outage would of course not be covered.

Dependent (also known as contingent) business interruption provides reimbursement coverage for the insured for actual lost income caused by a network security failure of a business on which the insured is dependent, as well as associated extra expense. The greater of a dollar amount retention or waiting period retention of between 8 to 24 hours usually applies.

These events are less common, but as law firms move more of their data and operations to cloud providers and outsource functions such as eDiscovery to third party providers, the potential for such interruptions is increasing. A firm that has moved its Document Management system to a cloud provider such as NetDocuments, or that uses Microsoft 365 is wholly dependent on that provider. In the event that the provider is victim of a major cyberattack and is shut down for two or more weeks, it is possible that the firm will not be able to progress existing matters and more importantly will be unable to onboard new matters. This could lead to clients redirecting business to other firms or will see the firm incurring extra expense to develop workarounds so that they can accept new matters. Either way, there is likely to be both extra expense and a loss of revenue.

---

21. *NotPetya: A War-Life Exclusion?*, Ciab (May 2, 2019), https://www.ciab.com/resources/notpetya-a-war-like-exclusion/.

Provided the cause of the loss to the provider is an event that would have been covered under the firm's cyber policy, the Dependent Business Interruption coverage will be triggered.

Contingent coverage for the non-IT supply chain is also available under cyber insurance policies (for both cyber events and system failure events). This coverage provides loss of revenue and extra expense incurred as the result of a non-IT vendor suffering a cyber event or an unexpected system outage. Few, if any, professional services firms have a material exposure to a non-IT vendor and the coverage is usually subject to a low sublimit of $1 million or less.

Dependent business interruption is no longer a default coverage. Furthermore, insurers are requiring the insureds to list and vet the applicable third parties akin to "named perils" as opposed to an "all risk" coverage that would apply for all third-party vendors. The SolarWinds, Accellion, and Microsoft "Hafnium" compromises have caused insurers to review their overall exposure to systemic, aggregated, correlated risks related to the software supply chain (i.e., compromise of a single source supplier causes losses for multiple different clients of the insurer).

The breadth of coverage afforded for business interruption losses is being reviewed by several insurers with a specific mind toward limiting the financial exposure to a systemic event in the following ways:

- Reconsidering waiting periods. In many cases, waiting periods had been negotiated to between six and eight hours (and in some instances removed entirely). The marketplace is beginning to push for waiting periods closer to 24 hours, such as those seen in the Property marketplace.
- Limiting aggregate limit exposure. This is being achieved through the reintroduction of sublimits or requirement of coinsurance.

C. Extortion

Extortion covers:

- Hire of an expert ransom negotiation consultant to negotiate with a Threat Actor who is holding systems hostage via ransomware, denial of service or other attack, or who has stolen data and is threatening to publish, release, or sell it, or who is otherwise credibly threatening the safety and security of the firm's systems or the confidentiality, integrity and/or availability of the data held by the firm

- Payment of a ransom (whether in cryptocurrency or other consideration)

1. Concern and Restrictions around Ransomware

Extortion is another area of insurer scrutiny, especially with regard to the current epidemic of ransomware. Cyber extortion coverage provides reimbursement for the insured for expenses incurred in the investigation of a threat and any extortion payments made to prevent or resolve the threat. Ransomware events and their associated losses are cited by many insurers as a major factor impacting their cyber insurance loss ratios.

Professional services firms are being hit particularly hard by ransomware and other forms of extortion; according to Coveware (a major ransomware negotiation consultant), professional services firms are being victimized with ransomware more frequently than any other sector.[22] In Q3 of 2020, 25 percent of the attacks Coveware responded to were against Professional Services firms with Public Sector and Health Care (the sectors most in the news) accounting for only 11.6 percent and 11.3 percent, respectively.

Insurers are therefore subjecting their clients to particular scrutiny with regard to technology solutions and implementations that reduce exposure to and harden systems against ransomware. The major front-line cyber insurers for law firms now require specific Ransomware Supplemental Questionnaires to be completed. These questionnaires focus on controls and technologies that have been demonstrated to harden systems against:

- Initial intrusion into the system (denying entrance is the best safeguard of all)
- Lateral movement within the system (once in the system, segregation of the network means threat actors cannot easily access other parts of the system to steal information and plant malware)

---

22. *Why Small and Medium-Sized Professional Service Firms Are a Big Target for Ransomware Attacks*, COVEWARE (Jan. 3, 2021), https://www.coveware.com/blog/2020/11/30/why-small-professional-service-firms-are-ransomware-targets.

- Escalation of credentials (if the threat actors cannot get authority to control systems they cannot install and run malware, greatly limiting the damage they can do)
- Theft of sensitive data (minimum access privilege and Data Loss Prevention systems reduces threat actors' ability to steal data that they can hold to ransom)
- Access to backups (if threat actors cannot access and encrypt backups, ransomware is an inconvenience not a crisis)

Insurers are also looking for practices and protocols that are shown to reduce the chances of an attack and to prepare the insured to respond rapidly and effectively to a systems incursion, thereby minimizing the damage, such as:

- Patching systems promptly, managing the patching process to ensure that critical patches are identified and prioritized, and ensuring that patching cadence is monitored and measured
- Phishing training for employees, helping employees to identify attempts to steal credentials or install malware (in addition to phishing simulation training, this can include providing systems for identifying e-mails from external addresses, flagging suspicious e-mail addresses such as those from domains that have been created within 90 days of the e-mail being sent, and "sandboxing" e-mails with malicious attachments, etc.)
- Incident response plan exercises (such as "tabletop simulations") that train the firm to respond rapidly and effectively to specific types of attack (particularly ransomware attacks)

Insurers are adopting a variety of strategies in response to varying standards of preparedness and controls within client systems. The level of losses being incurred by insurers has deteriorated to the extent that insurers are taking sometimes drastic action to control their exposure. Among these strategies:

- In extreme cases, insurers may decline to provide coverage at all. Several leading cyber insurers are reshaping their "book" of clients; this can involve declining to renew clients that do not fit their preferred profile (e.g. firms below or above a particular size, firms with a particular exposure profile such as large quantities of Personally Identifiable Information, etc.) and of course declining to renew or to provide terms to insureds whose controls are seen as inadequate.

- Many insurers are also implementing a limit deployment strategy by which they cap the total aggregate limit they offer to any insured; this takes a variety of forms, including:
  - Capping the maximum limit that they will offer to any insured (for instance up to Q4 2020 limits of $10 million were commonly available to law firms; in 2021 primary limits of $5 million and lower have become more usual).
  - Sublimiting certain coverage grants (for instance an insurer may be willing to offer full limit for most risks but with an aggregate sublimit for Ransomware; for example, they may offer a $5 million limit for Cyber but restrict the available aggregate limit for ransomware claims to $2.5 million).
  - Applying differential deductibles (also called retentions); insurers may offer a policy with a $25,000 deductible across the policy but apply a $250,000 deductible to ransomware claims.
  - Coinsurance is also being proposed, in some cases, in conjunction with a sublimit. This means that the insured is required to share the cost of a ransomware claim with the insurer in addition to the policy deductible. This means that after the deductible is paid the insured may have to pay between 10 percent and 50 percent of the cost of a ransomware claim (this is usually combined with an aggregate sublimit, so on a $5 million policy an insurer may sublimit ransomware to $2.5 million and require the insured to bear a 50 percent coinsurance. This coinsurance provision will usually state that the insured is not allowed to purchase additional insurance to fill the gap).

It is critical to note that while insurers are using these approaches to limit their exposure, these coverage restrictions are not designed to apply solely to a ransomware or cyber extortion insuring agreement (i.e., the restriction is not limited to just the amount of ransom paid). The restrictions are written to apply to ransomware as an attack vector (a "ransomware event"), and therefore the restriction will apply to all costs incurred in connection with a ransomware event.

Case Study

An insured has a $5 million cyber policy with a $100,000 per event retention, a $2.5 million ransomware sublimit and 50 percent ransomware coinsurance. The insured has a ransomware event and pays a $2.1 million ransom but also incurs costs of Breach Counsel, Forensic Investigation, Data Remediation to a total of $1 million and on top of that incurs a loss of revenue of $1 million. The total loss to the insured is $4.1 million and after the deductible the amount of the claim is $4 million.

However, all the costs relate to a ransomware event, so the 50 percent coinsurance for ransomware applies. This means that for this event the maximum amount that the insured can be reimbursed is 50 percent of the $4 million loss, that is, $2 million. In this case, the total is within the ransomware sublimit of $2.5 million so the insurer would reimburse the insured the full $2 million and this would reduce the aggregate limit of the policy to $3 million (the policy aggregate of $5 million less the $2 million paid) and the sublimit for ransomware would be reduced to $500,000 (the ransomware aggregate sublimit of $2.5 million less the $2 million paid for this loss).

2. Restrictions on Extortion Payments

In addition to the limitations that insurers are putting on payments to the ransomware and extortion perpetrators, ransom payments have increasingly come under sanctions scrutiny. In October 2020, the U.S. Department of Treasury's Office of Foreign Asset Compliance (OFAC) issued an advisory alerting companies to the potential sanctions violations for paying or facilitating ransomware payments to foreign Specially Designated Nationals and Blocked Persons (SDNs). The advisory was largely a reminder that payments to these prohibited individuals or entities may result in civil penalties for sanctions violations based on strict liability. In other words, a person in the United States may be held liable even if they did not know they were engaging in a transaction with a prohibited person under sanctions laws and OFAC regulations.[23] This is particularly pertinent to ransomware as it is known that there is an extensive ecosystem behind every ransomware attacker, so even if the immediate attacker is not sanctioned, one of the "supporting entities" (the group that wrote the malware, the group that provided access to the network et al.) might be, so everyone involved in the response to a ransomware attack (the victim, breach counsel, the forensic incident response consultant, the ransomware negotiator et al.) is potentially exposed to sanctions if any of the extortion payment is ultimately received by a sanctioned entity.

The OFAC advisory is very specific in identifying that it is not just the victim that is at risk of breaching sanctions:

> Companies that facilitate ransomware payments to cyber actors on behalf of victims, including financial institutions, cyber insurance firms, and companies involved in digital forensics and incident response, not only encourage future ransomware payment demands but also may risk violating OFAC regulations. This advisory describes these sanctions risks and provides information for contacting relevant U.S. government agencies, including OFAC, if there is a reason to believe the cyber actor demanding ransomware payment may be sanctioned or otherwise have a sanctions nexus. . . .
>
> OFAC may impose civil penalties for sanctions violations based on strict liability, meaning that a person subject to U.S. jurisdiction may be held civilly liable even if it did not know or have reason to know it was engaging in a transaction with a person that is prohibited under sanctions laws and regulations administered by OFAC. . . .
>
> This also applies to companies that engage with victims of ransomware attacks, such as those involved in providing cyber insurance, digital forensics and incident response, and financial services that may involve processing ransom payments.

---

23. U.S. Dep't of Treasury, *Advisory on Potential Sanctions Risks for Facilitating Ransomware Payments* (Oct. 1, 2020), https://home.treasury.gov/system/files/126/ofac_ransomware_advisory_10012020_1.pdf.

OFAC recognizes that ransomware can have a catastrophic impact on the victim and, importantly, on the clients, employees, vendors, investors, and other stakeholders associated with the victim. There has been at least one case where a law firm permanently lost all its legal files, including all back-ups, to ransomware, which had a devastating impact on the firm and its clients.[24] The advisory recognizes that there are situations where the impact on the victim and associated parties is so disproportionately extreme that payment of a ransom may be the only viable strategy, and provides as follows:

> Under OFAC's Enforcement Guidelines, OFAC will also consider a company's self-initiated, timely, and complete report of a ransom-ware attack to law enforcement to be a significant mitigating factor in determining an appropriate enforcement outcome if the situation is later determined to have a sanctions nexus. OFAC will also consider a company's full and timely cooperation with law enforcement both during and after a ransomware attack to be a significant mitigating factor when evaluating a possible enforcement outcome.

It is therefore greatly in the victim firm's interests to involve the FBI at the very earliest stages of a ransomware incident. In addition to the OFAC considerations (and the FBI will be able to assist in identifying whether the attackers are a sanctioned entity), the FBI often has valuable information about the attackers: How reliable are they? Will they delete the information they have stolen? Will the decryption tool work and what percentage of data can the victim expect to recover? While the FBI will never approve or recommend payment of a ransom, they can provide a great deal of use-ful information that will assist the victim in the decision-making process of whether or not paying a ransom is a viable solution.

---

24. *American Law Firm Admits Entire Server of Legal Files Fell Victim to Cryptolocker*, WeLiveSecurity (Feb. 10, 2014, 10:29 AM), https://www.welivesecurity.com/2014/02/10 /american-law-firm-admits-entire-server-of-legal-files-fell-victim-to-cryptolocker/.

D. Additional First Party Coverages

Additional first party coverages can include (these are usually subject to a sublimit):

- "Bricking"—the cost of replacing physical equipment rendered inoperable and irreparable by malware
- Reputational Damage—loss of revenue resulting from adverse publicity arising from a publicly disclosed breach or other covered cyber event
- Voluntary Shutdown—loss of revenue resulting from a proactive decision to shut down systems in order to avert, prevent, or mitigate a cyber event
- eCrime—the theft of the firm's or its clients' money by deception (social engineering, business e-mail compromise, invoice fraud, etc.)
- Cryptojacking—the excess cost of utilities as the result of computer systems being hijacked to run software that mines cryptocurrency
- Telephone Fraud—the excess cost of telecommunications service as the result of the system being hijacked and used for long-distance telephony or for calling premium telephone services
- Proof of Loss Costs—the cost of hiring a forensic accounting firm to analyze and prove the firm's loss of revenue from a cyber event
- Betterment—additional costs incurred in enhancing systems to improve security after a breach

III. Third Party Coverages

A. Security Failure and Data Privacy Liability

Security failure and data privacy liability cover:

- Defense costs and damages arising from a lawsuit or claim for damages from a third party alleging that they were harmed by the firm's negligence in allowing or failing to prevent:
  - Unauthorized access, compromise, loss or theft of Personally Identifiable Information or Protected Health Information (from the firm's

systems or from the systems of a third party to whom the firm has entrusted the data for storage or processing)

- Unauthorized access, compromise, loss or theft of confidential data (from the firm's systems or from the systems of a third party to whom the firm has entrusted the data for storage or processing)
- Cross-infection of systems by malware, or use of the firm's systems to launch a Denial of Service Attack or other form of attack (e.g. use of the firm's website to launch a "watering hole" attack)
- Failure, outage, or other unavailability of the firm's systems causing them to be inaccessible to the third party for processing of data, provision of a platform or other service on which the third party was dependent
- Defense of a Regulatory Proceeding, including fines and penalties (where insurable by law) under HIPAA, GDPR, CCPA/CPRA, BIPA, and other privacy rights statutes. In some policies, it is possible to include coverage for Regulatory Proceedings arising from breach of the compliance requirements of statutes such as GDPR and CPRA
- Penalties levied under a Payment Card Industry Master Services Agreement as a result of breach of Payment Card Industry Data Security Standards (PCI-DSS)
- Wrongful collection of data

In the majority of cases, if a law firm suffers a cyberattack that compromises confidential information (whether Personally Identifiable Information, Protected Health Information or other confidential information, trade secrets, M&A deal information, or other sensitive data) the data will have been entrusted to the firm by clients in connection with the work or engagement that the firm is undertaking on behalf of that client. In some cases, the firm may have received the information from another law firm, again in connection with litigation or other consultative professional work. This implies that any compromise, loss, theft, or leak of that information will be an infringement of the firm's duty under ABA Model Rule 1.6 governing confidentiality of information and the requirement for client consent to any disclosure. This means that any demand or legal action by the client against the firm is most likely to be rooted in a breach of professional duty, malpractice, or negligence and is therefore most appropriately responded to by the firm's professional liability policy.

Lawyer's Professional Liability policies are typically broad in scope and often provide more advantageous terms and conditions than the Security & Privacy Liability section of a cyber policy; for example, many Lawyer's Professional Liability policies are structured as reimbursement policies, giving the firm control and management of the claim, whereas Cyber Policies are typically "Duty to Defend" in which the insurer appoints counsel and manages the claim.

Managing the interplay between the two policies is becoming more difficult as cyber risks are becoming larger and more complex. Some professional liability insurers are beginning to restrict coverage for cyber exposures (including some that are applying absolute exclusions of claims arising from cyber events). At the same time, many cyber policies have absolute exclusions for professional risks. It is important when arranging (or renewing) a cyber policy to determine what terms and conditions apply to each policy and to prescribe how each should respond when a cyber event gives rise to an accusation of professional negligence or malpractice.

The extent of Regulatory coverage in cyber policies varies considerably from those that provide broad coverage of actions from Regulators grounded in breach of any applicable privacy statute (including provisions regarding compliance), to those that take a more "named perils" approach and require that there (1) be a covered cyber event to trigger coverage and (2) a breach of a specified privacy statute. This is an important consideration when one takes into account that two of the largest fines levied against U.S. corporations (Amazon, $888 million;[25] Google, $57 million;[26] and Facebook, up to $366 million[27]) under GDPR related to compliance failures under the

---

25. Stephanie Bodoni, *Amazon Gets Records $888 Million EU Fine over Data Violations*, BLOOMBERG (July 30, 2021, 7:03 AM), https://www.bloomberg.com/news/articles/2021-07-30/amazon-given-record-888-million-eu-fine-for-data-privacy-breach.

26. Chris Brook, *Google Fined $57M by Data Protection Watchdog over GDPR Violations*, DIGITAL GUARDIAN (Sept. 17, 2020), https://digitalguardian.com/blog/google-fined-57m-data-protection-watchdog-over-gdpr-violations.

27. Neil Hodge, *Facebook Reserves $366M for Expected GDPR Fines in Ireland*, COMPLIANCE WEEK (Dec. 11, 2020, 3:13 PM), https://www.complianceweek.com/gdpr/facebook-reserves-366m-for-expected-gdpr-fines-in-ireland/29829.article.

statute, not breaches of data by cyber hackers. Many cyber policies would not consider covering the defence costs and penalties in these cases because neither involved a covered cyber peril.

The proliferation of new privacy statutes together with questions regarding the extent to which regulatory inquiries and actions might be covered under the various insurance policies (Cyber, Professional Liability, Media Liability, Commercial General Liability, Employment Practices Liability, etc.) makes it important to understand the extent of coverage under the cyber policy and the availability of coverage under other policies.

One of the more problematic statutes is the state of Illinois' Biometric Information Privacy Act (BIPA). This act is intended to protect individuals who have been asked to provide biometric information to facilitate identification (from facial recognition in the workplace to providing fingerprint identification to enter a theme park). The act has a number of novel features, including:

- Requirements for notice to individuals who are being asked to provide Biometric Information, including how the information will be used and stored as well as how long it will be kept.
- Companies collecting Biometric Information must receive written informed consent from the individual.
- Penalties for failure to comply with the notice, consent, storage, and other compliance requirements.
- Statutory standing for individuals whose information has been compromised or whose data was collected without appropriate compliance steps being followed. Statutory standing opens the door to class action lawsuits, and since the law was passed, the number of such lawsuits in the state of Illinois has escalated rapidly.

Most policies are silent on the specific definition of Biometric Information, relying on a definition of Private Information that references definitions of such information as provided by the applicable statute under which action is being brought (whether by a regulator or individual). However, as legal actions accumulate with regard to Biometrics, some insurers are beginning to express concern about the costs and impact not only of defense but the sometimes extremely substantial settlements and penalties being levied. For example, a Northern District judge in California approved Facebook's $650 million class-action settlement for the lawsuit regarding its photo-scanning feature.[28]

As companies reeled from Illinois' Biometric Information Privacy Act (BIPA) liability (with New York in the process of imitating),[29] they turned to their insurance for redress, only to be met by a solid wall of coverage denials. But insurance coverage for BIPA liability may exist under several different types of policies: general liability, directors' and officers', employment practices, as well as cyber.

How will a cyber insurance policy respond to a BIPA complaint? As with most answers in insurance, it depends. A robust cyber insurance policy, properly designed, may afford the policyholder coverage provided the definition of Private Information is sufficiently broad and also provided the policy grants coverage for compliance wrongs as well as those arising from a data breach. Policies vary considerably on this latter issue; some cyber policies have this language written into the policy wording, some will endorse it on (often for payment of an additional premium) while some insurers will not provide this coverage at all. Some cyber policies may contain an exclusion for Biometric Information, so it is important to pay close attention to all aspects of the wording.

Currently, there is not a stand-alone policy specifically designed to address BIPA claims, and given the increase of claims in Illinois, it is unlikely that such a policy will arise.

Coverage for regulatory fines and penalties, like those that could be issued under BIPA, is typically available in cyber policies in some form or another; however, it is important to note that in some states insurance of such fines and penalties is illegal and while many policies contain a "most favorable venue" provision that may allow these to be covered if the firm is resident in a liberal state where fines are legal and the fine was levied in a more restrictive state, some states have "long arm" provisions that effectively

---

28. Patel v. Facebook, 932 F.3d 1264 (9th Cir. 2019), *cert. denied*, 140 S. Ct. 937 (2020). In *Patel*, the plaintiff sued Facebook for its use of facial recognition software without the consent of the users. The Court found that there was either actual harm or a material risk of harm to privacy interests.

29. While the New York bill has not yet been enacted, it does bear striking similarities to BIPA. If the litigation maelstrom in Illinois serves as an example, New York business owners should be wary of potential exposure should the bill ultimately become law.

prohibit the insurance of fines and penalties anywhere in the USA. There is a specialist insurance market for Fines and Penalties insurance in Bermuda, which being outside the jurisdiction of the United States is able to write such policies; but these policies are expensive, complex, and few insurance brokers have access to those markets.

The biggest hurdles for companies seeking insurance coverage for liabilities arising from Biometric Information (or indeed for liabilities arising from compliance wrongs arising from the provisions of may newer Data Privacy Acts) under a policy not specifically designed to address data breaches are the many exclusions added in recent years by insurance companies to their policies for disclosure of confidential information and data-related liability. For example, in one case in which a policyholder sued its insurance company for BIPA liability under the "invasion of privacy" coverage, the insurance company relied on an exclusion for claims arising from violations of a statute that "addresses, prohibits or limits the printing, dissemination, disposal, collecting, recording sending, transmitting, communicating or distribution of material or information" to deny coverage. Insureds who do not have cyber insurance that would explicitly cover such "wrongs" frequently rely on creative interpretations of other policies in order to try to obtain coverage for something that was not the intent of the policy; by the same token insurers are being more rigorous about imposing exclusions on non-cyber policies and invoking other exclusions that might excuse them from covering cyber exposures under a non-cyber policy.

In another case brought under an EPLI policy, the insurance company relied on an "Access to or Disclosure of Confidential or Personal and Data-related Liability" exclusion, which denied coverage for "[d]amages arising out of (1) [a]ny access to or disclosure of any person's or organization's confidential or personal information, including patents, trade secrets, processing methods, customer lists, financial information, credit card information, health information or any other type of non-public information; or (2) the loss of, loss of use of, damage to, corruption of, inability to access, or inability to manipulate electronic data."[30] The impact of this is to clarify the intent of coverage and to reduce the scope of coverage as it relates to

---

30. Pamela Hans, John Lacey & Marc Schein, *Maximizing Coverage amid the Biometric Liability Wave*, ABA (May 19, 2020), https://www.americanbar.org/groups/litigation/committees/insurance-coverage/articles/2020/maximizing-coverage-biometric-liability/.

Private Information. Policyholders should be aware of these exclusions as they renew or place coverage, especially if they already use or plan to use biometric information.

B. Media Liability

Media liability covers:

- Defense costs and damages arising from a lawsuit or claim for damages from a third party alleging that they were harmed by the firm via publication (electronic or hard copy) or broadcast (including via traditional analogue broadcast media), of:
  - Defamation, libel, or slander (including product defamation)
  - Copyright, trademark, or trade dress infringement
  - Invasion of privacy, false light
  - Eavesdropping or other invasion of the right to private occupancy
  - Negligent or intentional infliction of emotional distress

Media Liability coverage has been a part of cyber insurance policies for many years, although for law firms it is the least-used section of the policy, largely because it substantially overlaps with the Advertising Injury coverage granted in typical Commercial General Liability (CGL) policies.[31] CGL policies typically have no deductible and no "Other Insurance" clause and are therefore automatically called on first for any claim that might be made against the insured, with the cyber providing coverage excess of that. In many cases, particularly defamation cases, the Lawyer's Professional Liability policy may also be called on to respond if the actions that gave rise to the claim arose in the context of a professional engagement.

This section of the policy could develop more prominence as CGL underwriters are narrowing the coverage grant under their policies, largely as a result of some unfavorable decisions and settlements that have pushed interpretation of coverage beyond the limits of underwriters' intent. As media

---

31. Kevin Kallnich & Laura Grabouski, *Evolution of Insurance Coverage for Intellectual Property Litigation*, ABA LITIG. SECTION (Feb. 20, 2020), https://www.americanbar.org/groups/litigation/committees/insurance-coverage/articles/2020/insurance-intellectual-property-litigation/.

content and activity is increasingly digitized there is an inevitable logic to the coverage for a non-physical damage / injury coverage to move to the policy that is explicitly designed to address these types of risk.

Examples of situations that have led to law firms reporting incidents to their cyber insurers (in all of these cases the CGL policy responded first, but the claim was accepted by the cyber insurer on an excess basis). None of these incidents went to court so there is no public record, but they serve as examples of how law firms can incur media liability:

- A law firm hired a web-designer to create a new website for them. The firm was happy with the results, until another law firm accused them of copyright infringement. It turned out that the web-designer had copied the underlying code of the other firm's website and "repurposed" it with new graphics and information.
- A law firm was contacted by a commercial real-estate entity over a stock photograph of a distinctive building that was prominently displayed on the landing page of their website. The real estate entity was not a client of the firm and was concerned that the very recognizable building implied that they were (the firm changed the photograph).
- A member of the procurement staff of a large law firm posted some extremely disparaging comments about a supplier on social media. The individual thought that he had posted them in "private mode," but they were visible to the general public. The supplier very quickly found out and threatened to sue the firm for disparagement.
- An attorney was being interviewed about an old case that he had participated in; in the interview the attorney mixed up the names of the defendant and the defendant's attorney, stating by name that the defendant's attorney had committed multiple very serious crimes. The attorney in question sued for defamation.

Many law firms disregard media liability as an insignificant risk and some believe that they have no exposure; however, as the first two examples illustrate, as businesses move to the Internet and with social media becoming an increasingly important communication tool, the possibilities for infringement, defamation, and other media wrongs increase greatly;

and, if CGL insurers continue to limit and even remove the coverage from their policies, the emphasis will move to cyber to pick up these exposures.

It is important to note that while media liability insurance does provide the firm with some coverage for infringement of "Intellectual Property" in the form of copyright, trademark, trade dress, etc., the policies usually have explicit exclusions relating to other forms of intellectual property, particularly Patents and Trade Secrets.[32] Patents and Trade Secrets are typically the most valuable assets in a law firm's possession,[33] so the question is often asked as to how the law firm can protect itself and how these assets can be insured.

The Patents and Trade Secrets held by law firms generally belong to the firm's clients, who may insure them as an asset via one of the available intellectual property insurance entities. The issue for the law firm is what happens if these assets of their clients are stolen as the result of a breach of the law firm's servers? In this case, the client is most likely to take legal action against the law firm for failing to protect the confidentiality of the data (in breach of ABA Model Rule 1.6) and for negligence in the course of a professional engagement. The harm done to the client may be substantial and the negotiation and possible litigation arising is likely to be both complex and expensive; however, as this is a claim against the firm for professional negligence or malpractice, the firm's Professional Liability policy should respond.

The value of the law firm's own patents and trade secrets is not covered, and if the firm has such an exposure it can only be covered in the specialist intellectual property insurance market.

---

32. *Id.*

33. Madison Alder, Perry Cooper & Lydia Wheeler, *Corporate Secrets at Risk in Hack of U.S. Courts Documents (1)*, BLOOMBERG LAW (Jan. 7, 2021, 3:35 PM), https://news.bloomberg law.com/privacy-and-data-security/corporate-secrets-at-risk-in-hack-of-u-s-courts-docu ments. Trade secrets often the most valuable information assets: Financial Statement Impact of Intellectual Property & Cyber Assets: *Intangible Assets Strategy, Capital Markets and Risk Management*, AON, https://www.aon.com/thought-leadership/ponemoninstitutereport.jsp.

IV. Multiple Lines of Insurance Collaboration

Do we really need cyber insurance? Legal organizations need insurance that covers cyber exposures, but the form of coverage may not be the same for all lawyers. It is critical that we examine the financial damage from cyber perils and determine the cost-benefit analysis of each potential insurance policy so each legal organization can make a quantifiable, objective, fact-based decision with respect to whether, and how, to purchase cyber insurance coverage. In general, as law firms increasingly rely on digital assets and technology, cyber exposures are highly underinsured compared to physical assets (Property, Plant and Equipment or PPE) (see Fig. 16.2).[34] The majority of organizations do not assign the same priority to data assets as they do to physical assets.[35]

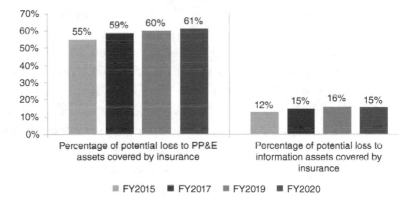

Figure 16.2 Percentage "Intangible Assets" versus "Tangible Assets" covered by insurance

There is not a standard cyber insurance policy form. It can be confusing because insurance carriers and cyber insurance policies are not consistent in how they address cyber perils. For instance, most cyber insurers exclude

---

34. *Intangible Assets Strategy, supra* note 33.
35. Robert Handfield, PhD, et al., 4th Annual Data Quality & Governance Study 2020, https://scm.ncsu.edu/wp-content/uploads/2021/02/4th-Annual-Data-Quality-Governance-Study-2020-1-1.pdf.

first party coverage for stolen laptops and other computer hardware from cyber policies. Therefore, insureds must look to their property policies for their first party loss to replace the hardware. However, cyber insurers will generally cover the potential third party liability owed to clients and other third parties for the unauthorized disclosure or loss of information from the stolen hardware.

In the following outline of other lines of insurance and the extent to which they may or may not provide some coverage for events triggered by a cyber peril, it is important to remember that this is a dynamic environment. Insurers are conducting extensive reviews of wordings with a view to eliminating unintended cyber coverage (so-called Silent Cyber) and making policies explicitly clear on the extent to which they will or will not cover events that are the result of a cyber peril. Lloyd's of London has a formal edict out to all Lloyd's insurers requiring them to carry out Silent Cyber reviews and to amend their policies so that they are clear as to the extent of cyber coverage provided.

The Silent Cyber issue is becoming less prominent over time, partly because insurers are paying attention to it and are issuing clarifying endorsements to non-cyber policies; but another dynamic is that more and more firms are purchasing dedicated cyber insurance and therefore there is less incentive for firms that are victims of an attack to seek coverage from a non-cyber policy. Nonetheless, the overlap of insurance policies and the severity of cyberattacks does mean that insureds should pay attention to this issue and ensure that insurance policies are appropriately structured to coordinate with one another to maximize coverage. Insureds should also consider carefully what limits of insurance are appropriate to the exposure. Experience has shown that when multiple lines of insurance could be applicable, non-expert judges could issue contradictory decisions that create confusion and unpredictability for insurance law,[36] which leads to

---

36. Emmis Commc'ns Corp. v. Illinois Nat'l Ins. Co., case no. 18-3392, in the U.S. Court of Appeals for the Seventh Circuit: The short-lived unanimous ruling, which held that a D&O liability policyholder could lose coverage by notifying multiple insurers about a claim, rattled some legal departments and led to a round of intense briefing but had little effect on the industry otherwise. Brandon Lowrey, *What One Scrapped Opinion Might Say about Judge Barret*, Law360 (Oct. 2, 2020), https://www.law360.com/privateequity/articles/1316104.

uncertainty for clients and avoidable situations where coverage proves to be unavailable, inadequate or illusory.

A. Professional Liability

Lawyers and law firms have historically been responsible for holding their clients' data and information private (ABA Model Rule 1.6), and in many cases client engagement letters or contracts have specific provisions relating to the confidentiality and protection of data and the return or destruction of data once the engagement is terminated. In the past, a standard lawyers' professional liability policy was all that was needed to provide liability protection from unintended disclosures. The most significant financial impact was the damages the firm's client would suffer and would seek compensation for in a suit for malpractice. However, technology has dramatically changed that exposure. Whereas a misplaced file or stolen briefcase in a paper-dominated world would normally not make much information available beyond an account or two, the average smartphone today can enable access to a client's or firm's entire history. Further, thumb drives that have the capacity to hold gigabytes of data dramatically expand the consequences of a breach, as well as the costs associated with responding to one, whether from a hacker or simple human error (for perspective, 1GB of data represents approximately 50,000 to 75,000 pages of data, as a stack of paper it would be the height of a utility pole[37]). Data privacy statutes now apply onerous obligations on firms that leak Personally Identifiable Information or Protected Health Information, requiring notifications to be issued, credit monitoring and ID Theft insurance to be provided. On top of these obligations, regulators can investigate the event and levy fines and penalties and under the terms of some statutes (e.g., the Biometric Information Privacy Act in Illinois) anyone whose data is compromised in an attack automatically gains standing to sue for damages, raising the prospect of lengthy and expensive class action litigation.

The good news for law firms and legal organizations is that a well-crafted professional liability insurance policy should address costs of defense for

---

37. Paulette Keheley, *How Many Pages in a Gigabyte? A Litigator's Guide*, DIGITALWAR ROOM (Apr. 2, 2020), https://www.digitalwarroom.com/blog/how-many-pages-in-a-gigabyte.

a claim against the firm, indemnity, and settlement expenses arising from professional services. Often, the only reason a firm has third-party information is because of an engagement on a matter, hence the connection to their professional services. The key for law firms is to maximize existing coverage and consider how to address the significant gaps that exist due to changes in technology and expenses of forensic and related costs that may not be covered by a professional liability policy. Some professional liability policies explicitly provide for first party costs incurred in the investigation of a claim, but with cyber events the first party costs are substantial and immediate and it cannot be known for some time (months to possibly years) whether the cyber event will give rise to a claim for professional negligence. It can therefore be difficult to know if costs incurred in the immediate response to a cyber claim will ever be part of a professional liability claim and no professional liability insurer will willingly pay substantial event response costs on the assumption that professional negligence claims might follow. To date there is remarkably little evidence of cyber events giving rise to professional negligence claims.

The key consideration, for large and small law firms alike, is what each firm considers to be its relative financial statement materiality impact, given that professional liability is unlikely to contribute significantly (if at all) to the first party costs of a cyber event. For instance, a $17,000 cyber ransomware attack on a firm of two to five lawyers may be considered "catastrophic" and an essential risk to be addressed by cyber insurance coverage. In addition to the cost of meeting the ransom payment, the firm will be faced with requirements for legal advice, forensic investigation, remediation of data and systems (when the cyber criminals provide a decryption key it is rare for all data and systems to be recovered; 80 percent is considered a good result), loss of revenue, and loss of reputation. In extreme cases, the firm may not, without the expert resources available through cyber insurance, be able to satisfy the ransom at all and could lose access to all of its data.[38]

---

38. *American Law Firm Admits Entire Server of Legal Files Fell Victim to Cryptolocker,* WᴇLɪᴠᴇSᴇᴄᴜʀɪᴛʏ (Feb. 10, 2014, 10:29 AM), https://www.welivesecurity.com/2014/02/10/american-law-firm-admits-entire-server-of-legal-files-fell-victim-to-cryptolocker/.

On top of these costs, many firms specialize in areas of law that involve large amounts of Personally Identifiable Information and Protected Health Information, compromise of which can result in enormous costs of complying with notification requirements under state privacy laws and there may be a regulatory investigation and fines and penalties on top of that. HIPAA penalties for data breaches can mount up very rapidly (penalties range from $100 to $50,000 per individual violation capped at $1,500,000 per calendar year[39]). Even a small firm can incur substantial costs from employee records when it is taken into consideration that Human Resources records can include family members, and historic records (that can contain up to 30 years of digitized records) will include employees, temporary workers, contract workers, job applicants, interns, summer associates, and so on.

Some law firms rely on extensions of coverage for cyber provided under a "Business Owner's Policy" without realizing that in many cases this coverage may be subject to a low sublimit and other restrictions of coverage. In one case such a firm was hit with ransomware and was effectively "unproductive" for three months, losing an estimated $700,000 in revenue. When they made a claim against their Business Owner's Policy they found that there was a sublimit of $20,000 for "computer virus" and the insurer's refusal to pay any more than this was upheld in litigation.[40]

In extreme cases, there is no question that a cyber incident can be catastrophically damaging to a law firm. The most famous case (so famous that it was turned into a Hollywood movie, "The Laundromat"[41]) was law firm Mossack Fonseca that closed down[42] as a result of the leak of their entire database of firm and client information to the International Consortium of Investigative Journalists. This event demonstrated the enormous and

---

39. Benjamin Elmore, *What Is a HIPAA Violation? The Cost of Penalties*, Accountable (May 12, 2021), https://www.accountablehq.com/post/cost-of-noncompliance.

40. *Law Firm Sues Insurer over $700K in Lost Billings Due to Ransomware Attack: eDiscovery Trends*, https://cloudnine.com/ediscoverydaily/electronic-discovery /law-firm-sues-insurer-700k-lost-billings-due-ransomware-attack-ediscovery-trends/.

41. *The Laundromat*, IMDb (2019), https://www.imdb.com/title/tt5865326/.

42. *Panama Papers Law Firm Mossack Fonseca to Shut Down after Tax Scandal*, Reuters (Mar. 14, 2018, 5:22 PM), https://www.reuters.com/article/us-panama-corruption /panama-papers-law-firm-mossack-fonseca-to-shut-down-after-tax-scandal-idUSKCN1GQ34R.

widespread impact that a cyber leak from a law firm can have, from the collapse of the firm itself to the resignation of the Prime Minister of Iceland.[43]

In the event of a cyber incident, any claim from a client alleging that they have been harmed by the leak or compromise of their data in that event should be addressed by your professional liability insurer. Insurance companies do not segregate professional liability coverage based upon the peril that created it. For example, law firms do not buy one policy for claims arising out of conflicts and another for claims arising out of missed statutes of limitations. Recall when facsimile machines were introduced and firms were transmitting documents electronically for the first time. If a firm sent a document to the wrong fax number and damages were suffered by a client, the resulting claim would be covered by a professional liability policy. These were the first digital "breaches" or unintended disclosure claims that law firms faced.

Lawyers' Professional Liability policies typically do not have cyber exclusions, although such exclusions are beginning to be seen in certain markets around the world in response to initiatives (particularly out of Lloyd's of London) to ensure that all policies are explicit in how they cover, or do not cover, cyber perils (the so-called Silent Cyber issue). This is something that needs to be watched with extreme care by insurance brokers and their clients, because it is quite possible for gaps to be created between professional liability policies that have a cyber exclusion and cyber policies that have a professional liability exclusion.

When it comes to data breaches, however, the traditional insurance coverages that most law firms typically have may not provide enough or, in some instances, any protection. Insurance Services Organization commercial property policies may provide a small and very limited amount of coverage for loss due to a virus, but this is increasingly being pared down as insurers move toward absolute exclusions. Standard property damage coverage typically offers very limited protection unless there is physical damage to or destruction of the equipment on which the data is stored.

---

43. Katrin Jakobsdottir, *Iceland's Prime Minister: "The Ice Is Leaving,"* N.Y. TIMES (Aug. 17, 2019), https://www.nytimes.com/2016/04/06/world/europe/panama-papers-iceland.html.

Cybercriminals, with the exception of ransomware attack methods, rarely irretrievably destroy data, because simple destruction cannot be monetized and therefore has no payoff to the criminals unless conducted for political reasons or is industrial sabotage. General liability policies typically only address physical injury to persons or tangible property, as well as the insured's liability arising from the publication of material that violates a person's right to privacy. Policies such as the Surety and Fidelity Computer Crime Policy, which are commonly assumed to provide coverage for cyber liability-like claims, generally exclude losses resulting directly or indirectly from the theft of confidential information, indirect consequential loss of any nature, and loss of potential income, including but not limited to interest and dividends.

Professional liability policies are, in the final analysis, a highly evolved product for a niche exposure and therefore are not an appropriate vehicle to address the many, varied, and wide-ranging exposures arising from a cyber event. While there are areas of overlap between professional liability and cyber policies, they are fundamentally intended to cover different risks and it should be recognized that each has its own specialty and value as a tool in a law firm's risk management toolkit:

- A professional liability trigger is generally an alleged error, omission, or negligent act (e.g., a demand against the firm based on the allegations) and responds to a demand made by a third party. A robust cyber insurance policy will be triggered by the cyber incident and cover first-party costs incurred prior to a third-party demand to help the firm respond and avoid a third-party claim or limit its magnitude.
- Professional liability policies are limited to claims due to the limited definition of "professional services," as compared to a cyber insurance policy's broader scope of coverage based on first party triggers such as a failure of security, a privacy event, or even a reasonable suspicion that such an event may have happened.
- Professional liability policies are not intended to address first-party business interruption or extra expense costs to the firm due to cyber incidents that knock out or cause degradation to the firm's computer system, or extortion payments demanded by ransomware operators or

cybercriminals that have stolen sensitive data. Cyber policies have specific affirmative coverage grants for such perils and damages.

- Cyber policies, unlike most professional liability policies, may include media/publication coverage, identified by insurance carriers as "advertising injuries," such as libel, slander, invasion of privacy, and misappropriation of advertising ideas, although insurers may differ in the breadth of coverage they provide in this area. Under cyber liability coverage, one would typically see coverage afforded for disclosure injury, reputational injury (even if limited), and content injury, such as trademark, service mark, and copyright infringement.[44]

- Some cyber insurance carriers offer increasingly expanded loss mitigation services with the policy, such as cyber assessments, mitigation services, and incident response. While this may not appeal to large firms that prefer to control the choice of outside vendors, the additional cyber risk mitigation may be quite valuable to smaller and mid-size firms, and available at a significantly reduced cost.

- The assessment of coverage and gaps can encourage an open dialogue about opportunities to shore up systems and procedures. It can also help identify holes in processes and protocols as well as gaps in the insurance portfolio that potentially could be filled with cyber insurance. When identifying cyber coverage gaps, it is useful to leverage external expertise. For instance, it is critical to partner with an insurer and insurance broker with expertise in cyber policy wording customization and claims handling.[45]

---

44. Evolution of Insurance Coverage for Intellectual Property Litigation: Policyholders and coverage practitioners should be aware of changes in available coverage. Kallnich & Grabouski, *supra* note 31.

45. Several cyber insurance coverage claims have been denied due to lack of a common understanding of the coverage between the insurer and the insured and/or inadequate policy wording customization:

- Columbia Cas. Co. v. Cottage Health Sys., C.D. Cal. No. CV 15-03432 2015 WL 4497730 (AGRx) (C.D. Cal. July 17, 2015) (CNA NetProtect360 policy coverage denied by CNA due to failure of insured to meet minimum required practices, misrepresentation in the application, and other defects; declination overturned after CNA lost a decision with respect to enforceability of the ADR clause).
- Travelers Prop. Cas. Co. of Am. v. Fed. Recovery Servs., No. 2:2014cv00170—Document 45 (D. Utah 2015) (CyberFirst policy coverage denied by Travelers due to alleged

B. Property Damage and Business Interruption

The traditional insurance coverages that most law firms typically have may not provide enough or, in some instances, any protection against a cyber event. Insurance Services Organization commercial property policies may provide a small and very limited amount of coverage for loss due to a virus, but this is increasingly being pared down as insurers move toward absolute cyber exclusions and clarifying language that explicitly defines data as non-physical property. Standard property damage coverage typically offers very limited protection unless there is physical damage to or destruction of the equipment on which the data is stored.

Cybercriminals, with the exception of ransomware attack methods, rarely irretrievably destroy data because simple destruction cannot be monetized and therefore has no payoff to the criminals (unless conducted for political reasons or is industrial sabotage; for instance the NotPetya attack of June 2017 appears to have been part of a Russian act of aggression against the government of the Ukraine, with multiple international firms being hit as collateral damage, including at least one major, global, law firm). However, ransomware in particular can lead to extensive impairment of the firm's ability to operate (multiple law firms have suffered periods of interruption of up to two weeks, followed by many more weeks of severely impaired operations as the result of ransomware or other virus attacks). In the absence of demonstrable physical damage to property, a property damage/business interruption policy is not likely to provide much if any compensation to

---

intentional excluded act of withholding distribution of information by insured; denial upheld).

- P.F. Chang's China Bistro, Inc. v. Fed. Ins. Co., No. CV-15-01322-PHX-SMM, 2016 U.S. Dist. LEXIS 70749 (D. Ariz. May 26, 2016) (coverage denied by Chubb for Payment Card Industry Fines & Penalties, which would seem to be the main vulnerability and damages that should be addressed for a restaurant that accepts payment via credit cards).

- New Hotel Monteleone, LLC v. Certain Underwriters at Lloyd's of London, Subscribing to Ascent Cyberpro Policy No. ASC14C00944, No. 2:16-CV-00061-ILRL-JCW (E.D. La. filed Jan. 5, 2016 (New Hotel Monteleone made claim against its insurer alleging lack of adequate limits for Payment Card Industry fines (insurer denied claim); Eustis Insurance Co. filed a third-party complaint against wholesale insurance broker R-T Specialty, Inc. after the broker allegedly failed to properly advise New Hotel Monteleone, Inc. about its cybersecurity exposures and coverage that R-T Specialty was tasked to procure).

the insured. The case cited earlier of the law firm that suffered a three-month interruption of its business as the result of a ransomware attack is an instance in point. The firm sued the insurer behind their Business Owner's Policy (BOP), hoping to recover $700,000 of lost revenue (the firm had no stand-alone cyber policy and their BOP had an extension for cyber events affording only $20,000 of coverage, which the insurer paid in full). The courts sided with the insurer holding that the policy was very clear that the only coverage for a cyber event was subject to the $20,000 sublimit.[46]

While ransomware demands have exploded, they are not the only harm inflicted by these attacks. In contrast to the 2017 decision just cited, a decision from 2020 indicates that policyholders may sometimes be successful in securing coverage for a cyber event from a property damage policy.[47] In this case, the court held that a policyholder that suffered serious damage and losses from a ransomware attack was entitled to all-risk property coverage for lost data, lost software, and a dysfunctional computer system and hardware. The court held:

> Here, not only did Plaintiff sustain a loss of its data and software, but Plaintiff is left with a slower system, which appears to be harboring a dormant virus, and is unable to access a significant portion of software and stored data. Because the plain language of the Policy provides coverage for such losses and damage, summary judgment will be granted in favor of Plaintiff's interpretation of the Policy terms.

This was a particularly influential decision in which the courts found that the computer system's impairment constituted property damage as defined in the policy, despite being still functional following a ransomware attack. This is an excellent example of "Silent Cyber" where a non-cyber insurance policy has no explicit statement of position on cyber perils and consequently has been held to afford coverage for the impact of a cyberattack.

There are two major takeaways from this case:

---

46. Moses, Afonso, Ryan, Ltd. v. Sentinel Ins. Co., Case No. 1:17-cv-00157 (D.R.I. Apr. 21, 2017).

47. Nat'l Ink & Stitch, LLC v. State Auto Prop. & Cas. Ins. Co., 435 F. Supp. 3d 679 (D. Md. 2020).

1. Despite the court finding that there was coverage, it is clear that the insurer believed that there was not and was prepared to fight the case to establish its intent (it is worth mentioning that the insured was offered two essentially identical Business Owner's Policies from the same insurer at inception, one that explicitly included cyber coverage at a higher premium than the one they purchased, that did not have explicit cyber coverage). It is notable that this is one of many lawsuits that have arisen when a firm that does not have a dedicated cyber insurance policy suffers a cyber event and finds itself faced with enormous and potentially uncovered costs as a result. No insured wants to be in the position of having to sue to make an insurance recovery, particularly when the suit is for coverage that is available on a policy that they have elected not to purchase. The lack of explicit coverage leaves them in an uncertain situation where they may make some recovery, or they may incur all the costs of a lawsuit and do not persuade the court of their case.

2. Insurers are very concerned about "Silent Cyber" and will continue to amend and endorse non-cyber policies to make it explicitly clear whether or not the policy will pay for a cyber event. In general, these endorsements are not absolute exclusions that resemble the pollution exclusions but define what constitutes "property" (specifically excluding data and software) and "property damage" more closely so that non-damage cyber events such as those caused by ransomware will not be covered, but a fire or other physical damage caused by malicious programming will continue to be covered. The loss profile associated with cyber risks is now so extreme and so adverse that insurers are keen to ensure that coverage is directly associated with appropriate underwriting and premiums and the best way for them to ensure that this happens is by excluding coverage from all but stand-alone cyber policies.

C. General Liability

General Liability policies are intended to provide coverage to the insured for Bodily Injury or Property Damage to a third party. General Liability policies have historically been silent on cyber events as a peril intending to pick up Bodily Injury or Property Damage even when caused by a cyber peril.

However, General Liability policies also provide "Advertising Liability" coverage and a certain amount of personal injury coverage, which as discussed previously, does overlap with coverage provided under the media liability section in many cyber policies.

In at least one case this has led to a similar situation to the one outlined in earlier in subsection B, where an insured was required to defend a claim arising from a Biometric Information Privacy infringement and did not have a cyber insurance policy. The policyholder in this case sought coverage under the policy provision providing coverage for liability arising out of "written publication of material that violates a person's right of privacy." The policyholder had provided customers' fingerprint data to a vendor. The insurance company argued that no "publication" had occurred because that term required dissemination to a wide audience. The court disagreed, holding that "publication" was also commonly understood to encompass a more limited sharing with a single party and found coverage.

The same considerations apply in this case as in the case quoted in subsection B, Property Damage and Business Interruption, in that insureds should have certainty of coverage and not have to pursue legal action to "find" coverage in policies that were not intended (and critically with cyber exposures, not priced) to grant that coverage. The case shown here is another "Silent Cyber" case that is leading to insurers of Commercial General Liability making changes to wording to ensure that their intent and the coverage is clear.

There has been concern in the market that as with the Property Damage insurance an absolute cyber exclusion, rather than providing clarity will actually force open gaps in coverage between Cyber (which explicitly excludes Bodily Injury and Property Damage) and General Liability and traditional Property Damage policies that are excluding all consequences of cyber events. It is therefore to the insured's advantage to work with brokers who understand the intricacies of coverage, including the interplay with other policies, as well as the threat environment and business of the insured. Then coverage can be arranged and coordinated in such a way as to minimize gaps and the uncertainty of leaving exposures uninsured on the assumption that coverage can be "found" if catastrophe strikes.

D. Commercial Crime

Long before ransomware was becoming a major threat, criminals refined "social engineering" and "phishing" techniques to dupe victims into transferring funds, whether by wire transfer, gift card, or invoice manipulation. For several years this was one of the major sources of cybercrime according to the FBI's Internet Crime Complaint Center (IC3), which includes these types of fraud within their statistics for cybercrime, classifying them under the general umbrella of "BEC" (Business Email Compromise). In 2019, according to IC3, BEC scams accounted for half of the cybercrime losses, averaging nearly $75,000 per complaint and totaling an estimated $1.77 billion.[48] In 2020, the total increased to $1.87 billion.[49] Law firms have proven to be a particularly attractive target for this type of crime as they are so often the hub of transactions involving millions of dollars being exchanged on an international basis.[50] Law firms are also often the fiduciary acting for clients in a transaction and therefore are vulnerable to "man in the middle" attacks where the client's e-mail system is hacked and, using an absolutely genuine e-mail address, the hacker instructs the law firm to pay the transaction funds to a fraudulent bank account.[51]

This type of crime, from an insurance perspective, fell into a gap between two policies.

- Cyber policies typically have specific exclusions for monies and securities and, on top of this, these crimes do not involve hacking systems

---

48. Catalin Cimpanu, *FBI: BEC Scams Accounted for Half of the Cyber-Crime Losses in 2019*, ZERO DAY NET (Feb. 11, 2020, 9:30 PM), https://www.zdnet.com/article /fbi-bec-scams-accounted-for-half-of-the-cyber-crime-losses-in-2019/.

49. *Internet Crime Report*, FED. BUREAU OF INVESTIGATION (2020), https://www.ic3.gov /Media/PDF/AnnualReport/2020_IC3Report.pdf.

50. *Why Are Social Engineering Attacks Targeting Law Firms?*, AON | PRO. SERVS PRAC. (Oct. 2020), https://www.aon.com/risk-services/professional-services/why-are-social-engineer -attacks-targeting-law-firm.jsp.

51. *In Deep Water. Phishing Risks for Professional Service Firms*, AON | PRO. SERVS PRAC. (May 2021), https://www.aon.com/risk-services/professional-services/in-deep-water-phishing -risks-for-professional-service-firms.jsp.

so there is rarely a triggering event for a cyber policy to respond to in the first place.

- Commercial crime policies traditionally had an exclusion for "voluntary parting" that is, when the victim voluntarily and willingly hands the money to the criminal (usually thinking they are the rightful recipient).

Crime insurers were initially willing to extend coverage for this risk although usually subject to a sublimit and for an additional premium. As the environment deteriorated and losses escalated rapidly, crime insurers began to pare back coverage, usually providing limits no greater than $250,000 for any one incident and in the aggregate. Underwriters, in a precursor to what has been happening in cyber insurance in 2021, started paying close attention to controls, policies, and procedures, providing more coverage to those with rigorous controls.

Nonetheless, these scams continue and in a pattern that has been seen with cyber insurance, entities that have been victims of one of these scams and that have not purchased the available coverage from their crime insurers have gone to court. One of the most influential cases, concerning a fraudulent transfer of more than $4.8 million was argued in court for more than four years before being decided in favor of the insured.[52] This immediately led to insurers revising and limiting coverage with clarifying endorsements that ensured that coverage was explicitly clear, often expressed as an absolute exclusion for social engineering crime losses, with a carve-back to the exclusion that provided a small aggregate limit.

Since that time, a number of cyber insurers have extended their policies to introduce some coverage for a variety of theft crimes based on social engineering techniques. Where the coverage is available, it can have great value in supplementing the limited coverage in the commercial crime insurance market, but the coverage available from cyber policies tends to be even more limited than in the commercial crime market, and subject to low sublimits. It is again important for the insured to work with advisers who understand the coverage and the interplay between crime and cyber policies in order to maximize available coverage, particularly as the coverage granted in cyber

---

52. Judy Greenwald, *Chubb Unit Must Cover Firm's Spoof Email Loss: Appeals Court*, Bus. Ins. (July 6, 2018), https://www.businessinsurance.com/article/20180706/NEWS06/912322505.

policies may use different language, terminology, and definitions than that in the commercial crime policy.

E. Kidnap, Ransom, and Extortion

Kidnap and ransom is the original form of corporate extortion, and a sophisticated insurance market developed around it (initially at Lloyd's of London but now with many major insurers participating in the U.S. domestic market). The coverage has evolved over the years and provides added value services, including emergency extraction from high risk areas (for instance during a coup or civil unrest).

One of the extensions of coverage Kidnap and Ransom insurers added early on as an additional benefit was Extortion coverage. This new addition emerged at the time when Distributed Denial of Service (DDoS) attacks were the major form of cyber extortion and these attacks were usually a relatively minor inconvenience with low ransoms being paid. Interruptions as a result of DDoS attacks were usually also very short and the Kidnap and Ransom insurers further expanded coverage to include loss of revenue from cyber extortion attacks.

The cyber extortion coverage in Kidnap Ransom and Extortion policies was typically to full limit and was not priced into the coverage, as it was rarely used, until 2017 and NotPetya.[53] NotPetya was possibly not intended to have the dramatic global consequences it launched, but many large international firms, including one global law firm, were brought to their knees by the attack, which used very sophisticated malware (in part derived from tools developed by the NSA) that portrayed itself as ransomware.

At that time, June 2017, uptake of cyber insurance in Europe, which was the epicenter of the attack, was very low (the Association of British Insurers estimated that in 2018 just 11 percent of UK corporations were purchasing cyber insurance,[54] and uptake in Europe was substantially lower). Many large corporations that were catastrophically impacted by NotPetya

---

53. Andy Greenberg, *The Untold Story of NotPetya, the Most Devastating Cyberattack in History*, WIRED (Aug. 22, 2018, 5:00 AM), https://www.wired.com/story/notpetya-cyberattack-ukraine-russia-code-crashed-the-world/.

54. *Cyber Insurance Payout Rates at 99%, but Uptake Still Far Too Low*, ABI (Aug. 8, 2019), https://www.abi.org.uk/news/news-articles/2019/08/cyber-insurance-payout-rates-at-99-but-uptake-still-far-too-low/.

did not have cyber insurance at all. However, as the malware displayed a ransomware note, these large firms very often did have Kidnap Ransom & Extortion coverage and were able to file claims. Not all of these claims were paid as there was some dispute as to whether or not NotPetya was truly ransomware or just "wiperware" (i.e. designed to encrypt all data with no functionality or capability to decrypt it). Nonetheless, the impact on the Kidnap Ransom and Extortion insurance market was catastrophic and the response was immediate. Insurers cut available limits for cyber extortion to $1 million, or eliminated it altogether. Kidnap Ransom and Extortion policies typically renew for a three-year period so the coverage lingered for a substantial period after the NotPetya event; however, at this point most insurers no longer offer coverage for cyber extortion at all.

F.   Employment Practices Liability

Employee data is one of the substantial data privacy exposures that all law firms are subject to; particularly as over the years the quantities of data can grow substantially and as law firms tend to keep all information forever, this compounds the issue. Many firms will think that as they have relatively few employees, the problem is not substantial, but the aggregation of information pertaining to everyone that touches the firm in an employment capacity over the years can be enormous:

- Partners and their family members (benefits plans)
- Associates and employees and their family members (benefits plans)
- Contract attorneys
- Summer associates
- Temps and interns
- Job applicants

This information on its own is a substantial exposure to law firms from a regulatory perspective (and associated costs), particularly where newer privacy statutes are granting automatic standing to plaintiffs whose data has been stolen; however, it is not the basis for an Employment Practices claim.

Employment practices liability policies are intended to cover the firm for lawsuits arising from the firm's wrongful behaviors toward specific individuals or groups, particularly to defend the firm against allegations of discrimination (on whatever basis, age, race, gender, orientation, religion, etc.), harassment, and so on.

This is another example of the intersection of cyber policies and other policies regarding liability to third parties who may have been harmed by actions of the firm that may also involve misuse or compromise of data. Cyber policies are usually written to be clear about the boundaries of the response to complaints from employees, with clear exclusions relating to employment-related complaints, particularly discrimination, a typical cyber wording excludes:

> any illegal discrimination of any kind, or any employment relationship, or the nature, terms or conditions of employment, including claims for workplace torts, wrongful termination, dismissal or discharge, or any discrimination, harassment, breach of employment contract, or defamation.[55]

There will often be a limited carve-back for emotional distress caused by the release of sensitive personal information as the result of a cyberattack, but such harm would have to be established on an individual, personal basis as the result of the specific cyber event, which does not lend itself to the type of workplace practices wrongs that are the subject matter of an employment practices policy.

Biometrics are increasingly in use in the workplace, and employee biometric claims have occurred—although not yet for law firms. Many manufacturers require employees to use their fingerprints to clock in. Similarly, warehouses often require truck drivers to scan their fingerprints when picking up or delivering loads. In one case, a former employee brought an action alleging that his employer violated BIPA by requiring employees to use a biometric scanner without obtaining their written permission. The employer asserted that it had deleted the data after it stopped using the technology in Illinois. The court recently approved a settlement involving the estimated class of employees.

---

55. *AIG Specialty Risk Protector, Form 91222* (Sept. 2016).

Similarly, in a case involving the Salvation Army, a former employee alleged that the organization violated BIPA by requiring employees to log their fingerprint or other biometric information when clocking in and out. The employee further alleged that the organization neither obtained written consent nor disclosed whether and how the information would be stored or used. The Salvation Army has agreed to pay approximately $898,000 to settle the class action.[56]

These cases are unlikely to trigger an employment practices claim as they appear to be founded in technical breaches of process requirements in the Illinois Biometric Information Privacy Act. There seems to be no allegation of discrimination or harassment on an individual basis or as part of workplace culture. Biometrics can be used in a discriminatory manner against individuals who might have religious or cultural issues with the process or may allege that the process invades their privacy, and this latter issue gets into the gray area where the specifics of the allegation are important in deciding which insurance policy will respond and whether it is an EPLI claim, a cyber claim, or possibly neither.

The preceding issues, however, do not appear to be allegations made in these cases, which illustrate the points made earlier concerning regulatory developments around biometric information and the importance of understanding the extent and limitation of the cyber policy. On one hand, some cyber policies now have specific exclusions relating to the use of biometric information, and in the absence of a cyber event trigger (theft or compromise of the information by a hacker), would not respond to cases of this type. On the other hand, there are cyber policies that provide broad coverage for wrongful acts that may trigger an investigation by regulatory authorities, fines and penalties, and legal defense and settlements.

The other type of policy that insureds might consider when facing allegations of personal injury as the result of a wrongful act by the firm are the commercial general liability and workers' compensation policies. General liability policies, like cyber policies, typically exclude claims by employees; bodily injury claims by employees are typically the province of worker's

---

56. Gebel v. Salvation Army, Settlement Memorandum (Aug. 2020), https://s3.amazonaws.com/jnswire/jns-media/64/7b/11517967/gebel_v_salvation_army_settlement_memo.pdf.

compensation policies. By the same token, as with cyber insurance, worker's compensation policies do not cover employment practices claims.

Employment practices liability insurance is an important coverage for law firms to have in their risk management portfolio, as it offers coverage for a broad range of employment torts. It may also have some application in gray areas where new regulations are introducing new wrongful acts concerning employee privacy. Given the evolution in privacy legislation and litigation, it is important to ensure that available insurance policies are purchased and the coverage structured in such a way to ensure as far as possible that gaps are minimized, coverage maximized, and any potential conflicts and overlaps between policies mitigated.

G. Alternative Risk Transfer/Captives

Demand for captive insurance is rising as commercial premiums soar.[57] A "captive insurer" is generally defined as an insurance company that is wholly owned and controlled by its insureds; its primary purpose is to insure the risks of its owners, and its insureds benefit from the captive insurer's underwriting profits.[58] Captive insurance is utilized by insureds that choose to (1) put their own capital at risk by creating their own insurance company; (2) work outside of the commercial insurance marketplace; and (3) set and achieve their own risk financing objectives. Insureds can either reinsure their captive or retain the risk (self-insure), which provides flexibility in coverage and premium options. Captives allow insureds to access international insurance and reinsurance markets in a more efficient way than through traditional insurance market structures, allowing them to structure complex risk financing mechanisms.

Captive insurance has traditionally been the province of very large organizations ($1bn+ revenue) that have the exposures and available finance to capitalize their own insurance company; however, other captive structures have been created that allow smaller firms to access the alternative

---

57. Alice Uribe, *Captive Insurance Seen as Covid-Era Remedy to Rising Premiums*, WALL ST. J. (Sept. 27, 2020, 8:00 AM), https://www.wsj.com/articles/captive-insurance-seen-as-covid-era-remedy-to-rising-premiums-11601208001.

58. *Revisiting the Captive Concept*, AON, https://www.aon.com/captives/insights/an-introduction-to-captives.jsp.

risk finance market, such as "Cell Captives," "Risk Retention Groups," and "Group Captives."

Structures like these have been used in the legal industry for conventional programs such as professional liability insurance and worker's compensation liability. Interest in captives for cyber insurance is being driven by both the rapidly hardening market and reductions in available capacity from the conventional market, dynamics that often drive interest in alternative risk finance structures.

One of the limiting factors for captives and cyber insurance is that the threat environment is changing so rapidly that it is difficult to model the risks so that the captive is appropriately capitalized and that the premiums and reinsurance required for sustainability are adequate. Captives rely on substantial actuarial support to create the models and underwriting parameters and these rely on historical trends and loss information. One of the distinctive features of cyber risk is that the exposures change over time and can fluctuate dramatically. In the three years from Q1 2018 to Q4 2020 privacy events went down by 57 percent, and in the same time period ransomware events increased by 486 percent.[59]

Group and cell captives are predicated on spread of risk and on events being limited in scope and scale in such a way that any one event is unlikely to victimize the entire group. However, as has been seen in recent years, cyber is extremely exposed to aggregation risks, from NotPetya to SolarWinds,[60] Accellion,[61] and Microsoft "Hafnium"[62] the cyber supply chain creates situations where a single vulnerability can cause material losses for multiple insureds (the White House estimated that NotPetya caused more than $10 billionn of losses worldwide). Group captives struggle to cope with material aggregation risks, and captives generally are not well suited to writing

---

59. *Cyber Insurance Snapshot*, *supra* note 1, at 3.

60. Isabella Jibilan & Kaie Canales, *The US Is Readying Sanctions against Russia over the SolarWinds Cyber Attack. Here's a Simple Explanation of How the Massive Hack Happened and Why It's Such a Big Deal*, Bus. Insider (Apr. 15, 2021, 1:25 PM), https://www.businessinsider.com/solarwinds-hack-explained-government-agencies-cyber-security-2020-12.

61. Lily Hay Newman, *The Accellion Breach Keeps Getting Worse—and More Expensive*, Wired (Mar. 8, 2021, 7:00 AM), https://www.wired.com/story/accellion-breach-victims-extortion/.

62. *HAFNIUM Targeting Exchange Servers with 0-Day Exploits*, Microsoft (Mar. 2, 2021), https://www.microsoft.com/security/blog/2021/03/02/hafnium-targeting-exchange-servers/.

risks with catastrophe potential because of the profile of the claims, which is both unpredictable and extreme (natural catastrophe is rarely written in captives).

Nonetheless, based on current trends, Aon expects that by 2024 cyber insurance will be the number one risk written by captives alongside commercial general liability (the risk of liability to third parties for bodily injury and damage to physical property).[63]

H.   Attorney Client Privilege and Work Product Doctrine

When a law firm is the victim of a cyber event one of the major concerns is that the firm may be investigated by regulators (if Personally Identifiable Information or Protected Health Information is compromised) and, perhaps more importantly, may be sued by clients whose confidential data has been compromised. These considerations make the issue of maximizing attorney-client privilege around all aspects of the breach and response a priority.

The decisions in the Capital One case[64] and in Wengui v. Clark Hill PLC[65] do not set precedent but are an important reminder that it is never safe to assume that privilege is in place and secure just because outside counsel has been engaged in the process. Ensuring that privilege is engaged to the maximum extent possible is a matter of preparation and planning. Addressing issues such as decisions on engaging counsel and which forensic investigation vendor to use after the cyber event has struck are unlikely to result in the firm being in the best position possible. Even the best-prepared firms have confirmed that a cyber event induces chaos and emergency decision making that may disrupt a carefully planned process; but with proper planning and rehearsal combined with a simple (hard copy, of course) Incident Response Plan (IRP), the firm can be assured that the key elements will be in place at the start to best protect the firm.

---

63. *Cyber Captive Survey 2019*, AON, https://www.aon.com/captives/insights/cyber-captive-survey-2019.jsp.

64. Gwenn Barney, *Protecting Your Organization. Lessons from In re Capital One for Third-Party Cybersecurity Incident Reports*, JD SUPRA (June 9, 2020), https://www.jdsupra.com/legalnews/protecting-your-organization-lessons-63963/.

65. Wengui v. Clark Hill, PLC, 338 F.R.D. 7 (D.D.C. 2021); Carole J. Buckner, *Responding to a Data Breach? Preserve Your Privilege and Work Product*, PROCOPIO (Mar. 2, 2021), https://www.procopio.com/articles/view/preserve-privilege-work-product-data-breach.

Cyber insurance policies vary in how they address notice of an incident and engagement of resources. Some policies insist that the firm's first call should be to the insurer and that the insurer will then provide advice and initial triage of the incident, and the insurer will engage the resources from their panel to respond to the incident. Needless to say, none of this engages privilege, and once these processes have been set in motion, achieving privilege protection afterwards will be at best haphazard and compromised in key areas. One other important consideration in addressing an insurer requirement to be the first to be notified is that the insured will be in a position of conflict with other entities who may also be claiming precedence either by contract (client contracts often specify notification protocols and priorities for a cyber event), by law (some states require victims of cyberattacks to provide notification to the attorney general's office and/or law enforcement depending on the nature of the event within a certain timeframe), or by regulatory edict.

The conflict of notification provisions, client contract requirements, and the potential for law enforcement involvement (particularly critical if ransomware or data extortion is in train) are generally subsidiary to the insured's right to engage legal counsel before taking any further action.

Best practice is that following the internal process of triage and escalation of an incident (and it is important that this be a defined process and part of the incident response plan), the firm should engage outside counsel (often referred to as Breach Counsel) before taking any further action. It is important that this process be agreed with the insurer and that the insurer will accept notice from Breach Counsel (some insurers have this written into the policy, others may require an endorsement or written agreement from the underwriter). It is critically important that the selected Breach Counsel be from the insurer's panel of approved vendors or, if not, that insurer's agreement to the selected preferred Breach Counsel has been secured and the rates agreed.

Breach Counsel, based on their extensive experience, will be able to further triage the situation and advise on a course of action. This may involve engagement of a Digital Forensic Investigation and Response (DFIR) firm and other resources (ransomware negotiator, data remediation consultant, cybersecurity consultant, crisis communications consultant et al.), and again these should all be insurer-approved vendors. The key point is that all of these engagements can be secured by Breach Counsel acting on behalf of the insured and thereby maximizing attorney-client privilege protections. Breach Counsel will be familiar with the insurer, policy wording, and vendor panels and will be able to advise on the best resources to engage for the type and scale of incident being encountered. They will also work with the insurer to secure prior consent where required and will host meetings with the insurer's loss adjuster and other resources, ensuring that privilege-sensitive information is appropriately guarded depending on the audience.

There have been several decisions in the courts where privilege protection has been challenged, particularly around the forensic investigation report, which courts have generally deemed to be for business purposes rather than for legal purposes. In *Wengui*[66] the U.S. District Court in the District of Columbia addressed the application of the attorney-client privilege and work product doctrine in the context of a data breach investigation involving a law firm. The plaintiff alleged that the law firm failed to take adequate precautions to protect his data, seeking discovery of all reports of the law firm's forensic investigations and information regarding other clients of the law firm that were impacted by the cyberattack. The case and the findings of the court provide some helpful insight into strategies that may be helpful in preserving privilege in such a situation.[67]

At the moment the amount of attorney-client privilege protection that can be achieved is being assessed by the courts (when challenged) on a case-by-case basis; but until firm guidelines and precedent have been established, there is a process by which the victim firm can maximize available protection as outlined previously.

I.   Coverage Scenarios

The following are examples of a cyberattack scenario, followed by an illustration of how the various types of commercial insurance policy typically purchased by a law firm might respond to such an event:

---

66. *See Wengui*, 338 F.R.D. 7.

67. Stephanie Diehl, *Lessons from Wengui v. Clark Hill: Structuring a Two Track Cyber Investigation*, NAT'L L. REV. (Feb. 8, 2021), https://www.natlawreview.com/article /lessons-wengui-v-clark-hill-structuring-two-track-cyber-investigation.

Scenario 1. Internet of Things Attack on Building Services
Event:

- Building control systems are infiltrated through a security vulnerability in a third party's systems.
- Hackers shut down all building systems, including lights, elevators, locks, and HVAC, and demand a ransom to restore access.
- Lack of HVAC causes firm's servers to overheat, resulting in smoke damage to all the equipment, destroying the servers and necessitating total replacement.
- An employee and an outside consultant on-site suffer smoke inhalation and other injuries.
- Switchover to backup systems takes longer than anticipated, and the firm suffers an interruption to e-mail, telephone, and document management systems.

Impact:

- Extra expense and lost revenue are incurred as a result of the inability to access the building and loss of servers.
- Firm engages experts to negotiate with the hackers and pays the ransom demanded to facilitate access to the building.

Scenario 2. Exfiltration of Client Data
Event:

- Phishing attack results in malicious external hackers gaining access to law firm's internal IT systems.
- Hackers steal confidential client data relating to M&A transactions.
- Information subsequently leaked by the hackers leads to the failure of several transactions and the forfeiture of agreed "break-up fees" by the law firm's clients.

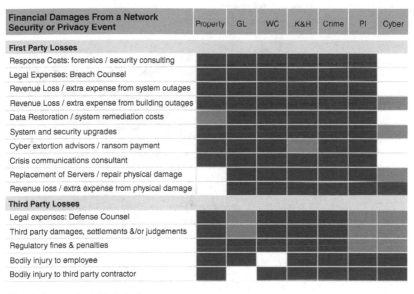

Financial Damages From a Network Security or Privacy Event	Property	GL	WC	K&H	Crime	PI	Cyber
First Party Losses							
Response Costs: forensics / security consulting							
Legal Expenses: Breach Counsel							
Revenue Loss / extra expense from system outages							
Revenue Loss / extra expense from building outages							
Data Restoration / system remediation costs							
System and security upgrades							
Cyber extortion advisors / ransom payment							
Crisis communications consultant							
Replacement of Servers / repair physical damage							
Revenue loss / extra expense from physical damage							
Third Party Losses							
Legal expenses: Defense Counsel							
Third party damages, settlements &/or judgements							
Regulatory fines & penalties							
Bodily injury to employee							
Bodily injury to third party contractor							

☐ Typically covered to full limit of policy

▨ Coverage maybe conditional on situation, subject to sublimit or may only be availible by a policy extension/endorsement

■ Typically not covered or excluded

Figure 16.3   Financial Damages from Network Security or Privacy Event (IoT Event Scenario)

Impact:

- Firm engages crisis communications consultancy to advise on and manage the reputational issues.
- Firm engages security consultants to investigate and remediate. Significant upgrades to data security systems recommended and implemented.
- Remediation involves shutting the systems down for several days; firm incurs loss of revenue and extra expense.

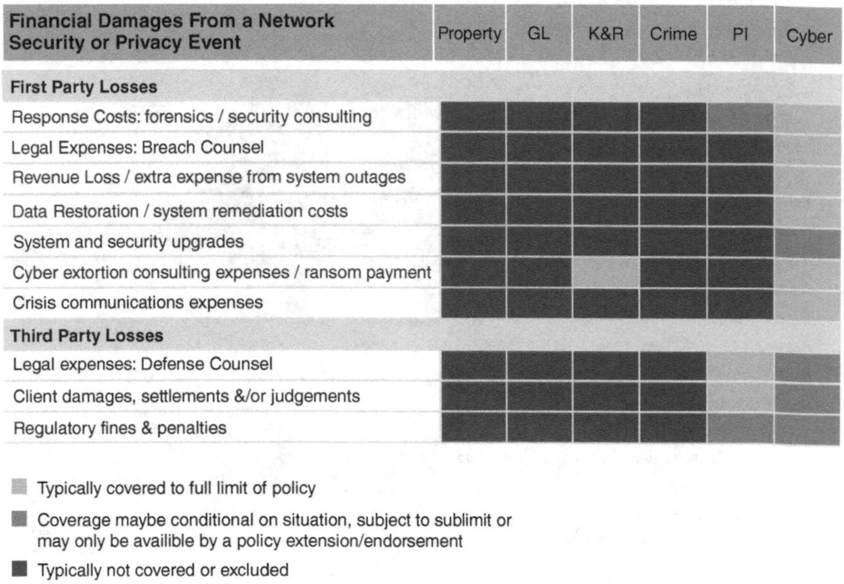

Financial Damages From a Network Security or Privacy Event	Property	GL	K&R	Crime	PI	Cyber
First Party Losses						
Response Costs: forensics / security consulting						
Legal Expenses: Breach Counsel						
Revenue Loss / extra expense from system outages						
Data Restoration / system remediation costs						
System and security upgrades						
Cyber extortion consulting expenses / ransom payment						
Crisis communications expenses						
Third Party Losses						
Legal expenses: Defense Counsel						
Client damages, settlements &/or judgements						
Regulatory fines & penalties						

Typically covered to full limit of policy

Coverage maybe conditional on situation, subject to sublimit or may only be availible by a policy extension/endorsement

Typically not covered or excluded

Figure 16.4   Financial Damages from Network Security or Privacy Event (Exfiltration of Client Data Scenario)

Scenario 3. "NotPetya" Wiperware attack

Event:

- Ransomware/malware attack infiltrates law firm's system and shuts down all access for more than two weeks, impacting:
  - E-mail communication
  - Telecommunications
  - Document management system
  - Financial management and billing system
  - Electronic docket scheduling system
  - Conflict management

Impact:

- No evidence of any data exfiltration.
- Substantial loss of revenue and extra expense incurred, potential liabilities to clients as firm missed critical filing dates for client matters.

- Firm engages forensic and security consultants to investigate.
- Firm engages a crisis communications consultant to advise on client communications and to control damage to firm's reputation.

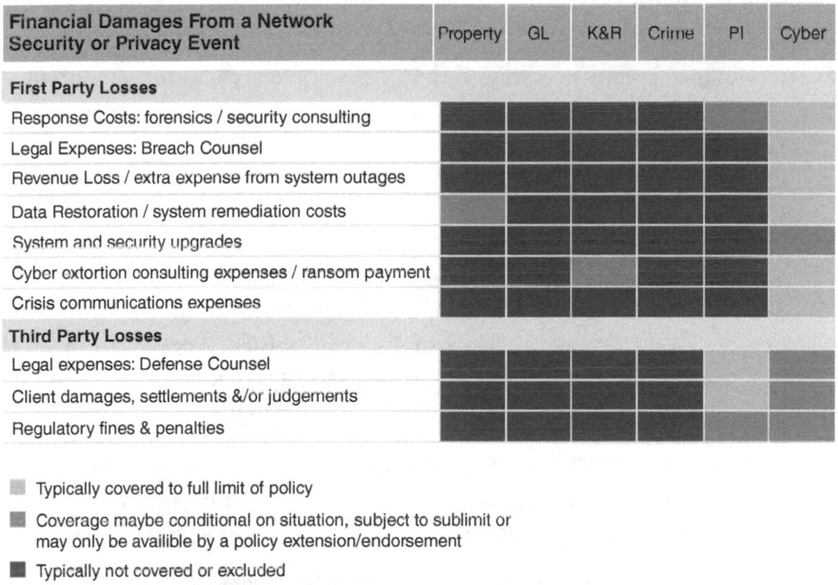

Financial Damages From a Network Security or Privacy Event	Property	GL	K&R	Crime	PI	Cyber
First Party Losses						
Response Costs: forensics / security consulting						
Legal Expenses: Breach Counsel						
Revenue Loss / extra expense from system outages						
Data Restoration / system remediation costs						
System and security upgrades						
Cyber extortion consulting expenses / ransom payment						
Crisis communications expenses						
Third Party Losses						
Legal expenses: Defense Counsel						
Client damages, settlements &/or judgements						
Regulatory fines & penalties						

▨ Typically covered to full limit of policy

▨ Coverage maybe conditional on situation, subject to sublimit or may only be availible by a policy extension/endorsement

■ Typically not covered or excluded

Figure 16.5   Financial Damages from Network Security or Privacy Event (Widespread systemic malware Scenario)

V. Specific Situations, Dynamics, and Scenarios[68]

Hackers see an opportunity to take advantage of large quantities of valuable and quality documents. By targeting law firms, they can quickly access information such as technical secrets, business strategies, and financial data for numerous clients. Law firms provide a quick detour around information

---

68. Alexandra Dattilo, *Cybersecurity Alert: Data Breaches Can Happen to Anyone*, Brouse McDowell (Feb. 5, 2021), https://www.brouse.com/cybersecurity-alert -data-breaches-can-happen-to-anyone.

of little value.[69] Personally identifiable information is a major issue that particularly impacts small firms (individual clients, trusts and estates, etc.), but also medium and large firms according to practices (mass tort litigation, employment, immigration, health care, etc.). Regulation is adding a multiplier effect—first it was the cost of notifications, and so on, then regulatory fines and penalties added to that; now there is the ominous threat of statutory standing adding mass tort litigation to the picture, although the U.S. Supreme Court's June 2021 decision in *Ramirez v. TransUnion* may reduce the risk.

Ransomware is a concern for all legal organizations, especially with the data exfiltration/extortion issue.[70] A ransomware attack on a boutique entertainment law firm in 2020, which became public news because of the firm's refusal to "pay cyber-terrorists" undoubtedly drew attention to the value of the information that law firms hold, in this case because the firm's client base included numerous "A-list" musicians and Hollywood stars. The event appears not to have been a major coup for the hackers (a group called REvil), as it appears they were unable to monetize the stolen information, but it was notable for the attention that it drew to the legal community and particularly the fact that firms of all sizes can be repositories of very valuable and sensitive information. Coveware, a leading provider of ransomware negotiation services, published a chart on their blog showing that as of Q3 2020 more than 25 percent of their assignments were with Professional Services Firms (with Public Sector at 11.6 percent and Health care at 11.3 percent).[71]

---

69. Aniket Bhardwaj, *Law Firms as Prime Targets for Hackers: 7 Steps to Reducing Cyber Risks*, WHOSWHOLEGAL (Dec. 18, 2020), https://whoswholegal.com/features /law-firms-as-prime-targets-for-hackers-7-steps-to-reducing-cyber-risks.

70. *Ransomware: REvil & the Increased Targeting of Law Firms*, AON | PRO. SERVS. PRAC. (Sept. 2020), https://www.aon.com/risk-services/professional-services/ransomware-revil -increased-targeting-law-firms.jsp.

71. *Ransomware Demands Continue to Rise as Data Exfiltration Because Common, and Maze Subdues*, COVEWARE (Nov. 4, 2020), https://www.coveware.com/blog/q3-2020 -ransomware-marketplace-report.

Common Industries Targeted by Ransomware in Q3 2020

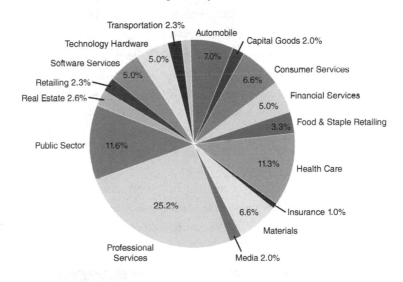

Figure 16.6   Ransomware Attack Frequency by Industry

The more recent events surrounding Accellion's FTA platform in Q1 2021 illustrate clearly the focus on law firms. Several major (AmLaw 100) firms were identified in the press as victims of this attack and there were undoubtedly other less noteworthy firms affected. In this case, the hackers had identified a vulnerability in a vendor platform; Accellion FTA was a legacy platform (now retired) for the sharing of very large files and was used by many firms as a means of transferring large documents between themselves and clients. The platform was partially cloud-hosted and it was here that the hackers were able to exfiltrate data, which by its presence on this "secure file transfer platform" was self-identified as very sensitive and confidential information. The hackers had no need to try to use ransomware, and one of the few silver linings to this attack is that they did not at any time have access to the firm's systems, instead being able to steal information directly from the platform in the cloud.

The $42 million ransom demand made against the entertainment firm was unusually high at the time (and extraordinarily high for the hacker, which previously had rarely demanded more than $2 million), although the demands made in connection with some of the ransomware attacks in early 2021 are known to be higher. In particular, the hacker group that successfully infiltrated insurer CNA initially demanded $60 million and the insurer eventually paid $40 million to the hackers.[72]

The material increase in average demand size and the increase in frequency of attacks against smaller firms cost insurers more in ransomware insurance payments for small- and medium-size law firms than large firms.

A few years ago, many insurers figured it was less risky to write cyber insurance for smaller firms and started avoiding cyber risks on large law firms solely due to size. However, 2020 showed that larger firms generally suffer fewer losses and practice superior cyber risk management than smaller firms due to the allocation of IT resources deployed.[73]

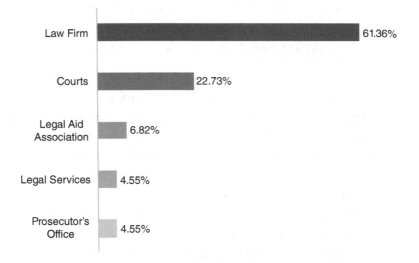

Figure 16.7   Ransomware Attack Frequency by Type of Legal Organization

The trend of vendor outsourcing and use of cloud is something that will affect all firms eventually, including legal services platforms, software as a

---

72. Lyle Adriano, *CNA Pays $40 Million Ransom to Lift Malware from Its Systems*, INS. BUS. MAG. (May 21, 2021), https://www.insurancebusinessmag.com/us/news/cyber/cna-pays-40-million-ransom-to-lift-malware-from-its-systems-255714.aspx.

73. *See* Figure 16.2, *supra*.

service, eDiscovery, document management outsourcing, and legaltech services. We already have examples like the 2020 Google outage that impacted numerous firms (particularly smaller firms that depend on Google productivity applications)[74] and the Epiq ransomware event that impacted numerous law firms (the legal services and eDiscovery platforms were down for two to three weeks).[75] Even seemingly innocuous "Business Process Outsourcing" functions such as HR and Health and Benefits Consulting can impact law firms, as they are repositories of extensive Personally Identifiable Information, which under state privacy law remains the responsibility of the firm (making the firm responsible for notifications and services to affected individuals as required by statute, although these responsibilities may be transferred to the vendor by contract). Furthermore, the creation of technology platforms and services (non-attorney-managed technology subsidiaries, technology services used by clients in engagements with other law firms) appears to be growing. All of these complex, allocation of liability issues need to be addressed from a cyber insurance standpoint.

A. Large Law Firms

Most large law firms, generally discussed in Chapter 8 of this Handbook, placed a greater emphasis on cyber resiliency the past few years following the WannaCry[76] and NotPetya[77] incidents of 2017 and subsequent major events that have specifically targeted large law firms, including ransomware and data exfiltration (particularly the Accellion FTA hack of Q1 2021 that impacted a number of large law firms). Most large law firm cyber policies are highly customized to fit their specific circumstances, although in the

---

74. *What Google Wants from Law Firm Websites in 2020*, LawLytics, https://www.lawlytics.com/blog/what-google-wants-law-firm-websites-in-2020/; Alex Hern, *Google Suffers Global Outage with Gmail, YouTube and Majority of Services Affected,* The Guardian (Dec. 14, 2020, 1:17 PM), https://www.theguardian.com/technology/2020/dec/14/google-suffers-worldwide-outage-with-gmail-youtube-and-other-services-down.

75. Tari Schreider, *Ransomware Attacks in the Legal Profession*, Law.com: Corporate Counsel (May 26, 2020, 1:39 PM), https://www.law.com/corpcounsel/2020/05/26/ransomware-attacks-in-the-legal-profession/.

76. *The Impact of Ransomware on Law Firms*, Lawyers Defence Group (Nov. 28, 2017), https://www.lawyersdefencegroup.org.uk/ransomware/.

77. Jonathan Crowe, *How One of the World's Largest Law Firms Was Paralyzed by NotPetya*, Barkly (July 2017), https://harryphillipsaic.com/wp-content/uploads/2018/10/How-One-of-the-World%E2%80%99s-Largest-Law-Firms-Was-Paralyzed-by-Petya-01810088.pdf.

current hard market of 2021 insurers are demonstrating considerably less flexibility in negotiating wording and are increasingly imposing restrictions on coverage.

Large law firms have always been a target of hackers with publicly disclosed attacks dating back to 2016 when several large law firms were revealed to have been among up to 15 firms victimized by hackers looking for information that could be used in financial trading (particularly M&A information). The subsequent investigation resulted in two Hong Kong citizens being found guilty of trading on stolen information, having profited to the tune of more than $3 million, and they were fined $8.8 million (the men were not extradited and were fined in absentia).[78]

Large law firms have the largest, most sophisticated, and most sensitive clients and, consequently, have to be very concerned about their connections to those clients; those that service government entities and government contractors (especially defense contractors) are a target and we may see this as the investigations resulting from the SolarWinds Orion hack play out.[79] Even those firms that were not exposed to the compromised version of the Solar-Winds Orion product may have been targeted, potentially through other known compromises such as the Microsoft "Hafnium" hack or through attacks that have yet to be discovered, and anything they shared with clients may have been exfiltrated at the client end. Clients of BigLaw giants and firms of any size are likely to demand answers about how such attacks unfolded and what steps firms took to prevent them, including whether they vetted the security of third-party products used to transfer sensitive data and whether they have cyber insurance to cover the cost of investigations, remediation of systems, and payment of extortion demands. In addition to this, the firms have to be concerned about the potential for professional claims from clients whose most confidential and sensitive information may have been compromised within the firm's technology environment.

---

78. *Chinese Hackers Must Pay $9m over Insider Trading Scam*, BBC News (May 11, 2017), https://www.bbc.com/news/technology-39883224.

79. Jonathan Greig, *US Court System Demands Massive Changes to Court Documents after SolarWinds Hack*, TechRepublic (Feb. 12, 2021, 12:50 PM), https://www.techrepublic.com /article/us-court-system-demands-massive-changes-to-court-documents-after-solarwinds-hack/.

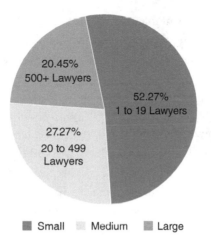

Figure 16.8   Ransomware Attack Frequency by Size of Law Firm

B.   Small Law Firms/Sole Practitioners[80]

Small firms do not typically have a dedicated IT security staff. That said, per Figure 16.8, ransomware attacks are targeting these small practices as much if not more than larger firms. One of the substantial benefits of cyber insurance is the availability from most cyber insurers of free or subsidized cybersecurity services that support the small firm's ability to strengthen its environment. Imagine a hacker scanning your law firm's digital presence searching for vulnerabilities. Where are you open to attack? Does your cybersecurity have flaws? Have your login credentials been compromised? Is your firm's data for sale on the dark web? Additional services offered by some insurers may provide as much, or more, value than the insurance defense and indemnity. For example, a cybersecurity assessment may include:[81]

- Scans infrastructure of publicly accessible servers, services, and technology
- Discovery of exploitable vulnerabilities and misconfigurations in the scanned infrastructure

---

80. For further discussion, see Chapter 9, *supra.*

81. *Cyber Liability Insurance,* AON, https://www.attorneys-advantage.com/Other-Insurance/Cyber-Insurance.

- Finding exposed/available user/employee information
- Uncovering existing threats hidden on the dark web
- Offering recommendations for taking immediate action to reduce cyber risks

Insurers are paying much more attention to technology implementations as part of the renewal process. This attention is largely the result of their own analysis of the claims that they have worked on, and they now have a good understanding of the techniques, strategies, technologies, and implementations that are most effective in hardening systems, particularly against ransomware attacks. In addition to the services available from preferred vendors, often at a discounted or sometimes complimentary price point, the expertise offered by the insurance companies themselves is adding value in making the firm and therefore its clients more secure.

There is also some evidence that cybersecurity has become a differentiator for small firms; some clients are concerned that large firms are more of a target and that a small firm with excellent cybersecurity offers an attractive value proposition. In an environment where there is a great deal of variability in security maturity and posture, a firm that is investing in best practices and best-in-class technological protections will differentiate itself within its peer group for clients that value security of their data. Smaller firms are best positioned to leverage the services and expertise provided alongside a cyber insurance policy and the fact that the firm has invested in a cyber insurance policy provides further reassurance to clients that the firm takes the risk seriously and has resources available to assist and protect the firm and its clients in the event of a cyberattack.

Many clients are now requiring outside counsel to carry cyber insurance. In January of 2017 the Association of Corporate Counsel published their "Model Information Protection and Security Controls for Outside Counsel"[82] guidelines. This included recommendations that all outside counsel should have and maintain cyber insurance with a limit of $10 million.

---

82. *Model Information Protection and Security Controls for Outside Counsel Possessing Company Confidential Information*, Ass'n of Corp. Couns. (Mar. 10, 2017), https://www.acc.com/resource-library/model-information-protection-and-security-controls-outside-counsel-possessing-0#.

In the current hard market, that level of insurance may be unrealistic for a small firm, but for many clients, the limit of insurance is a differentiator and the better the firm's cybersecurity controls and technology, the more insurance is available.

C. In-House Counsel[83]

Data breaches, while frequent in number and severity, remain big news events today. Even more newsworthy is when a corporate in-house attorney is criminally prosecuted in connection with his role in responding to a data breach event.[84] With the proliferation of data privacy regulations, regulatory attention (particularly the Department of Treasury Office of Foreign Asset Control), the potential for class-action lawsuits (particularly under BIPA and other proposed legislation), and of course the constant threat of employee and client litigation following a breach, internal counsel is now very much at the center of every cyber event.

The Office of General Counsel is by its nature "general," and few internal counsel have experience and expertise in cybersecurity and managing cyber events; even fewer have technological expertise and may be tempted to defer to the Information Technology experts within the firm on matters of cybersecurity.

This is no longer a viable strategy as cyber risk becomes more and more central to the well-being and even survival of the corporation. It is essential for internal counsel to be the "hub" of the cyber wheel and to ensure that the entity is prepared for a cyber event from the board level down. The IT function is an important part of the equation, but as outlined in previous sections, a cyber event will impact every aspect of the entity's work and therefore it is essential that cybersecurity strategy and preparedness be addressed at the highest level of the entity. The Office of General Counsel is the hub and coordinator and plays a critical role in event response as the liaison with external Breach Counsel (who is the specialist with experience

---

83. For further discussion, see Chapter 10, *supra.*

84. *What In House Counsel Can Learn from Criminal Prosecution of Uber's Former Chief Security Officer*, BLANK ROME (Feb. 18, 2021), https://www.blankrome.com/publications/what-house-counsel-can-learn-criminal-prosecution-ubers-former-chief-security-officer.

and expertise in breach response and who will act as guide and advisor through the process).

Internal counsel is in a position to ensure that the entity is purchasing its own cyber insurance and to manage the interplay between the cyber policy and all other coverages purchased. Cyber insurance is one of the critical elements in a cybersecurity program, but it is not enough just for it to be available, it has to be an integrated part of the entity's Incident Response Plan. Cyber insurance will typically only pay for pre-approved vendors, and communication with insurers and vendors should be to the extent possible protected by attorney-client privilege; it is internal counsel's job to ensure that this is communicated to all parties involved and appropriately managed through the event management process.

The other side of the equation is for internal counsel to ensure that the firm manages the external risk inherent in the work that it does. In January of 2017 the Association of Corporate Counsel published their "Model Information Protection and Security Controls for Outside Counsel"[85] guidelines. This included recommendations that all outside counsel should have and maintain cyber insurance. Similar considerations apply to all vendors used by the firm that are entrusted with the firm's sensitive data, and vendor contracts should maximize protections and indemnities in favor of the entity.

While Directors' and Officers' (D&O) insurance is typically inapplicable to most law firms, in-house counsel may obtain coverage under D&O policies, which is increasingly important given the exposure to data privacy events that can trigger:

- Notification costs
- Forensic investigation costs
- Loss of revenue
- Regulatory fines and penalties (which may be uninsurable)
- A class-action lawsuit as the result of the affected class having statutory standing under certain statutes (as is the case under BIPA)

---

85. *Model Information Protection and Security Controls for Outside Counsel Possessing Company Confidential Information, supra* note 80.

- Compliance penalties unconnected to a cyber event (several large corporations have incurred multimillion-dollar fines for failure to comply with process requirements under GDPR[86])

Public company D&O policies typically provide coverage for the entity for securities claims, which could include claims that, for example, the company failed to disclose in its SEC filings that it was subject to potential liability for biometric violations. Public company D&O policies also should apply to cover directors and officers facing lawsuits arising from company biometric and other privacy law compliance violations. Such a suit might allege that the value of company stock fell because of such violations and that the directors and officers failed to oversee corporate operations that resulted in the violations resulting in legal costs, fines and penalties, remediation, and compliance costs. Private company Management Liability policies also provide entity coverage that conceivably cover such stakeholder claims resulting from failure to comply with privacy legislation requirements. Thus, both public and private company policyholders should investigate D&O coverage in addition to cyber insurance for claims arising from the broad requirements and application of privacy legislation.

D. Government Lawyers[87]

In December 2020, it was discovered that SolarWinds' Orion software had been hacked and installed backdoors into the IT systems of its many federal government and Fortune 500 clients. Corporate and government investigations are still determining the full scope and origination of the cybersecurity attack.[88] Government entities typically enjoy sovereign immunity and often do not purchase insurance, although this is changing in the realm of cyber insurance as ransomware threat actors are targeting the sector. Govern-

---

86. Gabe Gumbs, *The Biggest GDPR Penalties for Noncompliance*, SPIRION (Feb. 23, 2021), https://www.spirion.com/blog/gdpr-fines-increase/#:~:text=A%20lower%2Dlevel%20 GDPR%20violation,annual%20revenue%2C%20whichever%20is%20greater.

87. For further discussion, see Chapter 11, *supra*.

88. Victoria Hudgins, *4 Ways the SolarWinds Hack Is Indirectly Impacting the Legal Industry*, LAW.COM: LEGALTECH NEWS (Feb. 2, 2021, 10:00 AM), https://www.law.com /legaltechnews/2021/02/02/4-ways-the-solarwinds-hack-is-indirectly-impacting-the-legal -industry/.

ment attorneys are therefore increasingly dealing with complex contractual issues, negotiating insurance and indemnity requirements with vendors and contractors, while at the same time facing the same pressures as in-house counsel to understand the threat environment and the available insurance solutions. Government entities may have the ability to finance response to a cyberattack from the public purse, but taxpayers are increasingly questioning whether purchasing available insurance is a more efficient way of managing the risk.

Contracts offered by government bodies are typically extremely onerous in their requirements on the vendors and contractors that work for them, but the divergence between what the contracts require and what insurance is actually prepared to provide is widening. Many contractors will agree to government contract requirements because they are non-negotiable, but are doing so sometimes not knowing the extent or provisions of their own insurance policies and sometimes in the knowledge that the insurer will not agree to respond on the terms required by the contractual indemnities and insurance requirements.

With the cyber market deteriorating, government lawyers, as with corporate in-house counsel, should be familiarizing themselves with the cyber insurance market and the availability and terms of coverage for both their own entities and the vendors/contractors they work with. The SolarWinds hack illustrated very clearly that cyber risk is escalating as a geopolitical issue, and the Colonial Pipeline hack demonstrated that the threat to society from the intersection of private utilities and societal function is a major concern for everyone. Government attorneys need to understand the dynamics of the threat environment, the technological environment, and the interplay of response strategies and risk finance solutions that are available.

E.   Public Interest Attorneys[89]

There was in the past an assumption on the part of many lawyers that no one could possibly be interested in the information that they held, so the cyber threat was perceived to be very low and as long as the firm had good

---

89. For further discussion, see Chapter 12, *supra*.

professional liability insurance that covered everything they needed to be concerned about. Events of the last 18 months have certainly demonstrated that these assumptions were incorrect in every respect. Lawyers' data in all sectors and in all sizes of firms have been targeted. For instance, there has been a string of bar association hacks as well as attacks on vendors that work with law firms (from the eDiscovery and legal services platform provider Epiq, to a health and benefits broker with many law firm clients).[90] Public interest attorneys are vulnerable to attacks from different types of hacker from those seeking personally identifiable information that can be monetized, to ransomware operators seeking a payoff to decrypt data, to "hacktivists" seeking to influence or disrupt social justice causes, or seeking information that may influence or disrupt causes.

Public interest attorneys are equally exposed to cyberattack as any other law firm and subject to the same data privacy laws and potential for paying for statutory notifications for breaches of Personally Identifiable Information and regulatory fines and penalties. It can be difficult for public interest attorneys to justify the high expense for the technological protections and cyber insurances to keep the firm and its data secure, but the firm is subject to the same ABA Model Rules and regulatory environment, and is equally exposed to the same threat environment as any other law firm. Arguably, the firm has an enhanced duty to protect the confidentiality and data of its clients because of the social justice and protection of the causes that the firm is supporting.

F. International Considerations[91]

The NotPetya attack of June 2017 impacted a large number of international corporations as well as two global professional services firms, one of them a law firm. The global impact of NotPetya was almost certainly unintended, although it is possible that the extent of the collateral damage

---

90. *Lawyers' Data Targeted in String of Bar Association Hacks*, LAW360 (Dec. 11, 2020, 8:01 PM), https://www.law360.com/insurance/articles/1335867/lawyers-data-targeted-in -string-of-bar-association-hacks?nl_pk=1c4af871-4228-4a8e-8f98-a3e025656b0e&utm_source _newsletter&utm_medium=email&utm_campaign=insurance.

91. For further discussion, see Chapter 5, *supra*.

achieved through the compromise of a tax preparation platform that was the nexus for the attack may have influenced the thinking behind the Solar-Winds and Microsoft Exchange attacks three years later. International firms are particularly exposed to cyber risks by virtue of a number of factors:

- Size and particularly the perimeter of the network. The technology and available solutions available to deliver functionality in multiple countries tend to introduce compromises that introduce vulnerabilities.
- Number of users/endpoints. Global firms have many more users and they are harder to train to the same level, particularly when standards, collateral, and training materials have to be translated into multiple languages. The majority of successful attacks against large law firms start with phishing; statistically the legal industry has a lower "click through" rate than most other sectors when it comes to phishing e-mails, but even at an exceptionally low rate of 5 percent that implies that as few as 20 e-mails are required to all but guarantee success for the hackers.
- Access. In many countries the Internet and Internet access are controlled by the government, making most if not all communication insecure. There are technological solutions available to increase security but the success of state actor hackers on a global basis indicates that if the firm has a presence in such a country and the government takes an interest, there may be little the firm can do to prevent an incursion. The possibility of accessing the firm's network-connected hardware in-country makes the hacker's job even easier.
- Delivering network updates and patches. The job of managing updates, upgrades, and patches on a global network is disproportionately harder because of the need to test against local technology solutions and implementations to ensure compatibility.
- International regulation. The world has a huge variety of Data Privacy legislation with provisions ranging from extremely onerous with severe penalties (GDPR) to countries with little or no regulation at all. For a firm with a presence in many countries, leveraging the global footprint to take advantage of the ability to serve global clients across multiple jurisdictions can be difficult, and it can be remarkably easy to fall foul of compliance rules, or breach contractual requirements imposed by

clients that may have different or very specific compliance rules that they must follow. The European Union's GDPR regulation has strong restrictions on the transmission of personal data from within the EU zone to other countries. For some destination countries, the transfer of such data may be simple, for others it may require a bureaucratic procedure and for others it may not be possible at all. It is easy to transgress and the fines can be extremely onerous; there will be situations where the firm is having to balance client needs and commercial pressures against the reality that providing best service to the client may put the firm into noncompliance with data privacy protection laws.

Cyber policies are typically global in their scope, but it is important for the firm to also consider jurisdictional issues; for instance the policy may provide coverage for fines and penalties, but this will always carry the proviso that such coverage can only be provided where not prohibited by law. In the European Union alone there is a spectrum of permissibility of insurance of fines and penalties, from countries where it is explicitly allowed, through countries where it varies according to situation, to those where it is prohibited absolutely. The same situation applies across the USA, with some states not only prohibiting the insurance of fines and penalties but having "long arm" laws that prohibit an insured from making a claim for reimbursement of fines and penalties in an overseas jurisdiction where it is permitted. Some policies have a "most favorable jurisdiction" clause that allows the insured to select under which jurisdiction the insurance will be interpreted and the reimbursement made, but such a clause may be of little value if the firm is based in a "long arm" state.

Cyber insurance, like any other form of insurance, is also subject to local insurance regulation and taxation. Arranging global insurance programs is an intricate process that requires knowledge of local laws and practices; in some countries, the provision of insurance is a government monopoly, in some locally arranged insurance is required, and in others it is sufficient to ensure that the relevant premium tax is paid. Working with an insurance broker that has a presence in all the territories as well as an insurer that can similarly accommodate local requirements in those jurisdictions is a necessity.

VI. Best Practices for Cyber Insurance Purchase Preparation[92]

Insurance markets move in cycles, and the current "hard" insurance market will pass. In the meantime, insureds can bolster chances at a better renewal by doing the following. Start with a strategic process to understand insurers' preferred standards of technology protections and implementations and measure the cost of improving the firm's stance against the benefits that doing so might confer in the insurance market. The higher the standards of protection the more opportunities the firm will have to consider cyber risk insurance alternatives. The process can be educational and improve law firm cyber resiliency—even if the firm determines not to purchase cyber insurance.[93] Beginning the renewal process early brings benefits, providing time to identify "low hanging fruit" of technology improvements, and allowing meetings with key underwriters, focusing on existing carrier relationships, and determining current renewal appetite, which will mitigate surprises. Phase 1:

- A "discovery process" is undertaken to understand the firm's exposures and primary data privacy and security concerns and to determine where possible coverage and gaps exist under existing insurance policies. This process will identify where the firm is missing coverage and or where coverage enhancements have become available, such as electronic crime (social engineering fraud) or "bricking." With a hardening market, there tends to be less control over the terms and conditions, exclusions, and premiums, but it is essential for the firm to understand what is and is not covered under the cyber program and how that coverage interfaces with the rest of the firm's policies (particularly the lawyer's professional liability).
- Increase risk assessment and management efforts as set forth in the previous chapters of this Handbook: know your losses and loss history and be prepared to discuss with the underwriter how those losses

---

92. "The status-quo habits for 'grandfathered' vulnerabilities do not legitimize them." —Stephane Nappo.

93. *Professional Services Practice Cyber Risk*, AON, https://www.aon.com/risk-services /professional-services/cyber-risk-cyber-insurance.jsp.

have been addressed by your firm. Draft and revise policies and procedures to address vulnerabilities in the firm's cybersecurity stance to reduce loss going forward. While no organization can eliminate the threat of a breach, being able to demonstrate basic steps to reduce the risk and significantly decrease the impact of a threat actor is critical. This requires proactive risk mitigation strategies, including assessment, testing, and practice improvement. It also requires incident response readiness, including conducting table-top breach simulation exercises (some insurers are requiring that firms not only conduct these exercises at least annually but that ransomware scenarios should be explicitly included in the exercises) and proactively retaining key third-party incident response providers. Leveraging resources available through an organization's insurer partners may improve the outcome should a loss arise. On February 4, 2021, the New York Department of Financial Services (NYDFS) released its Cyber Insurance Framework (the "Framework"). The first of its kind, the Framework lays out formal strategies for measuring and managing cyber risks.[94]

- Employee cybersecurity and phishing simulation training can demonstrate a culture of cybersecurity. No longer is this just an Admin/IT/Finance problem; employees should be trained to work to combat malicious actors and reduce common vulnerabilities. Without demonstrating adequate security training, insurers may struggle to provide competitive coverage terms or premium pricing.

- With carriers seeing both an increase in frequency and severity of ransomware-related losses, companies should be prepared to showcase preparedness for a ransomware attack. Insurers are reviewing this exposure via specific questionnaires and use of scanning technology. Focus is on business continuity/disaster recovery planning, privileged access controls, multifactor authentication, proactive scanning/testing, and overall incident response readiness. This attack vector is of utmost

---

94. *Cyber Insurance Risk Framework, Insurance Circular Letter No. 2*, N.Y. State: Dep't of Fin. Servs. (Feb. 4, 2021), https://www.dfs.ny.gov/industry_guidance/circular_letters /cl2021_02.

concern to underwriters and will continue to transform the insurance market for the next several years.

- Third-party contracts are of consideration from a technology supply chain and contingent/dependent business standpoint. After ransomware, loss of revenue is one of the major concerns of underwriters; one has only to look at the impact of NotPetya and other major ransomware incidents (such as that which hit CNA in Q2 2021) in which the victim firms were rendered "dark" (i.e., all computer systems, including telecommunications, completely shut down) for two weeks with restoration of full system functionality taking several weeks beyond the period of total shutdown. Considering the recent SolarWinds compromise, these critical supply chain and IT vendors are at heightened risk for "single point of failure" hacks impacting multiple organizations. It is critical to understand how both contracts and insurance respond in the case of a supply chain security breach.

- Based on the findings, alternative options are considered to address identified coverage gaps.

- Budget: Premiums are continuing to escalate rapidly and there are signs of contraction in capacity that will continue to drive further increases. There are signs that this cycle is unlikely to soften in 2021, so plan ahead.

Phase 2:

- An application for cyber risk insurance is completed. Given the 2021 "hard" market discussed at the top of this chapter, the information and diligence required has become much more specific and time-consuming to complete. Insurers are often requiring their own application forms and supplemental questionnaires to be completed before offering terms, resulting in clients having to complete multiple versions of similar forms. Average time for a small firm requires five to ten hours. Average time for a large firm is 20 to 30 hours to complete the application and submission process. Many insurers are requiring underwriting meetings with the IT staff of the firm to ask questions and learn in more detail about the firm's cybersecurity maturity and posture and specific technology implementations. The firm should leverage and highlight lessons learned from this Handbook to the extent implemented.

- A cyber risk submission matrix is prepared, which ranks most important coverage factors compared to what is available in the marketplace appropriate for each clients' individual needs.
- Create insurer competition by distributing your submission matrix "asks" to multiple cyber insurers.
- The firm should ask its broker for benchmark information to provide a cost-benefit analysis of retention, limits, and pricing against peer firms.
- A detailed comparison of the terms and conditions of each offering is presented.
- Establish mutual expectations for loss or claim response with insurers in advance (e.g., avoid Covid-19 business interruption-type disputes).
  - Retention or deductible figure your firm is comfortable paying prior to inception;
  - Selection of approved breach response vendors from the insurer panel, including breach counsel, Digital Forensic Investigation & Response experts, crisis communications firm, PII breach notification firms, and credit monitoring firms (if necessary); and
  - Business interruption "proof of loss" form and calculation.

Phase 3:

Notice provisions remain an omnipresent and important consideration for cyber insurance policyholders, particularly as technology and digital exposures continue to increase for many law firms that were not traditionally "technology companies." Understanding the distinction between "claims made" and "claims made and reported" notice provisions may be critical as late notice is among one of the most common causes of claims friction under cyber policies. Further complicating matters is the occasional inclusion of "occurrence" terminology within "claims made" and "claims made and reported" notice language, particularly with respect to technology failures or security issues that give rise to cyber claims. The inclusion of such "occurrence" parlance does not in and of itself convert these policies to "occurrence"-based forms, further underscoring the need for insureds to understand the various nuances of notice obligations under their policy.

VII. Top Ten Considerations

1. Start early. The cyber insurance renewal process is taking longer than in prior years. Underwriters are examining more issues, trends, and loss history. And insurers are waiting until the last minute to issue proposals.

2. Claims service is the most important element that insureds are buying; make sure your insurer has the resources you need and a reputation for excellent claims service.

   a. Ensure firm leadership has an appropriate governance structure, particularly with regard to a reporting protocol for insurable and non-insurable cyber risks.

   b. As cyber risks grow in complexity, it is important not only to ensure primary carrier engagement relative to coverage terms and conditions, but also to ensure excess carrier understanding of the primary policy provisions. Additionally, it is prudent to review exclusions that could come from other insurance lines such as Crime, Property, Casualty, and General Liability. Maintaining a clear and transparent relationship with both primary and excess insurers may better inform policy intent and improve claim outcomes.

3. Work with an expert to help you consider each of the issues raised in this chapter and the type of coverage you should consider for your organization. Cyber exposures and solutions are dynamic and fluid and so must be your approach. Retain a knowledgeable broker and attorney. A good broker, who knows your business, losses, and risks, can identify potential risks and appropriate products available. Emerging privacy regulations and requirements should be routinely reviewed with counsel.

4. Policy wording is important; cyber policy wordings are complex and differ greatly in their language and definitions. Work closely with someone who understands the nuances within the different types of policies.

5. Limits purchased should be a function of insured's overall risk management appetite, taking into account potential frequency and severity of the cyber risks faced by the insured. Position cyber insurance treatment solutions as a subset of enterprise risk management system capabilities for the organization to enable a firm-wide cyber risk management culture.

6. Cyber insurers are partners; they don't want you to have an event any more than you do. Use their expertise and resources, learn from their experience. Insurers' additional resources, such as cyber assessments, may be especially valuable to smaller firms.

7. Be aware of how your cyber policy interacts with other policies and work with a broker who is able to help you manage how the policies will respond; in the middle of a claim you don't want to be arguing about which insurer is going to help you.

8. Insurance is only part of risk management; it must integrate with the incident response plan. Test it regularly and analyze roles and scope of individuals engaged in the response plan; ensure that everyone involved is aware of and will work with internal and outside counsel to protect attorney-client privilege in communications.

9. Check that your preferred law firm and incident/breach response vendors are approved by your insurer. The worst time to learn that your incident response third-party vendor is not covered under your insurance is during an incident.

10. Remember that you are potentially liable for the acts of your vendors and suppliers, and that you are dependent on your vendors and outsourced service providers. Cyber maturity may be demonstrated via established and updated policies that address third-party contracts, online presence, service providers, supply chains, and each business unit.

Conclusion

You've just finished the third edition of the ABA's handbook on cybersecurity. Much has changed since the first edition was published in 2013, not to mention the second edition, published in 2018. The first edition was an introduction to the idea of cyberspace; today, most lawyers live in the cyber domain every day. Cybersecurity is no longer a separate topic for legal analysis; it has become the foundation for much of our professional success.

And that means we need to be more agile in our thinking, as the threats in cyberspace morph almost daily. Three years ago, few, if any, would have predicted the rise of the ransomware phenomenon. As this book goes to press (February 2022) the problem is rampant and ongoing. And so, we incorporate discussion of ransomware into various chapter throughout the book. We also have a new chapter on disinformation, which has become a mainstream problem for all enterprises. We could go on—but you get the idea. The only constant in the cyber realm is that nothing is constant.

Consider, by way of example, a favorite factoid about the Internet: seventeen years ago, Facebook didn't exist. Today, it boasts more than 2.8 billion users and is available in more than 110 different languages. If Facebook were a nation, it would be the largest on the planet and more than double the size of the next most populous nation, China. When founded, it aspired only to provide a venue for college students to socialize. Today, content on Facebook influences the politics of nations and the vaccination choices of the world.

This condition of change is endemic to the cyber network environment. Were the changes exclusively technological in nature and limited to the digital world we might be less concerned about their effect. But the cyber domain is, increasingly, one with real-world impact. In the 12 months prior to the publication of this edition, we saw real-world impacts on oil and gas pipelines, meat processing plants, and health care systems. It is not difficult to imagine cyber-initiated kinetic impacts on almost any physical entity. As one of us wrote in mid-2021, only half-jokingly, the most egregious threat that lies ahead is to the supply chain for the production of coffee.[1]

We know that, in many ways, this makes the volume you hold in your hands out-of-date almost at the moment it is published. But, in other ways, ones that are more important, the principles of good security and good lawyering are enduring and do not change over time—at least not nearly as rapidly as the underlying technology. But as technology changes, even changes in these more enduring principles are inevitable. And so, to ensure that our cybersecurity efforts are successful, it is useful in the end to try to plan for the future and anticipate the next iteration of threats in cyberspace.

Doing so is difficult. The network's remarkable pace of change will only accelerate. More change, more quickly and more frequently, is all that we can expect. Given this reality, it is a brave writer who ventures thoughts on what to expect in the future. Indeed, it is almost impossible and rather fool-hardy to look ahead in the cyber domain with a crystal ball. Nevertheless, in this conclusion we choose to brave the challenge (with a more forceful than is typical disclaimer that these views are ours alone and shouldn't be attributed to anyone but us). Here are a few things to keep in mind as you plan for the future:

First, and perhaps most obviously, connectivity will only increase. Today, we are at the very beginning of the deployment of a 5G network, and 6G is just getting on the drawing board. As the speed and ubiquity of communication increases, so too will the ability to do more and more things virtually. The Internet of Things will go global. Within the next five years, the currently novel self-driving cars and at-a-distance surgery will become commonplace.

And with connectivity comes vulnerability. It is often said that North Korea is practically invulnerable to cyberattack because so little of that country is connected to the network. By contrast, it is often thought that the United States has a cyber "glass jaw" because the ubiquitous nature of our connectivity to the network creates pervasive risk. If you think that the

---

1. Paul Rosenzweig & Bryson Bort, *Ransomware Attacks Put Everything We Depend on at Risk. What's Next, Foamy Coffee Lattes?*, USA TODAY (June 10, 2021), https://www.rstreet.org/2021/06/10/ransomware-attacks-put-everything-we-depend-on-at-risk-whats-next-foamy-coffee-lattes/.

glass jaw analogy is correct today, just imagine how much more vulnerable users will be if and when they are dependent on digital connectivity for an ever-greater fraction of their physical world activity. For lawyers, this means both increased vulnerability in their practice and more widespread vulnerability for their clients.

Second, we will continue to see the rise of well-resourced and enabled non-State actors. To be sure, the gravest threats in cyberspace will continue to arise from peer-competitor nations like Russia and China. But those nations are fundamentally logical in their approach to the world and, therefore, understandable at some level. And that which we can understand, we can deal with—we can cajole, coerce, or deter as necessary—if we have the will to do so.

Some non-State actors are also rational (almost mercenary in nature), and hence can be countered by deterrence or retaliation. But some other actors in the cyber domain appear (at least so far) to be irrational, and thus undeterrable. Many are at the borderline of becoming cyberterrorists who act for unfathomable ideological reasons. These sorts of threats are likely to multiply imagine, if you will, your least-favorite irrational political action/terror group with access to the network and sophisticated hacking tools. The nightmare of, say, an anti-capitalist group destroying the New York Stock Exchange cannot be discounted.

Third, the combination of ubiquitous connectivity and the rise of malicious actors means that more people will be more vulnerable to more bad events more regularly, and there is nothing we can do to change that. As Dan Geer, former CISO of In-Q-Tel, once put it, it's like having "every sociopath [in the world] as your next-door neighbor."[2]

The consequences of this manifestly new reality are hard to predict, but we can readily imagine any number of possibilities. For example, ransomware is now targeted at high-value vulnerable actors. Soon, ransomware will be democratized. It will move from being a global enterprise issue to affecting us in our daily lives (if you want proof, just consider the Kaseya attack that affected thousands of small- and medium-sized businesses who

---

2. Daniel E. Geer, Jr., *A Rubicon*, https://www.hoover.org/sites/default/files/research/docs/geer_webreadypdfupdated2.pdf.

relied on its product). If you want to start your car? That will be one bitcoin please. In response, we expect that enterprises will come to see cyber vulnerability as inevitable and continue the transition away from "prevention" to a model (similar to how we treat illness) of "detect, respond, and recover."

Fourth, the growth in connectivity will be married to an equivalent growth in the ability of machine learning to replicate human behavior in meaningful ways. We do not have to think of these systems as "intelligent" or "self-aware" to recognize that they are capable of completing many human tasks as readily as humans can, and at a quicker pace.

This means that, increasingly, human activities will become automated. As artificial intelligence improves, tasks as diverse as warfare and surgery will be done without human intervention, at least at the tactical level. This will have profound impacts on our lives and will raise questions of ethics, morality, and practicality for which, it seems, we are not well-prepared.

The risks of this change are speculative. They can range from simple problems (like AI bias) that can be address legally and practically to more difficult challenges. (How, for example, do we teach AI the laws of armed conflict when they involve questions of judgment?) Will even our cybersecurity responses be automated?

Fifth, privacy, in the sense of anonymity and freedom from scrutiny, will continue to erode. To begin with, technological advances allow governments to know more about citizens in ways that can leave the citizens uncomfortable and exposed. Large data aggregation and enhanced artificial intelligence analytics will enable the development of near-comprehensive personal profiles to allow the micro-targeting of influence and sanctions. In authoritarian countries, these effects will proceed almost without legal constraint. Even in Western democracies, where conceptions of individual privacy will find greater favor, legal protections will struggle to keep up with technological reality. It is hard enough to write rules for applications and systems as they exist today. In a regulatory environment where legal developments take a year or two to come to fruition, the pace of change magnifies the dissonance between capability and legal limitations. Even in the West, then, we can anticipate that legal protections of privacy will increasingly be seen as inadequate.

It is possible (perhaps even likely) that some jurisdictions around the world will respond with greater legal protections. For others, like the United States, the prospect of legal and regulatory response is more uncertain. Lawyers may be called upon to respond to the changing legal environment and also to think creatively about how to incorporate privacy protections into private (e.g., contractual) instruments.

Sixth, the trend toward ubiquitous connectivity will generate a significant real-world pushback of isolation and Internet balkanization. The fault lines of nation-state conflict will lead to multiple separate Internets that may be almost completely isolated, like North Korea, or very limited for regional control, like China. Meanwhile, even disputes between friends (like that between the United States and Europe over privacy and data transfer) will cause the unity of the network to fragment.

It is an interesting and existential question—which instinct will win out? Will the network become more comprehensive and seamless or will it become more balkanized and fragmented? One fears that the Western world will ultimately wind up with the worst of all possible futures, a network domain that is fragmented in terms of law and jurisdiction, but massively hyperconnected in terms of vulnerability and consequence. The result will be greater cyber risk to most Western enterprises.

Seventh, quantum computing may increase processing speeds exponentially. Both national governments and multinational corporations are investing billions of dollars in the development of quantum computers. If they are ever commercially developed (and that is, at this point, uncertain) their use would be transformative. To capture the nature of the change, consider this anecdote: it is said that a full-sized, working quantum computer could have the entire corpus of today's vast Internet in its internal storage. Unlikely? Maybe. But imagine if it were to occur.

There is truly no way of knowing what that change will portend. There are, of course, indications. Many are already concerned, for example, about the possible demise of current encryption systems that depend on the limited processing capability of current computing devices. And so it is easy to posit a world in which secure online communications or transactions (like banking) are no longer possible, and ponder the ramifications.

But that, we think, is but the tip of the iceberg. Exceedingly fast processing combined with ubiquitous connectivity is likely to be culturally transformative. Imagine, for example, a world in which each individual has computing power equivalent to that of a nation-state today at his or her fingertips; where each has access to the entire storehouse of human knowledge; and where currently difficult tasks are increasingly automated. And now, further imagine the malign possibilities behind such capabilities and you begin to see the problem. Perhaps this prediction is further off in the future than some of our others—but the youngest associates in a law firm today may live to see it become a reality.

Eighth, and perhaps most speculatively, reality itself will be contested—building on the disinformation campaigns of the past few years, the propagation of "deepfake" technologies that can mimic and mutate real-life experiences will make debates about facts and "fake news" ever more prominent. Virtual realities, today a novelty, will become more commonplace. This, too, will challenge settled cultural constructs. If the ground truth of all facts becomes contingent, then much of our shared experience will soon dissolve. You think the Yankees won the last World Series? Sorry, but here's the video of the Mets winning.

Unlikely? Probably—but the political events of the last few years in the United States and elsewhere are not encouraging. Transform our World Series example into, for example, a video of Hillary Clinton with a young child at a pizzeria and suddenly our most obscure and unreasonable conspiracy theories become fodder for a newly created reality. That's an especially scary prospect.

But although the future is uncertain, the principles set out in this book will remain critical for lawyers for years to come. These include:

- Lawyers have ethical and legal obligations to their clients relating to cybersecurity. While the specifics of those obligations may change, the basic principle will remain.
- Lawyers should anticipate cybersecurity problems with their clients and not wait for a crisis.
- Lawyers' concerns with cybersecurity should relate not only to their clients but to themselves.

- Lawyers are increasingly becoming targets of cyberattacks, and, even if not targeted, may be incidentally affected by an attack.
- The nature of the threat environment is constantly evolving. Competent lawyers need to keep abreast of the facts.
- The legal framework is equally evolving. Competent lawyers also need to keep abreast of the law.
- Cybersecurity problems are globalizing. While U.S. lawyers need not develop competence in the details of the laws of every country, they need to understand the basic legal framework in which their clients operate—and know when to seek assistance from competent local counsel.
- Cybersecurity is a process not an event.

We have one **final** prediction. One way to understand the transformative nature of the cyber domain is to think about how and when you will get the next edition of this book. The time of physical hardback books may be coming to an end. The fourth edition of this book, if there is one, will almost certainly be issued in a digital or virtual form. So, the next time you read this conclusion, it is likely to look very different and be on some sort of electronic device. That shift—from paper and print to e-readers and pixels—embodies the challenging nature of cybersecurity.

Jill Rhodes
Robert S. Litt
Paul Rosenzweig

Chapter 4 Appendices
Selected Data Security Statutes, Regulations, and Cases

Appendix A: Federal Statutes

COPPA: Children's Online Privacy Protection Act of 1998, 15 U.S.C. §§ 6501–6505.

CFPA: Consumer Financial Protection Act of 2010, 12 U.S.C. §§ 5531(a), 5536(a)(1) (prohibits unfair, deceptive, or abusive acts or practices in connection with a transaction for, or offer of, a consumer financial product or service).

E-SIGN: Electronic Signatures in Global and National Commerce Act, 15 U.S.C. § 7001(d).

FCRA/FACTA: Fair Credit Reporting Act, as amended by the Fair and Accurate Credit Transaction Act, 15 U.S.C. §§ 1681–1681x.

FISMA: Federal Information Security Management Act of 2002, 44 U.S.C. §§ 3541.

FTC Act: Federal Trade Commission Act, 15 U.S.C. § 45(a)(1) (prohibits unfair or deceptive acts or practices in or affecting commerce).

GLB Act: Gramm-Leach-Bliley Act, Pub. L. No. 106-102, 15 U.S.C. §§ 6081–6809, 6821–6827.

HIPAA: Health Insurance Portability and Accountability Act, 42 U.S.C. §§ 1320d-2, d-4. *See also* Subtitle D of Title XIII of the American Recovery and Reinvestment Act of 2009 (ARRA), Pub. L. No. 111-5, 123 Stat. 115, at §§ 13401 *et seq.*

Homeland Security Act of 2002: 44 U.S.C. § 3532(b)(1).

Privacy Act of 1974: 5 U.S.C. § 552a.

Sarbanes-Oxley Act: Pub. L. No. 107-204, § 302; 15 U.S.C. §§ 7241 (corporate responsibility for financial reports), 7262 (management assessment of internal controls), 7211–7266.

Federal Rules of Evidence 901(a): *See In re* Vinhnee, 336 B.R. 437 (B.A.P. 9th Cir. 2005); Lorraine v. Markel, 241 F.R.D. 534 (D. Md. 2007).

USA PATRIOT Act: 31 U.S.C. § 5318(l) ("Identification and Verification of Accountholders")

Appendix B: State Statutes

1. State Laws Imposing Obligations to Provide Security for Personal Information

Alabama	ALA. CODE § 8-38-3
Arkansas	ARK. CODE ANN. § 4-110-104(b)
California	CAL. CIV. CODE § 1798.81.5, .6 (credit reporting agencies); § 1798.91.04 (manufacturers of connected devices)
Colorado	COLO. REV. STAT. § 6-1-713 to -713.5
Connecticut	CONN. GEN. STAT. § 42-471; § 4e-70 (state contractors); § 38a-999b (health insurers); Conn. HB 6607, Pub. Act 21-119 (An Act Incentivizing the Adoption of Cybersecurity Standards for Businesses)
District of Columbia	67 D.C. Reg. 8039 (July 3, 2020)
Delaware	DEL. CODE ANN. tit. 6, § 12B-100
Florida	FLA. STAT. § 501.171(2); § 282.318 (state agencies)
Illinois	815 ILL. COMP. STAT. 530/45; 740 ILL. COMP. STAT. 14/1 (Biometric Information Privacy Act)
Indiana	IND. CODE § 24-4.9-3-3.5
Kansas	KAN. STAT. ANN. §§ 50-6, 139b
Louisiana	LA. STAT. ANN. § 3074
Maryland	MD. CODE ANN., COM. LAW § 14-3503; STATE GOV'T § 10-1304 (state agencies)
Massachusetts	MASS. GEN. LAWS ch. 93H, § 2(a)
Minnesota	MINN. STAT. § 325M.05
Nebraska	NEB. REV. STAT. § 87-801 to -807
Nevada	NEV. REV. STAT. § 603A.210
New Mexico	N.M. STAT. ANN. § 57-12C-4 to -5
New York	N.Y. GEN. BUS. LAW § 899-BB
Ohio	OHIO REV. CODE ANN. § 1354.01–.05
Oregon	OR. REV. STAT. § 646A.622
Rhode Island	R.I. GEN. LAWS § 11-49.3-2
Texas	TEX. BUS. & COM. CODE ANN. § 521.052
Utah	UTAH CODE ANN. § 13-44-201; § 78B-4-701 (Utah Cybersecurity Affirmative Defense Act)
Vermont	VT. STAT. ANN. tit. 9, §§ 2446–2447

2. State Laws Imposing Obligations to Provide Security for Credit Card Information

Minnesota	MINN. STAT. § 325E.64
Nevada	NEV. REV. STAT. § 603A.215
Washington	WASH. REV. CODE § 19.255.010

3. State Data Disposal/Destruction Laws

Alabama	ALA. CODE § 8-38-10 (was Ala. 2018 SB 318)
Alaska	ALASKA STAT. § 45.48.500–.590
Arizona	ARIZ. REV. STAT. § 44-7601
Arkansas	ARK. CODE ANN. § 4-110-104(a)
California	CAL. CIV. CODE § 1798.81
Colorado	COLO. REV. STAT. § 6-1-713
Connecticut	CONN. GEN. STAT. § 42-471
Delaware	DEL. CODE ANN. tit. 6, §§ 5001C–5004C; tit. 19, § 736 (employers)
Florida	FLA. STAT. § 501.171(8)
Georgia	GA. CODE ANN. § 10-15-2
Hawaii	HAW. REV. STAT. § 487R-2
Illinois	815 ILL. COMP. STAT. 530/40; 530/30 (state agencies); 20 ILL. COMP. STAT. 450/20 (state computers); 740 ILL. COMP. STAT. 14/15 (Biometric Information Privacy Act)
Indiana	IND. CODE §§ 24-4-14-8, 24-4.9-3-3.5l
Kansas	KAN. STAT. ANN. § 50-7a03
Kentucky	KY. REV. STAT. ANN. § 365.725
Louisiana	LA. STAT. ANN. § 51:3074(B)
Maryland	MD. CODE ANN., COM. LAW § 14-3502; MD. CODE ANN., STATE GOV'T § 10-1301–03 (government units)
Massachusetts	MASS. GEN. LAWS ch. 93I, § 2
Michigan	MICH. COMP. LAWS § 445.72a
Montana	MONT. CODE ANN. § 30-14-1703
Nevada	NEV. REV. STAT. § 603A.200
New Jersey	N.J. STAT. ANN. § 56:8-162
New Mexico	N.M. STAT. ANN. § 57-12C-3
New York	N.Y. GEN. BUS. LAW § 399-H
North Carolina	N.C. GEN. STAT. § 75-64

Oregon	OR. REV. STAT. § 646A.622
Puerto Rico	2014 P.R. Laws #234-2014
Rhode Island	R.I. GEN. LAWS § 6-52-2
South Carolina	S.C. CODE ANN. §§ 37-20-190, 30-2-310
Tennessee	TENN. CODE ANN. § 39-14-150(g)
Texas	TEX. BUS. & COM. CODE ANN. §§ 48.102(b), 72.004, 521.052
Utah	UTAH CODE ANN. § 13-44-201
Vermont	VT. STAT. ANN. tit. 9, § 2445
Washington	WASH. REV. CODE § 19.215.020
Wisconsin	WIS. STAT. § 134.97
Wyoming	WYO. STAT. ANN. § 9-21-101 (state agencies)

4. State Security Breach Notification Laws

Alabama	ALA. CODE § 8-38-1
Alaska	ALASKA STAT. § 45.48.010–.090
Arizona	ARIZ. REV. STAT. § 18-551 to -554
Arkansas	ARK. CODE ANN. § 4-110-101 to -108
California	CAL. CIV. CODE § 1798.82 (person or business); § 1798.29 (state agencies)
Colorado	COLO. REV. STAT. § 6-1-716
Connecticut	CONN. GEN. STAT. § 36a-701(b); § 4e-70 (state contractors)
Delaware	DEL. CODE ANN. tit. 6, § 12B-101 to 104; tit. 18, § 8606 (insurers)
District of Columbia	D.C. CODE § 28-3851 to -3853
Florida	FLA. STAT. § 501.171; § 282.0041, .318 (state agency additional requirements)
Georgia	GA. CODE ANN. § 10-1-910 to -912; § 46-5-214 (telephone records)
Guam	9 GUAM CODE ANN. § 48.10–.80
Hawaii	HAW. REV. STAT. § 487N-1
Idaho	IDAHO CODE § 28-51-104 to -107
Illinois	815 ILL. COMP. STAT. § 530/1–/10
Indiana	IND. CODE § 24-4.9; § 4-1-11-1 to -10 (state agency)
Iowa	IOWA CODE § 715C.1-2
Kansas	KAN. STAT. ANN. § 50-7a01 to -7a02
Kentucky	KY. REV. STAT. ANN. §§ 365.732, 61.931–.934 (state)

Louisiana	LA. STAT. ANN. § 51:3071–:3077; LA. ADMIN. CODE tit. 16, pt. 3, § 701 (reporting requirements)
Maine	ME. REV. STAT. ANN. tit. 10, §§ 1346 to 1350-B
Maryland	MD. CODE ANN., COM. LAW § 14-3501 to -3508; STATE GOV'T § 10-1301, -1305 (government units)
Massachusetts	MASS. GEN. LAWS ch. 93H
Michigan	MICH. COMP. LAWS § 445.63–.72b (see § 445.72)
Minnesota	MINN. STAT. §§ 325E.61, 325E.64, 609.891
Mississippi	MISS. CODE ANN. § 75-24-29
Missouri	MO. REV. STAT. § 407.1500
Montana	MONT. CODE ANN. § 30-14-1701 to -1705, § 33-19-321 (insurance-related); § 2-6-1501 to -1503 (state agencies)
Nebraska	NEB. REV. STAT. § 87-801 to -807
Nevada	NEV. REV. STAT. § 603A.010–.920 (see § 603A.220), § 242.183
New Hampshire	N.H. REV. STAT. ANN. §§ 359-C:19 to C:21, 332-I:1 to -I:6 (medical records); N.H. ADMIN. CODE § 3701 (insurance)
New Jersey	N.J. STAT. ANN. § 56:8-163
New Mexico	N.M. STAT. ANN. § 57-12C-1
New York	N.Y. GEN. BUS. LAW § 899-aa; N.Y. STATE TECH LAW § 208 (state entities)
North Carolina	N.C. GEN. STAT. § 75-61, -65
North Dakota	N.D. CENT. CODE § 51-30
Ohio	OHIO REV. CODE ANN. § 1349.19, .191, .192; § 1347.12 (state/local agencies)
Oklahoma	OKLA. STAT. tit. 24, §§ 161–166; tit. 74, § 3113.1 (state units)
Oregon	OR. REV. STAT. § 646A.600–.628
Pennsylvania	73 PA. CONS. STAT. §§ 2301–2329
Puerto Rico	P.R. LAWS ANN. tit. 10, §§ 4051–4055
Rhode Island	R.I. GEN. LAWS § 11-49.3-1 to -6
South Carolina	S.C. CODE ANN. § 39-1-90; § 1-11-490 (state agencies)
South Dakota	S.D. CODE § 22-40-20 to -26
Tennessee	TENN. CODE ANN. § 47-18-2107; § 8-4-119 (state agencies)
Texas	TEX. BUS. & COM. CODE ANN. § 521.002, .053
Utah	UTAH CODE ANN. § 13-44-101, -202, -301
Vermont	VT. STAT. ANN. tit. 9, §§ 2430, 2435
Virgin Islands (US)	V.I. CODE ANN. tit. 14, § 2209 (person or business), § 2208 (government agencies)

Virginia	VA. CODE ANN. § 18.2-186.6; § 32.1-127.1:05 (government entities, medical information)
Washington	WASH. REV. CODE § 19.255.010, § 42.56.590 (state/local agencies); WASH. ADMIN. CODE § 284-04-625 (insurance)
West Virginia	W. VA. CODE § 46A-2A-101 to -105
Wisconsin	WIS. STAT. § 134.98
Wyoming	WYO. STAT. ANN. § 40-12-501 to -502

5. State Social Security Number Laws

Alabama	ALA. CODE § 41-13-6 (government agencies); § 37-62-1 to -11 (insurers)
Alaska	ALASKA STAT. § 45.48.400, .430
Arizona	ARIZ. REV. STAT. § 44-1373
Arkansas	ARK. CODE ANN. §§ 4-86-107, 6-18-208
California	CAL. CIV. CODE §§ 1798.85, 1749.60; CAL. FAM. CODE § 2024.5; CAL. LAB. CODE § 226; CAL. ELEC. CODE § 2138.5; CAL. GOV'T CODE § 68107
Colorado	COLO. REV. STAT. §§ 4-3-506, 6-1-715, 13-21-109.5, 13-21-122, 23-5-127, 24-72.3-102
Connecticut	CONN. GEN. STAT. §§ 42-470, 8-64b
Delaware	DEL. CODE ANN. tit. 6, § 12B-102; tit. 9, § 9627 (state agencies); tit. 16, § 1009A (health care)
Florida	FLA. STAT. § 97.0585
Georgia	GA. CODE ANN. §§ 50-18-72, 10-1-393.8
Guam	5 GUAM CODE ANN. §§ 32704, 32705
Hawaii	HAW. REV. STAT. § 487J-1 to -4; § 12-3
Idaho	IDAHO CODE § 28-52-108(1)
Illinois	815 ILL. COMP. STAT. 505/2QQ, /2RR
Indiana	IND. CODE §§ 4-1-10-1 et seq., §§ 4-1-8 et seq., § 9-24-9-2, § 24-4.9-2-10
Kansas	KAN. STAT. ANN. § 75-3520
Louisiana	LA. STAT. ANN. §§ 17:440, 18:154, 32:409.1, 37:23, 44:11; LA. CIV. CODE ANN. art. 3352
Maine	ME. REV. STAT. ANN. tit. 10, §§ 1272, 1272-B
Maryland	MD. CODE ANN., COM. LAW § 14-3402
Massachusetts	MASS. GEN. LAWS ch. 167B, §§ 14, 22
Michigan	MICH. COMP. LAWS § 445 to 445.87, § 565.452, § 565.491
Minnesota	MINN. STAT. § 325E.59

Mississippi	MISS. CODE ANN. § 25-1-111
Missouri	MO. REV. STAT. § 407.1355
Montana	MONT. CODE ANN. §§ 32-6-306, 30-14-1702, 30-14-1703
Nebraska	NEB. REV. STAT. § 48-237
Nevada	NEV. REV. STAT. §§ 239, 239B, 603
New Hampshire	N.H. REV. STAT. ANN. § 382-A:9-528
New Jersey	N.J. STAT. ANN. §§ 47:1-16, 56:8-164
New Mexico	N.M. STAT. ANN. § 57-12B-1 to -4
New York	N.Y. GEN. BUS. LAW § 399-dd; N.Y. LAB. LAW § 203-d
North Carolina	N.C. GEN. STAT. §§ 75-62, 143-64.60
North Dakota	N.D. CENT. CODE § 39-33-01, -02
Ohio	OHIO REV. CODE ANN. § 1349.17
Oklahoma	OKLA. STAT. tit. 40, § 173.1
Oregon	OR. REV. STAT. § 107.840; § 646A.620
Pennsylvania	74 PA. CONS. STAT. §§ 201–204
Rhode Island	R.I. GEN. LAWS § 6-13-15, -17, -19
South Carolina	S.C. CODE ANN. §§ 7-5-170, 37-20-180, 30-2-310
South Dakota	S.D. CODE § 32-12-17.10, -17.13
Tennessee	TENN. CODE ANN. § 47-18-2110
Texas	TEX. BUS. & COM. CODE ANN. § 501.001–.002; TEX. ELEC. CODE ANN. § 13.004; TEX. BUS. & COM. CODE § 20.02
Utah	UTAH CODE ANN. §§ 31A-21-110, 13-45-301, 35A-4-312.5, 76-6-1102
Vermont	VT. STAT. ANN. tit. 9, §§ 2440, 2430; tit. 13, § 2030
Virginia	VA. CODE ANN. §§ 2.2-3808, 59.1-443.2, 24.2-416.5
Washington	WASH. REV. CODE § 19.146.205
West Virginia	W. VA. CODE §§ 17E-1-11, 16-5-33, 18-2-5f
Wisconsin	WIS. STAT. § 36.32

6. State Laws Requiring SSN Policies

Connecticut	Conn. Gen. Stat. § 42-471
Maryland	Md. Code Ann., State Gov't § 10-1301(d) (state agencies; broader than just SSNs)
Massachusetts	201 Mass. Code Regs. § 17.00 *et seq.* (broader than just SSNs)
Michigan	Mich. Comp. Laws § 445.84
New Mexico	N.M. Stat. Ann. § 57-12B-2 to -3
New York	N.Y. Gen. Bus. Law § 399-ddd(4)
Texas	Tex. Bus. & Com. Code Ann. § 501.051–.053 (also covers driver's license)

Appendix C: Federal Regulations

1. Federal Regulations Imposing an Obligation to Provide Security

COPPA Regulations: 16 C.F.R. § 312.8.

DHS Regulations: Electronic Signature and Storage of Form I-9, Employment Eligibility Verification, 8 C.F.R. § 274a.2 (e), (f), (g), (h) (requiring an effective records security program).

Exec. Order No. 14028: Improving the Nation's Cybersecurity, 86 Fed. Reg. 93, 26633 (May 12, 2021).

FCC Order re Pretexting: In the Matter of Implementation of the Telecommunications Act of 1996: Telecommunications Carriers' Use of Customer Proprietary Network Information and Other Customer Information IP-Enabled Services, CC Docket No. 96-115, WC Docket No. 04-36, Apr. 2, 2007, ¶¶ 33–36.

FDA Regulations: 21 C.F.R. pt. 11.

Federal Acquisition Regulations: 48 C.F.R. 52.204-21, Basic Safeguarding of Covered Contractor Information Systems.

Federal Acquisition Regulations: Defense Acquisition Regulations 48 C.F.R. 252.204-7012, Safeguarding Covered Defense Information and Cyber Incident Reporting.

Federal Financial Institutions Examination Council (FFIEC) Guidance: "Authentication in an Internet Banking Environment," Oct. 12, 2005. *See also* "Frequently Asked Questions on FFIEC Guidance on Authentication in an Internet Banking Environment," Aug. 15, 2006, at 5, and "Supplement to Authentication in an Internet Banking Environment," June 28, 2011.

GLB Security Regulations: Interagency Guidelines Establishing Standards for Safeguarding Consumer Information (to implement §§ 501 and 505(b) of the Gramm-Leach-Bliley Act), 12 C.F.R. pt. 30, Appendix B (OCC), 12 C.F.R. pt. 208, Appendix D-2 and 12 C.F.R. pt. 225, Appendix F (Federal Reserve System), 12 C.F.R. pt. 364, Appendix B (FDIC).

GLB Security Regulations (FTC): FTC Standards for Safeguarding Customer Information (Safeguards Rule) (to implement §§ 501 and 505(b) of the Gramm–Leach–Bliley Act), 16 C.F.R. pt. 314 (FTC).

HIPAA Security Regulations: HIPAA Security and Privacy Regulations, 45 C.F.R. pt. 164.

IRS Regulations: Rev. Proc. 97-22, 1997-1 C.B. 652, 1997-13 I.R.B. 9, and Rev. Proc. 98-25, and IRS Announcement 98-27, 1998-15 I.R.B. 30, and Tax Regs. 26 C.F.R. § 1.1441-1(e)(4)(iv).

Ratification of Transportation Security Administration (TSA) Security Directive Pipeline-2021-01: 86 Fed. Reg. 136, 38209 (July 20, 2021).

SEC Guidance: SEC CF Disclosure Guidance: Topic No. 2, Cybersecurity (Oct. 13, 2011);

SEC Regulations S-P, S-AM, and S-ID: 17 C.F.R. § 248.

SEC Regulations: General Rules and Regulations, Securities Exchange Act of 1934, 17 C.F.R. § 240.17a-4, and Preservation and Destruction of Records of Registered Public Utility Holding Companies and of Mutual and Subsidiary Service Companies, 17 C.F.R. § 257.1(e)(3).

SEC Regulations: 17 C.F.R. § 248.30 (procedures to safeguard customer records and information; disposal of consumer report information (applies to any broker, dealer, and investment company, and every investment advisor registered with the SEC)).

SEC Regulations: 17 C.F.R. § 242.1002—Obligations related to Systems Compliance and Integrity (SCI) events (upon any responsible SCI personnel having a reasonable basis to conclude that an SCI event has occurred, the SCI entity must provide the Commission with notifications pertaining to such event and regular updates until the event is resolved).

Defense Acquisition Regulations System (DFARS): 48 C.F.R. § 204.7300 (applies to contractors and subcontractors to safeguard covered unclassified defense information and also requires reporting of cyber incidents within 72 hours).

2. Federal Regulations Imposing Authentication Requirements

NACHA Operating Rules (2013): Section 2.5.2.5(d) ("Verification of Receiver's Identity").

Banking Know Your Customer Rules:

31 C.F.R. § 1020.220, Customer Identification Programs for Banks.

31 C.F.R. § 1023.220, Customer Identification Programs for Broker-Dealers.

31 C.F.R. § 1026.220, Customer Identification Programs for Futures Commission Merchants and Introducing Brokers.

31 C.F.R. § 1024.220, Customer Identification Programs for Mutual Funds.

FCC Order re Pretexting: Apr. 2, 2007—In the Matter of Implementation of the Telecommunications Act of 1996: Telecommunications Carriers' Use of Customer Proprietary Network Information and Other Customer Information IP-Enabled Services, CC Docket No. 96-115, WC Docket No. 04-36, Apr. 2, 2007, ¶¶ 13–25.

FFIEC Guidance: "Authentication in an Internet Banking Environment," Oct. 12, 2005. *See also* "Supplement to Authentication in an Internet Banking Environment," June 28, 2011.

3. Federal Data Disposal/Destruction Regulations

Fair Credit Reporting Act (FCRA) Data Disposal Rules: 12 C.F.R. pts. 334, 364.

SEC Regulations: 17 C.F.R. § 248.30 (procedures to safeguard customer records and information; disposal of consumer report information—applies to any broker, dealer, and investment company, and every investment advisor registered with the SEC).

4. Federal Security Breach Notification Regulations

FCC Order re Pretexting, In the Matter of Implementation of the Telecommunications Act of 1996: Telecommunications Carriers' Use of Customer Proprietary Network Information and Other Customer Information IP-Enabled Services, CC Docket No. 96-115, WC Docket No. 04-36, Apr. 2, 2007, ¶¶ 26–32.

GLB Security Breach Notification Rule: Interagency Guidance on Response Programs for Unauthorized Access to Customer Information and Customer Notice (Mar. 29, 2005); 12 C.F.R. pt. 30 (OCC); 12 C.F.R. pts. 208, 225 (Federal Reserve System); 12 C.F.R. pt. 364 (FDIC); 12 C.F.R. pts. 568, 570 (Office of Thrift Supervision, which merged with the OCC as of July 21, 2011).

IRS Regulations: Rev. Proc. 98-25, § 8.01.

HIPAA Breach Notification Rules: 45 C.F.R. § 164.400–.414.

SEC Guidance: SEC CF Disclosure Guidance: Topic No. 2, Cybersecurity (Oct. 13, 2011).

Appendix D: State Regulations

1. **Insurance:** National Association of Insurance Commissioners, Insurance Data Security Model Law (2017) now adopted in 13 states.
2. **Colorado:**
    a. Colo. Div. of Sec., Mortgage Broker-Dealer Cybersecurity, COLO. CODE REGS. § 704-1:51-4.6.1.
    b. Colo. Div. of Sec., Broker-Dealer Cybersecurity, COLO. CODE REGS. § 704-1:51-4.8.
3. **Delaware:** DEL. CODE ANN., tit. 10, § 301-13.0.
4. **Florida:** Fla. Dep't of Mgmt. Servs., Information Technology Security, FLA. ADMIN. CODE ch. 60GG-2.
5. **Georgia:** Ga. Elections Div., Standards for Security of Voter Registration System, GA. COMP. R. & REGS. § 590-8-3-.01.
6. **Maine:** Maine Insurance Regulation Bulletin No. 345 (Nov. 8, 2006), Notice of Risk to Personal Data Act.
7. **Massachusetts:** Standards for the Protection of Personal Information of Residents of the Commonwealth, 201 MASS. CODE REGS. 17.00.
8. **Michigan:**
    a. Pub. Serv. Comm'n, Security Reporting, MICH. ADMIN. CODE r. 460.2324.
    b. Pub. Serv. Comm'n, Technical Standards for Electric Service, Part 2: Records and Reports, MICH. ADMIN. CODE r. 460.3205.
9. **Minnesota:** Minn. Dep't of Com., Protection of Purchaser Information, Minn. R. 2876.3055.
10. **Mississippi:** Enterprise Cloud and Offsite Hosting Security Policy, 36 MISS. CODE R. § 3-a.5.
11. **New Jersey:**
    a. Exec. Order No. 178 (May 20, 2015), Creation of New Jersey Cybersecurity and Communications Integration Cell (NJCCIC).

    b. Exec. Order No. 44 (Nov. 1, 2018), An Order Directing the NJCCIC to Coordinate All Cybersecurity Efforts to Protect and Secure the State's Elections Infrastructure.

    c. N.J. ADMIN. CODE § 5:34-5.14, Cybersecurity and Data Ownership.

12. **New York:** N.Y. Dep't of Fin. Servs., Cybersecurity Requirements for Financial Services Companies, N.Y. COMP. CODES R. & REGS. tit. 23, §§ 500 *et seq.*

13. **Oklahoma:** Okla. Dep't of Sec., Information Security and Privacy, OKLA. ADMIN. CODE § 660:11-7-46.

14. **Texas:**

    a. Fin. Comm'n of Tex., Notice of Cybersecurity Incident, 7 TEX. ADMIN. CODE § 3.24.

    b. Pub. Util. Comm'n of Tex., Cybersecurity Monitor, 16 TEX. ADMIN. CODE § 25.367.

    c. Tex. Dep't of Banking, Notice of Cybersecurity Incident, 7 TEX. ADMIN. CODE § 33.30.

15. **Vermont:** Vt. Sec. Div., Cybersecurity Procedures, VT. CODE R. 7-8.

16. **Virginia:** Va. Bureau of Insurance, Insurance Data Security Risk Assessment and Reporting, 14 VA. ADMIN. CODE § 5-430 (2021).

Chapter 6 Appendices

ABA and State Bar Association Ethics Opinions and Other Resources Regarding Lawyers' Ethical Obligations to Provide Data Security to Their Clients

Appendix E: E-mail

Ethics Opinions on Lawyer Confidentiality Obligations Concerning E-mail

A) ABA Formal Ethics Opinions
The Opinion headnotes are reproduced below.

1) Formal Opinion 483 (Oct. 17, 2018)

Lawyers' Obligations After an Electronic Data Breach or Cyberattack
Model Rule 1.4 requires lawyers to keep clients "reasonably informed" about the status of a matter and to explain matters "to the extent reasonably necessary to permit a client to make an informed decision regarding the representation." Model Rules 1.1, 1.6, 5.1, and 5.3, as amended in 2012, address the risks that accompany the benefits of the use of technology by lawyers. When a data breach occurs involving, or having a substantial likelihood of involving, material client information, lawyers have a duty to notify clients of the breach and to take other reasonable steps consistent with their obligations under these Model Rules.

2) Formal Opinion 477R (Revised May 19, 2017)

Securing Communication of Protected Client Information
A lawyer generally may transmit information relating to the representation of a client over the Internet without violating the Model Rules of Professional Conduct where the lawyer has undertaken reasonable efforts to prevent inadvertent or unauthorized access. However, a lawyer may be required to take special security precautions to protect against the inadvertent or unauthorized disclosure of client information when required by an agreement with the client or by law, or when the nature of the information requires a higher degree of security.

3) Formal Opinion 99-413 (March 10, 1999)
   Protecting the Confidentiality of Unencrypted E-mail
A lawyer may transmit information relating to the representation of a client by unencrypted e-mail sent over the Internet without violating the Model Rules of Professional Conduct (1998) because the mode of transmission affords a reasonable expectation of privacy from a technological and legal standpoint. The same privacy accorded U.S. and commercial mail, landline telephonic transmissions, and facsimiles applies to Internet e-mail. A lawyer should consult with the client and follow her instructions, however, as to the mode of transmitting highly sensitive information relating to the client's representation. *See also* ABA Formal Opinion 477R (May 22, 2017) (interpreting later amendments to ABA Model Rules and providing advice on closely related questions).

4) Formal Opinion 11-459 (Aug. 4, 2011)
   Duty to Protect the Confidentiality of E-mail
   Communications with One's Client
A lawyer sending or receiving substantive communications with a client via e-mail or other electronic means ordinarily must warn the client about the risk of sending or receiving electronic communications using a computer or other device, or e-mail account, where there is a significant risk that a third party may gain access. In the context of representing an employee, this obligation arises, at the very least, when the lawyer knows or reasonably should

know that the client is likely to send or receive substantive client-lawyer communications via e-mail or other electronic means, using a business device or system under circumstances where there is a significant risk that the communications will be read by the employer or another third party.

5) Formal Opinion 11-460 (Aug. 4, 2011)
   Duty when Lawyer Receives Copies of a Third
   Party's E-mail Communications with Counsel

When an employer's lawyer receives copies of an employee's private communications with counsel, which the employer located in the employee's business e-mail file or on the employee's workplace computer or other device, neither Rule 4.4(b) nor any other Rule requires the employer's lawyer to notify opposing counsel of the receipt of the communications. However, court decisions, civil procedure rules, or other law may impose such a notification duty, which a lawyer may then be subject to discipline for violating. If the law governing potential disclosure is unclear, Rule 1.6(b)(6) allows the employer's lawyer to disclose that the employer has retrieved the employee's attorney-client e-mail communications to the extent the lawyer reasonably believes it is necessary to do so to comply with the relevant law. If no law can reasonably be read as establishing a notification obligation, however, then the decision whether to give notice must be made by the employer-client, and the employer's lawyer must explain the implications of disclosure, and the available alternatives, as necessary to enable the employer to make an informed decision.

B) ABA Treatises and Annotated Model Standards
1) ABA/Bloomberg Lawyers' Manual on Professional Conduct
http://www.americanbar.org/groups/professional_responsibility/publica
tions/aba_bna_lawyers_manual_on_professional_conduct.html
See the chapter from the treatise section of the Manual, "Confidentiality, Safeguarding Client Information, Electronic Communications, "55 Law. Man. Prof. Conduct 40.

2) Annotated Model Rules of Professional Conduct (ABA 9th ed. 2019).
https://www.americanbar.org/products/inv/book/364918796/
See the annotations to Rule 1.6 *Confidentiality of Information*.

3) Rotunda and Dzienkowski, Legal Ethics: The Lawyer's Deskbook
   on Professional Responsibility (ABA 2018-2019 ed.)
   https://store.legal.thomsonreuters.com/law-products/Statutes/Legal-Ethics
   -The-Lawyers-Deskbook-on-Professional-Responsibility-2018-2019-ed-ABA
   /p/106152833
   See Section 1.6-2 *Inadvertent Disclosure.*

*C) State and Local Bar Ethics Opinions that have
   addressed e-mail, cordless phone, and cell phone
   usage (with links to the full text where available)*

The following digests of state bar ethics opinions are excerpted with permission from the *ABA/Bloomberg Lawyers' Manual on Professional Conduct.*

1) Alaska Ethics Opinion 98-2 (Jan. 16, 1998)
   E-mail; Confidentiality; Internet.
   https://alaskabar.org/wp-content/uploads/98-2.pdf

A lawyer may use unencrypted e-mail to transmit client information, though lawyers are encouraged to use encryption software when communicating particularly sensitive or confidential matters by e-mail.

2) Arizona State Bar Opinion 95-11 (Dec. 1995)
   Confidentiality; Telephones.
   https://www.azbar.org/for-lawyers/ethics/ethics-opinions/

A lawyer may use a cellular or cordless telephone to contact a client or opposing counsel, but should exercise caution when discussing confidential matters as there is a genuine risk that a third party will intercept the information. Just as a lawyer would not discuss sensitive matters in a crowded restaurant, the lawyer should refrain from having such discussions when using a portable telephone. Rules 1.3, 1.4, 1.6.

3) Arizona Opinion 97-04 (April 7, 1997)
   Computer technology; Internet; Advertising
   and solicitation; Confidentiality.
   http://www.azbar.org/Ethics/EthicsOpinions/ViewEthicsOpinion?id=480

...(8) A lawyer may communicate with a client via e-mail even if the e-mail is not encrypted, although it is preferable to protect the attorney-client communications, if practical, through the use of encryption software or by having the e-mail encrypted with a password known only to the lawyer and the client. At minimum, e-mail transmissions to clients should include a cautionary statement either in the "re" line or at the beginning of the message, indicating that the transmission is "confidential" or "attorney-client privileged," just as is done when using facsimile transmittals. In determining whether to communicate with a client via e-mail, lawyers should consider that e-mail records, including the records of time and date of transmission and recipients, may be discoverable.

4)   Arizona Ethics Opinion 02-04 (Sept. 2002)
     Confidentiality; E-mail; Internet; Initial Consultation; Disclaimers.
https://www.azbar.org/for-lawyers/ethics/ethics-opinions/
A lawyer who simply uses e-mail, without having a Web site or advertisements on the Internet, does not owe a duty of confidentiality to an individual who unilaterally e-mails an unsolicited inquiry to the lawyer. However, lawyers who maintain Web sites or advertise on the Internet need to use "appropriate disclaimers" if they want to prevent unsolicited e-mail from having to be treated as confidential.

5)   California State Bar Opinion 2010-179 (undated)
     Computers; E-mail; Internet; Confidentiality;
     Communication with clients.
http://ethics.calbar.ca.gov/LinkClick.aspx?fileticket=wmqECiHp7h4%3D&tabid=837
Because the protection of confidentiality is an element of competent lawyering, a lawyer should not use any particular mode of technology to store or transmit confidential information before considering how secure it is and whether reasonable precautions such as firewalls, encryption, or password-protection could make it more secure. The lawyer should also consider the sensitivity of the information, the urgency of the situation, the possible effect of an inadvertent disclosure or an unauthorized interception, and the

client's instructions and circumstances, e.g., can others access the client's devices. A lawyer may use a laptop computer at home for client matters and e-mail if the lawyer's personal wireless system has been configured with appropriate security features. However, if using a public wireless connection—for example in a coffee shop—the lawyer may need to add safeguards such as encryption and firewalls. Opinions 1979-50, 2007-174; Orange County Opinion 97-0002; Los Angeles County Opinions 456, 514; 18 U.S.C. §§ 1030, 2510; Cal. Penal Code §§ 502(c), 629.86; Rule 3-110(C), ABA 95-398, 99-413.

6) Los Angeles County Bar Opinion 514 (Aug. 15, 2005)
    Internet; Communication with judges; Confidentiality; E-mail.
https://www.lacba.org/docs/default-source/ethics-opinions/archived-ethics
-opinions/eth514.pdf
A listserv, whether closed or open, is a public conversation. Participants in a listserv should take care not to divulge client confidences and secrets. Lawyers should also be mindful that their messages could be read by unintended recipients, such as judges, creating the possibility of unintended ex parte communications. A lawyer who posts comments about the merits of a particular expert witness does not necessarily breach confidentiality. However, the lawyer risks impairing his ability to continue representing the client because the lawyer could unintentionally be making improvident disclosures, or communicating ex parte with a judge, or waiving the work-product privilege by disclosing mental impressions. Judges, and lawyers acting as temporary judges or arbitrators, who participate in listservs that include lawyers who may potentially appear before them, must be mindful of the risk of engaging in ex parte communications and should expect from time to time to have to delete e-mail without reading it. Rules 1-710, 5-300; CJC Canons 2A, 4, 6D; ABA Rule 3.5; ABA 99-413.

7) San Diego County Bar Ass'n Legal Ethics Comm.
    Opinion 2006-1 (undated)
    Confidentiality; Prospective Clients; E-mail; Marketing.
https://www.sdcba.org/?Pg=ethicsopinion06-1
A lawyer has no duty to preserve the confidentiality of information e-mailed to her by a person who is seeking representation and locates the lawyer's

e-mail address on the California bar's Web site. The lawyer may represent the person's opponent in the matter and may even use the e-mailed information for that client's benefit. Inculpatory information in unsolicited e-mail from person asking for representation may be disclosed and used by the lawyer since the lawyer did not publish their e-mail address in marketing material and so "had no opportunity to warn" that communication would not be treated as confidential. However, a dissenting opinion argued that consumers have a reasonable expectation of confidentiality when they send an e-mail to an attorney with the information necessary to seek legal advice.

8) Connecticut Bar Association Opinion 99-52 (1999)

Under ordinary circumstances, a lawyer may use unencrypted e-mail to communicate with clients without violating Rule 1.6, since the risk of interception or inadvertent disclosure of the contents is minimal. However, in view of the lawyer's duty to receive, store, and transmit confidential client information using procedures that are reasonably designed and managed to ensure confidentiality, the lawyer must consult with the client regarding the risks involved in using unencrypted e-mail, must use good judgment in choosing the appropriate method for communicating confidential client information, and must counsel the client to do the same. Additionally, if the lawyer has reason to know that there is a greater than ordinary risk of interception or unauthorized disclosure, such as an e-mail address accessible to persons other than the intended recipient, the lawyer should not send e-mail to the client without the client's express consent. Similarly, client consent to using e-mail should be obtained prior to sending information that is extraordinarily sensitive or highly confidential, just as should be done when sending such information through telephone lines, fax machines, or regular mail. 18 U.S.C. § 2510(b); Rule 1.6; ABA 99-413.

9) Delaware Opinion 2001-2 (undated)
   Confidentiality; Communication with client;
   Attorney-client privilege; Computers; Telephones.
https://media1.dsba.org/public/media/ethics/pdfs/2001-2.pdf

Unless interception is reasonably suspected, a lawyer may transmit client information by e-mail or cellular phone. Extensive statutory protections make the prospect of being overheard on cellular phones in public places a far bigger problem than electronic interception of communications. 18 U.S.C. §§ 2510 et seq., 2701-2702; Rule 1.6; ABA 92-368, 94-382, 99-413.

10) District of Columbia Ethics Opinion 281 (Feb. 1998)
    Internet; E-mail; Confidentiality.
https://dcbar.org/For-Lawyers/Legal-Ethics/Ethics-Opinions-210-Present /Ethics-Opinion-281
Lawyers may transmit information by unencrypted e-mail; however, individual circumstances may require greater means of security. Rule 1.6.

11) Florida Opinion 00-4 (July 15, 2000)
    Internet; Lawyer-client relationship; Confidentiality; E-mail.
https://www.floridabar.org/etopinions/etopinion-00-4/
A lawyer may provide legal services over the Internet through the lawyer's firm with regard to matters that do not require in-person consultation or court appearances, provided the lawyer complies with the ethics rules including those relating to lawyer competence, communication, advertising, conflicts of interest, and confidentiality. If the client's matter is too complex to be easily handled over the Internet, the lawyer may not handle it if the client is unwilling to meet in person, and must withdraw if the representation has already begun. Legal services may be provided only through the law firm and not through a corporate entity other than a professional service corporation, professional association, or professional limited liability company. A lawyer may communicate with a client through the use of unencrypted e-mail in most situations, but must comply with the client's instructions when sending highly sensitive information. Opinion 88-13; Rules 4-1.1, 4-1.6, 4-1.7 through 4-1.12, 4-5.3, 4-5.5(b), 4-7, 4-7.6(b), 4-8.6(a); ABA 99-413.

12) Florida Opinion 07-3 (Jan. 16, 2009)

Confidentiality; Prospective Clients; E-mail.
https://www.floridabar.org/etopinions/etopinion-07-3/
A person seeking legal services has no reasonable expectation of confidentiality in information he unilaterally submits to lawyer by e-mail, regular

mail, telephone message, or facsimile transmission; lawyers should post a prominent statement to that effect on their websites.

13) Hawaii Opinion 40 (April 26, 2001)
Confidentiality; Communication with client; E-mail.

https://dbhawaii.org/wp-content/uploads/FO_40_-_E-MAIL_SECURITY.pdf

A lawyer may communicate with a client via encrypted or unencrypted e-mail. If the information is sensitive, the lawyer should consult with the client and follow the client's instructions. Rules 1.2(a), 1.6(a); ABA 99-413.

14) Illinois State Bar Opinion 96-10 (May 16, 1997)
(Affirmed Jan. 2010)
Electronic communications; Confidentiality;
Advertising and Solicitation.

http://www.isba.org/sites/default/files/ethicsopinions/96-10.pdf

In general, a lawyer may communicate with a client via electronic mail without encryption, since the expectation of privacy for electronic mail is the same as that for ordinary telephone calls and the unauthorized interception of an electronic message is illegal. Unusual circumstances involving extraordinarily sensitive information might warrant enhanced security measures like encryption, just as ordinary telephones and other normal means of communication would be deemed inadequate to protect confidentiality in such situations. A lawyer's use of an Internet web site is not "communication directed to a specific recipient" and is therefore governed only by the general rules regarding advertising and solicitation; a home page is the functional equivalent of a "yellow pages" entry of a telephone directory and the material included in the home page is the functional equivalent of the firm brochures and similar materials that lawyers commonly prepare for clients and prospective clients. A lawyer's participation in an electronic bulletin board, chat group, or similar service may implicate the rules governing solicitation to the extent that the lawyer seeks to initiate unrequested contact with a specific person or group through the use of such services. Furthermore, when a lawyer participates in a chat group or other on-line service that may involve offering personalized legal advice to anyone who happens to be connected to the service, the recipients of the advice become the lawyer's client.18 U.S.C. §§ 2510 et seq.; Opinions 90-07, 94-11; Rules 1.6, 7.1, 7.2, 7.3, 7.4.

15) Iowa State Bar Association Opinion 96-1 (Aug. 29, 1996)
   Confidentiality; Communication with client; E-mail; Advertising.
http://205.209.45.153/iabar/IowaEthicsOpinions.nsf/b6868944e3311dd087
2581100042934f/69139dea4264db38872581100042b586?OpenDocument
Lawyers' and law firms' home pages or web sites constitute advertising and must conform to ethics rules. Disclosures must appear in full, not by hypertext link, on first page or screen of the home page or web site and in any location where there is biographical matter other than the name, address, telephone and fax numbers for the lawyer or firm. If the home page or web site is sponsored by an entity other than the lawyer but contains references or links to a page or screen containing biographical matter (other than name, address, telephone and fax numbers), required disclosures must also appear on that page or screen. The foregoing does not apply to the pure exchange of legal information with another firm or other members of the home page or web site. It also does not apply to the pure exchange of information or legal communication with clients; however, if sensitive material is to be transmitted via e-mail, the lawyer must have written acknowledgment by client of the risk of the violation of Rule 4-101 and obtain consent for the communication via Internet or non-secure Intranet or other forms of proprietary networks. Otherwise the communication must be encrypted or protected by a password/firewall or other generally accepted equivalent security system. Opinion 95-30 is rescinded and replaced. DRs 2-101(A) (C)(D)(F), 2-105(A)(3), 4-101(B)(1),(C)(1).

16) Iowa State Bar Association Opinion 97-1 (Sept. 18, 1997)
   Confidentiality; Computer technology.
http://205.209.45.153/iabar/IowaEthicsOpinions.nsf/b6868944e3311dd0
872581100042934f/315d6205d531771e872581100042b88a?OpenDocu
ment&Highlight=0,97-1
Opinion 96-1 and 96-33 are amended to eliminate the board's determination of what is minimally appropriate e-mail security. Transmission of confidential information through e-mail or the Internet or other non-secure

proprietary networks requires written consent from the client after disclosure of the potential for loss of confidentiality. The means of protection should be determined after discussion between the lawyer and the client. Opinions 96-1 and 96-33 are amended. Opinions 96-1, 96-33.

17) Iowa State Bar Association Opinion 07-02 (Aug. 8, 2007)
    Confidentiality; Prospective Clients; E-mail; Internet.
http://205.209.45.153/iabar/IowaEthicsOpinions.nsf/b6868944e3311dd08
72581100042934f/bd12c617faff36c1872581100042b915?OpenDocument
Obligations that a lawyer generally owes prospective clients are not triggered by an e-mail or voicemail message that the lawyer receives out of the blue from a stranger in search of counsel, so long as the lawyer did not do or publish anything that would lead reasonable people to believe that they could share private information with the lawyer without first meeting with him and establishing a lawyer-client relationship.

18) Maine Board of Overseers of the Bar Opinion 195 (June 30, 2008)
    E-mail; Computers; Confidentiality; Communication with clients.
http://www.maine.gov/tools/whatsnew/index.php?topic=mebar
_overseers_ethics_opinions&id=63338&v=article
A lawyer generally may use unencrypted e-mail to communicate with clients, but should consider the content of the communication as well as the security of the e-mail address. If the information is of such a highly confidential nature that disclosure would significantly damage the client's interests, the lawyer should use reasonable judgment in selecting another means of communication. Opinion 134; 18 U.S.C. §§ 2510 et seq.; Rule 3.6(a), 3.6(f), 3.6(h)(1), 3.13(c); ABA Rule 1.6; ABA 99-413.

19) Massachusetts Opinion 2000-1 (July 15, 1999)
    Internet; Communication with client; Confidentiality.
http://www.massbar.org/publications/ethics-opinions/2000-2009/2000
/opinion-no-00-1
A lawyer's use of unencrypted e-mail to communicate with clients does not normally violate Rule 1.6(a), since legal and technical hurdles to the interception of e-mail give rise to a reasonable expectation that such communications

will remain private. However, a lawyer must not use unencrypted e-mail if doing so contravenes the express instructions of the client, and should avoid transmitting sensitive confidential information via unencrypted e-mail without the client's express consent. In addition, a lawyer should ensure that confidential e-mail messages, whether or not encrypted, are not sent to e-mail addresses that are reasonably accessible to persons other than the client. For instance, a lawyer should not send e-mail to a client's work address without the express consent of the client, since many employers reserve the right to review all e-mail messages sent through their systems. 18 U.S.C. §§ 2510 et seq.; Rule 1.6(a).

20) Minnesota Opinion 19 (Jan. 22, 1999; Amended Jan. 22, 2010)
Confidentiality; Communication with client; Internet; Computers.
http://lprb.mncourts.gov/rules/LPRBOpinions/Opinion%2019.pdf
A lawyer may use e-mail without encryption, or digital cordless and cellular telephones within a digital service area, to transmit and receive confidential client information; the use of analog cordless and cellular telephones for such purposes requires the consent of the client after consultation regarding the confidentiality risks associated with inadvertent interception. Client consent after consultation is also required when the lawyer knows or reasonably should know that a client or other person is using an analog cordless or cellular telephone, or other insecure means to communicate with the lawyer about confidential client information. Rule 1.6(a)(1).

21) Missouri Opinion 970161 (undated)
Internet; Confidentiality; Communication with
client; Advertising and solicitation.
http://www.mo-legal-ethics.org/Email%20Communications%20with%20
Clients%20and%20Email%20Disclaimers-body.php
A lawyer using the Internet to communicate with clients must comply with the ethics rules, including Rules 4-7.1 through 4-7.5. If e-mail communications are not secured through a quality encryption program in both directions, the lawyer must advise clients and potential clients that communication by e-mail is not necessarily secure and confidential. Rules 4-7.1, 4-7.2, 4-7.3, 4-7.4, 4-7.5.

22) Nevada Ethics Opinion 32 (March 25, 2005)
    Prospective Clients; Internet; E-mail; Confidentiality;
    Advertising and solicitation; Disclaimers.
https://www.nvbar.org/wp-content/uploads/opinion_32.pdf
Lawyers who have Web sites or advertise on the Internet should use disclaimers to avoid having to keep unsolicited e-mails confidential, and to ensure that prospective clients do not interpret the advertisement or solicitation as an invitation to form a lawyer-client relationship by simply responding. Nev. Sup. Ct. Rule 156; ABA Rule 1.18.

23) New York State Bar Opinion 709 (Sept. 16, 1998)
    Internet; Intellectual property representation; Confidentiality;
    Credit cards; Advertising and solicitation; Unauthorized practice.
https://nysba.org/opinion-709/
A lawyer may take orders for and conduct trademark searches, render legal opinions, and file trademark applications over the Internet, subject to ethical restrictions applicable to the practice of law via telephone or facsimile. A lawyer practicing over the Internet must check for client conflicts and should include on their web site the full text of the Statement of Client Rights and Responsibilities required by law. When relying upon legal research obtained through the Internet, the lawyer must insure the reliability of such information. In ordinary circumstances a lawyer may use unencrypted e-mail to transmit confidential information to clients; however, a lawyer must use a more secure means of communication if the lawyer is on notice that a specific e-mail transmission is at a heightened risk of interception or if the confidential information involved is of such an extraordinarily sensitive nature that it reasonable to use only a means of communication that is completely under the lawyer's control. A lawyer who uses e-mail must keep informed of the evolving technology to assess any changes in the likelihood of interception or in the availability of new technologies that would reduce such risks at a reasonable cost. A lawyer should discuss such risks with clients and abide by their wishes as to whether to communicate by e-mail. A lawyer may accept payment by credit card provided the fee is not excessive or does not otherwise violate the ethics code. A lawyer who accepts credit card payment over the Internet must insure the privacy of the client's credit

card information. A lawyer may advertise over the Internet provided the advertising is not false, deceptive, or misleading and otherwise complies with the ethics code. A lawyer must keep a copy of any Internet advertisement for at least one year following its last use, but need not file a copy with a departmental disciplinary committee. The copy may be maintained in electronic form. Lawyers may advertise to solicit clients residing outside of the state regarding matters that the lawyer may lawfully and competently handle; however, any Internet advertisement should inform potential clients of the jurisdictions in which the lawyer is licensed and should not mislead potential clients that the lawyer is licensed in a jurisdiction where the lawyer is not licensed. Whether a lawyer licensed only in New York may render legal opinions over the Internet to clients resident in another jurisdiction would depend on whether such conduct constitutes the unauthorized practice of law in the other jurisdiction. Similarly, if a lawyer licensed only in New York limits her services to trademark searches and filing trademark applications as nonlawyers are generally permitted to do, whether she may provide such limited services to clients resident in another jurisdiction with regard to matters arising in the other jurisdiction would be governed by the laws and rules of the other jurisdiction. Even though trademark searches and application filings may be performed by nonlawyers, a lawyer performing such services may not practice under a trade name if the lawyer exercises her professional legal judgment in performing such services, since the exercise of a lawyer's professional judgment would constitute the practice of law. Opinions 362, 375, 399, 557, 625, 636, 662, 664, 705, 768; 22 N.Y. Comp. Codes R. & Regs. Section 1210.1; DRs 1-102(A), 2-101(B)(F), 2-102(B)(D), 2-103(A), 2-106, 3-101(B), 4-101(A)(B)(D), 5-105(E), 5-108; ECs 2-10, 2-13, 3-5, 4-1, 4-4; Canon 4; ABA Rule 7.2(a).

24) New York State Bar Association Opinion 1076 (Dec. 8, 2015)
    Communication with clients; E-mail; Lawyer-
    client relationship; Communication with represented
    persons; Opposing counsel; Confidentiality.
https://nysba.org/ethics-opinion-1076/
A lawyer may blind copy ("bcc") a client on e-mail with opposing counsel even if opposing counsel objects; the lawyer is the client's agent and it is

unreasonable for opposing counsel to assume that the lawyer would not share the communication with the principal/client. Sending the client a copy by using "cc" would disclose the client's e-mail address and could be seen by opposing counsel as an invitation to communicate directly with the client. For practical reasons—such as avoiding the possibility of the client responding with the "reply all" button—the lawyer should consider forwarding the correspondence, rather than sending a blind copy. New York City Opinion 2009-1; Rules 1.4, 1.6, 4.2, 8.4.

25) New York City Bar Association Ethics
    Opinion 2001-01 (May 11, 2001)
    Confidentiality; E-mail; Conflicts.
https://www.nycbar.org/member-and-career-services/committees
/reports-listing/reports/detail/formal-opinion-2001-1-obligations-of-law
-firm-receiving-unsolicited-e-mail-communications-from-prospective-client
Information in unsolicited e-mail from potential client, generated in good faith after sender viewed lawyer's website which contained no disclaimer, does not disqualify lawyer from representation of current or future client adverse to sender but must be treated as confidential where lawyer had no meaningful opportunity to avoid receipt. DR 4-101 [22 N.Y.C.R.R. § 1200.19]; EC 4-1; DR 5-105(A) [22 N.Y.C.R.R. § 1200.20]

26) New York City Bar Opinion 2008-1 (Jan. 1, 2008)
    Files of client; Computers; E-mail.
http://www.nycbar.org/member-and-career-services/committees
/reports-listing/reports/detail/formal-opinion-2008-01-a-lawyers-ethical
-obligations-to-retain-and-to-provide-a-client-with-electronic-documents
-relating-to-a-representation
A lawyer is not required to organize or store electronic documents or e-mails in any particular manner or medium. E-mails present more difficulty than electronic documents because they often are deleted automatically after a certain period, and generally are not stored in a document management system. Because a lawyer may not charge a client file retrieval costs that could reasonably have been avoided, there is much to commend a practice of organizing saved e-mails for ease of retrieval. Opinion 1986-4; New York

State Opinions 460, 623, 780; DRs 2-106, 2-110(2), 9-102; ABA Rules 1.0(n), 1.16(d); ABA i1384.

27) North Carolina State Bar Association Opinion 215 (July 21, 1995)
    Confidentiality; Telephoning; Cellular telephones.
https://www.ncbar.gov/for-lawyers/ethics/adopted-opinions/rpc-215/
A lawyer using a cellular or cordless telephone, or e-mail or other unsecure method of communication, must minimize the risk of disclosing confidential information. If the lawyer has reason to believe that the mode of communication is susceptible to interception, the lawyer must so advise the parties to the conversation. Opinion RPC 133; Rule 4.

28) North Carolina Opinion 2012-5 (Oct. 26, 2012)
    E-mail; Computers; Confidentiality; Disclosure; Attorney-
    client privilege; Advice to clients; Government lawyers.
https://www.ncbar.gov/for-lawyers/ethics/adopted-opinions
/2012-formal-ethics-opinion-5/
A lawyer must avoid communicating with a client using the client's employer's e-mail system if there is a risk the employer will access the e-mails. A lawyer who represents an employer whose personnel policy states that use of the employer's e-mail system may be monitored must advise the employer as to its rights and responsibilities. If the employee accesses a personal e-mail account via the employer's computer, the lawyer may not advise the employer to change the password so it can access the employee's personal messages. If the employer notifies its lawyer that it has changed the password on the employee's personal e-mail account on its own initiative and has accessed e-mails between the employee and his attorney, the lawyer may not so notify the employee's attorney unless the lawyer has obtained the informed consent of the employer or believes that notification is reasonably required to comply with the law or a court order. The lawyer may not review the messages without a court order. If the employer notifies its lawyer that it has recovered e-mails between the employee and the employee's attorney that are marked "Attorney-Client Confidential Communication," the lawyer may not read the employee's e-mails unless the lawyer concludes in good

faith that the employee has waived the privilege. The lawyer who represents the employer has no duty under Rule 4.4(b) to notify the employee's attorney that the employer has copies of the employee's e-mail messages; the information is confidential pursuant to Rule 1.6(b)(1). A government lawyer may review e-mails between a government employee and his attorney to determine if the e-mails are public records. If they are not, the lawyer must treat them as privileged unless he can conclude that the privilege has been waived. Opinion 2009-1; Rules 1.2, 1.6, 4.4, 8.4; ABA 11-460.

29) North Dakota State Bar Opinion 97-09 (Sept. 4, 1997)
Confidentiality; Computers; Internet.
https://cdn.ymaws.com/www.sband.org/resource/resmgr/docs/for_law
yers/97-09.pdf
A lawyer may communicate with other lawyers or clients regarding routine matters using e-mail that is not encrypted and is sent on either a private network or on the Internet unless unusual circumstances require enhanced security measures. Rules 1.2(b), 1.6.

30) Supreme Court of Ohio Board of Commissioners
on Grievances and Discipline Opinion 99-2 (April 9, 1999)
Confidentiality; Communication with client; E-mail; Computers.
https://ohioadvop.org/wp-content/uploads/2017/04/Op-99-002.pdf
A lawyer may normally use unencrypted e-mail to communicate with clients. Particular matters or circumstances may, however, require choosing a different method of communication; the lawyer must use professional judgment. 18 U.S.C. § 2511; Ohio Rev. Code Ann. Section 2933.52(A)(B)(2); DR 4-101.

31) Pennsylvania Bar Association Opinion 97-130 (Sept. 26, 1997)
Confidentiality; Advertising and solicitation; Computers; Internet.
A lawyer may communicate with a client using electronic mail if the client consents after consultation. Encryption is generally not required, although in cases of sensitive information, it may be advisable. The lawyer should take appropriate steps under the circumstances to safeguard the confidentiality

of client information. If e-mail is used to solicit new clients for the lawyer, it is advertising and is similar to targeted mail and is subject to the restrictions set out in the ethics rules. Rules 1.6, 7.1 - 7.7.

32) South Carolina Opinion 94-27 (Jan. 1995)
Computers; Lawyer-client relationship; Confidentiality;
Communication with client; Advertising.
https://www.scbar.org/lawyers/legal-resources-info/ethics-advisory-opinions
/eao/ethics-advisory-opinion-94-27/
A lawyer may set up an electronic law office through an on-line service where the lawyer would provide legal information and advice to people throughout the nation. Although the operation of a law office via electronic media does not in itself violate the rules, the practice of law through such means raises several issues regarding communication, advertising, direct contact with prospective clients, and certainty of confidentiality. The lawyer's advertising would reach consumers in jurisdictions where the lawyer is not allowed to practice. Absent informed consent, confidential communications with clients would be jeopardized. The lawyer may also maintain a presence on the electronic media to generally discuss legal topics without giving advice or representing clients. Opinions 90-37, 91-4; Rules 1.6, 3.6, 7.1, 7.2, 7.3.

33) South Carolina Opinion 97-08 Opinion 97-08 (1997)
Internet; Communication with client; Confidentiality.
https://www.scbar.org/lawyers/legal-resources-info/ethics-advisory-opinions
/eao/ethics-advisory-opinion-97-08/
A lawyer may communicate with a client via e-mail, since the expectation of privacy is no less than that associated with regular mail, facsimile transmissions or land-based telephone calls and because the interception of e-mail is illegal under federal law. However, just as with other modes of communication, there is some information that a prudent lawyer would be hesitant to discuss via e-mail. In such situations, a lawyer should discuss with the client alternatives including encryption in order to safeguard against even inadvertent disclosure of sensitive or privileged information. 18 U.S.C. §§ 2701(a), 2702(a); Opinion 94-27; Rule 1.6.

34) State Bar of Texas Opinion 648 (April 2015)
   Confidentiality; E-mail; Communication with clients.
https://www.legalethicstexas.com/Ethics-Resources/Opinions/Opinion-648
.aspx
A lawyer may use e-mail to communicate with clients. The opinion enumerates circumstances under which the lawyer should consider using encryption
or another method of communication or advising the client regarding the
risks of communicating by e-mail. Opinion 572; 18 U.S.C2510 *et seq.*;
Rules 1.03, 1.05; ABA Rules 1.4, 1.6; ABA 11-459.

35) Utah Opinion 00-01 (March 9, 2000)
   Confidentiality; E-mail; Lawyer-client communication.
https://www.utahbar.org/wp-content/uploads/2017/11/2000-01.pdf
A lawyer usually may use unencrypted Internet e-mail to transmit confidential client information. However, if he has reason to believe greater
protection is necessary for a particular communication, or if the client has
a policy so requiring, the lawyer must use a means of communication with
higher security. Rule 1.6; ABA 99-413.

36) Vermont Bar Association Opinion 97-5 (undated)
   Communication with client; Advertising and Solicitation;
   Computers; Internet; Confidentiality.
https://www.vtbar.org/wp-content/uploads/2021/03/97-05.pdf
A lawyer may communicate with a client by e-mail without the use of
encryption. A lawyer who uses a web site to communicate with clients
and prospective clients must comply with rules relating to advertising and
solicitation. DRs 2-103, 2-104, 4-101; EC 4-4.

37) Virginia Ethics Opinion 1842 (Sept. 30, 2008)
   Prospective Clients; Confidentiality; E-mail; Internet; Marketing.
https://www.vacle.org/opinions/1842.htm
A lawyer does not owe any duty of confidentiality to a stranger who unilaterally divulges sensitive information to the lawyer in an uninvited e-mail
message to the lawyer's e-mail address provided on a law firm Web site or
in a voicemail message left on the law firm's telephone system via a phone

number listed in a public directory. However, circumstances other than the mere publication of contact information may invite contact from prospective clients and trigger a duty of confidentiality that could create a disqualifying conflict. The use of a disclaimer that warns against disclosure of confidential information may help prevent this scenario.

38) Washington Opinion 2175 (2008)
     Fee agreements; E-mail; Confidentiality.
https://ao.wsba.org/
A lawyer may arrange for a client to enter into a fee agreement by typing information into an e-mail and sending it to the lawyer. Absent special conditions, a lawyer's use of e-mail does not require any additional security precautions such as encryption. Formal Opinion 1962; Rules 1.0(n), 1.5, 1.6.

39) Washington Opinion 2217 (2012)
     Computers; E-mail; Internet; Communication with clients;
     Confidentiality; Attorney-client privilege; Advice to clients.
https://ao.wsba.org/
A lawyer must warn a client who uses public or employer-provided devices such as computers or cell phones or an employee e-mail account to communicate with the lawyer that the client's employer or other third parties may access those communications and attorney-client privilege may be waived. Rules 1.4(b), 1.6; ABA 11-459.

40) Wisconsin Formal Ethics Opinion EF-11-03 (July 29, 2011)
     Prospective Clients; E-mail; Internet;
     Confidentiality; Marketing; Disclaimers.
https://www.wisbar.org/formembers/ethics/Ethics%20Opinions
/EF-11-03%20final.pdf
Unilateral e-mails to a lawyer from people looking for representation do not trigger a duty of confidentiality or create conflicts of interest unless the lawyer has through a website or advertisements invited inquirers to share private information. Lawyers must use short disclaimers on their websites clearly warning that initial electronic communications create no lawyer-client relationship and that the e-mail message is not confidential.

Appendix F: Metadata

Ethics Opinions Concerning a Lawyer's Obligations to Prevent the
Inadvertent Disclosure of Confidential Client Information in Metadata

A)   ABA Formal Ethics Opinions
1)   Formal Opinion 06-442 (Aug. 5, 2006)

Review and Use of Metadata
The Model Rules of Professional Conduct do not contain any specific prohibition against a lawyer's reviewing and using embedded information in electronic documents, whether received from opposing counsel, an adverse party, or an agent of an adverse party. A lawyer who is concerned about the possibility of sending, producing, or providing to opposing counsel a document that contains or might contain metadata, or who wishes to take some action to reduce or remove the potentially harmful consequences of its dissemination, may be able to limit the likelihood of its transmission by "scrubbing" metadata from documents or by sending a different version of the document without the embedded information.

B)   ABA Treatises, Annotated Model Standards
     and other resources on Metadata
1)   ABA/Bloomberg Lawyers' Manual on Professional Conduct
http://www.americanbar.org/groups/professional_responsibility/publica
tions/aba_bna_lawyers_manual_on_professional_conduct.html
See the chapters entitled *Respect for Rights of Third Persons*, 71 Law. Man.
Prof. Conduct 801 and *Electronic Communications*, 55 Law. Man. Prof.
Conduct 401

2)   Annotated Model Rules of Professional Conduct (ABA 9th ed. 2019)
https://www.americanbar.org/products/inv/book/364918796/
See the annotations to Rules 1.6 *Confidentiality of Information* and 4.4
Respect for Rights of Third Persons.

3) Rotunda and Dzienkowski, Legal Ethics: The Lawyer's Deskbook
   on Professional Responsibility (ABA 2021-22 ed.)
https://store.legal.thomsonreuters.com/law-products/Treatises/Legal-Ethics
-The-Lawyers-Deskbook-on-Professional-Responsibility-2021-ed-ABA/p
/106722353
See Sections 1.6-2 *Inadvertent Disclosure* and 4.4-3(a) *Receipt of Privileged
Documents Through Inadvertent Disclosure.*

C) Digests of State Bar Ethics Opinions on Metadata
The following digests of state bar ethics opinions are excerpted with permission from the *ABA/Bloomberg Lawyers' Manual on Professional Conduct.*

1) Alabama Opinion 2007-02 (March 14, 2007)
   Computers; Internet; E-mail; Confidentiality; Discovery.
https://www.alabar.org/office-of-general-counsel/formal-opinions/2007-02/
A lawyer sending an electronic document must take reasonable steps to
safeguard confidential information in the document's metadata. A lawyer
receiving an electronic document from another lawyer must refrain from
trying to review that document's metadata. This opinion does not address
metadata in the context of discovery. Rules 1.6, 8.4.

2) Arizona Opinion 07-03 (Nov. 2007)
   Computers; E-mail; Confidentiality; Disclosure; Opposing counsel.
http://www.azbar.org/Ethics/EthicsOpinions/ViewEthicsOpinion?id=695
Lawyers who send documents electronically must take reasonable steps to
remove embedded metadata in order to prevent the unintentional disclosure of confidential client information. A lawyer who receives an electronic
communication may not search for embedded metadata unless authorized
to do so by law, rule, order, or court procedure. If a lawyer unintentionally
views metadata that reveals apparently confidential or privileged information, she must notify the sender and preserve the status quo for a reasonable
period of time. Rules 1.6(a), 4.4(b), 8.4; ABA 06-442.

3) California State Bar Opinion 2007-174 (Aug. 14, 2007)
    Files of client; Former clients; Computers; Client
    funds and property; Confidentiality.

http://ethics.calbar.ca.gov/LinkClick.aspx?fileticket=kiSRjKqnMBg%3D
&tabid=833

Upon termination of employment a lawyer must promptly comply with a client's request for any existing electronic versions of the following: e-mail correspondence, pleadings, discovery requests and responses, transactional documents, and databases of depositions and exhibits. The lawyer is not required to electronically create or reformat any materials in order to comply with the client's request. Before releasing the electronic items, the lawyer must take reasonable steps to strip them of any metadata reflecting other clients' confidential information. Opinions 1992-127, 1994-134; Los Angeles County Opinion 362; San Diego County Opinion 2001-1; San Francisco Opinion 1996-1; Cal. Bus. & Prof. Code §6068(e)(1); Rule 3-700(D).

4) Colorado Opinion 119 (May 17, 2008)
    Computers; E-mail; Confidentiality; Discovery.

https://www.cobar.org/Portals/COBAR/repository/ethicsOpinions/For
malEthicsOpinion_119_2011.pdf

A lawyer is permitted to search for and review metadata embedded in an electronic document received from opposing counsel or a third party, unless the lawyer has already been notified that confidential information has been inadvertently transmitted. The burden of protecting sensitive metadata rests with the lawyers who send the electronic documents. Opinions 90, 108; Fed. R. Civ. P. 34; Rules 1.1, 1.6, 4.4(b),(c), 5.1, 5.3, 8.4; ABA 06-442.

5) District of Columbia Opinion 341 (Oct.2007)
    Computers; E-mail; Confidentiality; Disclosure;
    Inadvertent disclosure; Opposing counsel.

https://www.dcbar.org/For-Lawyers/Legal-Ethics/Ethics-Opinions-210
-Present/Ethics-Opinion-341

A lawyer who sends electronic documents outside the context of discovery or subpoenas must take reasonable steps to prevent the disclosure of confidential information by removing embedded metadata. A lawyer who receives such an electronic communication from opposing counsel may not view its metadata if he has actual knowledge that the metadata was inadvertently provided, but must notify the sender and abide by the sender's instructions. In the context of discovery requests or subpoenaed information, the sender's removal of metadata from electronic documents may be impermissible. A recipient of such documents is generally justified in assuming that any included metadata was provided intentionally. Opinions 256, 318; Rules 1.0(o), 1.1, 1.3, 1.6, 3.4, 4.4(b), 8.4(c); ABA Rule 4.4; ABA 06-442.

6) Florida Opinion 06-2 (Sept. 15, 2006)
   E-mail; Confidentiality; Communication with
   adverse persons; Opposing counsel.
https://www.floridabar.org/etopinions/etopinion-06-2/
A lawyer sending an electronic document to another lawyer must take reasonable steps to safeguard confidential information in the document's metadata. A lawyer receiving an electronic document from another lawyer must not try to review that document's metadata; if the lawyer inadvertently does so, he must promptly notify the sender. This opinion does not address metadata in the context of discovery. Opinion 93-3; Rules 4-1.1, 4-1.2, 4-1.4, 4-1.6, 4-4.4(b).

7) Maine Opinion 196 (Oct.21, 2008)
   Computers; Internet; E-mail; Confidentiality; Opposing
   counsel; Communication with adverse persons.
http://www.maine.gov/tools/whatsnew/index.php?topic=mebar
_overseers_ethics_opinions&id=63337&v=article
A lawyer receiving an electronic document from a lawyer for another party may not attempt to "mine" metadata embedded in the document. A lawyer sending an electronic document must take reasonable care to safeguard confidential information in the document's metadata. Opinions 172, 194, 195; Rules 3.2(f)(3)(4), 3.6(a)(h)(1)(2); ABA 06-442.

8) Maryland State Bar Association Opinion 2007-09 (Oct. 19, 2006)
Computers; Confidentiality; Communication
with adverse persons; Discovery.

https://www.msba.org/ethics-opinions/ethics-of-viewing-and-or
-using-metadata/

A lawyer may review and use metadata in electronic documents produced in discovery. A lawyer producing electronic documents in discovery must take reasonable steps to remove confidential information and work product imbedded in the documents. Fed. R. Civ. P. 16(b)(5), 26(b)(5); Rules 1.1, 1.4, 1.6, 8.4(b); ABA Rule 4.4(b); ABA 05-437.

9) Minnesota Opinion 22 (March 26, 2010)
Metadata; Computers; E-mail; Confidentiality;
Communication with adverse persons; Opposing
counsel; Inadvertent disclosure; Competence.

http://lprb.mncourts.gov/rules/LPRBOpinions/Opinion%2022.pdf

A lawyer must act competently to prevent unauthorized disclosure of confidential information contained in the metadata of electronic documents. If a lawyer receives a document that she knows or reasonably should know inadvertently contains confidential metadata, she must promptly notify the sender. Rules 1.1, 1.6, 4.4(b); ABA 06-442.

10) Mississippi Bar Ethics Opinion 259 (Nov. 29, 2012)
Metadata; Inadvertent Disclosure; Confidentiality.

https://www.msbar.org/ethics-discipline/ethics-opinions/formal
-opinions/259/

A lawyer must take reasonable precautions to protect confidential information in metadata when transmitting electronic documents to opposing counsel.

11) Missouri Bar Informal Advisory Opinion 2014-02 (undated)
Inadvertent disclosure; Confidentiality; E-mail; Evidence; Discovery.

http://www.mobar.org/ethics/InformalOpinionsSearch.aspx

If a lawyer believes that metadata in a document sent by an opposing party or counsel was inadvertently sent, the lawyer must promptly notify the sender. Unless applicable law provides otherwise, the lawyer's ability to seek, review or use the metadata is left to the lawyer's professional judgment, as is the decision to return a document inadvertently sent. A lawyer must use reasonable care to ensure no confidential information is contained in metadata embedded in a document sent to an opposing party counsel. This may require "scrubbing" documents before transmission or using alternative means of transmission. Efforts to protect confidentiality must be exercised in light of the lawyer's duty under Rule 4-3.4(a) not to unlawfully obstruct another party's access to evidence or unlawfully alter, destroy or conceal evidence. Removing metadata with evidentiary value before transmission may violate laws governing discovery and therefore violate Rule 4-3.4(a). Rules 1.6, 3.4(a), 4.4(b).

12) New Hampshire Opinion 2008-09/04 (May 15, 2009)
    Computers; Internet; E-mail; Confidentiality; Communication
    with adverse persons; Opposing counsel.
https://www.nhbar.org/ethics/opinion-2008-09-04
A lawyer who sends a document electronically must take reasonable care to avoid improper disclosure of any confidential information that may be hidden in the document's metadata. A lawyer who receives a document electronically may not search for, review, or use any confidential information hidden in the document's metadata. Lawyers may, however, enter into agreements with each other that provide otherwise. This opinion does not address metadata in the context of discovery. Rules 1.1, 1.6, 4.4, 5.1, 5.3; ABA Rule 4.4; ABA 06-442.

13) New York State Opinion 782 (Dec. 8, 2004)
    E-mail; Confidentiality; Communication with adverse persons.
https://nysba.org/ethics-opinion-782/
A lawyer must exercise reasonable care when sending a document by e-mail to prevent the disclosure of metadata containing confidential client information. What constitutes reasonable care will vary with the circumstances, including whether the document was based on a "template" used for another client, and whether there have been multiple drafts of the document with comments from multiple sources. Opinions 700, 709, 749; DR 4-101; EC 4-5.

14) New York County Opinion 738 (March 24, 2008)
    Computers; Internet; Confidentiality;
    Communication with adverse persons.
http://www.nycla.org/siteFiles/Publications/Publications1154_0.pdf
A lawyer must exercise due care to prevent the disclosure of metadata when
sending a document electronically. A lawyer who receives documents electronically from an opposing lawyer may not search the metadata if he is
either looking for or likely to find confidential information. This opinion
does not address documents produced in the course of discovery. Opinion
730; New York State Opinions 749, 782; New York City Opinion 2003-4;
DRs 1-102(A), 4-101, 7-101, 7-102(A)(8); ECs 4-1, 7-1; ABA Rule 4.4(b);
ABA 06-442.

15) North Carolina State Bar Formal Ethics
    Opinion 2009-1 (Jan. 15, 2010)
    Metadata; Confidentiality; Computers; E-mail; Opposing counsel.
https://www.ncbar.gov/for-lawyers/ethics/adopted-opinions
/2009-formal-ethics-opinion-1/
A lawyer communicating electronically must use reasonable care to protect confidential client information that might be hidden in metadata. A
lawyer who receives an electronic communication from a party or a party's
lawyer may not search for or use any confidential information embedded
in its metadata. Allowing the use of found metadata is prejudicial to the
administration of justice. If a lawyer does unintentionally view metadata
he must notify the sender, and he may not use the information unless the
sender consents. Opinion RPC 215; Rules 1.6, 4.4(b), 8.4(d); ABA 06-442.

16) Oregon Opinion 2011-187 (Nov. 2011; Revised April 2015)
    Computers; Internet; E-mail; Confidentiality; Disclosure;
    Opposing counsel; Misrepresentation.
https://www.osbar.org/_docs/ethics/2011-187.pdf
If a lawyer communicates via electronic media, her obligations of competence and confidentiality require that she maintain a basic understanding
of the technology of metadata or use adequate technology support. A lawyer who receives a document with metadata she reasonably should know

was inadvertently included must inform the sender and then must consult with the client about the risks of returning the document versus the risks of retaining and reading it. Searching for metadata using special software when it is apparent that the sender has made reasonable efforts to remove the metadata may be analogous to surreptitiously entering the other lawyer's office to obtain client information in violation of Rule 8.4(a)(3). Opinion 2005-150; Rules 1.1, 1.2, 1.4, 1.6, 4.4(b), 8.4(a)(3); ABA 06-440.

17) Pennsylvania Formal Opinion 2009-100 (undated)
    Computers; Internet; E-mail; Confidentiality;
    Attorney-client privilege; Opposing counsel.

A lawyer transmitting electronic documents to opposing counsel or third parties must exercise reasonable care to remove unwanted metadata. A lawyer who receives electronic information that includes metadata and concludes that inclusion of the metadata was inadvertent must promptly notify the sender of the inclusion of the metadata. The lawyer must determine whether he is permitted under substantive law to use the metadata and must consult with his client about the appropriate course of action. Formal Opinion 2007-500; Rules 1.1, 1.2, 1.3, 1.4, 1.6, 4.4; ABA 06-442.

18) State Bar of Texas Opinion 665 (Dec. 2016)
    Confidentiality; Evidence; Opposing counsel;
    Competence; Computers.

https://www.legalethicstexas.com/Ethics-Resources/Opinions/Opinion-665
A lawyer transmitting an electronic document must take reasonable measures to remove metadata that would reveal confidential information. The receiving lawyer should explain the options and their consequences to the client, and if he reviews the information, he must not make any statements that would be misleading in light of what he has learned. Texas does not have a counterpart to ABA Model Rule 4.4(b) specifying how the receiving lawyer should treat the information but court rules or other applicable rules may apply in certain contexts, for example discovery. Opinion 664; Tex. R. Civ. P. 193.3(d); Rules 1.01, 1.05(a), 8.04(a)(3); ABA Rules 3.3, 4.4(b), 8.4(c).

19) Vermont Opinion 2009-1 (undated)

    Computers; Confidentiality; Communication with adverse persons;

    Opposing counsel; Inadvertent disclosure; Competence.

https://www.vtbar.org/wp-content/uploads/2021/03/09-01.pdf

A lawyer who transmits electronic documents to opposing counsel must use reasonable care to avoid including embedded metadata containing protected information; the rules regarding diligence and competence require this. No ethics rule prohibits the receiving lawyer from searching for and reviewing metadata in documents sent by opposing counsel; the duties of competence and diligence may require this. The committee expresses no opinion as to waiver of confidentiality or privilege, or as to discovery rights and obligations. Fed. R. Civ. P. 26(b)(5)(A); Fed. R. Evid. 502(b); Rules 1.1, 1.3, 1.6(a), 3.4, 4.4, 8.4; ABA Rule 4.4(b); ABA 92-368, 05-437, 06-442.

20) Washington State Bar Association Advisory Opinion 2216 (2012)

    Computers; Internet; E-mail; Confidentiality;

    Opposing counsel; Discovery.

https://ao.wsba.org/

A lawyer must safeguard confidential metadata from disclosure when exchanging documents with opposing counsel either by using formats such as hard copy, fax, or Portable Document Format ("PDF") that do not include metadata or by electronically "scrubbing" the documents. A lawyer may not remove metadata that has evidentiary value when producing electronic documents in discovery. A lawyer who receives an electronic document that contains confidential but readily accessible metadata must promptly notify the sender but, absent applicable court rules, an agreement, or a protective order, need not return the document or refrain from reading it. A lawyer may not use special forensic software to recover metadata that is not readily accessible. Wash. Rev. Code §5.60.060(2)(a); Rules 1.1, 1.6, 1.9, 3.4, 4.4, 8.4.

21) West Virginia Opinion 2009-01 (June 10, 2009)
   Computers; Confidentiality; Inadvertent disclosure; Communication
   with adverse persons; Opposing counsel; Attorney-client privilege.
http://www.wvodc.org/pdf/lei/LEI%2009-01.pdf
A lawyer who receives an electronic document may not unilaterally search
for or view hidden metadata that the sender apparently provided by mistake.
He should consult with the sender and abide by the sender's instructions
before reviewing any metadata. By the same token, lawyers who send electronic documents must use reasonable care to avoid transmitting embedded
information that is confidential or privileged. Rules 1.1, 1.6, 3.4(a), 8.4(c);
ABA 06-442.

22) Wisconsin Opinion EF-12-01 (June 15, 2012)
   Computers, Internet; E-mail; Confidentiality;
   Attorney-client privilege; Competence.
http://www.wisbar.org/newspublications/wisconsinlawyer/pages/article.asp
x?Volume=85&Issue=10&ArticleID=10222
A lawyer transmitting a document electronically must take reasonable care
to avoid the disclosure of confidential information contained in metadata.
The ethics rules neither prohibit nor require searching for and reviewing
metadata in documents received electronically. A lawyer who discovers
materially significant metadata must promptly inform the sender even if the
client says not to, but the ethics rules impose no further duty. A significant
minority of the committee believes that the Rules either prohibit or do not
clearly permit "mining" documents for metadata. Rules 1.1, 1.6, 4.4, 8.4;
ABA 06-442, 11-459.

Appendix G: Outsourcing

Ethics Opinions on Lawyer Confidentiality Obligations Concerning Outsourcing

A) ABA Formal Ethics Opinions
The Opinion headnotes are reproduced below.

1) Formal Opinion 08-451 (Aug. 5, 2008)
   Lawyer's Obligations When Outsourcing Legal
   and Nonlegal Support Services

A lawyer may outsource legal or nonlegal support services provided the lawyer remains ultimately responsible for rendering competent legal services to the client under Model Rule 1.1. In complying with her Rule 1.1 obligations, a lawyer who engages lawyers or nonlawyers to provide outsourced legal or nonlegal services is required to comply with Rules 5.1 and 5.3. She should make reasonable efforts to ensure that the conduct of the lawyers or nonlawyers to whom tasks are outsourced is compatible with her own professional obligations as a lawyer with "direct supervisory authority" over them.

In addition, appropriate disclosures should be made to the client regarding the use of lawyers or nonlawyers outside of the lawyer's firm, and client consent should be obtained if those lawyers or nonlawyers will be receiving information protected by Rule 1.6. The fees charged must be reasonable and otherwise in compliance with Rule 1.5, and the outsourcing lawyer must avoid assisting the unauthorized practice of law under Rule 5.5.

2) Formal Opinion 95-398 (Oct. 27, 1995)
   Access of Nonlawyers to a Lawyer's Data Base

A lawyer who gives a computer maintenance company access to information in client files must make reasonable efforts to ensure that the company has in place, or will establish, reasonable procedures to protect the confidentiality of client information. Should a significant breach of confidentiality occur, the lawyer may be obligated to disclose it to the client.

B) ABA Treatises and Annotated Model Standards

1) ABA/Bloomberg Lawyers' Manual on Professional Conduct

http://www.americanbar.org/groups/professional_responsibility/publica
tions/aba_bna_lawyers_manual_on_professional_conduct.html

See the chapters from the treatise section of the *Manual* entitled, *Multi-jurisdictional Practice*, 21 Law. Man. Prof. Conduct 2101; *Lawyers' Aiding Unauthorized Practice of Law*, 21 Law. Man. Prof Conduct 8201; *Super-visory and Subordinate Lawyers*, 91 Law. Man. Prof. Conduct 101; and *Supervision of Nonlawyers*, 91 Law. Man. Prof. Conduct 201.

2) Annotated Model Rules of Professional Conduct (ABA 9th ed. 2019).

https://www.americanbar.org/products/inv/book/364918796/

See the annotations to Rules 1.4 *Communication*, 5.3 *Responsibilities regarding Nonlawyer Assistants* and 1.6 *Confidentiality of Information*

3) Rotunda and Dzienkowski, *Legal Ethics: The Lawyer's Deskbook on Professional Responsibility*, American Bar Association (2018-2019 edition)

https://store.legal.thomsonreuters.com/law-products/Statutes/Legal-Ethics
-The-Lawyers-Deskbook-on-Professional-Responsibility-2018-2019-ed-ABA
/p/106152833

See § 5.3-2, *Sharing Client Information with Outside Contractors*

C) Bar Association Reports

1) The ABA Ethics 20/20 Commission's Report 105(c) concerning Outsourcing that was approved at the 2012 Annual Meeting.

http://www.americanbar.org/content/dam/aba/administrative/eth
ics_2020/2012_hod_annual_meeting_105c.authcheckdam.pdf

2) Association of The Bar of The City Of New York Committee on Professional Responsibility Report on the Outsourcing of Legal Services Overseas (2009)

http://www.nycbar.org/pdf/report/uploads/20071813-ReportontheOut
sourcingofLegalServicesOverseas.pdf

3) Council of Bars and Law Societies of Europe
Guidelines on Legal Outsourcing (2010)
http://www.ccbe.eu/fileadmin/user_upload/NTCdocument/EN_Guidelines
_on_leg1_1277906265.pdf

D) Digests of State Bar Association Ethics Opinions on Outsourcing
The following Digests of state ethics opinions are excerpted with permission from the *ABA/Bloomberg Lawyers' Manual on Professional Conduct.*

1) State Bar of California Opinion 2004-165 (2004)
Temporary lawyers; Contract lawyers; Lawyer-client
relationship; Communication with clients; Costs and
expenses of litigation; Fee agreements; Billing.
http://www.calbar.ca.gov/Portals/0/documents/ethics/Opinions/2004-165
.pdf
A private lawyer may hire a contract "appearance" lawyer to cover a court appearance, deposition, or arbitration proceeding. The contract lawyers are supplied by a lawyer-operated company that charges an hourly fee for their services. The rule requiring client consent to all fee divisions will not apply if the hiring attorney pays the contract lawyer an hourly rate, if the contract lawyer's fee is billed as a cost, if the fee is a separately identified entry on the hiring attorney's bill, or if the contract lawyer bills the client directly. However, if the arrangement will constitute a "significant development" in the client's matter the hiring attorney must tell the client about it, and if the contract lawyer's fees are going to be charged to the client as a disbursement the fee agreement must say so. Opinions 1981-63, 1993-133, 1994-138, 2003-161; Los Angeles County Opinion 473; Cal. Bus. & Prof. Code §§6068(c)(m), 6147, 6148; Rules 1-400, 2-200, 3-110, 3-310, 3-500.

2) Los Angeles County Bar Ethics Opinion 518 (June 19, 2006)
Legal research services; Out-of-state lawyers; Nonlawyers;
Division of fees with nonlawyers; Unauthorized practice of law.
https://www.lacba.org/resources/ethics-opinions

A lawyer may hire an out-of-state legal research company that employs only out-of-state lawyers to draft an appellate brief in a client's civil case if the lawyer reviews and remains ultimately responsible for the work. The lawyer must tell the client about the arrangement if it constitutes a "significant development" in the representation, as it normally will. The lawyer may directly pass on the company's fee to the client, mark up the cost and pass it on to the client, or charge a flat fee for the representation. If the attorney passes the company's fee on to the client, he must so identify it, and must also pass on any refund from the company. Opinions 374, 423, 457, 473; California Formal Opinions 1994-138, 2004-165; Cal. Bus. & Prof. Code 6125, 6126; Cal. Evid. Code §912(d); Cal. Rules of Court 227, 983; California Formal Opinions 1987-91, 1994-138, 2004-165; Los Angeles County Opinion 518; Orange County Opinion 94-2; Rules 1-300, 3-110(B), 3-500; ABA Rules 1.1, 5.1(b), 5.3(b). §§6068, 6125, 6126, 6147, 6148; Rules 1-100, 1-120, 1-200, 1-310, 1-320, 1-400, 2-200, 3-110, 3-310, 3-500, 4-200, 5-200.

3) San Diego County Bar Opinion 2007-1 (2007)
   Foreign lawyers; Unauthorized practice of law;
   Legal research services; Nonlawyers.
https://www.sdcba.org/?Pg=ethicsopinion07-1
A lawyer who hired foreign lawyers working in India to assist in the preparation of a successfully litigated matter, but supervised and remained ultimately responsible for the work performed, did not thereby aid the unauthorized practice of law. Because the work performed by the foreign lawyers was of the type reasonably expected to be performed by the lawyer himself, the lawyer was obliged to inform the client of the hiring. Before hiring foreign lawyers, a lawyer must also satisfy himself that they are competent for the work required and will preserve confidential information. Cal. Bus. & Prof. Code §§6067, 6068,

4) Colorado Bar Association Formal Ethics Opinion 121 (June 16, 2009)
   Temporary lawyers; Out-of-state lawyers; Foreign lawyers; Division
   of fees with nonlawyers; Division of fees with lawyers; Billing.
https://www.cobar.org/Portals/COBAR/repository/ethicsOpinions/For
malEthicsOpinion_121_2011.pdf

A Colorado lawyer who hires on a temporary basis lawyers admitted in
a foreign country or in a domestic jurisdiction other than Colorado must
make reasonable efforts to ensure that their conduct conforms to the
Colorado lawyer's ethical duties. The lawyer must take particular care to
supervise the work, and must confirm that the temporary lawyer is licensed
and in good standing in the home jurisdiction, is competent to undertake
the assignment, does not have a conflict, and will not thereby be engaging
in the unauthorized practice of law. Depending on how attenuated the outsourcing relationship is, the lawyer may need to secure the client's consent
before sharing any protected information. For conflicts purposes, the hiring lawyer must determine if he and the temporary lawyer are "associated
in a firm" according to the functional analysis of imputation in Opinion
105. Even if the lawyers are not "associated in a firm," payment of the
temporary lawyer will not constitute a division of fees if it is not tied to
payment by the client. The lawyer may mark up the temporary lawyer's
fees, but if the differential is excessive the fee might become unreasonable.
Although the lawyer is not required to disclose the amounts involved,
in some circumstances the lawyer may be required to tell the client that
certain work has been delegated. If the lawyer determines that a foreign
professional does not qualify as a foreign lawyer, the lawyer may hire him
as a nonlawyer and must supervise him in accordance with Rule 5.3. This
opinion incorporates relevant portions of Opinion 105, which addressed
the employment of temporary lawyers who are admitted in Colorado.
The Committee will issue an addendum to Opinion 105 addressing the
2008 amendments to the Rules. Opinion 105; Civ. Proc. Rules 220, 221,
221.1; Rules 1.1, 1.2(a), 1.4(a)(3),(b), 1.5, 1.6, 5.1(b), 5.3(b), 5.4, 5.5(a)(3);
ABA 01-423, 08-451.

5) Florida Bar Ethics Opinion 12-3 (Jan. 25, 2013)
   Client files; Internet; Confidentiality; Competence;
   Outsourcing; Record retention.
https://www.floridabar.org/etopinions/etopinion-12-3/
A lawyer may use cloud computing services to store, access and share client
files if the lawyer uses reasonable diligence to ascertain that the provider
has adequate measures in place to protect the security, confidentiality and

accessibility of the information. The lawyer should research the service provider and should consider taking additional security measures regarding proprietary client information or other particularly sensitive information. The opinion includes suggestions as to what the lawyer should consider in researching the service provider. Opinions 07-2, 10-2; Rule 1.6.

6) Illinois State Bar Association Opinion 10-01 (July 2009)
    Computers; Files of client; Confidentiality.
http://www.isba.org/sites/default/files/ethicsopinions/10-01.pdf
A law firm may use an outside administrator to manage the firm's computer network—even if the administrator accesses the network remotely—as long as it takes reasonable measures to ensure that the administrator will protect the confidentiality of client information on the network. Opinions 96-10, 03-07; 18 U.S.C. §2510; Rules 1.6, 5.3; ABA 95-398, 99-413, 08-451; ABA Rules 1.4(b), 1.6.

7) Maryland State Bar Association Opinion 2013-01 (Nov. 2, 2012)
    Outsourcing; Personal injury representation; Paralegals;
    Nonlawyers; Division of fees with nonlawyers.
https://www.msba.org/ethics-opinions/counsels-use-of-a-third-party-claims
-processing-service-to-assist-in-processing-personal-injury-claims/
A personal-injury law firm interested in subcontracting the paralegal function of its office to a third-party claims processing service must provide adequate supervision and quality control and must take steps to protect confidentiality, prevent conflicts of interest, and ensure against the unauthorized practice of law. The firm should obtain the client's informed consent to the arrangement and must pay the service based on the reasonable value of the work done, regardless of the size or outcome of the claims involved. Rules 1.5(e), 1.6(a), 1.7, 5.3, 5.4, 5.5(a); ABA 08-451.

8) Michigan State Bar Opinion RI-363 (June 28, 2013)
    Personal injury representation; Outsourcing; Fees; Costs
    and expenses of litigation; Business activities.
https://www.michbar.org/opinions/ethics/numbered_opinions?Opinion
ID=1198&Type=4

A law firm represents a plaintiff in a personal injury matter under a contingent fee agreement providing that the law firm will receive the maximum fee permissible under court rules. The firm asks whether it may "outsource" basic case-related administrative services traditionally deemed part of a firm's overhead, such as reviewing, copying, and organizing medical records and assembling case evaluations and demand letters, to a company wholly owned by one of the firm's lawyers and housed in the law firm's offices, and bill them to the client as if they were traditional case costs. The law firm may not enter into this arrangement and may not seek or obtain the client's consent to it; the services do not constitute "law-related services" as defined by Rule 5.7(b), and the arrangement would result in a clearly excessive fee. Opinion RI-346; MCR 8.121; Rules 1.5, 5.3, 5.7; ABA 93-379, 95-390.

9) New Hampshire Bar Association Opinion
   2011-12/05 (Dec. 14, 2011)
   Client files; Outsourcing; Computers; Internet; Nonlawyers;
   Confidentiality; Discovery; Foreign lawyers.
https://www.nhbar.org/ethics/opinion-2011-12-05
A law firm may contract with a local company to scan client documents and transmit them electronically to an overseas company for review as to relevance, confidentiality, and privilege. Document scanning and transmission are considered nonlegal support services. The firm must ensure that the service provider maintains client confidentiality. Scanning can probably be outsourced without notifying the client, but the firm must consult with the client about the method of transmission and must follow its security instructions. Document review is considered a legal support service; the firm must inform the client of the arrangements and must take reasonable steps to ensure that the overseas company performs its tasks competently and in compliance with the ethics rules. Opinions 1982-3/16, 1986-87/8, 1989-90/2, 1989-90/9, 1991-2/6, 1995-96/3; Rules 1.1, 1.2, 1.5, 1.6, 1.7, 2.1, 5.1, 5.3, 5.4, 5.5, 7.1; ABA 99-413, 08-451, 11-459.

10) New York State Bar Association Ethics Opinion 940 (Oct. 16, 2012)
    Client files; Confidentiality; Record retention; Outsourcing.
https://nysba.org/ethics-opinion-940/

A lawyer may store client information on equipment maintained offsite by outside service if lawyer exercises reasonable care to protect data's integrity and confidentiality. Rules: 1.6(a) & (c), 1.15(d).

11) New York City Bar Formal Opinion 2006-3 (Aug. 1, 2006)
     Foreign lawyers; Nonlawyers; Employees of lawyers; Temporary
     lawyers; Confidentiality; Unauthorized practice of law.
https://www.nycbar.org/member-and-career-services/committees
/reports-listing/reports/detail/formal-opinion-2006-3-outsourcing-legal
-support-services-overseas-avoiding-aiding-a-non-lawyer-in-the-unauthor
ized-practice-of-law-supervision-of-non-lawyers-competent-representation
-preserving-client-confidences-and-secrets-conflicts-checking-appropriate
-billing-client-consent
A lawyer may outsource legal support services to overseas lawyers and nonlawyers if the lawyer supervises the work rigorously. Overseas lawyers not admitted in any U.S. jurisdiction are regarded as nonlawyers for this purpose. The lawyer should obtain background information about any intermediary involved in engaging the nonlawyer and should obtain the nonlawyer's resume, conduct reference checks, and interview the nonlawyer by telephone, Voice Over Internet Protocol, or Webcast. The lawyer will not necessarily need to inform each client in advance about the arrangement but would need to do so if, for example, nonlawyers will be playing a significant role in the matter, or if the client expects that only law firm personnel will be handling the matter. In addition, the client's advance consent is needed if the lawyer will be sharing the client's confidences and secrets or if the lawyer will be billing for the outsourced work on a basis other than cost. Opinions 1988-3, 1989-2, 1995-11; New York State Opinions 715, 721, 762, 774; N.Y. Jud. Law §478; DRs 1-104(C)(D), 3-101(A), 3-102, 4-101, 5-105(E), 5-107, 6-101; ECs 2-2, 3-6, 4-2, 4-5; ABA 93-379.

12) New York City Bar Formal Opinion 2015-1 (Feb. 10, 2015)
     Outsourcing; Confidentiality; Independent professional
     judgment; Conflicts of interest; Non-lawyers; Fee-sharing.
https://www.nycbar.org/member-and-career-services/committees
/reports-listing/reports/detail/formal-opinion-2015-1-professional-employer
-organization-use-by-a-law-firm-of-a-professional-employer-organization

Lawyers may use professional employer organizations ("PEO") to provide human resource services to employees, under certain conditions. Lawyers must not allow the PEO to interfere with the lawyer's ethical obligations to exercise independent professional judgment or to supervise other lawyers and non-lawyers. Additionally, the PEO may not have access to confidential client information, the lawyer must avoid conflicts of interest, and the lawyer may not compensate the PEO in a way that would violate the prohibition against fee sharing with non-lawyers.

13) North Carolina Bar Ethics Formal Opinion 12 (April 25, 2008)
   Foreign lawyers; Unauthorized practice of law; Legal
   research services; Nonlawyers; Employees of lawyers.
https://www.ncbar.gov/for-lawyers/ethics/adopted-opinions/2007
-formal-ethics-opinion-12/
A lawyer may outsource certain legal support services to foreign lawyers or nonlawyers if the lawyer properly selects and supervises them, ensures the preservation of confidentiality, avoids conflicts of interest, discloses the arrangements, and obtains the client's informed consent first. Opinions RPC 70, 133, 215, 216, FEO 99-6, 2002-9; Rules 1.1, 1.6, 5.3, 5.5.

14) North Carolina State Bar Ethics Opinion 2011-14 (April 27, 2012)
   Outsourcing; Confidentiality; Communication with clients.
https://www.ncbar.gov/for-lawyers/ethics/adopted-opinions/2011
-formal-ethics-opinion-14/
A law firm may outsource clerical tasks, including transcription and typing, to a company outside the United States if the law firm obtains the client's informed consent, confirmed in writing. Opinions 2007-12, 2011-6; Rules 1.0, 1.6; ABA 08-451.

15) Ohio Advisory Opinion 2009-6 (Aug. 14, 2009)
   Legal research services; Foreign lawyers; Nonlawyers; Communication
   with clients; Billing; Fees; Costs and expenses of litigation.
https://www.ohioadvop.org/wp-content/uploads/2017/04/Op_09-006.pdf
A lawyer may outsource legal and support services domestically or abroad if the client gives informed consent. The lawyer is responsible for an outside lawyer's violation of professional obligations if the lawyer orders or ratifies

the outside lawyer's conduct. The lawyer must make reasonable efforts to ensure that any nonlawyer's conduct is compatible with the professional obligations of the lawyer; the lawyer is responsible for nonlawyer conduct that the lawyer orders or ratifies. The lawyer may bill the cost of the outsourced services either as part of the firm's fee or as a discrete expense so long as the basis of the billing is first communicated to the client; any charge in addition to the actual cost of the services must be reasonable. Opinion 90-23; Rules 1.2(a), 1.4(a)(2), 1.5, 1.6(a), 5.1, 5.3; ABA 93-379, 00-420, 08-451.

16) Pennsylvania Bar Association Formal Opinion 2010-200 (undated)
  Law firms; Internet; Advertising and solicitation; Letterhead.
A lawyer may practice in a "virtual law office" (VLO) in which all lawyers practice from their homes in several locales. Advertisements and firm letterhead must specify the city or town where the lawyers performing legal services principally practice law but need not include their physical addresses; a post office box in the city or town may be used. If a lawyer in Philadelphia sends local client files to VLO lawyers in Harrisburg and Pittsburgh, all firm lawyers are principally practicing law in Philadelphia for those clients. A lawyer practicing in a VLO may not state that the firm's fees are lower than other firms' fees, but may state that the firm's overhead costs may be lower. Opinions 91-176, 92-19, 2009-053; Rules 1.4, 1.6, 1.14, 1.18, 5.1, 7.1, 7.2, 7.5; ABA 08-451.

17) Utah State Bar Ethics Advisory Opinion 14-01 (Feb. 3, 2014)
  Outsourcing; Liens; Personal injury representation;
  Billing; Division of fees with lawyers; Creditors of
  client; Costs and expenses of litigation.
https://www.utahbar.org/wp-content/uploads/2017/11/2014-01.pdf
A plaintiffs' personal injury lawyer may retain a lien resolution company to assist in calculating, verifying and resolving health insurance liens and subrogation and reimbursement claims. The lawyer may treat the company's fee as a cost to the client if the services constitute nonlegal services, such as accounting and valuation, and if the lawyer's engagement letter so permits. If the company provides legal services, the arrangement must be

in writing, must state the method for determining the company's fees and must otherwise comply with Rule 1.5(c) and (d) respecting fee-splitting between law firms. The client must agree in writing to the arrangement, and the total fee must be reasonable. Utah Code Ann. §§38-7-1 et seq., 78B-1-152; Rules 1.5, 3.4.

18) Virginia Legal Ethics Opinion 1850 (Dec. 28, 2010;
    Amended Jan. 12, 2021)
    Legal research services; Foreign lawyers; Nonlawyers;
    Temporary lawyers; Communication with clients;
    Confidentiality; Costs and expenses of litigation; Billing.
http://www.vacle.org/opinions/1850.htm
A lawyer outsourcing legal or nonlegal services domestically or overseas must supervise and remain ultimately responsible for the work. Client consent is required unless only "tangential, clerical, or administrative" work is involved; client consent is also required before the lawyer discloses any confidential information. Written confidentiality agreements are strongly advised whenever outsourcing. Unless the client has agreed otherwise the outsourced services must be billed at cost, plus a reasonable allocation of supervision costs if the lawyer is not otherwise charging to review the work. Opinions 1712, 1735; Rules 1.1, 1.2, 1.4, 1.5, 1.6, 5.3, 5.5, 7.5(d); ABA 93-379.

E) *State Bar Ethics Opinions that address issues similar to those*
   addressed in ABA Formal Opinion 95-398; allowing outside
   computer maintenance firms access to law firm computer networks.
The following Digests of state ethics opinions are excerpted with permission from the *ABA/Bloomberg Lawyers' Manual on Professional Conduct.*

1) Illinois State Bar Association Advisory Opinion 10-01 (July 2009)
   Computers; Files of client; Confidentiality.
http://www.isba.org/sites/default/files/ethicsopinions/10-01.pdf
A law firm may use an outside administrator to manage the firm's computer network—even if the administrator accesses the network remotely—as long as it takes reasonable measures to ensure that the administrator will protect the confidentiality of client information on the network. Opinions 96-10,

03-07; 18 U.S.C. §2510; Rules 1.6, 5.3; ABA 95-398, 99-413, 08-451; ABA Rules 1.4(b), 1.6.

2) Massachusetts Opinion 2005-4 (March 3, 2005)
   Computers; Internet; Confidentiality; Files of
   client; Employees of lawyers; Nonlawyers.

http://www.massbar.org/publications/ethics-opinions/2000-2009/2005/opinion-05-04

A law firm may allow a third-party software vendor to have remote access via the Internet to the firm's computer system, which contains confidential client information, in order to service and update the software. The firm should make reasonable efforts to ensure that the vendor's conduct complies with the lawyers' obligations to their clients. "Reasonable efforts" on the firm's part could include notifying the vendor of the confidential nature of the stored information, reviewing the vendor's own policies regarding the handling of confidential information, obtaining written assurances from the vendor that the firm's computer system will be accessed only for technical support and only on an as-needed basis, and formulating additional policies and procedures to protect any particularly sensitive confidential client information. Opinions 89-3, 2000-01; Rules 1.6, 5.3; DR 4-101(D).

3) Michigan Opinion RI-328 (Jan. 25, 2002)
   Government lawyers; Confidentiality; Disclosure; Computers.

https://www.michbar.org/opinions/ethics/numbered_opinions?OpinionID=1198&Type=4

A law department of a governmental entity may use the services of the government's technical support department without violating the confidentiality rules. The use of technical support personnel to assist with computer-related issues does not in itself violate Rule 1.6(b). The law department should clearly communicate the requirements of the confidentiality rules to the technical support personnel. Steps should be taken to ensure that particularly sensitive client information is maintained outside the view of technical support personnel. This opinion assumes that there is no reason to believe that the technical support personnel have any particular interest in using, or would be likely to use, the confidential information involved. Opinions RI-77, RI-111, RI-311; Rule 1.6(b) (d); ABA Informal Opinion 1364.

4) Pennsylvania Opinion 2005-105 (Aug. 9, 2005)
   Confidentiality; Computers.

A lawyer may give a computer technology company access to client data in the course of upgrading and testing his software, provided that the lawyer makes reasonable efforts to ensure that the company puts in place reasonable procedures to protect the confidentiality of client information. Rules 1.6, 5.3; ABA 95-398.

5) Vermont Opinion 2003-03 (undated)
   Confidentiality; Computers; Employees of lawyer; Files of client.
   https://www.vtbar.org/wp-content/uploads/2021/03/03-03.pdf

A lawyer may engage an outside computer consultant to recover a lost database file containing confidential client information, provided that the lawyer (1) clearly explains to the consultant the confidentiality rules; (2) ensures that the consultant fully understands the rules and agrees to maintain the confidentiality of all information obtained in the course of assisting the lawyer; and (3) ensures that the consultant has implemented adequate safeguards to protect confidential information. The lawyer may satisfy the second requirement by obtaining a written acknowledgment from the consultant that he or she understands the confidential nature of the information and his or her obligation to protect it. The lawyer must inform the client if a significant breach of confidentiality occurs through the actions of the consultant. Opinions 91-06, 98-07; Rules 1.6, 5.3; ABA 95-398.

Appendix H: Cloud Computing

Ethics Opinions on Lawyer Confidentiality Obligations
    Concerning Cloud Computing

A) ABA Formal Ethics Opinions
The Opinion headnotes are reproduced below.

1) Formal Opinion 498 (March 10, 2021)
    Virtual Practice
The ABA Model Rules of Professional Conduct permit virtual practice, which is technologically enabled law practice beyond the traditional brick-and-mortar law firm. When practicing virtually, lawyers must particularly consider ethical duties regarding competence, diligence, and communication, especially when using technology. In compliance with the duty of confidentiality, lawyers must make reasonable efforts to prevent inadvertent or unauthorized disclosures of information relating to the representation and take reasonable precautions when transmitting such information. Additionally, the duty of supervision requires that lawyers make reasonable efforts to ensure compliance by subordinate lawyers and nonlawyer assistants with the Rules of Professional Conduct, specifically regarding virtual practice policies.

B) ABA Reference Material and Bar Association
    Reports on Cloud Computing
1) ABA Section of Law Practice Management website:
    Cloud Ethics Opinions Around the U.S.
https://www.americanbar.org/digital-asset-abstract.html/content/dam/aba/images/legal_technology resources/CloudEthicsOpinions2019/cloudethicsopinions2019.pdf

2) ABA Section of Law Practice Management
    Section: eLawyering Task Force
http://apps.americanbar.org/dch/committee.cfm?com=EP024500

The E-Lawyering task force has published "Guidelines for the Use of Cloud Computing in Law Practice" http://apps.americanbar.org/webupload/commupload/EP024500/related resources/cloudcomputingguidelines05.30.2011.pdfhttps://www .americanbar.org/content/dam/aba/administrative/ethics_2020/ethics_2020 _feb_2011_public_hearing_written_submissions.pdf

3) ABA Section of Science & Technology Law:
    Cloud Computing Committee
https://connect.americanbar.org/scitechconnect/communities/community -home?CommunityKey=95a000c5-7393-4a71-a446-bb2193eb7d0c

4) New York City Bar Report "The Cloud and the Small Law Firm:
    Business, Ethics and Privilege Considerations" (2013)
http://www2.nycbar.org/pdf/report/uploads/20072378-TheCloudandthe SmallLawFirm.pdf

5) Cloud Computing Guidelines from Canada:
http://www.lawsociety.bc.ca/docs/practice/resources/guidelines-cloud.pdf
http://www.lawsociety.bc.ca/docs/practice/resources/checklist-cloud.pdf

C) *Digests of State Bar Ethics Opinions on Cloud Computing.*
The following digests of state bar ethics opinions are excerpted from the *ABA/Bloomberg Lawyers' Manual on Professional Conduct.*

1) Alabama State Bar Opinion 2010-02 (undated)
    Client files; Computers; Confidentiality; Client
    funds and property; Disabled clients.
https://www.alabar.org/office-of-general-counsel/formal-opinions/2010-02/
A lawyer may outsource file storage to a service that uses cloud computing if he learns enough about the security issues to reasonably ensure that the service will protect the material's confidentiality. When disposing of electronic devices, lawyers should ensure that confidential information has been removed. A lawyer's obligation to retain client files and property

depends upon the category of material. First, there are certain intrinsically valuable documents that ordinarily must be retained indefinitely, be they originals or photocopies; these include wills, powers of attorney, advance healthcare directives, executed estate-planning documents, stock certificates, bonds, cash, negotiable instruments, title certificates and abstracts, deeds, official corporate or other business and financial records, and settlement agreements. Second is property that a client would normally expect to be returned, or whose premature or unauthorized destruction would be detrimental to the client; this includes tangible personal property, photographs, recordings, pleadings, correspondence, discovery, demonstrative aids, written statements, notes, memoranda, and business and financial records. The lawyer may destroy such items if the client consents; consent may be implied if the client fails to take possession within 60 days of a date specified in either the lawyer's written retention policy—which must be affirmatively acknowledged in writing at the outset or termination of the representation— or a separate written notice to the client. Property not belonging to either of these two categories and having no foreseeable value may be destroyed without notice after the lawyer has retained it for a reasonable time, which would be at least six years. If a client asks for a file in a particular format, the lawyer generally must comply and may not charge. However, if the client suffers from diminished capacity or has a propensity for violence and might use the information to endanger others, the lawyer may redact certain documents. Opinions 1986-02, 1993-10, 1994-01; Ala. Code §§6-6-574, 34-3-61; Rules 1.6, 1.15, 1.16(d); ABA i1376, i1384.

2) Alaska Bar Association Opinion 2014-3 (May 5, 2014)
   Internet; Client files; Client funds and property; Confidentiality;
   Competence; Outsourcing; Record retention.
https://alaskabar.org/wp-content/uploads/2014-3.pdf
A lawyer may use cloud computing services to store client files if the lawyer takes reasonable steps to ascertain that the cloud provider has adequate measures in place to protect the security, confidentiality and accessibility of the information and the lawyer knows where the client information is at any given time. At the conclusion of the representation, if the client does

not wish the file to be preserved, the lawyer must take reasonable steps to ensure that the information is deleted from the cloud. The opinion includes examples of appropriate security measures. Rules 1.1, 1.6, 1.15, 5.3.

3) Arizona State Bar Opinion 05-04 (July 2005)
    Electronic Storage; Confidentiality.
http://www.azbar.org/Ethics/EthicsOpinions/ViewEthicsOpinion?id=523
A lawyer may store information on computer systems that also connect to the Internet provided that the lawyer takes reasonable measures to prevent disclosure or destruction of the materials. If the lawyer lacks the requisite technological competence, he must hire a computer expert. Opinions 95-11, 97-04; Rules 1.1, 1.6(a), 5.1(a), 5.3(a,b).

4) Arizona State Bar Opinion 09-04 (Dec. 2009)
    Confidentiality; Maintaining Client Files;
    Electronic Storage; Internet.
http://www.azbar.org/Ethics/EthicsOpinions/ViewEthicsOpinion?id=704
A lawyer may offer clients online viewing and retrieval of their files if the lawyer takes reasonable security precautions. For example, the lawyer may use a "Secure Socket Layer" server that encrypts the files and stores them in online folders with unique, randomly generated alphanumeric names and several layers of password-protection. Competent personnel should periodically review the security precautions. Opinions 05-04, 07-02; Rules 1.1, 1.6(a).

5) State Bar of California Opinion 2012-184 (undated)
    Lawyer-client relationship; Internet; Competence;
    Confidentiality; Outsourcing; Communication with clients.
http://ethics.calbar.ca.gov/Portals/9/documents/Opinions/CAL%202012
-184-ADA.pdf
A lawyer may provide legal services via a secure internet portal going from her website to that of a third-party vendor (cloud computing) without telephone, personal, or e-mail contact. She may be required to take special measures in order to meet ethics obligations, for example those of confidentiality and competence. Among other concerns the lawyer must ensure

data security, and in some cases, she may need to verify the identity of the purported client. Opinions 1971-25, 1984-77, 2007-174, 2010-179; Los Angeles County Opinion 374; Rules 1-100, 1-300, 1-310, 3-100, 3-110, 3-310, 3-400, 3-500, 3-600, 4-200; Bus. & Prof. Code §§6068(e),(m),(n), 6125, 6126, 6127, 6147, 6148; Cal. Rules of Court 3.35-3.37, 5.70-5.71 (renumbered 5.425 as of January 2013); ABA 95-398, 08-451, 11-458.

6) Connecticut Bar Association Opinion 2013-07 (June 19, 2013)
   Internet; Computers; Record retention; Outsourcing; Competence;
   Confidentiality; Client files; Client funds and property.
https://www.ctbar.org/docs/default-source/publications/ethics-opinions
-informal-opinions/2013-opinions/informal-opinion-2013-07
A lawyer may use cloud computing, including software as a service (SaaS), for storing, transmitting, and processing client information if the lawyer uses reasonable efforts to prevent unauthorized access or disclosure, and ensures that the cloud service provider's policies and practices are consistent with the lawyer's obligations under the Rules of Professional Conduct. Opinion 99-52; Conn. Prac. Book §2-27(c); Rules 1.1, 1.6, 1.15, 5.1, 5.3.

7) Florida Bar Ethics Opinion 06-01 (April 10, 2006)
   Client files; Computers; Record retention.
https://www.floridabar.org/etopinions/etopinion-06-1/
A lawyer may store in electronic format any client documents he is required to retain. The main consideration in file storage is that the appropriate documents be maintained, not the method by which they are stored. Opinions 63-3, 71-62, 81-8, 88-11 (reconsideration); Rules 4-1.5(f)(4), 4-1.8(j), 5-1.2(d); ABA i1127.

8) Florida Bar Ethics Opinion 12-3 (Jan. 25, 2013)
   Confidentiality; Cloud computing; Outsourcing; Competence.
https://www.floridabar.org/etopinions/etopinion-12-3/
A lawyer may use cloud computing services to store, access and share client files if the lawyer uses reasonable diligence to ascertain that the provider has adequate measures in place to protect the security, confidentiality and

accessibility of the information. The lawyer should research the service provider and should consider taking additional security measures regarding proprietary client information or other particularly sensitive information. The opinion includes suggestions as to what the lawyer should consider in researching the service provider. Opinions 07-2, 10-2; Rule 1.6.

9)   Illinois State Bar Association Opinion 16-06 (Oct. 2016)
     Confidentiality; Competence; Internet; Computers; Client
     files; Communication with clients; Nonlawyers.
https://www.isba.org/sites/default/files/ethicsopinions/16-06.pdf
A lawyer may use an outside cloud-computing service to store and transmit client information if the lawyer understands the technology enough to be able to assess the risk of inadvertent disclosure or unauthorized access, and can act reasonably to protect the information. The lawyer must conduct a due diligence investigation before selecting a provider and must periodically review the chosen provider's security measures. The opinion suggests reasonable inquiries and practices. Opinion 10-01; Rules 1.1, 1.6, 5.1, 5.3.

10) Iowa State Bar Association Opinion 11-01 (Sept. 9, 2011)
     Confidentiality; Client files; Cloud computing.
http://205.209.45.153/iabar/IowaEthicsOpinions.nsf/b6868944e3311d
d0872581100042934f/a092fcd35bb508e0872581100042b927/$FILE
/Ethics%20Opinion%2011-01%20--%20Software%20as%20a%20Ser
vice%20-%20Cloud%20Computing.pdf
A lawyer may use "software as a service," known as SaaS, to store client information on the computers of an outside vendor. The lawyer must have unrestricted and reliable access to the data. In performing due diligence to ensure the information is protected, the lawyer may rely on the services of independent companies, bar associations and similar organizations, or the lawyer's own qualified staff, but the individuals must possess both the requisite technological expertise and an understanding of the ethics rules. As guidance, the opinion offers a list of questions lawyers should ask when considering whether to use outside vendors to store client information. Rule 32:1.6.

11) Iowa State Bar Association Opinion 14-01 (March 10, 2014)
    Confidentiality; Client files; Cloud computing; Competence.
https://cdn.ymaws.com/sites/iowabar.site-ym.com/resource/resmgr/IA_Law
yer_Weekly/IA_Ethics_Op_14-01.pdf
A lawyer must be aware of changes in computer operating systems that
could result in an increased risk to the security of confidential information.
Rule 1.6 imposes an ongoing obligation to exercise due diligence in assessing system security, but does not dictate how the lawyer should respond to
any particular risk. Opinion 11-01; Rule 1.6.

12) Kentucky Bar Association Opinion E-437 (March 21, 2014)
    Internet; Client files; Confidentiality; Outsourcing; Record
    retention; Competence; Supervisory lawyers.
https://www.kybar.org/resource/resmgr/Ethics_Opinions_(Part_2)_/kba
_e-437.pdf
A lawyer may use cloud computing to store confidential client information if the lawyer takes reasonable care to ensure that the confidentiality
and security of the information is preserved. The lawyer must use "reasonable efforts" to ensure that the cloud provider's conduct is consistent
with the lawyer's obligations under the Rules of Professional Conduct,
including investigating the cloud provider's qualifications, competence
and diligence. If the lawyer is a partner or manager in his law firm, the
lawyer must use "reasonable efforts" to ensure that his firm does so. If
a matter is particularly sensitive, the lawyer must consult with the client
about the use of cloud computing. Rules 1.1, 1.4, 1.6, 1.9, 1.15, 1.16,
1.18, 5.3; ABA Rule 1.6(c).

13) Maine Board of Overseers of the Bar Ethics
    Opinion 194 (June 30, 2008)
    Files of client; Computers; Confidentiality.
https://www.mebaroverseers.org/attorney_services/opinion.html?id=86894
A lawyer may use an outside provider to process and electronically store data
that include confidential client information only if the lawyer ensures that
the provider maintains appropriate standards for protecting confidentiality,

and has a legally enforceable obligation to do so. Opinions 74, 134; 45 C.F.R. §§164.302–318; Rules 3.6(a), 3.6(h), 3.13(c); ABA 95-398, 99-413.

14) Maine Board of Overseers of the Bar Ethics
   Opinion 207 (Jan. 8, 2013)
   Internet; E-mail; Record retention; Outsourcing;
   Competence; Confidentiality; Client files.
https://www.mebaroverseers.org/attorney_services/opinion.html?id=478397
A lawyer may use cloud computing and storage, including web-based e-mail, online document creation and data storage, software-as-a-service ("SaaS"), platform-as-a-service ("PaaS"), and infrastructure-as-a-service ("IaaS"), for client matters. The opinion enumerates recommended practices to reasonably ensure compliance with the obligation of confidentiality, including agreements to secure from cloud service providers, and observes that the standard of reasonable care in ethical conduct requires lawyers to periodically educate themselves on changes in technology. Opinions 74, 120, 134, 183, 194; Rules 1.1, 1.6, 1.15, 5.3.

15) Massachusetts Bar Opinion 12-03 (March 2012)
   Client files; Record retention; Confidentiality; Computers; Internet.
http://www.massbar.org/publications/ethics-opinions/2010-2019/2012
/opinion-12-03
A lawyer may store and synchronize confidential files using internet-based "cloud" storage offered by, for example, Google Docs, Microsoft's Windows Azure, Apple's iCloud, and Amazon's S3, if the lawyer makes reasonable efforts to ensure that the provider's policies, practices, and procedures are compatible with the lawyer's professional obligations, including the obligation of confidentiality. Opinions 00-01, 05-04; Rule 1.6(a).

16) Missouri Informal Ethics Opinion 2018-09 (undated)
   Computers; Internet; Client files; Record retention; Confidentiality
https://mobar.org/public/ethics/InformalOpinionsSearch.aspx
An attorney may use cloud computing as long as the attorney maintains competence in the use of relevant technology and makes reasonable efforts

to safeguard confidential information from inadvertent or unauthorized disclosure or access to client information. Rules 4-1.1; 4-1.6; 4-5.3.

17) State Bar of Nevada Formal Opinion 33 (Feb. 9, 2006)
     Files of client; Computers; Confidentiality.
http://ftp.documation.com/references/ABA10a/PDfs/3_12.pdf
A lawyer may store digital copies of client files on a server maintained by an outside contractor if the contractor agrees to keep the contents confidential and the lawyer takes reasonable steps to prevent unauthorized disclosure. Nev. S. Ct. R. 156; ABA Rule 1.6, ABA 95-398, 99-413; ABA i1127.

18) New Hampshire Bar Association Advisory
     Opinion 2012-13/04 (Feb. 21, 2013)
     Cloud computing; Confidentiality; Outsourcing;
     Non-lawyer assistants; Competence.
https://www.nhbar.org/ethics/opinion-2012-13-04
A lawyer may use cloud computing consistent with his or her ethical obligations, and must ensure that client information remains confidential. Other considerations include whether the cloud computing organization is reputable, whether the data is stored in a format that is retrievable and secure, whether the provider offers security measures, how long the provider will retain data, and whether the provider has an enforceable obligation to keep the data confidential. Rules 1.8(c), 1.0(e), 1.1, 1.6, 1.15, 2.1, 5.3.

19) New Jersey Advisory Opinion 701 (undated)
     Client funds and property; Files of client; Computers; Confidentiality.
http://www.judiciary.state.nj.us/notices/ethics/ACPE_Opinion701_Electronic
Storage_12022005.pdf
A lawyer may digitize and retain in electronic format copies of documents received by the lawyer in the course of a representation, except for wills, deeds, and other client documents that by their nature must be retained in their original form. If the lawyer entrusts the documents to someone outside the firm for storage, the outside person must be aware of the obligation to preserve the confidentiality of the information. Opinions 515, 692, 694; Rules 1.1, 1.4, 1.6, 1.15.

20) New York State Bar Association Opinion 820 (Feb. 8, 2008)
    Confidentiality; E-mail; Computers.
https://nysba.org/ethics-opinion-820/
A lawyer does not violate the duty of confidentiality by subscribing to
an e-mail service provider that gives him a discount in exchange for his
tolerance of targeted advertising displayed on his screen. The provider electronically scans e-mails the subscriber opens and looks for certain keywords;
the provider infers the subscriber's interests from the keywords and sends
him advertisements tailored accordingly. The process is entirely electronic
and does not entail any review of e-mails by human beings. Opinion 709;
DR 4-101; EC 4-3.

21) New York State Bar Association Opinion 842 (Sept. 10, 2010)
    Client files; Internet; Confidentiality; Attorney-client privilege.
https://nysba.org/ethics-opinion-842/
A lawyer who uses cloud computing provided by an online service as his
backup file storage system must take reasonable care to protect the confidentiality of the information. This may include: ensuring the provider
has an enforceable obligation to preserve confidentiality and security and
will notify the lawyer if served with process requiring production of client
information; investigating the adequacy of the provider's security measures
and recoverability methods; using available technology to guard against
reasonably foreseeable infiltration attempts; and investigating the provider's ability to purge, wipe, and move data. The lawyer should also monitor
changing law to ensure he is not jeopardizing any privileges applicable to
the material. Opinions 473, 709, 782, 820; New York County Opinion
733; C.P.L.R. 4548; Rules 1.4, 1.6.

22) New York City Bar Formal Opinion 2008-01 (Jan. 1, 2008)
    Files of client; Computers; E-mail.
http://www.nycbar.org/ethics/ethics-opinions-local/2008-opinions/799-a
-lawyers-ethical-obligations-to-retain-and-to-provide-a-client-with-elec
tronic-documents-relating-to-a-representation-
A lawyer is not required to organize or store electronic documents or e-mails
in any particular manner or medium. E-mails present more difficulty than

electronic documents because they often are deleted automatically after a certain period, and generally are not stored in a document management system. Because a lawyer may not charge a client file retrieval costs that could reasonably have been avoided, there is much to commend a practice of organizing saved e-mails for ease of retrieval. Opinion 1986-4; New York State Opinions 460, 623, 780; DRs 2-106, 2-110(2), 9-102; ABA Rules 1.0(n), 1.16(d); ABA Informal Opinion 1384 (March 14, 1977).

23) North Carolina State Bar Opinion 2011-6 (Jan. 27, 2012)
    Client files; Computers; Internet; Outsourcing;
    Confidentiality; Record retention.

https://www.ncbar.gov/for-lawyers/ethics/adopted-opinions/2011
-formal-ethics-opinion-6/

A lawyer may contract with a vendor of software as a service (SaaS) if the lawyer uses reasonable care to protect client information. Recommended options include an agreement with the vendor as to protection, retrieval, and disposition of confidential information during and after the contractual relationship and in the event the vendor goes out of business; evaluation of the vendor's security measures, including firewalls, encryption techniques, socket security features, and intrusion-detection systems; and evaluation of the extent to which the vendor backs up hosted data. The duties of diligence and competence require the lawyer to keep abreast of changes in technology and their impact on cloud computing and online security. Opinions RPC 133, 209, 215, 234, 1998-15, 2008-5; Rules 1.6, 1.15, 5.3(a).

24) State Bar of North Dakota Opinion 99-03 (June 21, 1999)
    Confidentiality; Internet; Files of client.

https://cdn.ymaws.com/www.sband.org/resource/resmgr/docs/for_law
yers/99-03.pdf

A law firm may subscribe to an online data backup service whereby the firm's computer server would periodically transfer data to the service's server, which would then transfer the data to disk or tape that would be stored offsite and the firm would be given a confidential password allowing members to retrieve firm data from the storage units. However, the firm must ensure that the security of the data transmission and storage are adequate for the sensitivity of the records. At minimum, the firm must limit the access to the data to authorized personnel only, usually by limiting disclosure of the password to those individuals. Opinion 97-09; Rule 1.6; ABA 99-413.

25) Oregon Opinion 2011-188 (2011; Revised April 2015)
     Outsourcing; Internet; Client files; Confidentiality;
     Record retention; Supervisory lawyers.
http://www.osbar.org/_docs/ethics/2011-188.pdf
A lawyer may contract with a third-party vendor to store client files and documents online on the vendor's remote servers (the "cloud") if the lawyer has taken reasonable steps to keep the information secure. This means the lawyer should investigate and periodically reevaluate how the vendor backs up and stores its data and metadata. The lawyer may include provisions in the service agreement requiring the vendor to preserve the confidentiality and security of the materials and to notify her of any unauthorized access. If industry standards relating to confidentiality and security meet the requirements of the lawyer ethics rules, ensuring the vendor's compliance with industry standards may satisfy the lawyer's obligation to take reasonable steps. Opinions 2005-44, 2005-129, 2005-141; Rules 1.6, 5.3.

26) Pennsylvania Bar Association Formal Opinion
     2010-14 (March 15, 2010)
     Client files; Confidentiality; Computers.
A lawyer may use an "off-site backup service" if he takes proper steps to safeguard client confidentiality; at a minimum the service should provide high levels of encryption. Rule 1.6.

27) Pennsylvania Bar Association Formal
     Opinion 2010-60 (Jan. 10, 2011)
     Client files; Computers; Internet; Confidentiality.
A lawyer may use cloud computing to access and store data, and may use smartphones synchronized through the cloud to remotely access the data, if the lawyer takes appropriate measures to protect client confidentiality. Rules 1.6, 5.1.

28) Pennsylvania Bar Association Formal Opinion 2011-200 (Nov. 2011)
    Client files; Internet; Outsourcing; Record retention;
    Confidentiality; Competence; E-mail.

A lawyer may store confidential client information off-site using "cloud computing" if the lawyer takes reasonable steps to protect data security. Generally, this will mean implementing mechanisms to back up data, install firewalls, limit unauthorized access, monitor all access, avoid inadvertent disclosure, and encrypt confidential data, as well as having a plan to address security breaches and having alternate ways to connect to the Internet. If using an overseas service provider, the lawyer must make sure the hosting jurisdiction has privacy protections, data security laws, and safeguards against unlawful search and seizure that are as rigorous as those of the United States and Pennsylvania. Similarly, lawyers using web-based unencrypted e-mail services must take reasonable precautions to protect confidential information; some communications may require special protection. Formal Opinions 2009-100, 2010-200; Informal Opinion 2010-60; 45 C.F.R. subpart 164.314(a)(2)(i); 73 Pa. Stat. §2303; Rules 1.0(e), 1.1, 1.4, 1.6, 1.15, 5.3; ABA 99-413, 08-451.

29) Tennessee Board of Professional Responsibility
    Opinion 2015-F-159 (Sept. 11, 2015)
    Internet; Confidentiality; Client files; Record retention;
    Competence; Supervisory lawyers; Communication with clients.

http://www.tbpr.org/ethic_opinions/2015-f-159
A lawyer may store confidential information in the cloud if the lawyer takes reasonable care to preserve its confidentiality and protect against loss and other risks. The meaning of reasonable care will depend upon the information, the technology and the circumstances. Rules 1.1, 1.6, 1.9, 5.1, 5.3.

30) Vermont Bar Association Opinion 2010-6 (undated)
    Client files; Internet; Confidentiality; Record retention; Competence.

https://www.vtbar.org/wp-content/uploads/2021/03/10-06.pdf
A lawyer may use Software as a Service (SaaS, also called cloud computing), to store, back up, and transmit confidential client information and

documents, and may use remote document synchronization systems and web-based e-mail and calendaring systems, but must take reasonable precautions to protect confidentiality and to ensure access to the materials. The nature of the precautions will depend on the circumstances and the technology. There may be circumstances in which using, or relying exclusively upon, a particular system would not be reasonable. The opinion invites the Vermont Supreme Court to examine whether technological changes have warranted changes in applicable procedural rules and ethics rules. Rules 1.1, 1.6, 1.15, 5.3.

31) Virginia Legal Ethics Opinion 1872 (March 29, 2013)
    Virtual Office; Cloud computing; Confidentiality; Internet.
https://www.vacle.org/opinions/1872.htm#:~:text=A%20partner%20in%20
a%20law,the%20Rules%20of%20Professional%20Conduct
Operating a virtual law office does not change a lawyer's ethical obligations but does require extra precautions to meet the obligations of confidentiality, client communication, and supervision of others in the firm. Lawyer must act with reasonable care to protect client information, which includes selection of third-party vendors who transmit and store client data and supervision of nonlawyer assistants and subordinate lawyers who work remotely or in shared office with nonlawyers who are not law firm employees.

32) Washington State Bar Association Opinion 2215
    (2012) Confidentiality; Client files; Record
    retention; Computers; Outsourcing.
https://ao.wsba.org/
A lawyer may contract with a third-party cloud computing vendor to store client files and documents on a remote server for access by the lawyer and the lawyer's clients if the lawyer takes reasonable steps to evaluate the risks of online data storage and ensure that the provider uses reasonable care to protect the information from loss or security breaches. The lawyer must monitor and regularly review the provider's security measures. Rules 1.1, 1.6, 1.15A.

33) State Bar of Wisconsin Opinion EF-15-01 (March
    23, 2015; Amended Sept. 8, 2017)

Cloud computing; Client files; Competence; Confidentiality.
https://www.wisbar.org/formembers/ethics/Ethics%20Opinions/EF-15
-01%20Cloud%20Computing%20Amended.pdf
A lawyer may use cloud computing to store and transmit client information if the lawyer uses reasonable efforts that are commensurate with the
risks presented to protect access and confidentiality and ensure that the
cloud service provider's actions are consistent with the lawyer's professional obligations. If the provider uses a server outside the United States,
the lawyer must ensure that the client information stored on that server is
protected by laws as stringent as those of the U.S. The opinion discusses
factors to consider in assessing risk and determining what constitutes reasonable efforts. Rules 1.1, 1.4, 1.6, 5.3; ABA Rules 1.6, 5.3.

Appendix I: Social Media

Ethics Opinions Relating to Judges and Social Media and Lawyers'
  Passive Communications with Jurors on Social Media

(I) Judges and Social Media

A) ABA Formal Ethics Opinions
The Opinion headnotes are reproduced below.

1) Formal Opinion 462 (Feb. 21, 2013)

Judge's Use of Electronic Social Networking Media
A judge may participate in electronic social networking, but as with all
social relationships and contacts, a judge must comply with relevant provisions of the Code of Judicial Conduct and avoid any conduct that would
undermine the judge's independence, integrity, or impartiality, or create an
appearance of impropriety.

2) Formal Opinion 478 (Dec. 8, 2017)
    Independent Factual Research by Judges Via the Internet
Easy access to a vast amount of information available on the Internet exposes
judges to potential ethical problems. Judges risk violating the Model Code
of Judicial Conduct by searching the Internet for information related to
participants or facts in a proceeding. Independent investigation of adjudica-
tive facts generally is prohibited unless the information is properly subject
to judicial notice. The restriction on independent investigation includes
individuals subject to the judge's direction and control.

B) ABA Treatises and Annotated Model Standards
1) ABA Annotated Model Code of Judicial Conduct (3rd ed. 2016)
https://shop.americanbar.org/ebus/Store/ProductDetails.aspx
?productId=263035570&sc_cid=2150064-SHR02
See the annotations to Canon 3, A judge shall conduct the judge's personal and extrajudicial activities to minimize the risk of conflict with the

obligations of judicial office (p. 367) and Canon 4, A judge or candidate for judicial office shall not engage in political or campaign activity that is inconsistent with the independence, integrity, or impartiality of the judiciary (p. 505).

2) Rotunda and Dzienkowski, *Legal Ethics: The Lawyer's Deskbook on Professional Responsibility*, American Bar Association (2018-2019 edition)
https://store.legal.thomsonreuters.com/law-products/Statutes/Legal-Ethics
-The-Lawyers-Deskbook-on-Professional-Responsibility-2018-2019-ed-ABA
/p/106152833
See § 10.2-2.11 *When the Judge Is a Friend of the Lawyer or Party or Witness*

3) Judicial Conference of the United States
http://www.uscourts.gov/about-federal-courts/governance
-judicial-conference

4) Resource Packet for Developing Guidelines on Use of Social Media by Judicial Employees (2010)
http://www.uscourts.gov/uscourts/RulesAndPolicies/conduct/SocialMedia
Layout.pdf

C) *Excerpts from State Bar Judicial Ethics Opinions on Judges' use of Social Media.*
1) Arizona Supreme Court Judicial Ethics Advisory Committee Advisory Opinion 14-01 (Revised Aug. 5, 2014) Use of Social and Electronic Media by Judges and Judicial Employees
http://www.azcourts.gov/LinkClick.aspx?fileticket=zNRP1
_l8sck%3d&portalid=137
"...[A] judge who uses social media must not make any public statement that might reasonably be expected to affect the outcome or impair the fairness of a matter pending or impending in any court. *See* Rule 2.10(A); *see also* Rule 4.1(A)(9) ('A judge or a judicial candidate shall not do any of the following: make any statement that would reasonably be expected to affect

the outcome or impair the fairness of a matter pending or impending in any court'). Although nonpublic statements are only prohibited under Rule 2.10(A) if they might substantially interfere with a fair trial or hearing, it is prudent to assume that even postings intended only for friends and family may be more broadly disseminated through social and electronic media."

2) California Judges Association Formal Opinion 66 (Nov. 23, 2010) Online Social Networking

http://www.caljudges.org/docs/Ethics%20Opinions/Op%2066%20Final.pdf

"Caution is essential when a judge goes onto an online social networking site. Internet communications are permanent and lack the privacy of in-person or telephonic conversations. Judges must be careful to avoid making remarks that would cast doubt on the judge's ability to act impartially. As the commentary to Canon 4A makes plain: 'Expressions of bias or prejudice by a judge, even outside the judge's judicial activities, may cast reasonable doubt on the judge's capacity to act impartially as a judge. Expressions which may do so include jokes or other remarks demeaning individuals on the basis of a classification such as their race, sex, religion, sexual orientation, or national origin.'"

3) Kentucky Formal Judicial Ethics Opinion JE-119 (Jan. 20, 2020) Judges' Membership on Internet-Based Social Networking Sites

https://kycourts.gov/Courts/Judicial-Ethics/Judicial%20Ethics%20Opinions/JE_119.pdf

"While a proceeding is pending or impending in any court, judges are prohibited from making "any public comment that might reasonably be expected to affect its outcome or impair its fairness ...." Canon 3B(9). Furthermore, full-time judges are prohibited from practicing law or giving legal advice. Canon 4G. Judges, therefore, must be careful that any comments they may make on a social networking site do not violate these prohibitions. While social networking sites may have an aura of private, one-on-one conversation, they are much more public than offline conversations, and statements once made in that medium may never go away."

4) Massachusetts Committee on Judicial Ethics
   Opinion 2016-01 (Feb. 16, 2016)
   Facebook: Using Social Networking Site
https://www.mass.gov/opinion/cje-opinion-no-2016-01
"A judge who uses Facebook must avoid violating the Code's restrictions, including those enumerated above. This requires a judge to be cautious concerning the judge's Facebook communications, that is, to think before engaging in electronic speech. A judge must avoid conduct that may interfere with the duties of judicial office (e.g., making improper comments on pending or impending matters, engaging in ex parte communications, suggesting that any person or party has special access to the court) or conflict with the dignity of judicial office (e.g., posting inappropriate photos)...."

"Moreover, a judge must consider all of the judge's Facebook communications to be potentially public and, once made, wholly outside of the judge's control. Postings, including comments on other's posts, may be transmitted without the judge's permission or knowledge to unintended recipients, and Facebook communications may be taken out of context or relayed incorrectly. Facebook communications may be saved indefinitely."

5) Massachusetts Committee on Judicial Ethics
   Opinion 2016-08 (Sept. 6, 2016)
   Linked In: Using Social Networking Site
https://www.mass.gov/opinion/cje-opinion-no-2016-08
"As the use of social media continues to grow, we again emphasize judges' obligations under the Code of Judicial Conduct, including the obligations to uphold and promote the independence, integrity, and impartiality of the judiciary; promote public confidence in the judiciary; avoid both impropriety and the appearance of impropriety in their professional and public lives; maintain the dignity of judicial office at all times; avoid abuse of the prestige of the judicial office; refrain from political activity; and conduct all personal and extrajudicial activities to minimize the risk of conflict with the obligations of judicial office. Judges must expect to be the subject of public scrutiny that might be burdensome if applied to other citizens. Each judge who uses social media must take steps to minimize the likelihood that

the manner in which that judge uses social media would lead a reasonable person to question the judge's impartiality."

"Judges must, of course, be aware that all social media communications may become public."

6) Missouri Commission on Retirement, Removal
   and Discipline Opinion 186 (2015)

"[W]hile the Commission does not think that judicial involvement in social media is per se unethical, it is conduct that exposes the judge to unnecessary danger of engaging in conduct that may be violative of the Code of Judicial Conduct....[I]n order to limit the potential of ethical violations and the number of cases in which the judge might be required to recuse, the judge should take care to adjust the privacy setting of the judge's personal Facebook or other social media account such that it could be viewed only by those who are the judge's listed 'friends' and not by the general public."

7) New York Advisory Committee on Judicial Ethics
   Opinion 08-176 (Jan. 29, 2009)

https://www.nycourts.gov/ipjudicialethicsopinions/08-176.htm
"The Rules require that a judge must avoid impropriety and the appearance of impropriety in all of the judge's activities (*see* 22 NYCRR 100.2) and shall act at all times in a manner that promotes public confidence in the integrity and impartiality of the judiciary (*see* 22 NYCRR 100.2[A]). Similarly, a judge shall conduct all of the judge's extra-judicial activities so that they do not detract from the dignity of judicial office (*see* 22 NYCRR 100.4[A][2])....A judge should thus recognize the public nature of anything he/she places on a social network page and tailor any postings accordingly."

8) The Supreme Court of Ohio Board of Commissioners on
   Grievances and Discipline Opinion 2010-7 (Dec. 3, 2010)

https://www.ohioadvop.org/wp-content/uploads/2017/04/Op_10-007.pdf
"A judge should avoid making any comments on a social networking site about pending or impending matters in any court. As required by Jud. Cond. Rule 2.10 "[a] judge shall not make any public statement that might

reasonably be expected to affect the outcome or impair the fairness of a matter *pending* or *impending* in any court, or make any nonpublic statement that might substantially interfere with a fair trial or hearing." Avoidance of any pending or impending case related comments is advised."

(II) Lawyers' Passive Communications with Jurors on Social Media

A) ABA Formal Ethics Opinions

1) Formal Opinion 466 (April 24, 2014)
   Lawyer Reviewing Jurors' Internet Presence

Unless limited by law or court order, a lawyer may review a juror's or potential juror's Internet presence, which may include postings by the juror or potential juror in advance of and during a trial, but a lawyer may not communicate directly or through another with a juror or potential juror.

A lawyer may not, either personally or through another, send an access request to a juror's electronic social media. An access request is a communication to a juror asking the juror for information that the juror has not made public and that would be the type of ex parte communication prohibited by Model Rule 3.5(b).

The fact that a juror or a potential juror may become aware that a lawyer is reviewing his Internet presence when a network setting notifies the juror of such does not constitute a communication from the lawyer in violation of Rule 3.5(b).

In the course of reviewing a juror's or potential juror's Internet presence, if a lawyer discovers evidence of juror or potential juror misconduct that is criminal or fraudulent, the lawyer must take reasonable remedial measures including, if necessary, disclosure to the tribunal.

B) ABA Reference Material and Bar Association Reports on Judicial Ethics and Social Media

1) New York State Bar Association Social Media Ethics Guidelines of the Commercial and Federal Litigation Section of the New York State Bar Association (Revised April 29, 2019; Released June 20, 2019) https://nysba.org/app/uploads/2020/02/NYSBA-Social-Media-Ethics-Guidelines-Final-6-20-19.pdf.

C) Digests of State Bar Judicial Ethics Opinions

The following digests of state bar ethics opinions are excerpted with permission from the *ABA/Bloomberg Lawyers' Manual on Professional Conduct*.

1) Colorado State Bar Opinion 127 (Sept. 2015)
   Social media; Investigations; Communication with judges;
   Communication with jurors; Communication with unrepresented
   persons; Communication with represented persons;
   Communication with witnesses; Competence; Advice to clients.

http://www.cobar.org/Portals/COBAR/repository/ethicsOpinions/FormalEth
icsOpinion_127.pdf

A lawyer may view the public portion of anyone's social media profile. The committee agrees with the majority view that "passive" browsing of a social media profile generally does not amount to contact or communication, even if the account-holder gets an automatic notification. Repetitively browsing a website knowing the account-holder is being notified could, however, amount to a violation of Rule 4.4(a) depending on degree and intent. A lawyer may never view or ask permission to view the restricted portion of a social media profile belonging to a judge presiding over the lawyer's case, or to a prospective or sitting juror. A lawyer needs counsel's consent before asking to see the restricted portion of a represented person's profile; if the person is unrepresented, the lawyer must first identify himself as a lawyer and disclose the general nature of the matter. A lawyer may never use deception to gain access to the restricted portion of a social media profile, and may not circumvent the rules by having someone else make "friend" requests. As a matter of competence, lawyers should keep abreast of technological developments relevant to their ethical obligations, and should advise their clients to expect opposing counsel to view the public portions of their profiles. Rules 1.1, 3.5, 4.1, 4.2, 4.3, 4.4(a), 5.1(b), (c), 8.4(a), (c); CJC Rules 2.4(B), 2.9; ABA 466.

2) New York State Bar Opinion 2012-2 (undated)
   Social media; Investigations; Internet; Communication with jurors.

http://www2.nycbar.org/pdf/report/uploads/20072303-FormalOpinion2012
-02JuryResearchandSocialMedia.pdf

A lawyer may research a potential or sitting juror using publicly available social networking websites such as Facebook, LinkedIn, or Twitter if no communication with the juror occurs, whether through a "friend" or connection request with the juror or an automated notification from the social media service that the juror's profile was viewed or followed. If the lawyer learns of juror misconduct through social media research, the lawyer must promptly notify the court. After the jury has been discharged, the lawyer may use social media to communicate with the jurors. Opinions 2010-2, 2012-1; New York State Opinions 246, 843; New York County Opinion 743; N.Y. Crim. Pro. Law §270.40; Rules 3.4, 3.5, 8.4; ABA 319.

3) New York County Lawyers' Association Opinion 743 (May 18, 2011)
   Communication with jurors; Social media; Internet; Investigations.
https://www.nycla.org/siteFiles/Publications/Publications1450_0.pdf
A lawyer trying a jury case may passively monitor jurors' postings on publicly available social networking sites that do not enable their account-holders to learn a website visitor's identity. The lawyer may not "friend" or tweet jurors, subscribe to their Twitter accounts, or otherwise contact them. If in the course of permissible monitoring the lawyer learns of juror misconduct, including deliberations that violate the court's instructions, he must promptly notify the court whether or not the client wants him to. New York State Opinion 843; Rules 3.5, 4.1, 8.4(a).

4) Pennsylvania State Bar Opinion 214-300 (2014)
   Social media; Internet; Advice to clients; Competence;
   Evidence; Investigations; Discovery; Communication with jurors;
   Communication with represented persons; Communication with
   unrepresented persons; Communication with judges; Confidentiality.
A lawyer should advise a client regarding the effects social media postings may have on a lawsuit or other matter. The lawyer may advise a client to remove matter that may be damaging from the client's social media page if it will not violate any law or court order, but must take appropriate action to preserve the material. A lawyer may contact persons through social networking websites to the extent permitted by applicable law and may request access to an unrepresented person's social networking website if the lawyer

identifies himself and states his reason for making the request. The lawyer may not use subterfuge to gain access to a person's nonpublic social media website. A lawyer may view the public portion of a juror's social networking website, even if the website generates a notification to the juror that the lawyer has viewed it, but may not ask the juror for access to the private portion of the website. A lawyer may connect with a judge on social media if the lawyer does not seek to improperly influence the judge and if there is no ex parte or other proscribed communication. A lawyer may endorse another lawyer and may accept an endorsement from a client on a social media website if the endorsements are not false or misleading and if the lawyer discloses whether any compensation was given for the endorsements, but a lawyer may not accept endorsements from celebrities or judges. A lawyer may respond to negative reviews of the lawyer's performance on social media websites if the lawyer does not disclose confidential client information. The opinion discusses lawyers' ethical obligations when using social media in a variety of contexts. Formal Opinions 90-142, 2005-200, 2014-200; Philadelphia Opinions 2009-2, 2014-5; Pa. R. Civ. P. 4011(b); Rules 1.1, 1.6, 3.3, 3.4, 3.5, 3.6, 4.1, 4.2, 4.3, 8.2, 8.4; CJC Canon 2.9; ABA 462, 466.

5) West Virginia State Bar Opinion 2015-02 (Sept. 22, 2015)
   Social media; Internet; Confidentiality; Competence; Prospective clients; Advice to clients; Communication with clients; Communication with represented persons; Communication with unrepresented persons; Investigations; Advertising and solicitation.
   http://www.wvodc.org/pdf/LEO%202015%20-%2002.pdf
Lawyers must comply with the lawyer ethics rules when using social media just as when using other forms of communication. A lawyer may advise a client about the content of the client's social networking website, including removing or adding information. A lawyer may connect with clients and former clients on a social networking website, but may not contact a represented person through a social networking website. A lawyer may contact an unrepresented person through a social networking website and may use information from a social networking website but may not use a pretextual basis to gain access to private information. A lawyer may review a juror's

Internet presence, and may connect with a judge on a social networking website. A lawyer may accept client reviews if he monitors them for accuracy, and may generally endorse other lawyers and comment on or respond to reviews or endorsements. A lawyer's interactions on a social networking website may create a prospective lawyer-client relationship. Rules 1.1, 1.6, 1.18, 3.3, 3.4, 3.5, 3.6, 4.1, 4.2, 4.3, 7.1, 7.2, 7.3, 7.4, 8.2, 8.4.

Author Biographies

SHELLEY BETHUNE is an associate attorney at Hinshaw and Culbertson LLP, where she defends professionals in a wide range of liability issues, focusing on counseling attorneys facing disciplinary and malpractice matters. Having worked as litigation counsel for the Illinois Attorney Registration and Disciplinary Commission (ARDC), Ms. Bethune has a deep knowledge and understanding of attorney disciplinary proceedings. During her tenure with the ARDC, she investigated hundreds of charges of lawyer misconduct, including the misappropriation of client funds, criminal conduct, conflicts of interest, and the neglect of client matters. She also represented the administrator of the ARDC in more than 20 proceedings before the Inquiry and Hearing Boards, handling all phases of the litigation, and before the Illinois Supreme Court. With her extensive experience, Ms. Bethune has frequently presented to Chicago-area law schools, bar associations, and other entities on ethics and professional responsibility. Currently, she is an inaugural member of the ABA New Lawyers Steering Committee.

BRYSON BORT is the founder of SCYTHE, a start-up building a next-generation, attack emulation platform, and GRIMM, a cybersecurity consultancy, and cofounder of the ICS Village, a nonprofit advancing awareness of industrial control system security. He is a senior fellow for Cybersecurity and National Security at R Street and the National Security Institute and an advisor to the Army Cyber Institute. As a U.S. Army officer, he served as a battle captain and brigade engineering officer in support of Operation Iraqi Freedom before leaving the Army as a Captain. He was recognized as one of the Top 50 in Cyber in 2020 by Business Insider. Mr. Bryson received his bachelor of science degree in computer science with honors from the U.S. Military Academy at West Point. He holds a master's degree in telecommunications management from the University of Maryland, a master's in business administration from the University of Florida, and completed graduate studies in electrical engineering and computer science at the University of Texas.

RUTH HILL BRO has focused her legal career on advising businesses on privacy and information management strategy, cybersecurity, global compliance, the electronic workplace, and e-business. She has been featured as a speaker more than 180 times and has published more than 90 works on these issues. Ms. Bro is a long-standing leader in the American Bar Association, where she is a special advisor to and immediate past co-chair of the ABA Cybersecurity Legal Task Force, for which she also serves as a liaison to the ABA's new Practice Forward initiative (designed to help move legal practice and the profession forward during COVID-19 and beyond). A leader in the ABA Science & Technology Law Section (SciTech), she is a senior advisor for the Privacy, Security, and Emerging Technology Division; a member of the planning committees for the annual Internet of Things (IoT) National Institute (since 2015) and annual Artificial Intelligence and Robotics National Institute (since 2019); and the Section's Liaison to the ABA Commission on Women in the Profession (since 2018). She also served as SciTech's Section Chair (2008–2009), Membership and Diversity Committee Chair (2009–2016), and E-Privacy Law Committee Founder and Chair (2000–2005). Ms. Bro served two three-year terms (2009–2015) on the ABA Standing Committee on Technology and Information Systems (the second term as chair), in addition to terms on the ABA Standing Committee on Continuing Legal Education (as a liaison, 2012–2015), the ABA Commission on the Future of Legal Services (2014–2016) (a two-year presidential commission to improve access to, and delivery of, legal services in the United States), the ABA E-Mail Stakeholder Committee (2017–2018), the ABA Standing Committee on Disaster Response and Preparedness (2016–2017), and the ABA Board of Governors Communications Task Force (2017). She also has served on many of the top advisory or editorial boards in the privacy, data security, and technology field and on the board of the Illinois Institute for Continuing Legal Education. She has been recognized as a leader by numerous organizations, including for four consecutive years in Ethisphere Institute's annual list of Attorneys Who Matter (data privacy/security). Now a consultant, Ms. Bro started her legal career at McBride Baker & Coles (now Holland & Knight) and then spent nearly a decade at Baker & McKenzie, where she was a partner in the Chicago office and founding North American member of the firm's Global Privacy Steering

Committee. She received her BA from Northwestern University and her JD from the University of Chicago.

ANGELINE G. CHEN has more than 30 years of legal and business experience, including as a general counsel and chief compliance officer. Her operational perspective and experience informs her practice area focus in corporate and business law, compliance, cyber, space, trade controls, risk management, national security, regulatory affairs, industrial security and FOCI, and investigations. Ms. Chen is currently of counsel with DLA Piper and a principal at Cynefin LLC. Previously, she served as the vice president, general counsel, chief compliance officer, and corporate secretary at Siemens Government Technologies and at Fincantieri Marine Group/Marinette Marine Corporation, and in leadership roles with Lockheed Martin, International Launch Services, the National Security Agency, and INTELSAT. Ms. Chen's legal career started in private practice where she specialized in complex litigation focused in the areas of antitrust and white collar particularly in the high technology and manufacturing sectors. She has served as a director on several boards. Her academic experience includes more than 15 years as an adjunct professor teaching national security and technology law at the Antonin Scalia Law School (George Mason University), as well as serving as an executive-in-residence and a professor for the University of Maryland's University College's MBA program. She holds a BA and JD from Villanova University, an LLM from the Georgetown University Law Center, and an MBA from the University of Maryland.

JOHN A. DIMARIA is the assurance investigatory fellow and research fellow with the Cloud Security Alliance (CSA). He has 30 years of successful experience in standards and management system development, including information systems, business continuity, and quality. Mr. DiMaria was one of the innovators and cofounders of the CSA STAR program for cloud providers, a contributing author of the American Bar Association's Cybersecurity Handbook, a working group member and a key contributor to the NIST Cybersecurity Framework. He currently manages all facets of the CSA STAR program, which includes security, privacy, continuous monitoring, and development of new solutions.

MATTHEW F. FERRARO is counsel in the Washington, DC, office of Wilmer Cutler Pickering Hale and Dorr LLP where he practices at the intersection of national security, cybersecurity, and crisis management. He counsels clients, writes, and speaks on the threats that digital disinformation and deepfakes pose to corporations, brands, and markets; on the positive-use applications of synthetic media; and on the evolving regulatory environment surrounding these issues. Earlier in his career, Mr. Ferraro was a U.S. intelligence officer and held staff, policy, and operational positions at the Office of the Director of National Intelligence and the Central Intelligence Agency. He is a term member of the Council on Foreign Relations and a visiting fellow at the National Security Institute at George Mason University. He writes widely on intelligence, national security, and legal issues, and his publications are available at www.matthewfferraro.com and through Twitter (@MatthewFFerraro). Born and raised in New York City, Mr. Ferraro was educated at Yale, Cambridge, and Stanford universities.

MICHAELENE E. HANLEY represents companies on cybersecurity, privacy, and data trust issues that arise in counseling and global compliance programs, regulatory inquiries and enforcement actions, internal investigations, data breaches, law enforcement compliance, transactions, and data review boards. Ms. Hanley started her legal career at ZwillGen PLLC as a fellow and then moved to Sidley Austin LLP, where she was a member of the Privacy and Cybersecurity group. Drawing on her experience, she has contributed to several books, including the *PLI Treatise on Cybersecurity* and the *ABA Cybersecurity Handbook*, 2d edition. She is a member of both Women in Privacy and ChIPs and was selected to be a member of the team representing Sidley Austin for the ChIPs 2018 Next Gen Summit Mock Pitch. Throughout law school, Ms. Hanley served as a research assistant to the director of the Center for Applied Cybersecurity Research, Professor Fred Cate. She also spent a summer as a law clerk in the U.S. Department of Justice's Office of International Affairs working on extraditions and mutual legal assistance requests. She holds a BA with honors from Indiana University and a JD from the Indiana University Maurer School of Law, where she served as the executive business editor for the *Indiana Journal of Global Legal Studies*.

SANDRA L. "SANDY" HODGKINSON is the senior vice president for Strategy and Corporate Development at Leonardo DRS, a wholly owned subsidiary of top-tier defense company Leonardo. In this role, she leads the Strategic Planning process and Mergers & Acquisitions (M&A) activities for the company. She is also currently Leonardo DRS sustainability ambassador. Ms. Hodgkinson previously served as a civil servant achieving the rank of senior executive in the U.S. government, including assignments at the Department of Defense (DoD), State Department, and White House. These assignments included special assistant (chief of staff) to Deputy Secretary of Defense William J. Lynn, III; deputy assistant secretary of defense; distinguished visiting research fellow at the National Defense University; deputy to the ambassador-at-large for war crimes issues; director for international justice at the National Security Council; and senior advisor at the Coalition Provisional Authority in Baghdad, Iraq. Among her awards are DoD's highest career civilian award, the Distinguished Civilian Service Award, and four State Department Superior Honor Awards. Prior to the civil service, Ms. Hodgkinson spent six years as a U.S. Navy Judge Advocate General Corps officer, as an appellate clerk at the Navy Marine Corps Court of Criminal Appeals, as a prosecutor and international law officer in Naples, Italy, and as a country program director, Defense Institute of International Legal Studies, where she trained foreign military and civilians in more than 30 countries. Following 15 years in the Naval reserves specializing in international, national security, and cybersecurity law, she retired from the U.S. Navy with the rank of Captain. Ms. Hodgkinson has written more than 15 legal articles and six book chapters and has been an adjunct professor teaching national security law at Catholic University's Law School since 2007. She is a member of the Council on Foreign Relations and a senior peace fellow at United States Institute of Peace (USIP) and serves on the board of directors for the Naval Submarine League. She has previously served on the Executive Council of the American Society of International Law, the ABA Cybersecurity Task Force, and ABA Standing Committee on Law and National Security. She has a JD from the University of Denver (DU), an MA from DU's Graduate School of International Studies, and a BA from Tulane University. She also studied abroad at the

Hague Academy of International Law and l'Institut d'Etudes Politiques (Sciences Po), Paris.

KEVIN P. KALINICH currently leads Aon's global practice to identify exposures and develop insurance solutions related to intangible assets, including intellectual property, technology errors and omissions, miscellaneous professional liability, media liability, and coordination of multiple lines of insurance related to cyber. A 2007, 2008, 2009, 2010, 2011, 2012 (Finalist), 2014, and 2016 (Finalist) Risk & Insurance "Power Broker," Mr. Kalinich writes frequent articles, blogs, and chapters for cyber insurance books such as "Cyber Insurance for Law Firms and Legal Organizations," included within *The American Bar Association Cybersecurity Handbook: A Resource for Attorneys, Law Firms, and Business Professional* (2d edition); "Treating Cyber Risks—Using Insurance and Finance," included within *Wiley Finance Series: The Cyber Risk Handbook: Creating and Measuring Effective Cybersecurity Capabilities*. He is also quoted in numerous publications, including Ted Koppel's 2015 book, *Light's Out* (with Ajit Jain of Berkshire Hathaway), the *Wall Street Journal, Time, Forbes,* and *Bloomberg.* He is a frequent speaker on professional liability–related issues in various venues, including CNBC, RIMS, PLUS, American Bar Association, American Bankers Association, FERMA, World Economic Forum, Stanford Program in Law, Science and Technology, CCH Computer Law Advisory Council, and Association of Financial Professionals. He advised the Department of Homeland Security regarding insurance requirements with respect to the Support Anti-Terrorism by Fostering Effective Technologies Act of 2002 (SAFETY Act). Mr. Kalinich joined Aon in September 2000, from Altima Technologies, where he served as chief executive officer and led the successful launch of an Internet of Things intelligent visualization of network equipment software product with respect to telecommunications, data, cables, and computers. Prior to Altima, Mr. Kalinich was a partner at Chapman and Cutler Law Firm, where he represented domestic and international technology-focused public and private entities in general corporate matters, intellectual property, M&A, venture capital and institutional investor transactions, and professional athletes. He also served as Chicago Bar Association Legislative Liaison (Corporations Committee). Mr. Kalinich earned a BA degree in economics and mathematics, cum laude, from Yale University (1984) and a JD from the University of Michigan Law School (1987).

MAUREEN T. KELLY is an assistant general counsel/corporate director at Northrop Grumman. In her current role, she is the lead lawyer for Northrop Grumman's Enterprise Services, which includes an array of internal corporate services, including next gen technology, information security, industrial security, privacy, mission and operational excellence, and flight operations. Ms. Kelly has been a member of the Northrop Grumman Corporate Security Council and serves on the company's Crisis Management team. In addition to supporting Enterprise Services, she provides cyber- and privacy-related support to the company's sectors and the Supply Chain and Contracts organizations. Previously, she was the lead operations counsel for multiple Northrop Grumman business divisions, including its cyber, intelligence, and defense divisions in its heritage TRW Mission Systems sector. She joined TRW in 1999 and became a member of the Northrop Grumman corporate law department when Northrop Grumman acquired TRW in 2002. Prior to joining TRW, Ms. Kelly was a senior counsel at NCR Corporation, where she supported NCR's Government Solutions business. She was also an associate in the Government Contracts practice groups at both Jones Day and Fried Frank. Ms. Kelly is a recognized expert in cybersecurity and privacy matters and speaks on these important topics frequently. She became the co-chair of the American Bar Association's Cybersecurity Legal Task Force in August 2020 after serving for three years as the Public Contract Law Section's representative to that task force. Previously, Ms. Kelly was a co-chair of the Public Contract Law Section's Cybersecurity and Privacy Committee for four years. She also is a long-time active member of the Georgetown Cybersecurity Law Institute Advisory Board, serving as the planning chair for the 2019 Institute and as co-chair for the 2020/2021 Institute. Ms. Kelly is a graduate of American University's Washington College of Law and Rutgers University, where she majored in history and English.

ROBERT S. LITT is of counsel in the Washington office of Morrison & Foerster LLP. He served as the second general counsel of the Office of the Director of National Intelligence (ODNI) from June 2009 until January

2017. Before joining the ODNI, Mr. Litt was a partner with the law firm of Arnold and Porter, LLP. He has served as a member of the governing body of the American Bar Association's Criminal Justice Section and a member of the Standing Committee on Law and National Security. He previously worked at the Department of Justice, where he served as deputy assistant attorney general in the Criminal Division and as the principal associate deputy attorney general; as special advisor to the assistant secretary of state for European and Canadian Affairs; and as an assistant U.S. attorney for the Southern District of New York. Mr. Litt started his legal career as a clerk for Judge Edward Weinfeld of the Southern District of New York and Justice Potter Stewart of the U.S. Supreme Court. He holds a BA from Harvard College and an MA and JD from Yale University.

KEVIN E. LUNDAY is a Rear Admiral and career judge advocate in the U.S. Coast Guard with more than 34 years of active service in legal, cyber, and operational assignments. He has been a member of the American Bar Association Advisory Committee to the Standing Committee on Law and National Security. Currently assigned in Washington, DC, he provides oversight of Coast Guard engineering and logistics, acquisitions and contracting, security, and information technology programs. Rear Admiral Lunday previously served from 2018 to 2020 as the commander of the Fourteenth Coast Guard District, where he was responsible for directing Coast Guard operations throughout Oceania, including Hawai'i, Guam, the Commonwealth of Northern Mariana Islands, American Samoa, and activities in Singapore and Japan. From 2016 to 2018, he served as the commander, Coast Guard Cyber Command, responsible for operating and defending Coast Guard networks and for protecting the U.S. marine transportation system from cyber threats. He also served as the assistant commandant for C4IT, performing the duties of the chief information officer where he directed policy and program management for all Coast Guard information technology, enterprise architecture, cybersecurity, and privacy functions. From 2014 to 2016, he served as the director of Exercises and Training (J7), U.S. Cyber Command, where he was responsible for the joint training of the Cyber Mission Force and delivery of trained and ready cyberspace forces for the Department of Defense. He is a distinguished graduate of the National War College and recipient of the 2005 American Bar Association Standing Committee on Armed Forces Law Career Judge Advocate Award.

EDWARD MARCHEWKA is the VP, IT and Quality Services, & Strategic Planning for Gift of Hope Organ & Tissue Donor Network. In this role, he provides leadership for information and technology services, quality and compliance, process improvement, data and reporting, education and training, and strategic planning. He also serves as the quality officer and HIPAA security and privacy officer. Mr. Marchewka is also the founder and creator of CHICAGO Metrics®, a platform to help manage a company's critical IT and information security risks enabling you to tell a better story. Before joining Gift of Hope, he was the Enterprise Information Security and Server Operations Manager (CISO) for Chicago Public Schools, the third-largest school district in the country. His IT background includes experiences from running his own business to field service to Fortune 250 experience with Thermo Fisher Scientific. Mr. Marchewka holds active certifications from (ISC)2, ITIL, PCI, PMI, ASQ, ISACA, Microsoft, CompTIA, and a designation from the NSA and legacy certifications from Cisco and HP. He is a member of (ISC)², PMI, AITP, ISACA, ASQ, and SIM. He is involved with the board of the InfraGard Chicago Members Alliance as president emeritus. From Northern Illinois University, Mr. Marchewka has completed an MBA and an MS in mathematics, and from Thomas Edison State University, a BS in nuclear engineering technologies and a BA in liberal studies. He also holds a certificate in nonprofit management and leadership from the Kellogg School of Management at Northwestern University and a certificate in applied project management from Northwestern University. Currently, Mr. Marchewka is pursuing a DBA from California Southern University.

LUCIAN T. PERA is a partner in the Memphis, Tennessee, office of Adams and Reese LLP. His practice includes commercial litigation and media law, and he also counsels and represents lawyers, law firms, and others on questions of legal ethics and the professional responsibility of lawyers. Mr. Pera is a graduate of Princeton University and Vanderbilt University School of Law. He served as a law clerk for Judge Harry W. Wellford of the U.S. Court of Appeals for the Sixth Circuit. Mr. Pera joined Adams and Reese in 2006 to help open the firm's Memphis office after practicing law for 20 years with Armstrong Allen, PLLC. As part of his national practice in the ethics field, Mr. Pera represents and advises lawyers, law firms, their clients, and businesses who deal with lawyers about all aspects of the law governing lawyers. Recent assignments have included defense of lawyers in disciplinary investigation, counseling clients with disciplinary and other claims against lawyers, advising law firms about loss prevention and claims, and defending and prosecuting motions to disqualify lawyers or for sanctions. Mr. Pera regularly provides expert witness testimony in matters concerning legal ethics, professional responsibility, and the standard of care for lawyers and law firms. He also advises businesses seeking to do business with lawyers about how they may do so legally and ethically. He writes and speaks frequently on legal ethics and professional responsibility and media law. He served for five years on the ABA Ethics 2000 Commission, which rewrote the ABA Model Rules of Professional Conduct. From 1995 through 2009, he led the ABA Standing Committee on Ethics and Professional Responsibility. Under his leadership, the committee developed and successfully proposed to the Tennessee Supreme Court new legal ethics rules for Tennessee based on the ABA Model Rules of Professional Conduct. Mr. Pera has served as president of the Association of Professional Responsibility Lawyers (APRL), the national membership organization of lawyers who work in the legal ethics arena. He has chaired and served as a member of the editorial board of the ABA/Bloomberg Lawyers' Manual on Professional Conduct, has chaired ethics committees for the Media Law Resource Center and the ABA Business Law Section, and serves as a member of the advisory board for the Miller-Becker Institute for Professional Responsibility of the University of Akron. He has also chaired the governing board of the ABA Center for Professional Responsibility. He is a member of the American Law Institute and the American Bar Foundation, and is recognized in The Best Lawyers in America in the areas of First Amendment law, ethics and professional responsibility law, commercial litigation, health care law, legal malpractice law, and appellate law. He is a past treasurer of the ABA and a past president of the Tennessee Bar Association.

CLAUDIA RAST is a shareholder in Butzel Long's Ann Arbor office, where she chairs the firm's IP, Cybersecurity and Emerging Technology Group.

Her areas of practice focus on domestic and international privacy and data protection, cross-border data transfers, the integrity of critical infrastructure, data breach response, cybersecurity standards addressing autonomous and connected vehicles, and technology licensing and protection. Her privacy and data protection practice reaches back more than 25 years, and she recently concluded a "mega" breach response, defined by the Ponemon Group as one involving more than one million affected individuals. In addition to her legal practice, she is a frequent author on issues of data privacy and security. Ms. Rast has been a longtime member of the American Bar Association's Section of Environment, Energy, and Resources, and was chair of that Section in 2008–2009. In August 2020, she received an ABA Presidential appointment to a three-year term to co-chair the ABA's Cybersecurity Legal Task Force—a task force on which she has served both as a liaison member and member-at-large since 2013. As part of that Task Force, she co-authored a chapter of the ABA's Cybersecurity Handbook (2d ed. 2018) and co-authored Vendor Cybersecurity Checklist, 2d edition, published in May 2021. Ms. Rast received her BS from the University of Michigan, majoring in natural resources, and her JD from University of Detroit School of Law, where she was the editor-in-chief of the law review and later clerked for the Chief Justice of the Michigan Supreme Court, G. Mennen "Soapy" Williams.

ALAN RAUL is the founder and leader of Sidley's highly ranked Privacy and Cybersecurity practice. He represents companies on federal, state, and international privacy, cybersecurity, and digital technology issues. His practice includes global data protection compliance programs, data breaches, and crisis management. Mr. Raul advises companies and boards regarding their cybersecurity preparedness, digital governance, transactional due diligence, and emerging data technologies like AI and facial recognition. He is also a lecturer on law at Harvard Law School where he teaches a course on "Digital Governance: Privacy and Technology Trade-offs." His practice involves litigation, regulatory defense, internal investigations, strategic counseling, and policy advocacy. He handles consumer class actions, enforcement matters, and public policy involving the FTC, state attorneys general, SEC, FCC, HHS, DOJ, international data protection authorities, and other government agencies. He also represents clients on cyber matters before the FBI, NSA, and DHS/CISA. Mr. Raul provides clients with perspective gained from extensive government service. He previously served as vice chairman of the White House Privacy and Civil Liberties Oversight Board, general counsel of the Office of Management and Budget, general counsel of the U.S. Department of Agriculture, and associate counsel to the President. Mr. Raul maintains an active national security clearance. He serves as a member of the Technology Litigation Advisory Committee of the U.S. Chamber Litigation Center (affiliated with the U.S. Chamber of Commerce). He also serves on the American Bar Association's Cybersecurity Legal Task Force by appointment of the ABA President, and as a member of the Practicing Law Institute's Privacy Law Advisors Group. He is a member of the governing board of directors of the Future of Privacy Forum. He is also a member of the Council on Foreign Relations. Mr. Raul is ranked by *Chambers USA* and *Chambers Global* among the first tier of privacy and data security practitioners. He has been named as a leading international Internet and E-Commerce Lawyer in *Who's Who Legal*. Mr. Raul was also named to *Ethisphere Institute's* "Attorneys Who Matter" in Data Privacy/Security, among *Washingtonian's* Best Lawyers: Cybersecurity, and as a *National Law Journal* "Cyber Security Trailblazer."

JILL D. RHODES is vice president and chief information security officer for Option Care Enterprises, Inc. Her responsibilities include the integration of information security governance, education, process development, and technology into all facets of this multibillion-dollar health care company. Prior to moving to the private sector, Ms. Rhodes spent 20 years working in and with the national security community of the federal government. She joined the Office of the Director of National Intelligence (ODNI) where she supported the intelligence community (IC) integration of data and security into the Cloud Environment for the IC Chief Information Office. In addition to other national security roles, Ms. Rhodes worked with data management, foreign language, and training matters on behalf of the National Clandestine Service of the CIA, addressing issues such as data security and exploitation. Before joining the national security community, Ms. Rhodes was a foreign service officer, stationed in Bolivia and Russia. She also worked extensively throughout Eastern and Southern

Africa. Ms. Rhodes was honored with the 2019 Chicago-area CISO of the Year award. She has written, published, and speaks nationally about cybersecurity issues. Ms. Rhodes was the co-editor of the first and second editions of the *ABA Cybersecurity Handbook: A Resource for Attorneys, Law Firms, and Business Professionals* and edited the book *National Security Law, Fifty Years of Transformation: An Anthology* (2012). In addition, she has written articles and chapters on various cybersecurity topics and is regularly interviewed about cybersecurity for different publications. She is a graduate of the University of Illinois at Urbana-Champaign, the University of Cincinnati College of Law (JD), and the George Washington University College of Law (LLM). She is also a certified information security manager and certified information privacy professional/IT.

TOM RICKETTS is a senior vice president and the cyber practice leader of Aon's Professional Services practice, providing cyber risk management advice and cyber insurance placement for more than 180 professional services firms across the country. Mr. Ricketts is on the faculty of Thomson Reuters Westlaw and of the UCLA Cybersecurity Certificate Extension program. He started his 30-year insurance broking career with Willis Faber & Dumas Ltd. in Sheffield, England, and subsequently worked for Sedgwick in London and New York before joining Aon in New York. As a founder of Sedgwick's Global Telecommunications practice, Mr. Ricketts became a leading provider of risk management and insurance advice to the global telecommunications and media sector. Among his innovations in the industry, he created and placed the very first open-market Technology Errors & Omissions program. He was recognized by *Risk & Insurance Magazine* as a power broker for his work in the telecommunications sector (2006) and in the construction sector (2011). Mr. Ricketts holds a master's degree in English literature from the University of St. Andrews, Scotland.

HARVEY RISHIKOF is a director of policy and cyber security research and visiting research professor at the University of Maryland (Applied Research Laboratory for Intelligence and Security), a visiting professor of law at Temple Law School, and senior counsel to the ABA Standing Committee on Law and National Security, having served previously as chair. Mr.

Rishikof is involved in a number of legal-policy projects sponsored by the MITRE, the MacArthur Foundation, the Center for Strategic International Studies, the Hewlett Foundation, the Congressional "Solarium" Project, the National Science Foundation, and the National Academy of Sciences. His most recent publications are "National Cyber Information Integration Network" (ARLIS Report 2021); The US Intelligence Community Law Source Book (2021, ABA Publications); "Deliver Uncompromised—Supply Chain" (MITRE Report 2018); and "The National Security Enterprise: Navigating the Labyrinth" (2009, 2d ed. 2017).

PAUL ROSENZWEIG is the founder of Red Branch Consulting PLLC, a homeland security consulting company. He is also a senior advisor to The Chertoff Group. Mr. Rosenzweig formerly served as deputy assistant secretary for policy in the Department of Homeland Security. He is a professorial lecturer in Law at George Washington University, a senior fellow in the Tech, Law and Security program at American University, an advisor to and former member of the American Bar Association Standing Committee on Law and National Security, and a contributing editor of the *Lawfare* blog. He is a member of the ABA Cybersecurity Legal Task Force. In 2011 he was a Carnegie Fellow in National Security Journalism at the Medill School of Journalism, Northwestern University. Mr. Rosenzweig is a cum laude graduate of the University of Chicago Law School. He has an MS in chemical oceanography from the Scripps Institution of Oceanography, University of California at San Diego, and a BA from Haverford College. Following graduation from law school he served as a law clerk to the Honorable R. Lanier Anderson III of the U.S. Court of Appeals for the Eleventh Circuit. He is the author of *Cyber Warfare: How Conflicts in Cyberspace Are Challenging America* and *Changing the World* and of three video lecture series from The Great Courses: Thinking About Cybersecurity: From Cyber Crime to Cyber Warfare; The Surveillance State: Big Data, Freedom, and You; and Investigating American Presidents. He is the co-author (with James Jay Carafano) of *Winning the Long War: Lessons from the Cold War for Defeating Terrorism and Preserving Freedom* and co-editor (with Timothy McNulty and Ellen Shearer) of two books: *Whistleblowers, Leaks and the*

Media: The First Amendment and National Security, and *National Security Law in the News: A Guide for Journalists, Scholars, and Policymakers*.

THOMAS J. SMEDINGHOFF focuses his practice on legal issues involving technology, digital information, and electronic business activities and is internationally recognized for his leadership in addressing emerging digital legal issues. He has been retained to structure and implement first-of-their-kind e-commerce initiatives, and identity management and information security legal infrastructures for the federal government and for national and international businesses. He also has been actively involved in developing e-business, e-signature, identity management, and data security legal policy both in the United States and globally. Mr. Smedinghoff is a member of the U.S. Delegation to the United Nations Commission on International Trade Law (UNCITRAL), where he participates in the Working Group on Electronic Commerce and helped to negotiate the United Nations Convention on the Use of Electronic Communications in International Contracts as well as the UNCITRAL Model Law on Electronic Signatures. He currently is working on UNCITRAL projects to develop legal rules for cross-border identity management and for artificial intelligence. He previously served as the American Bar Association's advisor to the Uniform Law Commission committee that drafted the Uniform Electronic Transactions Act in 1999. He also wrote the Illinois Electronic Commerce Security Act enacted in 1998 when he chaired the Illinois Attorney General's Commission on Electronic Commerce and Crime. He currently chairs the Identity Management Legal Task Force of the ABA Business Law Section and serves on the ABA Cybersecurity Legal Task Force (which he co-chaired from 2019 to 2020). A long-standing leader in the ABA Science & Technology Law Section, Mr. Smedinghoff served as the Section chair from 1999 to 2000 and the Electronic Commerce Division chair from 1995 to 2003. In addition to publishing numerous articles on electronic transactions, identity management, privacy, and data security law, he is the co-editor of the book *Guide to Cybersecurity Due Diligence in M&A Transactions* (ABA 2017), author of the book *Information Security Law: The Emerging Standard for Corporate Compliance* (IT Governance Publishing 2008), and the editor and primary author of the book *Online Law* (Addison-Wesley, 1996). Based in Chicago, Mr. Smedinghoff continues to consult on selected legal issues following his 2021 retirement from Locke Lord LLP.

SUZANNE SPAULDING is senior advisor for homeland security and director of the Defending Democratic Institutions project at the Center for Strategic and International Studies (CSIS). She also serves as a member of the Cyberspace Solarium Commission. Previously, she served as undersecretary for the Department of Homeland Security (DHS), where she led the National Protection and Programs Directorate, now called the Cybersecurity and Infrastructure Security Agency (CISA), managing a $3 billion budget and a workforce of 18,000, charged with strengthening cybersecurity and protecting the nation's critical infrastructure, including election infrastructure. Ms. Spaulding has served in Republican and Democratic administrations and on both sides of the aisle in Congress. She was general counsel for the Senate Select Committee on Intelligence and minority staff director for the House of Representatives Permanent Select Committee on Intelligence. She also spent six years at the Central Intelligence Agency, where she was assistant general counsel and the legal advisor to the director's Nonproliferation Center. She was executive director of two congressionally created commissions, on WMD and on terrorism. Following the attacks of 9/11, Ms. Spaulding worked with key critical infrastructure sectors as they reviewed their security posture, and advised the CEOs of the Business Roundtable. In 2002, she was appointed by Governor Mark Warner of Virginia to the Secure Commonwealth Panel to advise the governor and the legislature regarding preparedness issues. She was managing partner of the Harbour Group, a principal in the Bingham Consulting Group, and of counsel to Bingham McCutchen LLP. In addition to her work at CSIS, Ms. Spaulding currently serves on a number of corporate boards and advisory boards and is a member of the Homeland Security Experts Group (HSEG).

LUCY L. THOMSON is the founding principal of Livingston PLLC, Washington, DC, where she focuses her practice on legal and technology issues related to cybersecurity and global data privacy, and compliance and risk management. Previously a senior engineer at CSC, a global technology company, she conducted privacy and risk assessments and developed FISMA security plans on two of the government's largest technology modernization projects—Customs and Border Protection (CBP-ACE) and the IRS. While at CSC she was appointed a Department of Homeland Security (DHS) Information System Security Officer (ISSO). A career U.S. Department of Justice attorney, she managed and conducted complex litigation in the Criminal and Civil Rights Divisions. In the American Bar Association (ABA), Ms. Thomson is a past chair of the Science & Technology Law Section and an elected member of the House of Delegates (2004–present). She is editor of the *Data Breach and Encryption Handbook*, co-editor of the *Internet of Things (IoT): Legal Issues, Policy, and Practical Strategies*, contributing author to the *ABA Cybersecurity Handbook*, member of the program planning committee for six ABA Internet of Things (IoT) National Institutes, and serves on the Cybersecurity Legal Task Force. Since 2008, she has been appointed Consumer Privacy Ombudsman (CPO) in 31 federal bankruptcy cases. Responsible for evaluating the sale of "assets" consisting of sensitive personal information, she has overseen the disposition of more than 350 million electronic consumer records. Internationally, Ms. Thomson served as a legal advisor to the Asia-Pacific Economic Cooperation (APEC), Association of Southeast Asian Nations (ASEAN), and the United Nations Centre for Trade Facilitation and Electronic Business (UN/CEFACT). She was elected to membership in the American Law Institute (ALI) and is a past alumni trustee of Phillips Academy/Andover. Ms. Thomson received a master's degree from Rensselaer Polytechnic Institute, earned the CISSP and CIPP/US certifications, and holds a JD degree from the Georgetown University Law Center.

ROLAND TROPE is a partner in the New York City office of Trope and Schramm LLP and an adjunct professor in the Departments of Law and of Electrical Engineering and Computer Science at the U.S. Military Academy at West Point, where he has been teaching since 1992. He is public liaison on the ABA Cybersecurity Legal Task Force, vice-chair of the Intellectual Property Committee for the ABA Public Contracts Law Section, a member of the Intellectual Property Council of the New York City Bar Association, and co-host for the ABA-sponsored podcast series Mind the Gap:

Dialogs on AI. He has written more than 30 articles, has co-authored two books published by the ABA—*Checkpoints in Cyberspace: Best Practices for Averting Liability in Cross-Border Transactions*, and *Sailing in Dangerous Waters: A Director's Guide to Data Governance*—and was co-editor of the ABA's Guide to Cybersecurity Due Diligence in M&A Transactions. Mr. Trope has a national security practice in which he advises on government procurement, protection and licensing of intellectual property under government contracts, cross-border tech transfers, export controls, economic sanctions regulations, anti-corruption laws, reviews by the Committee on Foreign Investment in the United States (CFIUS), determinations of foreign ownership, control, and influence (FOCI), cyberspace law, cybersecurity, and artificial intelligence. Mr. Trope has successfully represented governments in international arbitrations of commercial contracts for design and development of advanced, computer-based systems. His international work includes significant experience in advising ministries of defense and aerospace and defense contract clients in Australia, New Zealand, Singapore, Thailand, Japan, the Middle East, Norway, the Netherlands, Brazil, and Canada. Mr. Trope earned a BA in political science from the University of Southern California. As a Marshall Scholar and a Danforth Fellow, he studied English language and literature at Oxford University, earning a BA and MA. He earned a JD at Yale Law School. He clerked on the Minnesota Supreme Court and began practicing law in New York City in 1982.

OZODA USMANOVA received an LLM from the Georgetown University Law Center in February 2022, specializing in national security law with cybersecurity and data privacy focus. Originally from Tashkent, Uzbekistan, Ms. Usmanova obtained her first law degree from Tashkent State Institute of Law and practiced law before immigrating to the United States. In 2018, she joined the DC Office of the Attorney General as a litigation technology paralegal specialist. There, Ms. Usmanova splits her time between Civil Litigation and Consumer Protection Divisions, where she assists in the technical management of complex civil litigation and governmental investigations, trains attorneys and staff on Relativity, and investigates consumer complaints against fraudulent business practices. Ms. Usmanova speaks four languages and is currently learning Chinese Mandarin. She was selected as a

Digital Sherlock Scholar and completed OSINT (Open Source Intelligence) training at the Atlantic Council's DFRLab (Digital Forensics Research Lab), where she focused her research on Russia's disinformation campaigns. Most recently, Ms. Usmanova received a Security Innovation Scholarship from ICMCP (International Consortium of Minority Cybersecurity Professionals) sponsored by Google for a six-month Red Team training. Ms. Usmanova obtained several certificates from National White Collar Crime Center in digital forensic analysis and cyber investigations.

MELISSA VENTRONE is on the cutting edge of data security and privacy, helping clients navigate emerging challenges related to today's digital economy. As leader of the Cybersecurity, Data Protection and Privacy Business Unit at Clark Hill, PLC, Ms. Ventrone directs her skilled, multidisciplinary team of first responders to minimize security risks, ensure regulatory compliance, and curtail damage in the event of a data incident. As a Marine Corps veteran, she understands the best defense is a strong offense, especially when it comes to risk mitigation, resiliency, and protection. Ms. Ventrone reviews data security policies, procedures, and incident response plans and works with clients to create a tactical action plan to establish compliance with state, federal, and international laws and regulations and minimize cyber risks. This action plan includes creating and facilitating executive training and simulation exercises to improve clients' cyber resiliency and ensure they are prepared to respond effectively and efficiently to data security incidents. Understanding technology and the related legal issues and complex challenges, where she helps clients manage data to minimize risks and ensure compliance with changing regulatory requirements. Ms. Ventrone is proficient in data security regulations including the European Union's General Data Protection Regulation (GDPR,) the California Consumer Privacy Act (CCPA), and the Health Insurance Portability and Accountability Act (HIPAA), among others. Leveraging her extensive knowledge, Ms. Ventrone helps clients collect, use, monetize, and protect data (including intellectual property and customer, financial, medical, and employee records) in a secure and compliant manner. When a damaging data breach or cybersecurity attack occurs, Ms. Ventrone and her team are available 24/7 to manage the end-to-end process from containment to recovery, minimizing operational disruption, negative repercussions, and costs. She has managed thousands of data security incidents across all industries, ranging from lost devices at small companies to high-profile cyberattacks impacting millions of customers' data. Ms. Ventrone's vast experience in cybersecurity preparedness and response allows her to swiftly identify the best strategies to protect clients' most critical assets.

Student Editorial Volunteers

Sydney Huppert is a law student at the George Washington University Law School in Washington, DC. She studied computer science at the University of Virginia and has previously worked as a software engineer.

Irene Kim graduated from Stanford University in 2019 with a degree in international relations and honors in international security studies. She is currently a senior analyst at a disputes and investigations-focused law firm in Washington, DC, and aspires to attend law school.

Veronica Lark is a third-year law student at the George Washington University Law School. She is interested in data privacy and communications law and is the senior articles editor for GW's *Federal Communications Law Journal*.

Index